P9-DYY-503

The Shaping
of the
American High School
1880–1920

The Shaping of the

AMERICAN HIGH SCHOOL
1880–1920

EDWARD A. KRUG

THE UNIVERSITY OF WISCONSIN PRESS

MADISON, MILWAUKEE, AND LONDON   1969

Published by
The University of Wisconsin Press
Box 1379, Madison, Wisconsin 53701
The University of Wisconsin Press, Ltd.
27–29 Whitfield Street, London, W.1

First UWP printing, 1969

Printed in the United States of America
Standard Book Number 299–05165–X
Library of Congress Catalog Card Number 64–12801

This book was first published
by Harper & Row

*To
Anne*

Contents

Preface   xi

1. A Decade of Transition   1
2. Toward the Committee of Ten   18
3. Dr. Eliot's Report   39
4. A Sea of Troubles   66
5. Harris, Hall, and the Herbartians   93
6. The High School and the College   123
7. The Rise of Accreditation   146
8. The Children of the Plain People   169
9. Electivism and the End of an Era   190
10. The Interlude of Vocationalism   217
11. Social Efficiency Triumphant   249
12. The Colleges Defied   284
13. The Call to Judgment   304
14. The Reshaping of the Studies   336
15. Mr. Kingsley's Report   378
16. The Impact of War   407
17. The Venture Reaffirmed   428

Bibliographical Note   449

Index   467

List of Abbreviations

CCER   *Report of the Committee on College-Entrance Requirements,* published by the National Educational Association in 1899.

CRSE   Commission on the Reorganization of Secondary Education. This is used both in the text and in the footnotes; in footnotes it refers to the reports of the Commission.

Commissioner   U.S. Commissioner of Education. This is used in footnotes only and refers to the annual reports of the Commissioner.

MSM   Association of Colleges and Preparatory Schools of the Middle States and Maryland. This is used in footnotes only and refers to the annual proceedings of the organization.

NC   North Central Association of Colleges and Secondary Schools. This is used in footnotes only and refers to the annual proceedings of the organization.

NEA   National Education Association. When used in footnotes with designation of year, this refers to the annual proceedings of the organization.

NSPIE   National Society for the Promotion of Industrial Education.

RSE   Commissioner's Office, Reorganization of Secondary Education, 1915–1923. This is used in footnotes only and refers to this collection in the National Archives.

SA   Association of Colleges and Preparatory Schools of the Southern States. This is used in footnotes only and refers to the annual proceedings of the organization.

Preface

*I*t was in the period between 1880 and 1920 that the American high school assumed its familiar shape and characteristics. This book is an attempt to tell the story of the high school in that period. It grew out of personal curiosity aroused by tantalizing but elusive interpretations made by various writers in education and in the larger domain of social and intellectual history. I began specifically with what looked like the simple question of the allegedly college-preparatory character of high school pupils around 1900. These inquiries led to others and ultimately to a vast and fascinating literature, published and unpublished, pertaining to high schools over the period of four decades.

The story necessarily involves the clash of doctrines and points of view of those who by dint of much speaking and writing were identified as leaders of this or that school of thought. Much of this, especially during the period after 1905, reflected what might be called an anti-academic bias, some of it expressed to an almost unbelievable degree. The interpretation of this bias, however, requires qualifications. One is that the high schools themselves did not necessarily and in all instances adopt the strong doctrines being advocated. This was reflected in the despairing utterances of some of the leaders about the reluctance of high school teachers to change. Another qualification is that the so-called new ideology was not an inevitable response to social and economic forces in American society. It was often proclaimed to be by those advancing the cause; unfortunately later writers have sometimes accepted these proclamations at face value.

The high school, like all other institutions, was caught in a vast complex of change, or as the terminology of the times would have expressed it, of reform. It was an age of criticism directed against established orders. The established order of the high school was identified as the academic program. It would be difficult to determine whether the criticisms of the high school were originated by the public and supported by educators, or originated by educators and supported by the public. In both groups, the expressions of criticism came from a relatively small number of articulate individuals. For the most part, the criticism came from advocates of social efficiency rather than from those who may have been identified with the conventional interpretation of progressive education as freedom for the child. The mood of the American people during the First World War made possible even more strenuous advocacy of education as social control.

Social control did not mean soft pedagogy or disregard of subject matter. In fact, the advocates of the new doctrines put more stress on subject matter than had the traditionalists who were identified with mental discipline. It was subject matter, however, that they claimed to be functional in the practical affairs of life. Associated with this position were two far-reaching consequences: one, that subjects—particularly academic subjects—had to prove their right to existence in the school program; the other, that subject matter would make its maximum contribution to social efficiency by being organized in differentiated programs of study designed for pupils categorized in groups. The first of these put the academic studies on the defensive; the second tended to channel some of them, particularly foreign languages and mathematics, into the programs identified as college-preparatory.

This was an age of remarkable individuals. Possibly they did not always manage to say exactly what they meant, but there were apparently few occasions on which they said less than they thought. Some of them, like William T. Harris, seemed to enjoy nothing more than a good platform fight at an NEA meeting. The zest and gusto, however, diminished somewhat after 1905. Controversy after that time remained intense, but it also became grim, in fact, much like the cheerless world of social efficiency that some of the participants were demanding.

The high school itself struggled through this period like a bewildered giant, accommodating itself as it could to a staggering degree of sheer physical growth, shaking off for the most part, as it still does today, the barbs of its critics and the free advice of its many well-wishers. As the image of the high school was a composite one derived from institutions varying much in size and in environment, so were the causes of its development necessarily multitudinous and complex. All of this— the emergence of the high school as an institution and the doctrines that accompanied it—makes a good story. If it does not appear so in these pages, the fault lies in the telling, not in the story itself. Much more remains to be learned and told. Particularly welcome would be studies of some of the less well-known participants, such as David Snedden, Augustus F. Nightingale, William H. Maxwell, and Clarence Kingsley.

For help in the location and use of unpublished materials, I am indebted to Lewis G. Vander Velde, F. Clever Bald, Robert W. Warner, and Mrs. E. S. G. Ehrmann of the Michigan Historical Collections of the University of Michigan; Alice H. Bonnell of the Columbiana Library, Columbia University; Edda Colombo of the Chicago Public Library; Kimball C. Elkins of the Harvard University Archives and William A. Jackson of the Houghton Library, Harvard University; Joseph Howerton and Jerome Finster of the Labor and Transportation Branch, Social and Economic Records Division, National Archives; Mildred Sandison Fenner and Irene F. Wolz of the National Education Association; the staff of the Ravenswood–Lake View Historical Association, Frederick H. Hild Regional Branch Library, Chicago; Josephine L. Harper of the State Historical Society of Wisconsin; Lucile Fry of the University of Colorado Libraries; Juliet Wolohan of the New York State Library, Albany; Bruce McClellan of the Lawrenceville School, Lawrenceville, New Jersey; Howard D. Williams, University Archivist, Colgate University; Superintendent Benjamin C. Willis of the Chicago Public Schools; and Elsa Wallenius of the Bureau of Vital Statistics, Evanston, Illinois.

Among my most pleasant and rewarding experiences in carrying on this study were conversations with Helen Tetlow and Frances Tetlow of Cambridge, Massachusetts, daughters of John Tetlow of the Committee of Ten, and with Dr. Augustus Nightingale Abbott of Shawano, Wisconsin, grandson of Augustus F. Nightingale, Chairman of the NEA Committee on College-Entrance Requirements. The Misses Tetlow made available to me some valuable unpublished documents, now on deposit in the Houghton Library, Harvard University. Dr. Abbott shared with me a number of delightful reminiscences of his grandfather and allowed me to examine an unpublished journal kept by Nightingale's daughter, Mrs. Harrison Angle. I am most grateful also to Mrs. Nathan Finch of Palo Alto, California, daughter of David Snedden, for her generosity in giving to the Memorial Library of the University of Wisconsin a copy of her father's privately printed *Recollections of Over Half a Century Spent in Educational Work*.

Permission to quote unpublished letters of Charles W. Eliot has been most kindly extended to me by Samuel Eliot, Jr., and Charles William Eliot, 2nd; of Nicholas Murray Butler by Mrs. Robert Whitelaw Wilson; of John Tetlow by Helen Tetlow and Frances Tetlow; of Michael Vincent O'Shea by Harriet O'Shea; of William T. Harris by Edith Davidson Harris; of Charles De Garmo by Kenneth De Garmo; and of Clarence D. Kingsley by Ernest P. Seelman. Institutional permission to quote from designated unpublished documents in their archives and collections has been granted by Harvard University, Columbia University, Colgate University, and by the Trustees of the Lawrenceville School. All these were gratefully received by me, as were also the permissions granted by Stanwood Cobb to quote from his letters in the State Historical Society of Wisconsin and by Thomas H. Briggs from a letter written to Walter H. Drost.

Permission to make extensive use of direct quotations from published materials has been granted to me by A.M.S. Reprint Company, New York, N.Y., for *Educational Administration and Supervision;* The Bobbs-Merrill Company, Inc., Indianapolis, Indiana, the holder of the copyright to *Education;* Boston University School of Education for *Journal of Education;* the Middle States Association of Colleges and Secondary Schools; the North Central Association of Colleges and Secondary Schools; the National Education Association; The Society for the Advancement of Education, Inc., New York, N.Y., for *School and Society* and *Educational Review;* and The University of Chicago Press for *School Review*. I appreciate their generosity.

Among the many people on whom I have imposed conversations pertaining to this study are past and present graduate students and fellow faculty members in the Department of Education at the University of Wisconsin. Special acknowledgment is due Father Roman Bernert, Walter H. Drost, Frances McPherson, and Solberg Einar Sigurdson, all of whom have been most generous in sharing with me materials pertaining to their own studies, and Ruth Simmons, who as research assistant in the summer of 1961 unraveled for me some of the complex threads in the reports of the U.S. Commissioner of Education for the period under study. I am indebted also to Theodore Sizer, Richard Whittemore, and Gayle Simmons, who during the course of this study were completing their investigations at graduate schools elsewhere. Gordon M. Seely, Jr., was most kind in sharing with me notes taken from unpublished manuscripts as part of his own study.

It is a happy privilege indeed to acknowledge my appreciation to the

Graduate School Research Committee of the University of Wisconsin for grants of summer-session support in 1960 and 1962 and to Dean Lindley J. Stiles of the School of Education of the University of Wisconsin for adjustment of teaching load and for warm encouragement and support throughout the study. As in the past, I remain indebted beyond measure to John Guy Fowlkes of the University of Wisconsin for penetrating editorial criticism and, at all times, inspirational guidance.

Portions of the material for this book have been used by me in "Charles W. Eliot and the Secondary School," *History of Education Quarterly*, September, 1961; "Graduates of Secondary Schools in and around 1900: Did Most of Them Go to College?" *School Review*, Autumn, 1962; and *Charles W. Eliot and Popular Education*, Classics in Education No. 8, Bureau of Publications, Teachers College, Columbia University, 1961.

E. A. K.

The Shaping
of the
American High School
1880–1920

Chapter 1

A decade of transition

> "The new era, the era of new things, is seemingly upon us."
>
> —HEADMASTER E. T. TOMLINSON,
> MARCH, 1885.

*T*hey had come with a grievance and were ready to do something about it. Assembled in Boston on April 12, 1884, for their seventeenth annual meeting, the members of the Massachusetts Classical and High School Teachers' Association unanimously passed two resolutions. The specific targets of these resolutions were the nineteen colleges and universities of the New England states.

"In the opinion of this Association," declared the first resolution, "the want of understanding and effective cooperation between the teachers of the preparatory and high schools and the faculties of colleges is a serious evil." Another age would call this a "problem," but the Association preferred to say what it meant. The second resolution asserted that "a meeting of delegates from this Association with representatives of the New England colleges would be productive of good."[1] Having identified evil and good, the members instructed their secretary to send a copy of the resolutions to each of the college presidents and went home to the pressing demands of their own schools to wait for the results.

A year later, the secretary announced that only three of the nineteen presidents had acknowledged the resolutions. "I do not remember," wrote Principal John Tetlow of the Boston Girls' High and Latin Schools, "that the result of this effort created any marked surprise. Indeed, this incident was only one among many manifestations of the attitude of reserve and isolation then maintained by the members of col-

[1] "Meeting of Classical and High School Teachers," *Journal of Education* (April 17, 1884), p. 252.

1

lege faculties towards the teachers of secondary schools. . . . College officers as a rule—though there were notable exceptions—did not attend the meetings of associations of teachers of secondary schools, and were generally credited with a disposition to view themselves as a sort of Brahmin caste in the educational system."[2] Perhaps it was surprising that even three representatives of this Brahmin caste had taken the trouble to reply.

Encouraged by this response, meager though it appeared to be, the Association created a committee "to devise and carry into effect such measures as should seem to them most likely to be efficacious."[3] To this committee were appointed John Tetlow; Ray Greene Huling, principal of the high school at Fitchburg, Massachusetts; and William C. Collar, the outspoken headmaster of the Roxbury Latin School, who eleven years before had startled his contemporaries by proposing that Greek no longer be required for college entrance.

One of the "notable exceptions" referred to by Tetlow—also one of the three presidents who had acknowledged the resolutions of 1884— was the controversial president of Harvard, Charles W. Eliot. Tetlow, who later was characterized as "the only school principal who could confront President Charles W. Eliot with an opinion diverging from that of Harvard's head and continue to function,"[4] decided to enroll this formidable personage in the cause. He was even successful in arranging for Collar and himself to have "an hour's talk" with Eliot. The main thing that Tetlow sought and received was advice, both of a general nature and about strategy. Perhaps he wanted the prestige of Harvard on the side of his campaign, although other colleges in New England did not always feel disposed to follow when Harvard led the way.

Presumably acting on Eliot's advice, the committee went ahead to make plans for a meeting of school and college men and diplomatically asked some of the college men to make speeches. Among the topics listed for discussion were the desirable modifications, if any, in requirements for admission to college; whether or not a greater degree of uniformity in requirements for admission to college was practicable; and the conditions

[2] John Tetlow, "The Colleges and the Non-Classical High Schools," John Tetlow Papers (Houghton Library, Harvard University, Cambridge, Mass.), pp. 2–3. [The manuscript is undated, but was probably written shortly after 1895.]
[3] *Ibid.,* p. 5.
[4] William T. Emery, *New Bedford Sunday Standard-Times* (Massachusetts), March 25, 1945.

under which admission to college by certificate might be permitted.[5] All the presidents except one replied to this proposal, and all except one of these "promised cordial cooperation."[6]

The meeting took place in October, 1885. Tetlow and his two associates were ready with a constitution for the permanent group they hoped might be formed. With this before them, the college officers forsook their aloofness and joined the secondary school teachers in organizing the New England Association of Colleges and Preparatory Schools. College men and school men working in the same region had fashioned a means of talking to each other. As the first such group to be formed in the United States, the New England Association not only anticipated the organization of similar enterprises in other parts of the country, but also set the stage for a new era of study and discussion.

II

This action did not usher in the millennium; old evils persisted and new ones were invented. It reflected, moreover, not only the mechanical difficulties in the relationships between schools and colleges, but also a broad range of questions about the aims and programs of institutions classified as secondary schools. The classification was a loose one indeed, and even though the New England school men regarded college men as exclusive and aloof, the boundary lines between so-called secondary education and college education—as well as between secondary and elementary education—were extremely fluid. Some colleges and universities maintained their own secondary or preparatory departments, and the distinctions between these and the higher departments were not always clear.

There were still many academies, probably more than 1600 of them in 1884–1885.[7] The term was applied not only to schools with the word *academy* in their titles, but also to some called seminaries, institutes, collegiate institutes, and, in a few instances, colleges. Although ridiculed at

[5] John Tetlow, W. C. Collar, and Ray Greene Huling, printed circular, May 23, 1885, Charles W. Eliot Papers (Harvard University Archives, Cambridge, Mass.).
[6] John Tetlow to Charles W. Eliot, June 14, 1885, Charles W. Eliot Papers (Harvard University Archives, Cambridge, Mass.).
[7] Commissioner of Education, *Report for the Year 1884–1885* (Washington, D.C.: Bureau of Education, 1886), pp. cxlix, clxiii, and 438–551. [These reports are referred to in subsequent notes as Commissioner, with the appropriate year: for example, Commissioner, 1884–1885.]

times for their pretensions, academies often won high regard in their communities; collectively, they occupied a cherished position in the pedagogical domain. "Many a man still in the vigor of life," wrote one observer as late as 1916, "looks back with an almost romantic affection to his academy days."[8]

Those who wrote about academies they had attended dwelt on such characteristics as flexible course offerings and what would later be called individualized instruction. According to one nostalgic citizen, recalling his academy days near Utica, New York, there had been "unlimited application of the elective principle," with each boy taking what subjects he pleased and with classes rarely numbering more than five or six persons. "Nearly all," he said, "recited alone in something. Three or four in algebra followed after each other, a few pages apart. . . . No one was dragged back by association with a sluggish companion."[9] Writing fondly in his autobiography of the academy he had attended in Maine, President James B. Angell of the University of Michigan noted that most of the pupils had been farmers' sons and daughters looking for something beyond their district schools. "A small number," wrote Angell, "were preparing themselves for college. I joined them in their classes with no such purpose distinctly formed. I also took nearly all the scientific instruction which was given, and given as well as it could be without laboratories or much apparatus. Many of the students were men in years. They were diligent students. Some of them were awkward and rustic in manners, but they were thoroughly earnest and gave a good tone to the school."[10]

Practically all academies taught Latin and mathematics, but not necessarily to prepare students for college. Those with special concern about preparation for college also offered Greek. Academies were noted for the breadth and variety of their offerings in the "moderns," that is, science, history, modern languages (German or French), and literature in English. Some gave work in "practical" subjects, including bookkeeping, surveying, and drawing. There were also subject titles now vanished from the secondary schools, such as political economy, ethics, moral philosophy, mental philosophy, mental science, and logic.

[8] Elmer E. Brown, "The Historical Development of Secondary Schools in the United States," *School and Society* (February 12, 1916), p. 228.
[9] E. B. Powell, "The New York Academy," *School Journal* (September 4, 1897), p. 189.
[10] James B. Angell, *Reminiscences* (New York: Longmans, Green & Co., 1912), p. 8.

It was probably some time during the 1880's that public high schools gained the numerical lead among the various institutions of secondary education. The Commissioner's *Report* of 1889–1890 listed 2,526 schools under this heading, and their 202,963 pupils greatly outnumbered the 94,391 in a total of 1,632 private secondary schools, including academies.[11] Just how a public high school differed from an academy was not always easy to tell, although the writers of the time used both terms with confidence. Many academies existed under charters granted by the states, and some of them received public funds. In the State of New York, the so-called literature fund was distributed both to academies and to high schools. Local governments in New England sometimes took over existing academies, but ran them under their old names. Still, with all these admitted qualifications, a distinction between academies and public high schools did exist, and it was one increasingly noted during the middle and latter 1880's.

The high schools reputedly offered a more restricted range of subjects than the academies and consequently gave their pupils less freedom of choice. A former agent of the Massachusetts Board of Education, for example, recalled a high school where every first-year pupil had been required to study Latin, algebra, and history. "There was," he stated, "absolutely no alternative. He must study these or nothing. . . . There were hundreds of boys and girls in that community who under the old conditions would have attended the academy one or two terms. Then they would have selected such studies as they chose."[12]

Many high schools, however, offered two programs, labeled Classical and English. The Classical courses of study included little but Latin, Greek, and mathematics; in some schools they were only three years in

[11] Commissioner, 1889–1890, II, pp. 1388–1389 and 1486–1487. As late as the middle 1880's, however, the *Reports* had given admittedly sketchy information about high schools. In 1884–1885, for example, only 148 high schools were identified, and these in a category labeled "city high schools," with only 35,307 pupils enrolled. Commissioner, 1884–1885, pp. clv–clvi and cxlviii. Another part of the same volume cited the Massachusetts Board of Education as claiming 224 high schools in that state alone. *Ibid.*, p. 124. Almost certainly the differences between the figures reported in 1884–1885 and 1889–1890 did not represent any such spectacular increase in the number of high schools. Still, it was taken for granted by educators at the time that a marked swing upward had occurred throughout the decade.

[12] George H. Martin, "Election of Studies in Secondary Schools: An Affirmative View," *Educational Review* (May, 1898), pp. 451–452. Martin did not supply a date for this state of affairs, although he referred to the change as one that had started about fifty years before. His tone implied that such was still the case in the years immediately preceding his article.

length, as contrasted with the English course of four years. Schools without Greek called their two courses Latin and English. The English courses were the home of the modern subjects. In these the high schools paralleled the proliferation of miscellaneous subjects found in the academies, including the range of "philosophies" and such strange-sounding subjects as "science of arithmetic." Bookkeeping appeared in many programs, and some high schools were adding manual training and household arts.

The larger schools presented pupils with a choice among three or more courses of study. The three-course pattern included a course variously called General, Latin, or Latin-Scientific. This was the Classical course with Greek left out and modern subjects added. In some schools a fourth course appeared, usually designated Modern Language, with German or French or both replacing the Latin of the General or Scientific course.[13] Additional courses were sometimes contrived and were designated by the names of the languages included, such as German-Latin or English-French. Courses called Commercial appeared when schools added subjects such as commercial law and commercial geography to the familiar offering in bookkeeping.

It was customary for pedagogical orators of the time to refer without discrimination both to the high schools and the academies as the people's colleges. The expression was accurate enough in at least one respect; most of the pupils went to no other. No figures were presented in the Commissioner's *Report* of 1884–1885 on the proportions of college-bound pupils in the city high schools. For the academies, less than 10 percent of the pupils were identified as preparing for college in either the Classical or the Scientific course.[14]

[13] The Jefferson Township High School, Cook County, Illinois, was one of those with a familiar four-course pattern, using the names Classical, General, Modern Language, and English. Its General course, with four years of Latin, but no Greek, was recommended "for those who do not expect to pursue Collegiate studies" and was believed to be "the best to select as a preparation for general business life." The English course was intended "for those who are averse to the study of 'Languages,'" but the announcement added that those who studied foreign languages were the best English scholars. In its second year was included a one-term class in "The Gates Ajar (Phelps)" and "Self-Help (Smiles)." "Fifth Annual Circular of Jefferson Township High School, Cook County, Illinois, for the Year Beginning September 5, 1887," James B. Angell Papers, Michigan Historical Collections (University of Michigan, Ann Arbor, Mich.).

[14] Commissioner, 1884–1885, pp. cl–cli. The *Report* added a special category of preparatory schools, 179 of them with 17,605 pupils. These were schools identified as giving special attention to preparation for college. Most of them were

For the most part, colleges did not depend on high schools and the ordinary academies to supply them with students. Admission was largely based on examinations, and these in a restricted range of subjects. The rigor of the examinations varied from one college to the next. Applicants did not have to present credits, and there were no stipulations about graduation from any kind of secondary school. It was possible to get ready for the examinations by private study or by attending a preparatory department of a given college. The connections between colleges and secondary schools were in consequence somewhat vague, and it was easy for colleges to maintain the isolation of which they were accused by the Massachusetts teachers.

On the other hand, neither the high schools nor the academies could ignore college requirements. Almost every one of them had at least a few college-bound pupils, and the principals were anxious to prepare these as well as possible for the examinations. Besides, they had the reputations of their schools to consider! They were also asking themselves and increasingly were being asked why more of their pupils did not seek further schooling. The members of the Massachusetts Classical and High School Teachers' Association were justified, therefore, in wanting the college officers to talk with them about matters they felt were of mutual concern.

The questions being raised about the relations between high schools and colleges testified to a growing awareness of both institutions. In September, 1880, the New England Publishing Company, with an ambitious educator named Thomas W. Bicknell as "conductor," launched a new journal, *Education,* on the strength of an apparently widespread interest in something called higher education. "Our first claim to public recognition and patronage," this journal stated in its first issue, "rests on the fact that the field which we propose to cover is but partially occupied. No educational paper or magazine in England or America proposes to devote itself exclusively to the domain of higher education, and to the philosophy which underlies all educational methods."[15] The term *higher education* was understood to include secondary schooling, although sometimes the high schools and the grades were thrown together into a category called the lower schools.

---

academies of the kind known as endowed preparatory schools. Of those pupils who had completed their work at these schools in 1884–1885, a total of 1,291 were identified as having gone to college. The entire number of those who had completed the work was not given. Commissioner, 1884–1885, p. cliii.

[15] "Editorial," *Education* (September, 1880), p. 88.

Six years later, in February, 1886, an organization called the Associated Academic Principals of the State of New York started a journal aimed especially at secondary schools. This new journal was called *The Academy: A Journal of Secondary Education.* "We propose," delared its editor, George A. Bacon, "to conduct a journal for those teaching youth in their teens, not forgetting the relation of that work with the earlier work, mindful also of the steps that may follow, but aiming chiefly, by suggestion and mutual aid, to raise the standard of secondary instruction and increase the efficiency of secondary schools."[16] Bacon, who was principal of the high school at Syracuse, New York, begged readers to overlook his mistakes, pointing out that the first number was issued "in the midst of examinations, promotions, and all the thousand details incident to the admission of an entering class and the reorganization of work for the second half of the school year."[17]

III

The decade began on a note of optimism. "We have entered upon an era of solid prosperity," proclaimed *Education* in 1880.[18] It was, at least, an age of promotion and expansion. For educators this was symbolized not only by the appearance of new journals but also by the rebirth of the National Educational Association at the Madison, Wisconsin, meeting in 1884. Although this organization dated back to 1857, its membership had remained small; only 300 or so had attended the national convention in Saratoga, New York, in 1883. The new president, elected for the following year, was Bicknell, editor of *Education* and prophet of prosperity. He set in motion such a gigantic publicity campaign that in 1884 the little convention city was almost buried under an attendance of seven thousand. "In 1884 a new era dawned upon the association," wrote one commentator seven years later.[19] The NEA grew so large that increasing use was made of its National Council of Education, a 60-member group of "leading educators" created for intensive study and discussion of educational questions.

Optimism about education was tempered, however, by criticism of the

[16] "Our First Word," *Academy* (February, 1886), p. 1.

[17] "Correspondence," *Academy* (February, 1886), p. 29.

[18] "Prosperity and Education," *Education* (November, 1880), p. 186.

[19] Z. Richards, "Historical Sketch of the National Educational Association," *Addresses and Proceedings of the National Educational Association, 1891* (Washington, D.C.: The Association, 1891), p. 128. [These volumes are referred to in subsequent notes as NEA with the appropriate year: for example, NEA, 1891.]

schools. Charles Francis Adams, Jr., descendant of presidents, had set the fashion for so-called lay criticism back in 1873 with his investigation of the grammar schools in his home town of Quincy, Massachusetts.[20] The changes he promoted in the Quincy schools had gained international fame as the Quincy plan. In 1883 Adams castigated the colleges for their devotion to Greek and their failure, as he saw it, to prepare their graduates for modern life.[21] These criticisms gained sympathetic response from many who were directly involved in the business of keeping school. Francis Parker, the professional educator brought in by Adams to effect the Quincy innovations, was rapidly becoming the hero of teachers identified with something called the New Education. The assaults of Adams on the colleges similarly evoked applause from educators who were demanding what they called practical reforms.

A more caustic and, from the point of view of school men, less constructive critic was Richard Grant White, who in 1880 charged that the public school system had failed "completely to accomplish the end for which it was established." Not only were most of the pupils "unable to read intelligently, to spell correctly, to write legibly, to describe understandingly the geography of their own country, or to do anything that reasonably well-educated children should do with ease," but public schooling in addition led to idleness, political corruption, and crime. He clinched his point to his satisfaction with statistics allegedly showing more crime in New England, with all its public schools, than in the South. Moreover, the whole business was expensive and in 1870 had cost more than $64 million. His remedy was in "a discontinuation of any other education at the public cost than that which is strictly elementary . . . and in the remission of all education higher than this to the parents." This was hardly an encouraging suggestion to those interested in public high schools, although he allowed for "some jealously guarded provision for the higher education of pupils who have exceptional ability and show special aptitude and taste for science and literature."[22]

School men were sensitive to what they regarded as hostile criticism.

[20] See Charles Francis Adams, Jr., *The New Departure in the Common Schools of Quincy and Other Papers on Educational Topics* (Boston: Estes and Lauriat, 1879), pp. 31–51.

[21] Charles Francis Adams, Jr., *A College Fetich,* an Address delivered before the Harvard chapter of the Fraternity of the Phi Beta Kappa in Sanders Theatre, Cambridge, Mass., June 28, 1883 (Boston: Lee and Shepard, 1883).

[22] Richard Grant White, "The Public-School Failure," *North American Review* (December, 1880), pp. 537–550.

An editorial in *Education* in 1887 probably expressed the feelings of many in declaring the age to be one "of indiscriminate and unwarranted fault-finding with the schools and the teachers." The critics were charged with holding the schools responsible "for all the evils now existing or anticipated, from the election of President Cleveland to the troubles of the fishery question and the refuge of so many defaulters in Canada."[23] Whether or not anybody really blamed the schools for the election of President Cleveland, there was a tendency to relate much of the criticism to a larger background of political, social, and economic affairs. School men were ready with answers. To the charge that people were being educated above their station, Principal Oscar D. Robinson of the Albany, New York, High School replied "that character and intelligence should determine station, and to develop these is the aim of our high school."[24] Fears of revolution from an educated proletariat were met by educators with the familiar and time-tested arguments that schooling produced better citizens and that popular government demanded citizens who had been to school, and preferably to high school.

In stressing the contributions of education to orderly government, the educators were touching a sensitive nerve in American public life. Despite the peace and prosperity of the times, there was apprehension about radical ideas and movements, and particularly—after the Haymarket Riot in Chicago in 1886—about those labeled anarchistic. Victor Lawson, proprietor of the *Chicago Daily News,* established a Public School Patriotic Fund of $10,000, the income from which was set aside for medals to be awarded for essays on patriotism. "Was ten thousand dollars ever more wisely invested?" asked one admirer, who went on to state that a boy who won a silver medal had entered the school two years before with an anarchist flag in his buttonhole.[25] A school man from New Orleans cried out in 1885 that a mob spirit was abroad in the land. He saw the possibility of "a mighty conflagration" of social conflict, but, like other educators, had the remedy in hand, namely, "a system of uniform, well-organized, and liberally supported public schools," adding that "the high schools, especially, should be the objects of the first solicitude."[26]

To many the fear of radicalism was linked to a fear of foreigners. Already abroad was the view of the early immigrants as industrious, or-

---

[23] "Editorial," *Education* (June, 1887), p. 722.
[24] Oscar D. Robinson, as quoted in "Editorial," *Education* (March, 1887), pp. 513–514.
[25] Mary E. Beedy, "Miscellany," *Education* (September, 1888), pp. 59–60.
[26] J. E. Seaman, "High Schools and the State," NEA, 1885, p. 175

derly, and law-abiding, in contrast to the more recent immigrants, characterized by a teacher from Philadelphia's Central High School as "alien in race and sympathies, or revolutionary in tendencies." He quickly made the point that "against the subversive influence of this element our common school is our tower of strength."[27] The high school in particular, declared a speaker in 1885, should be "fully sustained" to meet "the danger to this country . . . in the mass of uneducated people pouring into it from abroad."[28]

With such concerns as these in evidence, the preoccupation of the members of the Massachusetts Classical and High School Teachers' Association with the behavior of college officials may suggest a peculiar lack of awareness about what was going on in the world. Such a judgment, however, would be wide of the mark. Relations between colleges and secondary schools reflected the times in the context of the social and economic aspirations of parents for their children. Surrounded by anarchists and foreigners they might be, but Americans still wanted their children to get ahead in life. Whether or not attending high school would help in this was therefore a question of the utmost importance. Closely related to it was the question of the high school as a road to college for pupils who did not plan their studies specifically for college entrance. From another point of view, there were fears, expressed perhaps more by school men than parents, that the attention given to the few pupils who were preparing for college examinations might lead to the neglect of the many who, in the parlance of the times, were preparing not for college, but for life.

IV

Although high school attendance increased throughout the 1880's, the figure of 202,963 pupils in public high schools reported by the Commissioner for 1889–1890 represented less than 1 percent of the total population.[29] It was a rare thing to go to high school. The question then arises, Who did go? On one point the answer is clear—more girls than boys. According to the Commissioner's statistics in the 1889–1890 *Report,* 57.6 percent of the pupils and 64.8 percent of the graduates were

[27] George Stuart, "The Raison d'Etre of the Public High School," *Education* (January, 1888), p. 286.

[28] D. D. Metcalf, discussion, NEA, 1885, p. 180.

[29] Elmer E. Brown, *The Making of Our Middle Schools* (New York: Longmans, Green & Co., 1902), p. 468.

girls. In contrast, the private secondary schools showed about equal numbers of boys and girls enrolled.[30] The relative scarcity of public high schools in rural areas indicated that the high school population of the 1880's was largely representative of city youth. About intellectual qualifications little is known except that many high schools required applicants to take entrance examinations.

What the high schools represented in the way of social and economic selection became a matter of much controversy. They were attacked as institutions for the well-to-do supported by taxes on the poor. The Commissioner presented no figures on this point, but school men tried to refute the charge by making studies in local communities. In 1883 one writer brought together data on more than 1000 pupils in five Massachusetts communities, showing that one-fourth of the pupils were children of parents who paid only a poll tax or no tax at all, whereas only one-seventh had parents paying a tax (unspecified) on more than $10,000. "Does this prove," he queried, "that the high school is the school of the rich? Is it not rather the school of the poor, or at least of those who are worth but little besides the house that shelters them? The assertion, then, that in the high school the money of the poor man is paying for the education of the rich is defective in this one respect—it isn't true."[31]

Along the same lines, the principal of a midwestern high school, that of Lake View Township, Illinois, contended in 1887 that the majority of the graduates were "the children of those whom some were pleased to call the common people," half the pupils representing families who were not householders and less than one-quarter being "from homes where wealth abounds."[32] In 1889 the principal of the high school at Erie, Pennsylvania, reported that of 347 pupils in his school there were 200, or 57.6 percent, whose parents had property assessments of less than $500, including 54, or 15.5 percent, having no property assessment whatsoever. At the other extreme there were 111 pupils, or 32 percent, whose parents had property assessments ranging from $1,500 to a somewhat staggering figure of $32,000. Although this report did not disclose the procedure used in making these assessments, it indicated that high school pupils in Erie came from homes representing a wide range of eco-

[30] Commissioner, 1889–1890, II, pp. 1388–1389 and 1486–1487.

[31] John O. Norris, "The High School in Our System of Education," *Education* (March, 1883), p. 332.

[32] Lake View Township High School, Cook County, Illinois, *Thirteenth Annual Report,* year ending June 23, 1887, p. 10.

nomic circumstances.[33] In the Middle West the principal of the high school in Adrian, Michigan, identified 23 of his 151 pupils as children of farmers, 17 of railroad employees, 18 of widows, 13 of manufacturers, 6 of carpenters, 6 of traveling men, and 6 of physicians, and numbers of less than 6 apiece as children of a variety of small businessmen, such as butchers, saloonkeepers, and druggists.[34]

It was, in fact, one of the most cherished convictions among school men that high schools not only were free of class distinctions but also served to break down such distinctions where they did exist. "Here the children of the rich and the poor, the lords and the peasants, exercising a healthful influence upon one another, are fed from the same table," proclaimed one principal back in 1876.[35] A city superintendent in 1881 said: "It is necessary, then, to *abolish caste*. . . . Let the doors of the school-house, the 'brain factory,' be open to all the children; and the child once started on the career of learning, let him not find those doors ever closed against him till, if he so elects, he shall have completed not merely the course of study in the common English branches, but in the English high school, the scientific school, or the college."[36] One high school principal showed that when he said *caste,* he meant caste, by declaring: "Cut off from the masses the boon of higher education . . . and we take the first step in separating the people of our country into castes as permanent and as sharply defined, if not as numerous, as those of India."[37]

With such a point of view as this, school men, along with many of their fellow citizens, worried much about the low survival rate of children in the grades and in high school. The 202,963 pupils in high schools in 1889–1890 included only 21,882, or 10.7 percent, who had been graduated or had finished their courses that year.[38] State reports ran along similar lines. Wisconsin in 1884 had 7,531 pupils in high school, but only 475 graduates, or 6 percent of the total.[39] In 1890 Ohio re-

[33] H. C. Missimer, "Something for the Educational Iconoclast," *Academy* (April, 1889), p. 121.
[34] "Notes," *Academy* (March, 1891), p. 114.
[35] Lake View Township High School, Cook County, Illinois, *Second Annual Report,* year ending June, 1876, p. 6.
[36] W. A. Mowry, "The School Curriculum and Its Relations to Business Life," *Education* (November, 1881), p. 149.
[37] Missimer, *op. cit.,* p. 121.
[38] Commissioner, 1889–1890, II, pp. 1388–1389.
[39] "Editorial," *Wisconsin Journal of Education* (July, 1885), p. 299.

ported 13,995 pupils enrolled but only 1,089, or 8 percent of the total, graduated.[40] Not only did few youths enter the high school, but fewer still remained.

Possibly the drop-out rate was high among those whose parents had the lower property assessments, but educators who believed that their schools served the poor as well as the rich were not in a good position to use this as an explanation. Discussions of the question, therefore, tended to center on the suitability of existing high school programs. What was needed, argued many, was a more practical course of study, particularly for those who had to earn their living immediately after finishing high school. For many girls there was a specific vocational goal, namely, teaching in the grammar grades. The rest of the girls, ran the contention, and almost all the boys, could look forward only to college, or to the business and industrial world for which they were unprepared. Even the girls who married, it was further contended, were poorly prepared for household duties and for motherhood.

Although the intensive drive for industrial education lay nearly two decades in the future, there was a substantial amount of demand among educators and other public leaders during the 1880's for manual training and business subjects. The governor of Pennsylvania chose his inaugural address as the occasion for arguing that "the main fault of our present system is, that it leads directly and inevitably to that which is abstract, and away from that which is practical. It deals in words and signs, and not with facts and things. The graduate of our average high school, as all experience proves, is educated away from what are called industrial pursuits, and into a fitness for those employments which involve only mental training."[41] Some practical work, however, did exist. The Commissioner's *Report* for 1884–1885 reviewed the work in manual training not only in private schools but also in city public schools, such as those in Boston; Newark and Montclair, New Jersey; Peru, Illinois; Minneapolis; and Eau Claire, Wisconsin.[42] Business subjects, especially bookkeeping, existed in many high schools. The demand, however, was for more such work, in more places, and for more pupils.

Nevertheless, the circumstances of the 1880's were not favorable to vocationalism. Advocates of manual training, including even such a national figure as C. M. Woodward of the Manual Training High School

[40] James H. Blodgett, "Secondary Education in Census Years," *School and College* (January, 1892), p. 18.
[41] As quoted in Missimer, *op. cit.*, p. 115.
[42] Commissioner, 1884–1885, pp. ccvi–ccxvii.

of Washington University, St. Louis, argued their case less on the grounds of vocational training than on those of educating the whole boy.[43] Among public school educators, Principal Ray Greene Huling of Fitchburg, Massachusetts, favored manual training but was opposed to direct preparation for specialized trades.[44] Neither was there a clear demand for vocational training on the part of the public. The Springfield, Massachusetts, High School, for example, inaugurated a two-year business course in 1885. Forty pupils of the 367 enrolled in the school started this program in the first year, but this group produced only 15 graduates two years later. Subsequent graduating classes from this two-year program declined to eleven pupils in 1888, to seven in 1889, and to five in 1890, and the program was dropped in 1893. A manual-training school established there in 1886–1887 likewise attracted only small enrollments.[45] On the other hand, an enthusiastic report from Toledo, Ohio, pointed to increasing enrollments in the boys' program of its manual-training department since its establishment in 1884 and in the girls' program since the beginning of that work in 1886.[46]

Although local circumstances undoubtedly had much to do with responses to such programs, the demand for the practical tended to remain somewhat inconclusive. It was, however, loud and insistent and by no means directed only to the high schools. "Practical arithmetics, grammars, readers, and books of all kinds are in demand. Teachers at educational gatherings are hungering and thirsting for the practical. The profession of teaching has fairly run mad in search of the royal road which leads to the practical." So ran an editorial back in 1882.[47] There were perennial debates about the value of a college education, and college officials did not hesitate to defend their programs on the grounds that

[43] C. M. Woodward, "The Results of the St. Louis Manual Training Schools," NEA, 1889, pp. 73–91.

[44] Ray Greene Huling, "The American High School," *Education* (September, 1883), pp. 63–73.

[45] Gladys A. Midura, *A Critical History of Public Secondary Education in Springfield, Massachusetts* (Doctoral dissertation, University of Connecticut, 1961), p. 150. This was an early example of the failure of the people to respond to what some speakers and writers said the people were demanding. Then, as later, the proposed cure was to convince the people that they really wanted vocational education after all. The *Springfield Daily Republican* (Massachusetts) on April 6, 1896, pointed out that industrial education had to be sold both to the public and to the educators. Cited *ibid.*, pp. 159–160.

[46] H. C. Adams, "Domestic Economy for High Schools," *Academy* (May, 1890), p. 193.

[47] "The Practical," *Education* (January, 1882), p. 308.

they, too, led to practical success. Such a mood had ample justification. The period was one of industrial and business expansion, with ruthless competition, fantastic rewards for success, and, in some quarters at least, little sympathy for failure. Under such circumstances it was to be expected that the demand for the practical would be strenuously expressed; it was also understandable that it would remain vague, since no one could prove the superior merits of one kind of schooling over another for economic advancement.

The demand took many forms and involved matters other than worldly success. It was in part a manifestation of the very human and continuing tendency to direct school training toward a broad range of contingencies, especially the one or ones with which a given writer or speaker was at the moment most concerned. Among the school men who took issue with this, William T. Harris declared it "an error frequently made, to demand of the school all kinds of education—education for trades and business, education in religion, education in politics and statesmanship, education in habits which the nurture of the family should supply."[48] J. W. Macdonald, high school principal at Stoneham, Massachusetts, made an almost savage attack on these tendencies. Commenting on the demands of ministers for moral education, medical men for physical training, and temperance leaders for temperance education, he noted that "large numbers of children gathered daily into school rooms furnish tempting fields, if access to them can be obtained, to every hobby-horse rider and gibbous-headed reformer for doing what each considers the *sine qua non* in reforming the world."[49] Neither Macdonald nor Harris, however, could moderate the desires of their fellow citizens, including many of their fellow educators, to use the schools for reforming the world or for hosts of other good causes. In short, the simple business of keeping school—particularly a high school—was not so simple as it would look retrospectively to a later age.

Educators might deplore some of the specific demands made upon them, but for the most part they welcomed the changing times as opening new opportunities and responsibilities for the schools. Progress was a magic word in the 1880's, and the schools must have their share in it. "To conduct any kind of mercantile or manufacturing business successfully today, and for twenty-five years to come," wrote Superintendent

---

[48] William T. Harris, "The Education of the Family, and the Education of the School," *Journal of Social Science* (February, 1882), p. 1.
[49] J. W. Macdonald, "Educating the Whole Boy," NEA, 1888, p. 416.

W. A. Mowry of Providence, Rhode Island, in 1881, "will require a far greater discipline of mind, a more liberal culture, a more generous scholarship than were necessary a generation ago."[50] Edward S. Joynes of the University of Tennessee saw educational discussion and experiment as everywhere "the order of the day" and predicted even greater things ahead. "With undoubting faith in human progress and human destiny," he proclaimed, "as we survey the wonders and promise of the age in which we live, let us give glory to the century that is past, and hail! all hail! to the century that is to come."[51] The headmaster of Rutgers College Grammar School contented himself with the relatively moderate announcement that "the new era, the era of new things, is seemingly upon us."[52]

---

[50] Mowry, *op. cit.,* p. 149.
[51] Edward S. Joynes, "A Southern View of Education," *Education* (September, 1880), pp. 77 and 83.
[52] E. T. Tomlinson, "Progress in Teaching the Classics," *Education* (March, 1885), p. 400.

Chapter 2

Toward the Committee of Ten

"Think again of the different views entertained as
to the purpose of the high school itself."
—PRINCIPAL E. W. COY,
JULY 19, 1889.

*O*ratory proclaimed the advent of a new era, but the destiny of the high school was by no means clear. Beginning in 1887, events brought together the major figures who would seek to clarify it. At the July 11 session of the National Council of Education, Principal James H. Baker of the Denver High School seized the occasion to move "a thorough investigation" of the "rational selection and order of high-school studies with reference to uniformity in high-school work, and consequent uniformity in requirements for admission to college."[1] The following winter, on February 16, 1888, President Eliot of Harvard commanded the attention of the NEA in a forceful address to the Department of Superintendence on the work of elementary and secondary schools. In 1889 William T. Harris, former superintendent of schools at St. Louis, forsook his retirement at Concord, Massachusetts, to become the fourth Commissioner of Education of the United States. Two years later, in 1891, a young professor of philosophy at Columbia University, Nicholas Murray Butler, became a member of the National Council, thereby gaining a foothold for his ascent into the higher regions of the NEA.

It was Eliot who most effectively inspired and irritated people on the widest front. For at least a quarter of a century to come, discussion of public schooling, and of high schools in particular, was to involve being for or against something Eliot had said. To many it seemed a curious thing that a president of Harvard should occupy himself not only with the broad policies of the public schools but also with the most minute

---

[1] National Council of Education, Report of Secretary, NEA, 1887, p. 260.

details of their subjects and methods. Yet it was much in keeping with his background and personality. Shortly after his graduation from Harvard in 1853 Eliot had taught a night class at the Pitts Street School (his only teaching below the college level) and had served as a member of the Boston Primary School Committee. As a young assistant professor in mathematics and chemistry at Harvard he had experimented with methods of teaching, and when he went to Europe in 1863 for graduate work in chemistry, he spent much of his time studying educational policies and practices in Germany and France. In 1869, the year in which he left the Massachusetts Institute of Technology to become Harvard's president, Eliot published two articles espousing the cause of the modern subjects, especially English.[2]

All this was evidence of Eliot's intellectual and personal interest in the everyday work of schools. His critics, however, saw it in a different light. He was considered meddlesome at Harvard, and there were school men who felt that he had decided to meddle with the public schools as well. At one of the meetings of the Massachusetts State Teachers' Association, for example, Eliot's address "evoked," in the words of an unidentified reporter to the *Academy,* "the fiercest storm of denunciation that we have witnessed in some time." Significantly, the storm broke out not in the open session, but immediately afterwards, "when President Eliot's modest strictures were characterized as shameful and insulting and he himself was accused of insincerity, untruthfulness and various other characteristics not ordinarily possessed by a college president."[3]

Eliot's opening remarks in his speech to the NEA Department of Superintendence in 1888 seemed to support an accusation that was made frequently, that he wanted to change the public schools for the benefit of Harvard. He began by calling attention to the advancing age of entrants to that institution. College men, he declared, wanted school work shortened to permit "boys" to come to college at eighteen instead of nineteen, and they wanted it "enriched" so that these same boys might "bring to college at eighteen more than they now bring at

---

[2] Charles W. Eliot, "The New Education: Its Organization," *Atlantic Monthly* (February, 1869), pp. 203–220 (March, 1869), pp. 358–367.

[3] "The Massachusetts State Teachers' Association," *Academy* (January, 1891), pp. 558–559. On the other hand, one of the leaders of the Massachusetts Classical and High School Teachers' Association said: Eliot "has been almost constantly with us, a most original, stimulating, inspiring, and I may almost say, provoking force." [Samuel Thurber], "Opening Remarks by the President," *Academy* (May, 1892), pp. 190–191.

nineteen, so that the standard of the A.B. may not be lowered."[4] This unfortunate beginning, at least for school men suspicious of college domination, was partly corrected by his pointing out the "broader scope" of his remarks, namely, his conviction that improving the schools for the college-bound would also do so "for the less fortunate children whose education is to be briefer."[5] To justify his contention that programs could be both shortened and enriched, he called for the elimination of what he considered useless work, especially in arithmetic, a subject he regarded with particular abhorrence,[6] and for improvement in methods of teaching.

Before finishing this address, he managed to get himself in trouble in several other directions. He dwelt on what he felt to be the superiority of French and German schools to those in the United States, suggesting that the way to get better teaching in our country was to increase the proportion of male teachers.[7] Although he related this to the tendency of women to undertake teaching as a temporary occupation only, he left the impression, as he did on other occasions, that he believed women to be intellectually inferior to men. Finally, he suggested longer school hours and shorter vacations.[8]

This was hardly an auspicious entry into the national arena of public schooling, but Eliot preferred to make his views as plain and direct as possible, a virtue not always appreciated in an age of exaggerated rhetoric. Still it was an entry, and from this time on Eliot was to play a major role in the work of the NEA. Perhaps he stimulated an overwhelming curiosity in what he was going to say next. At any rate, the NEA and other groups in public schooling sought eagerly to give him every opportunity to say it.

In part, at least, the interest of school men in Eliot had been aroused by what he preferred to call the elective principle, but which unfortunately had become known as the elective system. He had not originated electives at Harvard, but he gave the idea his enthusiastic approval. This reflected his preoccupation with the expansion of knowledge that had taken place in the nineteenth century and his feeling that it was no longer

[4] Charles W. Eliot, "Can School Programmes Be Shortened and Enriched?" *Proceedings of the Department of Superintendence of the National Educational Association* (U.S. Bureau of Education Circular No. 6 [Washington, D.C. 1888]), pp. 101–102.

[5] *Ibid.*, p. 103.

[6] *Ibid.*, pp. 108–109.

[7] *Ibid.*, pp. 104–106.

[8] *Ibid.*, p. 110.

possible to make uniform programs for all college students. A less flattering interpretation, taken by some, was that electives served the cause of making Harvard easier for the newly rich of the Gilded Age.[9]

Increasingly, however, Eliot based the elective principle on his belief that mental discipline was best developed when people worked intensively on a few subjects which they liked and in which they had some talent. Electives, therefore, did not mean to him an aimless scattering of subjects, but an opportunity for the individual to pursue the subject or subjects to which he was best suited. Accordingly, he began to promote electives not only in the college, but also in the secondary and even the elementary schools.[10]

His identification with electives exposed Eliot to numerous attacks, not only from the Harvard faculty, but also from others. In the presidential address at the Madison meeting of the NEA in 1884, Bicknell saw the colleges "liable to go to pieces on the rocks and shoals of elective studies."[11] An editorial in *Education* in 1886 said that the public was weary of this "hobby" and "vagary" of the Harvard president.[12] Another writer that year attacked Eliot's ideas in an article entitled "The 'New Education' Run Mad."[13] There were few, if any, school men in the 1880's who shared Eliot's views on electives, especially as applied to the elementary and secondary schools. The idea was regarded as sufficiently outrageous, however, to keep them constantly aware of the man with whom it was associated.

The appearance of Eliot as a national leader in elementary and secondary education aroused mixed emotions and responses. On the one hand he seemed to represent the alleged autocracy of Harvard, the aristocracy of his Brahmin background, and the so-called traditional domination and aloofness of college men; on the other he appeared as a champion of the modern academic subjects, although this was interpreted by some as a desire to enroll schools in the cause of industrial and commercial expansion. Worst of all he was a radical whose elective

[9] See Charles A. and Mary R. Beard, *The Rise of American Civilization* (New York: Macmillan Co., 1930), II, 471–472.

[10] Charles W. Eliot, "Undesirable and Desirable Uniformity in Schools," NEA, 1892, p. 90.

[11] Thomas W. Bicknell, "The President's Address: the Annual Address before the National Educational Association of the United States, at Madison, Wis., July 18, 1884," *Education* (January, 1885), p. 295.

[12] *Education* (March, 1886), p. 452.

[13] Charles H. Levermore, "The 'New Education' Run Mad," *Education* (January, 1886), pp. 290–298.

principle threatened to destroy academic traditions. Little wonder, then, that he perplexed and confused most of the school men, not only in the late 1880's but also in the following decades.

Quite different was the response to William Torrey Harris, who, assuming his office as Commissioner on September 12, 1889, was, at least in one of his many images, a practical school man himself. From the point of view of those who toiled at the daily tasks of keeping school, Harris had earned the right to speak on such matters by serving successively in the St. Louis public schools as elementary teacher and principal, assistant superintendent, and, finally, superintendent. Born at North Killingly, Connecticut, in 1835, he had emigrated to the West in 1857. His formal schooling included three years at Yale, but he had left without finishing his course or taking his degree, presumably dissatisfied with the narrowness of the classical course. With or without a degree, Harris possessed the qualities needed to be appointed superintendent in 1868 and to carry out his duties in that post.

There was, however, another side to his personality, and he resigned his superintendency in 1880 to devote himself to scholarship in philosophy and letters. Already known as a leading exponent of Hegelian philosophy in America, he expressed his views through the *Journal of Speculative Philosophy,* which he had founded in 1867 as a means of offsetting the popularity in this country of Herbert Spencer. After his resignation as superintendent he returned to New England, joining Bronson Alcott in the School of Philosophy at Concord, Massachusetts, and serving for three years (1882–1885), at the special request of the citizenry, as superintendent of the Concord schools. He devoted himself to studies of Dante and in 1889 published *The Spiritual Sense of Dante's Divina Commedia.* It was from this official, but only partial, retirement that he was called by President Benjamin Harrison to become Commissioner of Education.

By this time Harris, like Eliot, was known as a proponent of the modern academic studies. As was also true of Eliot, this did not imply antagonism to Latin and Greek, for Harris had long since modified his earlier attitude of indifference to the classics and was even defending their right to survival in the curriculum. Harris believed in both modern and classical studies for passing on the wisdom of the race. While he supported the disciplinary value of certain subjects for training the will, he did not attach much importance to mental discipline and later disparaged formal training in the report of the Committee of Fifteen. He loved to refer to the school subjects as the windows of the soul. Like many of his fellow educators of this period, he was an enemy of "caste," and he dismissed the accusation that people were being dangerously educated beyond their station in life. His answer to the charge that schools made people discontented was not to deny it, but to insist that it was good. "The critics of our educational system are never done with telling us that its results are to make the rising generation discontented with its lot. As if this were a defect rather than the greatest glory of the educational system."[14] At the same time he believed in education as a stabilizing force and pointed out that "if you wish property safe from confiscation by a majority composed of communists, you must see to it that the people are educated so that each sees the sacredness of property and its service to the world in making available to each the industry of the entire population of the earth."[15]

The only possible flaw at that time in Harris' reputation as a forward-looking educator, at least to some, was his lack of enthusiasm for, and ambivalent attitude toward, the ascending star of manual training in the schools. This had drawn Harris into a controversy with Calvin M. Woodward of the Manual Training High School of Washington University, which culminated in a widely publicized interchange between the two men at the NEA convention in 1889, on the very eve of Harris' induction as Commissioner. The controversy was in part a reflection of the confusion between manual training and vocational education and in part of the militant temperaments of both Harris and Woodward. Harris already had a reputation of being a fierce opponent on the battlegrounds of NEA platforms, and Woodward, like other promoters of causes, had long felt that those who were not for his special interest were against it.

Woodward, like Harris, was a New Englander who had emigrated to the West, coming to Washington University, St. Louis, in 1865 as a teacher of Latin, Greek, and mathematics. His background included a bachelor's degree from Harvard, a brief period as a high school principal, and military experience in the Civil War. At Washington University he moved first to mathematics and then to mathematics and drawing; after making one more move to mathematics and applied

[14] William T. Harris, "Does the Common School Educate Children above the Station They Are Expected to Occupy in Life?" *Education* (May, 1883), p. 475.
[15] *Ibid.*, p. 466.

mechanics, he became dean of the newly created School of Engineering in 1871. He introduced shop work for the engineering students and was ready, along with others, to be impressed at the Philadelphia Centennial in 1876 by the Russian exhibits of work from their Imperial Technical Schools. In 1879 he started the Manual Training High School of Washington University.[16] Woodward was no enemy of academic studies, and his school included substantial work in these fields, as well as in manual training.

He became, however, an increasingly ardent, almost belligerent, enthusiast for the cause. By 1883 he was announcing that "one by one the outposts have fallen into our hands, and only a few citadels remain. An armistice has been asked for, and, if we can only arrange satisfactorily the terms of an honorable capitulation, the enemy is willing to march out and join our ranks."[17] He urged those who shared his views to lay their plans before "wealthy public-spirited men" in their communities. "Almost for the first time in America," he said, "we are harvesting a splendid crop of millionaires. They abound in every city."[18] Although insisting that manual training had vocational value, Woodward did not urge the subject on vocational grounds. Rather he demanded it as the rounding out of liberal education. "Manual training is essential to the right and full development of the human mind."[19] He was a persuasive speaker, and he won a particularly enthusiastic reception for his views when he addressed the general session of the NEA meeting at Chicago in 1887.[20]

In view of the position he took on the matter, Woodward was bound to be sensitive about the confusion in the minds of some between trade schools and his school at St. Louis. In his address to the NEA Department of Superintendence on March 6, 1889, he insisted emphatically

[16] "Calvin Milton Woodward," *School Journal* (January 5, 1895), p. 16.
[17] C. M. Woodward, "The Function of an American Manual Training School," *Education* (May, 1883), p. 517.
[18] *Ibid.,* p. 533.
[19] C. M. Woodward, "Manual Training in General Education," *Education* (July, 1885), p. 615.
[20] C. M. Woodward, "The Function of the Public School," NEA, 1887, pp. 212–224. In the discussion period, one of the participants called for a voice vote on the importance of manual training in public education. After hearing the *ayes,* this member declared it a favorable vote. Woodward, however, was not satisfied. The presiding officer restated the question, and this time there was "a unanimous response." *Ibid.,* pp. 234 and 237.

that a manual-training school was not a trade school.[21] On the following day Harris, speaking on the same general topic, cast doubt on the general value of manual training, but expressed qualified approval of it for vocational purposes. Even in this context he granted it only limited value, since, he declared, not more than 8 percent of employed people worked with metals or wood.[22] At the end of his address, Harris declared that whether manual-training schools should become industrial schools for trade training or be incorporated into the school system depended "upon the answer which educational psychology finally gives to the question."[23]

The discussion was resumed that summer at the Nashville meeting of the NEA: Harris reported as chairman of the Committee on Pedagogics of the National Council, and he and Woodward each gave a speech at a general session. Harris' report at the National Council declared "the moral education" in manual training to be a "far greater educational factor than the intellectual factor"[24] and particularly urged the development of industrial drawing.[25] In his general session address, Harris accorded "a permanently valid place" to manual-training schools for specific vocational training, but expressed doubt that manual training as a subject opened "any new windows of the soul."[26] It was with this bland skepticism about the general value of manual training that Woodward became most irritated and impatient. In his own speech, he again made a case for manual training on intellectual grounds and noted with pride that 87 of the 239 graduates of his St. Louis school had gone to college.[27]

As was often true of NEA controversies, there was no clear-cut decision on the field of battle itself. The continued growth of manual

[21] C. M. Woodward, "Relation of Manual Training to Body and Mind," *Proceedings of the Department of Superintendence of the National Educational Association* (U.S. Bureau of Education Circular No. 2 [Washington, D.C., 1889]), pp. 102–110.
[22] William T. Harris, "The Psychology of Manual Training," *Proceedings of the Department of Superintendence of the National Educational Association* (U.S. Bureau of Education Circular No. 2 [Washington, D.C., 1889]), pp. 129–130.
[23] *Ibid.*, p. 132.
[24] National Council of Education, Report of the Committee on Pedagogics, "The Educational Value of Manual Training," NEA, 1889, p. 421.
[25] *Ibid.*, p. 423.
[26] William T. Harris, "The Intellectual Value of Tool-Work," NEA, 1889, p. 97.
[27] C. M. Woodward, "The Results of the St. Louis Manual Training School," NEA, 1889, p. 74.

training in the schools may have indicated a practical victory for Woodward, but it did not resolve the issues under discussion. So far as Harris was concerned, he may have left the impression of being opposed to progress. Perhaps this marked the beginning of what eventually became his reputation as a traditionalist. There does not seem to have been any marked animosity between the two men on personal grounds, or if there was, Harris tried to conceal it. During the winter following the Nashville debate, Harris wrote several cordial letters to Woodward, explaining in one of them that he was critical not of manual-training schools but of manual training when held up as "a complete education," adding, "I cannot say that you have ever made any such claims for it."[28] In April, 1890, he wrote to Eliot praising Woodward for his "public services in the cause of education and scholarship" and recommended that Harvard grant him an honorary degree.[29]

Woodward's choice for Commissioner, however, had been not Harris, but Butler, and he had replied favorably to Charles H. Ham, an advocate of manual training, who was conducting a large volume of correspondence on Butler's behalf.[30] At that time, Butler was president of a philanthropic organization known as the Industrial Education Association of New York and had persuaded this group to establish the New York College for the Training of Teachers, subsequently Teachers College of Columbia University. He was pursuing a multitude of interests, and manual training was only one of them. His views on the disciplinary values of the subject, however, were similar to Woodward's. Nevertheless he had already attached himself to Harris and had attended a brief summer session at the School of Philosophy in Concord. According to his memoirs, Butler was actually offered the commissionership and, on declining, recommended Harris for it.[31] Certainly by 1891 Butler was far more concerned about his career in the NEA than he had been about the commissionership, if indeed he had been interested at all in what up to that time had been a somewhat nebulous and inconclusive position in the affairs of American schools.

[28] William T. Harris to C. M. Woodward, January 22, 1890, Letters sent by Office of Commissioner of Education 1870–1908 (National Archives, Record Group 12).
[29] William T. Harris to C. W. Eliot, April 2, 1890, Letters sent by Office of Commissioner of Education 1870–1908 (National Archives, Record Group 12).
[30] C. M. Woodward to Charles Ham, February 2, 1889, Nicholas Murray Butler Paper (Columbiana Library, Columbia University, New York, N.Y.)
[31] Nicholas Murray Butler, *Across the Busy Years* (New York: Charles Scribner's Sons, 1939), I, 189–190.

II

The NEA was clearly becoming the national arena for discussions of, and attempts to resolve, questions involving the secondary schools. Nerve centers of the NEA for this purpose were the Department of Secondary Education and the National Council. Much scorn has been directed against this latter group as an elite organization set apart from the general membership. Nevertheless, it was true that such a group of 60 people could pursue questions with a degree of attention not feasible in the larger NEA assemblies. Bicknell, who in 1884 had promoted the NEA into a large organization, was also the one who had instigated the creation of the National Council back in 1880; critics may have suspected him of developing the conditions that justified his earlier creation. At any rate, the Council was available for use, and it was at its 1887 session that the formerly unknown principal of the Denver High School, James H. Baker, put through his resolution calling for a study of uniformity in high school programs and admission requirements of colleges.

Baker's resolution stressed the matter of uniformity, but in the context of developing more effective relationships between colleges and high schools. It was in the same context that the New England Association had been organized two years before. Much had been made of an alleged choice between preparing for college and preparing for life, with the assumption that these were quite different things. Preparation for life was then, as it has been over many decades since, a slogan with much appeal, but exclusive commitment to it in the sense implied would have meant closing the doors of the college against thousands of American youth. Most high schools therefore tried to do both, but made a sharp distinction between the work of "finishing" pupils and those who were "fitting" for college work ahead. Although the distinction was widely accepted, the reasons for it were by no means clear. Its continued existence presented difficulties in practice to school men and their pupils alike.

Some of the prevailing convictions and their related difficulties were reviewed for the Council in its 1887 session by Principal E. W. Coy of the Hughes High School, Cincinnati, in a report for the Committee on Secondary Education. Evidently it was this report that stimulated Baker's resolution directing the committee to a further pursuit of the subject. In his presentation Coy testified to the popular belief that it was not the main purpose of high schools to prepare pupils for college and pointed out that "but few high schools in the country can count ten per cent. of their entering classes among those who intend to continue their studies beyond the high school." Nevertheless, he added, such preparation "was widely recognized" as a "legitimate and important part" of the high school's work.[32] A more satisfactory adjustment of the two aims was needed; to bring this about, thought Coy, would require closer relations between the better high schools and the better colleges.[33]

The discussion of this report on the floor of the Council reflected a tendency to leave things as they were, at least with regard to the duality of aims and their corresponding courses of study. Apparently Coy felt that he had not stated his points explicitly enough; near the end of the discussion he called the attention of the Council to the specific difficulties faced by the pupils in high schools. "It is very desirable," he argued, "that there should be college courses that will meet the ordinary high school courses; for many pupils who enter the high school with no intention of going further, decide, when half or three fourths of the way through the school, to take a college course. They receive, in the high school, the impulse or inspiration that leads them to this decision. Unless there be such courses in the college, it is necessary for the student to go back and begin a new course of study in the high school that will fit him to enter college. This is very often entirely impracticable."[34]

The question was whether or not colleges might accept pupils who had taken something other than what was then regarded as the college-preparatory course. This involved the gaining of social mobility through the schools. If admission to college meant Greek and Latin, pupils were called upon to make plans for this from the time of entrance into high school. Even those who started Latin in the first year (as did some who were not necessarily planning to go to college) had to decide in the second or third whether or not to take Greek. If they omitted Greek, they were not prepared for the entrance examinations at most of the reputable colleges. One pupil who had found himself in this position was none other than Nicholas Murray Butler, who, on being graduated from the high school at Paterson, New Jersey, in 1875 with neither Latin nor Greek, had been obliged to spend two years in private study for the examinations at Columbia. In Butler's case the reason for not taking these languages was a simple one; the school he attended did not teach them.

---

[32] National Council of Education, Report of the Committee on Secondary Education, "The Relation of High Schools to Colleges," NEA, 1887, pp. 282–283.
[33] *Ibid.,* p. 285.
[34] In discussion, NEA, 1887, p. 291.

His school, in short, did not prepare for college as such preparation was then understood.[35]

There was already under way, however, some modification of the stipulations for the classics, and it was possible under some circumstances for pupils to enter some colleges without Greek. Such attempts at flexibility in turn aroused the demand for uniformity implied in the resolution placed by Baker before the National Council. A few reputable colleges as far back as the 1850's had introduced the degrees of bachelor of science and bachelor of philosophy as parallel degrees to the bachelor of arts. It was the degree of bachelor of arts that required Greek for admission, although there were exceptions to this in the "West," and Harvard in 1887 began giving applicants to this program a choice between Greek and Latin. Requirements for admission to many of the new programs still included Latin, and the corresponding courses of study in the high school were often called Latin-Scientific. The tendency, however, was to regard such degrees as inferior even when Latin was required.

Modern subjects sometimes appeared among those required for admission to college, but they were not taken seriously for this purpose. In the traditional subjects the examinations were considered searching enough to warrant substantial preparation, although this did not necessarily have to be obtained in school. On the other hand, the examinations in English, history, modern languages, and science, when these were first introduced, were thought of as sketchy. The advocates of these modern subjects were nevertheless glad to have them recognized in the requirements, even on this basis, for therein lay the road to respectability. Colleges sought increasingly to include them, but in doing so each college decided for itself what subjects it would include.

This development was already under way by 1887, and for school principals it was producing new sources of confusion. "The subjects of the requirements are found to range from the merest rudiments of arithmetic, reading, and writing, up to the higher mathematics, Greek, moral philosophy, and the history of art," reported William C. Collar in 1891 from a survey he had made of 487 colleges. "It is hardly an exaggeration," he continued, "to say that the histories of all states and all times are included, from Babylonian and Assyrian history, specially designated, in the requirements of one college, and of Persian history, in those of

[35] Butler, *op. cit.*, pp. 52–58.

another, down to the history of Texas and North Carolina, the former required by three, the latter by two colleges."[36] The consternation of a principal on discovering that he had even one student to prepare for an examination in Babylonian history, sketchy though the examination might be, may well be imagined.

Even so, when the principal once identified the names of the subjects required by the colleges to which his pupils planned to go, his troubles had only begun. Next he had to find out what these subjects were supposed to include. This was an older difficulty, and complaints were numerous about variations even in such an established field as Greek. Selections from Xenophon, Herodotus, Homer, and the New Testament jostled one another in confusing and perplexing combinations. Colleges recognized this and tried to mitigate the difficulties by providing options. "Of colleges requiring Greek," reported Collar, "150 do not require Homer; but it would appear that sometimes a portion of Homer would be accepted in place of some of the prescribed Herodotus, or even of some of Attic prose. Some colleges allow New Testament Greek as an alternative."[37]

Keeping track of these variations was difficult enough in the traditional subjects; it was rendered even more so by the appearance of the modern ones. One modern field beginning to cause trouble along these lines was English. A faculty member at Vassar wrote in 1888: "There seems to be little reason why in English, for example, one college should require a specific examination on Burke, Landor, and Chaucer, another college one on Milton, Goldsmith, Shakespeare and Franklin, and a third no specified reading whatsoever. Thus it happens that if a girl who has decided to go to Bryn Mawr is preparing in a school which sends most of its graduates to Wellesley, she may have a good knowledge of the works selected by Wellesley while entirely ignorant of those required by the college she is to enter."[38] The principal of such a high school might have added that he would have to make special provision for the girl going to Bryn Mawr and probably would end by doing the coaching himself, and on "his own" time.

Under a system where each college devised its own examinations, there remained the unavoidable difficulty of various standards, even

[36] William C. Collar, "The Action of the Colleges upon the Schools," *Educational Review* (December, 1891), p. 429.

[37] *Ibid.*, p. 431.

[38] Lucy M. Salmon, "Unity of Standard for College Entrance Examinations," *Academy* (May, 1888), p. 229.

when the colleges involved specified the same books. "What the printed requirements of admission are," said Collar, "anyone can find out with time and patient search. What the real requirements are, nobody can discover, nor will any person be able to discover, so long as college reports are so meager, or should I say so discreet?" There was, he felt, no way of guessing the requisite degrees of attainment in knowledge and power. According to general belief, a performance of 40 percent was sufficient to gain admission to Harvard. Collar believed this himself and suggested that the level was no higher than 25 or 30 percent at "many other reputable colleges."[39] The meaning of these figures depended of course on what the examinations included from one college to the next, but not even Collar was bold enough to speculate on this kind of diversity.[40]

The whole question was further complicated by the presence of institutions called colleges (148 of them in Collar's survey) that stated no requirements whatsoever. Many of these undoubtedly fell in the category of "questionable" colleges to which sarcastic references were made in many articles and speeches. Some of them were "really" academies and had programs that paralleled the secondary schools. Furthermore, there were 42 colleges in Collar's list with "requirements for admission differing but little, except in a requirement of United States history, from those of a school in Boston with which I am tolerably well acquainted, that receives boys at eleven years of age, and of the grade of the third class in grammar schools."[41] All this, of course, added to the bewilderment of the principal and teachers, and it raised the persistent question of what a high school or a college was.[42]

Although the word *uniformity* was to have an abhorrent connotation

[39] Collar, *op. cit.*, p. 433.

[40] The preoccupation of the school men with examinations tended to obscure the fact that some colleges even at this time admitted pupils on certificate. Collar found 177 of them doing so for some or all subjects and believed there were more in spite of protestations to the contrary in catalogues. *Ibid.*, pp. 433–434. Admission by certificate, however, did not help relieve the chaos confronting the principal. Except in a few states, such as Wisconsin and Michigan, where certification was systematized by the state universities, the certificate plan operated as a series of private treaties between given colleges and given high schools. Principals were obliged to fill out long and apparently irritating forms testifying that the proper books had been read, these again being different for different colleges.

[41] *Ibid.*, p. 428.

[42] The high schools themselves also lacked the alleged virtues of uniformity, not only in the subjects offered but also in the order or sequence in which these subjects appeared in the program. E. W. Coy's survey, reported to the Depart-

to later generations of school men, it had for those of the late 1880's a sweet and pleasant sound indeed. Even Eliot regarded it with some favor, although insisting on giving it a special meaning, one that was to prove quite different, for example, from Baker's. There were many shades of meaning among those who invoked the virtues of uniformity in this period. It became a slogan and as such undoubtedly comforted many who were aware of being uncomfortable but did not know quite what to do about it.

The question, furthermore, involved differences in choice of subjects among those who were in reasonably close agreement about what uniformity meant. Classicists and modernists did not see eye to eye. Among modernists there were those who, like Spencer, followed the gospel of science; others who proclaimed the supreme virtues of history or philosophy; and still others who gave their devotion to modern foreign languages or English.

III

Baker's resolution at the National Council in 1887 therefore implied more than it expressed, but he was not being devious. By using the idea of unformity, he succeeded in getting a short resolution instead of a long one, for which his colleagues might well have been grateful.

So far as the subjects of instruction were concerned, the main question underlying Baker's resolution was the future of the classics. In his address to the Harvard Phi Beta Kappa chapter in 1884, Charles Francis Adams, Jr., had savagely lashed out at Greek and only grudgingly left a somewhat diminished role for Latin. Classicists in the secondary schools looked to the colleges to hold the line against the threats presented by allegedly inferior degrees, some of which did not call for preparatory work even in Latin. There were, of course, many pupils who took Latin with no intention of going to college; but the admission requirements were, nevertheless, regarded as the main stronghold of defense.

---

ment of Secondary Education in 1889, showed the various sciences and even algebra, geometry, and rhetoric appearing anywhere from the first year to the fourth. By this time, Coy was beginning to doubt that a uniform course of study could be, or even should be, achieved. "Think again," he said, "of the different views entertained as to the purpose of the high school itself." There were some, he felt, who saw culture as the main purpose, but others would make it "chiefly a business school," while "some would substitute for it a technical school; and I am not sure but some would turn it into a workshop." E. W. Coy, "Uniform Course of Study for High Schools—A Report," NEA, 1889, p. 525.

The college men valiantly attempted to strengthen the fortifications. At the same NEA meeting at which Baker presented his resolution to the Council, a committee of college representatives submitted a report to the Department of Higher Instruction. For admission to courses leading to the bachelor of arts degree, they proposed Latin through Vergil, Greek through the *Anabasis* and one book of the *Iliad*, algebra and geometry, history, and English. Here was a firm holding to Latin and Greek, but also some recognition of the modern subjects. It was on the "inferior" degrees that their determination was most clearly expressed. For admission to courses leading to the bachelor of philosophy or bachelor of science, they demanded Latin at least through Cicero; Greek was replaced by German or French at least to the same level as the Greek in the Classical course.[43] They had stated: There should be no admission to college without some Latin.

If this seems a blind adherence to tradition, it should be kept in mind that the classicists faced what in some quarters amounted to massive and almost insulting hostility. Charles Francis Adams, Jr., was not alone in this, and there were school men who echoed his sentiments in even more biting terms. Samuel Thurber of the Girls' High School, Boston, declared that the classical schools in Germany were "crowded with the sons of *parvenu* families anxiously aspiring to the social standing that, in the artificial system of Germany, gymnasial education confers" and suggested pointedly that such was also the case in the United States by saying that at Yale "fathers whose professions imply classical training send their sons in considerably larger proportion to the scientific school than do the fathers whose employments suggest the absence of such culture."[44] Such attacks aroused the militant defenders of the classics to fury and left the more moderate ones somewhat breathless and overwhelmed. At the meeting of the Massachusetts Classical and High School Teachers' Association in 1886, Moses Merrill, headmaster of the Boston Latin Grammar School, conceded the possibility that the classics might well disappear, but asked why there were "such heartless and bitter denunciations of them in so many quarters where we should expect a more generous treatment."[45]

[43] Department of Higher Instruction, Report of Committee of Seven, "Requisites for Admission to College, and for College Degrees," NEA, 1887, pp. 462–463.
[44] Samuel Thurber, "The Order and Relation of Studies in the High School Course," *Academy* (September, 1887), p. 254.
[45] Moses Merrill, "The Effect on Preparatory Schools of Optional Examinations for Admission to College," *Academy* (May, 1886), p. 131.

Some defenders of the classics were willing to let Greek go in order to save Latin. Others, such as Principal Augustus F. Nightingale of the Lake View Township High School in Cook County, Illinois, regarded the attack on Greek as the "entering wedge." To his listeners at the Department of Secondary Instruction of the NEA in 1887 he declared his conviction "that if a sufficient amount of public opinion can be maintained to push this claim to a successful issue, by substituting the modern-language route across the Isthmus for the Cape Horn route of Greek culture, the next step will be the subordination of Latin to make room for the claims of practicability involved in the study of the sciences, and a more extended knowledge of English literature." He noted also that "the State University of Iowa, which ought to be the educational star of the West . . . yielded some time since to this diseased public opinion, and no longer requires Greek for admission."[46] Perhaps the hopelessness of the cause was symbolized by the fact that ten years later Nightingale was using his highly ornamented prose not for, but against, the surviving requirements in Latin and Greek.

Greek, in fact, was in a peculiar position. The difficulty lay in persuading pupils to take it or the courses of study in which it appeared. In many schools Greek went out and came back in and went out again, depending on the persuasive powers of the principal. When enough pupils were gathered to make a class, the principal wrote about it with enthusiasm, as did the principal of Port Huron, Michigan, High School to Angell in 1887, pointing out that he had a group of excellent scholars engaged in the reading of Xenophon. He added his fears, however, that there was a move to abolish the study of languages in the school.[47] The principal at Monroe, Michigan, wrote proudly in 1885 that he had three very good scholars in the *Anabasis*, who had begun Greek the year before.[48] It was a struggle to keep Greek going, and only 3 percent of the pupils in public high schools were enrolled in it for the school year 1889–1890.[49] The state of affairs was not greatly different in private secondary schools, where only 7 percent were enrolled in Greek.[50] It

[46] Augustus F. Nightingale, "The Claims of the Classics," NEA, 1887, p. 408.
[47] Henry J. Robeson to James B. Angell, April 4, 1887, James B. Angell Papers, Michigan Historical Collections (University of Michigan, Ann Arbor, Mich.).
[48] John A. Stewart to James B. Angell, May 19, 1885, James B. Angell Papers, Michigan Historical Collections (University of Michigan, Ann Arbor, Mich.).
[49] Commissioner, 1889–1890, II, pp. 1390–1392.
[50] *Ibid.*, Table 6, pp. 1490–1491.

was understandable that school men not necessarily hostile to Greek would begin to welcome the placement of the subject on the optional, instead of the required, list for the bachelor of arts degree.

IV

Confronted by these questions pertaining to the classics, as well as by the other difficulties, the Committee on Secondary Education of the National Council, with Baker as chairman after 1888, went on with its study of uniformity. Such committees were not characterized by rapid action or movement. Baker in particular liked to work at a leisurely pace. There was, in fact, little possibility of working at any other. Members were widely separated geographically, and there were no funds for travel. About the only chance they had to get together was at the national summer convention of the NEA and then only for brief periods sandwiched in among the many and lengthy general sessions and those of the various departments. Everything else had to be done by correspondence. There was often a note of incongruity in the fervent summer oratory that demanded immediate action on this or that, followed by the break-up of the meeting with the members apparently forgetting all about it until the following year. Yet they did not forget. Remarkable patience and persistence were exhibited year after year, and the reports eventually did find their way to the floor of the Council. So it was with Baker's committee, which finally presented its work to the Toronto session in 1891.

The report itself was inconclusive and disappointing. In prose unusually turgid even for the NEA it wandered aimlessly around the various questions involved. There was a need, it seemed, for a "recommendation in creating a tendency toward uniformity," but the report supplied no such recommendation. Instead it suggested the holding of a conference between a dozen representative colleges and a dozen secondary schools for the purpose of achieving "a plan for complete adjustment between Secondary Schools and Colleges."[51] The Council accepted and commended the report, referring to the committee itself the responsibility of acting on its suggestion for a conference.[52]

[51] National Council of Education, Report of Committee on Secondary Education, "Uniformity in Requirements for Admission to College," NEA, 1891, pp. 315–316.
[52] National Council of Education, Secretary's Report, NEA, 1891, p. 279.

Perhaps feeling that destiny was close at hand, Baker moved more rapidly than he or his committee had during the preceding four years of their deliberations. By November he had obtained agreements from Harvard (meaning, very likely, from Eliot), Johns Hopkins, and the Andover Academy to attend such a meeting. On the strength of this he issued his invitation to the other colleges and schools, stating that the conference would be held July 7–11 of the following year, at the time of the NEA convention at Saratoga Springs, New York. Besides Harvard and Johns Hopkins, the colleges invited to send representatives (one each) were Amherst, Bowdoin, California, Columbia, Cornell, DePauw, Michigan, New Jersey College (Princeton), Northwestern, Oberlin, Vassar, Virginia, Wisconsin, and Yale. The secondary schools were Boston English, Chicago North Division, Cincinnati Hughes (Coy's school), Denver (Baker's), Kansas City, Minneapolis, Newark, Newport Rogers, Roxbury Latin, San Francisco Boys', St. Louis, Andover, Exeter, Lawrenceville, and the Norwich, Connecticut, Free Academy. This was the original list; possibly there were changes later. Baker's invitation pointed out that the work was "gratuitous," but added that much interest was already "manifested in many quarters."[53]

The sessions of the conference began at Saratoga on July 7, 1892. One of the participants was Nicholas Murray Butler, who the year before had joined the exclusive circles of the National Council at the age of twenty-nine. Presumably Butler was present at this conference as the representative of Columbia University. At some point he was named chairman of "the Committee of Conference between Colleges and Secondary Schools," and it was in this capacity that he appeared before the Council on July 9 to present the report.

What happened during those three days was not published in the NEA volume of proceedings. A manuscript by John Tetlow, who may have been present although his school was not in the original list, throws light on the part taken by President Eliot. According to Tetlow the discussions seemed to be heading toward a new association to promote uniformity along the lines of Baker's report in 1891. "At this point in the discussion, President Eliot, who had entered late, was invited to state

[53] James H. Baker, printed circular from him as Chairman, Committee on Secondary Education, National Council of Education, November 16, 1891, Charles W. Eliot Papers (Harvard University Archives, Cambridge, Mass.). Eliot's copy of the printed invitation contains the brisk notation, presumably by Baker, *"Important. Please reply at once,"* suggesting that Baker did not welcome procrastination on the part of his guests.

his views. He spoke in disapproval of the proposed formation of a new association, and expressed the belief that there were associations enough already existing for the accomplishment of the kind of work to which permanent associations were adapted." Eliot referred to the work in New England involving representatives of schools and colleges and, according to this manuscript, "recommended, therefore, that a committee, duly representative of colleges and secondary schools and of the different sections of the country, be appointed, with authority to call conferences, similarly representative, of experts in each of the several subjects or groups of subjects required for admission to college, and that the committee so constituted after receiving and digesting the reports of these conferences should make a final report to the national Council." The manuscript adds that "president Eliot's proposal met with a prompt and hearty acceptance" and that "the Committee of Ten was at once created."[54]

The general session of the National Council, meeting on July 9, amended and then adopted Butler's report. According to the amended version, it was the opinion of the conference, and of the Council, that conferences "by departments of instruction" consisting of teachers in colleges and secondary schools were desirable. "Ten persons," including Eliot as chairman, were named as an executive committee to call and arrange for such conferences during the academic year 1892–1893.[55] It was further suggested that the NEA grant $2500 for the work. Three days later, on July 12, the Board of Directors of the NEA voted 21 to 9 to approve the venture and to grant the $2500, although one member of the Board tried unsuccessfully to limit the amount to $1000.[56] The work apparently was no longer to be gratuitous; at least, expenses would be paid.

Eliot's associates among what was often later referred to as the "Ten" included James H. Baker, who at the beginning of 1892 had become president of the University of Colorado, and Commissioner Harris. The other seven members were John Tetlow, principal of the Boston Girls' High and Latin Schools; Oscar D. Robinson, principal of the high school

[54] John Tetlow, "The Colleges and the Non-Classical High Schools," John Tetlow Papers (Houghton Library, Harvard University, Cambridge, Mass.), pp. 13–15.
[55] National Council of Education, Report of the Committee on Conference between Colleges and Secondary Schools, NEA, 1892, p. 754.
[56] National Educational Association, Minutes of the Board of Directors, NEA, 1892, p. 31.

at Albany, New York; James C. Mackenzie, headmaster of the Law-renceville School, New Jersey; Henry C. King, professor, Oberlin College; President James M. Taylor of Vassar College; President Richard H. Jesse of the University of Missouri; and President James B. Angell of the University of Michigan.[57]

According to Tetlow's manuscript the Committee of Ten, at least in the form it assumed, was Eliot's idea, possibly called up on the spur of the moment to keep the conference from drifting into another direction. Butler leaves the impression in his autobiography, published more than 40 years later, that it was his idea.[58] That it was Baker who "proposed" the Committee of Ten is the confident assertion of the article on him in the *Dictionary of American Biography*. The specific decision to create the committee was certainly located in a sequence of events beginning with Baker's resolution in the National Council in 1887. Perhaps something like the Committee of Ten was bound to happen anyway. Looked at from today's perspective, it was an outgrowth of conditions or "forces" such as had led in 1885 to the New England Association of Colleges and Preparatory Schools. The combination represented by Baker's persistence, Butler's stage management, and Eliot's timely inspiration probably had much to do with the direction taken by these forces.

Possibly the creation of the Committee of Ten represented the human tendency to put off difficult questions by referring them to still another committee. In any case, the Council had come up with a new plan for action. With Eliot at the controls, the plan promised, if nothing else, at least the temporary suspension of oratory and the beginning of work.

---

[57] National Council of Education, *op. cit.,* p. 754.
[58] Butler, *op. cit.,* p. 17.

Chapter 3

Dr. Eliot's report

"Differences of opinion were numerous and in
some instances not easily harmonized."
—OSCAR D. ROBINSON,
JUNE, 1894.

*P*ractically everything about the Committee of Ten has been controversial. The
nature of its membership stirred up early attacks and continued to be a
target of later critics. Feminists have not overlooked the absence of
women from an enterprise representing thousands of women pupils and
teachers. Moreover, the ten men included six from the colleges, and five
of them were presidents. The three men from the secondary schools were
administrators too: one of these was headmaster of a reputedly exclusive
preparatory school and another was principal of a public classical school
for girls; only Robinson represented what would today be called a "regular" high school. The tenth and perhaps designedly neutral member,
Commissioner Harris, has long since been written off as a conservative,
and this evaluation of his stand has secured the Committee in its role
in pedagogical folklore as the group that fastened college domination on
the secondary schools.

Even those not critical of the Committee have been puzzled about
how it was selected. It was Butler who brought the list of names to the
National Council from the recesses of the Committee of Conference.
More than 40 years later he said on one occasion that he had nominated
Eliot as chairman and on another occasion that he had suggested him.[1]

---

[1] Nicholas Murray Butler, *Across the Busy Years* (New York: Charles Scribner's
Sons, 1939), I, 17 and 196; Nicholas Murray Butler, to Mildred Sandison Fenner,
March 18, 1942, as quoted in Mildred Sandison Fenner, *The National Education
Association* (Doctoral dissertation, George Washington University, 1942), p. 229,
footnote 20.

He did not say why the other members were chosen or who had chosen them. Perhaps Eliot selected the others himself. The records of the Council are noncommittal, and only speculation remains to fill in the gap. There was an attempt at geographical representation and, in spite of the unbalanced outcome, some desire to represent various kinds of colleges and schools.[2] Except for Eliot, Harris, and Angell, the men selected were not especially prominent outside their own regions.

The choices may have been more casual than has been assumed. In July, 1892, this was just another committee, on the surface no more far reaching in significance than others called into existence by the Council, and differing from them only in regard to its expense account. William T. Harris was a veteran of many committees, and he found his appointment to this one another incident in his busy life as Commissioner. Secondary education was not one of his main interests. He had been an elementary school principal and teacher, and as city superintendent in St. Louis was known for his work with elementary schools. Even as a philosopher, the appointment did not challenge him at the outset. "When Mr. James Baker, then principal of the Denver High School, made his report before the National Council of Education at Toronto in 1891, on the course of study in secondary schools, I did not see that any important results were likely to be secured by the discussion of his theme," he wrote in January, 1894, and he viewed the creation of the Committee as a result of "Mr. Baker's earnestness and persistence."[3]

It was Baker's earnestness as well as his previous involvement in affairs of the Council that probably brought him his place on the Committee. Those who were concerned about the alleged college loading of the Committee overlooked one important fact about Baker: He had become president of the 66-student University of Colorado in January, 1892, only six months before his appointment to the Committee and had previously served for eighteen years as principal of the Denver High School. In spite of their being fellow presidents, Eliot and Baker did not always agree. "I saw in my first intercourse with him [Baker], nearly two years ago," Eliot wrote to Angell in December, 1893, "that he believed it possible to invent a uniform high school programme for the entire country. That idea he still clings to—indeed, he thinks he can write that

[2] Nicholas Murray Butler, "The Reform of Secondary Education in the United States," *Atlantic Monthly* (March, 1894), p. 373.

[3] William T. Harris, "The Committee of Ten on Secondary Schools," *Educational Review* (January, 1894), p. 1.

programme himself, and that it would closely resemble his programme in the Denver High School."[4]

The other college presidents on the Committee of Ten represented a variety of institutions and interests. Jesse, like Baker, was newly come to his presidency, having been named to his position at Missouri in 1891 from a professorship in Latin at Tulane University. At one time he had served as teacher and principal in private secondary schools. Taylor had been President of Vassar College since 1886 and before that time had been a prominent Baptist clergyman. In November, 1892, four months after his appointment to the Committee of Ten, he was elected President of the new Association of Colleges and Preparatory Schools of the Middle States and Maryland;[5] there is no record of his previously having taken part in relationships between schools and colleges. Angell of Michigan brought a great name to the Committee. Both by age and by temperament he was well qualified for a possible role as the Committee's elder statesman. Angell was particularly identified with admission to college by certificate, and the Michigan system of accreditation through inspection was widely known and discussed. Eliot did not like admission by certificate. Fortunately for the relationships between Angell and Eliot, this question was not involved in the work of the Committee of Ten.

The college contingent was rounded out by King, a future president of Oberlin, but at this time a 33-year-old Professor of Philosophy at that school. At the NEA Convention in 1889 he testified that "ten weeks' experience in constant visitation of high schools brought the belief that more careful thought, and a better acquaintance with the work of the schools, will convince college men that there are points of some importance, in which the high schools generally are right, as against the requirements of many colleges."[6] His work on a committee of the Ohio College Association in 1890 involved him in a magazine controversy with a professorial defender of the classics from Buchtel College, who exclaimed, "if we believe in scholarship, let not Ohio lower the flag."[7]

[4] Charles W. Eliot to James B. Angell, December 8, 1893, James B. Angell Papers, Michigan Historical Collections (University of Michigan, Ann Arbor, Mich.).

[5] College Association of the Middle States and Maryland, *Proceedings of the Fourth Annual Convention,* November 25–26, 1892, p. 67.

[6] Henry C. King, discussion at July 19 session, Department of Secondary Education, NEA, 1889, p. 532.

[7] W. D. Shipman, "The Ohio College Association and the High Schools," *Ohio Educational Monthly* (April, 1891), p. 153.

Robinson of Albany had been connected with the high school of that city since 1870, first as a teacher of Latin and Greek, and after 1886 as Principal. He often disagreed with Eliot during the course of the Committee's work and was afterward openly critical of several aspects of the final report. Some of his criticism involved the place of music, drawing, manual training, and business subjects, on which Robinson expressed what many would regard as a modern or liberal point of view. Unfortunately for his reputation along these lines, Robinson subsequently joined the American Philological Association in its assault on the Committee of Ten for having reduced the amount of time for Greek.

Headmaster Mackenzie of the Lawrenceville School also refused to fit a stereotype, in his case that of a private school man. If he had a so-called private school point of view, it was a most unconventional one. At the International Congress of Education in Chicago in 1893, he urged supervision of private schools by state or municipal authorities and referred to "the strange and hurtful isolation of the private schools and academies from the public high schools—two classes of schools that should, in the necessities of the case, have very much in common."[8]

The third representative of secondary schools, John Tetlow of the Boston Girls' High and Latin Schools, had never lost his joy in teaching Greek and could not understand why some of his fellow principals sought to abandon the classroom entirely for the school office.[9] He believed in the modern subjects, however, and he was prepared not to insist upon Greek or Latin for admission to college. Judged by the delightful cartoons he drew of his Civil War experiences,[10] he was a man with a sense of humor, a virtue possibly denied to some of his colleagues on the Committee of Ten.

Eliot's fellow Committee members, then, presented a variety of back-

[8] James C. Mackenzie, "Supervision of Private Schools by the State or Municipal Authorities," NEA, 1893, p. 184.

[9] He expressed his views on this point to his fellow administrators at a meeting of the Massachusetts High School Masters' Club, December 10, 1898. "The principal, no matter how large his school," said Tetlow on this occasion, "has the right to teach. He should not, for many reasons, permit himself to be so engrossed by the cares of administration as to have no direct share in the work of instruction." He reminded his audience also that the term "principal" was a short form of "principal teacher." At this time he was teaching eleven hours a week himself. Some people, he suspected, felt he was "indulging a personal preference at the expense of more important duties." John Tetlow, "The High-School Principal: His Rights, Duties, and Opportunities," *Educational Review* (March, 1899), pp. 227–229.

[10] One of them is reproduced in *Brown Alumni Monthly* (March, 1962), p. 6.

grounds. It was by no means a council of the elders, for there was an age range from King at 33 to Angell at 63. Six of the members were less than 50 years of age. Whatever it may have meant for their breadth of outlook, five of them had studied in Europe. Although all of them except Harris were men with earned college degrees, only two of them, Tetlow and Angell, had gone to the same college, Brown University. The others represented Dartmouth, Lafayette, Rochester, Oberlin, Virginia, and Bates. With Eliot's Harvard added to the list, there were six New England colleges in the background, possibly giving a provincial tone to the proceedings. In addition, six of the members, including Eliot, were New Englanders born and bred. This was perhaps appropriate enough, since it was in New England that high schools had been originated and developed. Characteristically, it was two of the New Englanders, Robinson (from New Hampshire) and Baker (from Maine), who disagreed most with their fellow New Englander, Eliot.

The Committee members represented a broad range of ideas about education, but had some characteristics in common. The Committee included no enemy of the classics, such as Samuel Thurber of Boston, and nobody who felt the classics alone to be worthy of study. All members of the Committee wanted a larger place for the modern academic studies in school programs and in college admission requirements. This was the limit of agreement so far as the studies were concerned. On other matters pertaining to the studies they were in disagreement. Some of them were willing to admit pupils to college who had studied no classics at all, not even Latin, while others wanted to retain the classics in college admission requirements while including the new and modern subjects. Harris wanted everybody to study the classics, in both college and high school. Beyond this the members shared a desire to promote the development of high schools and to make it possible for more pupils to find a convenient route to the colleges in their high school work.

II

There remains, then, the aloof and enigmatic figure of the Chairman. Since his address to the superintendents in 1888 Eliot had been reformulating and making more explicit the ideas he was to use as working equipment on the Committee of Ten. His 1888 address had revealed his desire to get more and better work done in less time for the benefit of all pupils.[11] In his 1890 address to the same group he urged the

---

[11] Charles W. Eliot, "Can School Programmes Be Shortened and Enriched?"

building of more high schools, particularly in rural communities, and the development of state aids and supervision.[12] The third of this series of addresses was made to the superintendents at the Brooklyn meeting of 1892. Here he specifically recommended physics, algebra, geometry, and foreign languages in the upper grades of the elementary schools. To the potential objection that not all children were capable of pursuing these subjects, he had a ready answer. It was not necessary for all pupils to take the same subjects. Furthermore, the selection of subjects should not depend on how long the child was to stay in school. His proposals, he said, were "much more for the interest of the children who are not going to the high school," and for whom therefore the grammar school was to provide "all the systematic education" they would ever receive.[13]

It has become customary to regard some of Eliot's statements in these three addresses as the beginning of what was later called the movement for economy of time. Eliot did indeed refer to the shortening of the program, but it is important to note what he had to say and the context in which he said it. What he called for in the 1888 address was a period of schooling that would enable boys to come to college at eighteen instead of nineteen. Unlike many others who later became involved in the question, Eliot did not propose having pupils come to college earlier than eighteen, and in subsequent utterances he held to eighteen as the ideal age. The immediate context of his 1888 address was the nine-year —and in some instances, ten-year—programs of elementary education then existing in Massachusetts and other parts of New England. He made this explicit in the 1892 address, saying, "the number of grades may be reduced from ten to nine and from nine to eight, so that the combined primary and grammar school periods shall end at fourteen or thirteen."[14] It is a mistake, therefore, to enroll Eliot as an advocate of acceleration aimed at early entrance into college or as a prophet of what became the junior high school.

The central themes of his address to the superintendents in 1892 were individuality and diversity. "Every child," he proclaimed, "is a unique

Proceedings of the Department of Superintendence of the National Educational Association (U.S. Bureau of Education Circular No. 6 [Washington, D.C., 1888]), pp. 101–115.

[12] Charles W. Eliot, "The Gap between the Elementary Schools and the Colleges," NEA, 1890, pp. 522–533.

[13] Charles W. Eliot, "Shortening and Enriching the Grammar-School Course," NEA, 1892, p. 623.

[14] *Ibid.*, p. 617.

personality,"[15] an expression that unfortunately later was worn down to a slogan. In defiance of the almost universal demand for uniformity, he flatly declared: "Uniformity is the curse of American schools."[16] This was in February. In July of the same year he found himself chairman of an enterprise dedicated to uniformity.

Possibly Eliot or someone else felt that his curse on uniformity left the whole question in a somewhat unsettled state. Even Eliot believed in some kind of uniformity. At any rate, he was scheduled to address the summer meeting of the NEA in Saratoga Springs on the subject of undesirable and desirable uniformity in schools. This address was made to the general session on July 12, three days after his appointment to the Committee of Ten. He began with undesirable uniformity, noting how the systematizing of schools lost sight of the interests of the individual, "a great evil, particularly in a democratic society, where other influences, governmental, industrial, and social, tend toward averaging the human stock." He lauded democracy as a means of "discovering all the small, peculiar gifts and faculties which reside in individuals." With loving care he gave numerous examples of unusual individual talents, mentioning those of singers, verse-writers, surgeons, and wool-testers, but dwelling in particular on the craftsmen who made the models of glass flowers for the Harvard Botanical Musuem. "It is the mobility of democratic society —a new thing in the world—which has brought home to us the importance of discovering and training each least individual gift and power." Uniformity in the schools, he said, "crushes and buries" such "individual endowments."[17]

At this point Eliot's audience must have wondered how he was to find any virtues in any kind of uniformity whatsoever. He went on, however, to declare himself in favor of uniformity in defining the various studies and the manner in which they should be studied and taught. "Although it may not be best for all children to study algebra, geometry, zoology, physics, or a foreign language, there is probably a best way of studying each of these subjects, which best way all the pupils who attack any one of them should follow. Moreover, it is altogether probable that there are certain topics within each of these subjects which all children who take up the subject should study; and the expedient limits of each one of these topics can probably be defined with a good degree of precision."

[15] *Ibid.,* p. 621.
[16] *Ibid.,* p. 623.
[17] Charles W. Eliot, "Undesirable and Desirable Uniformity in Schools," NEA, 1892, p. 85.

These things, he felt, could be settled by conventions of experts in the teaching of the various subjects. He thought also that a "minimum standard for a given grade could probably be agreed on," but disclaimed any desire that all pupils "should move at the same rate through any subject" and insisted on "ample allowance for the very various aptitudes for each subject in any given group of children."[18] It was "wholly unnecessary," he said, for all pupils going from grammar schools to high schools to study the same subjects, and it was "neither necessary nor desirable that all candidates for admission to college" should have done so.[19]

This was, in effect, his declaration of principles for the Committee of Ten. So far as he was concerned, the goal was neither uniform offerings by schools nor uniform programs for pupils. Rather it was uniformity of topics, methods, and standards of attainment for any subjects that might be offered or taken. It was this kind of uniformity, at least with reference to college-admission examinations, that many school men were seeking, and Eliot undoubtedly struck a responsive chord when he complained in this address of the "curious little diversities within the same subjects" in requirements of different colleges. Perhaps it was his resolution of the conflict about uniformity that made Eliot more confident of the responsibility he had assumed. At any rate, he wrote to Butler: "The more I think of that undertaking [the Committee of Ten] the more promising it seems to me."[20]

III

Eliot lost little time getting the work started. Equipped with his $2500 expense fund, he called a meeting of the Committee in New York City for November ninth. To Butler's great satisfaction, this first meeting was held "in my own apartment on Stuyvesant Square."[21] The task of the Committee at this meeting was to identify the "departments of instruction" for the conferences and to make a tentative selection of the members. To guide the Committee in its identification of studies, Eliot had gathered information on subject offerings from 40 schools. This survey had yielded a total of 36 subjects, the miscellaneous nature of which

[18] *Ibid.,* p. 89.
[19] *Ibid.,* p. 90.
[20] Charles W. Eliot to Nicholas Murray Butler, July 21, 1892, Nicholas Murray Butler Papers (Columbiana Library, Columbia University, New York, N.Y.).
[21] Nicholas Murray Butler, *Across the Busy Years,* I, p. 197.

confirmed Eliot's feelings that too many subjects of an informational nature were being offered (see Fig. 1). Had he heard from all 200 of the schools to which he sent his inquiry, the list might well have been longer and more diversified.

This was the time—if there was any time—for Eliot or others on the Committee to propose a larger role than had been assigned to it by the Council. They did not do so, a fact interpreted by some critics to indicate a lack of sensitivity to the pressing problems of the times. The Committee of Ten was not, however, an 1892 version of the Educational Policies Commission of the 1930's or even of the Commission on the Reorganization of Secondary Education. The Council did not expect it to re-

FIG. 1.   Eliot's Summary of Subject Offerings and Time Allotments in Forty High Schools. [On the following four pages a copy of Eliot's table from the James B. Angell Papers of the Michigan Historical Collections of the University of Michigan is shown, printed from new-type composition. The term "hours" as used here means the number of hours of instruction in a given subject during an academic year. In the case of San Antonio High School, the total of 510 hours for Latin probably means an offering of 170 hours in each of the three years of Latin. Classes in each of the three years of Latin perhaps met five times a week during a school year of 34 weeks. Astronomy with its 51 hours for one-half year probably met three times a week for 17 weeks.]

[The following is the explanation, presumably written by Eliot, that is attached to the Table.]

In the table the figures against the name of each subject in the column under the name of the school indicate the maximum number of hours devoted to that subject in that school. When the school has two or more courses of study, the figures against each subject indicate the total number of distinct hours of instruction given in that subject in all the courses of the school taken together, excluding mere repetitions. They thus indicate roughly the proportional expenditure of the school on the several subjects named, except expenditure for repetition. In schools which maintain several courses—such as Classical, Latin-Scientific, English, and Commercial—the total number of hours of instruction given by the school in a single subject is often much greater than any one pupil can avail himself of.

The small figures at the left of the number of hours devoted to the several subjects indicate the number of years, or the part of a year, in which that subject occurs in the school programme; but these figures are in some cases approximate, not exact.

The recitation period, called an hour, varies in these schools from thirty to fifty-five minutes, the commonest periods being forty and forty-five minutes.

All the figures in the table have been verified by the masters or principals of the several schools, and have been reported to be correct so far as it is possible to exhibit the work of a school in such figures. In the majority of instances the figures are derived from the programmes of 1891–92,—in the rest, from the programmes of 1892–93.

School.	San Antonio High School, Texas.	Albany High School, N. Y.	Ann Arbor High School, Mich.	Battle Creek High School, Mich.	Bay City High School, Mich.	Cambridge High School, Mass.	Chicago High School, West Side, Ill.	Cleveland Central High School, Ohio.
No. of Years in the Course.	3	4	4	4	4	4	4	4
SUBJECT								
Latin	^{3}510	^{4}810	^{4}714	^{4}800	^{4}740	^{4}580	^{4}760	^{4}760
Greek	....	^{3}540	^{2}380	^{2}400	^{2}400	....	^{3}600	^{3}600
German	^{3}408	^{3}216	^{2}390	^{2}400	^{2}400	^{2}400	^{4}760	^{4}760
French	....	....	^{2}390	^{2}400	^{2}400	^{2}400	^{4}760	....
Spanish	^{3}408	....	....	.....	....	....	....	....
English	^{3}884	^{4}665	^{4}720	^{4}1000	^{4}680	^{4}480	^{3}280	^{4}800
Rhetoric	^{1}136	....	^{1}130	$^{1/2}$100	^{1}200	....	^{1}71	$^{1/2}$80
Arithmetic	^{2}34	$^{1/2}$55	^{1}125	$^{1/2}$100	^{1}300	^{1}160	....	^{1}200
Algebra	^{2}238	^{3}420	^{3}285	^{3}300	^{3}360	^{2}340	^{1}160	^{2}260
Geometry	^{2}238	^{3}300	^{1}160	^{2}200	^{2}240	^{3}300	^{1}240	^{1}200
Trigonometry	....	$^{1/2}$90	$^{1/3}$65	.....	$^{1/2}$100	^{1}80	^{1}80	^{1}60
Analytic Geometry	....	....	....	.....	....	....	....	....
Descriptive Geometry	....	....	....	.....	....	....	....	....
Surveying	....	....	....	.....	....	....	....	....
Drawing	....	....	....	.....	^{2}160	....	^{4}320	....
Mechanics	....	....	....	.....	....	....	....	....
Physics	^{1}170	^{1}180	^{1}273	^{1}200	^{1}200	^{1}200	^{1}200	^{1}200
Astronomy	$^{1/2}$51	....	^{1}95	$^{1/2}$100	$^{1/2}$100	^{1}72	^{1}80	$^{1/2}$60
Chemistry	^{1}119	$^{1/2}$90	^{1}95	$^{1/2}$100	$^{1/2}$100	^{1}120	^{1}200	^{1}120
Geography	^{1}68	$^{1/2}$90	$^{1/3}$63	^{2}200	$^{1/2}$100	^{1}24	....	^{1}120
Natural History	^{1}102	^{3}270	^{2}190	^{2}400	^{3}360	128	^{1}260	^{2}140
Music	....	....	....	.....	....	....	^{4}160	....
Physical Training	....	....	....	.....	....	....	....	....
Elocution	....	....	....	.....	....	....	....	....
Psychology	....	$^{1/2}$90	....	.....	....	....	....	....
Ethics	....	$^{1/2}$90	....	.....	....	....	....	....
History	^{3}527	^{2}132	^{2}520	^{3}400	^{4}600	^{2}272	^{1}160	^{1}160
Civil Government	....	^{1}60	$^{1/3}$63	$^{1/2}$100	$^{1/2}$100	^{1}48	^{1}80	$^{1/2}$64
Constitutional Law	....	....	....	.....	....	....	....	....
Commercial Law	....	....	....	.....	....	....	....	^{1}120
Political Economy	....	$^{1/2}$90	$^{1/3}$63	$^{1/2}$100	....	....	^{1}80	^{1}96
Stenography and	....	^{1}180	....	.....	....	....	....	....
Type-Writing	....	....	....	.....	....	....	....	....
Bookkeeping	....	$^{1/2}$90	^{2}380	^{1}200	^{2}200	^{1}160	^{1}80	^{2}200
Penmanship	....	....	....	.....	....	....	....	....
Sacred Studies	....	....	....	.....	....	....	....	....

Colgate Academy, Hamilton, N. Y.	Hillhouse High School, New Haven, Conn.	Kansas City High School, Mo.	Lawrenceville School, N. J.	Michigan Military Academy, Orchard Lake, Mich.	Newton High School, Newtonville, Mass.	Peoria High School, Ill.	Phillips Academy, Exeter, N. H.	Pittsburgh Central High School, Pa.	Providence High School, R. I.	Rochester Free Academy, N. Y.	Saginaw High School, East Side, Mich.
4	4	4	4	†4	4	4	4	4	4	4	4
[3]637	[4]880	[4]720	[4]741	[4]720	[4]920	[4]800	[4]792	[4]640	[4]1009	[4]1000	[4]800
[2]360	[3]600	[3]540	[3]494	[3]540	[3]640	[3]600	[3]504	[2]200	[3]658	[2]400	[2]400
[1]185	[2]400	[4]720	[2]266	[3]360	[3]600	[3]600	[2]324	....	.....	[4]800	[4]600
[1]45	[2]400	[4]720	[1]152	[2]360	[3]600	....	[2]288	....	[2]390	.....	....
....	....	[4]720	....	....	....	....	....	....	.....	.....	....
[1]125	[4]800	[3]540	[4]304	[3]252	[4]540	[4]1160	[2]234	[4]416	[3]351	[4]580	[4]1020
[2]150	....	[1]180	....	[1]180	....	[1]200	....	....	[‡]78	[1]200	[1]120
[1]185	[‡]67	[‡]90	[1]75	[‡]90	[1]120	[1]200	[1]120	[‡]60	[3]117	.....	[1]200
[2]230	....	[3]360	[4]381	[3]315	[3]400	[1]200	[3]216	[2]220	[3]233	[2]220	[2]300
[1]125	[3]300	[3]360	[1]228	[2]270	[2]240	[1]200	[3]276	[1]160	[‡]145	[2]220	....
....	....	[1]180	[‡]76	[‡]45	[1]120	....	[‡]72	[‡]60	[‡]49	.....	....
....	....	....	....	....	....	....	....	....	.....	.....	....
....	....	....	....	....	....	....	....	....	.....	.....	....
....	....	....	....	....	....	....	....	....	.....	.....	....
....	[3]240	[2]360	[4]380	....	[4]480	....	....	[4]320	.....	.....	[1]120
....	....	....	....	....	....	....	....	[1]80	.....	.....	....
[1]125	[1]200	[1]180	[1]152	[1]180	[1]160	[1]200	[1]72	[1]120	[2]195	[2]200	[1]200
[2]125	[‡]100	[‡]90	....	[‡]90	[1]54	....	....	[‡]80	[‡]98	.....	[‡]80
[1]180	....	[1]180	[1]114	[2]180	[2]200	[1]200	[1]216	[1]160	[1]224	[2]200	[1]120
....	[‡]100	[2]90	....	....	[1]134	[‡]140	....	[‡]60	.....	[‡]100	[3]200
[‡]50	[2]400	[4]630	[2]114	[1]180	[3]320	[1]200	....	[4]320	[‡]97	[4]500	[2]340
....	....	....	[4]152	....	....	....	....	....	[‡]78	.....	....
....	....	....	....	....	....	....	....	....	.....	.....	....
[‡]25	....	[1]180	[4]304	[2]72	....	[1]40	....	[4]160	[4]156	[1]80	....
....	....	[‡]90	....	....	[1]70	....	....	....	.....	.....	....
....	....	....	[‡]19	....	[1]50	....	....	....	.....	[2]150	....
[2]200	[2]300	[1]180	[2]76	[3]450	[3]420	[2]270	[1]72	[2]220	[4]190	[2]360	[1]260
[‡]50	[2]80	[‡]90	....	[‡]90	....	[‡]60	....	....	.....	[1]200	[‡]60
....	....	....	....	[‡]90	....	....	....	[‡]40	[‡]97	.....	....
....	[‡]67	[‡]90	....	....	....	[1]80	....	....	.....	.....	[‡]80
....	....	[‡]90	....	[‡]90	[1]80	....	....	....	[‡]98	[‡]100	[1]120
....	[‡]134	....	....	....	....	[2]360	....	....	.....	.....	....
....	....	....	....	....	....	....	....	....	.....	.....	....
....	[‡]67	[3]360	....	....	[1]120	[1]200	....	....	[‡]98	[1]160	[2]400
....	[2]134	....	....	....	....	....	....	....	.....	.....	....
....	....	....	....	....	....	....	....	....	.....	.....	....

School.	Somerville High School, Mass.	Thayer Academy, So. Braintree, Mass.	Vermont Academy, Saxton's River, Vt.	Williston Seminary, Easthampton, Mass.	Browne & Nichols's School, Cambridge, Mass.	Cambridge Latin School, Mass.	Girls' Classical School, Indianapolis, Ind.	Hopkins Grammar School, New Haven, Conn.
No. of Years in the Course.	4	4	4	4	†5	5	†5	5
SUBJECT								
Latin	[4]760	[4]760	[4]733	[4]737	[5]740	[5]1000	[5]820	[5]945
Greek	[3]600	....	[3]521	[3]547	[3]444	[3]600	[3]525	[3]560
German	....	[2]228	[4]570	[2]197	[4]370	[3]460	[4]350	[1]140
French	[2]240	[3]190	[4]570	[2]197	[5]444	[3]420	[5]455	[2]140
Spanish	....	....	....	....	....	.....	.....	....
English	[4]480	[4]276	[3]218	[4]480	[5]555	[5]380	[5]455	[5]420
Rhetoric	....	[1]40	‡135	‡75	....	.....	.....	....
Arithmetic	....	‡70	[1]75	[1]190	[1]37	.....	‡75	....
Algebra	[2]240	[3]275	[1]152	[2]213	[4]314	[2]300	[2]225	[2]265
Geometry	[2]280	[3]225	[2]190	[2]250	[4]333	[2]200	[2]250	[2]286
Trigonometry	....	[2]130	....	‡55	‡37	.....	‡100	[1]136
Analytic Geometry	....	‡60	....	‡65	[1]56	.....	.....	....
Descriptive Geometry	....	....	....	‡65	....	.....	.....	....
Surveying	....	....	....	‡121	....	.....	.....	....
Drawing	....	[1]66	....	[3]342	[2]148	.....	.....	....
Mechanics	....	....	....	‡75	....	.....	.....	....
Physics	[1]200	[2]146	‡202	[1]190	[3]407	[2]200	[1]175	....
Astronomy	....	....	‡36	‡65	....	.....	.....	....
Chemistry	....	[2]120	‡194	[1]358	[2]296	.....	.....	....
Geography	....	....	‡75	....	....	.....	‡85	[1]70
Natural History	....	[2]60	[2]170	[2]201	[2]222	‡48	[3]430	....
Music	....	[1]38	....	....	....	.....	.....	....
Physical Training	....	....	....	....	....	.....	.....	....
Elocution	....	....	....	....	....	.....	.....	....
Psychology	....	....	‡75	‡60	....	.....	.....	....
Ethics	....	....	....	[1]55	....	.....	.....	....
History	[2]200	[4]416	[4]455	[3]351	[5]555	[3]272	[2]175	[2]175
Civil Government	....	....	....	....	....	.....	.....	....
Constitutional Law	....	....	....	‡55	....	.....	.....	....
Commercial Law	....	....	....	....	....	.....	.....	....
Political Economy	....	....	‡55	‡75	....	.....	.....	....
Stenography and Type-Writing	....	....	....	....	....	.....	.....	....
Bookkeeping	....	[2]60	....	‡60	....	.....	.....	....
Penmanship	....	....	....	[1]38	....	.....	.....	....
Sacred Studies	....	....	....	....	....	.....	.....	....

Polytechnic Institute, Brooklyn, N. Y.	Albany Academy, N. Y.	Boston Public Latin School, Mass.	The Arthur H. Cutler School, New York City.	Groton School, Mass.	Roxbury Latin School, Mass.	St. Mark's School, Southborough, Mass.	St. Paul's School, Concord, N. H.	The Barnard School, New York City.	The Berkeley School, New York City	Free Academy, Norwich, Conn.	Central High School, Washington, D. C.
5	†6	6	6	6	6	6	†6	7	†8	4	4
923	[6]863	[6]1053	[6]1110	[6]900	[6]1159	[6]1073	[6]1925	[4]760	[6]850	[4]681	[4]582
550	[3]520	[3]566	[4]740	[4]540	[3]561	[4]777	[4]1120	[3]578	[4]680	[3]535	[3]438
[2 1/3]400	[4]291	....	....	[2]216	[3]449	[4]518	[3]455	[4]456	[8]697	[3]470	[4]582
[3]300	[6]583	[3]293	....	[4]396	[4]426	[5]370	[3]490	[4]456	[8]697	[3]470	....
....	....	....	....	....	....	....	....	[1]114	....	....	....
[5]1710	[6]800	[6]1053	[1]148	[5]432	[6]806	[6]851	[6]805	[7]1803	[8]1326	[4]325	[4]480
....	....	....	....	....	....	....	....	[1]76	[1]170	....	....
[4]800	[3]469	[3]332	....	[2]240	[2]191	[4]449	[3]420	[5]950	[4]680	....	....
[2]400	[2]384	[3]328	[2 1/3]464	[5]255	[2]225	[4]458	[3]805	[3]570	[3]510	[2]254	[1]150
[1/2]100	[3]337	[4]218	[1 1/2]278	[2]216	[3]283	[3]92	[3]716	[2]380	[2]340	[2]262	[1]144
....	[1]75	....	[1/2]92	....	[1]55	....	....	[1]190	[1]68	[1/2]48	[1]144
....	....	....	[1/2]92	....	....	....	....	....	....	....	[1]144
....	....	....	....	....	....	....	....	....	....	....	....
....	....	....	....	....	....	....	....	....	....	....	....
[5]500	....	....	....	....	[3]114	[2]74	[6]350	[5]190	[8]578	[4]270	....
....	....	....	....	....	....	....	....	....	....	....	....
[1/2]100	[2]185	[1]137	[3]296	....	[2]375	[3]296	[3]665	[1]114	[2]340	[1]204	[1]150
....	....	....	....	....	....	....	....	....	....	[1/2]12	....
....	[1]185	....	....	....	....	....	....	[1]114	[1]68	[1/2]144	[1]150
[2]500	[2]250	[2]176	....	....	[1]38	[2]148	[2]140	[5]646	[4]578	....	....
[1/2]100	[1]94	[3]48	....	....	[2]82	[1]37	....	[1]76	[4]136	[3]156	[3]396
....	....	....	....	[2]72	[6]125	....	[2]210	....	....	....	....
....	....	[6]468	....	....	....	....	....	....	[8]1156	....	....
....	....	....	....	....	....	....	....	....	....	....	....
....	....	....	....	....	....	....	....	....	....	....	....
....	....	....	....	....	....	....	....	....	....	....	....
400	[2]328	....	[2]370	[4]324	[3]215	[6]714	[5]560	[5]798	[3]272	[2]203	[4]540
[1/2]100	....	....	....	....	[1]44	....	....	[1]76	....	[1/2]34	....
....	....	....	....	....	....	....	....	....	....	....	....
[1/2]100	....	....	....	....	....	....	....	....	....	....	....
....	....	....	....	....	....	....	....	[1]76	....	[1/2]35	[1]144
[1]200	....	....	....	....	....	....	....	....	....	....	....
....	....	....	....	....	....	....	....	....	....	....	....
[1]200	[1]94	....	....	....	....	....	....	....	....	[1/2]69	....
[4 1/2]720	....	....	....	....	[2]76	....	[2]210	[6]684	[4]238	....	....
....	....	....	....	....	....	....	[6]175	....	....	....	....

† In this school there is a preparatory course below the one here given.

organize secondary education, but to achieve uniformity in the school subjects. It was the subsequent volume and intensity of discussion that made the report more significant than it had been expected to be.

Lacking this knowledge of the future, the Committee proceeded to group the studies into nine categories, each to be the topic of a conference. The categories selected were Latin; Greek; English; other modern languages; mathematics; physics, astronomy, and chemistry; natural history, including botany, zoology, and physiology; history, civil government, and political economy; and geography, including physical geography, geology, and meteorology. The prestige of the classics was indicated by the specification of separate categories for Latin and Greek, while French and German were combined as "other modern languages." Apart from this, the groupings gave full recognition to the modern academic subjects. No categories were provided for manual training, art, music, or business subjects, although these were mentioned in the final report.

In addition to naming the categories and suggesting people to participate in the conferences, the Committee prepared a set of questions for the conferences to discuss. These questions, eleven in number, seemed to deal with minor details of the mechanical arrangement of subjects, and great concern was shown for such matters as how many hours the subject should be taught per week, how many years it should be taught, and what division might be made in the subject for colleges that gave preliminary and final examinations for admission. Almost all these questions, however, were relevant to what Eliot had defined as desirable uniformity in schools.

The nine conferences met simultaneously, but in different places, December 28–30, 1892. This was little more than a month after the November meeting of the Committee. During that short period of time, it had been necessary to carry on correspondence with more than 90 people and to make the arrangements for the meetings, including provisions for transportation. Apparently Eliot was expected to take care of these matters himself. President Jesse, for example, wrote to Eliot on December 17, asking what route Professor Allen of his staff should take to the English conference at Vassar and how reduced railroad rates might be obtained.[22]

[22] Richard Henry Jesse to Charles W. Eliot, December 17, 1892, Charles W. Eliot Papers (Harvard University Archives, Cambridge, Mass.).

Of the 90 members of these conferences (10 for each one), 47 were from colleges or universities. Here was the opportunity for academic scholars, associated with practical school men, to make their mark on the school subjects. Taken together, the school men and the academic scholars constituted the experts from whom Eliot hoped to gain the agreements needed for his version of desirable uniformity in the schools.

Guided by Eliot's somewhat loaded questions, the conference sessions were held in their various localities, and those who had been assigned secretarial duties went home to write up what had taken place. Each conference was unique, but the way things moved may be indicated in part by the minutes of the conference on history, civil government, and political economy, held at Madison, Wisconsin. The group included among its college contingent President Charles Kendall Adams of the University of Wisconsin; Professor Albert Bushnell Hart of Harvard; Professor James Harvey Robinson of the University of Pennsylvania; and the young Professor Woodrow Wilson of what was then called the College of New Jersey. There were three school men in this conference, one of them being Ray Greene Huling, at this time principal of the high school at New Bedford, Massachusetts, who had worked with Tetlow in the founding of the New England Association.

As often happens when strangers get together on a somewhat vague assignment, the history conference began with aimless discussion, including the usual testimonials about how things were done back home. Inevitably, the conference participants talked about what history really was, one declaring it to be a branch of philosophy, another contending for it as the movement of organized society. The principal of the Albany Academy pointed out the dangers of "underrating the capacity of bright boys."

There was some doubt, however, about the expediency of teaching history in the secondary schools at all. President Adams thought poor teaching in the schools caused loss of interest in the subject. The implication was that pupils who went to college would study history in college anyway. "As for pupils who did not intend to go to College," state the minutes, "he [Adams] was inclined to let them pick up their historical information indirectly."[23] Professor Hart of Harvard did not agree with

[23] Minutes of the conference on History, Civil Government, and Political Economy, typescript submitted by Albert Bushnell Hart, secretary, Charles W. Eliot Papers (Harvard University Archives, Cambridge, Mass.). Material in this and the subsequent two paragraphs comes from this document.

this, but suggested detaching the question from that of preparation for college. So far as the colleges were concerned, they "could do their own historical work from the beginning and were not dependant on previous preparation in the schools." The conference, therefore, should "consider only how far history could be made a part of a good education in the lower schools." Woodrow Wilson supported Hart, reminding his fellow conferees that "they were not preparing for college in the secondary schools, but for life." He felt, however, that what he called scientific history, involving criticism and examination of evidence, had no place in the schools, for it tended to confuse young pupils. Scientific history, he declared, was college work and not school work; he recommended literary history in schools, for example, English history taught through Chaucer, Shakespeare, and Tennyson.

The conferees eventually agreed on teaching history in schools for eight years, including the four years of the high school. Separate resolutions were approved providing for various kinds of history, but without indicating any given order of these studies. It was left to Woodrow Wilson to bring in and gain approval for a program that called for French history in the first year of high school, English history in the second, American history in the third, and, in the fourth, a combination of civil government with "a special period pursued in an intensive manner." James Harvey Robinson had proposed the special-period study, but it was Ray Greene Huling who worked out the list of fourteen topics for it, including some from European and some from American history, as well as one labeled "some considerable phase of local history."

As the conference moved from one question to the next, it accumulated a total of 40 resolutions, condensed to 35 in the published version, all passed unanimously. One of these, moved by Wilson, excluded formal instruction in political economy from school programs. Correlation, a favorite word in this period, was recognized by resolving "that the teaching of history should be intimately connected with the teaching of English" and that history should "be constantly associated with" geography. Modification of Wilson's views about scientific history was achieved by a resolution "that in all practical ways an effort should be made to teach the pupils in the later years to discriminate betwen authorities and especially between original sources and secondary works." Since this also was unanimous, Wilson evidently voted for it. In another resolution, the conference declared "that the instruction in history and relative subjects ought to be the same for pupils on their way to college or the scientific school and for those who expect to stop at the end of the grammar schools, or at the end of the high schools."

It was not only the history conference, but six others as well that achieved unanimity. Only two conferences submitted minority as well as majority reports. The general report of the Committee of Ten found this unanimity "very striking" and added that "it should carry great weight."[24] It supported, of course, Eliot's previously expressed hopes that committees of experts could agree on the definitions of their respective subjects.

Furthermore, the conferences agreed with Eliot on important points. All of them recommended having "the elements of their several subjects taught earlier than they now are,"[25] opening the way particularly for Eliot's desire to have foreign languages, algebra, geometry, and physics introduced in the upper elementary grades. Probably most gratifying of all to Eliot was the unanimous response about not differentiating the treatment of subjects for pupils who were going to college and those who were not.[26] This has been interpreted by critics as a disregard for individual differences. Neither Eliot nor the conference members, however, were talking about differentiation as a general proposition, but solely as related to the plans of the pupil for further schooling. On the whole, Eliot had many reasons to be pleased by the results of the conferences. In future years he was to restate his conviction that their work was the most important part of the Committee of Ten.

In only one respect did the conferences disappoint him. Two of them failed to get their reports to him on time! Eliot had planned a tight schedule, according to which the final report of the Committee was to be presented at the summer meeting of the International Congress of Education. He had called for the conference reports by April 1, 1893, allowing time for the over-all Committee to prepare its summary. On April 11, however, he wrote to Angell noting the absence of two of the reports and commenting about the secretaries involved that "both these gentlemen now promise, three and a half months late, to take hold of the work assigned to them." In spite of the delay caused by "the two delinquents," he still felt "that our Committee will be able to contribute

[24] National Educational Association, *Report of the Committee of Ten on Secondary School Studies* (New York: American Book Co., 1894), p. 12.
[25] *Ibid.*, p. 14.
[26] *Ibid.*, p. 17.

largely to the improvement of American secondary schools."[27]

The two delinquents did not get their reports in until July. Late in September, Eliot sent printed copies to the other members, plus a printed tentative draft of an over-all report, presumably written by himself. This was printed "on wide paper," to allow room for proposed changes.[28] Evidently these were numerous and extensive, for he had the draft re-printed before the meeting of the Committee, from which only King was absent, November 8–11, 1893. Here the discussions "were vigorous and comprehensive."[29] Eliot and Tetlow then worked on a new revision that went out by mail for final criticism; of this Eliot wrote that he and Tetlow "found that a good deal of the old matter had to be modified and considerable new matter inserted."[30] By December 5 he had made his decisions about the last suggestions received by correspondence, and he wrote to Tetlow, "I send you by tonight's mail the final revise of the re-port in pages. Please read every word of it, and return it as soon as pos-sible. I shall read it too." He added: "This stage of our undertaking ap-proaches completion; but what vistas of debate open,"[31] indicating perhaps an anticipation of the controversy the report was to evoke.

The report was far from being a one-man affair. Robinson of Albany later wrote: "The major part of the work outside the committee meet-ings was done by the chairman, President Eliot. We might almost speak of the report as 'Dr. Eliot's report,' and yet this would be far from the truth, for I suppose no member of the committee conceded more than he —perhaps no one so much as he—in the various compromises reached."[32] Taylor's comment was: "Everyone knows certain opinions, published again and again, held by the chairman of the committee, for example, that would in his case modify the application of the principles agreed upon. It was not the least appreciated of his great services to the

[27] Charles W. Eliot to James B. Angell, April 11, 1893, James B. Angell Papers, Michigan Historical Collections (University of Michigan, Ann Arbor, Mich.).

[28] Charles W. Eliot to James C. Mackenzie, September 19, 1893, James C. Mackenzie Papers (Lawrenceville School, Lawrenceville, N.J.).

[29] National Educational Association, *op. cit.,* p. 12.

[30] Charles W. Eliot to James B. Angell, November 18, 1893, James B. Angell Papers, Michigan Historical Collections (University of Michigan, Ann Arbor, Mich.).

[31] Charles W. Eliot to John Tetlow, December 5, 1893, John Tetlow Papers (Houghton Library, Harvard University, Cambridge. Mass.).

[32] Oscar D. Robinson, "The Work of the Committee of Ten," *School Review* (June, 1894), p. 366.

committee that he could hold these in check, however cherished, for the sake of the general truth in which all could agree."[33]

This "general truth" was of necessity quite general, for there was more disagreement among the ten members of the Committee than among the ninety members of the conferences. With regard to the latter part of the report, according to Robinson, "differences of opinion were numerous and in some instances not easily harmonized."[34] As late as October 24, Eliot feared it would be impossible to reach agreement and thought the Committee might "find it necessary to do nothing but give an account of how the conferences were organized, and then present their work without recommendations. . . ."[35] Nevertheless, the disagreements were resolved, or at least they were smoothed over in the last stages of editorial revision.

Baker, though he did not withhold his signature from the report as a whole, submitted a minority statement, and it was printed in the final report.[36] His objections centered around what he felt to be an implied doctrine of equivalence of subjects, or the idea that one subject was as good as another for mental training. In dealing with this matter, Baker argued that the training furnished by subjects depended not on their form, but on their content. This was not an attack on disciplinary values in education. Baker, like many others, believed in these disciplinary values. The difficulty was that almost everyone had his own version of discipline, and the literature of the period abounded in hairbreadth distinctions set forth to enlighten, but for the most part obscuring, what was in any case a murky topic indeed! Baker sent a copy of his statement to Angell on November 28, "thinking of the possibility of a stray signature in addition to my own."[37] Angell did not oblige him. Eliot was not happy about the minority statement, particularly one part of it recommending a continuation of the Committee, but he did not suppress it.

It is probable that the notion of a general summary and interpretation had grown in importance as the work proceeded. The resolution creating

[33] James M. Taylor, "The Report of the Committee of Ten," *School Review* (April, 1894), pp. 198–199.

[34] Robinson, *op. cit.*, p. 367.

[35] Charles W. Eliot to unnamed committee member, October 24, 1893, as quoted *ibid.*, pp. 368–369.

[36] National Educational Association, *op. cit.*, pp. 56–59.

[37] James H. Baker to James B. Angell, November 28, 1893, James B. Angell Papers, Michigan Historical Collections (University of Michigan, Ann Arbor, Mich.).

the Committee mentioned only reporting the results of the conferences. In the report itself, the assignment was stated more fully,[38] but this was written after the event. Possibly Eliot was moved by his associates toward a more comprehensive general report. He never felt the general report to be as important as the results of the conferences, and he clung to his idea of the suggested courses of study as "but tentative."[39] Appropriately enough from Eliot's point of view the general report occupied only 59 pages of the 249-page volume that appeared as the product of the Committee of Ten.

IV

Prominently displayed in the general report was a series of tables, beginning with one that spread out the recommendations of all the conferences for eight years of elementary and four years of secondary schooling. Table II was an attempt to show what the high school program would look like if the time allotments recommended by the conferences for the various subjects were adopted. Table III was an adjusted version of Table II with some changes in the time allotments (see Fig. 2). According to the report Table III was presented without "judgment or recommendation of the Committee" as a "possible source of a great variety of good secondary school programmes,"[40] but in Table IV the Committee presented four "programmes" of its own. Harris and Mackenzie felt that the importance of Table IV was minimized by the prominence given to Table III.[41] Eliot preferred to see Table IV minimized. He did not like prearranged courses of study and preferred to think of those in Table IV as tentative only.[42]

The four "programmes" or courses of study were labeled Classical, Latin-Scientific, Modern Languages, and English (see Fig. 3). These

[38] National Educational Association, op. cit., pp. 3–4.
[39] Charles W. Eliot to James B. Angell, December 8, 1893, James B. Angell Papers, Michigan Historical Collections (University of Michigan, Ann Arbor, Mich.).
[40] National Educational Association, op. cit., pp. 40 and 42.
[41] William T. Harris to Charles W. Eliot, November 22, 1893, William T. Harris Papers (Library of Congress) Washington, D.C.; James C. Mackenzie to James B. Angell, December 2, 1893, James B. Angell Papers, Michigan Historical Collections (University of Michigan, Ann Arbor, Mich.).
[42] Charles W. Eliot to James B. Angell, December 8, 1893, James B. Angell Papers, Michigan Historical Collections (University of Michigan, Ann Arbor, Mich.).

Table III of the Report of the Committee of Ten

1ST SECONDARY SCHOOL YEAR.	2ND SECONDARY SCHOOL YEAR.
Latin .... 5 p.	Latin .... 4 p.
English Literature, 2 p.⎱ .. 4 p. " Composition, 2 p.⎰	Greek .... 5 p.
German [or French] .... 5 p.	English Literature, 2 p.⎱ .. 4 p. " Composition, 2 p.⎰
Algebra .... 4 p.	German, continued .... 4 p.
History of Italy, Spain, and France .... 3 p.	French, begun .... 5 p.

Applied Geography (European
   political — continental and
   oceanic flora and fauna) .. 4 p.
	Algebra,* 2 p.⎱ .... 4 p.
	Geometry, 2 p.⎰

	Botany or Zoölogy .... 4 p.
	English History to 1688 ..... 3 p.
25 p.	33 p.
	* Option of book-keeping and commercial arithmetic.
3RD SECONDARY SCHOOL YEAR.	**4TH SECONDARY SCHOOL YEAR.**
Latin .... 4 p.	Latin .... 4 p.
Greek .... 4 p.	Greek .... 4 p.

English Literature, 2 p.⎫
   "   Composition, 1 p.⎬ .. 4 p.
Rhetoric,   1 p.⎭
	English Literature, 2 p.⎫
	   " Composition, 1 p.⎬ .. 4 p.
	   " Grammar, 1 p.⎭

German .... 4 p.	German .... 4 p.
French .... 4 p.	French .... 4 p.
Algebra,* 2 p.⎱ .... 4 p. Geometry, 2 p.⎰	Trigonometry, ⎱ .... 2 p. Higher Algebra, ⎰
Physics .... 4 p.	Chemistry .... 4 p.

History, English and
   American .... 3 p.
	History (intensive) and Civil
	   Government .... 3 p.

Astronomy, 3 p. 1st ½ yr.⎱ 3 p.
Meteorology, 3 p. 2nd ½ yr.⎰
	Geology or Physiography,⎫
	   4 p. 1st ½ yr. ⎬ . 4 p.
	Anatomy, Physiology, and ⎭
	   Hygiene, 4 p. 2nd ½ yr.

34 p.	33 p.
* Option of book-keeping and commercial arithmetic.	

FIG. 2. The Range of Offerings for a High School As Set Forth by the Committee of Ten in Table III, p. 41, of the Report. [Table III represented the total program as derived from recommendations of the conferences, with some adjustment of periods per week. From it the programs of individual pupils could be derived. Eliot apparently preferred this to the set courses of study identified by the committee in Table IV.]

were familiar titles then being used in the schools. Taken in order from
Classical to English, they represented decreasing amounts of foreign languages. The English course, unlike many with that title in the schools,
was not confined to the vernacular, but required the study of one foreign
tongue, ancient or modern. All four courses, as was customary at that
time, included mathematics of the algebra-geometry sequence. The order
of courses from Classical to English also represented increasing amounts
of the modern academic studies. Even in the Classical course, 38 to
41 of the 80 allotted periods over four years were provided for subjects
other than Latin, Greek, and mathematics. Each course included some
foreign language, mathematics, English, science, and history.

These courses of study provided convenient objects for attack. For
one thing, though it was an age of enthusiasm for manual training and
other practical subjects, none of these appeared in Table IV at all, and
there had been no conferences to recommend these subjects. Robinson
wanted them included, perhaps as an independent action on the part of
the Committee, but Eliot said it was "absolutely impossible to make a
course valuable for training to which these varied and numerous subjects are admitted."[43] The report did declare, however, that "the omission of music, drawing, and elocution from the programmes offered by
the Committee was not intended to imply that these subjects ought to
receive no systematic attention" and left the matter to local school authorities to decide, "without suggestions from the Committee."[44]

Table IV also contained provisions that would later stir up the classicists. It recommended that Greek be started in the third year in the
Classical course, whereas the Greek conference had proposed starting
it in the second. Moreover, Table IV assigned Latin only four, instead
of five, periods per week in the third and fourth years. These recommendations on the classics, combined with the omission of the practical
subjects, succeeded in lining up the extreme right and left wings of opinion at that time against the report.

If anything, the report was calculated to appeal to the moderate center
composed of innovators who sought a larger place for the modern aca-

[43] Charles W. Eliot to unnamed committee member, October 24, 1893, as quoted
in Robinson, *op. cit.*, p. 368. Eliot's bias was not directed against practical subjects
as such, but against all of what he called short informational subjects, including
music, drawing, elocution, spelling, penmanship, political economy, mental science,
and ethics. He was later to campaign vigorously for manual training, drawing, and
music.

[44] National Educational Association, *op. cit.*, p. 48.

Table IV of the Report of the Committee of Ten

CLASSICAL. Three foreign languages (one modern).	LATIN-SCIENTIFIC. Two foreign languages (one modern).
YEAR I.	**YEAR I.**
Latin .... 5 p.	Latin .... 5 p.
English .... 4 p.	English .... 4 p.
Algebra .... 4 p.	Algebra .... 4 p.
History .... 4 p.	History .... 4 p.
Physical Geography .... 3 p.	Physical Geography .... 3 p.
20 p.	20 p.
YEAR II.	**YEAR II.**
Latin .... 5 p.	Latin .... 5 p.
English .... 2 p.	English .... 2 p.
*German [or French] begun .. 4 p.	German [or French] begun ... 4 p.
Geometry .... 3 p.	Geometry .... 3 p.
Physics .... 3 p.	Physics .... 3 p.
History .... 3 p.	Botany or Zoölogy .... 3 p.
20 p.	20 p.
YEAR III.	**YEAR III.**
Latin .... 4 p.	Latin .... 4 p.
*Greek .... 5 p.	English .... 3 p.
English .... 3 p.	German [or French] .... 4 p.
German [or French] .... 4 p.	Mathematics { Algebra 2 / Geometry 2 } .. 4 p.
Mathematics { Algebra 2 / Geometry 2 } .. 4 p.	Astronomy ½ yr. & Meteorology ½ yr. .... 3 p.
	History .... 2 p.
20 p.	20 p.
YEAR IV.	**YEAR IV.**
Latin .... 4 p.	Latin .... 4 p.
Greek .... 5 p.	English { as in classical 2 / additional 2 } .... 4 p.
English .... 2 p.	German [or French] .... 3 p.
German [or French] .... 3 p.	Chemistry .... 3 p.
Chemistry .... 3 p.	Trigonometry & Higher Algebra or History } 3 p.
Trigonometry & Higher Algebra or History } 3 p.	Geology or Physiography ½ yr. and Anatomy, Physiology, & Hygiene ½ yr. } 3 p.
20 p.	20 p.

* In any school in which Greek can be better taught than a modern language, or in which local public opinion or the history of the school makes it desirable to teach Greek in an ample way, Greek may be substituted for German or French in the second year of the Classical programme.

FIG. 3. The Four Courses of Study Recommended by the Committee of Ten in Table IV, pp. 46–47, of the Report.

Table IV (*continued*)

MODERN LANGUAGES.	ENGLISH.
Two foreign languages (both modern).	One foreign language (ancient or modern).

YEAR I.	YEAR I.
French [*or* German] begun... 5 p.	Latin, or German, or French . 5 p.
English .... 4 p.	English .... 4 p.
Algebra .... 4 p.	Algebra .... 4 p.
History .... 4 p.	History .... 4 p.
Physical Geography .... 3 p.	Physical Geography .... 3 p.
20 p.	20 p.

YEAR II.	YEAR II.
French [*or* German] .... 4 p.	Latin, or German, or
English .... 2 p.	French ....5 or 4 p.
German [*or* French] begun... 5 p.	English ....3 or 4 p.
Geometry .... 3 p.	Geometry .... 3 p.
Physics .... 3 p.	Physics .... 3 p.
Botany or Zoölogy .... 3 p.	History .... 3 p.
20 p.	Botany or Zoölogy .... 3 p.
	20 p.

YEAR III.	YEAR III.
French [*or* German] .... 4 p.	Latin, or German, or French.. 4 p.
English .... 3 p.	English { as in others 3 / additional 2 } ...... 5 p.
German [*or* French] .... 4 p.	
Mathematics { Algebra 2 / Geometry 2 } .. 4 p.	Mathematics { Algebra 2 / Geometry 2 } ...4 p.
Astronomy ½ yr. & Meteorology ½ yr. .... 3 p.	Astronomy ½ yr. & Meteorology ½ yr. .... 3 p.
History .... 2 p.	History { as in the Latin-Scientific 2 / additional 2 } 4 p.
20 p.	
	20 p.

YEAR IV.	YEAR IV.
French [*or* German] .... 3 p.	Latin, or German, or French.. 4 p.
English { as in Classical 2 / additional 2 } ... 4 p.	English { as in Classical 2 / additional 2 } ... 4 p.
German [*or* French] .... 4 p.	Chemistry .... 3 p.
Chemistry .... 3 p.	Trigonometry & Higher Algebra 3 p.
Trigonometry & Higher Algebra 3 / or / History } 3 p.	History .... 3 p.
Geology or Physiography ½ yr. and Anatomy, Physiology & Hygiene ½ yr. } 3 p.	Geology or Physiography ½ yr. and Anatomy, Physiology, & Hygiene ½ yr. } 3 p.
20 p.	20 p.

demic studies. Even they must have had some difficulty with a cloudy sentence proclaiming the unanimous opinion of the Committee "that, under existing conditions in the United States as to the training of teachers and the provision of necessary means of instruction, the two programmes called respectively Modern Languages and English must in practice be distinctly inferior to the other two."[45] This was not necessarily a concession to Harris' belief that every pupil should have Latin and Greek. In an address to the New England Association in October, 1893, before the completion of the report, Eliot deplored the representation of the modern studies by what he called "an extraordinary number of scraps of miscellaneous subjects, instead of a limited number of substantial subjects each treated with some thoroughness." He disparaged "the scrappy, ineffective programs" substituted for the classics, adding, however, that it was "one object of the conferences to show the way to make the so-called English, or modern, side of our high schools just as firm, substantial, and valuable as the classical side."[46] These sentiments were repeated in the report, with commendation of the conferences for having shown how every subject could be made "a serious subject of instruction, well fitted to train the pupil's powers of observation, expression, and reasoning."[47] It was with this qualification that the moderate innovators dedicated to the modern academic studies had to remain content.

Eliot's version of disciplinary values played a large part in what seemed to be his rather tortured locutions on this and other points in the report. Neither at that time nor in subsequent years did he show enthusiasm for information or content. The purpose of subjects was to develop power, particularly in observation, expression, and reasoning. On the other hand, he was at no time associated with the later stereotype of formal discipline as an exercising of mental faculties through difficult and unpleasant tasks. His belief in electives was based on the premise that superior mental training would result from permitting pupils to study those subjects in which they had interest and ability. At the same time he believed in the need for thoroughness and continued study in a subject. This is why he insisted with wearisome persistence on the importance of time allotments and why so much discussion of time allot-

[45] *Ibid.*

[46] Charles W. Eliot, Eighth Annual Meeting of the New England Association of Colleges and Preparatory Schools, October 12–13, 1893, *School Review* (December, 1893), pp. 616–617.

[47] National Educational Association, *op. cit.,* p. 53.

ments appeared in the report of the Committee of Ten. Therefore the modern academic subjects had to be rescued from the scrappy information guises in which they had hitherto appeared. In spite of the comment about the inferiority of the English and Modern Language programs, the net result of Eliot's thinking was strong advocacy of a larger place (with greater time allotments) for the modern subjects.

Near the end of the report, the Committee expressed its views on college admission. Here it stated that "the secondary schools of the United States, taken as a whole, do not exist for the purpose of preparing boys and girls for colleges. Only an insignificant percentage of the graduates of these schools go to colleges or scientific schools." This was neither a bold declaration for the independence of the high schools nor, as some have seen it, a piece of hypocrisy. It was a statement of fact. The main function of the high schools, continued the report, was "to prepare for the duties of life that small proportion of all the children in the country —a proportion small in number, but very important to the welfare of the nation—who show themselves able to profit by an education prolonged to the eighteenth year, and whose parents are able to support them while they remain so long at school." In this reference to economics, the Committee was not proposing wealth as a criterion for selection. It was expressing its opinion that not many parents could afford to keep children in school until eighteen years of age.

The Committee did not propose leaving the high schools without a preparatory function. It was obviously desirable, they declared, "that the colleges and scientific schools should be accessible to all boys or girls who have completed creditably the secondary school course." They called attention to the difficulties faced by pupils who could not anticipate college while they were in the beginning year of the high school. Therefore, colleges should accept "the attainments of any youth who has passed creditably through a good secondary school course, no matter to what group of subjects he may have mainly devoted himself in the secondary school." If the recommendations of the conferences were carried out, they "might fairly be held to make all the main subjects taught in the secondary schools of equal rank for the purposes of admission to college or scientific school." Finally, the Committee asserted that the satisfactory completion of any one of the courses in Table IV "should admit to corresponding courses in colleges and scientific schools."[48] Since two of these courses required neither Latin nor Greek, this was a break with

[48] *Ibid.*, pp. 51–53.

tradition, although some colleges were already doing what was here recommended.

On the whole, the message of the report ran along these lines: There should be no difference made in the teaching of any subject on the ground of whether or not a pupil was going to college. The modern academic subjects should be rescued from their scrappy inferiority; this could be done by following the recommendations of the conferences. With this done, colleges could and should accept these subjects for admission. One could get good mental training and should be admitted to college even though he had never studied either Latin or Greek. The elective principle was clearly endorsed, although not in the form Eliot would have preferred; still he clung to his hope that the four courses of study were only tentative and would, in time, be abandoned.

The report has been called an uninspiring document. It is on the whole a sober one, but also one far more readable than many produced by subsequent committees. It was bound to disappoint those who expected inspirational utterances about the mission of the high school in America's destiny. Eliot's style always fell short of what was expected in late nineteenth-century pronouncements. As one of his sympathetic critics declared in 1899, it had "little of that magic power to light up present facts with glowing reminiscences of kindred facts and fancies drawn from far-off lands and days and to set sentences to throbbing in rhythmic sympathy with the pulsations of the thought."[49] Furthermore, the report was not up to the level of Eliot's best writing in this period, such as the three addresses to the Department of Superintendence and the one on uniformity to the NEA. It was marked by the repetition and prolixity characteristic of attempts to incorporate suggestions from a committee. On the other hand, in view of the wide and furious subsequent discussion of the report, it is awesome to contemplate what might have happened had Eliot overstimulated the imaginations of his contemporaries with "glowing reminiscences of kindred facts and fancies drawn from far-off lands and days."

[49] William DeWitt Hyde, "President Eliot as an Educational Reformer," *Atlantic Monthly* (March, 1899), p. 348.

Chapter 4

A sea of troubles

> "I have never had any dealings with Mr. Nightingale of Chicago, and know nothing about him. If he has any malice against the members of the committee, I think it must be of some impersonal nature."
>
> —CHARLES W. ELIOT,
> MARCH 1, 1894.

"*A* deluge of discussion has overspread the entire world of secondary education," declared Professor Andrew F. West of Princeton in the year 1899. "When," he asked, "in the history of our land has there been anything like it?"[1] The waters of this flood had been released by Eliot and his nine associates. Moreover, the deluge overspread not only the world of secondary education, but several other pedagogical worlds as well. From 1894 to 1905 almost every treatment of matters educational was referred to, compared with, or distinguished from the report of the Committee of Ten.

Just why the appearance of this sober document, glutted with details about time allotments and methods of teaching, should have done all this has never been clear. Perhaps it was an accident, one of those events occurring at the right time to be associated with movements that would have taken place without it. Or it may have been in part the response of educators made sensitive by the critical articles of Joseph M. Rice that appeared in the *Forum* while the Committee was still at work. Possibly the International Congress of Education held in the summer of 1893 created an awareness of controversy not only about American schooling but also about schooling in other countries, where similar debates were taking place. Another possibility is that American educators

[1] Andrew F. West, "Is There a Democracy of Studies?" *Atlantic Monthly* (December, 1899), p. 821.

66

found in the report a conversation piece that unloosed their individual and collective tongues.

The report was quickly and widely distributed. Harris had arranged for the printing of it by the Bureau of Education, and 30,000 free copies were soon on their way to school men, school board members, and other interested parties. Without Harris the report might not have been printed at all, for the Committee had not only spent its $2500 grant from the NEA, but also an additional $2005.94 that had been raised by Eliot from private contributors,[2] these including Tetlow, Harris, and Eliot himself.[3] After the 30,000 copies were gone—and this happened within the first few months—the NEA made an arrangement with the American Book Company for a second edition, differing from the first in that it had a topical index. By 1901 this second edition had sold 10,538 copies,[4] making a total by that time of about 40,000 copies that had gone into personal libraries, school libraries, wastebaskets, and the stalls of second-hand-book stores. Apparently the report did get to a lot of people, and those who wanted to read it could do so in a convenient volume instead of trying to dig it out of the confused jumble of papers that constituted the annual proceedings of the NEA, where previous reports of the National Council had appeared. All of this probably contributed to the degree of attention given to, and the amount of discussion stimulated by, the report.

II

The first official airing of the report took place at the Richmond meeting of the Department of Superintendence on February 20 and 21, 1894. Although by this time Eliot was well known to the superintendents and had addressed them three times in preceding years, he did not attend these sessions. The only member of the Committee of Ten whose presence was recorded was William T. Harris. Butler came, probably to get an eyewitness account for his own satisfaction and for editorial comment in *Educational Review*. Some of the most prominent city

[2] N. A. Calkins, letter to the editor, *Public-School Journal* (May, 1895), pp. 515–516.
[3] Charles W. Eliot to John Tetlow, undated letter, between March 3 and April 26, 1893, John Tetlow Papers (Houghton Library, Harvard University, Cambridge, Mass.).
[4] Irwin Shepard, "First Annual Report of the Permanent Secretary to the Board of Trustees," NEA, 1901, p. 45.

superintendents in the country were there, including William H. Maxwell of Brooklyn, New York, and James M. Greenwood of Kansas City, Missouri. Maxwell had been a member of the conference on English, one of the few city superintendents who served in any of the conferences. If the superintendents resented not having been asked, this was their opportunity to hit back.

On the afternoon of February 20, Francis W. Parker of Quincy fame, but at this time principal of the Cook County Normal School, Illinois, talked on the use of the report at teachers' institutes and meetings, urging the preparation of study guides and questions for discussion. He was one of the few commentators who ever grasped the social meaning of the recommendations pertaining to pupils who were preparing to go to college and those who were not. "One unanimous conclusion of all the conferences," said Parker, "a conclusion without a single dissenting voice, or vote, is worth all the cost and all the pains that were necessary to produce the report. That conclusion is that there should be no such thing as class education. President Eliot is emphatic as to this." He went on to rebuke what he called "a rapidly growing sentiment in our large cities," namely "to reduce the common schools to charity schools, to give the poor a crumb when justice demands a full loaf." He pursued this with reference not only to science and history but also to the classics, declaring, "There is no reason why one child should study Latin and another be limited to the '3 R's.' "[5]

Parker's favorable comments were offset in the ensuing discussion by Superintendent Greenwood, who aimed his remarks particularly at the conference on mathematics. He was annoyed by recommendations for cutting out certain topics from arithmetic, such as "compound proportion," and by the suggestions for correlating arithmetic with other subjects. "To the Committee of Ten, and to the Committee of Ninety, I will say, that the only way a boy can learn arithmetic is to study in arithmetic and not to mix it up with other things." Personal resentment was indicated by his sarcastic reference to "the immense array of names and the positions of those that have made these reports." He contended that city teachers in a number of localities were doing excellent work, "better

[5] Francis W. Parker, "The Report of the Committee of Ten: Its Use for the Improvement of Teachers Now at Work in the Schools," NEA, 1894, p. 449. According to a present-day critic of the Committee of Ten, this was one occasion on which Parker was taken in: see Edgar B. Wesley, *NEA: The First Hundred Years* (New York: Harper & Row, 1957), p. 72.

than the gentlemen themselves can do," and tauntingly declared: "Let them take their own medicine first."[6]

The main show took place the next day, February 21, beginning with an introduction of the report by Commissioner Harris. This turned into one of the liveliest meetings in the history of the NEA, supplying an abundance of anecdotes, which grew as they were told and retold over many years. Harris dwelt on his favorite theme, the five windows of the soul, pointing out that the traditional Classical program had opened only two or three such windows. It was necessary therefore to include modern studies in the Classical program, but this was not easy to accomplish. The making of the Classical course of study, he said, had taken up nearly all the time in the discussions of the Committee of Ten. He explained and defended the decision to begin Greek in the third rather than the second year. At the same time, he again set forth the virtues of Latin and Greek, particularly with respect to their literature.[7]

Superintendent Maxwell praised the report but raised questions about what he felt to be Harris' excessive devotion to the classics.[8] At some later point Harris gained the floor to reply to Maxwell. The accounts of what then took place remain somewhat confusing, but it is clear that Harris provided what many regarded as the supreme example of effective platform warfare. "He was at his best, and so was the audience. . . . It was not only irresistibly amusing, but was in every way classic humor. It was wholly good-natured. There was not the shadow of a suspicion of viciousness in it; pure classic mischief, with an educational purpose —that was all. To report it is impossible. Every point that Mr. Maxwell had innocently presented merely furnished coloring for the vivifying of the historic painting by Dr. Harris. The audience was more convulsed than it has ever been before in its history."[9] So ran one account. Whether Maxwell agreed that it was "wholly good-natured" is not known, and just what Harris did say is not clear. The published version in the NEA volume of proceedings was no more than a garbled condensation. At the end, President Andrew S. Draper of the University of Illinois urged Maxwell to ask Harris another question; drawing the retort from Max-

[6] James M. Greenwood, discussion, NEA, 1894, p. 454.
[7] William T. Harris, "The Curriculum for Secondary Schools," NEA, 1894, pp. 496–508.
[8] William H. Maxwell, discussion, NEA, 1894, pp. 508–512.
[9] "The Harris-Maxwell Instance," *Journal of Education* (March 8, 1894), p. 153.

well that he should ask one himself, Draper further convulsed the meeting by saying he had a wife and children at home. "The most vivid imagination," continued the account in the *Journal of Education,* could not at that point have portrayed "the condition of that audience of dignitaries."[10]

Some of these dignitaries had enjoyed themselves earlier when Assistant Superintendent Augustus F. Nightingale of the Chicago public schools had turned loose his famous attack on the entire Committee of Ten. This speech was left out of the NEA volume of proceedings. It appeared condensed as a direct quotation in the *Journal of Education.* Nightingale declared it "a matter for congratulation that there were to be found so many eminent men who were willing to come together at the expense of the National Educational Association" and pronounced it "one of the wonders of the age that this committee was so unanimous upon every subject and every phase of every subject, upon every grade of work except that in which the majority of the committee had had any experience."[11] In his editorial comment in the April *Educational Review,* Butler said that Nightingale "in a blizzard-like voice" had made "an ignorant and indecent attack upon the Committee of Ten." The audience was much upset, according to Butler, and every serious-minded man present was shocked and ashamed. "Unfortunately, a group of noisy sensationalists encouraged the speaker by their laughter and shouts of approval . . . continuing their demonstrations for an hour."[12] On the other hand, the *Journal of Education* stated editorially that Nightingale had "made a brilliant charge upon the weak points in the Report of the Committee of Ten, receiving the most spontaneous and hearty applause of any speaker except, of course, Dr. W. T. Harris, who was applauded as no other man had been in the history of the department."[13]

After such a strenuous meeting, the superintendents consoled themselves at a midnight banquet at the "elegant" Masonic Temple where they enjoyed "oysters in the half-shell, oysters 'in patties,' and oysters fried, tenderloin and mushrooms, croquettes of chicken with genuine green peas, roast duck, sorbet de Virginia, Roman punch, creams and ices, fruit and cake, coffee and chocolate, with no end of accessories,

[10] *Ibid.*
[11] Augustus F. Nightingale, "The Committee of Ten: Five-Minute Speeches," *Journal of Education* (March 8, 1894), p. 150.
[12] *Educational Review* (April, 1894), p. 405.
[13] "Richmond Notes," *Journal of Education* (March 8, 1894), p. 152.

such as olives, celery, etc."[14] Southern hospitality apparently had triumphed, and the pedagogical animosities of the preceding hours dissolved in a brief era of good feeling.

Butler either did not attend the midnight banquet or succeeded in resisting its effects, for he soon wrote to Eliot expressing severe disapproval of "Mr. Nightingale of Chicago," who with one or two others, "apparently unacquainted with the courtesies of life, endeavored to substitute a malicious attack upon the members of the Committee for criticism of their report." More consolingly, he told Eliot that the report had been received "with almost unqualified admiration and with substantial approval by the large body of serious minded public school men."[15] Eliot replied that he was "more than content," and added: "I have never had any dealings with Mr. Nightingale of Chicago, and know nothing about him. If he has any malice against the members of the committee, I think it must be of some impersonal nature."[16]

Meanwhile the journals developed a campaign of uninhibited editorial exuberance about the report, both for and against. *Dial* began it on a low note, offering dignified approval, but warning against a "tendency" in the report to "countenance a dangerous latitude" with respect to the elective system.[17] Butler's *Educational Review* sustained a high statesmanlike tone in its praise of the report. Other journals in favor of the report were *Intelligence* and the *American Journal of Education*. The opposite side was taken by *Education,* which saw the report as an attempt "to capture the common school system of the country" in the interest of university aims and methods, and as evidence that leading educational thinkers were "still largely out of sympathy with the steady movement of the American Educational Public."[18] These men, continued the criticism in *Education,* did not know that there was "a vaster body than itself; broader, more far seeing, wiser and more humane . . . engaged in building up a proper system of education for American youth."[19]

The most vitriolic editorial critic of the report, however, was A. E. Winship in his *Journal of Education.* He began by predicting that the re-

[14] *Ibid.*

[15] Nicholas Murray Butler to Charles W. Eliot, February 26, 1894, Charles W. Eliot Papers (Harvard University Archives, Cambridge, Mass.).

[16] Charles W. Eliot to Nicholas Murray Butler, March 1, 1894, Charles W. Eliot Papers (Harvard University Archives, Cambridge, Mass.).

[17] "The Report on Secondary Education," *Dial* (January 16, 1894), p. 36.

[18] *Education* (March, 1894), pp. 432–433.

[19] *Education* (April, 1894), p. 498.

port would attract more attention than previous reports of the NEA or the National Council, these having "fallen flat," but characterized as "ludicrous" the attempts of those who knew "nothing except incidentally" about elementary education to recommend subjects for the elementary grades.[20] In subsequent issues, Winship published condensations or abstracts of the various conference reports. He found some "good wholesome truth" here and there, but said this was "hardly what was expected when the appropriation of $2500 was made to secure it."[21] In the February 8 issue Winship printed a portrait of Eliot and praised his services, "whatever difference of opinion there may be, regarding the wisdom and practical ability of the recommendations."[22] Several issues later, he scolded those who displayed "undue sensitiveness over the failure of school men to worship the Report."[23] Inviting his readers to compare, or rather to contrast, the report with the writings of Horace Mann, Thaddeus Stevens, and, presumably in his more inspired moments, William T. Harris, Winship declared that there was nothing sacred about the report, that it had nothing in it to be worshipped, and that it presented evidence of neither genius nor greatness. Winship finally moved to a triumphant outburst of indignation in which he said the report "only escaped being a gigantic fraud because it was so well intentioned."[24]

As the journalistic war progressed, so did the various local and regional meetings, held throughout the spring and summer of 1894. The recently founded Harvard Teachers' Association went over the report in March, and Eliot may well have felt like the prophet in his own country. Professor Nathaniel Shaler quoted Charles Darwin as having once said that his position might not be tenable but would be much talked about, and Shaler predicted the same future for the report.[25] This was perhaps the most perceptive remark made on the subject, and even the *Journal of Education* in its editorial comment on the meeting praised Eliot's ability to furnish ideas "that provoke limitless desire for discussion."[26]

[20] *Journal of Education* (January 18, 1894), pp. 40–41.
[21] "Committee of Ten," *Journal of Education* (February 8, 1894), p. 79.
[22] "President Eliot," *Journal of Education* (February 8, 1894), p. 88.
[23] "Reception of the Report," *Journal of Education* (March 22, 1894), p. 185.
[24] "Dr. Harris' Masterpiece," *Journal of Education* (February 21, 1895), p. 128. The reference in the title was to the report of the Committee of Fifteen on Elementary Education, to which Winship was contrasting that of the Committee of Ten.
[25] As quoted in "The Great Incubator," *Journal of Education* (March 15, 1894), p. 168.
[26] *Ibid.*

Superintendent Edwin Seaver of Boston was less charitable about the report, particularly the work of the conference on mathematics. The midwestern *Intelligence* found in his comments an example "of the petty and insincere Yankee schoolmaster, quibbling on statements in defiance of manifest substance."[27]

At the traditional April meeting of the Massachusetts Classical and High School Teachers' Association, Eliot attempted to calm down the discussion about the report by declaring it to hold "but a temporary position in educational history" and to be "but a temporary expedient in a transition period." It was, he said, "suggestive rather than decisive."[28] This made his position clear, but his words had little effect, either on his opponents or friends. Where Winship found the report almost a gigantic fraud, Superintendent Maxwell of Brooklyn had seen in it "the cloud by day and the pillar of fire by night that is to lead us into the promised land" and "the noblest monument" ever erected by the teachers of America through the NEA.[29] Apparently nobody was prepared to consider the report as merely "a temporary expedient in a transition period."

Not at all inclined to do so, from one side or the other, were the 391 school men and professors who gathered at Albany early in July for the University Convocation of the State of New York, known as the regents' convocation. Seeking, but not finding, the implications of destiny in the report, Superintendent John Kennedy of Batavia, New York, declared it "at once the greatest delight of the age, and the most supreme disappointment." He chided the Ten and their associates for having failed "to sound an inspiring trumpet call" and for not having "quickened our blood." Education, he said, still awaited its leader. "It is a headless host."[30] Robinson attended and spoke at this meeting, expressing some of his misgivings about the report.[31] On the whole, the tone of the meeting was very critical, and the *School Review*, in its editorial comment, said: " 'Giving it to the Committee of Ten' has been a popular recreation for the past six months. The convocation gave it to them all day Friday."[32]

[27] "Criticism of the Report of the Committee of Ten," *Intelligence* (April 1, 1894), p. 97.
[28] As quoted in "High and Classical Association," *Journal of Education* (April 12, 1894), p. 235.
[29] William H. Maxwell, discussion, NEA, 1894, p. 512.
[30] As quoted in "A Headless Host," *American Journal of Education and National Educator* (November 9, 1894), p. 4.
[31] C. H. T., "Summer Meetings," *School Review* (September, 1894), p. 432.
[32] *Ibid.*

Another group not in the mood to consider the report as a temporary expedient was its sponsoring agency, the National Council of Education. On July 9, 1894, two years to a day from the creation of the Committee, the Council assembled to receive and to discuss the report. Baker made the address of presentation. It did not suffer from excess of enthusiasm. He reminded the Council that the work of the Committee had taken a different turn from what had been anticipated, probably referring here to the report he had brought to the Council in 1891 from his Committee on Secondary Education. Nevertheless, he said, he did not doubt "the wisdom of the plan finally adopted."[33] Baker went on to express himself both for and against the results of this plan, setting forth twenty-two points in favor of the report and seven points against it. Among the aspects of the report he favored were what he called "the omission of industrial and commercial subjects" and "the desirability of uniformity," adding, however, that the latter had not been definitely recommended in the report. He expressed strong approval of postponing the choice between the Classical course of study and the Latin-Scientific, and he pronounced "the advantage of postponing the necessity of making a final choice of courses as long as possible" to be a very important principle recognized by the Committee.[34] Still on this point, he spoke against determining station in life by the differentiation in courses at an early period. Finally, he warmly endorsed the recommendation under which colleges would accept any one of the courses of study for admission.

In spite of his possible resentment of Eliot as Chairman, Baker agreed with what Eliot would have regarded as fundamental recommendations in the report. So far as his disagreements were concerned, Baker dwelt at length on the so-called equivalence of studies and the form-and-content distinction treated in his minority statement. Mere form, he argued again, was nothing; power came through knowledge; and the choice of studies was not a matter of indifference. At the end of his speech, he recommended the continuation of the Committee, a point he had also included in his minority statement.

At least fifteen people took part in the subsequent discussion. Woodward declared the report to have "great value," but he criticized the omission of specific provisions for manual training and the alleged pre-

[33] James H. Baker, "Review of the Report of the Committee of Ten," NEA, 1894, p. 646.
[34] Ibid., p. 650.

occupation with "literary high schools and academies."[35] Several persons expressed doubts about the competence of the Committee to deal with elementary schools and recommended the referral of that part of the report to a new committee of experts in elementary education. Mackenzie sought to meet both these criticisms halfway, but added: "Do not scalp the committee. Be good to them."[36] Robinson did not ask for such consideration and seemed more inclined to scalp the Committee himself. He called attention to the presence on the Committee of only one representative of a "typical high school." The most valuable thing he saw in the report was the number of programs, and he added the optimistic note that "criticism will have the effect of correcting their evils."[37]

The most portentous comments for the future reputation of the report were made by President G. Stanley Hall of Clark University, who declared the report "a fine thing" and found it "almost sacrilegious to oppose it." After heartily advising his audience to vote for it, he criticized its lack of coordination, the result of its having been inspired by a man "who believes in a mob of subjects." Severe judgment was passed on the "highly pernicious" doctrine of equivalence of subjects. Hall also pronounced the report "wrong" in its advocacy of teaching all pupils the same way, for this was considered "radical heresy" in Germany and France.[38] Others found too much European influence in the report, but on this point Hall apparently did not find it European enough. In the years to come, Hall would return again and again to his dislike of the report, culminating in the full-scale denunciation included in his two volumes on adolescence.

On the whole, the discussion throughout the long day of July 9 was critical of, in fact, almost hostile to, the report. The only spirited defense of it came from Butler, who, whether he had appointed the Committee or not, felt a proprietary interest in its product. "In listening to the discussion of the report of the Committee of Ten," he said, "not only as it has taken place in this Council, but in other educational bodies as well, I am reminded a little of the traditional attitude of the English peasant toward a new idea. It is said that when a new idea crosses the path of an English peasant, his first impulse is to ' 'eave 'arf a brick at it.' There

[35] C. M. Woodward, discussion, NEA, 1894, p. 661.
[36] James C. Mackenzie, discussion, NEA, 1894, p. 662.
[37] Oscar D. Robinson, discussion, NEA, 1894, p. 663.
[38] G. Stanley Hall, discussion, NEA, 1894, p. 663.

has been something of this disposition on the part of some participants in these discussions."[39]

The big question was whether or not to continue the Committee. Baker wanted it continued. Eliot, absent from the meeting in spite of an urgent personal invitation from the President of the Council, did not. He had requested the discharge of the Committee in an official letter to the Council several days before. The Council unanimously supported Eliot and put an end to the official existence of the Committee of Ten. Perhaps Eliot felt disinclined to spend more time on the matter, but he probably feared that further work by the Committee might lead to what he considered undesirable uniformity. At any rate, he did not want a seemingly endless reconsideration of theoretical or abstract questions, such as the so-called doctrine of equivalence. It has been said, and rightly, that Eliot was not a philosopher, and he clearly had a low level of tolerance for what people like Baker, Harris, and Hall considered to be philosophical discussion. The Council's action in discharging the Committee was evidently a great relief to him. Four days later, the NEA unanimously adopted a resolution thanking "the distinguished Chairman and his associates" for their "remarkable report," which was predicted to "stand for years to come as a monument of American scholarship and a source of inspiration to American teachers."[40] The chairman of the Committee on Resolutions was William H. Maxwell, who had pronounced the report a monument back at Richmond.

III

It was at Bethlehem, New Hampshire, on July 11, with the NEA still in session at Asbury Park, that Eliot broke his silence about criticisms of the report. His audience was the American Institute of Instruction, a pre-NEA organization dating back to 1830. What occupied him especially in this address was the criticism implied in the question, "What do college men know about schools?" His answer was an appeal to what he termed "the unity of educational reform," under which needed changes were common to all levels of instruction. According to this non-philosopher, the "artificial and arbitrary distinction" among levels had

[39] Nicholas Murray Butler, discussion, NEA, 1894, p. 666.
[40] Report of the Committee on Resolutions, NEA, 1894, p. 35.

"no philosophical foundation," and he predicted such distinctions would be modified or "altogether pass away."[41] So far as the specific content of the report was concerned, he dismissed as "temporary trestlework" the recommended programs of study in Table IV.[42]

In this address, Eliot identified seven major reforms common to all levels. One of these involved the "main object of education," which he declared to be giving the pupil "the power of doing himself an endless variety of things which, uneducated, he could not do."[43] Another main line of reform was the elective principle, defended here by Eliot as an "absolute necessity" in secondary schools, "and even in the later years of the elementary course."[44] On this occasion, however, he seemed to disregard his own strictures against distinctions among educational levels by recognizing "a serious limitation on the principle of election" in what he called "the very last stage of education," that of professional training.[45]

Eliot was not mistaken about the major criticism of the report. During the spring and summer of 1894 it was in fact the college men on the Committee and in the conferences, with their alleged ignorance of schools, who had drawn most of the popular fire. It should be noted, however, in view of the shift that later took place, what the nature of this criticism was at that time. It was largely that the college men were meddling with the elementary schools, especially by their recommendations for the introduction of subjects in seventh and eighth grades. This point was made by city superintendents. In many school systems in that period the relationships between the city superintendent and the high school principal were far from cordial, and city superintendents tended especially to identify themselves with the elementary or so-called grammar grades. Much of the criticism then was a defense of the independent province of elementary education, and it was directed to a large extent against specific recommendations by the conferences, especially those in mathematics and English. Furthermore, Eliot's advocacy of algebra, geometry, foreign languages, and physics in elementary schools was re-

[41] Charles W. Eliot, "The Unity of Educational Reform," *Educational Review* (October, 1894), p. 225.

[42] *Ibid.,* p. 224.

[43] *Ibid.,* p. 215.

[44] *Ibid.,* p. 216. The other five main lines of reform identified by Eliot in this address were the promotion of individual instruction; the need for developing the abilities of observation and reasoning; better motivation and more humane discipline; specialization of teaching; and the need for experts in school administration.

[45] *Ibid.,* p. 217.

sented by many superintendents who felt their programs already over-crowded.

The discussion about equivalence of subjects was less widespread, but it was persistent. Baker pointedly identified the expressions against which his minority statement had been directed as "due rather to the standpoint of the writer of the report than the resolutions of the committee."[46] Those who joined Baker on this point saw Eliot and the elective principle as the main targets of attack. In his general session speech to the NEA on July 12, Mackenzie defended the report by denying that it recommended equivalence of studies. "If the chairman is known to have a marked conviction to the effect that Choctaw or road-making have as much educational value as Latin," said Mackenzie, "there was nothing done or said by the committee in its official capacity, so far as I can recall, to give the slightest warrant of authority to such opinion."[47] So far as the text of the report was concerned, Mackenzie was right. All that was endorsed was equivalence of the subjects represented by the nine conferences, and this with particular reference to purposes of college admission.[48]

There were other criticisms made often enough to be identifiable and in some cases strongly enough to affect the general tone of discussion about the report. One referred to the omission of manual training and other practical subjects. Another line of attack centered on the twenty-period-per-week schedules in the four courses of study. Fears were expressed about the consequences on pupils of this amount of overwork. Of 247 high schools in Massachusetts, only 23 had as many as twenty exercises a week,[49] and it was felt in many quarters that more than fifteen constituted an unwarranted burden. Another criticism, although one not frequently made in the summer of 1894, was that of domination of high schools by colleges. J. Remsen Bishop of Cincinnati suspected for-

[46] Baker, op. cit., p. 653.

[47] James C. Mackenzie, "The Feasibility of Modifying the Programs of the Elementary and Secondary Schools to Meet the Suggestions in the Report of the Committee of Ten," NEA, 1894, p. 149.

[48] Eliot had little appetite for this particular discussion, and he advised William H. Smiley, Baker's successor at Denver High School, against including a meeting on the subject at the 1895 session of the NEA. In this letter Eliot stated his belief that the modern subjects would train the mind as well as Greek, Latin, and mathematics, but indicated it would be necessary to gain more experience with them before coming to firm conclusions. Charles W. Eliot to William H. Smiley, October 31, 1894, Charles W. Eliot Papers (Harvard University Archives, Cambridge, Mass.).

[49] Ray Greene Huling, School Review (December, 1894), p. 600.

eign influence in this and characterized the report as emanating from a "trans-oceanic" party seeking coordination of high schools and colleges, contrasting this group with those who were for the independent American high school.[50] In subsequent years little would be heard of the foreign influence, but much about the alleged college domination.

Relatively little was said about the application of the report to college admission until the October meeting of the New England Association of Colleges and Preparatory Schools. Tetlow wanted to open the colleges more widely to graduates of nonclassical programs. He therefore presented a resolution that "the satisfactory completion of any one of the four courses of study embodied in the programmes submitted on pages 46 and 47 of the Report of the Committee of Ten should be accepted as an adequate preparation for corresponding courses in colleges and scientific schools."[51] Tetlow's point was obscured in the ensuing discussion, but it was highlighted, although not in the manner he would have approved, in the evening general address by President William DeWitt Hyde of Bowdoin College. Hyde began by attacking equivalence of studies and contended that Latin was indispensable for liberal study worthy of the name. "Latin," he declared, "is the Thermopylae, where the modern Greeks must take their stand, determined to withstand the Barbarians or perish in the attempt."[52]

Since two of the four programs of the Committee of Ten included neither Greek nor Latin, the effect of Hyde's speech was to put Tetlow on the defensive. Apparently catching the mood of the meeting, Tetlow proposed modifying his resolution to read, "or at least any one of these programmes that includes Latin."[53] The half-loaf that might have been obtained under this modification was the compromise arrangement, already in existence in some colleges, for admission to programs leading to the degrees of bachelor of science or bachelor of philosophy. It would also have extended to other colleges the Harvard plan of 1887 under which a candidate might submit either Latin or Greek. Even this was not

[50] J. Remsen Bishop, "The Future of the American High School," NEA, 1894, pp. 789–790. Hall, on the other hand, had criticized the report for disregarding the wisdom of Germany and France.

[51] John Tetlow, discussion, Secretary's Report of the Ninth Annual Meeting of the New England Association of Colleges and Preparatory Schools, *School Review* (December, 1894), pp. 621–622.

[52] William DeWitt Hyde, "Educational Values as Assessed by the Committee of Ten," *School Review* (December, 1894), p. 640. It was Hyde who on another occasion criticized the allegedly barren qualities of Eliot's prose.

[53] Tetlow, *op. cit.,* p. 656.

to be won. After more discussion and speech-making, the Association postponed action on Tetlow's resolutions to a special meeting scheduled for December 29, about two months later.

The special meeting opened innocently enough, Tetlow now having incorporated his modification calling for endorsement of "at least" the programs with Latin. Suddenly and dramatically the atmosphere was changed by the appearance of, and the remarks made by, Professor M. H. Morgan of the Greek Department at Harvard. Morgan did not oppose the resolutions, but he moved the insertion of an official preference for three years of Greek in the Classical course. Had Tetlow agreed with his adversary quickly, no damage might have been done. Instead he rose to dispute the wisdom of reopening the Greek question. This drew a massive rejoinder from the Greek professors who were present, plus the reading of letters from their absent colleagues who, in anticipation of the debate, had prepared their statements in advance. The meeting was soon turned into a fury of controversy, damaging in its effect on those who had favored the resolutions to begin with, but who were now upset by this unexpected flank attack. As one member expressed it, he had come prepared to vote for the resolutions as drafted "and had not been moved by any of the considerations urged against them up to the moment of Professor Morgan's presentation of the protest against the classical course."[54]

Finally Eliot claimed the floor and with it the attention of the entire assembly. It was, after all, "his" Greek department that had started the attack. According to Winship's *Journal of Education,* Eliot " 'spanked' his Greek department with keen relish, and Greek never suffered more in debate than at his hands."[55] What Eliot did was to warn the Greek men that their rash demand would lead to the exclusion of Greek from "the immense majority of the secondary schools of the United States."[56] Somewhere in the course of his "harsh language," as termed by a later commentator,[57] Eliot suggested a revision of Tetlow's resolution to read

[54] Charles E. Fay, discussion, Secretary's Report of the Second Special Meeting of the New England Association of Colleges and Preparatory Schools, *School Review* (March, 1895), pp. 180–181.

[55] "Anti-Greek," *Journal of Education* (January 17, 1895), p. 44.

[56] Charles W. Eliot, discussion, Secretary's Report of the Second Special Meeting of the New England Association of Colleges and Preparatory Schools, *School Review* (March, 1895), p. 181. Spurning the use of Greek himself, Eliot reminded his audience " 'Quem Deus vult perdere prius dementat.' "

[57] Augustus F. Nightingale, "The Plan of a Six-Year Latin Course," *School Review* (June, 1895), p. 342.

that the subjects recommended by the Committee of Ten "to the extent and in the manner recommended by the Committee, should be allowed to count for admission to colleges and scientific schools." Tetlow moved the resolution with Eliot's substitute wording, and it was passed. Nothing was said in the resolution about Greek. *Journal of Education* interpreted this to be "the greatest victory that the anti-Greek men have had."[58]

Eliot knew better than to interpret his move as a victory. His substitution of "count for admission" for Tetlow's "should be accepted" represented a real change of meaning, and he knew it. Somewhat apologetically he wrote to Tetlow three days later, asking: "On the whole, were you satisfied with the outcome of Saturday's meeting?" Eliot said he had been partially prepared for the attack by notice of it given to him by Professor Morgan, but he had not been informed about "the other batteries which were brought up." The Association, he felt, had been "puzzled and staggered," and he had feared losing the "important principle" of the resolution. He ended by protesting lamely that he could not "at the spur of the moment" think of anything better to try, and once more asked, "Do you not think something was gained, if not all that you hoped to gain?" [59]

Tetlow's reply was courteous as always, but he did not succeed in concealing the degree of emotion he felt about the outcome. "I was and am," he wrote Eliot, "a good deal disappointed." He pointed out his strong desire to bring the nonclassical high schools into closer touch with the colleges, but this end "now seems to me a long way off." Conceding there was nothing to do but wait, he added his feeling very much as St. Paul must have when he said he was " 'troubled on every side, yet not distressed.' " In the postscript he assured Eliot: "You did the best thing possible, and at just the right time." He had moved the substitute wording himself "to have the privilege of accepting it graciously."[60]

IV

As it happened, the point of Tetlow's resolution was forgotten in the ensuing controversy about Greek. The American Philological Association, meeting in Philadelphia on December 28, the day before the

[58] "Anti-Greek," *Journal of Education* (January 17, 1895), p. 44.

[59] Charles W. Eliot to John Tetlow, January 1, 1895, John Tetlow Papers (Houghton Library, Harvard University, Cambridge, Mass.).

[60] John Tetlow to Charles W. Eliot, January 3, 1895, John Tetlow Papers (Houghton Library, Harvard University, Cambridge, Mass.).

stormy session at Boston, had passed a resolution denouncing the Committee of Ten for its two-year proposal and demanding three years of Greek in high schools.[61] A Committee of Twelve, with Professor William W. Goodwin of Harvard as chairman, was appointed by the Association to do something about it. This Committee prepared a lengthy "address" in which grievances were set forth in detail. It also collected signatures from school men, including Oscar D. Robinson of the Committee of Ten, Augustus F. Nightingale of the blizzard-like voice at the Richmond meeting, and surprisingly, William C. Collar of the Roxbury School.[62] This "address" was given wide publicity among school people and was presented by the Twelve to the Department of Secondary Education at the summer NEA meeting in Denver.

Winship's *Journal of Education* found in this a golden opportunity for further editorial criticism of the Committee of Ten. The address, according to Winship, "has utterly demoralized the 'Report of the Ten,' and makes it ridiculous in the extreme." Claiming that the *Journal of Education* alone had refused to bow the knee to "that farce" when "all the world" had seemed to shout " 'Great is the Report of the Ten,' " Winship now said he was "entirely content."[63] He kept his word, and from this point on tossed only minor barbs at the report.

The Committee of Twelve was by no means content. It now took up the cause of five-day-a-week Latin in the third and fourth years as opposed to the four-day-a-week Latin proposed by the Committee of Ten. The Department of Secondary Education of the NEA meeting in joint session with the Department of Higher Education unanimously passed a resolution to this effect at the summer meeting of 1896, expressing "cordial approval."[64] A year later at the summer meeting of the NEA in Milwaukee, the same departments received from the Committee of Twelve a reaffirmation of the original three-year position on Greek and had these printed in its official minutes.[65] Eventually the full reports on

[61] American Philological Association, "Address of the Committee of Twelve," *School Review* (September, 1895), p. 435.

[62] *Ibid.,* p. 440.

[63] "The Report of the Twelve," *Journal of Education* (September 19, 1895), pp. 196–197.

[64] Department of Secondary Education, Secretary's Minutes, NEA, 1896, p. 559. One of those speaking in favor of the resolution was Principal J. Remsen Bishop of Cincinnati, who two years before had denounced the Committee of Ten for representing a transoceanic influence and working for college domination of the schools.

[65] American Philological Association, Report of the Committee of Twelve, NEA, 1897, pp. 644–645.

Greek and Latin of the Committee of Twelve found their way into the 1899 report of the NEA Committee on College-Entrance Requirements.

In the end, the Committee of Twelve did not succeed in saving three years, or in fact, any years of Greek. Eliot had warned the advocates of Greek that clinging to the three-year course would in fact jeopardize the continued existence of their subject. It is difficult to see how even the friends of the classics felt they were promoting their cause by insisting on a third year of Greek, but it is not impossible to sympathize with their position. They felt like a beleaguered host defending the citadel of traditional culture against the onslaughts of barbarians. Repeated denunciations of the classics had made them sensitive to the point where they felt some kind of expression had to be made. Few of the enemies of the classics chose to defend the Committee of Ten in this controversy, and Eliot, who repeatedly protested his desire to save the classical studies, was left as the main object of attack.

It is more difficult to understand why so many school men found it expedient to support the Committee of Twelve. There was a strong suggestion that many of these found in it a new and usable basis for attacking the Committee of Ten. Probably the classicists were deceived when they congratulated themselves on finding so many supporters among school principals. On the other hand, these school men would not have supported something with which they were wholly out of sympathy. As previously noted, the school men for the most part were not trying to get rid of Greek, and many of them worked hard and long to keep that subject alive in their schools as long as any pupils could be persuaded to take it.

V

After this outbreak of the classicists, the criticisms of the report began to diminish in volume. They remained strong enough, however, to affect the future reputation of the Committee of Ten. Especially persistent was the charge of college domination. With this came a shift in the image of the Committee from ruthless destroyers of academic tradition to equally ruthless agents of reaction. After 1900 the most influential critic of the report was undoubtedly G. Stanley Hall; it was probably his attacks that fixed the reactionary label on the Committee.

Hall had disliked the report from the beginning, but it was only gradually that he unfolded the accusation of college domination. His main

target at Asbury Park in 1894 had been the alleged doctrine of equivalent values of subjects. This was still his object of criticism late that year
when he asserted that every study "awakens, strengthens, develops a
special area of the brain," claiming furthermore that "if we had a special
Tyrian dye for each study and its effect upon the brain was marked by
its coloring of the cells and fibres specially and strongly affected, we
should find that each had its own value and affected its own area."[66]

 * The main presentation of his college-domination theme was made by
Hall in a debate with Eliot at the New England Association in 1901.
Rising enrollments in Latin, he felt, were a sign of decadence, and he
blamed this on the Committee of Ten. According to Hall's interpretation,
the Committee had created a bias in favor of preparation for college,
with the consequence that more pupils were taking Latin.[67] College domination, Hall contended in this speech, was something uniquely American,
and he denounced the high school teachers who were ready "to sell their
birthright and independence." He called for a new association of high
school teachers acting independently of the college to work toward fitting
"for life and not for college."[68]

Eliot replied vigorously, but without indication that he had been stung
by Hall's criticisms. He reaffirmed his own convictions and those of the
Committee about not differentiating between the college-bound and other
pupils. Reminding his audience that thousands of pupils did not know
whether they were going to college or not, he urged postponement to the
latest possible point of "the forking of the ways in the high school." He
exhorted the group to "carry to the college or the scientific school every
child that can be led that way."[69] Those who agreed with Hall probably
felt that Eliot here furnished evidence of his own guilt. Out of this arose
the paradox. The idea of giving early and separate treatment to those
who could identify themselves as college-bound pupils became known as
a "liberal" point of view; while the opposite notion, that of providing the
broadest possible entry for all pupils to college, became known as "conservative."

The two pedagogical champions clashed once more, although not face

[66] G. Stanley Hall, "Educational Values," *Journal of Education* (December 27,
1894), p. 424.
[67] G. Stanley Hall, "How Far Is the Present High-School and Early College
Training Adapted to the Nature and Needs of Adolescents?" *School Review* (December, 1901), pp. 662–663.
[68] *Ibid.,* p. 664.
[69] Charles W. Eliot, discussion, *School Review* (December, 1901), p. 671.

to face, before this tournament of debate was closed. In his mammoth volumes on adolescence, published in 1904, Hall assembled his criticisms under three categories of "extraordinary fallacies"—that subjects should be taught the same way to all pupils regardless of their educational plans for the future, that all subjects were of equivalent value if taught equally well, and that fitting for college was the same as fitting for life.[70] He also taxed the committee with disregarding "the great army of incapables, shading down to those who should be in schools for dullards or subnormal children."[71]

This time Eliot was aroused, and he showed it in his address at the July, 1905, meeting of the American Institute of Instruction, the same group before which he had defended the report of the Committee of Ten back in 1894. He contended that early classification of children into "future peasants, mechanics, trades-people, merchants, and professional people," although "common in Europe," was unacceptable in "a democratic society like ours."[72] He explained again that the doctrine of equivalent values in the report referred to equivalence for purposes of college admission. Again he rejected the dualism of fitting for life and fitting for college and expounded his conviction that the objective of all schools was to fit pupils for life. So far as Hall's incapables were concerned, Eliot argued that such pupils formed only an "insignificant proportion" of the children in school and "that any school superintendent or principal who should construct his program with the incapables chiefly in mind would be a person professionally demented."[73]

Except for his strictures against Latin, even Hall did not identify college domination with choices of subjects, but rather with their treatment. Such identification with particular kinds of subjects did begin to appear after 1905, possibly as an extension of Hall's criticisms. A speaker at the NEA meeting in 1908 said the ideals of the Committee of Ten had been "only for those subjects then deemed acceptable for college preparation."[74] The following year, John Franklin Brown in his book *The American High School* criticized the Committee for having recognized the fact

[70] G. Stanley Hall, *Adolescence* (New York: Appleton-Century-Crofts, 1904), II, 510–515.
[71] *Ibid.*, p. 510.
[72] Charles W. Eliot, "The Fundamental Assumptions in the Report of the Committee of Ten," *Educational Review* (November, 1905), p. 330.
[73] *Ibid.*, pp. 331–332.
[74] Eugene W. Lyttle, "Report of the Committee on Six-Year Course of Study," NEA, 1908, p. 625.

that the school population was composed largely of pupils not bound for college and for having recommended, nevertheless, courses of study "prepared from the view point of the higher institution"; he said there seemed to be "a tacit underlying assumption" that courses for college were also the best preparation for life,[75] an interesting reversal of Eliot's position. This criticism of inconsistency was to be repeated many times for at least a half century to come. It has been a fascinating anachronism, for most of the subjects included by the Committee of Ten were in 1892–1893 regarded as preparatory for life, rather than college. Eventually, modern languages, the physical sciences, and history came to form part of what has been understood since then as a college-preparatory course, but this was not true at the time of the report. Even J. Remsen Bishop of Cincinnati in his 1894 speech denouncing college domination of the schools was careful to charge the so-called transoceanics with promoting those subjects "traditionally required for college work or gradually being introduced as college requirements."[76]

VI

Some of the gentler critics over the years have been inclined to excuse the Ten for their deficiencies on the ground of their not knowing any better. Harvard's Paul Hanus found the explanation in the Committee's lack of "an illuminating, well-defended educational doctrine."[77] Ella Flagg Young in 1907 felt the Ten had come along when "the academic idea was beginning to lose command of the whole education in the high school."[78] In the same year a young psychologist at Columbia, Edward Lee Thorndike, expressed the view that the Committee had assumed a typical high school to be one with from six to twelve teachers, whereas most high schools then had only one or two.[79] Briggs, in 1931, found the Committee hampered by doctrines of formal discipline.[80] In 1954 Alan Thomas, Jr., thought the Committee had not anticipated the

[75] John Franklin Brown, *The American High School* (New York: Macmillan Co., 1909), p. 59.
[76] Bishop, *op. cit.*, p. 791.
[77] Paul H. Hanus, "Obstacles to Educational Progress," NEA, 1902, p. 162.
[78] Ella Flagg Young, "The Educational Progress of Two Years, 1905–1907," NEA, 1907, p. 394.
[79] Edward L. Thorndike, "A Neglected Aspect of the American High School," *Educational Review* (March, 1907), pp. 245–246.
[80] Thomas H. Briggs, "The Committee of Ten," *Junior-Senior High School Clearing House* (November, 1931), pp. 134–141.

immigrants and their children, who "were to sweep through and over the traditional operative concepts of formal education."[81] Somewhat more severely, Theodore Sizer chided them in 1961 for not taking into account the great social, political, and economic forces of their time.[82]

It is largely for their alleged conservatism that the gentle critics have sought ways of excusing the Committee of Ten. Unfortunately, the term "conservatism" is as difficult to define in the field of education as in other human enterprises. This charge of conservatism leveled against the Committee of Ten has dealt largely with college domination, but not with that alone. It has also involved the question of disciplinary values, or the training of the mind and other aspects of personality. Here the Ten were conservative in that they followed the point of view of the preceding several decades. When they sought to promote the modern subjects, it was on the ground that these subjects, too, could train the mind. Eliot repeatedly defined education as training in various mental qualities or processes. As the doctrines of mind training went out of fashion, the point of view of the Committee of Ten came to be out of date and hence conservative in the negative sense.[83]

It is doubtful that the report can be claimed as an endorsement of the so-called new educational conservatism of the late 1950's. If the Ten were not calculating villains imposing the evils of college domination on the schools, neither were they the heroes of an early campaign against life-adjustment education. To the extent they represented an ideology, it was that of the moderate innovators who were seeking to establish,

[81] Alan M. Thomas, Jr., "American Education and the Immigrant," *Teachers College Record* (February, 1954), p. 257.

[82] Theodore R. Sizer, *The Committee of Ten* (Doctoral dissertation, Harvard University, 1961), p. 209.

[83] Emphasis on mental discipline in the 1880's and 1890's was usually associated with disparagement of subject matter, particularly of what was referred to as mere information. Even the idea of subject matter for practical everyday living was accepted only by a few followers of Herbert Spencer. The notion of subject matter as communicating moral ideals was one of the tenets of the American disciples of the German philosopher Herbart. William T. Harris valued subject matter as an agency for revealing the environment to the pupil. Sociologist Lester Frank Ward was one of the very few in that period who talked about subject matter or knowledge as the intellectual or cultural heritage and about the duty of the school to transmit it. See Lester Frank Ward, *Applied Sociology* (Boston: Ginn and Co., 1906), pp. 310–312. He was, on these grounds, properly critical of the report of the Committee of Ten. All these views on the value of subject matter, however, were in those days minority views. As the doctrines of mental discipline lost ground, subject matter came into its own, particularly subject matter for social efficiency.

clarify, and strengthen the modern academic subjects of science, history, English, and the nonclassical foreign tongues. For the most part, the Committee's ideology was rather implied than explicit and had to be extracted from the hundreds of details about time allotments and similar matters that make up the bulk of the report. Again, it must be kept in mind that the Committee had a limited assignment from the Council and rightly or wrongly did not go much beyond it. The Committee could not anticipate the future, in which people would be seeking larger propositions about the reorganization of secondary education. Had the Ten realized how sweeping their report would be regarded, they might have tried to have something more sweeping to say. The irony of it is that had they done so, as was attempted by some subsequent national committees, the educational world might have given it brief applause and then proceeded to forget all about it.

The reputation of the Committee of Ten has, for the most part, been unfavorable. This is not to say that it was, or has been, entirely friendless in a hostile world. Most of the favorable expressions of opinion, however, were vague. Terms such as "a great achievement," or "a noble monument," rolled easily off tongues and pens. Few of the professed admirers of the report stated specifically what they admired. Charles De Garmo,[84] president of Swarthmore College, and Francis W. Parker[85] both hailed the report for its stand against social caste in education, but they were notable exceptions in this. Only occasionally did someone commend the report for its attempt to render the modern academic subjects acceptable for college admission, although this perhaps was taken for granted since the process was already under way.

On the other hand, there has been a tendency both among its friends and enemies to see the report as having had that elusive something known as great influence. The Committee of Ten has left many questions to puzzle subsequent generations, and the question of its influence is one of the most puzzling of all. It has been much easier to assert that it had great influence than to present evidence of it. The president of the Association of Colleges and Preparatory Schools of the Middle States and Maryland said in 1902, for example, that the Committee had had "a profound influence on American education," but he admitted that its programs would "not be found in many schools." He added: "Some of

[84] Charles De Garmo, "Report of the Committee of Ten," *Educational Review* (March, 1894), p. 276.
[85] Parker, *op. cit.,* p. 449.

its conclusions . . . have not been accepted by the sober judgment of the educational world." According to this speaker, the Committee had "formulated and stated in concrete shape many of the problems that up to that time had been vague and formless."[86] Many of the statements about great influence were even vaguer than the problems to which this speaker referred.

It would not be unfair to say that on the matter of treating pupils alike regardless of their educational destinations, the Committee was almost without influence. Not only did the school world of that period continue the traditional distinction, on the basis of the classics, between the curricula of pupils who were preparing for college and those who were not; it also began to look with favor on more refined versions of that distinction, involving the modern academic subjects as well. Over the years the idea of a college-preparatory curriculum became as rigidly fixed from this point of view as it had ever been with reference to Greek.

The promotion of the modern academic subjects for college admission did prosper, but this had already been under way before the Committee began its work. Its first specific attempt to push this ahead with more speed met with disaster at the meeting of the New England Association of Colleges and Preparatory Schools. The acceptability of the modern subjects probably moved along at a reasonably certain, though also somewhat slow, pace independently of the recommendations of the Committee of Ten. When the movement gained speed and momentum, as it did after 1905, it also included the practical subjects not found in the report.

So far as the courses of study in Table IV were concerned, there were movements in various states, particularly in the South, to adopt these, at least in part, and to ascribe the pattern to the Committee of Ten. Kentucky,[87] Mississippi,[88] and Missouri[89] were some of the states in this group. The pattern laid down by the Ten in Table IV, however, was one already in use in many parts of the country. What the Commit-

[86] Wilson Farrand, "The Existing Relations between School and College," *Educational Review* (February, 1903), p. 183.

[87] Kentucky Educational Association, "Report of the Kentucky 'Committee of Ten,'" Lexington meeting, July 3, 1895, Charles W. Eliot Papers (Harvard University Archives, Cambridge, Mass.).

[88] R. W. Jones, "Our Proposed New Requirements for Admission to College," *School Review* (February, 1901), p. 106.

[89] "Report of the Committee of the State Teachers' Association of Missouri," *School Review* (September, 1896), pp. 546–548.

tee had done was to accept the four-course pattern with some internal modifications. To the extent that the courses represented a version of the elective principle, the Committee probably reinforced some tendency to electives, but not according to Eliot's views.

Some aspects of the report appeared in local programs here and there. Almost inevitably, there were local systems that claimed they were already doing what the report had recommended. "In the recent recommendations of the Committee of Ten," wrote the Chicago superintendent of schools, Albert G. Lane, in 1894, "it has been gratifying to know that our High School system is fully abreast of the demands for change and improvement, which that committee recommended."[90]

The Chicago superintendent, however, also itemized certain changes that looked on the surface like a partial response to the Committee of Ten. Latin, for example, was to be introduced in the seventh grade in some of the schools.[91] Since the motive was to give college-preparatory pupils a chance for additional study of the subject, this move was hardly in the direction of the Committee's point of view about differentiation of programs on the basis of the presumed educational destinations of high school pupils. Furthermore, the Chicago schools had been teaching German in the elementary grades for some time, as had been at least a dozen or so other city school systems in the country. Lane's comments on arithmetic were probably more reflective of the influence of the report. Many topics, he said, had been eliminated from arithmetic to make way for elementary algebra in the eighth grade.[92] Other systems were also revising their work in mathematics for the seventh and eighth grades in this period; whether or not this was in response to the Committee report cannot, in most cases, be known.

Specific recommendations for topics in arithmetic and algebra, of course, had come from the conference report on mathematics, and it was on these reports as a whole that Eliot centered his hopes, especially with reference to uniformity in definitions of the subjects. From the volume and intensity of the continued complaints about annoying diversities in college-admission specifications, this hope apparently was not realized. True, some uniformity was achieved in the identification of "classics" for English literature, but this movement had grown out of the Commission

---

[90] Albert G. Lane, "Report of the Superintendent," *Chicago Board of Education Fortieth Annual Report,* year ending June 29, 1894, p. 45.
[91] *Ibid.,* pp. 46–47.
[92] *Ibid.,* pp. 58–59.

of Colleges in New England on Admission Examinations dating back to 1886. It may be said, however, that the report fostered an atmosphere favorable to the creation in 1900 of the College Entrance Examination Board. This Board succeeded in establishing uniform definitions of subjects at least for the examinations recognized by its member colleges, and to this extent the Committee of Ten probably had some indirect influence. On this point, Eliot's personal influence was probably of more importance than that of the report.

So far as the specific recommendations of the conference reports were concerned, Edwin G. Dexter concluded in 1906 on the basis of comparisons of course outlines of 1895 with those of 1906 that the reports seemed "not to have influenced directly to a marked degree the curriculum of public high schools." Dexter granted the report an important part in directing thought to the important problems, "but with the shaping of its details it has had little to do." He went on to say that "more of the specific recommendations of the committee have been actually violated by the trend of high-school organization, or have proved inert, than have been followed."[93] In his comment on Dexter's study Butler said that the statistical method of inquiry was "a broken reed to lean upon in judging matters so intangible as influences." Partly acknowledging the force of Dexter's statistics so far as the secondary school "program" was concerned, Butler insisted upon holding to a broader point of view on the influence of the Committee "upon secondary education generally."[94]

One kind of influence, however, cannot be denied the Committee of Ten, that of having aroused the educational world to discussion and controversy. As Shaler had predicted at the Harvard Teachers' Association in 1894, the report was "much talked about,"[95] and it has continued to be talked about. For a report allegedly steeped in tradition, it has had a peculiar fascination for writers and speakers into our own time. Even those most irritated by it may be said to have fallen in some way under its influence. The 1918 report on *Cardinal Principles of Secondary Education* by the Commission on the Reorganization of Secondary Education has been regarded as somewhat archaic even by those who profess to believe in its recommendations. The Report of the Committee of Ten,

[93] Edwin G. Dexter, "Ten Years' Influence of the Report of the Committee of Ten," *School Review* (April, 1906), p. 269.
[94] "Notes and News," *Educational Review* (June, 1906), pp. 106–107.
[95] As quoted in "The Great Incubator," *Journal of Education* (March 15, 1894), p. 168.

in spite of Eliot's allegedly uninspired prose, has rarely failed to arouse what Winship called "limitless desire for discussion."[96]

Even Eliot could not keep away from a report that contained much of what he had called only temporary trestlework. What he continued to stress, however, was the presumed contribution of the conference reports. In 1921, at the age of 87, he wrote a major paper on American education since the Civil War, devoting nearly half this paper to the report of the Committee of Ten.[97] He especially praised the conference reports, and in this context he made explicit reaffirmation of his faith that a given subject should be taught the same way to all pupils regardless of their educational destinations.

[96] *Ibid.*
[97] Charles W. Eliot, "American Education Since the Civil War," *A Late Harvest* (Boston: Atlantic Monthly Press, 1924), pp. 121–148.

Chapter 5

Harris, Hall, and the Herbartians

> "To dissent from an Herbartian is to take your life in your hand."
>
> —ALBERT BUSHNELL HART,
> DECEMBER, 1895.

*T*he high school did not live unto itself. Its fortunes and destiny were linked not only to the college but also to the elementary school. Moreover, whereas only a small fraction of the pupils in high school went to college, practically all of them came from the grades. According to Eliot many questions were common to all levels of instruction, and he did not overlook the elementary school in the report of the Committee of Ten.

Nevertheless, even when the same problem affected the grades and the high schools and colleges, the specific questions were different. Schools on all levels, for example, faced the problem of organizing the daily schedule and arranging for the use of the teaching staff, but in elementary schools of the 1890's this problem gave rise to the question whether departmentalization or the single teacher was to be preferred. By 1895 various kinds of departmentalization were being tried in a number of school systems[1] including Utica, New York; Springfield, Massachusetts; and Boston.[2] There were speeches and articles on both sides of the question. Among others, Superintendent William H. Maxwell of Brooklyn favored departmentalization,[3] while Francis W. Parker of the Cook County, Illinois, Normal School opposed it.[4] Butler pushed it vigorously in his *Educational Review*.

[1] J. M. Fendley, "Departmental Teaching in Grammar Grades," NEA, 1895, p. 577.

[2] *Educational Review* (April, 1895), pp. 424–426.

[3] William H. Maxwell, "The Grammar School Curriculum," *Educational Review* (May, 1892), p. 481.

[4] Francis W. Parker, "Departmental Instruction," *Educational Review* (November, 1893), pp. 342–350.

Similarly, the question of what to teach took on a different character in relation to the elementary schools. The issue in the high schools was that of balance between the classics and the modern subjects; in the elementary schools it was that of balance between arithmetic and English grammar on the one hand and the "content" subjects like history and the sciences on the other. There was also the question whether or not to accommodate the elementary school program to the so-called practical subjects, such as manual arts. Elementary school teachers and administrators, especially city superintendents, were deeply aware of their crowded curricula, and it was from this point of view that some of the recommendations of the Committee of Ten were most bitterly resented. "There is not a clear-headed superintendent in the United States who does not know that the common schools are crowded with too many studies already," wrote James M. Greenwood of Kansas City, Missouri, in 1894, "and yet to adopt the recommendations of the committees would be to double the work the children are doing."[5] Winship's *Journal of Education* scolded the Ten for proposing twelve new studies "without so much as asking what the elementary schools have in hand already by way of manual training, sewing, cooking, drawing, physiology, physical culture, reading, language, geography, music, arithmetic, grammar, nature study, etc."[6]

Elementary school people felt their work hampered by domination from the high schools. Many high schools admitted pupils by examination only. These examinations placed much stress on complicated exercises in arithmetic, especially those in which the pupil was amusingly directed to "simplify" expressions in which fractions appeared as numerators and denominators of fractions.[7] The terminology of English grammar, often inconsistent from one book to the next, also came in

[5] James M. Greenwood, "Supt. Greenwood Sharpens the Point of His Criticism," *Intelligence* (May 15, 1894), p. 146.

[6] *Journal of Education* (January 18, 1894), p. 41.

[7] For example:

$$\frac{\left(\frac{2}{3} + 4.2\right) \div \left(.125 \times \frac{5}{2}\right)}{.375 \times \left(\frac{3}{5} - .16\frac{2}{3}\right)}$$

From Lake View Township High School, Cook County, Illinois, *Tenth Annual Report*, year ending June, 1884. The same entrance examination called for the cube root of 2,571,353, presumably without benefit of logarithms.

for a large share of attention. Consequently, the elementary school people resented, or appeared to resent, the amount of time devoted to preparing for the high-school-admission examinations. Just who was responsible for the nature of these examinations is not clear; in city
systems they were often prepared and administered by the superintendent's office. Many elementary school people ardently defended the
arithmetic and grammar they were teaching, especially in the face of
critics like Eliot. At any rate, the secretary of the Connecticut State
Board of Education in the late 1880's condemned the influence of secondary schools as "disastrous," since it had "directed the energies of
teachers and scholars to the one end of passing examinations to enter
secondary schools."[8] In some cities there were arrangements for admission "by certificate" or principal's recommendation, with examinations
stipulated for those not recommended or otherwise judged to have done
poor work in the grades.[9]

Criticisms of the elementary schools were somewhat specialized in
character and, if anything, more numerous and caustic than those made
of the high schools. One of the charges repeatedly leveled at elementary
education was that of waste: too long a period of time was said to be
taken to accomplish too little. This charge was not invented by Eliot. As
far back as 1873 a similar note had been sounded in the *Massachusetts
Teacher*.[10] The denunciation of waste resounded throughout the country,
but it was especially sharp in New England, with its nine-year and, in
some cases, ten-year programs of elementary schooling, producing first-
year high school pupils fifteen and sixteen years of age, or more.

Involved in the question of waste, however, was not only the length
of time for elementary schooling, but also the nature of the curriculum.
Here the critics, such as Eliot, called for programs both shortened and
enriched, the latter term usually meaning the introduction of algebra,
geometry, and foreign languages. Also under attack was the alleged
rigidity of the grade system, under which pupils deficient to some extent
in one subject had to repeat all subjects, and for an entire year. This was
not unique to the elementary school, but the public and the critics were
most aware of it there. Various school systems experimented with plans
for flexible promotion, and Cambridge, Massachusetts, in 1892 inaugu-

[8] Charles D. Hine, as quoted in Commissioner, 1888–1889, I, p. 602.
[9] "Promoting to the High School," *School Journal* (June 14, 1902), p. 689.
[10] A. B. (Mrs.) Martin, "What Is Accomplished in Our Grammar Schools?"
Massachusetts Teacher (October, 1873), pp. 349–357.

rated what would today be called a "three-track" plan, under which three groups of pupils, identified in terms of their abilities, would proceed through elementary school at different rates.[11]

Another matter that caused concern and occasioned criticism was the shockingly large number of children who left elementary school without completing the course. Compulsory-attendance laws were in many states chaotic in nature and poorly enforced. The high school had its dropouts by the thousands, the elementary school by the tens of thousands. Statistical information on these matters was not always dependable, and there were disputes about what kinds of figures should be used as the basis for reckoning and over what periods of time. It was clear, however, that what later came to be called holding power was weak both in the high schools and in the grades. Whereas the high school people exhorted grade school graduates to come to high school, the elementary school people begged their pupils to stay and be graduated from the grade school course.

Furthermore, there was the persistent charge that the grade schools failed to turn out pupils who could read, write, and compute. The elementary school took most of the punishment from widely publicized "lay" critics such as Charles Francis Adams, Jr., Richard Grant White, and Joseph M. Rice. Allegedly poor teachers and inadequate provisions for the training of teachers were explanations frequently offered for the states of affairs periodically "exposed." School people often responded by pointing to the sizes of classes in the elementary schools. In 1900 the Boston School Board extended itself and its budget in an attempt to reduce the number of pupils per elementary teacher from 56 to 50.[12] The Chicago Board of Education in 1898 congratulated itself on reducing the number from 63 to 54.[13] In addition, the elementary school day included both morning and afternoon sessions, and the nervous state of the teachers by closing time may well be imagined. In comparison with the high school teachers of this period, many of whom worked in schools that closed at one or two o'clock in the afternoon,[14] elementary school teachers were indeed the overworked and oppressed proletariat of the

[11] Albert Bushnell Hart, "Reform in the Grammar Schools: an Experiment at Cambridge, Mass.," *Educational Review* (October, 1892), pp. 253–269.

[12] Charles Marsh Clay, "High School Reform," *Education* (November, 1900), p. 145.

[13] M. E. Fitzgerald, "Mrs. Young's Lecture," *School Journal* (February 26, 1898), p. 237.

[14] "Single Sessions," *American School Board Journal* (January, 1893), p. 6.

pedagogical enterprise. Under these conditions, they might well have been excused for wondering how they could meet the demands for perfection set by detached critics who wrote for popular magazines.

II

Elementary education, then, did have difficulties and concerns of "its own." There was strong feeling that these difficulties and concerns had been neglected by the NEA. True, there was a standing committee on elementary education in the National Council, but the title of its major report, "Waste in Elementary Education," presented in 1888, was hardly an encouraging one from the point of view of people already sensitive to criticism. What the grade school people felt they needed was a special project of their own, comparable to the Committee of Ten in scope and especially in the possession of a substantial expense account.

In February, 1893, the Department of Superintendence at its Boston meeting created a Committee of Fifteen on Elementary Education. This took place just seven months after the creation of the Committee of Ten, and the work of the two committees overlapped and ran side by side for more than a year. Where the Committee of Ten had only a limited assignment, however, the Committee of Fifteen was charged with investigating the organization of school systems, the coordination of studies, and the training of teachers. The superintendents asked the NEA Board of Directors for $2500 for all this work, but were put off with $1000, a fact that occasioned further comments about the attitude of the NEA.

The general chairman of the Committee of Fifteen was Superintendent William H. Maxwell of Brooklyn, Harris' victim at Richmond in 1894. Born in Stewartstown, Ireland, in 1852, Maxwell had taken his bachelor's degree at Queen's College, Galway, in classics and English and had taught in the Royal Academical Institution, Belfast, before his move to the United States in 1874. He had started in Brooklyn as a teacher in the evening high schools, becoming Associate Superintendent in 1882 and Superintendent in 1887. Maxwell was one of the city superintendents not distinctly associated with elementary schools, a fact that may have accounted for his friendly reception of the report of the Committee of Ten. He developed the Brooklyn high school program from a three-year course that had been offered at the Central Grammar School.[15] In spite

[15] "City Superintendent Maxwell of New York," *Educational Review* (January, 1904), pp. 1–18.

of this high school background he was well accepted by the superintendents as Chairman of the Committee of Fifteen.

His fellow members for the most part were superintendents of the largest city systems in the country. In fact, the Committee of Fifteen, within its context, was far more a group of "big names" on a national basis than the Committee of Ten. The group included W. B. Powell of Washington, D.C., James M. Greenwood of Kansas City, Missouri, E. P. Seaver of Boston, A. G. Lane of Chicago, and Edward Brooks of Philadelphia. Greenwood and Seaver were to be among the leading critics of the Committee of Ten. Colleges were presumably represented by President Andrew S. Draper of the University of Illinois. Inevitably and, in relation to the consequences, fatefully, the membership included Commissioner William T. Harris.

The Fifteen organized themselves into three subcommittees, one on the training of teachers, one on the organization of city school systems, and the third, with Harris as chairman, on "the correlation of studies in elementary education." With Harris on this subcommittee were Maxwell, Greenwood, L. H. Jones of Indianapolis, and Charles B. Gilbert of St. Paul. There was little doubt about who was the dominating force on this subcommittee. Writing about the sessions ten years later, Greenwood, not intending any disparagement of Harris, wrote, "Dr. Harris was unswerving in his views. . . . Dr. Harris must have said 'yes, yes, yes,' a thousand times during the week, but his 'yesses' did not always mean 'yes'—he was just getting wind to pitch into something or to demolish someone's position."[16] Still there were disagreements, and the other four members ended by writing separate statements clarifying their views on details.

In his resolution calling for the creation of the Committee of Fifteen at Boston in 1893, Maxwell had used the term "coordination of studies." The change in wording to "correlation of studies" was in this instance freighted with more significance than is often true of changes in wording. *Correlation* was becoming a popular term. On the surface, it referred simply to the relationships among the studies and to arrangements for bringing out and developing these relationships. It was neither "conservative" nor "liberal." It was used freely by the Committee of Ten. The important point for the Committee of Fifteen and especially for Harris' subcommittee was that it was also used by the Herbartians.

[16] James M. Greenwood, "Some Educators I Have Known," *Educational Review* (April, 1903), pp. 410–411.

The name *Herbartians* was assumed by or applied to a relatively small group of American educators, mostly with interests in elementary schooling, affected through several degrees of relationship by the German philosopher Johann Friedrich Herbart, who had died back in 1841. Some of them had studied in Germany. Herbart himself had not been strictly or solely a philosopher of education, but his general philosophy was applicable to that field. Two of his disciples, Stoy and Ziller, developed these educational implications, which were carried still further by one of their students, Wilhelm Rein, who succeeded Stoy at Jena in 1885. It was probably Rein who was directly best known by the American Herbartians, including those who had themselves studied in Germany. *Herbartian* was a loose term, and there were some so labeled who protested they were not, while others who aspired to the term had their credentials questioned by the purists. With these qualifications in mind, it was possible nevertheless to identify the McMurry brothers, Frank and Charles, of the Illinois State Normal University, as leading Herbartians. Charles De Garmo, President of Swarthmore College, was considered a Herbartian at this time and in fact organized the Herbart Club at the Asbury Park meeting of the NEA in 1894. Others associated with the movement were C. C. Van Liew of Illinois Normal and Wilbur S. Jackman of Cook County Normal, Illinois. Francis W. Parker was not, in strict parlance, one of the Herbartians, but he had friends among them, often joined them in their discussions, and on one occasion at least was one of their most militant allies.

Just what constituted true Herbartianism was a point of contention even among the Herbartians themselves. There was common rejection of the idea of mental faculties and the related theories of mental discipline. Herbartians placed greater value on the substance or content of studies than on formal training. This put them in a minority among educators of their time. The major purpose of content, as they saw it, was to develop moral understanding and conduct. Overcrowding and congestion in the curriculum were to be remedied by emphasizing particular subjects or groups of subjects. These were the content subjects, as distinguished from the formal subjects, such as grammar and mathematics. The formal subjects and some of the content subjects were to be learned in their relationship to the central subjects, topics, or units. Arithmetic, reading, writing, and other formal or process subjects were to be related to history, literature, or science. One difficulty was that the Herbartians could not always agree among themselves about what the central subjects should be. Charles De Garmo at one point advocated "three co-ordinate cores, or centers, of unification," bound together by the "universal correlating study" of geography,[17] but other Herbartians had ideas of their own.

Since no Herbartian ever stated the doctrines in a form acceptable to his fellow disciples, the foregoing oversimplification of one aspect of these doctrines would probably not have been accepted by any of them. They represent, however, much of what was understood by Herbartianism in the discussions of the 1890's. The doctrines involved consideration of what was known as Herbartian psychology, a central element of which was the importance of interest as a motivating force and direction-setter for the learning process. Methods of teaching consequently demanded stage management to identify and build on pupil interests. This was not meant in the superficial sense of entertainment, but involved the psychological foundations, background, or "apperceptive mass" that the pupil brought to the study of any given topic. The so-called "five formal steps" of teaching were designed to facilitate this building upon and adding to the stock of pupil knowledge and interest. They did not, however, occupy more than a minor share of attention in the discussions of Herbartianism at this time.

Within this general context, the term *correlation* was used by Herbartians to mean the relationship of some of the subjects of study to the central subjects or, as they were sometimes called, the centers of concentration. Often correlation served simply to mean concentration, but whether it did so before 1895 was one of the points later disputed by Harris. When the Committee of Fifteen set up a subcommittee on the correlation of studies, the Herbartians responded as to a fire bell in the night. Parker claimed later that he had made the motion for a committee on correlation at the Boston meeting of the superintendents in 1893,[18] but according to the report of the Committee of Fifteen, the subcommittees were not set up until a year later at Richmond.[19] At any rate, the use of the term aroused the hopes and the fears of the Herbartians. Harris and his subcommittee had taken on a small but extremely critical national audience that would go over every word in the ensuing report. Herbartians at this time were zealots, and as was perceptively noted by

[17] Charles De Garmo, "A Working Basis for the Correlation of Studies," *Educational Review* (May, 1893), p. 458.

[18] Francis W. Parker, discussion, NEA, 1895, p. 344.

[19] National Educational Association, *Report of the Committee of Fifteen on Elementary Education* (New York: American Book Co., 1895), pp. 8-9.

historian Albert Bushnell Hart, "to dissent from an Herbartian is to take your life in your hand."[20]

III

Throughout 1894 there developed in the pedagogical world a gradual awareness of differences between the Herbartians and the Committee of Fifteen. This meant, specifically, differences between the Herbartians and Harris. Actually they were not far apart in their evaluation of the importance of content. Harris did not reject discipline, but he attached far more importance to his windows of the soul as providing understanding of the human environment. As is often the case, the heretics were more intolerant of what appeared to the outsider to be minor differences among themselves than they were of the orthodoxy against which they were protesting. Harris and the Herbartians were heretics with reference to the formalistic pedagogical theories of their time. There was one fundamental point, however, on which differences might have been expected: Harris was a firm believer in the freedom of the will, and he considered the Herbartian psychology of interest to be in conflict with that freedom. The emerging differences, nevertheless, were centered rather on the meaning and application of the term *correlation of studies*.

The presentation of the report of the Committee of Fifteen was scheduled for the February 20, 1895, session of the Department of Superintendence at Cleveland. As this date approached, word spread that the Herbartians would be there in force to take on the king of NEA platform warfare. Harris' supporters hoped the Herbartians would do exactly this, for they had all confidence in the prowess of their chief. Winship provoked the Herbartians to the attack, declaring editorially that they "must meet the issue squarely . . . or strike their colors." The Herbartians, he said, "must silence the heavy artillery," but he tauntingly reminded them to "remember Maxwell at Richmond!"[21] Harris was by no means averse to a good fight himself. He wrote to President Calkins of the NEA Board of Trustees that the report was "written in such a form as to cut to the quick many of the favorite opinions advocated so much in newspapers and books just at the present time."[22]

[20] Albert Bushnell Hart, "College Entrance Requirements in History," *Educational Review* (December, 1895), p. 421.

[21] "Dr. Harris' Masterpiece," *Journal of Education* (February 21, 1895), p. 128.

[22] William T. Harris to N. A. Calkins, February 14, 1895, Commissioner's Office Outgoing Correspondence, 1880–1895 (National Archives, Record Group 12).

It was necessary at the February 20 meeting for Harris and the chairmen of the other subcommittees to read substantial portions of their reports to the audience. Only a few people had seen the reports in advance, and copies were not available for general distribution. Accusations abounded about the responsibility for this state of affairs. The reading was a long and, to many, an irritating affair. Even those who agreed with Winship that Harris' report had "the richness of cream, the tonic of Colorado air, the spark and tingle of champagne"[23] must have found it a lengthy discourse indeed.

Harris' report covered not only correlation but also a variety of other topics. It assumed an eight-year elementary school and presented a program of studies including reading, writing, spelling, English grammar, arithmetic, United States history, general history, geography, vocal music, natural science, physical culture, and, perhaps surprisingly in view of Harris' ideas, manual training or sewing plus cookery. Overtones of the Committee of Ten were suggested in the recommendation for Latin in the eighth year and algebra and geometry in seventh and eighth.[24] On the question of departmentalized instruction, the subcommittee recommended "that the specialization of teachers' work should not be attempted before the seventh or eighth year of the elementary school and in not more than one or two studies then."[25] With regard to educational values, the report disparaged the disciplinary view of education and took a firm stand on behalf of the content of studies to "make the individual acquainted with physical nature and with human nature."[26]

Correlation, however, was the main business at hand, and the report plunged into it. Four notions of correlation were stated as representing what the subcommittee understood by the term: the logical order of topics and branches; the symmetrical whole of studies in the world of human learning; psychological symmetry; and the correlation of the pupil's course of study with the world in which he lives.[27] None of these fit the Herbartian use of the term. Up to this point Harris was guilty only of omission. Later in the report, however, he referred to "another sense" in which the term was "sometimes" used, namely, as "an artificial center of the course of study." As an example of this he gave the use of

[23] A. E. Winship, letter to the editor, *Cleveland Leader*, February 19, 1895, William T. Harris Papers (Library of Congress, Washington, D.C.).
[24] National Educational Association, *op. cit.*, p. 94.
[25] *Ibid.*, p. 95.
[26] *Ibid.*, pp. 42–43.
[27] *Ibid.*, pp. 40–43.

Robinson Crusoe as a reading exercise connected with lessons in geography. This he characterized as "shallow and uninteresting."[28] From the point of view of the Herbartians this was not only an attack on their doctrine but a caricature of it.

The Herbartians rose to the challenge, Frank McMurry leading the charge. *Intelligence* editorially said the report had sounded "very innocent" as read by Harris, "but when Mr. Frank McMurry, with a warmth which his earnestness could hardly keep from being amusing, began to read his paper . . . it began to appear from his citations what a horrible thing the committee had done. They had really, and with malice aforethot, not only shown no sympathy for 'the concentration of studies,' but had actually ignored it in a large part of their report and had discounted it in the rest."[29] Charles McMurry, Charles De Garmo, and others joined the attack, but the most spectacular oration evidently was the one made by Francis W. Parker. According to the published proceedings, Parker deplored the failure of the members of the Committee to familiarize themselves with Herbart, Ziller, Stoy, and Rein. Instead, "they have ignored the very subject which they were intended to treat. The report . . . is like the play of 'Hamlet' with Hamlet left out; or, as I might better say, with Hamlet kicked out." He promised, however, to take it home and to study it prayerfully.[30] The *American Journal of Education,* one of Harris' supporters, caricatured Parker's speech as a bundle of contradictions and compared it to the beating of drums at a meeting of the Salvation Army.[31]

Harris broke into the discussion several times. He criticized Herbart's doctrine of interest and said that to make use of Herbart in pedagogy it was necessary to ignore his philosophy. "His usefulness in education," said Harris, "is proportioned to his uselessness as a philosopher."[32] He was surprised at the accusation that the report had ignored its assigned topic and complained about the assumption that correlation meant concentration. "There is no such definition," he contended, "to the word correlation in any dictionary; only four or five obscure books in the English language give the word correlation the meaning of concentra-

---

[28] *Ibid.,* p. 84.
[29] "The Cleveland Meeting of the Department of Superintendents," *Intelligence* (March 1, 1895), p. 66.
[30] Parker, *op. cit.,* p. 344.
[31] "The Cleveland Circus," *American Journal of Education* (April 9, 1895), pp. 6–7.
[32] William T. Harris, discussion, NEA, 1895, p. 345.

tion."[33] *Intelligence* noted editorially "that the authors of three of these 'obscure books' were present and among the critics of his report" and wished "they had saved themselves from such a punishment. But the audience enjoyed it."[34]

It was undoubtedly a severe blow to Harris in the discussion to find Nicholas Murray Butler among the critics of his report. Butler said bluntly that he was disappointed and that the definition of the term *correlation* in the report was not the one in current use. He cited the *Century Dictionary* as supporting the definition of the term as that of "orderly connection or reciprocal relation." Finally, he dismissed the report as "an elaborate defense of the status quo."[35] Several weeks later, in a letter to Harris, he still held to his understanding of correlation, but said the whole discussion had been a purely verbal one. He added that the question of correlation was "a subordinate one to that of educational values and selection of studies."[36]

The immediate response to what came to be known as "the great debate" favored Harris and indicated that he had routed his opponents. Most of the superintendents and the journals were undoubtedly on Harris' side. State Commissioner G. R. Glenn of Georgia in an interview reported in the *Atlanta Constitution* said that "a great many new-fangled ideas" had crept into American education "from across the water." The "young men" who attacked the report "talked learnedly about herbartianism, hegelianism, apperception, psychology and a lot of other 'ologies' and 'isms,' " but Harris had "literally demolished the followers of these foreign creeds."[37] Superintendent A. P. Marble of Omaha said Harris had "left the opposition, as he always does, in the plight of the boy who had tickled a mule's heels with straws, and whose father remarked to him later that he would never again look so well as he had before, but he would know more."[38] This witticism was joyously repeated by Harris' admirers in their comments on the debate. The *School Bulletin*

---

[33] *Ibid.*

[34] "The Cleveland Meeting of the Department of Superintendents," *Intelligence* (March 1, 1895), p. 66.

[35] Nicholas Murray Butler, discussion, NEA, pp. 347–348.

[36] Nicholas Murray Butler to William T. Harris, April 8, 1895, Nicholas Murray Butler Papers (Columbiana Library, Columbia University, New York, N.Y.).

[37] G. R. Glenn, as quoted in *Atlanta Constitution,* February, 1895, William T. Harris Papers (Library of Congress, Washington, D.C.).

[38] A. P. Marble, letter dated March 23, 1895, *Northwestern Journal of Education,* April, 1895, William T. Harris Papers (Library of Congress, Washington, D.C.).

of Syracuse, New York, said the Herbartians "must have a new appreciation of the slangy aptness of the phrase that attempts to dissuade the
tyro from monkeying with a buzz-saw," but expressed disappointment
that the report had not dealt more fully with Herbartian theories.[39]

Yet with all this applause resounding from his admirers, Harris was
not sure himself that he had emerged the victor. During the following
weeks and months he wrote to a large number of educators seeking to
justify his position and in some cases almost imploring their aid. He
particularly resented the charge of conservatism made against the report.
"I unhesitatingly claim," he wrote to C. W. Bardeen of the *School Bulletin,* "that there were more radical departures in my part of the report
than have been put forward in any one paper for many years." He characterized as "the strangest possible view of the situation" the idea that
his report was conservative "simply because it was not devoted to the
Herbartian doctrine of concentration."[40] In a reply to John MacDonald,
editor of the *Western School Journal* of Topeka, Kansas, he claimed that
German Herbartians never used correlation in the sense of concentration
and denied further that his report was an expression of Hegelianism.[41]
To George P. Brown of the *Public School Journal,* Harris denied that
Germans ever used the term "correlation" at all.[42] To Butler he protested
that he had not encountered correlation as concentration before reading
Parker's *Talks on Pedagogics* on the train the day of the Cleveland meeting.[43] He even appealed to De Garmo to help him track down the definitions.[44] To William H. Maxwell, his victim at the Richmond meeting in
1894, Harris expressed the fear that he might have misunderstood entirely the intention of the Department of Superintendence.[45]

[39] C. W. Bardeen, editorial comment, *School Bulletin,* March, 1895, William
T. Harris Papers (Library of Congress, Washington, D.C.).
[40] William T. Harris to C. W. Bardeen, March 7, 1895, Commissioner's Office
Outgoing Correspondence, 1879–1901 (National Archives, Record Group 12).
[41] William T. Harris to John MacDonald, March 30, 1895, William T. Harris
Papers (Library of Congress, Washington, D.C.).
[42] William T. Harris to George P. Brown, April 4, 1895, Commissioner's Office
Outgoing Correspondence, 1880–1895 (National Archives, Record Group 12).
[43] William T. Harris to Nicholas Murray Butler, April 5, 1895, Nicholas Murray
Butler Papers (Columbiana Library, Columbia University, New York, N.Y.).
[44] William T. Harris to Charles De Garmo, April 8, 1895, Commissioner's
Office Outgoing Correspondence, 1880–1895 (National Archives, Record Group
12).
[45] William T. Harris to William H. Maxwell, April 9, 1895, Commissioner's
Office Outgoing Correspondence, 1880–1895 (National Archives, Record Group
12).

Harris may have demolished his opponents at Cleveland, but he was probably right in his feeling that pedagogical opinion was reacting against him. The Herbartian ideas were regarded as new and advanced, and it was old fashioned to oppose them. Conservatism was becoming disreputable. E. E. White of Columbus, Ohio, was stung by a characterization of his part in the Cleveland debate as "traditional conservatism" and protested against making acceptance of Herbartian doctrine a test of "conservatism" or "progressiveness."[46] Nevertheless, the labels stuck. Almost 40 years afterward, Charles De Garmo wrote to Butler about his memories of the past, in which "no scene recurs to me more vividly than on the immortal day at Cleveland, which marked the death of an old order and the birth of a new."[47] The children's children of the educators of 1895 developed an even sharper image of Harris as the archconservative. Because of Harris' membership on the Committee of Ten, this may have affected the reputation of that group as well.

Furthermore, Herbartianism as an advanced view was especially identified with elementary education. The notion grew that elementary schools were particularly receptive to advanced views. This was a departure, for they had been severely criticized for devotion to the old-fashioned and the traditional. It became customary to regard the high school as the institution needing to catch up. The idea of correlation also became an important symbol of progress in thinking about the curriculum. So far as the high school was concerned, this became obscured after 1905 by the drive toward social efficiency, but it was revived later to become involved in the changes proposed in the 1930's.

While Harris was searching his own mind and motives in connection with the controversy, the Herbartians proceeded to consolidate their position. Even Winship conceded that Harris had "by indirection, given Herbart an importance not heretofore admitted in this country."[48] At the Denver meeting of the NEA in July, four months after the Cleveland meeting, the Herbartians organized the Herbart Society for the Scientific Study of Teaching, with Charles De Garmo as president. The Executive Committee included the two McMurrys; Nicholas Murray Butler; Wilbur Jackman; C. C. Van Liew; Elmer Ellsworth Brown, later to succeed

[46] "Dr. E. E. White on 'The Correlation of Studies,'" *School Journal* (March 23, 1895), p. 308.

[47] Charles De Garmo to Nicholas Murray Butler, December 15, 1933, Nicholas Murray Butler Papers (Columbiana Library, Columbia University, New York, N.Y.). In this letter, however, De Garmo also recalled his friendship with and esteem for Harris.

[48] "Herbart," *Journal of Education* (April 25, 1895), p. 285.

Harris as Commissioner of Education; and a 35-year old professor from the University of Chicago named John Dewey. Not all these men remained identified with Herbartianism, but an organization that could enroll both Dewey and Butler on its Executive Committee must have had wide appeal indeed. The Society continued over the next several years to have spirited meetings and to publish yearbooks. By 1902, however, it had dropped the word "Herbart" from its name to become known as the National Society for the Scientific Study of Education.

Harris characterized the material in the Society's yearbooks as "a dreary sort of stuff."[49] Actually the sessions of the Society as reported in the yearbooks showed a good deal of intellectual vigor and much disagreement among the Herbartians themselves. The 1895 session was marked by a sharp dispute between the advocates of nature study on the one side and of history and literature on the other—the former represented by Francis Parker and Wilbur Jackman, the latter by Frank McMurry and by R. H. Beggs of Denver. Parker contended that nature study was excluded from the schools to keep the "masses" from rising against the "classes,"[50] and he maintained that "through history and literature, the child can be adjusted to the society, state, and government," but "through the proper study of nature he can only be adjusted to the truth of the Eternal God."[51] Beggs insisted that the Prussians were mistaken if they thought nature study conflicted with authoritarianism, for nature study led to the doctrine of the survival of the fittest.[52] The second supplement to the 1895 yearbook contained John Dewey's *Interest as Related to Will,* gaining for its author an audience not large in number but national in scope. This was Dewey's attempt to resolve the dilemma that Harris had previously noted. The third yearbook of the Society, appearing in 1897, contained a paper by Harris himself, on the relation of school discipline to moral education.

IV

Herbartianism was not the only evangelical movement at this time. Another, and one representing far greater numbers of people, was that

[49] William T. Harris to B. A. Hinsdale, October 15, 1896, Commissioner's Office Outgoing Correspondence, 1880–1895 (National Archives, Record Group 12).

[50] Francis W. Parker, *First Supplement to the Yearbook* (National Herbart Society for the Scientific Study of Teaching, 1895), p. 181. The *National* was added to the society's name shortly after its organization.

[51] *Ibid.,* p. 183.

[52] R. H. Beggs, *First Supplement to the Yearbook* (National Herbart Society for the Scientific Study of Teaching, 1895), p. 184.

of child study. Here again elementary education was directly affected and became further identified with newness and progress. The child study movement also made some impact on discussions about the high school. Even so, the high school people responded slowly and with some skepticism, lending more support to their reputations as laggards in the race toward the new.

Child study as a scientific movement dated back to the 1870's. It had attracted enough attention by 1880 to become the major topic of the education section in the meeting that year of the American Social Science Association. A letter was read at this meeting from Charles Darwin, who had published a paper, "A Biographical Sketch of an Infant," in the British journal *Mind* in 1877.[53] A letter was also read from Bronson Alcott.[54] At this meeting, the education department of the Association drew up a broadside calling on parents to observe and record the behavior of their children. "We have been familiar with the habits of plants and animals from the careful investigations which have from time to time been published. . . . Recently some educators in this country have been quietly thinking that to study the natural development of a single child is worth more than a Noah's ark full of animals."[55] The broadside included a "register" to be used by parents for recording observations on such matters as when the child first smiled, recognized mother, followed a light with its eyes, and spoke, and what the child said on first speaking. It was predicted that such records from "many thousand observers" would be of great value to the educator and the psychologist.[56]

Among those who had papers read at this meeting were William T. Harris[57] and G. Stanley Hall,[58] but while Harris later regressed toward conservatism, Hall took up the new cause and made himself its leader. Born in Ashfield, Massachusetts, in 1846, Hall had attended Williston Seminary and Williams College. After a year at the Union Theological Seminary, he spent three years of study at Bonn and Berlin, returning to Union to take his degree of bachelor of divinity. A brief turn as Professor of English literature at Antioch College was followed by study at Harvard and the taking in 1878 of one of the early American Ph.D.'s.

[53] As quoted in *Journal of Social Science* (February, 1882), pp. 6–8.
[54] *Ibid.,* pp. 8–11.
[55] *Ibid.,* p. 189.
[56] *Ibid.*
[57] William T. Harris, "The Education of the Family, and the Education of the School," *Journal of Social Science* (February, 1882), pp. 1–5.
[58] G. Stanley Hall, "The Moral and Religious Training of Children," *Journal of Social Science* (February, 1882), pp. 56–76.

Still thirsting for the word from Germany, Hall spent two more years at Berlin and Leipzig. In 1882 he became a member of the faculty at Johns Hopkins University.[59] Here he began more or less officially his long, inspirational, and controversial career as the prophet of child study and the critic of almost everything else, including the report of the Committee of Ten. In this he was helped, no doubt, by the prestige of his presidency of Clark University, to which he was appointed in 1888.

Hall made enemies, but he also attracted the devotion of thousands of teachers. Several expressions about him indicated the complex nature of his reputation. A poem addressed to him in 1894 began,

> How tell the debt we owe the toiling seer
> Who strives, and by his impulse helps us all
> To grasp with him, the outstretched hand of Mind?

and ended,

> Oh friend, unflinching, undismayed
> Thought Captain, on the march of Time
> That leads through strife to peace, and final goal
> The beauty of His holiness in Man.[60]

In an almost brutal review of Hall's writing in 1909, Paul Shorey, the embittered classicist, found Hall guilty of "aberrations of taste and logic which the educated opinion of older civilizations would not tolerate, and which almost justify Kipling's sneer at the 'picture-writing of a half-civilized people.' "[61] With somewhat less heat, Edward L. Thorndike wrote in 1925 that Hall had been "interested in philosophy, psychology, education and religion in every one of their aspects which did not involve detailed experimentation, intricate quantitative treatment of results, or rigor and subtlety of analysis."[62]

Thorndike's disdainful appraisal of Hall was in some ways an accurate one, although one is not obligated to interpret Hall's lack of interest in "quantitative treatment" as a defect. Apart from a few studies, such as "The Contents of Children's Minds on Entering School," Hall left to others the task of compiling observations. He preferred to become the "philosopher" or the larger interpreter of child study, and he was con-

[59] Edward Lee Thorndike, "Biographical Memoir of Granville Stanley Hall: 1846–1924," *Biographical Memoirs* (Washington, D.C.: National Academy of Science, 1925), Vol. XII, pp. 132–180.
[60] "To Dr. G. Stanley Hall," *Journal of Education* (August 23, 1894), p. 119.
[61] Paul Shorey, "Hippias Paidagogos," *School Review* (January, 1909), p. 9.
[62] Thorndike, *op. cit.*, pp. 139–140.

stantly in search of and proclaiming its implications. These were often romantic and inspirational in character. In an article published in 1885, he pronounced that the new education held one thing alone "fit to inspire," and this was "the soul and body of the healthy young child."[63] He predicted that when child study was fully organized, it would do much "toward making education more of a science, or rather, which is far better, a profession."[64]

By the 1890's the process of developing and organizing the child study movement was in full blast, enrolling thousands of disciples among teachers and others interested in education. Inevitably it soared into the high and, to some people, dry regions of the NEA. The Department of Child Study of that organization came into being at the Asbury Park summer meeting of 1894. The NEA had assigned the new group a small hotel room with only nine chairs, but so many devotees arrived that the meeting had to be shifted three times and finally filled a church.[65] Hall provided the oratorical flourishes, proclaiming "that unto you is born this day a new Department of Child Study" and referring, probably figuratively, to "the little child now standing in our midst,"[66] who was to regenerate education, to moralize it, to make it religious, and "to bring the child . . . home to the hearts of men and women, where children should always find a warm place."[67]

This action of the NEA provided a national platform for the child study people, supplementing their efforts in large and active state congresses, such as the one in Illinois. The movement was by no means confined to the public schools, and a Catholic Child Study Congress was held in New York City late in 1897, with G. Stanley Hall as one of the principal speakers.[68] Furthermore, universities other than Clark began to accord a somewhat official status to investigations of child life. Professor Earl Barnes of Stanford in 1896 announced a series of "Studies in Education," the topics of which were indicative of the range of the field, including children's interests, children's superstitions, children's ambitions, children's sense of propriety, children's time sense, the intellectual habits of college students, the rise of the social instinct, children's

[63] G. Stanley Hall, "New Departures in Education," *North American Review* (February, 1885), p. 145.

[64] *Ibid.,* p. 150.

[65] Sarah E. Wiltse, letter to the editor, *Educational Review* (January, 1897), p. 104.

[66] G. Stanley Hall, "Child Study," NEA, 1894, p. 173.

[67] *Ibid.,* p. 175.

[68] "Child Study Congress," *School Journal* (January 15, 1898), p. vii.

play, and children's inferences.[69] With its origins in England and Germany, the movement was also international in scope, and child study organizations in various countries maintained correspondence with one another and exchanged fraternal messages at their meetings.

Such a powerful movement was bound to arouse criticism and antagonism, especially among those previously identified as leaders of educational thought. Butler was initially sympathetic, at least to the rhetorical possibilities. During the Cleveland debate in 1895, he demanded a system based on the child and forced on the philosopher.[70] Later, however, he called for someone to save child study from its "unscientific and hysterical friends" and wrote off much of the movement as "the sending-out of silly questionnaires" and the pronouncing of "ponderous platitudes and never-denied propositions."[71] The State Commissioner of Common Schools of Ohio, O. T. Corson, ridiculed the common-sense or commonplace findings of child study investigations. "To a teacher who really studies children as they are, some of the so-called modern discoveries resulting from original investigation are, to say the least, very humorous. To be told that a careful and scientific investigation has revealed the wonderful fact that Santa Claus appears to have a strong hold upon the hearts of boys and girls of all ages makes us tremble at the dense ignorance in which we have all been living."[72]

William T. Harris had many questions about the movement and feared that its activities often constituted a kind of human "vivisection," a charge indignantly denied by Hall.[73] In gentler moods, Harris referred to the movement as "so much mere froth."[74] He felt that child study could legitimately devote itself to what he called the dangers of "arrested development,"[75] a phenomenon he believed to occur when children were kept too long on materials and tasks already learned. It was significant that neither Butler nor Harris could repudiate child study as a whole and

---

[69] *School Review* (February, 1896), p. 117.

[70] As quoted in *School Journal* (March 23, 1895), p. 304.

[71] "Editorial," *Educational Review* (November, 1896), pp. 412–413.

[72] O. T. Corson, "Educational Extremes," NEA, 1897, p. 150.

[73] William T. Harris to Hugo Muensterberg, May 10, 1895, Commissioner's Office Outgoing Correspondence, 1880–1895 (National Archives, Record Group 12).

[74] William T. Harris to Nicholas Murray Butler, October 8, 1896, Nicholas Murray Butler Papers (Columbiana Library, Columbia University, New York, N.Y.).

[75] William T. Harris, "The Study of Arrested Development in Children As Produced by Injudicious School Methods," *Education* (April, 1900), p. 455.

found it necessary to protest their belief in aspects of it considered sensible and good.

Probably the central issue between Harris and the child study movement was identified in his statement made in 1900: "We do not begin, therefore, with child-study in our school education. But next after finding the great branches of human learning we consider the child, and how to bring him from his possibility to his reality. Then it becomes essential to study the child and his manner of evolution."[76] Child study wanted the curriculum to evolve from the nature of the child; Harris saw child study as a means in the teaching of a curriculum determined on other grounds. Harris was concerned about the content of studies in relation to human experience and wisdom. For years he had contended against the disciplinarians to gain this end; and now his possible victory was threatened by the claims of child study.

V

The Herbartians, like Harris, also believed in the primacy of content. They were able, however, possibly through their doctrine of interest, to make a better accommodation to child study, and there were many loosely known as Herbartians who also marched in the child study movement. The issue of content versus the child became a very real one in the Herbart Society. Parker had early pronounced himself on the side of the child. Nevertheless, in the Society's meeting in 1895 he defended nature study and science as the basis of the curriculum against the literature and history advocated by the McMurrys. This opened him to the accusation of advancing a science-centered curriculum. To clear himself of this, he had it placed on the record in 1896 that he and Jackman did not claim that science was the center of their work, but rather had "urged that the child is the center of all education."[77] The Herbartians and others continued to be bothered by the relationship between the child and the curriculum, and it was with this background in mind that Dewey attempted to resolve the issue in his essay, *The Child and The Curriculum,* published in 1902.

Herbartians and child study people also became involved with each other in connection with the doctrines of recapitulation and culture

[76] *Ibid.,* p. 466.
[77] Francis W. Parker, "A Few Corrections," *Education* (January, 1896), p. 306.

epochs. The first, as a biological doctrine involving the development of individual characteristics in relation to those of the species or the race, was identified with child study. The second, as a doctrine of curriculum that called for units of study paralleling the alleged culture epochs of man in the march toward civilization, found favor with some of the Herbartians. Child study people preferred to use recapitulation in the study of the individual and the identification of children's characteristics, and often reacted against the attempt to carry this over to units or subjects of study. Dewey was in this period identified with culture-epoch theory, and there was much in his 1899 essay, *The School and Society,* to justify this identification. Hall found the recapitulation of industrial history through "cooking, spinning, weaving, dyeing, drawing, and so forth," as exhibited in "Dewey's school," to be of interest, but he preferred to keep his own judgment "still suspended" on this "most fascinating experiment."[78] Other child study people were more critical, W. N. Hailmann stating that he could admit the validity of recapitulation in biological evolution, but could not "appreciate its application to cultural development."[79] He also identified Dewey with culture epochs.

Dewey was in this period, as always, unclassifiable. He served on the Executive Committee of the National Herbart Society, but was considered a Herbartian only in the very large and general sense in which the term was understood by many who circulated through the movement. While he sympathized with child study, he was not numbered among the disciples, certainly not among the disciples of G. Stanley Hall. At the Milwaukee meeting of the NEA in 1897 he both defended and criticized child study. His criticism, as was the case with the criticisms of others, was directed against the "exaggerations" resulting partly from "the misdirected gyrations of those camp-followers who, hanging about education as about all other progressive forces, attempt to use child study for their own advertising and aggrandizement."[80] The major difficulty, he found, was the expectation that the child study movement would produce a revolution in educational practice. It would have been equally mistaken, said Dewey, to expect early pioneers in the study of electricity to provide "us off-hand with the telegraph, telephone, electric light, and transporta-

[78] G. Stanley Hall, "Some Social Aspects of Education," *Educational Review* (May, 1902), pp. 442–443.

[79] W. N. Hailmann to Michael Vincent O'Shea, April 26, 1906, Michael Vincent O'Shea Papers (State Historical Society of Wisconsin, Madison, Wis.).

[80] John Dewey, "Criticisms Wise and Otherwise on Modern Child Study," NEA, 1897, p. 867.

tion."[81] In the same speech he quoted William James on the isolation of child study from related sciences.

These remarks were perhaps designed to offset some of the disillusionment about child study that appeared during the latter part of the decade. Such disillusionment was based on the alleged failure to produce applications. Child study was a fine thing, but grade school teachers still working with 50 or more children at a time might have found it difficult to appreciate. The Department of Superintendence, meeting in February of 1897, discussed a committee report that sought "to emphasize the generally recognized desirability of securing or preserving vital contact between school instruction and the life of the child at every point and in every phase of the work."[82] On the basis of this report, the Department appointed a new committee to formulate a detailed plan for a report on elementary education, but this came to little and was gradually lost in the growing volume of activities in which the Department became engaged.

The impact of both Herbartianism and child study on elementary education in this period, then, was not to be found in any revolution in classroom practice, at least not on any extended basis. Elementary school people gained their forward-looking reputation from the discussions and the debates. It was largely in the meetings of elementary school groups that the new doctrines found favorable reception, and many elementary school teachers were kept busy recording observations of children as the basis of the new science. So far as Herbartianism was concerned, there were many discussions and undoubtedly some use of the units of study that appeared in print to illustrate the doctrine of concentration. Some of these attracted ridicule from the critics, Harris commenting adversely on one article that made a tree the unity for a day's work, "so that the pupil reads a description of a tree, makes an arithmetic lesson a tree, and draws a tree."[83] These "unity lessons" stimulated the writing of ludicrous caricatures, such as the fish-centered curriculum, that have continued to amuse students of pedagogy down through the years. The lack of application of Herbartianism and child study to immediate class-

[81] *Ibid.,* pp. 867–868.

[82] W. N. Hailmann, "Report on Plans To Collect Data Concerning Methods and Courses of Work in Elementary Schools, Tending To Promote a Vital Connection between School Studies and the Educational Development of the Child," NEA, 1897, p. 199.

[83] William T. Harris to Charles De Garmo, May 14, 1895, Commissioner's Office Outgoing Correspondence, 1880–1895 (National Archives, Record Group 12).

room practice does not, however, support the notion that the classroom practice was necessarily rigid, traditional, or "formal." An English visitor to American classrooms in 1908 commented on the freedom and flexibility she saw in them and on what was to her the self-reliance of American pupils.[84] These may or may not have been among the fruits of the child study movement.

In the later 1890's and in the early 1900's, skeptics were asserting that both Herbartianism and child study had lost their driving force. "Correlation and coordination have had their day," wrote J. L. Pickard of Iowa in 1898.[85] By 1907 Principal Charles S. Chapin of the Rhode Island Normal School felt safe in saying that "the literature of this once popular cult rests in peace on our upper shelves, except when the student of bygone theories blows away the dust from the nearly forgotten volumes."[86] Butler welcomed "the decreased attendance at the child-study department" at Milwaukee in 1897 as an indication that the movement was passing "from the emotional to the rational stage."[87] The president of the Child Study Department, Michael Vincent O'Shea, a year later agreed that the movement had seemed to be slackening off in 1897, but optimistically noted what he considered to be signs of revival.[88] In 1901, the *School Journal* decided that the movement had reached "flood tide" four years before and had since then been declining. This editorial said that the child study people would be missed, for "in the main they were sweet-tempered souls who took themselves seriously—optimists all, viewing the world as it is to be thru rose-colored spectacles."[89]

Herbartianism as a slogan was probably fading away by 1900, as may have been evidenced by the renaming of the national Herbart Society, but the skeptics were premature in their judgments about child study. At the Cleveland meeting of the NEA in 1908 Hall showed no signs of defeat. He pronounced the child "the consummate flower of the cosmic process"[90] and felt that child study, "like the revolution of Copernicus," had made men realize "that the school is for the child and not

---

[84] Sara A. Burstall, *Impressions of American Education in 1908* (New York: Longmans Green & Co., 1909), pp. 22, 24–25, 34, 66.

[85] J. L. Pickard, "Co-operation in Education," *Education* (September, 1898), p. 44.

[86] Charles S. Chapin, "Departmental Teaching in the Grammar Grades," *Education* (April, 1907), pp. 505–506.

[87] "Editorial," *Educational Review* (September, 1897), pp. 192–193.

[88] Michael Vincent O'Shea, "President's Address," NEA, 1898, p. 894.

[89] "The Passing of Child Study," *School Journal* (December 21, 1901), p. 665.

[90] G. Stanley Hall, "Recent Advances in Child-Study," NEA, 1908, p. 952.

the child for the school."[91] When Hall spoke at the Boston NEA meeting in 1910, the meeting scheduled for the New Old South Church attracted so many people that it had to be marched across the street to the public library.[92] Hall's speech on this occasion made clear what had really happened to the child study movement. He celebrated the recently held second annual Child Welfare Conference, pointing out that child study was now so specialized in various departments—medical, hygienic, criminological, legal, religious, pedagogic, linguistic, social—that "no one can master all its fields." The Child Welfare Conference sought to unite all these specialties into a national "organization of organizations."[93] What Hall was saying was that child study of the primitive evangelical sort had been caught up in the larger movement for social reform and was having its rebirth as child welfare.

VI

Unlike Herbartianism, the child study movement had a definite impact on the discussions of secondary education, particularly as it enlarged its scope of activities from the study of very young children to include that of adolescents. Although it was G. Stanley Hall who eventually became the major figure of what some called the adolescence cult, he was not particularly identified with this aspect of child study during the early period. His first criticisms of the Committee of Ten, such as those made at Richmond, did not involve adolescence or any aspect of child study, but were based on his admiration of secondary schools in Germany and France.

One of the first to proclaim the discovery of adolescence was Professor James Earl Russell of the University of Colorado, later dean of Columbia's Teachers College. In a letter written to the *School Review* in 1895, Russell identified the ages twelve and thirteen as the critical time when intellectual and physiological changes took place in the child. "He becomes, in short, speculative, philosophical. The child lives in a world essentially realistic; the world of the youth is essentially idealistic."[94] Secondary education, he argued, should begin at that time. This

[91] *Ibid.,* p. 948.

[92] Department of Child Study, Secretary's Minutes, NEA, 1910, p. 873.

[93] G. Stanley Hall, "The National Child Welfare Conference: Its Work and Its Relation to Child Study," NEA, 1910, p. 893.

[94] James Earl Russell, "What Constitutes a Secondary School," *School Review* (September, 1896), p. 529.

point was echoed by the NEA Committee on College-Entrance Requirements, which identified "the seventh grade, rather than the ninth" as
"the natural turning point in the pupil's life."[95]

It was at the 1897 meeting of the New England Association, however,
that the idea of adolescence as the determiner of the secondary school
curriculum was vigorously advanced. Most of this session was dedicated
to adolescence. Principal Fred W. Atkinson of the Springfield, Massachusetts, High School made the opening address, in which he asserted
that the vital questions of secondary instruction were not "how much
algebra shall be exacted of the college preparatory pupil, or how many
pages of this or that Latin author translated, or how many English
books *read,* and how many *studied,* but do college requirements tend to
impoverish secondary education and are they based on a proper knowledge of the limitations and capacities of secondary pupils; are the present
demands of the secondary schools too great for the physical and mental
forces of any considerable number of pupils, and, is secondary instruction adapted to the needs and interests of the individual?"[96] Declaring
that child study needed to enter secondary education,[97] he distributed
copies of blanks used in the study of entering pupils at the Springfield
High School. Atkinson was followed by Professor William H. Burnham
of Clark University with a paper entitled, "Suggestions from the Psychology of Adolescence." Burnham referred to at least five investigators
who had conducted studies of adolescent growth and physiological
change, and suggested that the evils of secondary and college education
were "due to lack of appreciation and knowledge of adolescence rather
than to an unwise choice of subjects in the curriculum."[98] He ended by
contrasting the ideal of education as intellectual attainment and its tendency "to sacrifice pupils for the sake of subjects," with one that would
"even sacrifice the symmetry of curricula, systematic articulation of
grades, and logical method and sequence, whenever necessary in the interests of healthy growth and the development of character."[99] These
sentiments were received with enthusiasm by the same group, with much

---

[95] National Educational Association, *Report of the Committee on College-
Entrance Requirements* (Washington, D.C.: The Association, 1899), p. 31.

[96] Fred W. Atkinson, "The Capacities of Secondary School Students," *School
Review* (December, 1897), p. 642.

[97] *Ibid.,* p. 648.

[98] William H. Burnham, "Suggestions from the Psychology of Adolescence,"
School Review (December, 1897), p. 664.

[99] *Ibid.,* p. 665.

the same membership, that had only three years before gagged at Tetlow's pleas to admit pupils to college without Latin or Greek.

Several months later, in February, 1898, C. H. Thurber, editor of the *School Review,* declared that the addresses by Atkinson and Burnham had "opened a new era of thought and discussion for secondary-school teachers." Whereas the principal as "Programme Maker" had been "the hero of the hour," Thurber asked whether the next "hero" might not well be "the Principal as Pupil Student."[100] There were some who were skeptical about all this, just as there were others who were skeptical about other aspects of child study. Julius Sachs, headmaster of Sachs Collegiate Institute, New York City, later of Teachers College, Columbia University, took satisfaction in the fall of 1898 "in knowing that with hardly an exception the teachers of preparatory schools stood out firmly against the subversion of all the results of experience in favor of the new dispensation," and rejoiced in believing that the schoolroom was "definitely rid of the incubus of the psychological experiment."[101] Sachs was speaking for a losing cause, however, even in what he called the "preparatory" schools. The proclaimers of adolescence were abroad in the land. E. G. Lancaster of Colorado Springs College told the Department of Child Study of the NEA a year later that the mental life of the adolescent was "as distinct from the mental life of the child or adult as botany is distinct from chemistry or geology."[102] Preston W. Search of Holyoke, Massachusetts, foresaw a great era of high school improvement, "the greatest factor of which is due to the scientific study of children, emanating from the great throbbing heart of Clark University."[103]

In 1899 Myron T. Scudder, working under the inspiration of William H. Burnham and Fred Atkinson, described an elaborate project at his Hillhouse High School, New Haven, Connecticut, involving high school teachers, grammar school teachers, and parents in the study of pupils. He also presented a new form of reporting to parents in which teachers

[100] Charles H. Thurber, "Outlook Notes," *School Review* (February, 1898), p. 134.

[101] Julius Sachs, "Position of the Preparatory Schools in the Present Educational Movement," *Proceedings of the Twelfth Annual Convention* (Association of Colleges and Preparatory Schools of the Middle States and Maryland, 1898), p. 118. [In subsequent notes, these proceedings are referred to as MSM, with the appropriate year: for example, MSM, 1898.]

[102] E. G. Lancaster, "The Adolescent at Home and in School," NEA, 1899, p. 1039.

[103] Preston W. Search, "The Larger High School," *School Review* (April, 1900), p. 221.

marked such matters as lack of earnestness and purpose, lack of powers of expression, capacity to do better work, and annoying others. One of Scudder's teachers characterized this as the most " 'human' " report she had ever seen.[104] The pupils were also asked to respond to questionnaires on their problems and their ideas of what made a good teacher. All this new ferment attracted the attention of William T. Harris, who lived up to his reputation as a conservative by writing to Frank McMurry "that this continual allusion to adolescence in such sentimental, thoughtless and factless modes is disgusting." He added that he knew of nothing that had been brought out "by anybody that is really enlightening as to education in the adolescent period."[105]

By this time Hall had begun to give special attention to adolescence, possibly stimulated by the efforts of Burnham on his own faculty at Clark. In an address to the National Council at Detroit in July, 1901, he said that high school teachers as a class cared less than those of any other grades for problems of child development, "if, indeed, they suspect their existence." Disregarding the 1897 session, Hall criticized "the representatives of New England high schools and colleges" for centering their discussions "more and more in the details of how to fit in this and that study."[106]

It was in the fall of the same year and at the annual meeting of the New England Association that Hall and Eliot met to debate about the Committee of Ten. Hall related his criticism partly to child study and adolescence. Distinguishing between what he called the "scholiocentric" and "paidocentric" points of view, he proposed to consider "a few high-school topics" from the genetic standpoint.[107] He blamed the Committee of Ten for the relative decline of enrollments in physics, explaining it on the basis of an alleged failure to take into account the nature, needs, and interests of high school boys and girls: the mistake of the Ten with regard to physics was in making it too mathematical. The normal boy, he proclaimed, "would like to see hundreds of demonstrative experi-

---

[104] M. T. Scudder, "A Study of High School Pupils," *School Review* (April, 1899), p. 209.

[105] William T. Harris to Frank McMurry, November 26, 1901, Commissioner's Office Outgoing Correspondence, 1897–1901 (National Archives, Record Group 12).

[106] G. Stanley Hall, "The Ideal School as Based on Child Study," NEA, 1901, p. 486.

[107] G. Stanley Hall, "How Far is the Present High-School and Early College Training Adapted to the Nature and Needs of Adolescents?" *School Review* (December, 1901), pp. 649–651.

ments made in physics and the liberty to repeat most of them himself, without being bothered about mathematics." Physics, he said, should emphasize what he called "hero-ology." According to Hall, the high school pupil was "essentially in the popular science age" wanting "great wholes, facts in profusion, and very few formulae."[108] This was the same address in which Hall deplored the increase in Latin enrollments, but he did not indicate what principles of child study were violated by this tendency.

Several months later he made this point more explicit. The classics evidently lacked the proper moral values for the upbringing of adolescents. He recommended in place of Homer, the use of King Arthur, Siegfried, and Lohengrin, exemplifying "chivalry and honor—the noblest thing in feudalism." The purpose of literature in high school, he said, is "supremely ethical, and the talk of art for art's sake here is degeneration."[109] In the subsequent discussion at this meeting, William T. Harris, with a flash of his old platform fire, congratulated Hall for helping "us to think and to see once in a while how absurd some of his views are!"[110]

In 1904 Hall proclaimed his views in the two volumes of *Adolescence,* the work most identified with him in the years to come. Here he included his complete attack on the Committee of Ten, and made reference to the "vast army of incapables" in the schools. In reply to this Eliot not only addressed himself to Hall's specific criticisms, but also paid his respects to "that psychological pedagogy" in which development was marked off into "distinct, sharply defined periods, bearing separate names like childhood and adolescence." He urged in contrast a view of growth as a continuous series of shaded transitions, "liable, to be sure, to occasional accelerations, but in the main a continuous enlargement without breaks or explosions."[111] Eliot's view was the one later adopted by most students of human development, but it was Hall who gained the reputation as the liberal who forced the secondary school to consider the nature and needs of the adolescent.

Hall's book on adolescence was hailed with enthusiasm when it appeared in 1904, even though Thorndike in his review referred to "the

[108] *Ibid.,* pp. 652–653.
[109] G. Stanley Hall, "The High School as the People's College," NEA, 1902, pp. 264–265.
[110] William T. Harris, discussion, NEA, 1902, p. 271.
[111] Charles W. Eliot, "Fundamental Assumptions in the Report of the Committee of Ten," *Educational Review* (November, 1905), pp. 343–344.

book and the ideas it presents" as "plainly in the adolescent stage."[112] The president of the Department of Child Study in 1905, E. G. Lancaster, then of Olivet College, Michigan, stated his opinion that "no single publication has ever influenced education to the extent which Hall's *Adolescence* is influencing it" and that no work of the past century could be compared with it save Darwin's *On the Origin of Species*.[113] A speaker at a meeting of the Child Study Society of the Nebraska State Teachers' Association celebrated its "erudite and researchful fifteen hundred pages, which soar into the sublime realm of poetry, mount the white height of subtlest philosophy" and "bankrupt the latest edition of the Century dictionary."[114] Many people rapidly forgot the other and earlier investigators and students of adolescence and began to think of Hall as the only one who had been involved in the movement. By 1909 Charles Hubbard Judd could write that "with the exception of President Hall's volumes . . . the literature of education strikes below the high school age," adding, however, that there was "so much mythology in Dr. Hall's books that one can hardly wonder at the reluctance of high-school teachers to read or follow their teachings."[115] Even as late as 1917 a writer stated that there were few sources of information about early adolescence apart from Hall's volumes and hailed Hall "as the great pioneer and master in this special field."[116]

Hall's writings, along with the entire child study movement, combined with the brief but furious episode of Herbartianism to fill out the image of something increasingly known as "the new education." This term was by no means a new one, for Eliot had used it in the title of his articles in the *Atlantic Monthly* back in 1869. During the 1890's, however, it was taken over largely by elementary education, and it was through child study that it returned to secondary and higher education in connection with the emphasis on adolescence. It was the child study movement in particular that placed upon the high school the burden of proving that it was not falling behind in the onward march of educational progress.

[112] Edward Lee Thorndike, "The Newest Psychology," *Educational Review* (October, 1904), pp. 226–227.

[113] E. G. Lancaster, "President's Address," NEA, 1905, pp. 708–709.

[114] Harriet H. Heller, "The Social Life of the Adolescent," *Education* (June, 1905), p. 579.

[115] C. H. J., "Editorial Notes," *School Review* (October, 1909), p. 570.

[116] Chester R. Stacy, "The Junior High School Movement in Massachusetts," *Educational Administration and Supervision* (June, 1917), p. 349.

Just what the so-called typical school man made of all this lofty philosophizing and psychologizing is open to conjecture. So far as the philosophizing went, Butler wrote to Harris in 1895, concerning the journalistic controversy the latter was conducting with Charles De Garmo on the freedom of the will, that the school men were "utterly perplexed by what has already been published." He added his opinion that the experts did not appreciate "the utter lack of 'apperceptive material' for such analyses on the part of the average school master, even when he is an intelligent and educated man."[117] At the NEA convention of 1903, one of the members in attendance recorded some of the informal comments he overheard in the halls. From one school man he obtained the judgment that "Dr. Hall's influence, conjoined with that of President Eliot and his elective system" had "done untold injury to sound mental discipline in the schools." Another school man bracketed Hall with John Dewey and wished they might both "be shut up in an iron cage," thereby keeping them "from doing further harm to American schools."[118] Merciful to both, he did not propose the same cage for Hall and Eliot.

[117] Nicholas Murray Butler to William T. Harris, December 10, 1895, Nicholas Murray Butler Papers (Columbiana Library, Columbia University, New York, N.Y.).
[118] Charles Cornell Ramsay, "Impressions of the NEA Convention for 1903," *Education* (September, 1903), p. 47.

Chapter 6

The high school and the college

"And still will the people of the future be able to
say, 'There were giants in those days.' "
—SECOND ANNUAL REPORT OF THE NEA COM-
MITTEE ON COLLEGE-ENTRANCE REQUIREMENTS,
JULY, 1897.

*C*olleges and universities abounded in the
land. Some of them were old, Eastern,
and distinguished; but there persisted even in the 1890's an image of
colleges supposedly housed in log cabins, naturally with low academic
standards, and invariably located in the broad and undefined region of
the West. This geographical identification was admittedly unfair, for
there were dubious colleges in all regions, and even the most provincial
educators of the Atlantic seaboard recognized the prestige of such Western universities as Wisconsin and Michigan. Many of the state universities had good reputations, but not all of them were large. Sparse populations meant small enrollments. When James H. Baker became president
of the University of Colorado in 1892, that institution had only 66 students, and it had been in existence for fifteen years.

The 415 colleges and universities listed by the Commissioner of Education for 1889–1890 enrolled 59,249 students,[1] or an average of 143
students per college or university. In addition, there were 179 women's
colleges, presented in a separate category, the collegiate departments of
which enrolled 11,811 students.[2] This made a total of 71,060 students
in 594 institutions. Excluded from this total were students in preparatory
departments and those in professional schools not connected with colleges or universities. Many of these professional schools did not require
preparation beyond the grades for entrance,[3] as was the case also with
most normal schools in this period.

[1] Commissioner, 1889–1890, II, p. 760–763.
[2] *Ibid.*, II, p. 747.
[3] *Ibid.*, II, pp. 875–876.

Even among the institutions classified as colleges or universities, there was much diversity in the requirements for admission, as indicated by William C. Collar's survey reported in 1891,[4] and much flexibility in the administration of such requirements. There were complaints that colleges admitted pupils to collegiate studies without the preparation represented by a good secondary school course, a term often undefined. Many were admitted on condition. Where these circumstances prevailed, colleges tended to become competitors with secondary schools for the available students, and the boundary lines between secondary schools and colleges remained fluid even in the 1890's and early 1900's. In 1893, *Educational Review,* perhaps with some overstatement, characterized half the colleges and universities in the Commissioner's lists as "secondary schools giving more or less instruction of collegiate grade."[5]

On the other hand, there were some colleges with well-defined standards applied with consistency and rigor. During the 1890's school men noticed that the requirements of such colleges were being increased. This increase occurred in the number of subjects in which applicants were required to take examinations and was also manifested in a tendency to add to the amount of material covered in the required subjects. One subject so affected was algebra. In the 1870's the usual requirement had been algebra to quadratics; by 1900 algebra had been extended through quadratics and in some cases beyond. The geometry requirements were increased by the addition of more books of Euclid. In the classics there was more stress on sight translation from the books designated.[6]

School men then felt what they considered to be a dual threat from the colleges. Some colleges were taking, or seemed to be taking, their pupils away from them when they had not had adequate preparation or had not finished the school course. This could be, and was, a serious matter for private secondary schools and for those high schools seeking to become established. Other colleges were taking the opposite course of adding to the burdens of principals and teachers in getting pupils ready for the admission examinations.[7] Again, this did not mean that prepara-

---

[4] William C. Collar, "The Action of the Colleges upon the Schools," *Educational Review* (December, 1891), pp. 422–441.

[5] *Educational Review* (January, 1893), p. 102.

[6] Edwin Cornelius Broome, *A Historical and Critical Discussion of College Admission Requirements* (New York: Macmillan Co., 1903), pp. 64–69.

[7] See Wilson Farrand, "Are College Entrance Requirements Excessive?" *Official Report of the Twenty-Second Annual Meeting* (New England Association of Colleges and Preparatory Schools, 1907), pp. 12–13, for an inventory of the complaints being voiced by school men on this point.

tion for college was the primary task of the secondary school, but the college-preparatory pupils could not be neglected or ignored. The school men did not want to neglect them, and, in fact, sought to encourage the college ambitions of their pupils, especially among those who were undecided.

College men at the same time were becoming increasingly aware of the secondary schools. The issue of school-and-college relations, to which attention had been explicitly directed by the Massachusetts school men back in 1885, was felt to be overwhelming by the time of the Committee of Ten. Within this context, there was plenty of opportunity for irritation on both sides. It was easy for school men to blame their difficulties on college domination, just as it was for college men to complain about poor preparation in the schools. After listening to complaints from college men about the schools at the Middle States meeting of 1896, Charles H. Thurber, then Dean of the Morgan Park Academy in Illinois, a visitor to the convention, said: "It is our habit to sit still in such gatherings and absorb wisdom; but I tell you, you college gentlemen have no idea how we give it to you when we are by ourselves and you can't hear us."[8] "During the last two hours," declared a representative from the Boys' High School, Brooklyn, "we have listened to many compliments paid to the teaching done in secondary schools. Several of the speakers have taken the trouble to state that they knew little or nothing about secondary schools. This is a point upon which I am sure we can all agree. . . . They state that they know but little of secondary school work. That saves me the trouble of proving it."[9]

Optimistic and pessimistic views were advanced on whether the relations between school and college were getting worse or better. Tetlow's two associates in the forming of the New England Association, Ray Greene Huling and William C. Collar, expressed contradictory views about the long-term success of their venture. Huling opened the Congress of Secondary Education at the Columbian Exposition in 1893 by recalling the days when there had seemed to be "a wide, impassable gulf" between school and college teachers. "I have come," he went on, "to find the professors taking a deep interest in the secondary work, and declaring that their own work depends very largely upon the success of secondary teaching. I have come to see the professors and school-teachers, men and women, united in discussing secondary subjects, and find

[8] Charles H. Thurber, "Standards of Admission to College," MSM, 1896, p. 130.
[9] O. D. Clark, MSM, 1896, pp. 66–67.

the men of the colleges asking the opinions of those of the secondary schools concerning these difficult questions that relate to passages on one side or the other."[10]

Collar in 1904 referred to the days of twenty years before, when he, Tetlow, and Huling, "assisted in launching this Association," saying he had dreamed and hoped it would bring schools and colleges together in heart and purpose. "I am sorry to say it," he went on, "but my conviction is today that the chasm that separates the schools and the colleges is as wide and deep as ever it was." He granted that many conferences had been held with college men, "and I am bound to say that their reception of us schoolmasters has always been gracious, polite and respectful. They have listened to our representations with a certain benignant condescension." Nevertheless, he felt their real attitude to have been one of "partial amusement," disposed "to grant, if they could, something, but not very much."[11]

If Collar was right, then he, with Huling and Tetlow, indeed had failed. The New England Association, like those subsequently formed in other regions, was based on the presumed values of bringing the school and college men together. Collar's resolution back in 1884 had said that a meeting of the two groups would be "productive of good." It is not unlikely that Huling in 1893 overstated the case for success, while Collar in 1904 exaggerated the argument for failure. There was no indication, at least in the published proceedings, that the college men and school men tended to line up against each other in the consideration of decisions. The necessity of compromise on Tetlow's resolutions of 1894, dealing with the acceptance of any of the four programs of the Committee of Ten, was not brought about by the college men, although it was a Greek professor from Harvard who initiated the confusion. It was only two years later, in 1896, that the Association passed a resolution calling for an enlargement of options in admission requirements with special reference to a closer connection between the colleges and the nonclassical schools.[12] Again this did not reflect a clash of interest between the two groups in the Association.

[10] Ray Greene Huling, NEA, 1893, p. 181.

[11] William C. Collar, discussion, *Official Report of the Nineteenth Annual Meeting* (New England Association of Colleges and Preparatory Schools, 1904), p. 26. This statement was made eleven years after Huling's, but the difference probably lay in the contrasting temperaments of the two men rather than in the dates of their utterances.

[12] Ray Greene Huling, "Report of the New England Association of Colleges and Preparatory Schools," *School Review* (December, 1896), p. 783.

II

School and college men in other parts of the country evidently felt that the New England experiment had been productive of good, for three new associations were formed between 1893 and 1895. In practice, these did not work the same as the New England group, but the motive was the same, namely, to bring college men and school men together. Each association reflected a somewhat distinctive way of working toward this end. The initiative in New England had been taken by the school men, but in the Middle States and Maryland it came from the colleges. In the formation of the Association of Colleges and Preparatory Schools of the Southern States, the initiative also came from the colleges, but not from all of them as a group: it was a small group of colleges that carried along both the secondary schools and the other colleges as well. The North Central Association of Colleges and Secondary Schools was an outgrowth of initiative taken by colleges and schools together.

The Association of Colleges and Preparatory Schools of the Middle States and Maryland was the successor of a college association with the same regional designation, which itself had developed out of the College Association of Pennsylvania, organized back in 1887. In November, 1892, this College Association of the Middle States and Maryland opened its membership to secondary schools. James M. Taylor of Vassar, already a member of the Committee of Ten, was elected president for 1892–1893 and in this capacity gave the presidential address to the first meeting of the expanded group, held at Columbia College in December, 1893.[13]

An address given at the 1892 convention by President George W. Atherton of Pennsylvania State College sheds light on his own reasons for wanting the secondary schools included, and it may have been representative of the thinking of other college men in the region. The high schools, at least in his own state of Pennsylvania, were from his point of view not sending enough pupils to college. Only 31 out of the 57 high schools in his state, he declared, were engaged in college-preparatory work, and of 8608 high school pupils in the state in 1891–1892, a mere 619 were preparing to enter college, while only 236 actually entered.

[13] James M. Taylor, "The Neglect of the Student in Recent Educational Theory," MSM, 1893, pp. 65–77.

If this situation was to be corrected, Atherton went on, "the colleges must themselves take the initiative." This would mean that colleges must maintain two parallel courses, to one of which students might be admitted "without a knowledge of Greek, and possibly without a knowledge of Latin." He reminded his college audience of the influential place the high schools had come to occupy in the general system of education, a place that fifty years before had been "almost exclusively held by academies and other secondary institutions, from which Colleges mainly drew their supply." If the colleges would make "a frank and cordial recognition of this fact," he said, and "concede the proper status" to high schools, better understanding might come about. The time was "fully ripe" in Pennsylvania "to make the High School an integral and characteristic feature of the public school system," a condition he said was already characteristic of many states.[14]

Such an expression was open to various interpretations. On the one hand, it sounded as though the colleges were seeking to use high schools for their own ends. The reference to schools as sources from which colleges "drew their supply," suggested a processing firm interested in raw materials or a business concerned about obtaining customers. Possibly he had this in mind; certainly colleges in those days could not exist without students—and self-preservation is not necessarily an unworthy motive.

Another interpretation might be that President Atherton thought that a college education was a good thing and that as many people as possible should have one. This idea was fully in accord with the American dream of equal opportunity, to some a romantic delusion, but one not necessarily conservative, aristocratic, or "mediaeval." At any rate, he was prepared to make concessions and to open the colleges to nonclassical pupils, a goal vainly sought by Tetlow in the New England Association the following year. There was, perhaps, a tone of condescension about the address, and a firebrand like William C. Collar might have found in this something to resent. The general drift, however, was consistent with the objectives for which Collar, Tetlow, and Huling had worked in founding the New England Association nine years before.

During the years after 1893, the Middle States Association developed into a serious, workmanlike, and highly creditable educational venture. Its major distinctive contribution—though to some a major disaster—

[14] George W. Atherton, "Proposals for the Middle States," *Proceedings* (College Association of the Middle States and Maryland, 1892), pp. 12–14.

was the creation in 1899–1900 of the College Entrance Examination Board. With regard to the program of studies, there was steady support of the modern academic subjects, although without antagonism toward the classics. For the most part, the published proceedings lack the sparkle and zest characteristic of the New England Association and seem more like the product of competent organization men. The list of presidents of the Association over the years included many distinguished names, such as Nicholas Murray Butler, who made it in 1894; James C. Mackenzie, of Lawrenceville School and the Committee of Ten; President J. G. Schurman of Cornell; Julius Sachs of Sachs Collegiate Institute in New York City; Wilson Farrand of Newark Academy, New Jersey; and, in 1907, Woodrow Wilson. There seemed to be a policy of electing a school man one year and a college man the next. Apart from this, and in contrast again to the New England Association, the impression left by the *Proceedings* is that the college men did most of the talking, though not necessarily to the disadvantage of the schools.

The Southern Association was another matter. It was a minority movement, led by a few colleges, with much of the initiative assumed by the young Chancellor of Vanderbilt University, J. H. Kirkland. Only twelve colleges were represented at the first meeting, held at the Georgia School of Technology, Atlanta, on November 6, 1895. The group drew up a constitution and bylaws providing for admission of both colleges and secondary schools, but the conditions for colleges were stringent and indicative of the purposes of the founders of the Association. Article I of the bylaws, for example, bluntly stated, "no college shall be eligible to membership in this Association which furnishes preparatory instruction in any subject as part of its college organization," while Article II stipulated minimum college admission requirements to be binding on all members. Article IV excluded colleges admitting students under fifteen years of age.[15]

What the leaders of this group evidently had in mind was to eliminate the tendency of colleges in the South to compete with secondary schools. This was by no means unique to the South, but it seems to have been especially prevalent there. Back in 1885 Charles Forster Smith of Vanderbilt had deplored the scarcity of high schools in the South, attributing this to the practices of the colleges. "All the colleges publish require-

---

[15] Association of Colleges and Preparatory Schools of the Southern States, *Proceedings of the First Meeting* (The Association, 1895), p. 6. [In subsequent notes, these proceedings are referred to as SA, with the appropriate year: for example, SA, 1895.]

ments for admission; very few enforce them. Since the boy is not required to prepare for college, he comes to college without preparation."
His own state of Tennessee at that time had only four public high
schools, but was equipped with twenty-one "male colleges and universities" and sixteen "female colleges and seminaries," with ten of the latter conferring college degrees.[16] The South appeared to be abundantly or
even overabundantly supplied with colleges of various kinds, but in the
same year, A. D. Mayo, a friendly observer, declared that in sixteen
southern states there were 4 million white and nearly 2 million colored
children and youth of school age, not more than one-third of whom were
"in any effective school." Southerners often blamed these conditions on
the Civil War and reconstruction, and Mayo himself agreed that the
amount of money available for education "in a country just rising from
utter prostration" was comparatively small.[17] Under these conditions
the number of colleges in the South—and, according to southern writers
themselves, of colleges with low standards and of dubious status—represented a tragic lack of balance in the use of personnel and funds.

Kirkland and his associates had undertaken what looked like a hopeless task. Twelve colleges sent representatives to the first meeting in
1895, but only six assumed the obligations of what Kirkland called "the
compact": namely, Vanderbilt, North Carolina, Mississippi, The University of the South, Washington and Lee, and Trinity, later Duke University.[18] There was little motivation for colleges to bind themselves by
the rules set forth, and they could stay in business without them and
without the Association. In fact, there appeared to be more danger of
going out of business if they did follow the rules.[19] By 1898 only two
more colleges had been added to the group, Alabama and Tennessee;

[16] Charles Forster Smith, "Southern Colleges and Schools," *Atlantic Monthly*
(October, 1884), pp. 543–544.
[17] A. D. Mayo, "The New Education in the New South," *Education* (September,
1885), p. 49.
[18] J. H. Kirkland, "The Association of Colleges and Secondary Schools of the
Southern States," *School Review* (February, 1913), pp. 103–111.
[19] Vanderbilt itself lost students under Kirkland's commitment to standards.
"From the standpoint of educational policy Kirkland at once put himself firmly
behind the efforts of himself and his colleagues to maintain high standards of
admission and graduation. Despite the loss of students and the consequent decrease
of income, he did not waver. For more than fifteen years the college attendance
hovered around two hundred students, but as the number of preparatory schools
increased, the attendance at Vanderbilt increased slowly—very slowly." Edwin
Mims, *Chancellor Kirkland of Vanderbilt* (Nashville, Tenn.: Vanderbilt University
Press, 1940), p. 104.

twenty-six secondary schools were represented at the annual meeting, but only three of these were identified as high schools, Nashville, Tennessee, and Norfolk and Bellevue, Virginia.[20]

The delegates at the initial meeting in 1895 had drawn up a statement of minimum requirements for college admission. Latin, Greek, and mathematics were stipulated only for those who expected to take these subjects in college. History, geography, and English were to be required of all applicants except those "pursuing technical studies in not more than two subjects," a mysterious reference not explained in the minutes. Examinations were assumed to be the normal means of meeting the requirements, but provision was also made for admission by certificate.[21]

Kirkland and his associates were evidently among the moderates who welcomed the modern subjects, but without antagonism toward the classics. Although willing to admit nonclassical students, they urged public high schools to offer four years of Latin and, "as soon as practicable," two years of Greek. This recommendation, according to the resolution, was made "in the best interests of popular education," and the Association declared itself strongly in sympathy "with the development of the State public school system."[22] To some, this may have implied college domination, but the founders of this Association were hardly in a position to dominate anybody, whether high schools or other colleges. What they believed was that Latin and Greek, for whatever values they possessed, belonged in popular education as well as in education considered more exclusive.

Mississippi was one state in particular where this conviction about Greek was strongly held. Conferences between the University and public school teachers had led in 1894 to a system whereby certain schools were affiliated with the University and their students admitted on certificate. A one-year requirement of Greek was to go into effect for the years 1897–1899, and a two-year requirement after that time, presumably for students in the bachelor of arts program, but this was not explicitly stated. The affiliated schools were urged to introduce Greek, but few teachers were qualified in that language and only "three or four" schools had been attempting to teach it. This led to a venture in what would later be called "in-service" education. The University in the summer of 1896 offered a course in Greek, both for those who had made

[20] SA, 1898, pp. vi–vii.
[21] SA, 1895, p. 6.
[22] *Ibid.*, p. 8.

some study of it previously and for those who had not, and "more was accomplished than one not present could realize." According to the report of this venture, "sixty teachers returned to their classrooms with a desire to teach Greek, and many with a fair idea of how it should be taught to beginners." It was pointed out that "those teachers who had not studied Greek before did not become capable instructors from one course. For these a correspondence course was offered. . . . About twenty-five took this course and many of them did excellent work." Eighteen schools introduced Greek during the year following the summer course. By 1899 there were 44 schools teaching Greek in the state, of which 31 were affiliated with the University.[23]

To enemies of the classics and possibly even to some friends there may have been something ludicrous about this promotion of Greek in a poverty-stricken state burdened with widespread illiteracy in English, to say nothing about turning loose on pupils teachers who had studied the language in one summer session and by correspondence. Whether the same amount of money and time would have reduced illiteracy cannot be known. At any rate, it was a brave attempt, one revealing an unusual phase of what European visitors in this period referred to as the great American faith in education.

The fortunes of the Association itself prospered but slowly. Only four more colleges—West Virginia, Missouri, Texas, and the College of Charleston—joined the group between 1898 and 1901, making twelve in all.[24] In 1902 Professor Paul Saunders of the University of Mississippi reviewed the progress made by the Association toward its goals. He felt that substantial gains had been made in his own state and in Texas. Mississippi by that time had 59 high schools doing work of which he approved.[25] He attributed this to the abolition by the University of its preparatory department back in 1892. Texas, he noted, had about one hundred high schools following "in whole or in part the course outlined by the University."[26] He compared public high schools to an infant industry needing protection from colleges that offered secondary school work.[27] Unfortunately, from his point of view, the high schools in many parts of the South were suffering from competition not only with general

[23] Paul Hill Saunders, "Greek in Mississippi Schools," SA, 1899, pp. 63–71.
[24] SA, 1901, p. vi.
[25] Paul Hill Saunders, "The Outlook of the Public High School in the South," SA, 1902, p. 82.
[26] *Ibid.*, p. 85.
[27] *Ibid.*, p. 74.

colleges and universities but also with agricultural, industrial, and normal colleges.[28] He quoted several replies made by school men to his inquiries, one of them saying, "they enter college classes from even our seventh grade," and another lamenting that while he offered work of the tenth grade, there were no pupils. They had "gone to college."[29]

Another speaker at the 1902 convention, Professor Edwin Mims of Trinity College, was more pessimistic than Saunders. He said that the meetings of the Association had been on the whole "confessions of failures," and he declared, "we have scarcely held our ground." Granting that many felt a prior need to establish elementary education, he added that accomplishment of this goal would still mean having "colleges and universities that are the laughing-stock of the world."[30]

Four years later, Professor Joseph Stewart of the University of Georgia contended that high schools in the South were still suffering "in attendance and local prestige from the attempt of the colleges to persuade fond parents that their sons and daughters could do much better if sent to . . . college before completing the high school course." During the years following 1906, the hand of the Association was strengthened by the national movement toward standards and accreditation.[31] Nevertheless, Chancellor Kirkland as late as 1913, while recognizing "great improvement in the past seventeen years,"[32] still felt obliged to admonish colleges against inviting students to leave high school after two years of work.[33] Perhaps the Southern Association was a failure with reference to its own goals, at least during those early years. Its successes, such as they were, varied from state to state. Year after year the same handful of men came back to their sparsely attended meetings to make inventories of discouragement and to express hopes for the future. To those who believed in public high schools, these men were valiant workers in a great cause. To others, the venture may have represented the efforts of well-established colleges and universities to aggrandize themselves at the expense of smaller and weaker institutions and to build up the public high schools toward this end.

By way of contrast, the career of the North Central Association was

[28] *Ibid.,* pp. 75–76.
[29] *Ibid.,* p. 79.
[30] Edwin Mims, SA, 1902, p. 6.
[31] Joseph S. Stewart, "The High School Population of the South and a Plan for the Correlation of the High Schools and the Higher Institutions," SA, 1906, p. 18.
[32] J. H. Kirkland, *op. cit.,* p. 104.
[33] *Ibid.,* pp. 109–110.

a success story, although not all would be in agreement about the desirability of the success achieved. It began with a resolution passed by the Michigan Schoolmasters' Club at its Ypsilanti meeting in December, 1894, calling upon the presidents of Michigan, Wisconsin, Chicago, and Northwestern to join them in forming an association for the North Central States.[34] A meeting of 36 delegates from various states was held at Northwestern University on March 29, 1895. James B. Angell was elected President, and a constitution was adopted that proclaimed the name of the new organization to be "the North Central Association of Colleges and Secondary Schools,"[35] not, as was the case with the other associations, of colleges and preparatory schools. This choice of a word may have had some doctrinal significance.

The Michigan Schoolmasters' Club, within which this movement had originated, had been founded back in 1886. Apparently the Club was open to college men as well as school men, for John Dewey, then at the University of Michigan, had been one of the founding group and had served as vice-president in 1887–1888. At the 1886 meeting he had presented a paper on "psychology in high schools from the standpoint of the college,"[36] a title that may have implied college domination. The Michigan school men, however, had long been used to working with their own state university. In 1895 the Schoolmasters' Club sponsored a Classical Conference, at which one of the major addresses was given by Princeton's Andrew F. West.[37] This meeting took place in the midst of the campaign of the American Philological Association against the Committee of Ten, and the delegates passed a resolution favoring three years of Greek.

The newly formed North Central Association moved quickly and easily into its business, with its leaders soon identified: Angell of Michigan, Jesse of Missouri, Charles Kendall Adams of Wisconsin, and G. N. Carman of Lewis Institute among the college men; A. F. Nightingale of Chicago, Frederick L. Bliss of Detroit, and E. W. Coy of Cincinnati among the school men. For the first five years it dealt largely with mat-

---

[34] North Central Association of Colleges and Secondary Schools, *Proceedings of the Preliminary Meeting for Organization* (The Association, 1895), p. 5.

[35] *Ibid.*, pp. 6–11.

[36] Leslie A. Butler, *The Michigan Schoolmasters' Club* (Ann Arbor, Mich.: University of Michigan, 1958), pp. 21–23.

[37] Classical Conference, Ann Arbor, Michigan, Proceedings, *School Review* (June, 1895), pp. 354–396.

ters that were becoming the set pieces of discussion at associations. At the outset it had no special mission, such as the one undertaken by the Southern Association. In 1897 it passed resolutions against "short courses" in secondary schools and in favor of developing the powers and faculties of the pupils. One resolution, unusual for the times but prophetic of the future, characterized as an "evil" the tendency to entrust college freshman classes to inexperienced teachers "often inferior to those in the high schools."[38] College men presumably joined school men in voting for this resolution, and it had been proposed by a committee including several college men.

Another resolution proposed at the 1897 meeting stirred up some lively controversy and in particular aroused Nightingale to deliver a speech that matched his oratorical effort against the Committee of Ten back at Richmond. This proposed resolution called for the study of foreign language and mathematics throughout the secondary school course and through the second year of college, accompanied by the study of English, but with no other studies being "allowed to interfere with the preëminence of the studies here designated."[39] Nightingale, who only two years before had supported the American Philological Association in its demand for three years of Greek, denounced the proposed resolution as "weighty with the odor of resurrected graveclothes." He acknowledged "no little remorse" for what he called his once "too uncompromising attitude toward all but the traditional subjects." To advocate this resolution, he said, would be "such a crime against the youth of our country" that he would expect "to answer for it on the great day of assize." He went on to contemplate the direful consequences of the passing of such a resolution by the leading educators of the Northwest. "When I see boys turning their backs upon the schools, and girls fainting by the way because language and mathematics are made the be all and the end all of fundamental culture, I feel like crying out again with the Virginia delegate to the house of burgesses—'Give me liberty in courses of instruction or give me death!'"[40] He proposed a substitute resolution calling in effect for a strong application of the elective principle, with

[38] North Central Association of Colleges and Secondary Schools, *Proceedings of the Second Annual Meeting* (The Association, 1897), p. 10. [In subsequent notes, these proceedings are referred to as NC, with the appropriate year: for example, NC, 1897.]

[39] *Ibid.,* p. 82.

[40] Augustus F. Nightingale, NC, 1897, pp. 82–83.

courses arranged under the headings of language, mathematics, science, history and literature, and civics and economics, but with "alternative options, with a view to their adaptation to the individual capacities and purposes of students."[41]

The Association deferred action on the original resolution and Nightingale's substitute until the 1898 meeting. During the intervening year's time, Nightingale sought support by correspondence from various educators throughout the country, including Eliot. The reply from Eliot, who by now presumably had heard of Mr. Nightingale of Chicago, was especially favorable. Eliot characterized the proposed resolution as "distinctly archaic" and called Nightingale's substitute a great improvement, noting that it recognized "the indispensableness of election of studies and individual instruction."[42] At the 1898 meeting, where he was elected president of the Association, Nightingale triumphantly read the letter from Eliot, defended his substitute, and referred to a national trend to emancipate "the race from the narrowing and degrading influences of outgrown mediaevalism."[43] His oratory, or perhaps his oratory combined with Eliot's support, carried the day, and his substitute was adopted.[44] The North Central Association had committed itself to the elective principle.

It was at this 1898 meeting that the Association made an effort to define uniform college-admission requirements in relation to prescribed subjects. The proposed resolution on this point called for two years' work each in English, mathematics, Latin, and physical science, plus additional studies up to a total of a four years' course. In this case the opposition came from a college man, President Henry M. Rogers of Northwestern University, who spoke against the absolute requirement of Latin and physical science.[45] Although he did not, like Nightingale, quote Eliot directly, he expounded Eliot doctrine in proclaiming that desirable uniformity consisted, not in naming the subjects, but in defining the standards in the subjects.[46] The Association agreed with him and voted a substitute resolution providing for commissions to formulate uniform entrance requirements in the separate subjects, but saying nothing about

[41] *Ibid.*, p. 86.
[42] As quoted in Augustus F. Nightingale, "Discussion of the Fourth Resolution of 1897," NC, 1898, p. 156.
[43] Nightingale, *op. cit.*, p. 148.
[44] NC, 1898, p. 160.
[45] Henry M. Rogers, NC, 1898, p. 82.
[46] *Ibid.*, p. 84.

what subjects should be required.[47] Eliot, therefore, had in a sense scored two victories in this 1898 meeting of the North Central Association.

III

In the meantime, there had been in existence since 1895 a new venture of the NEA, the Committee on College-Entrance Requirements, sponsored jointly by the Departments of Secondary and Higher Education. Its formation had been prompted at the Denver meeting of the NEA in 1895 by Professor William Carey Jones of the University of California in a speech, reported under two different titles, calling for action to promote the introduction of programs recommended by the Committee of Ten.[48] The Department of Secondary Education appointed a committee of five members to work toward better understanding between schools and colleges about requirements for admission.[49] The Department of Higher Education concurred and added five members of its own to the Committee.[50] Later, members were added to represent the regional associations. Some of these seem never to have served actively, while others came in through unspecified channels. The result was that the over-all Committee never settled at a precise size, thereby failing to become known as a committee of "Twelve" or "Thirteen," although attempts were made in this direction, and going into history as the Committee on College-Entrance Requirements.

In the end, the group of twelve members who submitted the final report was made up of six from the schools and six from the colleges, although the classification in some cases was an arbitrary one. The school men were Ray Green Huling, one of the pioneers of the New England Association; J. Remsen Bishop of Cincinnati, an articulate opponent of the Committee of Ten; William H. Smiley, who was Baker's successor at the Denver High School; John T. Buchanan of Kansas City; George B. Aiton, state inspector of high schools in Minnesota; and Augustus F. Nightingale. Colleges were represented by professors only, namely, Paul Hanus of Harvard; Burke A. Hinsdale of Michigan; Wil-

[47] NC, 1898, p. 111.
[48] William Carey Jones, "The Prospects for a Federal Educational Union," NEA, 1895, p. 599.
[49] Department of Secondary Education, Secretary's Minutes, NEA, 1895, pp. 579–580.
[50] Department of Higher Education, Secretary's Minutes, NEA, 1895, p. 637.

liam Carey Jones of California; James Earl Russell of Colorado; and Edmund J. James and Charles H. Thurber of the University of Chicago.[51] Four of these—Hanus, Hinsdale, Thurber, and Russell—were professors of pedagogy. Jones was listed as a professor of jurisprudence, and James of public administration.[52] The list of names at the end of the report also included a professor of mathematics, Henry B. Fine of Princeton.[53] The Committee was devoid of college presidents and had on it only one professor of a traditional subject.

No chairman was designated in the resolutions, and Augustus F. Nightingale apparently was chosen for this position by the group itself. The man who had delivered the "intemperate" attack on the report of the Committee of Ten was now in the anomalous position of being chairman of a committee set up in part to take action on behalf of that report. He was also exposing himself as a target for attacks similar to the ones directed against the Committee of Ten, one of which, of course, he had delivered himself. The prospect of being the center of controversy did not, however, frighten Nightingale. Rather it seemed to stimulate him, and he threw himself into his new responsibility with determination and zest.

Although Eliot had never heard of Nightingale before the Richmond meeting of 1894, the Chicago administrator was himself a New Englander, a distant connection of the Adams family, born only a few miles from Eliot's Beacon Street in the Adams stronghold of Quincy, Massachusetts. His love of a good fight, particularly when he thought he represented a minority point of view, was perhaps a reflection of his New England individuality. Nightingale had been prepared to enter Harvard, but his wife-to-be persuaded him to go to Wesleyan instead. Those who enjoy historical might-have-beens might speculate on the possible consequences if Nightingale had stayed with his original intention. Perhaps Harvard would have inhibited the development of his oratorical style.

In 1866, Nightingale began teaching Greek and Latin at a small Iowa college that did not permit him to play croquet on Sundays or to smoke. During the next several years he taught at two other colleges

[51] National Educational Association, *Report of the Committee on College-Entrance Requirements* (Washington, D.C.: The Association, 1899), p. 5. [In subsequent notes, this report is referred to as CCER, with the appropriate page numbers.]

[52] *Ibid.*, pp. 48–49.

[53] *Ibid.*

and served briefly as Superintendent of Schools in Omaha; from there he came in 1874 to become principal of the new Lake View Township High School near Chicago. There he enjoyed himself for fifteen years, teaching Latin and Greek, playing ball with the pupils, and watching his semi-rural environment gradually being encroached upon by the big city.[54] When Chicago annexed the entire township and its schools in 1889, Nightingale joined the city school staff as Assistant Superintendent in charge of high schools. He was no stranger to the NEA, having addressed the Department of Secondary Instruction back in 1887, but it was in his new capacity that he attended the Richmond meeting of the Department of Superintendence in 1894 to make himself known to Butler, and through Butler, by correspondence, to Eliot. He also stayed with the Department of Secondary Instruction (renamed The Department of Secondary Education in 1888) and was led thereby to the Committee on College-Entrance Requirements and the chairmanship.

As he acknowledged in his North Central speech in 1897, Nightingale at one time had been an archconservative about the classics. At some point, probably before the 1894 Richmond meeting, he ceased to believe in Greek as a universal prescription in college admission, but he joined the attack made by the American Philological Association on the Committee of Ten for having recommended only two years of Greek in the high school program. His attitude toward the Committee of Ten itself seemed to fluctuate. Having denounced the report at Richmond in February of 1894, he turned to a partial defense of it in a general-session speech at Asbury Park in July of the same year.[55] In all these utterances, he proved himself the king of NEA oratory, just as Harris was of NEA platform warfare. There were many pedagogical orators in this period, in which Eliot's style was considered hopelessly drab. Regardless of one's taste, however, Nightingale's high-altitude prose compels admiration as the most nearly perfect example of the art as practiced at the NEA. Even through the yellowed pages of the NEA *Proceedings,* one can feel that he thoroughly enjoyed himself in giving his virtuoso performances and that he delighted his audiences as well. Butler's comments on Nightingale's remarks at Richmond were probably ill-founded;

[54] Esther Van W. Tufty, " 'Millionaire of Love,' " *News-Index* (Evanston, Illinois), December 4, 1925; also unpublished journal written in 1945–1946 by Jessie Irma Nightingale (Mrs. Harrison Angle), made available for examination through the courtesy of Dr. Augustus N. Abbott.

[55] Augustus F. Nightingale, "Discussion of Reports of the Committee of Ten," NEA, 1894, pp. 155–160.

the Chicago editor of *Intelligence* responding to the editorial in *Educational Review* declared that it was just "not in the man" to do anything justifying Butler's "castigation."[56]

As Chairman of the Committee on College-Entrance Requirements, Nightingale fostered the widest possible cooperation with existing scholarly groups in the academic fields of study, including the American Philological Association, the Modern Language Association, the American Mathematical Society, and the American Historical Association. The report of the last of these groups, the American Historical Association, known as that of the Committee of Seven, became especially widely known and was long remembered. Nightingale's march to the elective principle, like Eliot's, did not imply antagonism toward the academic studies, and like Tetlow, he retained his love of Latin and Greek.

The Committee on College-Entrance Requirements worked more slowly, and possibly more thoroughly, than had the Committee of Ten. Nightingale and other members presented progress reports to various NEA groups in 1896 and 1897. In his introductory remarks about the progress report in 1897, he declared: "The fires are already lighted, and they need but the added fuel of intellectual common sense to kindle a conflagration that shall consume the time-worn, the age-shattered conservatism of the past."[57] Both he and the Committee were moving rapidly to an extreme position of electivism in college-entrance requirements. The progress report itself, presumably written by Nightingale, proclaimed that, one after another, "the old idols" were being broken. "The giants that stood in the path and said to every student, 'Let him who enters here' leave all behind but Latin, Greek, and mathematics are growing limp and lifeless." Harvard, Cornell, Vassar, Michigan, California, and Stanford, declared the report, were already "unfurling their banners of freedom." In a magnificent outburst, the progress report concluded: "There is already a path blazed thru the thicket and jungle of conservatism and tradition, and before the twentieth century dawns in its glory there will be a broad highway thru which a pupil may walk unfettered, amid attractive associations, from the kindergarten to a degree at the end of the postgraduate course of the university, and still will the

[56] *Intelligence* (April 15, 1894), p. 117.
[57] Augustus F. Nightingale, "The Committee on College-Entrance Requirements: Report of the Chairman," NEA, 1897, p. 648.

people of the future be able to say, 'There were giants in those days.' "[58]

Still it was not easy to work out a practical application of the elective principle either to the school program itself or to college-admission requirements. Nightingale's Committee, like the Committee of Ten, wanted to proceed from a program designed for "preparation for life" and to use that as a basis for "preparation for college." They wanted to hold fast to the principle enunciated by Eliot of not differentiating pupils' programs on the basis of their presumed educational destinations. The members of this Committee, like the Ten, were moderate revisionists who wanted to strengthen and gain acceptance for the modern academic studies, but they did not propose to throw the high school program open to any and all possible studies. Furthermore, while the Committee did not believe in unlimited election, it had no desire to set up election by courses of study only. In particular, they did not wish to follow the Committee of Ten in recommending parallel courses of study, which Eliot himself had written off as only temporary trestlework.

In its final report, therefore, the Committee set forth a program they believed defensible for good secondary schooling regardless of the pupil's destination, one designed for life while at the same time being one that colleges would presumably accept. The major categories of study presented were English; foreign languages and literatures, based on the reports of the Modern Language Association and the American Philological Association, the latter with its controversial recommendation for three years of Greek; history, civics, and economics, with the history program incorporating the recommendations of the Committee of Seven; mathematics, with a four years' offering of algebra, geometry, and trigonometry; and the sciences, including physical geography, biology, physics, and chemistry.[59]

The policy recommendations were contained in a series of fourteen resolutions. The first one declared the principle of election,[60] and the sixth the inadvisability of unlimited election.[61] Here then was the dilemma. To resolve it the Committee proposed a device unusual for those times, namely, a set of constants or studies to be taken by all pupils without reference to courses of study, with the rest of the program for

[58] Augustus F. Nightingale, "The Committee on College-Entrance Requirements: Report of the Chairman," *School Review* (June, 1897), p. 331.
[59] CCER, pp. 12–27.
[60] *Ibid.*, p. 27.
[61] *Ibid.*, p. 32.

each pupil filled out by free electives. The constants recommended were four "units" or years of foreign languages, two of mathematics, two of English, one of history, and one of science.[62] In a sixteen-unit program for four years this left free electives to the extent of six units.

The pattern was to apply to all pupils whether college bound or not, and the colleges were to accept the pupils who had fulfilled such a program. With a single stroke the Committee had cut away the cumbersome devices of parallel courses of study. This arrangement represented a greater degree of application of the elective principle than had been set forth in the four courses of the Committee of Ten. According to Elmer Ellsworth Brown of the University of California, later Commissioner of Education, the Committee "had thrown a real Copernican suggestion into the midst of our confusion on this matter," one which served "to show how the Ptolemaic tables of courses which many large high schools present may be simplified."[63]

Apart from the elective principle and its application, the Committee on College-Entrance Requirements covered a variety of matters. In its fourth resolution it favored "a unified six-year high-school course of study beginning with the seventh grade,"[64] mentioned without commitment by the Committee of Ten as a possibility. The seventh resolution recommended what would today be called "advanced placement," that is, credit toward a college degree for work done in secondary schools.[65] The ninth resolution recognized the existence of "gifted students" and suggested encouraging them to complete secondary school studies in less time than required by most students.[66] In the fourteenth resolution the Committee recommended a longer school day, with supervised study, but tactfully recorded its appreciation of "the almost unanimous and perhaps enlightened opposition on the part of teachers" to such a proposition.[67]

The Committee frankly acknowledged its omissions. One of these was lack of consideration given to the place of "commercial instruction" in college admission requirements. The report noted, however, that the recognition of commercial studies for this purpose would "soon have immediate practical importance" and recommended it for special study,

---

[62] Ibid.
[63] Elmer Ellsworth Brown, "Present Tendencies in Secondary Education," School Review (September, 1901), p. 449.
[64] CCER, p. 30.
[65] Ibid., p. 33.
[66] Ibid., p. 35.
[67] Ibid., p. 40.

possibly by another committee.[68] Nothing was said about manual training. In the section of the report where the Committee acknowledged
what it had left undone, an observation was made to the effect that it
had received only $500 from the NEA. Note was made of the fact that
some of the Committee members, as well as other people, had contributed money to carry on the work.[69]

On the whole the report was straightforward and clear. Nightingale,
James, and Thurber had served as an editorial committee of three to
prepare the report for publication. The result was probably a more sober
document than might have come from the chairman alone, although
Nightingale did insert as quoted materials portions of his impassioned
progress report of 1897, including the reference to the giants there were
in those days. Perhaps the clearness of the report reflected the lack of
serious controversy among the Committee members themselves, although
Nightingale shortly afterwards referred to it as a "judicious compromise"
among "thirteen different opinions."[70] In the sense that it did not attack
the classics or propose a place for the so-called practical subjects, it was
what many might call a conservative report, but its advocacy of free
electives outside the confines of set courses was far from conservative
even in 1899. It continued the drive of the Committee of Ten for more
recognition of the academic modern subjects, and it reflected Eliot's
convictions that programs of pupils should not be differentiated on the
basis of whether they were or were not planning to go to college. Although the Committee did not follow Jones's original intention back in
1895 of bringing about acceptance of the programs of the Committee of
Ten, it stayed more or less within the official charge of the departments
that created it, namely to seek a better understanding between schools
and colleges on requirements for admission.

Nightingale made the official presentation of the report to the joint
session of the Departments of Secondary and Higher Education at the
Los Angeles NEA convention on July 13, 1899. He began by praising
the report of the Committee of Ten and noting the rapid progress in
education made even since his own Committee had begun its work four
years before. The report he was presenting, he said, would a half decade
afterward be considered only a "faint prophecy."[71] Much of his presen-

[68] *Ibid.*, p. 47.
[69] *Ibid.*, p. 48.
[70] Augustus F. Nightingale, discussion, NC, 1900, p. 21.
[71] Augustus F. Nightingale, "Presentation of the Report of the Committee on
College-Entrance Requirements," NEA, 1899, p. 625.

tation speech was occupied by comments on the recommendations in the separate subjects. He declared "the one central thought in the report" to be that of wide options in schools and in requirements for colleges.[72]

His speech finished, Nightingale braced himself for the storm, but no storm came. Several speakers praised the report, and Baker expressed himself in "general sympathy" with it. Coy of Cincinnati offered a mild criticism to the effect that the report recommended "at least one half-year's work more in Greek and some work in Latin beyond what was now customary or desirable," an interesting observation in view of the coals of fire that had been heaped upon the Committee of Ten for its recommendation on Greek. On the whole the discussion was favorable to the report. Like a teacher disappointed in the way a lesson has gone in class, Nightingale closed the discussion with an expression of regret that more opposition had not developed.[73]

Neither did it develop outside the halls of the NEA. Winship in his *Journal of Education* called it a report of great value, much more satisfactory than the report of the Ten, but predicted "in the nature of the case" that it would not "have so much weight or influence."[74] Chancellor Kirkland of Vanderbilt praised it but said it would not be received with the same "enthusiasm" as the report of the Ten, simply because educators had "grown accustomed to investigations of this character."[75] Inevitably it was compared to the report of the Committee of Ten. This was to be expected. What was striking, however, was that the report of the Committee on College-Entrance Requirements seemed to arouse practically no controversy at all. Many of the doctrines it presented continued to be attacked, but they were still being blamed on the Committee of Ten. Possibly nobody on the Committee on College-Entrance Requirements was sufficiently disliked. At any rate, its report was soon forgotten, and the giant-killers of the twentieth century have occupied themselves with the Committee of Ten instead.

The most striking disagreement with the report of the Committee on College-Entrance Requirements came from Nightingale himself. Within eight months of his presentation at Los Angeles in 1899, he told the North Central Association that the country had moved "far beyond the report of the committee of thirteen since last July." Possibly he was reflecting the distance he had moved from the report, for he had been

[72] *Ibid.*, p. 628.
[73] *Ibid.*, p. 632.
[74] *Journal of Education* (August 24, 1899), p. 128.
[75] J. H. Kirkland, discussion paper, *School Review* (September, 1899), p. 405.

rapidly changing his point of view to favor unlimited election of studies. What he criticized specifically in his own report was the provision of constants. "I want to say personally that I do not believe we should have any constants as such in our secondary school." The diploma, he said, should be granted to any pupil who had taken a good four years' curriculum in line with his interest and aptitude, regardless whether he had taken any mathematics, foreign language, science, or history. Furthermore every college in the country should accept such a pupil. "It is not what our young people study, but how they study and how they are taught, that gives them power." Moreover, he declared himself in favor of adding manual training, cooking and sewing, and commercial studies in every high school, these presumably being included in the subjects open to election.[76] This speech probably represented the extreme limit of advocacy of electives in American schools, for even Eliot usually favored English as a constant.

It has been suggested that Nightingale's views changed because of his experience as an administrator in a large city school system after 1889. There was little or no indication of this in his official annual reports. He was concerned about the drop-out rate, in the grades as well as in high school, but he had expressed himself on this point in the summer of 1889 before assuming his duties in Chicago.[77] Possibly he was influenced by Eliot, for his arguments closely paralleled Eliot's line of thought, especially on the elective principle in the development of power. Like Eliot he felt a deep sense of mission for the public high school, and he wanted it to provide the fullest possible opportunities for American youth under conditions of maximum freedom.

[76] Augustus F. Nightingale, discussion, NC, 1900, pp. 21–23.
[77] Augustus F. Nightingale, "The High School," NEA, 1889, pp. 501–506.

Chapter 7

The rise of accreditation

> "It [the need for coordination] is as true of an association of colleges and secondary schools as it is of an association of ants and bumble-bees."
>
> —S. A. FORBES,
> MARCH 29, 1901.

*N*ightingale's Committee had intended to say something about "the best methods of admission to college, whether by examination or by some form of certification," but it did not do so. This question, said the Committee in its final report, seemed "not so fundamental" as the matters to which it had "advocated its labors."[1] Many people today might agree with the Committee, but to the school and college men of the 1890's, the question was fundamental indeed. Possibly this was another reason why the Committee report did not arouse much interest.

Those who considered the question important gave it full and vigorous attention. From their efforts developed two parallel movements; one to clarify the examination system, the other to strengthen that of admission by certificate. The first led to the College Entrance Examination Board. The second, identified particularly with the North Central Association, led to organized inspection and accreditation. These became known, respectively, as the systems of the East and of the West. Each claimed the loyalty and enthusiasm of its devoted followers. In the end, both were involved in a larger movement to establish standards and to define more precisely the roles of colleges and secondary schools.

The College Entrance Examination Board was Eliot's idea and Butler's triumph. From 1891 Butler had been seeking a role in the formation of large-scale policy. He identified himself with the Committee of Ten but sought other ventures as well. Some of these brought him more

[1] CCER, p. 47.

censure than praise, in particular, his arrangement in 1895 to have the report of the Committee of Fifteen published by his *Educational Review,* with his fellow journalists of pedagogy interpreting this as an attempt to monopolize the report. One of them, the editor of *School,* dubbed him "Nicholas Miraculous," and this was perhaps the first instance of a long-lived academic joke. At the time of this controversy, however, Butler was more occupied in looking forward to his appearance at the Denver meeting as President of the NEA. On July 9, 1895, he delivered his presidential address, the title of which repeated Spencer's query about what knowledge was of most worth. Beginning with references to the complexity and confusion of modern life and the self-doubts of man in the universe, he identified "two great masters of thought" who had come forward "offering, like Ariadne of old, to place in our hands the guiding thread that shall lead us through the labyrinth—the German Hegel and the Englishman Herbert Spencer." Drawing on these two masters and enriching his discourse further with references to and quotations from Lamarck, from Hawthorne's *The Marble Faun,* and from Browning's *Paracelsus,* he paid tribute to spirit and reason on the one hand and to immediate utility on the other.[2] Thus did the higher learning come to the NEA.

Winship referred to Butler as "an exquisite gentleman" and as an educationist with a mission, "but without experience."[3] Butler was truly an educationist and one with a mission. He shared with Eliot and other moderate revisionists the desire to assure a great future for the public high school. More inclined than some of his fellow moderates toward the details of organization and planning, he sought at all times for definite machinery that would make his mission a success. He was by no means averse to talking, but he wanted other kinds of action as well.

In the College Entrance and Examination Board, Butler succeeded in creating a mechanism to bring into reality Eliot's two-fold vision of uniformity of standards and flexibility of programs. Butler had introduced a resolution to the Columbia faculty in 1893 calling for correspondence with other schools to establish such a board, but he did not succeed in getting it approved. In 1894 Eliot made a proposal for a "board of examiners" to the Association of Colleges of New England, also without success. The Columbia Conferences, held in New York on February 1,

[2] Nicholas Murray Butler, "What Knowledge Is of Most Worth?" NEA, 1895, pp. 69–80.
[3] "President Butler Once More," *Journal of Education* (May 16, 1895), p. 337.

1896, at the invitation of President Seth Low, established a context favorable to the idea. College men worked at these conferences with secondary school representatives to attempt uniform definitions of standards in Latin, Greek, mathematics, German, French, and history. In the same month Butler finally gained approval of his resolution from the Columbia faculty. On March 7 Eliot repeated his convictions on the matter to the Harvard Teachers' Association.[4] Still no definite steps were taken.

The matter hung fire until the 1899 convention of the Association of the Middle States and Maryland, where Butler gave a paper calling for the Association to sponsor such a board.[5] Fortunately for the cause and not without design, Eliot was present for the discussion. President F. L. Patton of Princeton rose first to speak, and he declared himself against Butler's proposal. Patton misunderstood the intent and spent much of his time criticizing the proposal as an attempt to place colleges under state supervision. He also feared colleges would lose the right to decide whom to admit and whom to exclude.[6] Eliot complimented Patton for having entertained the audience while the carbonic acid gas was being removed, a reference to a call previously made for opening the ventilators, but said he had "utterly misunderstood the proposition of Dr. Butler." The matter had nothing to do with supervision by the state. Furthermore, declared Eliot, each college could decide what it wanted to do about any applicant after receiving his scores.[7]

Discussion continued, for and against, much of it repetitious. Eliot remained silent until President Ethelbert D. Warfield of Lafayette expressed fears that the plan threatened the freedom of his college.[8] According to the published proceedings of the meeting, Eliot made a serious and earnest reply to Warfield, assuring him that complete freedom for Lafayette and any other college would be preserved under a joint examination board.[9] According to Butler's memoirs, written more than 30 years later, Eliot made the same point, but in a quite different manner. Eliot, in this account, "always stood perfectly erect with heels tight

[4] Charles W. Eliot, "A Wider Range of Electives in College Admission Requirements," *Educational Review* (May, 1896), pp. 425–426.

[5] Nicholas Murray Butler, "Uniform College Entrance Requirements with a Common Board of Examiners," MSM, 1899, pp. 43–49.

[6] F. L. Patton, discussion, MSM, 1899, pp. 64–67.

[7] Charles W. Eliot, discussion, MSM, 1899, p. 67.

[8] Ethelbert D. Warfield, discussion, MSM, 1899, pp. 80–82.

[9] Charles W. Eliot, discussion, MSM, 1899, pp. 85–86.

together, and began to speak with his hands lowered, with fingers and thumbs closely touching. His habit was to start slowly, coldly, with no sign of emotion of any kind, but with the greatest precision and definiteness." This time, said Butler, Eliot turned to Warfield with "just a suspicion of a smile on his face," saying, " 'It will be perfectly practicable, under this plan, for Lafayette College to say, if it so chooses, that it will only admit such students as cannot pass these examinations. No one proposes to deprive Lafayette College of that privilege.' " After a "roar of laughter" at Warfield's expense, the convention passed Butler's resolutions for the creation of the board. "This might never have happened," said Butler, "if President Eliot had not come down from Cambridge to support the proposal and make that kind of a speech."[10]

Butler moved swiftly to carry the resolutions into effect. Throughout 1899 and 1900 he conducted extensive correspondence and held meetings. In December, 1899, various college presidents from the Association met at Columbia to work out the details for the College Entrance Examination Board of the Middle States and Maryland. The Board was to consist of one representative from each cooperating college, plus five representatives of the secondary schools. In May, 1900, a subcommittee of this meeting came back with a constitution, and the Board thereby created came into official existence, holding its first meeting on November 17 of that year. The first examinations were held in June, 1901, having been prepared by committees of college men and secondary school teachers in the various subjects.

The original college members of the Board were Barnard, Bryn Mawr, Columbia, Cornell, Johns Hopkins, New York University, Rutgers, Swarthmore, Union, Pennsylvania, and Vassar. Invitations were sent to colleges throughout the country to accept the certificates of the Board, and a number of them agreed to do so. One that did not was Harvard. In spite of Eliot's advocacy of the plan, Dean Clement Smith reported action on the part of the Harvard Faculty of Arts and Sciences to the effect that it was "inexpedient . . . to accept the proposed certificates of the board." He added that it was an important experiment to be followed with interest, "but the fact must be recognized that it is as yet only an experiment."[11] Undaunted, the Board remained in business,

[10] Nicholas Murray Butler, *Across the Busy Years* (New York: Charles Scribner's Sons, 1939), I, 199–200.

[11] College Entrance Examination Board of the Middle States and Maryland, *First Annual Report of the Secretary* (New York: The Board, 1901), p. 4.

and even Harvard finally came around. On May 18, 1904, Eliot wrote triumphantly to Butler: "The Harvard Faculty moves slowly, but it moves. It will be ten years next November since I outlined a general admission examination board to the N. Eng. Assoc. of Colleges and could not interest the Assoc. at all, or the Harvard Faculty. Yesterday our Faculty voted by a large majority to go into your Board. You and Mr. Low have done this thing. See Educ. Rev. May, 1896. The country will thank you twenty years hence. I want to congratulate you now."[12] In 1905 the Secretary reported that the Board had administered the spring examinations to more than 2000 students. By this time colleges from other regions were included, the specific identification with the Middle States and Maryland Association having been dropped in 1901; and provision was made for membership of representatives of secondary schools from all four of the regional associations.

The Board and the idea it represented were not without critics. In October, 1900, an unsigned article in *Pedagogical Seminary* said the Board reflected "uniformity, over organization, and official and mechanical perfection which smacks of French methods and tends toward those of China." It sarcastically recommended that the Board construct 12,000 Chinese examination cells, "which will be necessary for the crowning effectiveness of this scheme."[13] Some of the misunderstandings expressed at the 1899 meeting persisted for many years. In view of these, it is perhaps appropriate to repeat the fact that the College Entrance Examination Board did not set up a pattern of subjects for admission to college and that it did not tell high schools what subjects to teach. It has existed to prepare and to administer examinations on a uniform basis and to report scores for colleges to interpret in relation to their own specifications. For principals and teachers it disposed in large measure of the old problem of having to prepare different pupils going to different colleges in different amounts and different books of Latin, Greek, or other subjects. If inevitably it motivated some coaching, so had the previous system of separate examinations conducted by each college. To Eliot it was an almost perfect system. Under it, no high school, for example, was obliged to teach Latin, or its pupils to study it. No college was expected to require Latin for admission. If, however, a pupil did take Latin for a college that required it and that was a member of the

[12] Charles W. Eliot to Nicholas Murray Butler, May 18, 1904, Nicholas Murray Butler Papers (Columbiana Library, Columbia University, New York, N.Y.).
[13] *Pedagogical Seminary* (October, 1900), pp. 449–450.

Board, there was machinery available for testing achievement in that subject according to defined standards. Some proposals were made to use the examinations in relation to graduation from high school, but these did not take hold.

II

The contrasting plan for college admission by certificate was by no means a new one in the 1890's, and it was not confined to the West. Procedures were poorly defined and haphazardly applied. They often depended on the relationship between a given college and a given school or even a given teacher. It was the University of Michigan that had started back in 1869–1870 to introduce some order and system into the plan. Provision was made in that year for admission to the University of pupils with diplomas from schools conducted "by a sufficient number of competent instructors," as determined in some way by the University faculty. This movement had been initiated by Acting President Henry S. Frieze, but for many years afterward it received encouragement and support from James B. Angell as well.

As the system developed at Michigan, it became the practice for committees from the University faculty to visit schools to determine the eligibility of their graduates. Schools thus accepted were known as diploma schools, and the plan was referred to as the *diploma system*. Purists insisted on this term instead of *certificate system*, but theirs was a losing cause. Actually the purists were wrong, for a diploma from a diploma school was by no means automatically a ticket of admission to the University. As Professor A. S. Whitney pointed out, the system involved recommendation from the high school principal, plus a regulation certificate "properly filled and signed," with itemization of courses taken, textbooks used, and teachers' estimates of scholarship.[14] It should be noted also that the system was not confined to schools within the state. Any school that wanted to send pupils to the University of Michigan was eligible, regardless of its location, and a substantial number of schools outside the state became part of the system, in fact, 75 of them by 1901.[15]

The high school visitors wrote brief reports in which they recommended acceptance or rejection of given schools. One report on a re-

[14] A. S. Whitney, MSM, 1902, p. 24.
[15] A. S. Whitney, NC, 1901, p. 25.

jected school of 65 pupils criticized the library and called for a revision of the course of study. It called also for a change in textbooks and a reduction in the size of classes.[16] Another report recommended that a school of 73 pupils be approved for one year, but noted that the local authorities had taken a backward step by removing one teacher. Relations with this school, warned the report, would be severed unless the people showed that they wanted good schools.[17] Criticisms were frequently made of the attitudes of local boards of education; some of the school men appreciated this as a help in getting what they wanted. One superintendent told President Angell that the diploma system had strengthened the high schools of the state by providing support against lukewarm school board members.[18] Nevertheless, the system was not always favorably received by its constituents, and it was another superintendent who complained in a letter to Angell that the specifications demanded by the visitors were unrealistic and had the effect of separating the university from the people.[19] For the most part, however, the exchange of correspondence between the school men and Angell indicated a cordial and mutual confidence in one another and in the system.

The Michigan plan was adopted by the University of Wisconsin and other state universities in the Middle West, as it was also by the University of California and by some of the state universities in the South. Indiana and Minnesota on the other hand went over to accreditation by state departments of education. By the time the North Central Association was founded in 1895, state-wide accreditation on the basis of the diploma or certificate system was found in various parts of the country, and especially in the North Central States.

It remained then to bring these various state systems together on some kind of regional basis. This was becoming a practical necessity, especially in the Middle West where a given school might easily have been accountable to, and subject to visits from, a half dozen different universities. At the 1901 convention of the North Central Association,

---

[16] C. O. Davis, December 15, 1905, The University of Michigan, Bureau of School Services, Records of High School Accrediting, Michigan Historical Collections (University of Michigan, Ann Arbor, Mich.).

[17] A. S. Whitney, February 13, 1902, The University of Michigan, Bureau of School Services, Records of High School Accrediting, Michigan Historical Collections (University of Michigan, Ann Arbor, Mich.).

[18] J. A. Stewart to James B. Angell, December 4, 1895, James B. Angell Papers, Michigan Historical Collections (University of Michigan, Ann Arbor, Mich.).

[19] J. A. Hathaway to James B. Angell, January 6, 1896, James B. Angell Papers, Michigan Historical Collections (University of Michigan, Ann Arbor. Mich.).

Dean S. A. Forbes of the University of Illinois made a long speech advocating coordination of these various efforts. Things poorly coordinated, he said, were weak, and this was as "true of an association of colleges and secondary schools" as it was of "an association of ants and bumble-bees."[20] What the state universities had done, he said, the colleges of the Association could also do as a unit, if they were so disposed.[21] A committee was immediately appointed to work out the details, and it came back the following morning with a proposal for the establishment of a permanent Commission on Accredited Schools. The convention quickly adopted the committee report, and the presiding officer, George B. Aiton of the state department of education in Minnesota, immediately named the members, including Baker of Colorado, Nightingale of Chicago, and President G. E. MacLean of the University of Iowa.[22]

The Commission met three times during the subsequent year and was back in 1902 with recommended standards and procedures. An acceptable high school was defined as one requiring fifteen units for graduation, each unit covering a school year of not less than 35 weeks with four or five periods of at least 45 minutes per week. Three units of English and two of mathematics were to be specified as constants.[23] Detailed statements were made for various subjects. The Commission, following its instructions, modeled the definitions of subjects on those of the Committee on College-Entrance Requirements. This was especially noticeable in history, Greek, German, and French. The Commission also presented the report of a subcommittee on high school inspection, recommending standards with respect to teachers and facilities and the creation of a board of five inspectors. The chairman of this subcommittee was A. S. Whitney of the University of Michigan, and the recommendations tended to reflect the Michigan system.[24]

Discussion of the report was preceded by an address by Nicholas Murray Butler, apparently a visitor for this meeting. Butler said that the College Entrance Examination Board system was better than a system of accreditation.[25] President Andrew S. Draper of the University of Illi-

---

[20] S. A. Forbes, "The Desirability of So Federating the North Central Colleges and Universities as to Secure Essentially Uniform or at Least Equivalent Entrance Requirements," NC, 1901, p. 12.

[21] *Ibid.,* p. 15.

[22] NC, 1901, pp. 70–71.

[23] Report of the Commission on Accredited Schools, NC, 1902, Appendix, p. 8.

[24] *Ibid.,* pp. 35–38.

[25] Nicholas Murray Butler, NC, 1902, p. 37.

nois reproached Butler for having gone over to the enemy, saying the teachers of the West had looked on Butler as a friend in the East.[26] There was possibly some justice in the reproach, for Butler, in a speech entitled "Is There a New Education?" delivered to the Middle States and Maryland Association in 1896, had criticized college-entrance examinations.[27] This did not mean, however, that he was against a properly conducted examination system, such as he felt was represented by the College Board. Butler evidently felt that he had been somewhat inconsistent, for he revised his 1895 speech for publication in his 1915 collection, *The Meaning of Education.* Moreover, he included a footnote in the 1915 version stating that "the important reform" that had been called for had "been admirably accomplished."[28]

The recommendations of the Commission, warmly applauded by Nightingale in spite of the stipulated constants,[29] gained the approval of the delegates, although a provision demanding at least five teachers for school approval was cut out in the process.[30] North Central was launched on its career as the major center of accreditation and inspection. From that point on, a large part of the proceedings was taken up by detailed consideration of standards for accreditation. Membership in the Association, under the amended constitution of 1904, was open to high schools requiring fifteen acceptable units for graduation,[31] whereas accreditation depended on meeting the additional specified criteria of the Commission on Accredited Schools. In 1908 the Association voted to begin accrediting colleges as well.[32]

So far as coordination was concerned, the North Central system did not necessarily replace the existing arrangements within the various states. Over a period of time these became less important in some states, as various kinds of relationships developed between North Central and the state systems. State universities accepted North Central accreditation as the equivalent of their own. Sometimes the two systems ran side by side, with schools choosing to be accredited by either or both. Eventually

[26] Andrew S. Draper, NC, 1902, pp. 42–43.
[27] Nicholas Murray Butler, "Is There a New Education?" MSM, 1895, pp. 107–108.
[28] Nicholas Murray Butler, in *The Meaning of Education* (New York: Charles Scribner's Sons, 1915), footnote 1, p. 91.
[29] Augustus F. Nightingale, NC, 1902, pp. 37–41.
[30] NC, 1902, p. 43.
[31] NC, 1904, pp. 105–106.
[32] NC, 1908, pp. 121–122.

North Central worked out a system of state committees using the common standards of the Association.

Advocates of the system became zealous in the cause and seemed, in the words of President Draper, almost to regard any plan of admission by examinations, particularly that of the College Board, as an enemy to be overcome. The ideological tone of North Central was expressed in the 1901 meeting by Professor F. N. Scott of the University of Michigan Department of English. He contrasted two ideas of the relationship between colleges and schools, "the feudal conception" and "the organic conception." The former, he said, had originated at Oxford and Cambridge and had been "transplanted bodily" to this country at the founding of Harvard and Yale. Under this feudal conception, the university was to the secondary schools as an ancient baron was to the common people. The feudal conception was characterized by arbitrary admission requirements and entrance examinations.[33] By way of contrast, the organic idea had originated in Prussia and had received "its first concrete expression in America in the school system of the State of Michigan." He felt that the organic system in the United States, rather than reproducing that of Prussia, would become something American, "probably something western." Admission by certificate was only part of the whole organic idea. In its entirety it involved agreement "as to what constitutes the normal course of development of young persons of high school age."[34] Under it the term *entrance requirements* was a misnomer borrowed from the feudal conception.[35] He granted that the organic system was not an unmixed good as actually practiced, but he insisted that it escaped the evils of the feudal system.[36] Many North Central enthusiasts went beyond this point and could never see anything but unmixed good in their system of accreditation.

In practice each system offered its own kind of freedom. Under the accreditation system principals and teachers were freed from the pressure of getting pupils ready for examinations. They did not feel the compulsion to coach. Pupils were freed from the tensions involved in preparing for "the college boards." On the other hand, the examination system freed the local school from conforming to defined standards of accreditation committees or other outside groups. Granted that many of these

[33] F. N. Scott, "College-Entrance Requirements in English," NC, 1901, p. 37.
[34] *Ibid.*, pp. 40–41.
[35] *Ibid.*, p. 45.
[36] *Ibid.*, p. 42.

standards were good, they still represented domination of the local school, and even some of the North Central leaders complained that the criteria for accreditation often involved unimportant administrative details. The North Central Commission in 1903, for example, debated whether or not a unit course might be interpreted as one meeting five times weekly for only 40 minutes each, instead of the stipulated four or five times weekly for 45 minutes each.[37] They agreed it could be done.

Under the examination system, the pupils were on their own. Their fate did not depend on the accreditation of their school. True, pupils within the accreditation system faced nothing worse than examinations if their schools fell from grace, but these were scourges from which the organic system had promised to deliver them. As time went on, the pupils, teachers, communities, and especially the principals came to view the loss of North Central accreditation as the final disaster that might be visited upon a school. This sometimes made it possible for the local administrator to put pressure on the board or community for needed facilities, but the tensions were there nevertheless. The expression "the fear of the Lord and the North Central Association" was much more than a witticism in schools of the Middle West.

There was developing during this period, however, a rival or compromise system that did promise the best of both possible freedoms. It was that of the New England College Entrance Certificate Board, organized in 1902, a group that included many of the colleges of that region, but not Harvard or Yale, these wanting no traffic whatsoever with certificates. Under this New England plan, secondary schools were approved, not on the basis of inspection and the meeting of uniform requirements, but more simply on the records their pupils had made in the member colleges. This system freed the local school both from examinations and from inspection. By 1907 there were 189 secondary schools of the 610 in New England that had gained the approval of the Board.[38]

Still even this system had its defects. Schools that previously had not sent pupils to the member colleges had to work their way up, although the Board eventually made provision for tentative or probationary approval of such schools. Moreover, a succession of poor performers from a given school could endanger the chances of better pupils coming along

[37] NC, 1903, p. 179.
[38] Walter H. Young, "The High Schools of New England, As Judged by the Standard of the College Certificate Board," *School Review* (February, 1907), p. 135.

later. The ones who suffered most under the system were the principals, for it was up to them to recommend the pupils on whom they were willing to gamble, knowing that bad choices would jeopardize the continued approval of their schools. A pupil might be "well prepared" for college, but still fail to do good college work for other reasons. There were many criticisms of the work of the Board. Principal Isaac Thomas of Burlington, Vermont, for example, called it "the same old, tattered system," and he could see in it "on the part of the colleges no sign of repentance, no sorrow for sins committed, no evidence of consciousness of offense."[39] Notwithstanding all these defects, the North Central Association regarded the New England Board with some affection. At least it did not give examinations. In 1905 President George E. MacLean of the University of Iowa referred to it as a "rudimentary form," but moving in the direction of the western plan.[40]

III

By this time, the various regional associations were well aware of one another's existence and characteristics. With four of them in the country, it was inevitable that some one would propose federating them in the interest of establishing a national plan for standardization. The initiative in this direction was taken in 1905 by the National Association of State Universities in a resolution calling for a conference with delegates from the four regional associations and the College Entrance Examination Board. MacLean earnestly supported this at the North Central meeting of 1906, declaring: "In this no longer the mid-west, but the magnificent mid-lands of our nation, solemnized by our opportunities and responsibilities, with renewed zeal and with the prophet vision as broad as that of humanity, let us continue by deeds more than by words to promote an American Federation of Learning."[41] This title, he argued, would be appropriate in its parallelism to the American Federation of Labor, since "learning and labor go hand in hand."[42]

[39] Isaac Thomas, "The New England Entrance Certificate Board from the Standpoint of Schools," *School Review* (November, 1904), pp. 701–702.

[40] George E. MacLean, "Which Is Better: the Western Plan of Admitting Students to Colleges and Universities by Certificates from Duly Inspected Secondary Schools, or the Eastern Method of Admitting Only by Examinations Conducted by Representative Boards or Otherwise?" NEA, 1905, pp. 506–507.

[41] George E. MacLean, "An American Federation of Learning," NC, 1906, pp. 24–25.

[42] *Ibid.*, p. 4.

Five delegates, accordingly, came together at Williamstown, Massachusetts, in August, 1906, joined by President George Fellows of the University of Maine, Secretary of the Association of State Universities. MacLean was there in person to represent North Central. The New England Association was represented by one of its founders, the irascible and irrepressible William C. Collar. The group passed six resolutions, one of them calling for a permanent national commission representing the groups present and the New England College Entrance Certificate Board as well.[43] The commission was formed during the subsequent year, and a group of delegates returned to Williamstown in June, 1907. Though known officially as the National Conference Committee of the Associations of Colleges and Preparatory Schools, the group was usually called the Williamstown Conference.

At its 1906 meeting, the Conference noted that North Central had its full-blown system of accreditation and that the New England region had its Certificate Board, rudimentary as it was. The Middle States and Maryland Association and the Southern Association were the two delinquent ones. True, the Middle States Association had sponsored the College Board, but that agency had now gone its own way. In any event, the College Board was no true substitute for an accreditation system. Accordingly, the Conference recommended that the Middle States Association and the Southern Association consider organizing either a college entrance certificate board or a commission for accrediting schools.[44] What Collar said on this point was not recorded.

At any rate, the delegates from these two associations carried the recommendations back to their groups. The Southern Association started machinery going in this direction, and it eventually produced, by 1913, a commission on accreditation similar to that of North Central, but including a provision, borrowed presumably from the New England Board, for checking on the records of pupils from approved schools after they went to college.[45] The Middle States Association also began work along these lines, but produced only a long comedy of frustration. Its College Entrance Certificate Board was created in 1908, designed to work along the lines of the one in New England, but it was not to go into effect

[43] F. W. Moore, "Report on the Williamstown Conference on Admission to College," SA, 1906, p. 8.
[44] *Ibid.*, p. 9.
[45] *School Review* (March, 1913), p. 202.

until ratifications from fifteen of the colleges were obtained.[46] In 1909 the chairman reported that only thirteen had done so; hence no action was possible at that time. A year later he reported that one more college had ratified, but this made only fourteen. In 1911 the score still stood at fourteen; hence no action. The same was true in 1912. By 1913, however, the University of Pennsylvania had decided to ratify. This produced the necessary fifteen, but the committee decided, in view of the lapse of time, to check back with those that had ratified before. St. Stephen's College of Annandale, New York, decided to withdraw its ratification.[47] The unhappy committee then disappeared from the recorded proceedings, and the Association did not begin accrediting secondary schools until 1928.

The restless quest for standardization, classification, inspection, and accreditation reflected several kinds of conditions and tendencies. In one sense, it was the desire for uniformity that had arisen in the late 1880's, perhaps by then gone to seed. It was a desire for being busy with affairs in an age that groaned under the weight of associations and commissions in almost every walk of life. To many it represented a sincere desire to improve the quality of schooling by every possible means.

Yet there was one thing more. Involved in all these maneuvers was the fluidity of the boundaries presumed to separate the various levels of schooling one from another. This should not have bothered someone like Eliot, who objected to artificial distinctions, but the boundary lines were in some respects too fluid even for him. Elementary education had been on the verge of achieving stability with an eight-year program, but the Committee of Ten, although expressing no preference, had suggested a different arrangement. The Committee on College-Entrance Requirements had flatly recommended beginning secondary schooling in the seventh grade. At the other end of the secondary school domain confusion was even more pronounced. The lines between school and college had been uncertain in the 1880's and were no less so throughout the 1890's. In part, then, standards meant definitions, and definitions promised a deliverance from confusion.

The notion of college as something preceded by graduation from a four-year secondary school, familiar as it has been in recent times, was

[46] Edwin S. Crawley, "Report of the Committee on College Entrance Certificate Board," MSM, 1908, p. 105.
[47] MSM, 1913, p. 94.

slow in developing, only partly understood, and in some quarters by no means appreciated. Even the Southern Association, with its hope of eliminating the competition between colleges and schools, did not make this idea explicit, although it was, of course, implied in its actions. It was made explicit by the North Central Association in 1900, when it adopted a resolution "that no student be received who has not completed the equivalent of a four years' curriculum by a secondary school."[48] The first report of the Commission on Accredited Schools, in 1902, recommended that colleges require no less than fifteen units;[49] its second report, 1903, proposed amending the constitution of the Association to exclude colleges requiring less than fifteen units and high schools having less than fifteen units in their programs. This amendment was adopted in 1904.[50] Discussions of the minute details involved in the definitions of units, such as the length and number of periods and weeks, constituted the attempt to enforce the broad provision for a four-year high school course as a condition for college admission.

When the Carnegie Foundation for the Advancement of Teaching was established in 1905, with Eliot becoming the first Chairman of its Board of Trustees, the movement for defining a four-year high school program in relation to the college was already under way. In the first annual report of the Foundation, 1906, the Trustees defined a college as an institution that, among other things, required for admission what they called "the usual four years of academic or high school preparation or its equivalent in addition to preacademic or grammar schools." This statement was prompted in part by the need of the Foundation to identify colleges for the Carnegie pensions. President Henry S. Pritchett commented in connection with the foregoing definition that the terms *college* and *university* had, at that time, "no fixed meaning on this continent" and that it was "not uncommon to find flourishing high schools" that bore "one or the other of these titles." To recognize colleges "without some regard to this fact would be to throw away whatsoever opportunity the Foundation has for the exertion of educational influence."[51] With Eliot as Chairman of the Board of Trustees, it was not likely that the

[48] NC, 1900, pp. 55–56.
[49] Report of the Commission on Accredited Schools, NC, 1902, Appendix, p. 8.
[50] NC, 1904, pp. 105–106.
[51] Henry S. Pritchett, "Report of the President," *First Annual Report of the President and Treasurer* (New York: Carnegie Foundation for the Advancement of Teaching, 1906), p. 38.

Foundation would throw away any such opportunity. Professors in non-approved colleges were not denied pensions, but were eligible for them as individuals rather than through their institutions.[52]

The expression "four years of academic or high school preparation" required explanation, at least in the minds of the Foundation Trustees. To clarify its meaning, the Board made use of the term *unit,* one that had been employed in the report of the Committee on College-Entrance Requirements back in 1899. North Central had also used this term as representing a year's work in a subject. Other terms in circulation to represent the same general notion were *points* and *counts,* the former being used by the College Entrance Examination Board to define the amount of work covered in the various subject examinations. The Carnegie Foundation Board defined a unit as a course of five periods weekly throughout an academic year, and a four-year high school course as fourteen units. The Board did not demand that every subject in high school be taught five days a week. It stipulated, for example, that a course taught two days a week should count as two-fifths of a unit.[53] There was nothing in its recommendations, then, except possibly some complicated arithmetic, to prevent any high school from being as flexible as it wished with regard to the arrangement and scheduling of subjects. Various refinements of the definition were made in subsequent years, involving, as in the efforts of the North Central Association, precise definitions of weeks and minutes. These refinements, although accepted by the Board, grew largely out of the work of the various Williamstown Conferences. By 1909 the Conferences and the Foundation agreed to consider the unit as approximately one-fourth of a year's work and discouraged the acceptance of more than four full studies in a given year.[54]

Thus was the unit sent forth on its long and controversial mission in the annals of American schooling. It was never officially designated *the Carnegie unit.* Sometimes it was referred to by the Carnegie Foundation and at the Williamstown Conferences as *a standard unit.* Usually, in the reports of these groups, it was simply called *the unit.* Pritchett of the Foundation insisted it was only a "counter" and in no way a limitation on the freedom of either the high school or the college.[55] As people began to react against the whole movement for standardization, however,

[52] *Ibid.,* p. 80.
[53] *Ibid.,* pp. 38–39.
[54] Henry S. Pritchett, "The Use and Limitations of a Standard Unit in Secondary Education," MSM, 1909, pp. 64–65.
[55] *Ibid.,* p. 64.

they found in the unit the most convenient symbol to attack. While the unit itself did not limit freedom, some of the policies related to it did have a limiting effect. For example, the attitude taken by the Carnegie Foundation, as well as by the Williamstown Conferences, against recognizing more than four units in a given year, imposed definite control on the local school. Moreover, it created a general bias on this point that has taken many years to overcome.

The Board of Trustees and President Henry Pritchett continued to stress their purpose throughout the first series of annual reports. In his 1907 report, Pritchett declared: "It is not easy to keep in the upper classes of the high schools boys who are free to try their luck at the university."[56] Tables presented in the 1908 report showed many colleges, not all of them in the South, still requiring less than the recommended fourteen units.[57] In 1909 Pritchett severely chided some of the colleges in the South, citing a report made by the state inspector of South Carolina to the effect that half the colleges of that state had "last year's tenth grade pupils in their sophomore classes."[58] In the same report, he censured colleges guilty of admitting too many pupils on condition. These were colleges officially requiring fourteen units, but admitting pupils deficient by three or more units. Several colleges of high repute and not located in the South were admitting as much as one-eighth to one-fifth of their freshman classes on this basis.[59]

From the point of view of secondary schools engaged in a struggle to exist, this drive toward standardization was commendable indeed. It represented a desire to extend opportunities to pupils who might otherwise have had no secondary schools to attend; it helped to define the boundary line between the school and the college. Nevertheless, something was lost in the process. Under the old system, those who were denied the opportunity for schooling could prepare themselves for the college examinations in several ways. If they passed the examinations, they could enter college regardless of previous years of study, secondary

---

[56] Henry S. Pritchett, "Report of the President," *Second Annual Report of the President and Treasurer* (New York: Carnegie Foundation for the Advancement of Teaching, 1907), p. 67.

[57] Henry S. Pritchett, "Report of the President," *Third Annual Report of the President and Treasurer* (New York: Carnegie Foundation for the Advancement of Teaching, 1908), pp. 92–94.

[58] Henry S. Pritchett, "Report of the President," *Fourth Annual Report of the President and Treasurer* (New York: Carnegie Foundation for the Advancement of Teaching, 1909), pp. 136–137.

[59] *Ibid.,* pp. 145–147.

school graduation, or accumulation of units. The possibilities of doing so were being reduced, although the foundation apparently did not object to special provisions for those over 21 years of age. Doors were never entirely closed, and the common sense of teachers and administrators found ways of mitigating the rigors of academic bureaucracy. It cannot be denied, however, that the machinery of standards and accreditation destroyed much of the flexibility that had once existed.

IV

At the same time that colleges were being discouraged from raiding the secondary schools, there was under way a powerful movement, led by men from the universities, to modify or shorten the period of college education itself. There were at least two motives behind this. One was to clarify the relationship between general and special studies. This usually involved a proposal to allocate part of the general college work to the secondary school. Sometimes the proposal was to cut out the college entirely and have pupils move from extended secondary schools into professional studies or graduate work. The other motive was to save time for the student.

The awkward combination of general and special studies in the American college had long been a source of concern to some engaged in higher education. Back in 1885 Princeton's Andrew F. West had defined secondary education as the period between the common school and the university. By the university, he said he meant the period of "self-directed activity" where the object was "the advancement of knowledge." He noted the longer periods devoted to secondary education in Prussia, England, and France.[60] Under the American system, students did two more years of secondary work in college. "If this secondary instruction now pursued in college can be relegated gradually to the schools, whither I believe it will eventually go, then our secondary instruction will be kept together instead of being broken in two between schools and colleges."[61] President C. K. Adams of Wisconsin anticipated in 1890 that ultimately college students would complete their collegiate work at the end of the second year, take the bachelor's degree at that point, and go on to specialized and professional studies.[62] President Richard H. Jesse

[60] Andrew F. West, "The Relation of Secondary Education to the American University Problem," NEA, 1885, pp. 195–196.
[61] *Ibid.*, pp. 200–201.
[62] C. K. Adams, "The Co-ordination of Colleges and Universities," *Proceedings* (College Association of the Middle States and Maryland, 1890), p. 14.

of Missouri in 1892 asked: "If . . . the high schools and academies continue to advance their instruction, may not three years of college curriculum be some day shortened to two, and finally abolished altogether?"[63] In 1896, James C. Mackenzie of Lawrenceville School said: "After America has had sufficient experience with her present costly and wasteful system, she will reach the same conclusion British and Continental people have reached, and commit to the 'Academy' or 'School' all merely disciplinary work, and end the long drawn farce in which our boys and girls pass from the increasingly large number of princely teachers of our schools to the increasingly large number of inexperienced tutors of our colleges."[64] President William Rainey Harper of the University of Chicago used the term *junior college* to refer to the first two years of college work regardless of where these were offered, and suggested these might be part of an extended period of secondary education.[65]

One way of bringing this about was to add college studies to the programs of local high schools. This provided additional schooling for those who could not attend college. For it to make an impact on the school-and-college relationship, it was necessary for colleges to recognize such work for advanced college standing. Principal E. C. Warriner of East Side High School, Saginaw, Michigan, reported in 1897 that his school for the past three years had been offering "courses corresponding to freshman work at the University of Michigan" in Latin, trigonometry and algebra, "paragraph writing," and English history. Many of his school's graduates, he said, added Greek or German to the courses in which they received their diploma. "We have sent to Ann Arbor eight or ten students who have received sufficient credit for work done in our high school to enable them to complete their college course in three years. This has, of course, been highly satisfactory to these students, as they are able to live more cheaply at home than at college, and, as far as I am informed, the work done in our graduate courses has been satisfactory to the university authorities."[66] Principal J. Stanley Brown of

[63] Richard H. Jesse, "University Education," NEA, 1892, p. 124.

[64] James C. Mackenzie, "Note by Dr. Mackenzie," *School Review* (September, 1896), pp. 533–534.

[65] William Rainey Harper, "The Small College: Its Prospects," NEA, 1900, pp. 82–83. See also his address, "The Length of the Baccalaureate Course and Preparation for the Professional Schools," NEA, 1903, pp. 505–506.

[66] E. C. Warriner, discussion, Twenty-seventh Semi-Annual Meeting of the Michigan Schoolmasters' Club, *School Review* (February, 1897), p. 127.

Joliet, Illinois, in 1905 mentioned Philadelphia, Muskegon, Saginaw, St. Joseph in Missouri, and Goshen in Indiana, plus his own school as places where such advanced work was being conducted. The Joliet High School, he said, had sought and received advanced credit at one college or another in mathematics, French, German, Latin, physics, chemistry, English and American Literature, and history, although no one college granted it in all these fields.[67] A year later he reported that the first graduate of his six-year high school course had finished a bachelor's degree after two years of work.[68]

Saving time for the students was the other motive involved in the general movement for shortening the college course. The man who had made the first dramatic announcement about the need for saving time was President Eliot. Back in 1892 he had recommended cutting one year from the nine-year elementary schools in New England.[69] He did not, however, favor reducing the period of elementary and secondary schooling beyond this point, and he wanted to keep an over-all program of twelve years. He believed eighteen to be a good age for college entrance.[70] The place to save the time, in his opinion, was the college, and he flatly advocated a three-year course. This was the goal he worked toward at Harvard, but he achieved it only in part. In 1902 Eliot sent Butler a list of his published references about the three-year course, saying: "You will see plainly that I have been pushing that way for about twenty-years; but I have had to be content with slow progress at Harvard."[71]

The Harvard faculty was not alone in being doubtful about the shortening of the college course. They had many supporters among men in other colleges and universities, and among school men as well. Some of these were concerned about saving time for the students, but they wanted to do it in the school rather than in the college. At the Middle States meeting of 1896, Superintendent Edward Brooks of Philadelphia proposed

[67] J. Stanley Brown, "Present Development of Secondary Schools According to the Proposed Plan," *School Review* (January, 1905), pp. 15–16. This constituted one application of Harper's term, *the junior college*.

[68] "Editorial Notes," *School Review* (October, 1906), p. 609.

[69] Charles W. Eliot, "Shortening and Enriching the Grammar School Course," NEA, 1892, p. 617.

[70] Charles W. Eliot to Nicholas Murray Butler, March 4, 1890, Nicholas Murray Butler Papers (Columbiana Library, Columbia University, New York, N.Y.).

[71] Charles W. Eliot to Nicholas Murray Butler, July 31, 1902, Nicholas Murray Butler Papers (Columbiana Library, Columbia University, New York, N.Y.).

separating college-bound students from others at the age of twelve so that they could have a shorter course aimed at earlier college entrance.[72] Eliot was present at this meeting and disagreed with Brooks's proposal because of his conviction that pupil programs should not be differentiated on the basis of plans for college. In the course of his comments he repeated his conviction that eighteen was a good age for college entrance.[73] At the New England Association meeting of 1897, Professor Thomas D. Seymour of Yale asked: "May not the student spend four years in the preparatory school and three years in college, as well as three years in the academy and four years in college?" His answer to this question was a blunt "No," and for two reasons—one that many secondary schools were not so well prepared as the colleges to give good instruction and the other that college was "felt to be the entrance upon a more manly and independent manner of work."[74] Others who favored reducing the secondary school course but not that of the college were Presidents Daniel C. Gilman of Johns Hopkins,[75] Andrew D. White of Cornell,[76] and S. C. Bartlett of Dartmouth.[77]

By 1900, then, there was fairly widespread agreement that time should be saved, but disagreement about where and how to save it. Many were confused by the issue and scarcely knew what to think. To President Baker of Colorado in 1903 it seemed time for the NEA to come up with another major committee, and he proposed that the National Council appoint one "to inquire into the contemporary judgment as to the culture element in education and the time that should be devoted to the combined school and college course." The Council appointed a committee to define the question and make recommendations.[78] Two years later, this group, with Eliot as chairman, supported Baker's suggestion in part, recommending a study of "the best period for the high school" and "the devices already in use for shortening the college course, or the combined courses of college and professional school," adding that these topics were

[72] Edward Brooks, "Standards of Admission to College," MSM, 1896, pp. 71–79.
[73] Charles W. Eliot, "Standards of Admission to College," MSM, 1896, pp. 79–80.
[74] Thomas D. Seymour, "The Three Years' College Course," *School Review* (December, 1897), p. 718.
[75] Daniel C. Gilman, "The Shortening of the College Curriculum," *Proceedings* (College Association of the Middle States and Maryland, 1890), pp. 16–20.
[76] Andrew D. White, "The Future of the American Colleges and Universities," *School and College* (February, 1892), pp. 68–69.
[77] S. C. Bartlett, "Shortening the College Course," *Education* (June, 1891), pp. 588–589.
[78] National Council of Education, Secretary's Minutes, NEA, 1903, pp. 306–307.

related "to economy of time in education."[79] Still the Council took no action, indicating possibly that interest in the whole matter had already passed its peak by 1905.

Baker, however, did not let the matter drop, and three years later the Council finally appointed its Committee on Economy of Time in Education, with Baker as Chairman. In 1909 Baker announced the intention of the Committee to prove or disprove the thesis that two years could be saved in the entire period of general education.[80] Eventually, in 1913, the Committee reported that it could be done. It did not, however, resolve the question whether to save the time during the high school or the college course. Elementary education, according to the Committee, should be completed by the age of twelve and college by the age of twenty. Within these limits the reader was invited to choose between a combination of a four-year high school and a four-year college course on the one hand and a combination of a six-year high school and a two-year college course on the other.[81]

The question of the relative merits of shortening one period or the other was never settled. In practice neither was shortened, except in isolated instances. The general movement toward standards and definitions, of which Baker's Committee was one tangential example, did not result in economy of time. Neither did it make a clearer distinction between the periods of general and special studies. Resolving these problems, however, was probably more a dream of enthusiasts than a tangible goal of the hard-headed practitioners who guided the Williamstown Conferences and the work of the Carnegie Foundation.

One thing was achieved, at least in part, and the pressures of stand-

[79] National Council of Education, Secretary's Minutes, NEA, 1905, p. 279.
[80] James H. Baker, "Report of Progress by the Committee on the Culture Element and Economy of Time in Education," NEA, 1909, p. 374.
[81] *Report of the Committee of the National Council of Education on Economy of Time in Education* (U.S. Bureau of Education Bulletin No. 38 [Washington, D.C.: 1913]), p. 10. Like Baker's earlier committee (*supra*, p. 35), this one worked at a leisurely pace, making its final report in 1919, eleven years after it had been created. See James H. Baker, "Final Report of the Committee on Economy of Time in Education," NEA, 1919, pp. 132–134. The important report, however, was the one made in 1913. In the meantime, the Department of Superintendence in 1911 had confused matters by creating its own committee with the same title. This second Committee on the Economy of Time in Education ran parallel to the first, but for the most part did not duplicate its work. It concentrated rather on the identification of minimum essentials, particularly in the elementary school subjects. Its first report appeared in the fourteenth yearbook of the National Society for the Study of Education, 1915, and was a phase of the movement for scientific management in education (*infra*, Chapter 13).

ardization apparently had something to do with it. Colleges were withdrawing from direct competition with high schools in the domain represented by what are now called the eleventh and twelfth grades. There were still many high schools not offering the work of those grades, but the new definitions both encouraged them to do so and helped to make it possible. The twelfth grade was perhaps not the best place to establish the line. Still a line was established, and high schools had gained a more assured place in the scheme of American schooling.

The movement toward standards and definitions, in this stage of its development, was an authentic phase of the movement represented by the Committee of Ten. Most of the men who struggled with minutes, weeks, and units were committed to the retention of the classics, to the admission of the modern academic subjects, and to some form of the elective principle. They wanted to extend the opportunities for this kind of schooling to the largest possible number of pupils throughout the land. It was necessary, therefore, to give high schools a chance to exist. Beyond this, there were those who wanted to add college studies to the local high schools. On this further extension of opportunity, general agreement was not reached.

Chapter 8

The children of the plain people

> "Whether agreeable or not, we must recognize the fact that it is the children of the plain people, in city and country, who are crowding our schoolrooms today, and these will always be in the majority."
> —STATE SUPERINTENDENT CHARLES R. SKINNER,
> JULY 6, 1897.

During the 1890's and early 1900's, teachers and pupils in the high schools lived their lives and carried on their work in a domain bounded pedagogically by accreditation, Herbartianism, child study, the elective principle, and the Committee of Ten. The larger world beyond this was defined by the financial panic of 1893, the Pullman and other strikes, the free silver campaign, the Spanish-American War, the return of prosperity, alleged dangers from immigrants and radicals, political corruption, and the stirrings of reform. Traditions of self-reliance and free enterprise were being pressed by theories of improvement through social control; philosophers and scientists were seeking further understanding of the nature of man and the society in which he lived.

It was an age in which many more young people than ever before decided to go to high school—or had it decided for them—possibly to develop power, possibly to absorb the heritage of their civilization, or perhaps just to get ahead in the world. At the beginning of the decade, in 1890, there were 202,963 pupils in 2,526 public high schools. By 1900 there were 519,251 pupils, and it took 6,005 public high schools to house them.[1] This expansion demanded more schools, many more teachers, more facilities and equipment, and, of course, more money.

The increase in enrollments, with the totals of 1900 running more than

---

[1] Commissioner, 1889–1890, II, pp. 1388–1389, and 1899–1900, I, p. liv.

two-and-one-half times those of 1890, was perhaps the most striking feature of public secondary education in that period. Just why this up-surge took place is a question not easily answered; compulsory-attend-ance laws for the most part did not affect children beyond fourteen years of age.[2] Economic explanations are popular, but necessarily controversial and complex: for example, good times make it possible for youths to go to school, but they also provide jobs to lure them away. The decade of the 1890's provided good times and bad, and the good times would not be considered very good today. Wages and prices were both low, but "even with prices so low . . . the income of many American families was meager and that of some was barely adequate to survival."[3] There was little general increase in prosperity in that decade to account for a large increase in high school attendance. Moreover, the greatest single annual increase in enrollments took place in 1894–1895, hardly the most favorable time of the decade from the point of view of economic prosperity, or even well-being.

According to another explanation, the increase in enrollments was a result of growth in technology, with consequent demands for more ad-vanced training and skills. For the most part, however, high schools were not providing technical skills for industry and commerce; in fact, they were accused by critics of being hopelessly out of joint with the times in that they provided allegedly useless studies. It seems reasonable, how-ever, that the expansion of industry and commerce should have fostered a demand for more education. The difficulty is that of relating the specific demands to what was learned in school. Perhaps the public believed the claims of school men that general power could be applied to many di-verse tasks.

The relationship of increased enrollments to technology may have been more indirect than is usually assumed. Population movement from

[2] See Commissioner, 1888–1889, I, pp. 470–471, and 1899–1900, II, pp. 2598–2599. Even in the period between 1900 and 1920, compulsory-attendance laws were not necessarily an important element in the enrollment increases in high schools. In 1917–1918, for example, 38 states had nominal upper limits beyond fourteen years of age, but in all except five of these states provisions existed for granting work permits at fourteen years of age, or, in some states, at even lower ages. The age of fourteen, therefore, remained the practical upper limit of compulsory at-tendance. See H. R. Bonner, "Compulsory Attendance Laws," *American School Board Journal* (December, 1919), pp. 37–39, 103; (January, 1920), pp. 39–40; (February, 1920), pp. 46–47, 106.

[3] Harold U. Faulkner, *Politics, Reform and Expansion: 1890–1900* (New York: Harper & Row, 1959), p. 93.

the country to the cities, for example, brought more youths to places where high schools were available, and this migration was in itself a reflection of industrial and commercial development. Possibly city life created a mood favorable to the notion that high school education was a prerequisite for success, even though such schooling did not lead immediately to well-paying jobs through direct vocational preparation. The strong drive toward social and economic advancement is a well-attested feature of the period, and schooling, rightly or wrongly, was viewed as one way to get ahead.

Only rarely is the possibility suggested that more people thought schooling was a good thing in itself. This possibility is a remote one, since the temper of the 1890's was at least as severely practical as had been that of the preceding years. Still, there has been in American life a quest for culture running side by side with a demand for practical results. As reflected in the Chautauqua movement, in the development of lyceums, in the growth of evening schools, in the popularity of public lectures, and in the development of public libraries, there was in the latter days of nineteenth-century America an appetite for knowledge, or at least for information. Much of this, it has been charged, was at bottom an appetite for entertainment, but it is at least significant that many people chose to be entertained through cultural activities. The expansion of knowledge in the sciences, both natural and social, provided more sustenance for, and undoubtedly whetted, the public appetite, pseudo-knowledge though some of it may have been. In all this, of course, it was necessary to defy the school and college men who proclaimed that the object of education was not information, but training.

In several respects, the pupil population of the 1890's was similar to that of the preceding decade. The proportion of girls stayed about the same, 57.6 percent in 1890[4] and 58.4 percent in 1900;[5] and the complaints on this score continued. Explanations were offered and remedies set forth. There were too many women teachers. Women feminized the course of study, with "the constant tendency to overvalue the softer and more showy arts at the expense of the hard essentials."[6] According to another critic it was "little short of monstrous" that boys in high school received "almost all of their intellectual and moral impulse from female

[4] Commissioner, 1889–1890, II, pp. 1388–1389.
[5] Commissioner, 1899–1900, II, p. 2119.
[6] As quoted in *Educational Review* (June, 1904), p. 102.

teachers," and it was for this reason that boys left high school without finishing the course.[7] Boys, it was also said, were more perceptive than girls of the sham of the academic studies. One explanation of the greater number of girls in the high schools was based on economics: girls used the high school as the route to teaching in the grades.

In spite of the preponderance of girls in the high schools, there were grave discussions about whether the program was suitable for girls and whether their delicate nerves could stand the strain of the advanced studies. "Many a one," said Supervisor Stratton D. Brooks of Boston in 1903, "has traded her birthright of health and strength, and happy and useful living for a mess of pottage made of sheepskin, and wrapped in blue ribbon."[8] Superintendent George E. Gay of Malden, Massachusetts, referred to "the sweet girl graduates who stagger through the ceremonies of diploma-giving to return to their homes condemned to invalidism for life."[9] Yet the girls were not only more venturesome in going to high school but also displayed more hardihood in finishing the course: comprising nearly three-fifths of the pupils enrolled, the girls made up two-thirds of the graduates.

Still, there were many pupils, girls as well as boys, who did not finish high school, and the drop-out question continued to vex the consciences of school men. In 1890 the number of graduates of public high schools came to only 10.7 precent of the number of pupils enrolled;[10] the corresponding figure of 11.9 percent for 1900[11] showed that little change had taken place. Most of the reasons given by pupils fell into three large categories, namely, poor health, lack of interest in school, and "services required by family." The large number of responses in the category of poor health suggests that this may have been merely a convenient reply for many pupils. Lack of interest in school suggested to some educators the need for what was called a more practical curriculum. Evidence on this point from existing manual-training high schools was not conclusive, and varied from one place to the next. In Kansas City, Missouri, the boys dropped out from the Manual Training High School at a higher

[7] Julius Sachs, "Coeducation in the United States," *Educational Review* (March, 1907), p. 301.

[8] Stratton D. Brooks, "Causes of Withdrawal from School," *Educational Review* (November, 1903), p. 377.

[9] George E. Gay, "Why Pupils Leave the High School without Graduating," *Education* (January, 1902), p. 303.

[10] Commissioner, 1889–1890, II, pp. 1388–1389.

[11] Commissioner, 1899–1900, II, p. 2122.

rate than from the academic school.[12] The category of "services required by family," however, seemed to point directly to economic circumstances as a possible major cause.

Another possibility was that of failure in studies, although this was rarely stated by the pupils. The practice in some schools of requiring those who failed in two or more subjects to repeat all subjects the following year, including the ones passed, certainly did not make failure easy to accept.[13] Yet there were, then as now, dropouts who had not failed, just as there were others who were not in poor health, or whose families were not short of money, or who were not particularly bored by school. In his report on dropouts to the National Council in 1900, Superintendent James M. Greenwood of Kansas City, Missouri, concluded, as would so many who struggled with the same question in subsequent years, that "instead of one or two factors determining this question, there are many causes operating."[14]

Dropouts made up one part of the school-age population not in some kind of secondary school. There were, of course, thousands of others who never entered at all. The large number of young people not enrolled inevitably raised the question whether or not the existing secondary schools, public and private, were serving all the youth they should have served. Later calculations, based on the age distributions in the census reports, have indicated that only 8.4 percent of the youth 14–17 years of age were in public high schools in 1900.[15] If private school enrollments are added to those of the public high schools, the total enrollment in secondary schools in 1900 came to 10.2 percent of the youth 14–17 years of age, about one in ten. This fact has contributed to the present-day notion of the high school population at that time as being highly selected, and the accompanying speculation about the kinds of selection represented, whether intellectual, economic, social, or perhaps geographical or regional.

In the period around 1900, criticisms of high schools for their failure to attract and hold pupils were based not on statistics similar to those given here, but on the contention that the public high schools enrolled

---

[12] James M. Greenwood, "Report on High-School Statistics," NEA, 1900, p. 347.
[13] Charles S. Hartwell, "Economy in Education," *Educational Review* (September, 1905), p. 168.
[14] Greenwood, *op. cit.*, p. 341.
[15] Table A, "Historical Statistics of Public Secondary Day Schools: 1890–1952," in "Statistics of Public Secondary Day Schools, 1951–52," *Biennial Survey of Education in the United States 1950–52* (Office of Education [Washington, D.C.: 1954]), Chapter 5, p. 6.

only 5 percent of the total number of pupils in the public schools. School men of that time were sensitive to this criticism and argued that the 5 percent figure did not reveal the true state of affairs. In 1902 Superintendent F. D. Boynton of Ithaca, New York, claimed that the enrollment in high schools should be compared not with the total public school enrollment, but with one-third of that figure, this representing the potential enrollment for the four-year high school period. He cited the case of Ithaca, with 2180 pupils in all grades of its public schools. The potential high school enrollment, he argued, was 726 pupils; with an actual enrollment of 671, he claimed, the high school in this community was serving 92.1 percent of its constituency.[16]

Boynton also sought to show how the degree of service varied from one community to the next. Applying his approach to several other places, he showed that Utica, New York, was serving 16.5 percent of its potential high school group and presented corresponding figures of 38.4 percent and 12.3 percent for Worcester and Fall River, Massachusetts, respectively.[17] He contended, too, that it was unfair to judge high schools in general on the basis of statewide figures because these did not take into account rural areas where high schools did not exist. "High schools are not found in country districts or small villages, and yet the thousands of children in these localities are reckoned in as part of the divisor in this problem, when by their geographical location they are excluded from the possibility of high-school enjoyment."[18]

Two years later, in 1904, James Russell Parsons, Jr., of the New York State Department of Education used a similar approach, modified to account for deaths and nonpromotions in grade schools, to make state and national comparisons. He concluded that the actual high school enrollment in the state of New York came to 57.9 percent of the total possible enrollment. By this he did not mean that the high schools of New York enrolled 57.9 percent of the relevant age group, but rather of the group eligible to attend high school through having completed the work of the grades. Calculating along the same lines, he estimated the national high school enrollment to be 38.8 percent of the possible enrollment, and that of the state of Massachusetts to be 83.8 percent.[19]

---

[16] F. D. Boynton, "High-School Attendance," *School Review* (September, 1902), p. 562.

[17] *Ibid.*, p. 564.

[18] *Ibid.*, p. 560.

[19] James Russell Parsons, Jr., "High-School Attendance," *Educational Review* (March, 1904), p. 298.

Public high schools in 1900 may then have been less selective than is sometimes assumed, at least with reference to grade school graduates. Perhaps the most significant point made by Boynton and Parsons was that of local and regional variations. A certain kind of intellectual selection was still represented by the surviving high school entrance examinations. Beyond this, geographical variation probably reflected economic circumstances; or, conversely, economic selection was tempered by local and regional availability of schools.

All this may help explain the extent to which school men and others in this period were impressed by the appearance in the high schools of some vast category of the population known as "the masses." The increase in the numbers attending high school, a phenomenon observed in the 1880's as well as the 1890's, would, of course, have served by itself to arouse comment and to stimulate discussion of what the attendance of these "masses" might imply. As early as 1890, E. A. Steere of Butte City, Montana, declared that five-sixths of the pupils in high schools came from the homes of what he called "the laboring classes," and he asked, "What influence does it [the high school] have upon the masses?" He thought it was a good influence because he saw education as "the wedge that lifts the curtain from benighted minds, and the working classes," he said, "stand upon a higher plane the more they use this wedge."[20] In 1897 State Superintendent Charles R. Skinner of New York in his presidential address to the NEA said, "Whether agreeable or not, we must recognize the fact that it is the children of the plain people, in city and country, who are crowding our schoolrooms today, and these will always be in the majority. The children of the masses and not of the classes will rule us."[21] A speaker at the Massachusetts Superintendents' Association in 1901 attributed the alleged decline in scholarship to "the admission of many pupils into the high school who formerly would not have been allowed there," but he felt the condition could be remedied by reducing the number of pupils assigned to a single teacher.[22] "Our High School population has greatly changed in character within the last ten or fifteen years," said a classroom teacher from the Philadelphia High School for Girls in 1904. "To quote a Salvation Army phrase, we

[20] E. A. Steere, "The High School as a Factor in Mass Education," NEA, 1890, p. 646.
[21] Charles R. Skinner, "The Best Education for the Masses," NEA, 1897, p. 53.
[22] "Massachusetts Superintendents' Meetings," *School Journal* (February 23, 1901), p. 203.

are 'getting deeper down' in the masses."[23] She expressed satisfaction in having "some small share in this great work of lifting the masses"[24] as part of her daily task.

Many of these expressions were well within the tradition of popular education for popular government, with the implied extension of popular education from grade schools to high schools. The Philadelphia teacher who felt the high school population had changed recommended, nevertheless, a thorough course in mathematics, Latin or German, English, history, and perhaps one of the physical sciences, with the aim of teaching pupils "to think logically, to speak and write clearly and correctly, and to act uprightly."[25] On the other hand, James Earl Russell of Columbia's Teachers College, in an address delivered in 1905 at the University of Cincinnati, asked: "If the chief object of government be to promote civil order and social stability, how can we justify our practice in schooling the masses in precisely the same manner as we do those who are to be our leaders?"[26]

Enrollments in Latin during this period are possible indicators of how "the masses" themselves felt about the matter. Latin was not a general requirement, but the enrollments went from 34.7 percent in 1890 to 50.6 percent in 1900.[27] Presumably either the pupils or their parents, or both, wanted Latin, a desire helped along perhaps by the persuasion of principals and teachers. This was a distressing state of affairs to those who doubted the value of Latin, particularly those who did not see Latin as meeting the needs of the majority of the pupils, or of "the masses," during this period of increasing high school attendance. Back in 1887 Samuel Thurber had interpreted the taking of Latin as a yearning for the

[23] Louise H. Haeseler, "The Simplification of the Secondary-School Curriculum," MSM, 1904, pp. 84–85.

[24] *Ibid.,* p. 89.

[25] *Ibid.,* pp. 85–86.

[26] James Earl Russell, "The Trend in American Education," *Educational Review* (June, 1906), p. 39.

[27] Commissioner, 1889–1890, II, p. 1390; 1899–1900, II, p. 2123. Small high schools with single programs did not always offer a choice, but neither did they always teach Latin. Such schools, although numerous, did not enroll a correspondingly large part of the pupils in high school. In 1904, 72 percent of the high schools had fewer than four teachers each, but these enrolled only 36 percent of the pupils. Edward L. Thorndike, "A Neglected Aspect of the American High School," *Educational Review* (March, 1907), p. 254. As a subject usually started in the first year of high school, Latin showed relative enrollments that were somewhat inflated by the high drop-out rate, but this would not have accounted for a sharpe increase during a period when the drop-out rate stayed about the same.

trappings of social status.[28] After 1900 G. Stanley Hall found the Latin enrollments "calamitous to the point of pathos," and he blamed them in part on what he called the "enormous bribe" of college-entrance requirements.[29] Latin, he said, was so "inexorably demanded by the college gatekeepers that to omit it on entering the high school has often meant to abandon all chance of going to college, however faint the prospect might be."[30] Hall was exaggerating his case here, for by 1900 it was no longer necessary for pupils without Latin to abandon hope of entering even respectable colleges.

As Hall himself recognized, most of the pupils were not preparing for college, and most of the graduates did not go there. No matter what else the educators in this period disagreed about among themselves—and they disagreed on many matters acrimoniously and at great length—they were of one voice on this point. So far as official figures were concerned, the Commissioner's *Report* for 1900 stated that 10.8 percent of the pupils in public high schools were preparing for college and that 30.8 percent of the graduates were so prepared. For private schools the corresponding figures were 31.9 percent and 46.5 percent.[31] These figures were not questioned or challenged at that time. There were, of course, regional variations. Unfortunately for the East-West stereotype, the reported rates were higher for the West; according to the *Report* for 1900, 32 percent

[28] Samuel Thurber, "The Order and Relation of Studies in the High School Course," *Academy* (September, 1887), p. 254.

[29] G. Stanley Hall, "The High School as the People's College," NEA, 1902, p. 261.

[30] G. Stanley Hall, "How Far Is the Present High-School and Early College Training Adapted to the Nature and Needs of Adolescents?" *School Review* (December, 1901), p. 656.

[31] Commissioner, 1899–1900, II, pp. 2122 and 2125. The *Reports,* however, did not state how many went to college, and no national figures are available on this point. One recent book has stated that two-thirds of the graduates in 1900 went to college, basing this figure on a comparison of 232,000 students in various categories of so-called higher education at that time with 700,000 in secondary schools. American Association of School Administrators, *The High School in a Changing World,* thirty-sixth yearbook (Washington, D.C.: The Association, 1958), pp. 156 and 166. As noted above, this would have been electrifying news to the school men of 1900. It cannot be assumed that most, or even many, of the 232,000 students in higher education referred to were graduates of secondary schools, and there is much evidence against such an assumption. I have summarized the arguments on this point and have also dealt with possible errors in the Commissioner's *Reports* in an article, "High School Graduates in and around 1900: Did Most of Them Go to College?" *School Review* (Autumn, 1962), pp. 266–272. On the basis of the evidence furnished in the period under consideration, there is no reason to believe that more than one-third of the graduates of public high schools went to college.

of the graduates of public high schools in the north central region were prepared for college, as contrasted with 25.3 percent in the northern Atlantic region. In Michigan, for example, 37 percent were so prepared, but only 25.8 percent were in Massachusetts.[32]

II

Whether bound for college or not, more and more pupils kept coming to the high schools, and the number of new schools increased throughout the decade in about the same ratio as the pupils. There were about two-and-one-half times as many of both in 1900 as there had been in 1890. New schools appeared at an average rate of 316 per year, or nearly one a day. This was less than the alleged two-a-day increase in the number of Methodist churches, but it was rapid enough to excite comment, satisfaction, and in some cases alarm.

"Of all the departments of education the high school is the most firmly entrenched," wrote the editor of the *School Bulletin* in 1899, in his comment on a speech delivered by Secretary Melvil Dewey of the New York Regents. "The stone which the builders at one time seemed likely to reject has become the head of the corner. The high school is the people's college. Its principal should be an educational bishop for the community. The building should be in the best location, and the handsomest in town."[33] Principal George W. Benton of the Indianapolis Shortridge High School, however, viewed the rapid development of the high school as grounds for anxiety about its future. People were willing, he said, to accept the gradual development of the elementary school, but the high school was different. "In some cities," noted Benton, "within the same time that the population has doubled, the attendance upon high schools has quadrupled; whereas, high school teachers could be readily engaged a few years ago, at anywhere from $700 to $1200, today these figures do not begin to express the expense."[34]

Some critics expressed doubts about the desirability, or even the morality, of free high schools at public expense. James P. Munroe, a Massachusetts paper manufacturer, regarded them as manifestations of what

[32] Commissioner, 1899–1900, II, p. 2130.
[33] *School Bulletin* (January, 1899), pp. 97–98.
[34] George W. Benton, "Since High Schools Are Costing So Much What Can Colleges Do to Assist Them in Meeting the Demands of the Public?" NC, 1906, p. 49.

he called socialistic tendencies in education. "The maintenance of free high schools," he declared, "is unwise, first, because it obliges a whole community to pay for what only a limited number can enjoy; second, because, necessarily expensive, it robs the lower schools of funds essential to them; and third, because it offers to boys and girls wholly unfit for secondary education, a temptation to exchange the actual benefit of remunerative work at 15 years of age for the doubtful advantage of a training that can have no direct bearing upon their life work, and which, at the time of life it occurs, may do decided harm." He did not object to the existence of public high schools, but felt they should charge a graded system of fees.[35]

Probably more characteristic was the feeling that local communities should not attempt too much. "The school," said a Pennsylvania board member in 1907, "sometimes takes on unnecessary expense by attempting too much—a high school course in a small town, including most of the 'ologies' and many of the modern languages and approaching a college course and electives the value of which is little and the expense great. Let the effort of our public schools be directed rather to the elementary education of the great number." Like others of all generations who deplore the cost of schools but want to foster their own projects, he went on to advocate spending more money for manual training and gymnasiums.[36]

In contrast to those who felt the high schools to be well entrenched and those who disliked this entrenchment, there were others who felt the need for a much greater expansion than was taking place. Principal A. W. Bacheler of the Gloucester, Massachusetts, High School declared in 1900 that "instead of the six thousand high schools stintingly feeding the appetite of a seventy-five million population we ought to have twelve thousand today, and even that quota should be doubled within the next twenty-five years."[37] Eliot had called for more high schools back in 1890, and he called for still more in 1903. With Eliot it was not a matter of spending more money for one aspect of public schooling than another. He wanted more for a great many things, such as kindergartens, enriched

[35] James P. Munroe, "Certain Dangerous Tendencies in Education," *Educational Review* (February, 1892), pp. 148–149.

[36] S. R. McClure, "School Board Economy," *Pennsylvania School Journal* (April, 1907), pp. 460–461.

[37] A. W. Bacheler, "The Problems Which Confront High Schools," *Education* (November, 1900), p. 142.

grade school programs, better and safer school buildings, reductions of teacher-pupil ratios, and vacation schools, but he included the expansion and improvement of high schools as well.[38]

By general agreement, the great lack was in rural areas and communities. In 1889 the Committee on Secondary Education of the National Council concluded that "for all secondary education, the mass of the rural population is generally dependent upon chance, or the favor of some city."[39] According to Eliot in 1890, the mass of the rural people, identified by him as comprising three-fourths of the population of the United States, was "unprovided" with secondary schools.[40] Throughout the decade the complaints continued, and at its end the note was still being sustained by expressions such as those of Henry R. Corbett of the University of Chicago. Opportunities of the country boy or girl for free schooling, he said, "have generally come to an abrupt end with the elementary course."[41]

As on other matters, conditions varied from one state and from one locality to the next. In some states, the development of county and township high schools offered basis for encouragement. Professor S. J. Hunter of the University of Kansas in 1904 proudly described one county high school in his state, that of Sumner County, with 377 pupils, 244 of them from rural districts. Even in such schools, however, most rural youth in attendance had to live away from home during the week. "The great majority of the students," he said, "secure unfurnished rooms in the town where the school is located, at about a dollar per month, bring their furniture and provisions from home, in some instances turning these provisions into a common boarding table called a club. They return to their homes each Friday evening to bring with them new supplies the following Monday morning." He admitted that many of these pupils could have gone to a city high school on the same basis, but claimed they would not do so. "And among the reasons for this is to be found, the country boy and girl do not feel at home in the city high school. . . .

[38] Charles W. Eliot, *More Money for the Public Schools* (Garden City, N.Y.: Doubleday & Co., 1903).
[39] National Council of Education, Report of the Committee on Secondary Education, "The Opportunities of the Rural Population for Higher Education," NEA, 1889, p. 387.
[40] Charles W. Eliot, "The Gap between the Elementary Schools and the Colleges," NEA, 1890, p. 522.
[41] Henry R. Corbett, "Free High Schools for Rural Pupils," *School Review* (April, 1900), p. 213.

The conditions are totally different in the country high school. The most truly democratic spirit prevails."[42]

By 1903 Indiana had 580 township high schools, making up 76 percent of the 763 high schools in the state.[43] Township high schools were usually smaller than those serving an entire county, but they were closer to home, and the pupils did not as a rule have to board out during the week. This did not mean less inconvenience, for pupils often had to walk long distances to such schools. Principal Milford F. Pletcher of Blanchard, Pennsylvania, reported to the State Teachers' Association in 1906 that he was proud to have seen pupils in his part of the state walking ten miles a day to the township high schools, graduating, and then securing admission to some of the strongest colleges.[44] Even in this pre-bus age, some schools transported their pupils, usually in horse-drawn wagons, and one Pennsylvania principal took advantage of the technology of his age by conveying pupils to his school by trolley, this service costing "us about $500 a year."[45] The development of the township high school in Pennsylvania was evidently somewhat spotty, for State Superintendent Nathan C. Schaeffer declared in 1908 that at least 40 percent of the children in the state had no access to high schools at all.[46]

It was not always easy to establish township high schools in rural areas, even in states like Illinois where provisions for such schools had existed since the early 1870's. Nightingale's Lake View Township High School, founded in 1874, had been one of the first organized under the law. He became deeply committed to the idea and sought to promote township high schools at every opportunity. On one occasion, presumably in his capacity as Cook County Superintendent of Schools, to which office he had been elected in 1902, Nightingale presented his arguments for a township high school to the people of a rural community. The next day, he said, "the chief landowner" of the community wanted to know "what anarchist was he who came over here to stir up my tenants to vote

[42] S. J. Hunter, "The Mean Proportional in the Problem of State Education," *Education* (April, 1904), pp. 491–492.

[43] Fassett A. Cotton, "The Township High School in Indiana," *School Review* (April, 1904), p. 279.

[44] Milford F. Pletcher, "The Township High Schools and Their Problems," *Pennsylvania School Journal* (September, 1906), p. 122.

[45] High School Department of the Pennsylvania State Teachers' Association, July 5, 1906, *Pennsylvania School Journal* (September, 1906), p. 122.

[46] Nathan C. Schaeffer, discussion, MSM, 1908, p. 80.

taxes on my property." Nightingale persisted, however, and the measure later passed, with the school becoming, in the words of his account, one of the best in the state.[47] In Illinois the township form of organization was also used in areas containing cities, and the Joliet Township High School, dedicated in 1901, with 87 rooms to accommodate 1400 pupils,[48] became one of the show-pieces of the Middle West.

Many rural high schools, as well as some considered nonrural, were small and, in relation to the ideal of having teachers work in only one or two instructional fields, inadequately staffed. Indiana's 580 township high schools in 1903 averaged 23 pupils and one and one-half teachers per school.[49] Such schools have often been the despair of educational leaders, but they have had defenders as well. In 1898 the report of the State Superintendent in Indiana contained an account of one such school, that of Nineveh Township in Johnson County, written possibly by the principal or a member of the local board. "It is one of the most potent factors in our community for good," wrote this unknown author, "and has unquestionably raised the standard of intelligence, of morality, of taste, and therefore, of life among the people." He pointed out that the principal had a master's degree and that the assistant was a high school graduate who had, however, "made other special preparation for her work." A four-year course was provided, but with terms of only six to seven months, and it served ten pupils in the first-year class, three in the second, four in the third, and five in the fourth. The pupils ranged in age from fourteen to twenty-two. The program included Latin, mathematics, and some of the modern academic subjects. "In Latin . . . we read two books of Caesar and three of Virgil. In mathematics we completed Milne's *High School Algebra* and Wentworth's *Plane Geometry*. We give two years to English literature, two years to general history, one year to geology, one year to physics, one year to rhetoric, one year to physical geography, and three months to civil government."[50]

Schools of this size were more numerous than many realized, at least if judged by those who took part in discussions at NEA and other meetings, or perhaps they were just taken for granted. Thorndike, using figures drawn from the Commissioner's *Report* for 1904, sought to direct

[47] Augustus F. Nightingale, "The Place of the High School in Our System of Education," *School Review* (February, 1906), p. 150.

[48] J. Stanley Brown, "The Joliet Township High School," *School Review* (September, 1901), pp. 417–432.

[49] Cotton, *op. cit.*, p. 279.

[50] Quoted *ibid.*, p. 276.

the attention of his contemporaries to this state of affairs. Among 7199 public high schools, there were 2175 with only one teacher each and 1807 with only two teachers. Only 1356 of these schools had five or more teachers, the standard proposed for accreditation, but judiciously withdrawn by the North Central Commission on Accredited Schools in 1902. The proportions of schools with one teacher each ranged in the various states from 58 percent in Nebraska and 56 percent in Oregon down to 3 percent in Minnesota and 2 percent in California.[51]

In contrast, there were 280 schools with thirteen through forty teachers each, and 28 schools with faculties of more than forty teachers.[52] The large cities, moreover, even with their larger schools, were confronted by their own kinds of difficulties. A committee of the Chicago Board of Education complained in 1894 that it could not keep up with the growth in attendance and deplored the necessity of setting up temporary branches. "The West Division High School, erected only a few years ago, to accommodate 1200 pupils, has completely outgrown its capacity. Four rooms will be used in the Grant School, a mile away, in September, and several additional rooms must be secured to accommodate the overflow. There will be, therefore, under the supervision of the school, about 500 pupils more than the main building has capacity for, a number sufficiently large for an entirely new school." The Lake View Township High School, which had been rebuilt under the township organization in 1886 to accommodate 250 pupils, had become part of the city system, enrolling 500 pupils in 1893–1894, with an additional 100 pupils expected for 1894–1895.[53] The committee noted with satisfaction, however, that the first-year programs of the Chicago high schools were enrolling 59 percent of the eight-grade graduates.

III

Cities faced not only the difficulties of providing enough space for the increased attendance, but also the question of general versus special high schools. So far as public schools were concerned, Boston had maintained the tradition of special-function institutions in its Latin Grammar School and its English High School, paralleled by its Girls' Classical High School and its High School for Girls. (John Tetlow had been principal of both

[51] Thorndike, *op. cit.*, pp. 253–255.
[52] *Ibid.*, p. 253.
[53] Chicago Board of Education, *Fortieth Annual Report,* year ending June 29, 1894, pp. 104–105.

girls' schools since 1885.) Other high schools in Boston, like those in most other communities, were, in effect, merged schools, with the two functions represented by the Classical course and the English course. Cambridge, Massachusetts, in 1886 took the step, unusual for the times, of dividing its merged high school into two distinct schools, one Classical and one English. This was brought about in part by the pressure of increasing numbers, but the way of resolving the dilemma was, according to an unsigned correspondent in the *Academy,* "quite out of harmony with the tendency of the time" and would "ultimately be regretted."[54]

Not out of harmony with some of the tendencies of the time was the demand for separate high schools of manual training, modeled on Woodward's experimental school at Washington University, St. Louis. Proponents of these schools did not overlook the precedent for special-function schools implied in the Latin and English schools of Boston. Most of the existing manual-training schools of the 1880's were conducted under private auspices, thereby raising the question why their advantages should be made available only to the children of well-to-do parents. There were public high schools, however, that taught manual training, in some cases, such as that of Toledo in 1884, through separately identified departments referred to as manual-training schools. The line between a "department" and a "school" was a thin and variable one, rendering difficult the questions where and when the first public manual-training high schools were established.

In 1890, however, Chicago opened its "English High and Manual Training School," an institution regarded as distinctly separate and by itself. This school offered shop courses and academic studies, but excluded foreign languages, both ancient and modern. Only 70 pupils enrolled in this school in September, but the number increased to 152 during the year.[55] Boston followed with its Mechanics Arts High School in 1892. Butler's *Educational Review* hailed this as a forward step, proclaiming that manual-training work was most successful when "isolated in a building specially prepared for the purpose" and "conducted by specially trained teachers."[56] When Denver faced the prospect of building a second high school in 1892, the authorities there, unlike those in Cambridge back in 1886, decided to establish a high school of manual

---

[54] *Academy* (March, 1886), p. 68.

[55] Chicago Board of Education, *Thirty-Seventh Annual Report,* year ending June 30, 1891, pp. 124–126.

[56] *Educational Review* (October, 1892), p. 310.

training. Brooklyn also joined the ranks of city school systems with manual-training high schools. The movement was sufficiently under way by 1894 for Charles De Garmo to ask the Committee of Ten why it had ignored manual-training schools in its report.[57]

Next came the demand for high schools of commerce, for which the leading spokesman was Edmund J. James of Philadelphia, later of the University of Chicago, and eventually President of the University of Illinois. In 1894, James advocated four kinds of high schools: one for manual training; a second for business; a third for language, literature, and mathematics; and a fourth for mathematics and natural science.[58] A vigorous discussion of high schools of commerce took place at the North Central Association meeting of 1899, with James defending them as a fourth road to liberal education.[59] He argued that the need could not be met by commercial courses in existing high schools, but agreed that a high school of commerce should provide general, not specialized, training.[60] The issue was not formally resolved in this session, and James did not appear the following year to press his arguments. Interest shifted to accreditation, and the Commission on Accredited Schools had committees at work in 1905 to define units in commercial education that might be included in the curriculum of any school. By this time several cities had established separate high schools of commerce, one of the most physically impressive being that of the City of New York. In 1904 a committee of the NEA Department of Business Education declared itself in favor of separate high schools of commerce when possible, but was willing to settle for commercial courses in the other high schools.[61]

The drive toward special high schools aroused opposition as well as support. Dean E. A. Birge of the University of Wisconsin spoke against the separation of technical and literary schools, fearing that the former might be regarded as distinctly a school for the working people.[62] In some quarters the idea was regarded as undemocratic, and Frederick E.

[57] Charles De Garmo, discussion, NEA, 1894, p. 512.

[58] Edmund J. James, "The Commercial High School As a Part of Secondary Education," *School Review* (November, 1894), p. 579.

[59] Edmund J. James, "Commercial Training and the Public High School," NC, 1899, pp. 50–52.

[60] *Ibid.,* pp. 59–60.

[61] James J. Sheppard, "Report of the Committee of Nine, Considered from the Standpoint of the Independent School of Commerce," NEA, 1904, pp. 719–725.

[62] E. A. Birge, "Should Industrial and Literary Schools Be Combined or Encouraged to Separate?" NC, 1901, pp. 51–55.

Bolton of the University of Iowa went so far as to accuse the advocates of separate high schools of being "wittingly or unwittingly" the enemies of "true democracy."[63] Principal J. Stanley Brown of Joliet Township High School, Illinois, in 1908 anticipated the discussions of subsequent years by arguing for the mixing of various groups in the high school, keeping "in close touch the boys who know they are going to be lawyers and those who know they are going to be farmers, mechanics, engineers and business men."[64]

So far as most communities were concerned in the period between 1890 and 1905, the debate was unrealistic. It was not so in the larger cities, however, faced as they were by the building of more than one school. The debate was nevertheless relatively mild in character before 1905. For the most part it only indirectly involved the question of vocational training that was to dominate consideration of this matter between 1905 and 1915. Although not denying the vocational implications, advocates of separate high schools in the 1890's and the early 1900's agreed with James that these should be regarded as different pathways to liberal education—and they were not actually very different. Programs of the special-function high schools contained substantial amounts of the modern academic studies. True, some manual-training schools omitted modern languages, but, on the other hand, the high schools of commerce placed particular stress on the study of modern languages.

The great majority of the 5050 new high schools created between 1890 and 1905 were just high schools. If the issue represented by manual-training high schools and high schools of commerce was unreal to the principals and teachers of these new schools, the older issue involving classical and English high schools was even more so. There was, as Thorndike pointed out, no such thing as a typical high school during this period, an observation that could equally well be made of all other periods in American secondary education. Still, there were more one-teacher schools than those in any other category, and the one-and-two-teacher schools made up more than one-half of the high schools in the country—objects of pride, no doubt, to the communities they served, but increasingly objects of concern to those educational leaders who noted their existence.

[63] Frederick E. Bolton, "Agricultural High Schools," *School Review* (January, 1908), p. 58.
[64] J. Stanley Brown, "Commercial and Industrial High Schools vs. Commercial and Industrial Courses in High Schools," NC, 1908, p. 138.

IV

The allegedly low level of formal schooling attained by the teachers themselves, whether in schools large or small, was another object of concern. According to Elmer E. Brown, the development of high schools had outrun the available supply of college-trained teachers as early as the 1870's and 1880's. In the South and West at that time many high schools had been taught by teachers who "had graduated from the grammar school into a teaching position in some lower school, and after experience which was deemed successful in the lower position, were graduated into the coveted occupation of high school teachers." He confessed that he had himself taught ten or twelve different high school subjects, "ranging from chemistry and astronomy to rhetoric and Caesar," on the strength of a normal school diploma and before he had entered college.[65]

During the period between 1890 and 1905, the number of high school teachers rose from 9,120 to 28,461, a staggering increase in relation to the resources from which they could be drawn. Comprehensive national statistics on the preparation of teachers during the period are lacking, but one survey indicated that about 70 percent of the men and 53 percent of the women teachers in high schools were college graduates.[66] There were substantial variations even among neighboring states. Only one-half the high school teachers in Wisconsin in the late 1890's were college graduates, as contrasted with two-thirds in Minnesota.[67] In Maine, as in Wisconsin, about one-half of the teachers were college graduates, while in neighboring New Hampshire the fraction was two-thirds.[68] As late as the 1890's some high school teachers had not been to college at all. In the New England states, the proportions of those with no more than high school or normal school training ran from 15 percent in New Hampshire to 32 percent in Vermont.[69]

[65] Elmer Ellsworth Brown, "The Need of Better Preparation of Teachers for Secondary Schools," *Education* (December, 1913), pp. 201–202.

[66] Edwin G. Dexter, "The Present Status and Personnel of the Secondary Teaching Force in the United States," *The Education and Training of Secondary Teachers,* National Society for the Scientific Study of Education, fourth yearbook (The Society, 1905), Part I, pp. 49–62.

[67] Michael Vincent O'Shea, "The Training of the High-School Teacher," NEA, 1898, pp. 709–710.

[68] Charles H. Douglas, "Status of the High School in New England," *Educational Review* (January, 1893), p. 33.

[69] *Ibid.*

It is not always clear in the surveys of that period whether or not the principals were included. In most cases they probably were, for the 1890's were not far from the days when the full title of a principal had been *principal teacher,* with the other members of the faculty known as the assistants. Only in the larger schools was it becoming the practice for principals not to teach at all. Even among the principals, however, there was not always a high proportion of college graduates. About 70 percent of the principals of the high schools and academies in the State of New York, surveyed as a separate group in 1892, had been to college, but only 47 precent of the total number had college degrees, some of these being, in the words of one commentator, "evidently honorary."[70] Those who had been to college but held only honorary degrees shared this distinction, or lack of distinction, with none other than the Commissioner of Education himself.

Then as now, there were teachers who felt keenly their own alleged shortcomings and low status and those of their colleagues. "Although morally the status of the teacher is high," said Principal F. W. Atkinson of the Springfield, Massachusetts, High School in 1896, "socially it is found to be lower than the status of the average lawyer, the physician, or the theologian." He was speaking of all public school teachers, but did not exclude high school teachers from his observations. Intellectually, he said, teachers had "not attained a high status," and he concluded that the group as a whole lacked culture, scholarship, and professional training.[71] One teacher in reply to Atkinson's articles tended to accept these conclusions, but insisted that the nature of American life and the conditions of work limited the chances of teachers for social and intellectual status.[72] Had Atkinson himself looked further, he might have found equally low or even lower proportions of college graduates among the lawyers and physicians. Higher proportions of college graduates probably would have been found only among college teachers in some colleges and among clergymen of some churches.

On the whole, then, this period of the first major expansion of the public high school was a mixture of things both good and bad. The increase in attendance was gratifying to those who believed it was a good thing to go to high school, but this was offset by the high drop-out rate

[70] Lucy M. Salmon, "Letters to the Editor: Certain Hindrances to Progress," *School and College* (March, 1892), p. 180.

[71] F. W. Atkinson, "The Case of the Public Schools: the Teacher's Social and Intellectual Position," *Atlantic Monthly* (April, 1896), p. 535.

[72] Harriet H. Heller, "The System," *Education* (November, 1896), pp. 165–172.

that did not diminish throughout the period. There were many new high schools, but among these were the thousands of one-and-two-teacher schools that to some educational leaders seemed hardly worthy to be called high schools. To make an assessment of all this, particularly in view of the low level of the formal schooling of the teachers, would be difficult indeed. U.S. Commissioner Elmer E. Brown, however, expressed the view in 1913 that the imperfect high schools of the earlier period had met a real need and had paved the way to better things. "Many a teacher," he said, "who had himself dreamed of a college course which he had never been able to achieve, went on preparing boys for college, and a few girls along with them, and doing it so well that college faculties took notice and approved of what he had done." He concluded with a comforting thought, and a perhaps somewhat less-than-comforting figure of speech. "It was," he observed, "the old story of Peter the Great, who civilized his people, though himself remaining a barbarian."[73]

[73] Elmer Ellsworth Brown, *op. cit.*, p. 202.

Chapter 9

Electivism and the end of an era

"When students in their 'teens' have a choice they will simply take the easiest."
—PRINCIPAL JOHN GREER,
1901.

*T*he doctrines of secondary education during the period between 1890 and 1905 did not break sharply from those of the past. This was an age of revision, but the shift in ideas was moderate rather than extreme. For the most part, the leaders of the revision fostered the modern subjects without disparaging the classics; both groups of subjects were considered appropriate for pupils of all social classes and vocational destinations. Programs of pupils were to be individualized and preferably governed by some version of the elective principle. There was, according to these tenets, no valid distinction between preparing for college and preparing for life. Necessarily, any graduate judged competent in the studies he had pursued should be judged competent to enter college.

These beliefs were far from universally accepted. It was opposition to them that produced much of the outcry against the Committee of Ten. They did, however, define the issues for discussion, and they could not be ignored. School men who wanted to be heard had to be for them or against them, or to present some compromise directed to the same or similar questions. Neither Herbartianism nor child study, widespread as they were, competed successfully with the moderate revision so far as the secondary school was concerned.

It was the elective principle that aroused the greatest interest, and there were various schemes or plans for its application. Some school men rejected the principle as such, while others defined it in their own terms and gave it qualified endorsement. Only a few accepted Eliot's version, although Nightingale eventually went beyond it.

190

Those who accepted the principle broke into two main groups, one favoring election by courses, the other by subjects. It was election by courses that appeared—and against Eliot's inclinations—in Table IV of the Committee of Ten. The four courses or "programmes" of the Committee closely paralleled existing arrangements in many schools. According to its advocates, this device represented electivism guided by adult wisdom and experience. A pupil might choose a course, but he would find the subjects prescribed within it, perhaps with an option here or there. Moreover, some subjects would be common to all the courses, thereby guaranteeing a body of constants. Defenders of election by subjects could also specify constants if they wished, but beyond these, they extended more choice to the pupil. Such was the arrangement proposed by the Committee on College-Entrance Requirements, with its ten units of constants and six of free electives.

One of the most articulate spokesmen for election by courses was Principal Oscar D. Robinson of the Committee of Ten. He felt that high school pupils were too limited in their ideas to do more than choose one from several set courses. "To abolish courses of study," he said, "because there are evils connected with them is to adopt the plan of the anarchist, who, because there are defects in organized society, would have organized society abolished."[1] Possibly in response to one of Eliot's strictures against courses of study, Robinson argued that the various courses did not differ greatly from one another. Those recommended by the Committee of Ten, he pointed out, differed primarily in the languages prescribed. This was only partly true, because the preponderance of language study did limit the number of modern subjects included in the Classical course. He was right, however, in pointing out the existence of common elements in the four courses of the Committee of Ten.[2] Seven years later, in 1901, he still defended election by courses, but was willing

[1] Oscar D. Robinson, "Should Electives in the High Schools Be by Courses or Subjects?" NEA, 1895, p. 590.

[2] *Ibid.*, pp. 587–588. Under the four courses of study of the Committee of Ten, all pupils were obliged to take four years of English, four years of foreign language, three years of mathematics, two years of history, and three years of science. Not all of these, however, were full years of five recitations a week. Second-year English, for example, was only a twice-a-week subject in the Classical, Latin-Scientific, and Modern Language courses. The work in each course came to twenty periods a week. Of the eighty periods for the four years of study, the common elements were eleven periods of English, seventeen of foreign language, eleven of mathematics, seven of history, and nine of science, making a total of fifty-five periods.

to grant substitutions and options, particularly in the upper high school years.[3]

Election by subjects was usually advocated by those who had few reservations, if any, about the validity of the elective principle itself. One of the most radical advocates of almost unlimited election by subjects was Samuel Thurber of the Girls' High School, Boston, who declared that "the aim of the school should be to discover, to respect, and to develop individual aptitudes." He did not fear the possibility of a so-called one-sided education in which a pupil might devote himself "almost exclusively" to one branch of study. Like Eliot, he did not approve the courses of the Committee of Ten, and he was one of the few critics who attacked the report on these grounds. "The Committee of Ten," he said in 1895, "failed to utilize its golden opportunity." It should have allowed so many options, he contended, "that the idea of a course should have disappeared."[4]

Thurber felt the abolition of courses to be the first step toward what he considered an ideal high school, one "which will have a large and pleasant room for study, where there shall be a sufficient library and teachers ever on duty to preside over discipline and to give aid and guidance in the use of books." In such a school, there would be "freedom of movement and conversation, so far as these freedoms are natural and inevitable in associated work."[5] Along with many others, Thurber talked of the high school as the people's college, but he drew from this the inference that the school "must not prescribe to the people what the people shall study." Election of studies, he argued, would bring out what the people wanted and would constitute "a sort of referendum" wherein the "verdict" of the people would be expressed. While the school could not provide all subjects, it should "within reasonable limits" offer what the public wanted. The people, he said, would make an emphatic demand "for the purely cultural subjects—for literature, history, economics, ethics, art." Thurber, unlike Eliot, had some bias against the classics, but he was prepared to offer them and to have them elected by the pupils. "There ought," he said, "to be the best possible teaching of

[3] Oscar D. Robinson, "Constants and Electives in the High Schools," *School Review* (April, 1901), pp. 249–251.

[4] Samuel Thurber, "Rigid Courses *versus* Optional Studies," *School Review* (April, 1895), pp. 207–209.

[5] Samuel Thurber, "Courses of Study in Secondary Schools," *Journal of Education* (February 14, 1895), p. 99.

Latin and Greek open to all comers, whether intending to apply for admission to college or not."[6]

Most advocates of election by subjects, including Thurber, were willing to have some constants. Thurber accepted constants as safeguards that would keep the elective principle from outrunning "the ability of governing bodies to give it wise direction," but said they could be easily modified or dropped.[7] He and other advocates of election by subjects expressed satisfaction with the provision for constants in the report of the Committee on College-Entrance Requirements. The idea of constants as presented by the Committee even won support in some quarters for election by subjects.

Both versions of the elective principle—election by courses and election by subjects—had been practiced in schools for some time before the principle became a major object of discussion with reference to secondary education. Election by courses was the easier to identify, since the courses themselves were often printed in the school catalogs or bulletins. Election by subjects was a less tangible proposition and depended on the informal arrangements made in local schools. Academies were famous, or to some notorious, for their flexibility. Public high schools apparently had no such general reputation, but it is difficult to imagine a high degree of rigidity in those that were growing up as extensions of the grades in the common school districts.

One of the first public school systems in this period to make official provision for election by subjects was Newton, Massachusetts, in 1886. This action came about partly in response to protests from parents and pupils against the existing requirements in algebra and geometry. Under the Newton plan, every pupil had to take English, history, and "the elements of physics and chemistry." Meeting this requirement involved nine exercises a week, with every pupil required to have twelve per week "exclusive of elocution, calisthenics, and military drill." There was apparently no upper limit on the number of exercises, apart from the natural one imposed by the school schedule, and pupils were allowed to take as many electives as they liked. Electives were chosen from the foreign languages, algebra, geometry, drawing, bookkeeping, and other subjects offered by the school. According to a report made in 1893, the average

[6] Samuel Thurber, "Election of Studies in Secondary Schools: Its Relation to the Community," *Educational Review* (May, 1898), pp. 430–433.

[7] Samuel Thurber, discussion of Report of the Committee on College-Entrance Requirements, *School Review* (September, 1899), p. 398.

number of exercises taken per week ranged from 13.5 for seniors to 15.5 for the first-year pupils. Only 19 percent of the first-year pupils restricted themselves to the stipulated twelve exercises per week, but 45 percent of the more cautious seniors did so. Latin was elected by 39 percent of the first-year pupils, but by only 6 percent of the seniors. Evidently the protests against algebra and geometry had been real ones, for 70 percent of the first-year pupils avoided algebra, and 77 percent of the second-year pupils resisted whatever inducements there were to take geometry.[8]

In 1895, the high school at Galesburg, Illinois, went over to a plan under which, according to the city superintendent, all the subjects were made elective. This step was motivated in part by a drop-out rate of 40 percent in the freshman year, and in part by the conviction of the superintendent that algebra should no longer be required. Under the new plan a pupil received one credit for each month's work in a subject meeting for twenty recitations a month, a year's work in that subject thereby yielding nine credits. "When the pupil gets one hundred credits," said Superintendent W. L. Steele in his address to the NEA in 1899, "he is given a diploma, in which is written the entire list of subjects completed and the value of each—making not only an intelligible diploma, but an honest one." He confessed that the school provided illustrative courses called Scientific, Latin, and Commercial, but these, he insisted, were "simply suggestive to the pupil," who was free at any time, "with the consent of his parents," to take something else. The first class under the new plan was graduated in June, 1899. During the four-year period between 1895 and 1899, the attendance of the school increased from 234 to 518 pupils, although the grade school enrollment at the same time went up only 9 percent.[9]

Advocates of election by subjects gained major victories in Chicago and Boston. The Chicago plan, adopted in 1900, required only seven units or years of constants, made up of two in English, two in one foreign language, one in algebra, one in history, and one in science.[10] By this time Nightingale had repudiated all constants, including those recommended by his Committee on College-Entrance Requirements, but ap-

[8] Edward J. Goodwin, "Electives in the High School: An Experiment," *Educational Review* (February, 1893), pp. 142–145.

[9] W. L. Steele, "To What Extent Should the High-School Pupil Be Permitted to Elect His Work?" NEA, 1899, pp. 331–336.

[10] Augustus F. Nightingale, "Report of Assistant Superintendent in Charge of High Schools," *Forty-Seventh Annual Report,* Chicago Board of Education, year ending June 30, 1901, pp. 81–82.

parently he was not able to persuade the authorities in Chicago to adopt this more extreme view. He contented himself by pointing out that the Chicago program was "purely elective for those who are not candidates for graduation."[11] Charles H. Thurber of the *School Review* congratulated Nightingale and the Chicago principals for having realized in practice "the sound doctrine" of Nightingale's NEA committee.[12] The Boston plan, adopted in 1901, was more extreme. All studies in the regular Boston high schools were made elective, except gymnastics or military drill, hygiene, and music.[13] However, both Chicago and Boston subsequently retreated from the positions taken then. Chicago reverted to multiple courses of study in 1910,[14] and in 1907 Boston stipulated constants in English, history, and science, and required pupils to choose in one instance between foreign language and "phonography" and in another between mathematics and bookkeeping.[15]

According to a survey made by D. E. Phillips of the University of Denver in 1901, the tendency among those he called the "reformers," by which he seemed to mean those favoring election by subjects, was to require "a certain 'core' of subjects . . . with all other subjects elective." The average extent of these constants, he declared, was three years of English, one and one-half of algebra, one of history, and one of science or geometry.[16] Phillips also noted the appearance of another device for safeguarding election by subjects, namely, the group system as illustrated by the Lyons Township High School, Cook County, Illinois.[17] This school required pupils to choose, not courses, but departments of study and to complete stipulated amounts of work in those chosen.[18]

The high point of electivism was probably reached between 1900 and 1905. Even at that time, advocacy of election by subjects was prob-

[11] *Ibid.*

[12] Charles H. Thurber, "Outlook Notes," *School Review* (February, 1900), p. 69.

[13] Edwin P. Seaver, "Elective Studies," *Educational Review* (May, 1902), p. 483; City of Boston, *Annual Report of the School Committee*, 1901, p. 15; also City of Boston, *Twenty-First Annual Report of the Superintendent of Schools*, March, 1901, pp. 49–54.

[14] John Wesley Bell, *The Development of the Public High School in Chicago* (Chicago: University of Chicago Libraries, 1939), pp. 195–197.

[15] *School Review* (June, 1907), p. 479.

[16] D. E. Phillips, "The Elective System in American Education," *Pedagogical Seminary* (June, 1901), pp. 228–229.

[17] *Ibid.*, p. 223.

[18] E. G. Cooley, "Limited Election in High-School Work," *School Review* (February, 1901), pp. 76–77.

ably no more than a minority point of view. In 1901, the year in which Phillips made his survey of practice, James H. Baker of the Committee of Ten collected and reported opinions about electives from forty administrators in large city systems. Of these, only five favored what Baker called "free election," and three of these stipulated constants. This was the group clearly committed to election by subjects. Perhaps a partial commitment was indicated by nine others who advocated one course, "with more or less electives." The remaining twenty-six respondents consisted of fifteen who favored election by courses and eleven who favored "little or no election in any form."[19] This was obviously not a scientifically drawn sample, but the names of the respondents indicated that Baker had reached many of those who had much to do with the making of policies in the larger cities. At any rate, Baker concluded that the prevailing judgment was "against very large election in secondary schools."[20]

Certainly most of the superintendents he quoted in his report were doubtful about it. Among these were W. F. Slaton of Atlanta; E. H. Mark of Louisville; James M. Greenwood of Kansas City, Missouri; Francis Cogswell of Cambridge, Massachusetts; and R. H. Webster of San Francisco. Baker himself favored election by courses and characterized what he called the "pursuit of inclination" as a "doctrine of Romanticism, so successfully carried out by Faust under the guidance of the devil."[21] Those who favored election by subjects included Superintendents James H. Van Sickle of Baltimore, R. G. Boone of Cincinnati, and W. C. Martindale of Detroit, and, of course, Assistant Superintendent Nightingale of Chicago. Nightingale proudly flew the flag of electivism, declaring in his reply that the Chicago program was working very well and that he expected it to "go on from glory to glory."[22]

Opponents of electivism attacked it from several different points of view. Some feared that pupils would pick easy subjects and avoid hard ones. "Pupils always take the subjects requiring the least preparation and the least study," confidently asserted Superintendent E. H. Mark of Louisville in his reply to Baker's inquiry.[23] "When students in their 'teens' have a choice," said Principal John N. Greer of Minneapolis, "they simply will take the easiest."[24] One principal of an unidentified

[19] James H. Baker, NC, 1901, p. 61.
[20] Ibid., p. 67.
[21] Ibid., p. 68.
[22] Ibid., p. 64.
[23] Ibid., pp. 64–65.
[24] Ibid., p. 65.

"large Eastern High School" declared his scientific course to be "the refuge of all the lame and lazy of the school."[25] The case of Newton, Massachusetts, where only 30 percent of the first-year pupils elected algebra, was submitted by one speaker at the Southern Association as an example of the dangers involved.[26] Others felt that pupils had little basis for making any choices whatsoever and consequently elected smatterings of subjects and ended up with miscellaneous collections of bits and fragments. Eliot shared their dislike of such a result, but felt it would not take place in a properly administered system.

Those who preferred to deal in pedagogical theory attacked the elective principle on the ground that it implied equivalence of subjects. This was the rallying cry of many who had joined the attack on the Committee of Ten. In vain did Eliot protest that he did not hold to the doctrine. What he had meant and what had been set forth in the report of the Committee of Ten was that all well-organized and thoroughly taught subjects should be accepted as equivalent for purposes of admission to college. Still, Eliot did believe that many human activities might some day be developed into worthy subjects of instruction. When Princeton's Andrew F. West asked whether even "the most hardened ignorer" of differences in the worth of studies could believe in the possibilities of "the Hawaiian language, or Christian Science, or bird-stuffing," there was little doubt about the identity of the "most hardened ignorer" of them all.[27]

Even West had to acknowledge the increase in relative enrollments in Latin as the elective principle was more widely applied. This he attributed to the common sense of parents and pupils, an explanation that contradicted the fears of those who believed the pupils to be lacking in the judgment needed to select their studies. West, however, was not entirely reassured even by his own confidence in the common sense of parents and pupils. Although he granted that Latin without Greek would prove "adequate to the wants of a majority of the scholars," he feared that it would "not prove so satisfying to those who want the best Latin."[28]

[25] *Ibid.*
[26] C. D. Schmitt, "The Proper Limitation of Elective Work in School and College," *School Review* (February, 1901), p. 97.
[27] Andrew F. West, "Is There a Democracy of Studies?" *Atlantic Monthly* (December, 1899), p. 823.
[28] *Ibid.*, p. 827.

II

Closely related to the controversies about electives was the assumed distinction between preparation for college and preparation for life. Traditionally, the distinction between college-preparatory and non-college-preparatory programs in American secondary schooling had been made on the basis of the Classical and English courses. Under extreme interpretations, the Classical course contained much Greek and Latin, plus mathematics, with a little ancient history, while the English course was made up of "information courses" in various sciences, fragments of philosophy, history and political economy, some English literature, and perhaps a modern foreign language. In some schools a Classical course extended only three years and consisted only of the three traditional subjects each year. Some of the English courses, as Eliot often said, were scrappy, including subjects representing such fields as astronomy, geology, and logic taught for only eight weeks. The compromise course called the Latin-Scientific was in effect a non-Greek Classical course, but it was also considered non-college-preparatory throughout the 1880's, and in some places into the 1890's as well. In practice, regardless of the names applied to the courses or programs, the one really distinguishing college-preparatory subject was Greek.

Among those who believed in the validity of the distinction between college-preparatory and non-college-preparatory work were many who considered the Classical course too restricted for the finishing pupils. Preparatory pupils would get the modern subjects in college, but the finishing pupils needed to take them in high school. "Present college preparatory courses," said W. R. Butler of Waltham, Massachusetts, in 1896, "are too narrow to meet the needs of present civilization and society; and, while it may always be necessary for the preparatory pupil to lay a deep foundation in the classics and mathematics, to the pupil whose formal education is to cease with his graduation from the high school the rudiments of civics, economics, and at least four sciences should be presented."[29] Superintendent Edward Brooks of Philadelphia in 1896 said that the pupils not bound for college needed "more mathematics and physical science, a course in English and history, in music, drawing, manual work, etc.," all of which he felt would be difficult to

[29] W. R. Butler, "Should Preparatory and Non-Preparatory Pupils Receive Identical Treatment in High Schools?" *Educational Review* (December, 1896), p. 485.

fit into his idea of a college-preparatory course. Separation of the two groups would, from this point of view, provide better schooling for the finishing pupil and at the same time render more convenient the preparation of those being prepared for college.[30]

Other defenders of election by courses, however, felt that the traditional college-preparatory program needed protection against the invasion of the modern subjects. Clear separation of the fitting and finishing functions would make it possible to divert the modern subjects into the non-college-preparatory programs. This notion was made explicit by Paul Shorey, a classicist from the University of Chicago, at the North Central Association meetings of 1897. The work of the college-preparatory program, he felt, should not be "interrupted by experimental attempts to find a place in the curriculum for the ten or fifteen departments that are descending from the university to compete in this arena." While holding out for "some central core of disciplinary study" even for the finishing pupils, he was in their case "inclined to make concessions to the alleged popular demand for obviously practical and informational courses."[31]

All of this was consistent with, and in fact demanded, election by courses. For the most part, however, these arguments involved the traditional distinction between the classical and the modern subjects, with the implied possibility of the kind of compromise represented by the Latin-Scientific course, this being recognized as preparation for technical or scientific schools. In this sense, the distinction between finishing and fitting courses that was made in the 1890's differed from the later point of view according to which some of the modern academic subjects themselves would be placed in the college-preparatory category and regarded as inappropriate for the finishing pupil.

III

Most of the advocates of election by courses with reference to preparation for college made only indirect reference to the occupational fu-

---

[30] Edward Brooks, "Standards of Admission to College," MSM, 1896, pp. 76–77.

[31] Paul Shorey, "Discipline vs. Dissipation in Secondary Education," *School Review* (April, 1897), pp. 221–222. He agreed sufficiently with the Eliot point of view to concede that divergence between the two courses of study should not begin until after the first year of high school. Also, he hoped to work out the courses in a manner "to reduce to the practicable minimum the difficulties of readjustment in case of a change in plan."

tures of the pupils. The indirect reference involved a vague assumption that the pupils bound for college were preparing themselves for the professions. Since such professions as medicine and law were then freely open to people who did not attend college at all, this identification could not be closely made. More specifically, the Classical course was allegedly designed for those aspiring to the ministry, to law, or to so-called literary careers, while the Latin-Scientific course was thought of as preparation for engineering, medicine, or leadership careers in the industrial world.

In the late 1890's and early 1900's, however, there was beginning to develop an idea of election by courses more closely related to the occupational futures of the finishing pupils. This was not necessarily an outgrowth of the early manual training high schools. The advocates of such schools, particularly C. M. Woodward, resented the implication that their programs of studies were specifically designed for those entering the mechanical trades. In the case of commercial schools, some of the early proponents, particularly Edmund J. James, also tried to stay clear of rigid vocational identification and insisted that their programs were one sort of pathway to liberal education.

Still, the vocational implication was there, and it proved difficult to separate the idea of manual training and commercial schools from the related occupations. The same difficulty applied to the manual training and commercial courses in the general or regular high schools. As such programs took shape, election by courses came to be thought of more and more in relation to presumed occupational choice. The lives of people in different vocations, argued Harlan Updegraff of the Baltimore Girls' Latin School in 1903, were "totally different, and the preparation for them necessarily as much so." He proposed therefore a set of courses called college preparatory, commercial, industrial, and "general culture," the last for those who had not yet made up their minds. "The complexity of the environment," he said, "demands the choice between four distinct secondary school courses." He could find no grounds for permitting election of subjects within these courses, but would permit some alternatives. The courses were, he felt, sufficiently diverse for the development of "peculiar aptitude."[32]

Updegraff was not arguing for specialized vocational training, and the key to his contention was that the lives of people in different vocations

[32] Harlan Updegraff, "The Elective System in Secondary Schools," MSM, 1903, pp. 18–20.

were "totally different." This was a much larger proposition than that of specialized training for particular kinds of jobs. There was a similar implication in an article by William T. Foster, Professor of English at Bowdoin College, in 1905. Foster wanted to award a high school diploma to every pupil who suitably completed a course valuable for a "particular community," but did not want such a diploma used for admission to college. While he granted the excellence of such an education "for the rank and file," what it represented to him was "various kinds of preparation for various lives."[33]

Another question was that of the comparative abilities of finishing and fitting pupils. G. Stanley Hall condemned the position of the Committee of Ten with reference to these two groups as one that disregarded "the great army of incapables" allegedly in the schools.[34] W. R. Butler found "a natural plane of cleavage" to exist between the non-college-preparatory and college-preparatory sections of a class, with the latter "comprising, generally, the more able part." He attributed this to a lack of zeal and ambition on the part of the finishing pupils, but also felt such pupils to be "as a rule of less natural ability."[35] Alfred H. Hitchcock of the Hartford Public High School considered the college-preparatory group to be "better timber" and "more ambitious."[36] Then, as at all times, there was a tendency to consider averages and to disregard possible overlapping between the two groups.

The alleged distinction between the needs and capacities of the two groups was applied not only to choice of courses and subjects, but, by some, to the treatment of subjects as well. Professor W. L. Cross of Yale endorsed the segregation of non-college-preparatory pupils in English to make possible the avoidance of books stipulated for the college-entrance examinations. When this was done, he said, "both instructors and students . . . enjoyed their freedom." The non-college-preparatory pupils should read a lot of books, some of which, he said, were "not quite literature, perhaps," but were interesting. Among these he listed

[33] William T. Foster, "Should the High School Diploma Admit to College?" *Education* (December, 1905), pp. 205–206.

[34] G. Stanley Hall, *Adolescence* (New York: Appleton-Century-Crofts, 1904), II, 510.

[35] W. R. Butler, *op. cit.,* p. 482 and p. 485.

[36] Alfred H. Hitchcock, "The Crisis in English: the Needs of the High-School Pupil Who Does Not Go to College," *Report of the Twenty-Third Annual Meeting, New England Association of Colleges and Preparatory Schools* (The Association, 1908), p. 27.

the works of John Fiske; the life of Henry Clay, by Carl Schurz; and Sir Charles Lyell's *Travels in North America*.[37] Hitchcock of Hartford felt the prescribed books did "not fully meet the needs of many who are destined never to advance in education beyond the high school." The thing to do, he said, was to have an elective course in the senior year for the non-college-preparatory group that would include the prescribed books, plus many more; pupils bound for college did not need this, since they would study the other books in college.[38] In another field of instruction, John C. Packard defended the existence in the Brookline, Massachusetts, High School of a class or section in applied physics for the non-college-preparatory pupils. This class, he said, differed from the college-preparatory physics class in paying less attention to mathematical problems, except those arising naturally in everyday life.[39]

There were many, then, who believed in a different kind of secondary education for finishing pupils, but they were by no means agreed among themselves on what the differences should be or on the reasons for such differences. Some took exception to the alleged narrowness of the traditional college-preparatory program. Pessimistic about the chances of modifying this program, they turned instead to a separate program for the non-college-preparatory pupils, one that would give more place to the modern subjects. Among these were some who feared a narrow college-preparatory treatment of the modern subjects as well and who advocated separate sections in English and physics. Common to men with these points of view was the hope that the work in college would correct the narrowness of the college-preparatory program, but they favored a broader program for the finishing pupils who, presumably, would never get another chance.

Rather different in spirit was the idea held to by others that secondary schooling should anticipate the different kinds of lives assumed to be characteristic of people in different kinds of occupations. This was the spirit of the future, at least part of the future beyond 1905. Some advocates of this position disclaimed the implication that one program was superior to another. Others considered the traditional college-preparatory program to be the best, although unsuitable for most of the pupils.

[37] W. L. Cross, discussion, *Report of the Twenty-Third Annual Meeting*, New England Association of Colleges and Preparatory Schools (The Association, 1908), pp. 35–36.

[38] Hitchcock, *op. cit.*, pp. 29–30.

[39] John C. Packard, "Physics for the Boys and Girls: an Introductory Course," NEA, 1903, pp. 880–883.

"Not even our intensely democratic spirit," said William T. Foster of Bowdoin, "can . . . blind us, ostrich-like, to the fact that only a small minority are fit for the higher education."[40]

Against this entire body of thought were the positions taken by the Committee of Ten and by the Committee on College-Entrance Requirements. Even though the Committee of Ten recommended the four specimen courses of study, it did not differentiate among these on the basis of preparation for college. Nightingale's report was perhaps clearer on this point. The constants set forth by his Committee on College-Entrance Requirements were intended to apply equally to graduation from the high school and college admission. Neither report succeeded in winning over the opposition. Perhaps Eliot, Nightingale, and Butler had their allies in the "masses" who invaded the high schools after 1890 and insisted on taking Latin against the advice of G. Stanley Hall, or possibly among the teachers who counseled the new high school population on choices of programs and subjects.

The alignments on the college question partly corresponded to, and partly cut across, positions taken on electives. Most of the advocates of election by subjects tended to reject distinctions based on the presumed destinations of the pupils. In this they were strangely allied to those who did not believe in election at all. Election by courses, on the other hand, provided a convenient device for differentiating between finishing pupils and those preparing for college. Just what was "conservative" or "liberal" in these various positions it would be difficult to establish. From the pedagogical point of view, the idea of separate programs for college-preparatory and non-college-preparatory pupils has seemed very liberal indeed. Yet it has never been easy in any realistic consideration of school practice for advocates of this position to shake loose the implications of caste education. What Eliot sought was a device that would avoid both caste education and uniform programs for all pupils. Election by subjects seemed to be this device.

IV

Another question on which positions both intersected and ran parallel to the college-preparatory controversy was whether training or information was the proper object of schooling. Throughout the 1890's mental training was clearly the preferred object, except among the Herbartians

[40] Foster, *op. cit.,* p. 206.

and a few independent dissenters, including, to a degree, William T. Harris himself. Information studies, so-called, were written off as inferior vehicles of education, if indeed they had anything to do with education at all. There were, of course, the usual comments to the effect that both training and information were important—the latter sometimes identified as knowledge or understanding. Still, training remained the standard by which the worth of studies was judged.

In the secondary school, the training subjects were Greek, Latin, and mathematics. The modern subjects could not easily break into this company, particularly when represented by such miscellaneous subjects as ethics, political economy, and a scattering of sciences. They were, in consequence, information subjects, considered to have nothing but information to impart. They were also the stuff of the old English course of study, that is, the non-college-preparatory course. Preparation for college then meant training, while finishing courses meant information.

It was against this differentiation that Eliot directed much of his effort before, during, and after the time of the Committee of Ten. All subjects, he felt, should become training subjects. Information could be acquired outside the school and in adult life. The ability of the adult to get information depended on his training. Proper training could not easily be had outside the school. It was critically necessary for the pupils not bound for college to get all the training they could while they had the chance. Furthermore, if they changed their minds and decided to go to college after all, it was the obligation of the college to admit them.

Eliot had no particular objection to the imparting of some information in the secondary school, provided, of course, it did not interfere with training. Here he made an interesting distinction between the humanities and the sciences. "If we are looking for information only," he said in 1896, "we had better get our information in what are called the 'humanities'—that is, in languages, politics, and philosophy, in the story of the development of the race, and of its home on the crust of the earth." The pupil bound for college, furthermore, needed "a just kind of information quite as much as the boys who are going into shops or offices." On the other hand, he was contemptuous of information in the sciences, being in this respect by no means a follower of Herbert Spencer. He denounced as "mischievous delusions" the idea that high school graduates must "know something about" this or that science. "The less we know about the chemistry and biology of the air of this room," he declared to an audience in a crowded convention hall, "the more comfortably we shall breathe it. We can ride quite happily in an electric car without having the slightest conception of what electricity is. Indeed, that is the condition in which we all ride." If a pupil did study science, what he should get from his study was "training in the power to observe accurately, describe correctly, and reason justly."[41] In fact, this is what he should get from any subject well taught. To these Eliot added on other occasions the power of "expressing cogently the results of these mental operations."[42]

Eliot and other advocates of training only rarely referred to "mental discipline" as such. They used the terms "disciplinary" and "formal" as separate modifiers applied to school studies, such as "disciplinary studies" and "formal studies." The word "formal" simply meant form as contrasted with content. Very few people used the term "formal discipline," in print at least, before 1900. "Formal culture" was used occasionally and perhaps meant what was later understood as formal discipline.

The idea of training or disciplining the mind through properly selected studies goes back at least as far as Plato and has appeared and reappeared in various guises throughout the history of pedagogy. In American education, a full-dress presentation of one version of this idea was made in the Yale report of 1829. This document proclaimed the two great points of "intellectual culture" to be the discipline and the furniture of the mind, with discipline considered "perhaps, the more important of the two." Much of the discussion in this report was taken up by the consideration of mental processes, or what would today be called behaviors, largely as the development of habits. It also referred, however, to the necessity of bringing "all the important mental faculties" into "exercise." As examples of these faculties, it mentioned such things as "reasoning powers," "imagination and taste," "fervid and impressive eloquence," "memory," and "the powers of invention."[43] The classics were defended as employing every faculty of the mind, including memory, judgment, reasoning powers, taste, and fancy.[44]

Throughout the nineteenth century, the term "mental faculties" was

[41] Charles W. Eliot, "Standards of Admission to College," MSM, 1896, p. 86.

[42] Charles W. Eliot, "Wherein Popular Education Has Failed," *Forum* (December, 1892), p. 421.

[43] *Reports on the Course of Instruction in Yale College by a Committee of the Corporation, and the Academical Faculty* (New Haven, Conn.: printed by Hezekiah Howe, 1830), p. 7.

[44] *Ibid.,* p. 36.

freely used, for the most part about as loosely as in the Yale report. The idea of faculties was almost as old as that of mental training itself. As used in the Yale report and in subsequent discussion, the term was practically synonymous with what would later be called mental functions. The idea did not involve the analogy of the mind as a muscle, and it did not require that the studies used for mental training be vexatious or dull. Some of these points were made from time to time in what might be called the intellectual underworld of the mental-training movement. When the writers of the Yale report wanted a comparison, they used instead the "dexterous performance of the manual operations, in many of the mechanical arts." If these required an apprenticeship with diligent attention, argued the writers of the report, the training of the powers of the mind even more demanded "vigorous, and steady, and systematic effort."[45]

Such general notions as these were later bundled together into a single stereotype called formal discipline, but not fully so until after 1900. In 1894 Professor B. A. Hinsdale of the University of Michigan presented to the National Council a criticism of what he called "the dogma of formal discipline." He was not, however, attacking mental training. What he did attack was the idea of "the mutual convertibility of the different kinds of mental activity of power," in other words the notion of an all-inclusive or general mental function. This was what he understood as formal discipline, and it was the very opposite of faculty psychology. In fact, while he protested that he was not trying to rehabilitate what had by then become "the much derided 'faculty' psychology," he defended it as having furnished "a convenient mode of describing mental phenomena." The main point of his protest was that mental power was more special than general and that no one kind of mental exercise could develop the whole mind. Different subjects were needed to train different mental powers, or to use the term Hinsdale did not reject, *mental faculties*.[46] Hinsdale's speech against formal discipline was by no means an attack on mental training as an object of education.

Neither were Thorndike's early studies, such as the one conducted with Woodworth in 1901. What Thorndike did in this period was to use

[45] *Ibid.,* p. 7. For an instance of the mind-as-muscle analogy see Report of the Committee of the Educational Value of Common-School Studies, NEA, 1886, p. 408.
[46] B. A. Hinsdale, "The Dogma of Formal Discipline," NEA, 1894, pp. 625–635.

the term *mental functions* in a more specific and narrow sense.[47] So far was Thorndike from repudiating mental training that he even mentioned it as a desirable by-product of a good course in psychology in secondary schools, one that would differ from existing courses in emphasizing the study of human behavior on a scientific basis. "The disciplinary value of such a course," he wrote in 1902, "would be great, for it would teach the student good habits of thought about matters which he would otherwise settle by guess work, or the acceptance of conventional opinion." He was not optimistic that such a course would be established and feared sarcastically that it would be preceded by the introduction of "entomology, Anglo-Saxon, counter-point, the history of fancy work and tatting, and Latin epigraphy."[48]

Various refinements of the doctrine of mental training were stated in 1908 by Alexander Meiklejohn of Brown University. He accepted the term *formal discipline* as representing the ideas he defended. His argument was that formal discipline, or mental training, depended not on psychology, but on logic. He rejected faculty psychology and the mind-body analogy implied in the idea of mental exercise. What was important, he claimed, was the distinction between form and content. He tried to define form, but in the end identified it largely with method. Formal discipline to him was "the theory that the mind can be trained to do well certain kinds of work, to follow successfully certain methods of procedure."[49]

In spite of their conflicting uses of the term *formal discipline,* both Hinsdale and Meiklejohn favored the same proposition, namely, the training of mental powers or functions. This was also the proposition of the Committee of Ten. Neither this proposition nor the idea of formal discipline attacked by Hinsdale in 1894 resembled what subsequent writers would call the "exploded" doctrine of formal discipline, namely, the idea of exercising the mind as a muscle, through tasks preferably distasteful.

In their insistence on mental training as an object of education, the

[47] Edward L. Thorndike and R. S. Woodworth, "The Influence of Improvement in One Mental Function upon the Efficiency of Other Functions," *Psychological Review* (May, 1901), p. 249.

[48] Edward L. Thorndike, "Psychology in Secondary Schools," *School Review* (February, 1902), pp. 120–123.

[49] Alexander Meiklejohn, "Is Mental Training a Myth?" *Report of the Twenty-Third Annual Meeting,* New England Association of Colleges and Preparatory Schools (The Association, 1908), pp. 47–55.

educational leaders of the 1890's were not clinging to a doctrine subsequently repudiated by psychological research. Perhaps, however, they put too much stress on training. Certainly they were guilty of a disdainful attitude toward content that went far beyond the Yale report itself. Theirs may have been, however, a kind of unconscious exaggeration, rendered necessary by the campaign to establish the modern subjects. To have left these subjects as vehicles of information only would at that time have invited defeat. If they saw the mind as something to be trained rather than furnished, they at least avoided the opposite conviction that the mind was not to be trained, but stuffed.

V

Although much of the discussion of this period was directed to psychological pedagogy, the moderate revision also involved social considerations. Its leaders were, of course, concerned about social and economic mobility through schooling, and they shared with many others the belief in popular education as essential to popular government. Their social aims, however, included another point as well. They rejected specific kinds of education allegedly suited to the presumed "lives" people would lead and assumed that good education would dignify and ennoble any life. All who could manage it should go through high school and college regardless of future work or station. Increasing enrollments were welcomed. The so-called masses were invited, almost beseeched, not to content themselves with what Francis Parker had called a "crumb," but to partake of the "full loaf."[50] It was not a new social order that was being aimed at, but a new cultural and intellectual order in which the dualism of class education would be replaced by "aristocratic" education for all.

So far as views on specific social questions were concerned, the men of the moderate revision did not fall into any particular category. As a group they were no more and no less conservative than other educators of their times. Butler abhorred any suggestion of violence, and the emotional intensity of the free-silver campaign reminded him of Wat Tyler's rebellion and the Paris mob howling on its way to Versailles.[51] He was consistent enough to oppose the war with Spain and courageous enough

[50] Francis W. Parker, "The Report of the Committee of Ten: Its Use for the Improvement of Teachers Now at Work in the Schools," NEA, 1894, p. 449.
[51] *Educational Review* (November, 1896), p. 404.

to condemn in May, 1898, "the barbarous and artificially stimulated war spirit which is now sweeping over the country."[52] Like most of his contemporaries, he was appalled by anarchism, but he opened the columns of *Educational Review* to articles by anarchists.[53] After the assassination of McKinley, he wrote that society owed no protection to those who teach "that there should be no society at all," advocating deportation to Guam or the Philippines for anarchists who had "not yet stolen or killed."[54]

William T. Harris has become in the minds of many the archetype of political and social conservatism. He certainly believed in an orderly society and felt that a good education would protect its recipient from the errors of anarchism. To write this off as conservatism in a negative sense would be to restrict almost to a vanishing point the potential range that might be occupied by liberals. On some matters Harris was liberal in the present-day sense of the term. He saw perhaps more clearly than any other educator of his time what advancing technology would do to the nature of employment and urged broad education that would enable workers to adjust more readily to changes in the market for jobs.[55] In 1898 he called for an end to isolationism, stating that the vocation of the schoolmaster "in the coming time" would be indicated by the need for study of the history, customs, and literatures of "European nations."[56] His scope was limited, but the words were much like those later used by others for the whole world. In connection with another matter, he defended higher education for Negroes,[57] including nontechnical higher education, when serious doubts were being expressed about the wisdom of making such provisions.

Eliot's social views were consistent with the value he placed on the individual. This led him into positions some would call conservative, such as his opposition to strikes, boycotts, and the closed shop, although he did defend the right of labor to organize. It also led him into other positions, such as his hatred of racial and religious persecution and his dislike for restrictions against immigration. "The restriction of immigration by the present occupants of the United States," he wrote in 1892,

[52] *Educational Review* (May, 1898), p. 515.
[53] See *Educational Review* (January), 1898, pp. 1–16.
[54] *Educational Review* (October, 1901), pp. 321–322.
[55] As reported in *Education* (February, 1899), pp. 375–376.
[56] William T. Harris, "Address of Welcome," NEA, 1898, pp. 49–51.
[57] William T. Harris, "Higher Education for Negroes," an address to students of Atlanta University, October 29, 1895, William T. Harris Papers (Library of Congress, Washington, D.C.).

"seems to me to be a peculiarly ungenerous and ungrateful proposal; because these present occupants are all themselves descendants from immigrants of very recent times."[58] Eliot has been identified as devoted to big business, but he was also opposed to monopoly and trusts.

Butler, Harris, and Eliot were by no means the only educators who expressed themselves freely on social issues. Judged by the quantity of their utterances on topics of the day, many school men of the period between 1890 and 1905 possessed a high degree of what was once called social sensitivity. They were often relatively conventional in their views, although the editor of the *Public School Journal* dared to praise Governor John Peter Altgeld of Illinois just two years after the pardon of the Chicago anarchists.[59] They were particularly concerned about radicals and immigrants, often associating one with the other. One enterprising teacher presented data from chiefs of police in 37 large cities on the presence of anarchists, anarchist Sunday schools, and anarchist organizations. She reported 880 known anarchists and one presumed anarchist Sunday school, but pointed out that three other cities "in which this leprous disease showed itself most prevalent" several years before had not yet replied to her questionnaire.[60] An alleged Sunday school for anarchists was referred to at the Department of Child Study in 1894,[61] but it turned out to be a school "started by German free-thinkers for the instruction of their children in morality."[62]

The pronouncements of educators about immigrants were not always consistent. An editorial in *Education,* May, 1891, viewed with horror the coming of immigrants from Hungary, Italy, and Russia and said that the leading industries of the great Northern states were "in a state of perpetual siege by an army of semi-savages."[63] Three years later, another editorial in the same magazine rejoiced in the presence of immigrant children, especially Italians, at the John Hancock School in Boston, noting that one of the recent graduating classes at that school had distinguished itself with an exhibition entitled "A Morning Hour with Oliver Wendell Holmes." Out of the 2100 pupils in this school, declared the editorial, was being developed a new American life, "certainly

[58] Charles W. Eliot to *Home Journal,* November 21, 1892, Charles W. Eliot Papers (Harvard University Archives, Cambridge, Mass.).
[59] "Gov. Altgeld," *Public School Journal* (February, 1895), p. 340.
[60] Laura Donnan, "The High School and the Citizen," NEA, 1889, p. 519.
[61] NEA, 1894, pp. 184–185.
[62] *School Journal* (August 11, 1894), p. 89.
[63] *Education* (May, 1891), p. 573.

broader than the ancient Puritanism of old Boston, with such an outfit of intelligence and executive power as no generation this side of the water has yet known."[64] In 1905 the same magazine referred to "undisciplined and uncouth hordes of foreigners," whose "hope of salvation" lay in the work of the schools.[65] These editorials may have been penned by different writers, or the policy of the magazine may have shifted from time to time. They were not, however, unusual among utterances of this period in the degree of emotional intensity revealed or the inconsistency of swings from one extreme position to another. There were, of course, more moderate and practical positions. In areas where immigrants lived under appalling social and economic deprivation, some of the schools undertook to relieve distress wherever they could. This was particularly true in New York City, where District Superintendent Julia Richman and Superintendent William H. Maxwell, following the example set by the settlement workers, promoted the development of vacation schools, the use of schools as neighborhood centers, and the provision of public baths in school buildings.

Crime, corruption, divorce, graft, and scandals also occupied the attention of educators in this period. Various causes of crime were identified, among these being the prevalence of impure literature, the liberty accorded youth by parents too busy with their own affairs, and the sparing of the rod, "often to the undoing of home and society."[66] Sometimes the schools were blamed for crime, and statistics were presented to show high crime rates in regions well equipped with schools and with a high degree of school attendance. Educators were on the alert to refute these statistics and inferences.[67] When pressed about the failure of the schools to prevent social evils, educators would point to the "brimstone journalists," but would admit that "these purveyors of scandal, these recruiters for the army of crime" were themselves the products of schools.[68]

On the whole the educators of the 1890's, including those both for and against the moderate revision, were far from dwelling in an ivory tower where they engaged in quibbles about the elective principle, training versus information, or Herbartian correlation, to the exclusion of

[64] *Education* (November, 1894), pp. 174–175.
[65] *Education* (October, 1905), p. 116.
[66] *Education* (April, 1901), pp. 503–504.
[67] A.B.A., "Education and Crime," *School Review* (January, 1900), pp. 42–45.
[68] D. S. Wright, "Complete Education," *Proceedings of the Fiftieth Annual Session,* Iowa State Teachers' Association (The Association, 1904), p. 17.

the social world about them. If their responses to social evils were naïve, so were those of many people in other walks of life, including some engaged directly in reform. Perhaps it was naïve to rely on education as a cure for social ills. Such reliance has always aroused the scorn of sophisticates like Barrett Wendell, professor of English at Harvard, who in 1904 characterized education as "our national superstition," saying: "Let social troubles declare themselves anywhere—lynchings, strikes, trusts, immigration, racial controversies, whatever you chance to hold most threatening, and we are gravely assured on every side that education is the only thing which can preserve our coming generations from destruction."[69] Somewhat different was the idea of Harvard's Eliot, who, although far from believing in education as the cure for all evils, trusted that popular education aimed at "strengthening of reasoning power" and freed from "reliance on the principle of authority" would play some part "in developing universal reasonableness."[70] Even he, however, did not want education thought of as "a measure of police."[71]

Some educators during the late 1890's were beginning to see the school as a positive social force in relation to the community. One of these was Samuel Train Dutton, Superintendent of Schools at Brookline, Massachusetts. A close friend of Francis Parker and a follower of William T. Harris, Dutton was an experimentally minded educator with a many-sided interest in the social aspects of the school. He was not specifically identified with the moderate revision, but he accepted and practiced some of its doctrines. Both at New Haven, where he had served as superintendent between 1881 and 1890, and at Brookline, he sought to build up and to strengthen the high schools as good institutions in themselves and as routes to the college. When he came to Brookline, he was appalled to find the high school the "Cinderella" of the system, with only 115 pupils in a community of 50,000 inhabitants, and with some of the leading citizens arguing that the community had no responsibility beyond the grammar grades. Four years later he had the high school in a new building and was beginning to establish the idea that it was no longer necessary to go to a special preparatory school be-

---

[69] Barrett Wendell, "Our National Superstition," *North American Review* (September, 1904), p. 389.
[70] Charles W. Eliot, "Wherein Popular Education Has Failed," *Forum* (December, 1892), p. 428.
[71] Charles W. Eliot, "The Function of Education in Democratic Society," *Outlook* (November 6, 1897), p. 570.

fore entering Harvard. Dutton also sponsored kindergartens, the introduction of manual training, and the teaching of French and Latin in the grammar grades.

In 1895, Dutton organized the Brookline Education Society, aimed at correlating the work of the schools with other agencies, such as churches, libraries, and museums. This was modeled in part on the Public Education Society of Philadelphia. The mission of the public school, he felt, was closely related to all forms of social work, and the "humanitarian spirit of the social reformer" was essential to the life of every good school.[72] In 1898 he argued for the high school as a "social institution" with a social aim, acknowledging his indebtedness to Dewey's *My Pedagogic Creed,* published the year before. He called for more work in the modern subjects, plus manual training, but said he was not in sympathy with "the demand that Latin should be excluded from our High Schools." Neither was he opposed to Greek, provided it could be furnished without "crippling other departments."[73]

By 1899 Dutton was ready to pull his ideas together and did so in a book entitled, *Social Phases of Education in the School and the Home.* Here he roamed over a variety of topics, including his conviction that the cultural and vocational aims could be harmonized "in a larger purpose" of socializing children and youth. He referred to Bellamy's *Looking Backward* as suggesting a time when the altruistic spirit would be dominant. "The whole life of the school," he said, "must be fashioned somewhat after this ideal community to which I have referred."[74] In another part of the book he commended the Committee of Ten for seeking to make the modern academic subjects "fully equivalent in value to Latin, Greek, or Mathematics."[75] He also referred favorably to an article by Horace E. Scudder urging that the schoolhouse become the center of community life.[76] Finally he described the work of the Brookline Education Society, noting that one of the outcomes of its activity had been the building of a public bath.[77] A reviewer praised this book

[72] Samuel T. Dutton, "The Correlation of Educational Forces in the Community," *Educational Review* (April, 1897), p. 347.

[73] Samuel T. Dutton, "The Place and Function of the High School," *Education* (June, 1898), pp. 588–591.

[74] Samuel T. Dutton, *Social Phases of Education in the School and the Home* (New York: Macmillan Co., 1899), pp. 16–18.

[75] *Ibid.,* p. 114.

[76] *Ibid.,* p. 232.

[77] *Ibid.,* p. 247.

as a summary of "the best current sentiment," although not "exactly a pathfinder."[78]

The year 1899 was also the year of John Dewey's essay, *The School and Society*. Although Dewey approached the question in somewhat different terms, there are points of intersection with Dutton's book, especially on the place of the school as an ideal community. In neither of these books was it suggested that the social aim demanded the repudiation of the academic studies. Dutton fully accepted both the classics and the modern subjects, while Dewey's school made much use of art, history, and science. Both these books went beyond the thinking of Eliot, Harris, and Butler, but they were consistent with the moderate revision as far as it went, more so than with the doctrines that ruled later.

Meanwhile, an era was coming to an end. "The change," declared Butler in his memoirs, "became plain to every one after 1905."[79] Like all dates marking the ends and beginnings of eras, the year 1905 is an arbitrary selection. In this case, as in many others, it is a useful one. By 1905 the moderate revision was no longer setting the issues for discussion. It was the year of the Douglas Commission in Massachusetts, with its assertion that vocational training was the issue to be discussed. It was also the year of Eliot's last formal defense of the Committee of Ten. This did not mean that the moderate revision had been accepted. Attacks continued against the Committee of Ten, but they lacked the verve and enthusiasm of times past. No longer viewed as an upsetter of tradition, the Committee itself was blended into a vague background of something called traditional education.

The old leaders were leaving the platforms where the issues of secondary education were under debate. William T. Harris retired as Commissioner of Education in 1906. His successor, Elmer E. Brown of the University of California, was a man of the moderate revision, but as such was largely out of touch with the new men. He resigned in 1911 to become Chancellor of New York University and was succeeded in the Commissionership by Professor Philander P. Claxton of the University of Tennessee. Nightingale left the Chicago schools in 1902 to become Superintendent of Schools for Cook County, a post he held in relative obscurity until his retirement in 1912. Eliot retired from Harvard in 1909 to devote himself to reform on many fronts, retaining, however,

[78] Henry R. Corbett, in *School Review* (October, 1899), p. 490.
[79] Nicholas Murray Butler, *Across the Busy Years* (New York: Charles Scribner's Sons, 1939), I, 204.

direct connection with educational affairs through the Carnegie Foundation and the General Education Board. Tetlow retired from his Boston principalship in 1910 after 32 years service in that city.[80]

Butler began withdrawing from affairs directly pertaining to secondary education after his succession to the Columbia presidency in 1901. His withdrawal was accelerated by his growing conviction that something had gone wrong with the NEA. As early as the Milwaukee meeting of 1897 he had referred to "a small but dangerous element of educational politicians and anarchists that has crept into the Association as it has grown larger."[81] He was upset by the Denver meeting of 1909, appalled by the Boston meeting in 1910, and so horrified by the San Francisco meeting in 1911 that he resigned from the Board of Trustees. Perhaps all this was only personal resentment over his own loss of leadership. More probably it represented his lack of sympathy with the pedagogical tenets being expressed. Butler came to feel that the year 1905 represented not only the end of an era, but the end of progress. In his memoirs he looked back with nostalgia to the days "when Harris ruled the educational philosophy of the United States and when Eliot was leading men on to strengthen and elevate the thought of the American people and to build sound and progressive policies not only for the schools but for the country."[82]

The moderate revision had stirred up much discussion and, along the way, had achieved a few victories. Among these was the winning of respectability for the modern academic subjects, not only in the high schools, but also for admission to college. Perhaps this would have come about anyway; nevertheless, a great deal of work was done to move it

[80] Perhaps nothing so clearly symbolized the ending of the era as the judgments passed by Winship's *Journal of Education* on the controversy between Tetlow and Boston's Superintendent Stratton D. Brooks in 1907–1908. Brooks had transferred Miss Griswold, one of Tetlow's teachers, to the Dorchester High School on the ground that she had thwarted the plans of the board for modernizing the Girls' High School. Tetlow protested this action, but was overruled. According to Winship's *Journal,* Miss Griswold was the "stronghold of the old standards as opposed to progress," and it was "the faith of the fathers" for which Tetlow was fighting in seeking to prevent the transfer. "The Griswold Incident," *Journal of Education* (January 30, 1908), p. 132. "Not since the days of Horace Mann," continued the *Journal* two weeks later, "has there been such a clear-cut issue between the new and the live against the hold of the old." *Journal of Education* (February 13, 1908), p. 184. Only little more than a decade before, Tetlow had been voted down and shouted down by the New England Association for his efforts to facilitate admission to college of pupils who had taken no Latin.

[81] *Educational Review* (September, 1897), p. 197.

[82] Butler, *op. cit.,* p. 206.

along. Other consequences of the movement were the creation of the College Entrance Examination Board and the definition of the roles of the colleges and the secondary schools.

Some of the most cherished proposals met with only limited success. Much skepticism remained about the elective principle. Even among those who did accept it, there was a tendency to restrict its application to election by courses, a practice that had been long established. Many school and college men continued to believe there should be a difference between the programs of pupils who were bound for college and those who were not. Eliot's ideas on this point, however, did survive in some quarters and later turned up in the reports of the Committee on the Articulation of High School and College in 1911 and the report on *Cardinal Principles of Secondary Education* of the Commission on the Reorganization of Secondary Education in 1918.

The movement as a whole had failed to win over two important groups. Extreme classicists were against it, partly because of the threat they felt was posed by the elective principle. On the other hand, some of the school men felt the campaign to broaden the curriculum had not gone far enough. They wanted immediate recognition not only for the modern academic subjects but also for such practical fields as manual training, business, and home economics. Although Eliot had little enthusiasm for business subjects in high school, he did look with favor on manual training, as, of course, did Butler. Neither was prepared in this period to make the case for manual training in relation to acceptance for college admission. Harris was viewed as an opponent of manual training, at least by its more ardent advocates.

Regardless of the positions taken, this had been a great era of discussion. Not even the published proceedings of the NEA could conceal the zest of those who had taken part. This was true not only of the debates on secondary education but also of those on other matters as well. Herbartians and child study enthusiasts, along with their opponents, seemed to be engaged in some kind of sport. The antics of the Richmond meeting of 1894 and the exhilaration at Cleveland in 1895 (that immortal day at Cleveland, as De Garmo called it, more than 30 years later) remained green in the memories of those who had been present, and undoubtedly improved as time went on. Perhaps those who took part in these debates may have accomplished little, but they had a good time. In this latter respect, if in none other, they differed from many of their successors.

Chapter 10

The interlude of vocationalism

"Our school system is gravely defective in so far as it puts a premium upon mere literacy training and tends therefore to train the boy away from the farm and the workshop."

—THEODORE ROOSEVELT,
DECEMBER 3, 1907.

*I*t was, declared one observer, a mental epidemic, much like the free-silver crusade and the Klondike gold rush:[1] he was talking about the sudden and widespread demand for industrial education, voiced by school men and other leaders in public life. The precipitating event for this particular campaign was the report in April, 1906, of the Massachusetts Commission on Industrial and Technical Education, known also as the Douglas Commission, from the name of the governor who had appointed its members the year before.

Industrial education covered a variety of pedagogical activities, and its earlier identification with manual training had by then gone out of fashion. Sometimes it meant training for industries or trades only. For the most part, however, the term had come to be used interchangeably with *vocational education,* especially in connection with preparation for such occupations as the manual trades, business, farming, and home-making. It was in this sense that it usually appeared in the everyday speech-making and writing of the school men themselves.

Much vocational education had existed before the launching of this particular campaign. Commercial subjects, partly vocational in purpose, had been established in many high schools. Minnesota and Alabama had started special state schools of agriculture for work below the

---

[1] John J. Marrinan, "Vocational Education for the Rural School," *Educational Review* (June, 1913), p. 40.

college level. Private schools, such as the Pratt Institute in Brooklyn and the New York Trade School, taught the mechanical trades. Large cities maintained evening schools both for commercial and shop training. Massachusetts had three publicly supported schools for textile workers. In addition there were the public manual-training high schools, although purists on their faculties strenuously denied teaching the trades.

Even before 1906, some of the school men had been demanding more explicit recognition of the need for industrial or vocational training in secondary schools. "The chief modification of the secondary school curriculum which is demanded by the conditions that surround us today," said President Charles H. Keyes of the Throop Polytechnic Institute of Pasadena, California, in 1895, "is the general introduction of industrial education."[2] Superintendent Thomas M. Balliet of Springfield, Massachusetts, called upon manual-training high schools throughout the country to assume responsibility for what he called technical training.[3] There were similar expressions from some of the manual-training men, although one of them, Principal C. F. Warner of the Mechanics' Arts High School of Springfield feared he would be "stigmatized as a deserter from the ranks of true educational manual training."[4] He was joined by Principal B. A. Lenfest of the Manual Training High School in Waltham, Massachusetts, who expressed the feeling in 1900 that vocational education at public expense, including trade schools, was bound to come.[5]

These were the kinds of sentiments drawn together by the Douglas Commission in its widely publicized report. Called into existence by a resolution of the Massachusetts legislature, this body consisted of nine leading citizens of the Commonwealth, including school man George H. Martin, a supervisor in the Boston system and former agent of the State Board of Education. The chairman was Carroll D. Wright, former United States Commissioner of Labor. Twenty public hearings were held by the Commission, during the course of which it listened to 143 "different persons." In addition, one of its subcommittees employed "an

[2] Charles H. Keyes, "The Modifications of Secondary School Courses Most Demanded by the Conditions of Today, and Most Ignored by the Committee of Ten," NEA, 1895, p. 731.
[3] Thomas M. Balliet, "Manual, Trade, and Technical Education," NEA, 1903, pp. 67–68.
[4] Charles F. Warner, "Teaching Trades in Connection with the Public Schools," NEA, 1900, p. 494.
[5] B. A. Lenfest, "Character, Content, and Purpose of High-School Courses in Manual Training," NEA, 1900, p. 497.

expert investigator" named Susan M. Kingsbury to conduct a special inquiry on the relation of children to industries and schools.

Martin's presence on the Commission not only provided representation for the school men, but served as a check on extreme points of view. He probably had much to do with the moderate tone of the general report, a document far less sweeping than many of the speeches later made in its name.[6] Martin had not gone to college and had relatively little direct experience with secondary schools. He was an elementary school man who had come up through the Bridgewater Normal School, part of the system that had been initiated by Horace Mann. With this background, he represented a group different from the college-trained New England schoolmasters like Tetlow and Collar. He was, however, deeply committed to the importance of secondary schools in Massachusetts and had worked as an agent of the State Board to foster their development.

The general report of the Commission began with a cautious acknowledgment of what it called widespread interest in its subject on the part of educators, wage earners, and manufacturers: "Men and women who have been brought into intimate contact with the harder side of life as it appears among the poorer people of the cities," it declared, "think they see in some form of industrial education a means of securing earlier and greater efficiency as wage earners, more self-reliance and self-respect, steadier habits of industry and frugality, and through these the opening of avenues to better industrial and social conditions."[7] These were the accents—in fact, practically the words—of Horace Mann, applied here to the possibility of adding industrial subjects to the ones Mann had used in the pursuit of the same goals.

According to the witnesses heard by the Commission, the schools had remained too literary to meet the demands of contemporary social and economic conditions. Still, said the report, these witnesses were loyal to, and proud of, their schools; and, in addition, had few, if any, specific ideas about how to remedy the situation.[8] Massachusetts already had laws requiring cities of 20,000 or more population to include manual-training work in the high schools and in the grade schools. These laws

[6] According to one statement, Martin drafted the report himself. Joseph Asbury Pitman, "George Henry Martin, a Biography," *Essentials of Education: George Henry Martin* (Boston: Richard G. Badger, 1932), p. 16. This probably needs qualification, especially in view of his later disagreements with some of the recommendations.

[7] *Report of the Massachusetts Commission on Industrial and Technical Education* (Boston: The Commission, 1906), p. 4.

[8] *Ibid.,* pp. 5–6.

were only spasmodically enforced, however, and, in any case, the Commission had doubts, either its own or those gathered from the witnesses, about manual training as the solution. Manual training, according to the Commission, had "been severed from real life as completely as . . . the other school activities," presumably the literary ones. The advocates of manual training were to blame for this, since they had, in the opinion of the Commission, taken a "narrow view" of their subject and had promoted it as a "cultural subject . . . without reference to any industrial end."[9] Thus had the schools, with or without manual training, fallen short of meeting their obligations in modern society.

As a result of this delinquency, neither the children who left school early nor those who stayed until they were sixteen or eighteen were equipped with "industrial intelligence." Industries, continued the report, had to depend on chance and on the few systems of apprenticeship still in existence. The consequences were increased production costs, limited output, and lowered quality, these combining to weaken the position of American industry in competition for world markets. "The State," declared the report, "needs a wider diffusion of industrial intelligence as a foundation for the highest technical success." Moreover, "the latest philosophy of education" was showing that education aimed at industrial intelligence would be the best for other purposes as well.[10]

The Commission made several broad, or perhaps vague, recommendations for the regular public schools. Elementary schools, it said, should include work in the elements of productive industry, including agriculture and the mechanic and domestic arts. How the work in the mechanic arts should differ from traditional manual training was not explained. The high school was called upon to apply the teaching of mathematics, botany, chemistry, and drawing more specifically to industrial life, "with especial reference to local industries, so that the students may see that these subjects are not designed primarily and solely for academic purposes, but that they may be utilized for the purposes of practical life."[11] Perhaps this recognition of what schools might accomplish through existing programs was a concession to Martin's presence on the Commission.

In its major recommendation, however, the Commission called for the establishment in local communities of "independent industrial schools"

[9] *Ibid.*, p. 14.
[10] *Ibid.*, pp. 18–19.
[11] *Ibid.*, p. 20.

or for the introduction of new day or evening industrial courses in the high schools. It also proposed the creation of a permanent "Commission on Industrial Education" to succeed itself and to foster the establishment of the new schools and courses. As a summary of its own work, the Commission declared that it had "endeavored to preserve the integrity of the public school system, to enrich it along industrial lines, and expand it along vocational lines through independent industrial schools."[12] The legislature of 1906 acted promptly to establish the new commission, and Paul Hanus, Harvard's professor of the art and science of teaching, was appointed chairman.

The report of the Douglas Commission was clear and for the most part restrained. It condoned the shortcomings of the so-called literary schools and only mildly reproached the manual-training people for not taking full advantage of the potential offered by their subject. No hostility was displayed toward the classics or any other part of the academic program. The report did, however, suggest points destined to become major arguments in the vocational campaign. One of these was the alleged decline of apprenticeship. The report also struck a note of fear about the position of the United States on the competitive world market. In its comments about the bettering of social and industrial conditions, the Commission presented industrial education as a part of the general program of social reform.

The paper of Susan M. Kingsbury, the special investigator, on the relation of children to industries attracted fully as much attention as the main report itself. According to her calculations, there were 25,000 children in Massachusetts who were fourteen and fifteen years of age and not in school, five-sixths of whom had not been graduated from the grammar schools and one-half of whom had not gone beyond the seventh grade.[13] Many of these were at work, largely in jobs without prospect of future advancement.

Conditions varied from one industry to the next and even within industries. The large and important textile industry presented a mixed picture of the employment of children. Textile mills in three cities, North Adams, Lowell, and New Bedford hired children at the ages of fourteen and fifteen, but half the firms who did so expressed a preference for young people sixteen to twenty. Mills in other cities of the state em-

12 *Ibid.*, pp. 21–23.
13 *Ibid.*, pp. 30–31.

ployed only a few children. "Evidently," said Miss Kingsbury, "the industry can thrive without child labor and thrive better with educated labor."[14]

The question, then, was why there were children in the mills at all. Many who left school for the mills, declared Miss Kingsbury, came from "good-grade families," and the parents of 40 percent of this group wanted their children to stay in school. Children themselves made the decision. "It is the dissatisfaction of the child which takes him from school, and ignorance on the part of the parent which permits him to enter the mill."[15] The theory that parents put children to work, said Miss Kingsbury in her general summary for conditions throughout the state, was "not tenable, except for the lower foreign element."[16]

Employers in the textile industry allegedly did not need or even want the children, and the parents did not want to send their children to work. Moreover, the children were not to blame for their own dissatisfaction. Still something had to be blamed. Miss Kingsbury consulted "35 to 40 superintendents," and all except three felt the great lack was in "the system, which fails to offer the child of fourteen continued schooling of a practical character."[17] Apparently then it was the schools that fostered child labor in Massachusetts. The Commission in its main report observed more soberly that further schooling for these children, if practical, would be attractive.[18]

These 25,000 children became a powerful symbol and were referred to over and over again in the campaign for industrial training. Miss Kingsbury's paper gave wide publicity to the guilt feelings of the "35 or 40 superintendents." Perhaps school men in other states felt guilty too, but even if they did not, they were encouraged to keep up with their colleagues in Massachusetts. Civic leaders who might not otherwise have blamed the schools for this state of affairs were inclined to accept the verdict the school men pronounced upon themselves.

This verdict did not immediately involve or affect the high schools. In fact, Miss Kingsbury noted that 81 percent of those who were graduated from the grammar grades went on to high school, although this enrollment was offset by a drop-out rate of 50 percent within one or

[14] *Ibid.,* p. 46.
[15] *Ibid.,* p. 44.
[16] *Ibid.,* p. 86.
[17] *Ibid.,* p. 87.
[18] *Ibid.,* p. 18.

two years.[19] The elementary schools were the culprits, and Miss Kingsbury's paper laid the groundwork for later advocacy of differentiated courses of study in the seventh and eighth grades. On the other hand, the Commission involved the high schools of Massachusetts at once, especially because of its recommendation for independent industrial schools and because of the difficult question it raised about administration by separate boards.

The distribution of the Douglas Report not only in Massachusetts, but throughout the country, was paralleled during the spring and summer of 1906 by the organization of the National Society for the Promotion of Industrial Education (NSPIE). It has been assumed that this enterprise was motivated by employers, particularly by big industrialists and manufacturers. Perhaps they were behind the scenes. The initiative, however, was assumed by two educators—manual-training men at that—James Parton Haney, Director of Art and Manual Training in the New York City Schools, and Charles Richards, a professor of the pedagogy of manual training at Teachers College, Columbia University. It was at their instigation that a small group came together at the Engineers' Club in New York City early in June to explore the possibilities. This produced the appointment of a subcommittee for intensive work aimed at a large meeting in the fall.

The subcommittee did its work well. On November 16, some 250 industrialists, labor leaders, social workers, and educators assembled at Cooper Union, New York City, to ponder about what was needed in industrial education. The Society was formally organized, with Henry S. Pritchett of the Massachusetts Institute of Technology, and also of the Carnegie Foundation, as president. Nicholas Murray Butler was there with a speech. So was Jane Addams, who tied industrial education to social reform by pointing out that Germany had not only established great technical schools but also "waked up to the fact that human welfare is a legitimate object for Governmental action." German educators, she said, had made it their business to uncover and develop power in the people.[20] Industrialist Milton P. Higgins of Massachusetts paid tribute to Haney and Richards as the originators of the idea for the Society.[21] Samuel B. Donnelly, Secretary of the General Arbitration Board

[19] *Ibid.,* p. 31.
[20] Jane Addams, "Address," *Proceedings of the Organization Meetings,* National Society for the Promotion of Industrial Education, Bulletin No. 1 (New York: The Society, 1907), p. 39.
[21] Milton P. Higgins, NSPIE, Bulletin No. 1, 1907, pp. 15–16.

of the New York Building Trades, spoke in favor of industrial schools and expressed optimism about a change of mind toward them on the part of labor.[22]

According to its constitution, the objects of the Society were "to bring to public attention the importance of industrial education," to provide for study and discussion of "the problem," to draw on experience in the field, and "to promote the establishment of institutions for industrial training."[23] The kinds of institutions were unspecified, but the Society, in a note to the constitution, disclaimed the intention of moving immediately toward trade schools, since there was at the moment no agreement about the form such schools should take.[24] Some educators accepted industrial education, but did not favor trade schools. Among these was still enrolled the doughty champion of manual training, C. M. Woodward, who objected to public trade schools and to the conversion of manual-training high schools to the purposes of trades training. Richards himself had written only two years before that trades training was impracticable in the public schools.[25]

II

Soon NEA meeting halls were ringing with oratory and resolutions on behalf of industrial education. At the winter meeting of the Department of Superintendence in Chicago, February, 1907, Superintendent F. B. Dyer of Cincinnati said that "the trade school in some form will come shortly to every city."[26] Superintendent L. D. Harvey of Menomonie, Wisconsin, gave the same audience a detailed report on Miss Kingsbury's paper and spelled out what he considered to be its implications. Although he said that the 25,000 children had left school "for a variety of reasons," he argued that industrial education would induce many to remain in school. For this "class of children," he said, trade schools were needed. He discounted the alleged opposition of labor leaders, saying that many of them had already committed themselves to trade schools. What he meant by trade schools were institutions whose

[22] Samuel B. Donnelly, NSPIE, Bulletin No. 1, 1907, p. 35.
[23] Constitution, NSPIE, Bulletin No. 1, 1907, p. 10.
[24] Note, NSPIE, Bulletin No. 1, 1907, p. 8.
[25] Charles R. Richards, "Is Manual Training a Subject or a Method of Instruction?" *Educational Review* (April, 1904), p. 371.
[26] F. B. Dyer, "Is There Need for Industrial Schools for Pupils Unlikely To Complete the Regular Elementary-School Course and Go on to the High School? Should It Provide Trade Instruction?" NEA, 1907, p. 315.

prime purpose would be "to fit boys and girls between the ages of four-teen and sixteen to earn a living," places where the pupils could "begin the mastery of some trade."[27] Terminology was not exact, and Harvey's definition of the trade school was to make it more fluid still. Soon it would be difficult to tell what the advocates and opponents of trade schools were for or against. Nevertheless, at its summer meeting the NEA called for trade schools at public expense whenever conditions justified their establishment. It was the duty of the state, according to the NEA, not only to teach citizenship, but to qualify children to be useful mem-bers of the community.[28]

The next major pronouncement came from none other than the Pres-ident of the United States. "Our school system," declared Theodore Roosevelt in his annual message to Congress on December 3, 1907, "is gravely defective in so far as it puts a premium upon mere literacy train-ing and tends therefore to train the boy away from the farm and the workshop. Nothing is more needed than the best type of industrial school, the school for mechanical industries in the city, the school for practically teaching agriculture in the country."[29] Two months later he addressed the Department of Superintendence at its winter meeting, de-manding that education be "directed more and more toward training boys and girls back to the farm and the shop."[30] Roosevelt's words indi-cated his awareness of the agrarian reform movement as a possible force in the direction of industrial education.

By 1908 the vocational issue was clearly dominant in the schools. "We are besieged," wrote the State Superintendent of New Hampshire, "with public documents, monographs, magazine articles, reports of in-vestigations too numerous to mention, etc., etc."[31] It was truly an amaz-ing phenomenon. So far as the educators were concerned, particularly those in the NEA, industrial education provided an exciting subject to talk about. The school men were now in a new mood, one in which the so-called "academic subjects," whether classical or modern, no longer commanded first attention.

Probably no single event more clearly demonstrated the new mood

[27] L. D. Harvey, "Is There Need for, etc.?" NEA, 1907, pp. 310–313.

[28] Declaration of Principles, NEA, 1907, p. 29.

[29] Theodore Roosevelt, "Annual Message, December 3, 1907," in *The Abridge-ments 1907*, Vol. 1, pp. 30–31.

[30] Theodore Roosevelt, address, *Educator-Journal* (April, 1908), p. 382.

[31] Henry C. Morrison, "Vocational Training and Industrial Education," *Educa-tional Review* (October, 1908), p. 242.

than the speech delivered by Eliot at the Chicago meeting of the NSPIE in 1908. The appearance of Eliot was, of course, a major triumph for the leaders of the campaign. He began by advocating trade schools, defining these as part-time or full-time continuation schools "for those children who are unfortunately obliged to leave the regular public school system by the time they are fourteen, or even earlier."[32] This did not necessarily contradict his long-maintained opposition to early differentiation of school programs. Presumably the children he had in mind would get the same program as others up to the time they had to leave "the regular public school system." He did not explain how they could then afford to go to full-time trade school.

Up to this point in the speech Eliot had been talking about children who were "unfortunately obliged" to leave school at an early age. Then he suddenly switched his line of thought to consider how children should be selected for industrial schools, ordinary high schools, or mechanic-arts high schools. "Here we come upon a new function for the teachers in our elementary schools," declared Eliot; these teachers "ought to sort the pupils and sort them by their evident or probable destinies." This kind of early selection, based on "probable destinies," was the very doctrine he had so eloquently attacked in his speech defending the Committee of Ten less than three years before. Moreover, he said, such selection was democratic, since it was practiced in democratic Switzerland.[33] "We must guide each child," he concluded, "into that path in which he can be most successful and happy," with each child "put at that work which the teacher believes the child can do best." This would give each child "the happiness of achievement," and it would be consistent thereby with "the best definition of democracy."[34]

This was indeed a new Eliot, with a few overtones, somewhat strangely recast, of the old. It would perhaps be an exaggeration to say that the age of Eliot was here ended by Eliot himself. Still, the speech was an enigma.[35] Less than three months later he presented to the

[32] Charles W. Eliot, "Industrial Education as an Essential Factor in Our National Prosperity," NSPIE, Bulletin No. 5, 1908, p. 9.

[33] *Ibid.*, pp. 12–13.

[34] *Ibid.*, pp. 13–14.

[35] Evidently there were some protests against this speech, for *School Journal* claimed Eliot had been misrepresented by newspapers "with a scent for the sensational possibilities." *School Journal* (April, 1908), p. 687. The above summary and quotations, however, have been taken from the official version published by the NSPIE in its proceedings. As was his practice in most controversies, Eliot did not seek to justify himself. Many years later, he reaffirmed his earlier point of

Northern Indiana Teachers' Association a somewhat modified version of his new commitment, saying that boys at thirteen should have opportunity to choose industrial occupations and that teachers should help in such choices.[36] Furthermore, he insisted before the Indiana teachers, industrial education at that age should be theoretical, with emphasis on the sciences underlying "the universal trades" and on the historical aspects.[37] This was not necessarily a repudiation of what he had said at Chicago, but it was a substantial modification of it.

III

Whether he intended it or not, what Eliot did in his Chicago speech was to bring out for explicit discussion the central issue of the campaign. Few educators cared to support the proposition that industrial education was designed for the purpose of furnishing employers with a supply of skilled labor. Presumably it was for the benefit of the pupils. Then the question was, Which pupils? One of the difficulties with Eliot's speech was that he presented two answers to this question. His first answer pointed to pupils who had to leave school anyway because of circumstances, mainly economic; his second answer pointed to pupils selected by teachers on the basis of their aptitudes.

There were other possible answers. Miss Kingsbury's paper implied that industrial education should be provided for pupils who left school because it did not provide what they wanted; these dissatisfied pupils would remain if they could get industrial education. This was a sort of application of Eliot's second answer, differing from it in that the selection would be made by the pupils themselves, allegedly on the basis, not of their aptitudes, but of their dissatisfactions. In this way, industrial education, like manual training earlier, was summoned as a solution of the drop-out problem, not in the high school itself, but in the grades immediately preceding high school.

Neither Eliot nor Miss Kingsbury viewed industrial education as a haven or dumping-ground for academically inept or unscholarly pupils. This suggestion, however, had great appeal and kept turning up like the

---

view about postponing as long as possible "the partings of ways." See his "American Education since the Civil War" in *A Late Harvest* (Boston: Little, Brown and Co., 1924), pp. 136–138.

[36] Charles W. Eliot, "The Elements of a Liberal Education," *Educator-Journal* (June, 1908), p. 501.

[37] *Ibid.*, pp. 503–504.

proverbial bad penny. "Few boys," said one eager proponent of the cause back in 1893, "are mentally fitted to be scholars or to take a University course. The majority are well-constituted mentally to be good artisans, men of business, agriculturalists."[38] James Parton Haney, one of the founders of the NSPIE and a manual-arts man himself, recommended that schools organize "preparatory vocational courses for boys in the lower grades who are duller mentally than their mates."[39] On another occasion Haney said that some who could do excellent manual work were not "attracted by work which demands much mental activity, and fall behind in classes where a high standard of mental achievement is set."[40] Another used the term "academic misfits" for pupils who ought to be directed to trade schools.[41] Through industrial education, then, the unscholarly pupil could be saved from dropping out of school or worse. Some saw it as a preventive of truancy. Superintendent Lorenzo D. Harvey felt it would make useful citizens of "those who otherwise would quickly and surely pass to the parallel path of crime with its entailment of expense to the public, of public demoralization, and of individual debasement."[42]

Another body of opinion saw industrial education, not as the haven of refuge for pupils of low academic ability, but as particularly appropriate for certain social and economic classes in society. Here, it seemed, was the answer to education for the "masses." In part, this was a twentieth-century extension of Horace Mann's ideals of social uplift through education, calculated to improve the economic conditions of the poor. It also reflected the feeling, however, that it was necessary to find some kind of education the masses would appreciate and understand. "Education, today," said a teacher in the Boston English High School in 1905, "demands that industrial and commercial training be given in the schools, to the common people, for their immediate and practical benefit and for their future welfare and development."[43] James Earl Russell, of

[38] Herbert Miller, "The Differentiation of the High School, the Coming Movement in Education," *School Review* (September, 1893), p. 422.

[39] James Parton Haney, "Manual Training as a Preventive of Truancy," *Education* (June, 1907), p. 640.

[40] James Parton Haney, "Vocational Work for the Elementary School," *Educational Review* (November, 1907), p. 335.

[41] George W. Benton, "Some Problems of Secondary Education," NC, 1911, p. 13.

[42] L. D. Harvey, "The Need, Scope, and Character of Industrial Education in the Public-School System," NEA, 1909, p. 59.

[43] Frank O. Carpenter, "Phases of Modern Education," *Education* (December, 1905), p. 194.

Teachers College, Columbia, felt that universities and professional schools were doing their job, but that the next step was to see "the common man" equally well provided for.[44] Principal J. Remsen Bishop of Cincinnati urged the development of the high school as "distinctively a preparatory school for men and women who are to enter at once into the industrial life of the community"[45] and hoped that "the strange increase" in Latin enrollments would cease as business courses absorbed more pupils. He was not, like Dewey and Jane Addams, seeking a new synthesis of cultural and practical education. "It is just as important," he declared, "that the few should devote themselves to the classics and keep alive for us the sacred fire of pure taste, as it is that the many should be fitted for some active labor."[46]

One of the questions that continued to perplex educators was that of education, vocational or otherwise, for girls. It was assumed by many that girls, allegedly ineligible for professional careers, particularly stood in need of practical education. The proponents of this practical education for girls, however, could not agree among themselves on the relative merits of preparing girls for paid jobs or for unpaid homemaking. Some argued for both. The school subject that started out as *cooking and sewing,* and that went through a long career of terminology including *housewifery, domestic science,* and *home economics,* was usually categorized among the industrial, practical, or vocational studies. Although training in this field did sometimes lead to paid jobs, it was for the most part aimed at homemaking. Nevertheless it ended up in the later Smith-Hughes Law as a full-fledged partner in the vocational enterprise, eligible for federal grants though business education, to prepare girls for paid jobs, was not. This was partly a result of its connection with vocational agriculture in the rural reform movement. It was also a reflection of the persistence and determination of leaders in the field of home economics, such as Ellen H. Richards, who believed that woman's place was truly in the home but wanted to establish homemaking itself on a technical or scientific basis. Work, said Mrs. Richards in 1909, could be put back into the home (a statement that might have surprised many housewives who thought it was still there), but it was the work of the brain. Technical homemaking training, including manual arts, was

[44] James E. Russell, "The Trend in American Education," *Educational Review* (June, 1906), p. 40.
[45] J. Remsen Bishop, "The Function of the High School of Today," NEA, 1901, p. 572.
[46] *Ibid.,* p. 574.

therefore needed for girls. "Woman will then choose the household as her profession," continued Mrs. Richards, "not because she sees no other way of supporting herself, not because it is a traditional inheritance; but because she will there find the means to give the best of strength and skill and knowledge for the betterment of mankind."[47] The triumph of home economics did not, however, prevent the development of the business subjects. In the meantime many girls continued to use the academic programs of the high schools as direct vocational preparation for the teaching positions they could get immediately after graduation.

IV

In addition to selecting their clientele, the proponents of industrial education had to decide who should administer this new venture. The Massachusetts law passed at the instigation of the Douglas Commission provided for separate state-wide administration of industrial education under the new Commission for Industrial Education as well as for separate boards in the local communities. It was up to Chairman Paul Hanus and his associates to persuade local communities to set up the new "independent industrial schools" on this basis. Even with the inducements provided by state aid, in some instances up to one-half the cost, this did not prove to be an easy task. George H. Martin, then Secretary of the Massachusetts State Board of Education, did not welcome the development of a whole system of schools under separate auspices.[48] Martin had been a member of the Douglas Commission himself, but apparently had not foreseen the consequences of establishing a new and permanent Commission.

The dispute was reminiscent of the earlier and abiding one about whether or not there should be separate high schools for manual training

---

[47] Ellen H. Richards, "Influence of Industrial Arts and Sciences upon Rural and City Home Life: from the Standpoint of Domestic Science," NEA, 1909, p. 639.

[48] "From time to time," wrote Chairman Hanus, "when we tried to get a community interested in founding a vocational school (with a separate local board in immediate control as specified by the law), we found that an agent of the state board had been before us and had cultivated public opinion against such a school under our auspices, the agent having stated in effect, that there was no need of a separate local board under the commission to do what the local school committee could do with the help of the state board." Paul H. Hanus, *Adventuring in Education* (Cambridge, Mass.: Harvard University Press, 1937), p. 171.

or for commerce. It had, however, a new dimension, a frightening one to many of the school men. Though the manual-training high schools were separate from other high schools, they came under the administration of the regular board and superintendent; these new schools were to be controlled by somebody else. Moreover, the advocates of separate administration plainly showed their lack of confidence in the disposition or ability of the regular school men to conduct vocational education. This was part of the current disdain for the manual-training schools and the manual-training people who were still unreconstructed. Industrial schools under the regular system, said Commissioner Andrew S. Draper of the State of New York, had "been arranged by men who were essentially theorists and not specially skilful as craftsmen themselves."[49] He warned that "the 'culturists' must not be allowed to appropriate the technical and trades schools to their own refined uses."[50]

The deadlock in Massachusetts led in 1909 to the abolition of the Commission on Industrial Education and a change in the membership of the State Board. Jurisdiction over vocational as well as other kinds of education was assigned to the State Board, its membership now including Paul Hanus, Chairman of the abolished Industrial Education Commission. An office of Commissioner was created to replace the old position of Secretary first held by Horace Mann. It was one of the new men in education, David Snedden of Teachers College, Columbia, who became the first Commissioner under the reorganized system.

Regardless of who gained control of the new enterprise, there remained the question of the kinds of schools suitable for the purposes of industrial education. Manual-training high schools were no longer in favor, but many school men continued to be fearful of anything called a trade school. The Superintendent of the Cleveland Public Schools carefully explained in 1908 that the technical high school in his city was neither "a manual-training school nor . . . a trade school," but was "allied to each."[51] The school provided wood-turning and cabinetmaking, pattern-making, foundry, blacksmithing, tool-forging, and machine-shop practice. The Superintendent said that it should also relate the academic subjects to vocational ends and suggested that "the study of the great

[49] Andrew S. Draper, "From Manual Training to Technical and Trades Schools," *Educational Review* (April, 1908), p. 403.
[50] *Ibid.*, p. 410.
[51] William H. Elson, "The Technical High School of Cleveland," *School Review* (June, 1908), p. 353.

industrial authors such as Carlyle, Ruskin, and William Morris" could "supplant in part the more purely literary authors."[52]

New York City had three public evening trade schools for apprentices sixteen to twenty years of age. In September, 1909, however, it opened what was called a "day vocational school," designed for boys who left school at fourteen. The Associate Superintendent, like his colleague in Cleveland, took pains to emphasize what this school was not, although he eventually got around to saying what it was. "This school," he said, "is not to be a manual training high school; it is not to be a technical high school; it is not to be a combination of an academic school, a commercial and a trade school under one head; it is not to be a compromise; it is not to be a tail to any kite; it will not emphasize scholarship; it will not be narrowly utilitarian; it will not graduate finished journeymen or skilled mechanics, but, it will be a preparatory trade school."[53] Entering pupils were required to state their intention to pursue some handicraft trade. The course was one or two years in length. Elementary school graduates were admitted without examination, fourteen-year-old non-graduates under certain conditions. The work was exploratory for those who had not decided on a given trade, but those who had decided were allowed to specialize. Trades were grouped in the broad categories of metal work, wood work, and printing. Metal work included machine shop and sheet metal work, forging, plumbing, and electrical wiring and installation. Academic work was provided in mathematics, from arithmetic through trigonometry; English; industrial history and geography; and applied physics and chemistry. Bookkeeping and commercial law also appeared in the program.[54]

This New York school met many of the criteria implied in the vocational movement and avoided some of the dilemmas. It was designed specifically for the fourteen-to-sixteen-year-old group, to which Miss Kingsbury's paper had called attention. Substantial work was provided both in shop subjects and in related academic fields. Obviously it was not a dumping-ground, for it required either the completion of elementary school or the meeting of other requirements for entrance. Neither was it explicitly aimed at any particular social class. It was not a trade school, but it helped pupils get ready for trades. Presumably those who finished this school were qualified to become apprentices and to enter

[52] *Ibid.*, pp. 354–355.

[53] Gustave Straubenmuller, "Industrial Education as Embodied in the New Vocational School in New York City," *Education* (April, 1910), p. 519.

[54] *Ibid.*, pp. 521–524.

the evening trade schools. On the whole, this school came about as close as anything in existence to the ideal "independent industrial school" so much under discussion at the time.

Nevertheless, it presented some difficulties insofar as general application to other communities was concerned, as well as some that applied even in the City of New York. In general it was only large metropolitan or industrial centers that could maintain a school of this kind. Costs were prohibitive unless fairly large numbers of pupils could be involved. There were exceptions, such as the all-day trade school in the public school system of Saginaw, Michigan, with its two-year course for entrants at least fourteen years of age. Over a four-year period, however, only 32 pupils finished the course in this school—but a private citizen had contributed $180,000 for the building of the manual-training high school in which the trade school had its quarters.[55] The difficulty that applied even in the larger centers was an economic one of another kind. In spite of Miss Kingsbury's optimistic statistics, many pupils at fourteen could not afford to attend a full-time day school of any kind without the opportunity of earning money at the same time.

One proposed solution to these dilemmas was offered in the work-study plan inaugurated with 60 pupils in 1908–1909 in the public schools of Fitchburg, Massachusetts. The idea for this had been picked up by "several Fitchburg industrialists" from a widely discussed plan used at the University of Cincinnati to provide shop experience for students of engineering. Pupils enrolled in the program at Fitchburg spent the first year entirely in the high school and the following three years both studying in school and working in local shops, during alternating weeks. The academic part of the course included English, history, algebra, physics, chemistry, commercial geography, business methods, and shop mathematics.

Since the pupils did their shop work in the industrial plants of the community, the school did not have to provide expensive equipment for the practical part of their training. Moreover, the pupils were paid at a wage scale running from 10 cents an hour during the first year to 12½ cents during the third year of the work-study part of the course. According to calculations, the pupils were able to earn $552.75 during the three-year period.[56] If these wages seem low (and they were not in relation to children's wages at the time), it should be kept in mind that

[55] E. C. Warriner, "The All-Day Trades School," NEA, 1915, pp. 313–319.
[56] W. B. Hunter, "The Fitchburg Plan of Industrial Education," NC, 1910, p. 48.

the over-all sum of more than five hundred dollars may have consti-tuted for many families a sufficient amount to enable them to allow their children to remain in school.

The essential feature of such plans as this was that children and youth could go to work and continue their schooling at the same time. With some modifications, this combination of study and work was also a fea-ture of what were coming to be known as continuation schools. Prior to serving as Chairman of the Massachusetts Commission on Industrial Education, Paul Hanus of Harvard had spent the winter of his sabbatical year (1904–1905) in Munich, Germany, where he observed continu-ation schools being operated under the direction of Superintendent Georg Kerschensteiner. Under the Munich plan, elementary school grad-uates who went to work attended these schools for six to twelve hours a week during a period of three years. The schools were aimed directly at the trades and provided a combination of academic studies and trades training. Hanus found much to admire in these schools, but criticized the system on the ground that training for managerial or executive po-sitions was not available to graduates of elementary schools.[57]

Soon the term *continuation schools* became a popular one in the United States. At first it was loosely used to mean any kind of continued education beyond the end of formal schooling, whenever that might occur. Eliot used the term in this sense in his Chicago speech to the NSPIE in 1908. It came, however, to mean, more specifically, a part-time school for employed children and youth below a designated age, usually sixteen, preferably during time released from the scheduled hours of work.

The Cincinnati Public Schools, under the direction of the regular board of education, established such a school for machine-shop ap-prentices in September, 1909. Pupils attended the school one half-day each week and were paid by their employers for the time. Both the Cen-tral Labor Council of the city and a committee of manufacturers gave their approval to the plan. Proponents of it succeeded in getting the Ohio legislature to pass a law in 1910 authorizing local boards to es-tablish such schools and to require attendance of those who went to work at less than sixteen years of age.[58] Cincinnati was one of the first cities to take action under the law, and so also was Cleveland.

[57] Hanus, *op. cit.*, pp. 166–167.
[58] F. B. Dyer, "Industrial Education in Cincinnati," *School Review* (May, 1911), p. 294.

Boston, never far behind on new ideas, opened several continuation schools in 1910. There also the plan involved the cooperation of employers in providing released time during working hours, with pay. One school established in Boston was designed for boys and girls working in retail stores as stock clerks, bundle clerks, and cashiers. Another school was devoted to banking and one, presumably for girls who were employed, to household arts.[59]

During 1910–1911, the NSPIE sponsored a series of lectures given by the man whose name had become practically synonymous with continuation schools, Georg Kerschensteiner of Munich. Although he talked on other aspects of vocational education as well, Kerschensteiner concentrated on continuation schools, and his lectures, published in 1911 by the Commercial Club of Chicago, helped give wide publicity to the idea. There were few, if any, who held out against it. Both the American Federation of Labor and the National Association of Manufacturers endorsed the idea in their 1911 conventions.

It was not long, however, before continuation schools became entangled with the perplexing question whether or not there should be separate boards. The Ohio law permitted their establishment under the regular local administrations. In Wisconsin a comprehensive law passed in 1911 for vocational education, including a system of continuation schools, required separate local boards. A proposal for a similar law in Illinois a year later revived all the acrimony of the earlier conflict in Massachusetts and created, for educators at least, a national issue. There the Commercial Club of Chicago, joined by three other organizations, sponsored what became known in the state legislature as the Cooley bill, so named from its author, Edwin G. Cooley, a former Superintendent of the Chicago Public Schools. Labor leaders and educators joined forces to resist the bill, with its proposal for separate vocational boards, and it was never passed. In October, 1913, in its seventh annual convention, held at Grand Rapids, Michigan,[60] the NSPIE sponsored a full-dress debate on what had by then become known as "unit versus dual control." John Dewey appeared as a speaker against dual control, and he was to continue from then on his resistance to what he considered to be a threat to the unity of the public school system.

Continuation schools kept on thriving in spite of the controversy in

[59] Documents of the Boston School Committee, as quoted by Frank M. Leavitt, *Examples of Industrial Education* (Boston: Ginn and Co., 1912), pp. 230–234.
[60] *School Review* (December, 1913), pp. 701–702.

which they had become involved. Perhaps the school men were encouraged by what many of them considered to be the successful outcome of the battle in Illinois. So far as employers were concerned, they continued to back the idea even though it cost them money. Organized labor did not object, especially when adequate safeguards were established and maintained for the apprenticeship system. Furthermore, those who sought to raise the age for compulsory schooling found in continuation schools a mechanism for partial achievement of their aims. It was to them a compromise that promised much not only for industrial education, but for a wider extension of popular schooling as well.

In the movement for social welfare, the continuation schools also represented a great step forward. They registered telling blows against long hours of child labor at a time when even the most advanced states permitted these for children fourteen years of age. In 1907 an enlightened Massachusetts manufacturer, in a speech on industrial education before the Harvard Teachers' Association, had taken great pride in the fact that his state permitted children of fourteen to be worked only 58 hours a week and that his own plant had cut this voluntarily to 55; he warned, however, that Massachusetts must not become hysterical on the subject and that it could not afford to move too far ahead of other states.[61] Three years later, employers in Boston were releasing their child workers four hours a week with pay for continued education. This was not much by today's standards, but it was significant at the time.

V

The success of the continuation school movement did not settle the question of how to fit vocationalism into the high schools. In the new climate after 1905, many educators joined those who had previously drawn a sharp distinction between finishing and fitting pupils. However, the distinction was now being drawn, not between the modern subjects and the classics, but between subjects called practical and academic. The high school enrollment increased mightily between 1905 and 1910, but many pupils continued to take what more and more of the school men regarded as the wrong subjects. Latin still claimed half the enrollment at a time when doubts were being expressed even about German

61 Charles W. Hubbard, "Industrial Education," *School Review* (May, 1907), pp. 392–393.

and French. There was little enthusiasm, however, for creating more high schools of commerce or manual arts. The favored device, especially in the large cities, was to add vocational and semivocational courses of study to the already overloaded course structure of the general high schools. One writer in 1914 rejoiced in noting that, although the Los Angeles high schools eight years before had offered only four courses of study, they now boasted 48 such courses or "curriculums,"[62] as they were coming to be known in some quarters. In consequence of this proliferation, the elective principle came increasingly to be understood as election by courses rather than subjects. The vocational courses of study were the ones being thought of as designed for finishing pupils, but at the same time there was an increasing demand for the recognition of vocational subjects for college admission.

Neither did continuation schools resolve the difficulties pertaining to elementary education. Ideally, they were designed to serve elementary school graduates, but more than half the children in Miss Kingsbury's study had not finished the seventh grade. One question, therefore, was how to attract more children to stay in elementary school until they finished. Another was how to make the work of the elementary school more immediately practical for those who would not, or could not, stay. Still another involved the appropriateness of the regular elementary school studies for pupils who, after graduation, would go to work and continuation school or who would enter a full-time trade or industrial school. Meanwhile there remained the pupils who intended to take, or who might take, the conventional high-school programs.

Out of all this came an advocacy of what was called *differentiation,* a term applied particularly in relation to the seventh and eighth grades. Just as the high schools distinguished between pupils who were and were not preparing for college, so would the grade schools in turn distinguish between those who were and were not preparing for high school, and even between those planning to take academic and vocational courses of study. This was by no means a new idea. The Latin Grammar School in Boston had provided such differentiation, and in separate schools. Proponents of the new differentiation used the Boston example as an argument in their cause. If the community, they asked, could provide differentiated elementary schooling for those planning to enter

---

[62] Charles Hughes Johnston, "Curriculum Adjustments in Modern High Schools," *School Review* (November, 1914), p. 590.

"professions," why should it not do so for those who would immediately enter business or industrial life?

An early proposal for this came from James Parton Haney in 1907. Proceeding, as did many others, from the findings of the Douglas Commission in Massachusetts, Haney recommended a modified program for certain elementary schools in the sixth, seventh, and eighth grades. Shop work, he said, should occupy about one-fourth of the time in the sixth and seventh grades and slightly more than one-third in the eighth —many elementary schools already required some manual training of all pupils, but in smaller amounts. In addition, American history should be taught with "particular emphasis on the industrial development of the country, on inventions and discoveries and their results." Other subjects included in his program were English, geography, arithmetic, drawing, physics, nature study, business law, and physical training. This was an ambitious program indeed, one that involved a school week of 2100 minutes or an average of seven solid hours per day.[63]

In 1910 the Cleveland Public Schools announced the inauguration of dual programs in grades five through eight. "The needs of children destined to terminate their school education with the elementary school," said the Superintendent and Assistant Superintendent in a joint statement, "are very different from children so situated that they may continue their schooling in higher institutions." They also declared it obvious that the educational needs of children "in a district where the streets are well paved and clean, where the homes are spacious and surrounded by lawns and trees, where the language of the child's playfellows is pure, and where life in general is permeated with the spirit and ideals of America" were different from those of children in foreign and tenement sections.[64] The differences were not specified.

Similar arguments, increasing in volume and number, continued to be advanced in the years following 1910. Secretary Charles A. Prosser of the NSPIE, the future initiator of the "life-adjustment" movement, said in 1912 that the usual elementary schools in cities of 50,000 or more "might well offer for the seventh and eighth years a high-school preparatory course, a commercial course, a household arts course for girls and a practical arts course for boys."[65] Professor Frank M. Leavitt of

[63] Haney, op. cit., pp. 343–346.

[64] William H. Elson and Frank P. Bachman, "Different Courses for Elementary Schools," Educational Review (April, 1910), pp. 359–362.

[65] Charles A. Prosser, "Practical Arts and Vocational Guidance," NEA, 1912, p. 650.

the University of Chicago felt that the selection of a differentiated course in the seventh and eighth grades should not bar the pupil from further schooling, but that the possibilities should be entrance into a trade school or into a vocational course in a high school. "Pupils should *not* expect," he said, "to enter upon the classical high-school course with the same chances of success as those who did not differentiate their work at the seventh grade."[66]

The point of view of some advocates of differentiation was indicated in the statement of Professor E. V. Robinson of the University of Minnesota that children differentiated themselves. "We do not put them on the scrap-heap; they put themselves there. We do not pick them out to go into the professions or to go into the shop. They pick themselves out, or circumstances sort them out." To provide for this, he said, there must be differentiation and as low as the seventh grade.[67] Charles Hubbard Judd of the University of Chicago approached the matter in more humanitarian terms, declaring that "the boy who is going into the trades and has no thought of high school cannot with equity be required to do the same work that is required of the boy who is going to become a clergyman and looks forward to a college education."[68]

In the meantime a new possibility emerged, that of intermediate industrial schools, serving pupils who would otherwise be in the upper grades and in the first year or two of high school. Charles De Garmo in 1909 advocated what he called a "junior industrial high school" with a four-year course beginning after the sixth grade. This, he felt, would provide "a new type of education needed for the millions."[69] Like so many others, De Garmo summoned the Douglas Commission as a witness for his point of view. A year later, a subcommittee of the NEA Committee on the Place of Industries in General Education, deploring what it called a tendency in school administration to deflect vocational education "toward general or liberal ends," recommended intermediate industrial schools.[70] Professor Frank M. Leavitt of the University of Chicago in 1910 cited the existence of schools along these lines, par-

[66] Leavitt, *op. cit.,* p. 66.
[67] E. V. Robinson, discussion, NC, 1913, pp. 123–125.
[68] Charles Hubbard Judd, "The Meaning of Secondary Education," *School Review* (January, 1913), p. 13.
[69] Charles De Garmo, "Relation of Industrial to General Education," *School Review* (March, 1909), pp. 150–153.
[70] Carleton Gibson, "Report of Subcommittee on Intermediate Industrial Schools," NEA, 1910, p. 720.

ticularly the Secondary Industrial School of Columbus, Georgia, identified as a new type of secondary school.

By this time, however, few school men were inclined to accept separate or special schools, even those called intermediate. What proved more attractive to them was the creation of separate courses of study, including those that were vocational or semivocational in nature, in a general intermediate school, thereby providing for election of courses below the ninth grade without creating separate schools. In January, 1910, Superintendent Frank Bunker of Berkeley, California, possibly responding to local circumstances in the distribution of pupils and buildings, started what were called introductory high schools, including grades seven through nine. Ben W. Johnson, Director of Manual Training in Seattle, was quick to see the possibilities and to point them out in a speech to the Department of Superintendence. Expressing his disapproval of separate academic and industrial schools at the intermediate level, he pointed out that the Berkeley arrangement could be used to provide preapprenticeship or industrial work in a general intermediate school.[71] Intermediate schools, some of them with seventh and eighth grades only, had existed before that time, but the movement took hold after 1910, with the term *junior high school* rapidly gaining in popularity. By 1912 Los Angeles had five intermediate schools of the three-year type. Each intermediate school provided three courses of study designated, respectively, as general, commercial, and elementary industrial.[72] In the minds of many, the ideal solution had been found for children like the 25,000 in Miss Kingsbury's report.

Enthusiasm for early differentiation reached its peak at the Cincinnati meeting of the Department of Superintendence in 1915, with the passing of a resolution that bestowed approval on "the increasing tendency to establish, beginning with the seventh grade, differentiated courses of study aimed more effectively to prepare the child for his probable future activities." According to the record, the only member to speak against this resolution was William H. Maxwell, Superintendent of Schools in New York City, one of the few men of the moderate revision still active at this time. What Maxwell found unacceptable was the theory that children of twelve years of age were "prepared to elect their future course of instruction and presumably their future life

[71] Ben W. Johnson, "Industrial Education in the Elementary School," NEA, 1910, pp. 254–255.
[72] J. H. Francis, "A Reorganization of Our School System," NEA, 1912, p. 371.

work."[73] One of the new men in education, Charles Hughes Johnston of the University of Illinois, confessed himself unable to understand Maxwell's point.

VI

One important by-product of the campaign for industrial education was vocational guidance. The need for guidance or counseling had, of course, been implicit in the elective principle, whether election was by courses or subjects; terms such as *counselor* and *counseling* were in use before 1900. Whether election was by course or subject, practically everyone agreed on the need for "wise direction" of pupils by parents, teachers, and principals. Eliot's speech to the NSPIE in 1908 was, in effect, an extreme view of the wisdom of direction by teachers. Few shared this view with him, but there were many who agreed with the modified version of assistance by teachers that he presented shortly afterward.

Vocationalism, of course, presented more strenuous demands on the counseling process; and "vocational guidance" as a planned enterprise began to take over the informal arrangements. As in so many other matters, the major initial thrust took place in Boston, although a teacher in New York City named Eli Weaver was referred to as "the father" of vocational guidance.[74] In Boston the work had its origin in the social welfare movement, and the Vocation Bureau was founded as a private philanthropic venture by Mrs. Quincy A. Shaw and other "liberal-minded men and women" in 1908, under the direction of Frank Parsons. Mrs. Shaw had previously been active in the promotion of kindergartens and manual training. The Boston Public School established a "Vocational Direction Committee" to work with the Vocation Bureau. Soon the Bureau was training those teachers who were being appointed to serve as "vocational counselors" in the elementary and secondary schools.

In June, 1910, twice as many graduates of the elementary schools in Boston as could be admitted stated their desire to enter the High School of Commerce and the High School of Practical Arts. Prior to this time the pupils had been selected by lot "on the basis of scholarship," but

---

[73] Department of Superintendence, Secretary's Minutes, NEA, 1915, pp. 256–257.
[74] *School and Society* (March 22, 1919), p. 354.

now the "existence of the vocational counselors rendered possible a different and a better procedure." The newly created vocational counselors did the selecting, using as bases the tastes and aptitudes of the pupils as displayed in the elementary school.[75]

The inevitable First National Conference on Vocational Guidance took place in Boston in November, 1910, under the joint sponsorship of the Vocation Bureau and the Chamber of Commerce, with several hundred persons present. There were delegates from 45 cities, including New York, Baltimore, Pittsburgh, Chicago, and Grand Rapids.[76] One of the participants was Principal Jesse B. Davis of Grand Rapids, who was already at work on the matter. In March of 1911 he reported to the North Central Association his plan of using six "session-room teachers" as vocational counselors, with teaching duties limited to three recitations a day, each in charge of about 250 pupils. These teachers worked with him as "a sort of cabinet" on vocational guidance, serving as vocational counselors, while he assumed the responsibilities of "chief counselor."[77] He did not, however, see vocational counseling as a new profession and advocated that it be regarded as "a broadening out of the opportunity and duty of the school principal."[78]

Throughout 1911 and 1912 there was much speech-making and other activity on behalf of this new offshoot of industrial education. Vocational guidance came to Chicago when the Association of Commerce, "seeking for some field not now occupied by other associations," involved the Board of Education and other groups in the creation of a bureau for vocational guidance.[79] The NSPIE, under the leadership of its new secretary, Charles A. Prosser, also took up vocational guidance, and its 1913 convention at Grand Rapids became the occasion for forming a new society, the National Vocational Guidance Association. Prosser urged the particular importance of vocational guidance at age fourteen, on the grounds that children had to decide at that age whether or not

[75] Stratton Brooks, "Vocational Guidance," *School Review* (January, 1911), pp. 46–47.

[76] Paul H. Hanus, "Vocational Guidance and Public Education," *School Review* (January, 1911), p. 51.

[77] Jesse B. Davis, "Vocational Guidance a Function of the Public School," NC, 1911, p. 98. Davis later became dean of the School of Education at Boston University. His charming and informative autobiography, *The Saga of a Schoolmaster* (Boston: Boston University Press, 1956), contains a good deal of material on the early movement for vocational guidance and other matters pertaining to high schools during his long teaching career.

[78] *Ibid.*, p. 100.

[79] *School Review* (February, 1913), pp. 146–147.

to remain in school, and if so, in what kind of school. The responsibility for vocational guidance, said Prosser, came to the school "as the agent of the state for the welfare of childhood."[80]

Vocational guidance fit readily the desires of many school men to absorb the vocational purpose into a larger realm of practical education. Even though the major victory represented by the Smith-Hughes legislation was yet to come, the vocational campaign by 1913 was losing force among the educators themselves. There was little question that vocational education in some form was a responsibility of the public schools. School men wanted vocational education, but they wanted it under control. The "cosmopolitan high school" serving a variety of purposes was rapidly gaining favor, and a recommendation by the NSPIE in 1913 for separate vocational schools had little chance for popular support among school men. Even less acceptable was the movement for separate boards. As late as 1920, the *School Review* commented bitterly on this as a device to separate industrial education from the common schools.[81]

VII

The movement on the whole was an exceedingly complex one, as is also the task of assessing its value. What is difficult to judge is not vocational education itself—this had already been in progress before 1906—but the intensive campaign of discussion and publicity that followed the Douglas Report. Perhaps vocational education might have developed more satisfactorily without it. Obviously the promoters of the campaign did not think so, and they were impatient for results. By 1913 some developments that may have been results of the campaign could be discerned. Among those pertaining to its direct object—namely, getting more vocational education into the public schools—the most important and enduring were continuation schools and vocational guidance.

Beyond these were some by-products affecting the general work of schools, good or bad depending on the bases used for judging. The campaign undoubtedly reinforced election by courses and, through the advocacy of early "differentiation," thrust this kind of election into the grades preceding the high school. It contributed also to a widespread bias against the so-called academic side of school work, particularly for

[80] C. A. Prosser, *op. cit.,* pp. 646–650.
[81] *School Review* (December, 1920), pp. 721–723.

the alleged "masses." This bias flowed from the attempt to promote industrial education by disparaging the work of what were referred to as the "literary" schools. Those with commitment to the academic tradition found themselves on the defensive. Some of them proudly took up the claim that their subjects were for the chosen few, reflecting perhaps the ancient view of liberal education as something for free men only. In either case, the existence of a sharp conflict between the academic and the practical was accepted; once accepted, it could not easily be removed. The efforts of Dewey and others to create a definition of culture involving both elements were valiant indeed, but it is not possible even now to judge their success.

The campaign could also be judged in relation to need. This question had two aspects. One was the need for skilled workmen to man the labor force of American industry. Such industry, however, had been expanding mightily since the Civil War and without benefit of the industrial education advocated after 1906. Yes, agreed the advocates, but American industries, they continued, had depended on skilled workmen from Europe, the kind allegedly not represented in the "new" immigration. Also, ran the argument, the apprenticeship system under which industry had developed was in a state of collapse and about to disappear. These forebodings about apprenticeship were expressed in several different periods. In the end, apprenticeship did not disappear, but survived as a feature of programs in continuation schools.

Relatively few schools were started for the specific purpose of teaching trades, or even of furnishing preparatory work for trades, as did the day vocational school of New York City. Had American industry depended on getting large numbers of craftsmen from these schools, it would have been in bad shape indeed. There was, in addition, the perennial difficulty of deciding which trades to train for, especially in the face of rapidly changing conditions in the labor market itself. More to the point was the need to develop what the Douglas Commission had called "industrial intelligence." This presumably could have been done by the slighted high schools of manual training. In fact, something very much like this was what Woodward and other advocates of manual training claimed was accomplished in such schools.

The other aspect of need had to do with the pupils themselves. Some pupils, it was claimed, were hand-minded rather than book-minded. The schools had long served the book-minded, preparing them for law, the clergy, and other allegedly bookish professions. Now, ran the argument, they should serve the hand-minded in their occupational goals. This did not represent the idea that industrial education was to absorb the "academic misfits," for it did not imply that one was superior to the other. In effect, this was an argument for the rights of the individual. Again, it is difficult to see why this need could not have been met by the further development of manual training. It so happened that manual training, renamed, with some modification of theory, *industrial arts,* did return to favor, and it was expected to serve pupils with manual interests and talents. Always there was the assumption, underscored by Miss Kingsbury's contentions, that the provision of practical work would encourage such hand-minded children to stay in school. This would have economic value as well as others, for, presumably, children who stayed longer in school would be able to compete more effectively for better-paying jobs.

From another point of view, the need of many pupils was specifically economic. Some children had to leave school early no matter how attractive the program. Whether or not pupils who left school early were helped to get better jobs through the prevocational work of the seventh and eighth grades would be difficult to establish. Continuation schools probably did help those who possessed talents and interest in mechanical trades and who could find apprenticeships to enter. The motive was a worthy one. If the campaign for industrial education helped even a few children along these lines, this was a positive result.

Although the campaign for industrial education based its case in part on the rights of the hand-minded individual, it tended in one respect to disregard individual differences. The difficulty lay in the assumption that all children of the working classes were alike and that all could be helped economically through industrial education, particularly through hand work. Vocational guidance, however, bore the promise of considering all children of all classes as individuals with unique talents to be developed in school. This was always Eliot's ideal and explains in part what he was trying to say in his perhaps ill-chosen words to the NSPIE at Chicago in 1908.

Among other unresolved questions about the vocational campaign is why it came about, particularly why it came about when it did. If it represented a genuine need, was this more true in 1906 than it had been in 1900 or even in 1895? To some extent, it may be interpreted as a pedagogical aspect of the general reform movement. Another possible explanation is that industrialists and political and civic leaders had been waiting for the educators to do something and finally decided to do it for themselves.

Still, educators were active both in the initiation and in the promotion of the campaign. The leadership assumed by Richards and Haney in the organization of the NSPIE may have been designed to keep the movement from falling entirely under the control of employers. "Industrial wealth," wrote Principal William McAndrew of the Washington Irving High School of New York City in 1908, "has proved itself no special friend of children, or of their education. The greed that lures children to the coal mine and cotton mill by the seductive temptation of early wage-earning would be a sorry influence in schools detached from the old system. The business avarice that first brought Africans as slaves to our shores, and then Chinese, and now Italians, because their labor is cheap, is scarcely a power to be trusted with the direction of any public schools."[82] A harsh judgment indeed, but one that, if widely felt, might account for the sudden interest in the subject on the part of school men.

Some assumed that the NSPIE, as an organization including manufacturers and industrialists, possessed great wealth and used it to promote the campaign. "Money will never be lacking for the promotion of this society," wrote Winship in his *Journal of Education* in 1908. "It was born under a golden star." Even Winship, however, could account for no more than $2500 in membership fees plus $5000 in contributions during the first year.[83] This was more, but not much more than had been spent by the Committee of Ten. Whatever force was exerted in the early years did not come from money, although the Society did have a few prosperous years later on.[84]

[82] William McAndrew, "Industrial Education from a Public-School Man's Point of View," *Educational Review* (February, 1908), p. 128.

[83] *Journal of Education* (February 13, 1908), pp. 175–177.

[84] Between November, 1913, and October, 1916, the Society received nearly $34,000 in gifts, these amounting to about half the total receipts for this period. Robert Ripley Clough, *The National Society for the Promotion of Industrial Education: Case History of a Reform Organization, 1906–1917* (Master's thesis, University of Wisconsin, 1957), p. 31. This came, however, after the campaign was well under way. By 1920 the Society, then known as The National Society for Vocational Education, was apparently in financial trouble; an editorial writer in *School Review* rejoiced to see it pleading with its members for special donations of three dollars each. *School Review* (December, 1920), pp. 721–723. Even in its most affluent period, however, the NSPIE came nowhere near matching the income of another reform organization, the New York Bureau of Municipal Research, which spent almost a million dollars in the five-year period between 1909 and 1914. Rockefeller alone gave $125,000 to the Bureau. Lorin Peterson, *The Day of the Mugwump* (New York: Alfred A. Knopf, 1961), pp. 50–51.

Neither can it be taken for granted that industrialists as a group were zealous promoters of the campaign. The proceedings of the National Association of Manufacturers leave no impression that most of the members were greatly interested in the committees generated by a few leaders, such as Milton Higgins of Worcester, Massachusetts, and Anthony Ittner of St. Louis. In fact, the members of the 1909 convention agreed readily to a motion that the reading of Ittner's report be dispensed with. Only the urgent pleas of a member who particularly wanted to hear the report led to the reversal of this action.[85] Certainly the demand did not come from organized labor. Unionists were originally skeptical of the movement and sometimes hostile to it, although by 1910 an AFL committee endorsed industrial education as a corrective for the one-sided education then allegedly being given by the schools.[86]

According to some interpretations, the demand came from the vague entity known as "the people." Yet there were irritated expressions from impatient educators about the slowness of the people in making such demands. This was a point of special concern at the Directors' Department of the Pennsylvania State Education Association in 1907. Mrs. Gertrude B. Bittle of the State Federation for Women urged the educators "not to wait until public opinion demands better methods and facilities," but to go ahead at once with manual training, trade schools, schools of domestic science, and schools for the teaching of practical farm work.[87] A superintendent in the same meeting said that considerable sentiment could be found "in opposition to the movement," but that public opinion could "be changed to favorable support as the work progresses.[88] Another told how "everyone was against" him when he had started manual training several years before, but that sentiment had become favorable to his program.[89] Director A. C. True of the U.S. Office of Experimental Stations, a leading advocate of vocational education for rural youth, said that influential persons and groups were in favor of the movement, although beneath the surface there was "a vast mass of stag-

[85] National Association of Manufacturers, *Proceedings of the Fourteenth Annual Convention*, May 17–19 (The Association, 1909), p. 17.

[86] American Federation of Labor, *Proceedings of the Thirteenth Convention*, 1910, pp. 40–41, as quoted in American Federation of Labor, *Labor and Education* (The Federation, 1939), p. 13.

[87] Gertrude B. Bittle, "Views of State Federation of Women," *Pennsylvania School Journal* (April, 1907), p. 439.

[88] H. E. Trout, "Instruction in Music, Manual Training and Domestic Science in the Public Schools," *Pennsylvania School Journal* (April, 1907), p. 444.

[89] Quoted *ibid.*, p. 446.

nant or recurrent water." The problem, he said, was "to increase agitation to such an extent that not only the leaders but the great mass of rural people" would be profoundly stirred. Agitation had already done some good, he declared, but it was necessary "to make this agitation deeper, as well as wider," until it thoroughly permeated "all the mass of our rural population."[90]

There was nothing wrong with such evangelical efforts. The need for them, however, casts some doubt on the many statements about a popular demand for industrial education as well as other innovations in the schools. It was easy to mistake the articulate expressions of the advocates for the demand of the public. One educator who tended to be skeptical about public demand was John Dewey, who in 1901 spelled out the process of introducing a new study in a community. "Someone feels," he said, "that the school system of his (or quite frequently nowadays her) town is falling behind the times. There are great rumors of great progress in education making elsewhere. Something new and important has been introduced; education is being revolutionized by it." At this point, he continued, the superintendent would become uneasy, and the matter would be taken up by individuals and clubs, with letters to the newspapers and appeals to the editor. "Finally the school board ordains that on and after a certain date the particular new branch—be it nature study, industrial drawing, cooking, manual training, or whatever —shall be taught in the public schools. The victory is won, and everybody—unless it be some already overburdened and distracted teacher —congratulates everybody else that such advanced steps are taking [place]."[91] This description, put in a national context, might explain the campaign for industrial education.

[90] A. C. True, "Agriculture in the Public Schools," *Pennsylvania School Journal* (April, 1907), pp. 448–449.
[91] John Dewey, "The Situation as Regards the Course of Study," NEA, 1901, p. 334.

Chapter 11
Social efficiency triumphant

> "Social efficiency is the standard by which the
> forces of education must select the experiences that
> are impressed upon the individual."
> —WILLIAM C. BAGLEY,
> 1905.

*V*ocational education was not enough.
The spirit of reform in American society
demanded an explicit social mission for the schools, and many sought to
supply its definition. From this came supposedly new doctrines of schooling, reflecting latter-day efforts to resolve the perennial dilemma of the
individual and the group. One expression of this quest was education for
social control; the other, education for social service. Soon they came
together in one slogan, education for social efficiency. These new brands
of enthusiasm involved schooling on all levels, but in the prevailing
opinion of the times, it was the high school that stood in particular need
of their ministrations.

The term *social control,* popularized by sociologist Edward A. Ross in
a book published in 1901, represented an idea as old as society itself.[1]
Implied in it has always been the management, and even the restraint, of

---

[1] Edward A. Ross, *Social Control* (New York: Macmillan Co., 1901). This
book was an accumulation of papers previously published by Ross in *American
Journal of Sociology,* the chapter on education having appeared in the January,
1900, issue, pp. 475–487. According to A. B. Hollingshead, the term *social control*
was first used in "sociological literature" by Albion W. Small and George E.
Vincent in their book *An Introduction to the Study of Society* (New York: American Book Co., 1894), p. 328. A. B. Hollingshead, "The Concept of Social Control," *American Sociological Review* (April, 1941), p. 217. In a recent statement,
H. C. Brearley has defined social control as "a collective term for those processes
and agencies, planned or unplanned, by which individuals are taught, persuaded,
or compelled to conform to the usages and life values of the group to which they
belong." H. C. Brearley, "The Nature of Social Control," *Sociology and Social
Research* (November-December, 1943), p. 95.

individual behavior on behalf of the group. No society, in fact, can exist without it. The persistent question, however, is whether to endure or to embrace it. In the period between 1900 and 1920 it was embraced, as was also its corollary, education for social control, this representing the production of habits and beliefs consistent with the desired kinds of behavior.

Although nineteenth-century education in the United States had stressed individualism, it was by no means void of social purpose. Many an orator had testified to the faith in popular education as the support of popular government. Schooling was expected to produce responsible citizens, and among the fruits of democratic education listed by Eliot were such qualities as "courage, self-denial, and zeal, and loyal devotion to the democratic ideals of freedom, serviceableness, unity, toleration, public justice, and public joyfulness."[2] There was even much precedent in practice for the more severe view of schools as agencies of social control. Schools were called upon, for example, to Americanize immigrants, to abolish drink, and to control crime; school men from time to time felt obliged to protest against the tendency of reformers to claim the service of education for the achievement of their specific goals.

During the 1880's and 1890's sociologists began to make specific criticisms of the highly individualistic doctrine of mental training as an object of school work. To Lester Frank Ward it was knowledge, particularly knowledge directed toward social ends, that was all-important. "Those who possess most knowledge," he wrote in 1883, "upon an average possess most intelligence, the average capacity being everywhere the same."[3] He enumerated the various notions of education as involving chiefly experience, discipline, culture, research, and information; of these, he concluded, education as information was the most important. It was a system for extending the most important knowledge to all members

---

[2] Charles W. Eliot, "The Function of Education in Democratic Society," *Outlook* (November 6, 1897), p. 575.

[3] Lester Frank Ward, *Dynamic Sociology* (New York: Appleton-Century-Crofts, 1883), II, 537. Ward himself had a Jeffersonian passion for acquiring knowledge. At the time he was writing *Dynamic Sociology,* he was assistant geologist with the U.S. Geological Survey, and within the next several years he published two books on palaeobotany. He had little formal schooling below the college level, but had studied a great variety of subjects by himself. A good deal of his study was in Latin and Greek literature, and he was committed both to the classics and the modern subjects. His early period of self-education is described in his fascinating diary, kept between 1860 and 1870. See Bernhard J. Stern (ed.), *Young Ward's Diary* (New York: G. P. Putnam's Sons, 1935).

of society.[4] "The distribution of knowledge," he said, "underlies all social reform,"[5] and the necessity for this was so crucial that it should be a direct function of the state.[6] The American Herbartians had not yet opened their attack on formal training, and Ward's voice at that time was a lonely one indeed. Naturally Ward did not like the report of the Committee of Ten when it appeared in 1894.

It was in an address to a general session of the NEA meeting of 1896 that one of Ward's disciples, Professor Albion W. Small of the University of Chicago, delivered a sweeping indictment of the Committee of Ten. Speaking broadly in the name of "sociology," Small condemned "the naïvely medieval psychology" he found inherent in the doctrine of training. Unlike Ward, however, Small did not define education as the transmission of knowledge, but rather as the "completion of the individual." Implied in this, he said, was the "adaptation of the individual to such cooperation with the society in which his lot was cast that he works at his best with the society in perfecting its own type."[7] Nowhere, he said, did he find in the report of the Committee of Ten, "recognition that education, when it is finished, is conscious conformity of individuals to the coherent cosmic reality of which they are parts."[8] He was perfectly right in not finding this in the report. At the end of this speech, Small made a leap to the farthest boundaries of his doctrine: "Sociology demands of educators, finally, that they shall not rate themselves as leaders of children, but as makers of society."[9]

At this time (1896), a young California teacher named David Snedden was in the process of finishing his work at Stanford for the bachelor's degree. Among his teachers was Edward A. Ross, who was then assembling his views on social control. Alert and intelligent, eager for new ideas and on the threshold of his career, Snedden absorbed what Ross had to teach and from this began to formulate his own version of social doctrine in education. In 1900, after a three-year principalship at Paso Robles, Snedden used the occasion of an address to the Stanford alumni association to present his formulation. The nineteenth century, he de-

[4] Ward, op. cit., pp. 568–571.

[5] Ibid., p. 598.

[6] Ibid., pp. 588–591.

[7] Albion W. Small, "Demands of Sociology upon Pedagogy," NEA, 1896, p. 174. The evolutionary phraseology here represented the idea of society as guiding its own evolutionary processes. Apparently it was not nature, but society, that would be "so careful of the type."

[8] Ibid., p. 175.

[9] Ibid., p. 184.

clared, had given the world "a new conception of society." This evidently meant late nineteenth century, for he declared that "only within our generation have we become accustomed to think of society as being governed by natural laws." With this scientific knowledge available, he said, the growth of society was subject to "conscious and intelligent human direction." Institutions of society would be examined from "the sociological standpoint," that is, in relation to their impact on society's general welfare. Public education was an institution of society and, like others, should be so examined, particularly with reference to what Snedden called the "rank and file."[10]

From this point, Snedden went on to attack what he called the traditional ideal of education, with special reference to the classics and English literature for anyone and mathematics and physical science for girls. Unlike Ward who sought to distribute knowledge to all, Snedden had in the mind the selective distribution of knowledge to various groups. Girls apparently constituted one such group, the so-called "rank and file" another. Ward himself would have rejected portions of traditional schooling, but he did not see these, or indeed any body of knowledge, as appropriate for one group and inappropriate for others. Snedden, however, was willing to concede that the traditional curriculum might be the best preparation for college; he could not believe it was "the best preparation for the place in society to be occupied by those who do not go beyond."[11]

It was in the following year that Professor Ross brought out his book on social control. Ross spoke frankly in this book of education as "an economical system of police" and quoted Webster as one who had let the cat out of the bag by so referring to the public schools. Education was also to succeed religion "as the method of indirect social restraint."[12] So potent were education and other forms of social control that these should be considered as esoteric doctrines not to be widely shared. "To betray the secrets of ascendancy," he said, was "to forearm the individual in his struggle with society." The mysterious processes were not to be bawled from housetops, and "the wise sociologist" would not let "the street Arab, or the Elmira inmate" into the secret of how he was managed. Rather, he would "address himself to those who administer the moral

[10] David Snedden, "The Schools of the Rank and File," *Stanford Alumnus* (June, 1900), p. 185.
[11] *Ibid.,* p. 195.
[12] Ross, *op. cit.,* pp. 174, 176.

capital of society—to teachers, clergymen, editors, law-makers, and judges, who wield the instruments of control; to poets, artists, thinkers, and educators, who guide the human caravan across the waste."[13]

Nonetheless, Ross had his moments of doubt, even in this book. "The coalescence of physical and spiritual forces in the modern state," he wrote at one point, "may well inspire certain misgivings. When we note the enormous resources and high centralization of a first-class educational system . . . when we consider that the democratic control of this formidable engine affords no guarantee that it will not be used for empire over minds—we may well be apprehensive of future developments." To offset the force of "this educating modern state," it would be necessary, he thought, to maintain voluntary associations such as the "free church" and "the republic of letters."[14]

For the most part untroubled by such apprehensions, other sociologists went on to hammer home with relentless logic the meaning of education for social control. One of these was Ross's pupil, David Snedden, who went to Columbia for his doctorate and taught there prior to becoming the first state Commissioner of Education in Massachusetts under the new system. In 1909 while visiting Great Britain, Snedden stopped to share his views with the members of the West Riding (Yorkshire) County Council Teachers' Vacation Course. America was attempting, he said, to define education as an integral process, "ministered to by many social institutions." The schools were of particular importance, for they were "the only educational institutions which society, in its collective and conscious capacity, acting thru the state, is able to control." Other institutions, such as the family, the church, the street, the stage, and the like, were "only indirectly under collective control," but the school was "completely so." This larger conception of education, he said, grew out of modern social economy and proceeded "from the broadest possible conception of society reconstructing itself."[15]

Another sociologist who took up the cause was Professor Charles A. Ellwood of the University of Missouri. Ellwood had faith in social science and a distrust of individualism, although he recognized the danger of going so far as "to suppress individuality and . . . to adapt merely to a static condition of things." It would be necessary, therefore, to provide

[13] *Ibid.*, p. 441.
[14] *Ibid.*, pp. 178–179.
[15] David Snedden, "Educational Tendencies in America," *Educational Review* (January, 1910), pp. 24–25.

for change, and education was to be viewed "as the conscious instrument of social reconstruction."[16] When it came to specific applications, however, Ellwood tended to forget the danger of going to extremes. In 1914 he decided that the laws on compulsory education were failures since they were based on age rather than on achievement. State and national committees, he declared, should decide on the minimum education to be required of pupils before they were allowed "to go forth into our complex social life." With this decided, he went on: "Then let every child in the state be 'sentenced', as it were, by a rational compulsory education law, to complete this minimum requirement of education in our public schools." This, he said, would offer the additional advantage of identifying the feeble-minded so they could be turned over to "proper institutions" for their care and training.

Evidently a disciple of eugenics, Ellwood deplored the fact that the feeble-minded were allowed to pass on their defects to future generations and "even diffuse them in the population as a whole." He felt, however, that it was difficult "even with a Binet-Simon test" to detect "the higher grades" of the feeble-minded if they were allowed to leave school at fourteen. "No such difficulty in detecting the feeble-minded would be experienced," he argued, "if all pupils were in the public schools for an indeterminate period, until they had completed the minimum prescribed for graduation. Thus, an indeterminate compulsory education law would have a eugenic value for the race, as well as social and economic value for individual success and good citizenship." This was the only kind of compulsory education that could be "approved of scientifically," and he asked, "Why should we not have it?"[17]

By this time the doctrine had arrived at a reasonable degree of completeness, and it was in 1915 that Professor Ernest R. Groves of New Hampshire State College expressed it in its most naked or perhaps most naïve form. "Any definition of education in terms of the individual," he said, "begins with a fallacy. . . . Society can largely determine individual characteristics, and for its future well-being it needs more and more to demand that the public schools contribute significantly and not incidentally to its pressing needs by a social use of the influence that the schools have over the individual in his sensitive period of immaturity."

[16] Charles A. Ellwood, "The Sociological Basis of the Science of Education," *Education* (November, 1911), pp. 134–137.
[17] Charles A. Ellwood, "Our Compulsory Education Laws," *Education* (May, 1914), pp. 575–576.

Sociology alone could settle purposes. To throw light on the question would require the study of primitive sociology and primitive education, and he asked how educators could fail to have an interest in the study of social control as it appears in its most clear and simple form among primitive peoples.[18]

II

In comparison with these strong doctrines, the social views of education taken by Samuel T. Dutton and John Dewey in this period were moderate indeed. Dutton had explored the meaning of the high school as a social institution and, in his work with the Brookline Education Society, had tried to establish realistic connections between the schools and the community they served. Dewey's *The School and Society* essay (1899) set forth the classroom as a community in which the ideal social processes he imagined had existed in earlier and simpler times could be reproduced and in which the child would be trained to "the spirit of service" and provided with "the instruments of effective self-direction" to bring about a "worthy, lovely, and harmonious" society itself.[19] This was also a kind of social control, but the spirit and the accents of Dewey in this essay differed fundamentally from those of Small, Snedden, Ellwood, and Ross.

Social control was one aspect of the reform movement, but social service was another. The writings of Dewey and Dutton in this period presented the school much more as an agency of social service than as an agency of social control. One expression of this view was the movement to establish schools as social or community centers. This movement had several sources, one of which was the development of settlement houses in the large metropolitan centers such as New York and Boston, aimed particularly at the problems and needs of the immigrant poor. According to one proponent of the movement, however, the real ancestor of the social center was "not the social settlement but the little red school house back home, which, in the evenings was used for a common meeting place for the neighborhood."[20] Horace E. Scudder in 1896 had also used the

[18] Ernest R. Groves, "Sociological Aspects of Public Education," *School and Society* (February 13, 1915), p. 245.

[19] John Dewey, *The School and Society* (Chicago: University of Chicago Press, 1899), p. 40.

[20] Edward J. Ward, "The Little Red School House," *Survey* (August 7, 1909), p. 641.

symbol of the little red schoolhouse in his advocacy of social centers. "The common schoolhouse," wrote Scudder, "is in reality the most obvious centre of national unity, and, with the growing custom of making it carry the American flag, it is likely to stand for a long time to come as the most conspicuous mark of a common American life."[21] The social-center movement had, however, ample precedents in other institutions as well, such as the Grange, the lyceums, and the Chautauqua circuit.

Shortly after 1900, the subject of social centers began to appear on the programs of the NEA. Dewey addressed the National Council on this subject in 1902, and Eliot followed early in 1903 with an address to the Department of Superintendence. Both spoke within the traditional context of the school as a center of community life. Dewey reviewed the usually mentioned changes in communication, transportation, and industrialization and deplored the fact that in some ways these had brought about what he called the decay of reverence and an increase of hoodlumism and flippancy.[22] More positively, he saw these changes as also bringing a closer connection of intellectual life with other affairs than there had been previously. With all this, there was the need for "providing, thru the school as a center, a continuous education for all classes of whatever age."[23] Dewey saw the school as a social center providing classes for study, specialized instruction for adults, and "reasonable forms of amusement and recreation," from which would flow the sharing by all people in the "intellectual and spiritual resources of the community."[24] Eliot endorsed the idea of the schoolhouse as "the most active social center of the neighborhood, kept so by the interest in the music, recitations, plays, readings, and illustrated lectures which there can be enjoyed." Where Dewey included "reasonable" amusement and recreation in his program, Eliot gave enjoyment the central place, contending "that the adding of pleasures, joys, and satisfactions to human life ought always to have been recognized as the principal function of every school and of all education."[25]

Social centers developed rapidly, with Edward J. Ward, Supervisor of Social Centers and Playgrounds in the Rochester, New York, Public

[21] Horace E. Scudder, "The Schoolhouse as a Centre," *Atlantic Monthly* (January, 1896), p. 103.
[22] John Dewey, "The School as a Social Center," NEA, 1902, pp. 376–378.
[23] *Ibid.*, p. 380.
[24] *Ibid.*, pp. 381–383.
[25] Charles W. Eliot, "The Full Utilization of a Public School Plant," NEA, 1903, p. 246.

Schools becoming identified as a major figure in the movement. The Rochester centers were started in 1907. Some of them were in neighborhoods including immigrants, but the West High School Center, according to Ward, was located in one of the most native-American, well-to-do districts. The spirit of the Rochester centers, said Ward, was the true democracy of the little red schoolhouse, battering down walls of class distinction, color prejudice, nationalistic hatred, and religious contempt.[26] Ward subsequently joined the Extension Division of the University of Wisconsin and established a Bureau of Social Center Development. In 1911 the university city of Madison became the scene of a National Conference of Civic and Social Center Development, financed in part by two philanthropic ladies in Pittsburgh. The conference was attended by 200 delegates and was addressed by three governors, including Woodrow Wilson, and six mayors. A magnificent time was had by all, and "no two people agreed as to just what a social center really is."[27]

It was clear, nevertheless, that the social-center movement had become part of the general campaign for political reform, or perhaps political brotherhood. The dominant note at the Madison conference was that of community study of social problems, cutting across party lines. At the closing banquet, the assembled disciples of the social-center movement sang as follows:

> There are several parties in this community,
> Republican and Democrat and Socialist, that's three;
> We never got together just because we disagree,
> But there's a place where all of us can talk things over free.
>
> It's at the center,
> The social center,
> The place where everybody feels at home,
> Forgets the external,
> Becomes fraternal,
> And knows the time for friendliness has come.[28]

At this point, continued the account, the music stopped, and the spotlight was thrown upon the Republican Mayor of Prescott, the Democratic Mayor of Madison, and the Socialist Mayor of Milwaukee, "sitting side

[26] Ward, *op. cit.*, p. 641.
[27] George B. Ford, "Madison Conference on Social Centers," *Survey* (November 18, 1911), p. 1229.
[28] Edward J. Ward, "Civic and Social Center Development," NEA, 1912, p. 1361.

by side, just as tho they had something in common." The final ceremonies of the conference included the singing of the following song, one that underscored Ward's contentions about the roots of the movement in American tradition:

> Come close and let us wake the joy
> Our fathers used to know,
> When to the little old schoolhouse
> Together they would go,
> Thus neighbor's heart to neighbor warmed
> In thought for common good;
> We'll strike that fine old chord again—
> A song of neighborhood.[29]

Whether or not their fathers had in fact gone together with joy to the little old schoolhouse, the enthusiasts for social centers were at any rate determined to link their passion for the future with nostalgia for the past. Apparently songs helped the movement along. In 1916 the U.S. Bureau of Education published and distributed five songs, all of them written by E. J. Ward himself, who was by that time a specialist in Community Organization with the Bureau. One of these was "It's a Short Way to the Schoolhouse," sung to the tune of "Tipperary"; another, "Neighborhood," sung to that of "Die Wacht am Rhein."[30]

High schools came in for their share of attention as social centers. Although some of these were located in cities, such as the ones in Rochester, the main development of high schools for this purpose took place in rural communities. According to one writer in 1914, the modern country high school was "opening its doors for all sorts of neighborhood meetings, entertainments, illustrated talks, exhibitions, and educational institutes."[31] There was nothing in this of antagonism toward the traditional academic studies, but it implied a shift of purpose toward social service, although not necessarily toward social control. Advocacy of social centers in city high schools became involved in the antivice aspect of reform, and they were set forth as wholesome substitutes for the bad environments of brothels, dance halls, saloons, pool-rooms, gambling resorts, and motion picture theaters. Practically only one phase

[29] Ford, *op. cit.*, p. 1231.
[30] *Education* (September, 1916), pp. 65–66.
[31] Arthur C. Perry, "The High School as a Social Centre," Charles Hughes Johnston (ed.), *The Modern High School* (New York: Charles Scribner's Sons, 1914), p. 523.

of life, the religious, was omitted from the scope of high schools, wrote one enthusiastic advocate in 1914, and this was represented "in the schemes for moral education . . . projected or in operation."[32]

All this activity was directed toward the idea of having the school serve the community. Meanwhile, a corresponding movement, known as *social education* was evolving to reflect Dewey's idea of the school as a model community in itself. Just as some people did not know just what a social center was, there were those in this parallel movement who were not sure how to define social education. To some extent it overlapped the movement for social centers and called for the active involvement in education of all the good forces in the communities. More specifically, however, the movement concentrated on what would later be called "the climate of the classroom," aimed at the development of skills and attitudes needed for cooperative effort both in school and in society. Like other movements, it had a leader—Colin A. Scott of the Boston Normal School—and it was soon to have an association, a congress, and a journal. The Social Education Congress met, inevitably, in Boston, in the fall of 1906. It had a long list of sponsoring agencies, including the American Institute of Instruction, the Catholic Union of Boston, the Harvard Teachers' Association, the Massachusetts State Teachers' Association, the Women's Education Association, the Women's Educational and Industrial Union, and The Fathers' and Mothers' Club.[33] Leading citizens, including President Frederick P. Fish of the American Telephone and Telegraph Company, Archbishop William O'Connell of Boston, and G. Stanley Hall delivered addresses and exhortations on behalf of social education.[34] Among other things, the Congress endorsed industrial education, but it was more preoccupied with such topics as social training in infancy and early childhood, self-organized group work, the school as a social organism, and the school and the family. The Congress gave birth to the Social Education Association and to a short-lived journal called the *Social Education Quarterly*.

Although the initial enthusiasm for the organization itself died down, Scott continued to promote social education through writing and through his work at the Boston Normal School. Much of his work paralleled the ideas of Dewey in *The School and Society,* including his stress on the

[32] *Ibid.,* p. 529.
[33] Social Education Association, announcement and prospectus of, undated, presumably December, 1906.
[34] *Education* (January, 1907), p. 305.

social values of handwork and domestic-science projects in the elementary grades. In 1908 however, he took issue with some of the practices that had been developed under Dewey at the laboratory school of the University of Chicago.[35] Perhaps he sought to avoid identification as a Dewey follower. At any rate, he persisted in his contention that "the mere occupation," such as cooking or play-making, was not the "educative feature" of the children's activities; it was rather "the impulse which by itself might become mere caprice, coming into contact with other impulses, and organizing itself socially, with care of and responsibility for others whom the children have chosen to work with, that is truly typical." It was this "socializing" that revealed the varying individuality of the children, and he insisted that one could not "be an individual by himself."[36] For the most part, the movement did not directly affect high schools, although Scott referred favorably to the practice in some schools of granting credit for home activities, such as dish-washing and bed-making, as an example of social education.[37]

III

Social centers and social education were seen largely in the context of social service. Much the same idea of social service, possibly with overtones of social control, tended to appear in the humanitarian aspects of general reform, particularly in settlement work for immigrants. Some of the activities of settlement houses found their way into the schools and undoubtedly contributed further to the developing ideology of social purpose in education.

New York City has often been used as a major example of the impact of settlement houses on education. It serves also to clarify the question of the nature of this impact on the ideology of the schools. Settlement houses, such as the Neighborhood Guild established by Dr. Stanton Coit, began to appear in New York City in the late 1880's and early 1890's. The settlement-house people, along with the New York Association for Improving the Condition of the Poor, promoted a number of specific and practical ventures, such as vacation schools and public baths, designed to mitigate the hard conditions of life on the Lower East Side. It was hoped

[35] Colin A. Scott, *Social Education* (New York: Ginn and Co., 1908), Chapter 5.
[36] Colin A. Scott, "Social Education," *Education* (December, 1909), p. 215.
[37] Colin A. Scott, "Socialized High School Curriculums and Courses of Study," Charles Hughes Johnston, *op. cit.*, pp. 233–234.

that the public schools would take over some of these ventures, or at least add to the available facilities for them. The schools were not slow to respond. In 1895 the Association for Improving the Condition of the Poor started vacation schools in buildings borrowed from the Board of Education. Four years later, the Board decided to operate such schools itself. Soon the New York Public Schools, largely under the direct leadership of Julia Richman, District Superintendent of the area including the Lower East Side, but with the active support of Superintendent Maxwell, were engaging in a variety of social services designed to meet immediate and practical needs.

The school baths were a fascinating chapter in the history of pedagogical services. They were by no means unique to New York City or to the United States. Neither were they unique to neighborhoods with immigrants. The modern movement for public baths had originated in Europe, and one writer declared in 1893 that the United States was 50 years behind the times in making such provisions.[38] School baths were "a settled feature of popular school organization in Germany," and German engineers, true to their stereotype of efficiency, had developed ingenious arrangements under which the most children could take the most baths in the least time and with maximum sanitary precautions.[39] The New York City Board started making plans for school baths in 1900, and by 1906 the school system had them in fifteen schools, not all of them on the Lower East Side.[40] In 1907 the Board of Education in Pittsburgh decided to install baths in its Riverside School,[41] and there were baths in the Jefferson School of St. Louis.[42] The greatest immediate need, of course, was in the slums, and the slum children apparently took their baths with enthusiasm.[43] An observer of the vacation program at one of the New

[38] Goodwin Brown, "Public Baths," *Charities Review* (January, 1893), pp. 143–152. The Association for Improving the Condition of the Poor had opened its public baths in New York City two years before. Suburban Brookline, Massachusetts, also had its public bath. J. A. Stewart, "The Model Public Bath at Brookline," *American Journal of Sociology* (January, 1900), pp. 470–474.

[39] "School Baths in Germany," *School Journal* (March 2, 1907), p. 230.

[40] "Baths in New York Schools," *Charities Review* (March, 1900), pp. 4–5. "Shower Baths in Public Schools," *School Journal* (February 3, 1906), pp. 111–112.

[41] "School Baths," *School Journal* (June 29, 1907), p. 690.

[42] *School Journal* (November 23, 1907), p. 473.

[43] "Last year one school had free baths; 1000 baths were taken in that school in one week. Every school in the thickly settled districts should have free baths." Marie Adele Shaw, "The True Character of New York Public Schools," *World's Work* (December, 1903), p. 4205.

York City schools told the story of a pupil who was missing from class. "Finally the youngster appeared and, when asked where he had been, replied, 'Just been takin' a bath, it's fine; ever had one?' "[44]

At all times it should be kept in mind that the New York City Board of Education was responding to a set of living conditions nothing less than tragic. In one part of Julia Richman's district there were 23,000 school children "crowded into a space covering less than three hundred acres, practically all of them foreign-born or of foreign parentage, under housing conditions at times intolerable, in an environment un-American at all times, unhygienic often, generally unfavorable to the best moral, physical, and mental development of the child."[45] The visitor to the vacation school where the absent pupil had been taking a bath found hundreds of children waiting for the doors to open in the morning. "The heat of an August sun," he wrote, "smote the district like a blast from a fiery furnace. The air was heavy with foul odors from unclean streets and dark basements. The windows and fire-escapes of the tenements were filled with mothers and babies, eager to catch any breeze that might sift thru the alleys and open streets below." In an average week "the aggregate attendance at the school, roof garden, and the near-by playground combined, was 41,072."[46]

It did not require a revolution in educational philosophy to motivate the provision of such critically needed services and facilities. Neither did the provision of them imply commitment to a new philosophy. Superintendent Maxwell was one of the leaders of the moderate revision in secondary education and one of the staunchest defenders of what might be called the traditional or academic curriculum. At the same time he consistently supported the social-service program of the New York City Public Schools. "To his support and advocacy," wrote the *School Journal* in 1908, "are due most of the credit of the present medical inspection of schools, the introduction of school nurses, the development of common-school athletics, the organization of special classes for defective children, the increase of playgrounds and recreative centers, and the insistence upon the supply of glasses for pupils with defective eyesight. He has

[44] George J. Kneeland, "The Largest Summer School in the World," *School Journal* (October 7, 1905), p. 341. Some skeptic, however, might add that the schools had merely provided a new excuse for cutting class.

[45] Julia Richman, discussion, NEA, 1910, p. 324.

[46] Kneeland, *op. cit.,* p. 339.

been one of the few men who had the courage to plead for the feeding of hungry school children."[47]

Furthermore, the children of the slums and their parents were by no means in conflict with "the traditional program" and were not inclined to accept the station in life to which some of the proponents of special education for "the masses" saw fit to assign them. One account of the work at P.S. 188, a school with 96 classrooms in a building five stories high in a square block on Houston Street, described a class of 39 pupils in the eighth grade, most of them Jewish immigrants. Of these 39 pupils, there were, according to the expressed intentions of the children themselves, nine prospective lawyers, six civil engineers, three dentists, three doctors, and two teachers.[48] Whether all these children had the talents needed for their choices or ever succeeded in realizing them will not be known, but the aspirations were there. Certainly there were among immigrant children many who would not profit from an exclusively academic education, but this was also true among the native born, including those of the purest Brahmin ancestry in New England. In all schools there was a need for the consideration of pupils as individuals, and there was nothing in the nature of immigrants, new immigration or old, that demanded a reformulated program aimed at them as a group.[49]

Although social workers and those engaged in settlement-house activity

[47] "Health Is First," *School Journal* (February, 1908), p. 607.

[48] "Largest Public School," *Pennsylvania School Journal* (November, 1906), pp. 208–209.

[49] Even where group statistics were used, the evidence did not suggest the need for a different kind of education aimed at immigrants as such. In the elementary school grades, for example, retardation rates were high for all groups, but those for children of foreign-born fathers did not differ markedly from those for children whose fathers were native-born whites. In the 37 cities studied by the Immigration Commission of 1910, the retardation rate in the fifth grade for children of immigrants was 48.3 percent, but that for children of native-born whites was 45.2 percent. In the seventh grade, the children of native-born whites showed a higher rate of retardation, 37.2 percent as compared with 34 percent for children of the foreign-born. The rates were higher for those from countries or regions identified with the so-called new immigration, but even among them there were many children who were not retarded. The group labeled "South Italian," for example, had a rate of 48.6 percent for all grades, as contrasted with the over-all figure of 36.1 percent for all grades and all groups. Apparently, then, at least half the children of fathers classified as "South Italian" were making normal progress, indicating that the focus of attention belonged on the individual child, not on the group. For retardation rates of the various groups see *Abstracts of Reports of the Immigration Commission,* 61st Congress, 3rd Session, Senate Document No. 747, (Washington, D.C., 1911), II, 29.

favored the assumption by the schools of some services, they were not trying to force a social program on the schools. On one occasion, at least, the charity workers of New York City felt that Maxwell and the schools were going too far. The point at issue was that of supplying free eyeglasses to children who could not afford them. None other than Jacob Riis himself attacked the schools on this point and sarcastically asked why they did not go further and supply children with watches. "It was to be expected," said the *School Journal,* "that the charity workers would attack Dr. Maxwell's plan." Furthermore, predicted the editor, "the common school of the future will be a truer charity organization than any now in existence."[50]

Settlement-house workers were by no means agreed that all their functions should eventually be taken over by the schools. Although Mrs. Vladimir Simkhovitch, a prominent leader in the movement and an active worker at Greenwich House, defended the work of the Board of Education in establishing school baths and vacation schools[51] and felt that many settlement activities, such as kindergartens, libraries, and evening classes, might well be incorporated into school programs, she set forth a continuing role for the settlements themselves. It would be a difficult task, she declared, "in any not far distant future to give the school that free and homelike character which makes the settlement a popular neighborhood center. . . . The idea in any case that the school will wholly supplant the settlement does not seem probable."[52] In 1917 David Rosenstein called on social workers to force schools forward to "complete socialization of their activities,"[53] but he also challenged the notion that

[50] "A Fair Deal for All the Children," *School Journal* (April 27, 1907), pp. 419–420. The affair had some of the overtones of a jurisdictional dispute, and the charity organizations proposed a compromise under which the children's eyes would be examined by school doctors and nurses and the children who needed glasses would be referred to "one of the four societies which makes offers of assistance or to other charitable societies, churches, settlements, etc." The dispute aroused interest outside New York and was commented on by newspapers as far apart as New Orleans and Boston. It would be difficult, if not impossible, to untangle the rights and wrongs of the dispute itself. The fact that it took place shows that social workers were not in all instances nudging the schools into an expansion of social services, or even approving such expansion.

[51] Mary Simkhovitch, "The Enlarged Function of the Public School," *Proceedings of the National Conference of Charities and Correction,* Thirty-First Annual Session (The Conference: 1904), pp. 479–480.

[52] Mary Simkhovitch, "The School and the Family," *Social Education Quarterly* (January, 1908), p. 17.

[53] David Rosenstein, "The Educational Function of the Social Settlement in a Democracy," *School and Society* (September 29, 1917), p. 377.

settlements were "romantic relics" that had been superseded by "socialized schools" and argued that there was still an important place for them in society.[54]

What did happen, however, was that some of the new men in education became engaged, directly and indirectly, in social work and incorporated some of the elements of that enterprise into their own thinking, with modifications in a direction away from social service and toward social control. David Snedden's major professor on his Columbia doctorate was Edward T. Devine, who was also Executive Officer of the New York Charity Organization Society. In his doctoral study of juvenile reform schools, Snedden concluded that the "work represented by these institutions has represented more fully the idea of state education than has the work of any other part of the educational system." In the reform schools, "the entire round of educational effort must be compassed." The public schools, he felt, had failed to "learn from juvenile reform schools," and these schools constituted "the most persistent, comprehensive, and effective experiment in the domain of education that is available to the student."[55] These extensions of social work into the domain of the schools were Snedden's own interpretations, not necessarily the ideas of Devine himself.

Another young graduate student in this period was Clarence Kingsley, a former instructor in mathematics at Colgate, who took his master's degree at Teachers College, Columbia, in 1904. During part of his period of study, Kingsley served as an agent of the New York Charity Organization Society. Kingsley's career is of special interest because he later became chairman of the NEA Commission on the Reorganization of Secondary Education, the group that produced the *Cardinal Principles* report of 1918. Although thoroughly imbued with the spirit of social service, he also moved somewhat toward social control, but not so much as Snedden.

IV

The impulse for humanitarian reform expressed itself partly in settlement houses and other varieties of social work. In addition, it involved two matters of great concern to school people, namely public health and

[54] David Rosenstein, "The National Federation of Settlements," *School and Society* (July 21, 1917), p. 72.

[55] David Snedden, *Administration and Educational Work of American Juvenile Reform Schools* (New York: Faculty of Philosophy, Columbia University, 1907), pp. 7–8.

child labor. Probably nothing brought home the meaning of social interdependence more sharply than the spread of contagious disease. The
nation was then suffering an average of 138,000 deaths per year from
tuberculosis alone. "A great deal of attention," said an editorial in
Education in 1908, "is being given of late to the subject of the public
health, and naturally the public schools are expected to contribute to the
movement."[56] With the increase in knowledge about the spread of
disease, this was both inevitable and desirable. Schools with overcrowded
classrooms and unsanitary drinking fountains and toilets undoubtedly
contributed at least their share to the tragic state of affairs prevalent at
that time. One response to the increased concern about public health was
the improvement of conditions in old school buildings and the making of
better provisions for sanitation in the new ones. Another was the provision of school doctors and nurses, a program in which Superintendent
Maxwell of New York City played a conspicuous part. Greater attention
was given, and on a more scientific basis, to teaching pupils about health
and hygienic habits. Much faith, perhaps an exaggerated faith, was placed
in the correction of physical defects as a means of reducing nonpromo-
tion and failure. To the extent that regular attendance was involved, the
campaign for health probably helped many children to achieve at least
the academic success of which they were capable. The movement for
public health affected many everyday and practical aspects of school
work, and it registered its ideological impact with the appearance of
health as one of the major objectives of schooling in the *Cardinal Principles* report.

In spite of Miss Kingsbury's conclusions in the Douglas Report of
1906, there was not a great deal the schools could do through their
curricula and practices about child labor. School people, however, could
and did support the campaigns to regulate or to prohibit child labor,
especially through the indirect device of compulsory school attendance.
A great deal of progress had been made in some of the states, but even
as late as 1906 the law in Massachusetts permitted the employment of
youth fourteen to eighteen years of age to the extent of 58 hours a week,
and included a special provision for longer hours in retail establishments
during December.[57] Compulsory education was a proposition that involved several kinds of possible motives. It could represent a humani-

---

[56] *Education* (November, 1908), p. 190.
[57] John W. Perrin, "Indirect Compulsory Education—the Factory Laws of
Massachusetts and Connecticut," *Educational Review* (April, 1906), p. 394.

tarian impulse to keep children out of mines and factories. From another point of view, it was a way of safeguarding the right of every child to gain the advantages of schooling. Beyond these traditional motives, compulsory education could be advocated as a form of social control. In some instances, all three motives were combined. Regardless of motive, however, compulsory-attendance laws when adequately enforced did mitigate the horrors of the industrial revolution with respect to children. These horrors, even in an age of progress, were by no means figments of the allegedly overheated imaginations of educators and social workers.

Humanitarian reform in all its phases, including those of social work and service, was part of a protest against the harsh conditions of the laissez-faire way of life. Even Nicholas Murray Butler, who suspected concealed potential tyranny in many proposals for reform, argued in 1910 that the theory of the survival of the fittest could not be directly applied to human affairs and that it was necessarily modified "by higher forms of interdependence."[58] He said that real and permanent successes were to be found in social systems of mutual cooperation, and that "participation in . . . society changes the whole character of the human struggle." He cited Huxley's warning against the fallacy that men as social and ethical beings must depend on the processes of survival proper to animals and plants.[59] Such a concession from a staunch defender of individualism and liberty shows that social reform was well established in American affairs. Perhaps Butler realized, like his friend Maxwell, that reform could be selective, that some movements were better than others, and that the installation of school baths did not necessarily demand the abolition of Latin, or possibly even of Greek.

Reform wore many guises. These were various kinds of political and economic reform, uplift reform, and the muckraking reform that persistently sought out evils to be suppressed. In one way or another, discussions of these matters inspired suggestions for something to be done by or through the schools. When Theodore Roosevelt exhorted the Department of Superintendence in 1908 to provide for industrial education, he also declared that there was no excuse if there was a failure "to war against rottenness and corruption, . . . to contend effectively with the forces of evil."[60]

[58] Nicholas Murray Butler, "The Revolt of the Unfit: Some Reflections on the Doctrine of Evolution," *Educational Review* (February, 1911), pp. 109.
[59] *Ibid.,* pp. 112–113.
[60] Theodore Roosevelt, address to the Department of Superintendence, NEA, February 26, 1908, *Educator-Journal* (April, 1908), p. 381.

Campaigns for political reform in local communities inevitably brought up issues pertaining to the schools, sometimes limited to the handling of funds, but at other times involving the nature of the school program. It might be assumed that conscientious school men and conscientious reformers got on well together, but this was not always the case. There was, for example, a good deal of tension between the New York City Board of Education and the New York Bureau of Municipal Research, a reform organization with laudable aims, a large budget, and a restless desire to concern itself about all phases of civic life. This tension culminated in a massive controversy involving the New York Schools Survey of 1911–1913, with Harvard's Paul Hanus, the Survey director, as the victim.

It was quite otherwise in Rochester, New York, where political and school reform rose and fell together. Both kinds were solidly established in 1905, and the introduction of commercial courses and manual training in the high schools was viewed as the result of reform. Social centers multiplied under the leadership of Edward J. Ward. This state of affairs, however, did not persist. In 1909–1910, "the spoils politicians" returned to power and with them a new administration in the schools. Sand-table work and clay-modeling in the primary grades were among the first casualties of the new regime. Miss Ada Van Stone Harris, who had been brought in to inaugurate such "construction (or expression) work" resigned.[61] Edward J. Ward left Rochester for Wisconsin, but it is not known whether this was motivated by the upsetting of local reform. So-called political liberalism and alleged liberalism in pedagogy have not always borne a one-to-one relationship. Perhaps here was one instance where such was the case.

The usual difficulties about identifying liberalism and conservatism apply to the reform movement as a whole. Political reform in local communities was often conservative or neutral with respect to economic questions, as were also many of the social-service campaigns for community recreation and health. In 1914 Edward A. Ross, then a professor at the University of Wisconsin, expressed impatience with much that had been done in the name of social service. He called for hard-hitting economic

---

[61] "A School Reform That Transformed a City," *School Journal* (October 7, 1905), pp. 353–355; "Miss Harris Resigns," *ibid.* (May, 1910), p. 338. For an account of the relationship between civic and pedagogical reform in another setting see Robert L. McCaul, "Dewey's Chicago," *School Review* (Summer, 1959), pp. 258–279.

reform and expressed the fear that too many women teachers had produced "too many sissies," a generation with "an alarming willingness to
take oppression and robbery lying down." What he called "trivial social
service" was, in his opinion, sidetracking economic reform. "The kept
newspaper," he said, "is strong for 'swat the fly,' anti-roller-towel, and
'clean-up' movements," and "petty charities" were diverting the public
mind "from big reforms involving questions of fares, prices, wages, hours,
and conditions of work." The promoters of social service were being
taught, he said, to " 'ask for reading-rooms, or fresh air, or teddy-
bears,' " but not for " 'less risk, or less hours, or for more pay, or more
rights.'"[62] Ross underestimated the importance of what he called
"trivial social service," but he did identify the essential neutrality of
much of the reform movement toward what he called "big reforms."
There was, of course, much suspicion of big business, this being one of
the by-products of muckraking reform. The mayor of Cleveland in 1907
denounced as sordid the motive of John D. Rockefeller in giving $32,-
000,000 to the General Education Board and charged that the gift was
made to perpetuate the privileges of the Standard Oil Company.[63] Such
hostility to big business, however, was not necessarily a demand for the
big reforms referred to by Ross.

Muckraking reform found many exciting evils to denounce, and the
schools were called upon to help correct these evils. There were other
possible kinds of interaction between muckraking reform and the schools.
According to one recent book, the growth of high schools had produced
"a larger readership" that supplied a market for the popular magazines
in which many of the muckraking articles were published.[64] Big business
and allegedly fraudulent businesses were frequently targets of attack.
Perhaps one consequence of this was the development in some educators
of hostility to industrialists, an attitude that played a part in the reaction
against vocational schools under separate boards.

In addition to the onslaughts against political corruption and big business, reformers campaigned against a variety of conditions, ranging from
cigarette smoking to organized vice. Schools were sometimes blamed
for creating the evils. Back in 1890 the *Arena* asserted that in New York
City 20,000 working girls were each year driven to "lives of shame" and

[62] Edward A. Ross, "Education for Social Service," NEA, 1914, pp. 105–106.
[63] "Johnson Criticises Rockefeller," *School Journal* (February 23, 1907), p. 199.
[64] Arthur and Lila Weinberg, *The Muckrakers* (New York: Simon and Schuster,
1961), p. xiv.

that this was a result of "training the intellect at the expense of ethical education"; *Arena* called for more ethical and industrial training in schools. The editor included dishonest and corrupt officials, trusts, and the selfishness of capital among other examples of the "moral torpidity" of education at that time.[65] In 1907 James Earl Russell of Columbia's Teachers College found "anarchy and immorality" to be "the direct results of our inadequate public school system." The typical American boy and girl, he said, looked forward to high positions in which they could wear handsome clothes. "It has been said," he continued, "that no agency in the country turns more girls into the streets than our public schools. These young women have no decent way to earn their own living. The boys whom we fail to attract to our schools are the ones who make the anarchists, and it is not strange, considering the upbringing they have had."[66] Industrial education was again seen as the remedy.

A more specific attack on vice was represented in the movement for sex education. In 1907 a number of leading educators met at the New York Academy of Medicine "in the interests of scientific teaching of sex subjects in the public schools." Included in the group were Dean Thomas M. Balliet of New York University's School of Pedagogy, formerly Superintendent of the Springfield, Massachusetts, schools; John R. Elliot of the New York Ethical Culture Schools; and Superintendent William H. Maxwell. According to the editorial in *Education,* Professor Burt C. Wilder of Cornell University "gave some dreadful statistics and said that he had brought with him a great many other documents showing the wide prevalence of sexual vice, but had not the heart to present them." Inevitably, "it was agreed that the schools must face the problem and solve it."[67]

Among other problems the schools were summoned to solve were those of impure music and reading matter. Addressing the NEA Department of Music Education in 1913, Editor Winship of the *Journal of Education* called upon his audience to combat ragtime and other music of what he called "the lower world." He compared the spread of ragtime to that of blue Canadian thistle in an orange grove. Like the Canadian thistle, the ragtime would be conquered by changing the conditions of the

[65] "A Broader Education Required," *Arena* (April, 1890), p. 627.

[66] James Earl Russell, address at the Manhattan Trade School, January 17, 1907, as quoted by William McAndrew, "Industrial Education from a Public-School Man's Point of View," *Educational Review* (February, 1908), p. 118.

[67] *Education* (February, 1907), pp. 370–371.

soil, and it was the "mission of the school" to provide the child with "all that is best, purest, noblest in music."[68] At the same meeting, Music Supervisor Lucy K. Cole of the Seattle Public Schools summoned her art to the cause of education for social control. "The wonderful success of municipally controlled music in New York and other eastern cities," she declared, "has opened a new field of responsibility for our civil authorities and has shown us also, in this short time, the great value of music as a sociological factor in community life. The moral results upon the masses are sure to follow."[69]

Those who attacked impure literature decided to provide themselves with the benefits of an organized group. In 1904 Julia Ward Howe joined Washington Gladden and Henry Van Dyke in Boston to form the Pure Literature League, one purpose of which was to discourage "the reading of weak and vicious literature by the young." The way to do this, declared the League in its advice to parents and teachers, was by giving children "the best in literature, that has nourished the great men and women of the race,"[70] a laudable aim indeed, but perhaps one of which teachers did not need to be reminded.

V

The Pure Literature League symbolized one of the most widespread and persistent characteristics of the reform movement, namely organization. Almost every phase of reform was represented by a league, a committee, an association, a congress, a society, or by a department in the NEA.[71] "The multiplication of societies and associations for the betterment of the physical, the mental, and the spiritual man," declared President Edward T. Fairchild of New Hampshire College in his presidential address to the NEA in 1913, "is the glory of the age."[72] Many of these were by-products of, or at least closely related to, the earlier movement for child study, and in 1910 the Child Welfare Conference was seeking,

[68] A. E. Winship, "Music and Ethics," NEA, 1913, p. 603.
[69] Lucy K. Cole, "Music and the Social Problem," NEA, 1913, p. 607.
[70] *Education* (December, 1904), pp. 239–240.
[71] Eliot alone was identified with more than 200 such organized groups, and he had at one time or another carried demanding responsibilities in the National Committee for Mental Hygiene, the Carnegie Endowment for International Peace, the American Social Hygiene Association, the General Education Board, and the National Civil Service Reform League. Henry James, *Charles W. Eliot* (Boston: Houghton Mifflin Co., 1930), II, 189.
[72] Edward T. Fairchild, "President's Address," NEA, 1913, p. 33.

in the words of G. Stanley Hall, to unite them into a national "organization of organizations" with headquarters at Washington.[73] These groups
concerned themselves with practically all phases of child welfare, both
inside and outside the school, and were often actively engaged in the
promotion of practical studies and industrial education.

Much of the reform movement, particularly in relation to education
and child welfare, was a women's crusade. During the last two decades
of the nineteenth century, philanthropic women had been active in the
promotion of manual training, cooking, and sewing. Women were prominent in the various congresses of child study in the 1890's. Soon there
were reform organizations exclusively for women. In 1897 Mrs. Alice
McLellan Birney, Mrs. Grover Cleveland, Mrs. Adlai Stevenson, and
Mrs. Phoebe Apperson Hearst, mother of Willian Randolph Hearst,
took the lead in forming the National Congress of Mothers. The first
meeting, held in Washington, D.C., attracted 2000 people and was addressed by G. Stanley Hall. There was a strong desire to include teachers, and in 1899 Kansas City became the birthplace of the first parent-
teachers association. The national organization changed its name in 1908
to *National Congress of Mothers and Parent-Teachers Associations,* one
destined to be changed again in 1924 to *National Congress of Parents
and Teachers.* It was in 1908 that the organization held its First International Congress on the Welfare of the Child, attended by delegates
from twelve countries, and it opened with "a ringing address of welcome" by Theodore Roosevelt.[74]

A woman speaker at the NEA meeting in 1907 said there were in
Chicago alone about 50 organizations of women engaged in social and
educational work.[75] The NEA in that year created the Department of
National Organizations of Women. Organizations which had joined in
requesting such action included not only the National Congress of
Mothers, but also the General Federation of Women's Clubs, the Association of Collegiate Alumnae, the Woman's Christian Temperance
Union, the National Council of Jewish Women, the Southern Association
of College Women, and the Daughters of the American Revolution.

The keynote of the first meeting in 1908 was socialization. "We have

[73] G. Stanley Hall, "The National Child Welfare Conference," NEA, 1910, p.
893.
[74] National Congress of Parents and Teachers, *Jubilee History* (Chicago: The
Congress, 1947), p. 60.
[75] Cited by Elmer E. Brown, NEA, 1907, p. 232.

been relieved by the new social order of what seems a dozen women's work," declared Mrs. O. Shepard Barnum of Los Angeles, "and have been left with our own time comparatively free. This time is due and should be devoted to the new social order." Here apparently was one instance where a connection could be established between modern technology and the new education. Mrs. Barnum presented a summary of women's work "for the socialization of the school," citing in particular the advocacy and promotion of "domestic science, manual training, industrial training, school gardening, agricultural training, vocational studies, technical and trade schools." Even the washing of hands, she said, would have to be socialized, for the rush of modern life prevented mothers from seeing, as had those of old, that children washed their hands before eating. She promised, however, that women's groups would not criticize local schools or interfere with them. "The aim should always be," she concluded, "to find out in any locality *what the schools want* and help them get it."[76]

State-by-state reports to this Department in 1911 (by then renamed the Department of School Patrons) further indicated the interests of women's groups in practical subjects, socialized activities, and social service. Projects included vacation schools, school lunches, the use of visiting housekeepers to teach women to prepare food properly, manual training, domestic science, sanitation and hygiene, and kindergartens. The local PTA's were evidently becoming vehicles for communication between women's organizations and school faculties. "In one suburb," said the report from Illinois, "the ladies of a parent-teachers association take turns at the high school in serving afternoon tea to the teachers. 'Over the tea-cups' a delightful and helpful social spirit is being developed between teacher and school patron."[77]

VI

It was largely in the domain of social service that most of the women's organizations carried on their work. This was true of much of the reform movement. Attempts to right obvious wrongs were by no means inconsistent with traditions of individualism. Neither was belief in an education

[76] Mrs. O. Shepard Barnum, "Women's Work in the Socialization of the Schools," NEA, 1908, pp. 1232–1235.
[77] Department of School Patrons, Summary of State Reports of Joint Committees and Affiliated Organizations, 1910–1911, NEA, 1911, p. 1098.

designed for the service of humanity. Even in the service aspects of reform, however, so much emphasis was placed on the social side of life that the result was a massive shift away from individualistic school purposes. The various elements of "socialization" became interwoven to such a degree that it was difficult to tell them apart. Within the fabric were the threads of education for social control. Speakers and writers who started out with "social aims," often included both service and control before they finished.

Meanwhile, it was becoming increasingly fashionable in pedagogical circles to talk of education for social efficiency. This was not a new expression, but it took time to develop. In 1904 Charles Scribner's Sons turned down a manuscript entitled "Education for Social Efficiency" on the ground of uncertainty about "the number of readers to whom the subject will appeal sufficiently to make them wish to possess the book."[78] They would not have had long to wait. The term served a useful purpose by covering all possible aspects of socialization. It swept in not only the two major aspects of reform—service and control—but also the various submovements, such as social centers and social education, as well. "Social efficiency," wrote William C. Bagley, then a young professor in the Dillon, Montana, Normal School, "is the standard by which the forces of education must select the experiences that are impressed upon the individual. Every subject of instruction, every item of knowledge, every form of reaction, every detail of habit, must be measured by this yardstick."[79] Here was the basic thought later to appear, perhaps somewhat more moderately expressed, in the doctrine of the *Cardinal Principles* report.

The large domain of education for social efficiency gave promise of making the everyday tasks of schooling appear more exciting, at least superficially, than they had been before. It seemed to meet the challenge to educators, expressed by Albion Small back in 1896, to be not leaders of children, but makers of society. Lewis M. Terman of Stanford enthusiastically declared in 1911 that the future belonged to the educator. The war lords, he said, no longer existed in the ancient sense, and clergymen and lawyers were waning in their influence. As society realized the importance of education, he concluded, "our prophecy will be fulfilled,

[78] Charles Scribner's Sons to M. V. O'Shea, December 14, 1904, Michael Vincent O'Shea Papers (State Historical Society of Wisconsin, Madison, Wis.).
[79] William C. Bagley, *The Educative Process* (New York: Macmillan Co., 1905), p. 60.

and the educator will come to his own. The common teacher will be rediscovered and the superintendent or principal will rank with judge or congressman in honor and reward."[80] Actually, the educators did not need to seek this role for themselves. There were many political and civic leaders in this period, including President Roosevelt himself, who seemed determined to have educators accept such responsibilities.

Whether for this or other reasons, testimonials for social efficiency poured in from all parts of the land. Nathaniel Butler of the University of Chicago declared that the definition of education as "a training for social efficiency" was "one beyond which it seems we shall hardly advance."[81] The primary aim of the public school, declared Arthur Deerin Call of Hartford, Connecticut, in 1909, was "not to promote academic training," but rather "to enable the pupils by means of free, fair and genial social intercourse, under the leadership of friendly and large-spirited men and women, to obtain practice in real life, to become socially and serviceably efficient."[82] The tendency in 1909, said G. H. Patterson of Salem, Oregon, in an address to the western division of the Oregon State Teachers' Association, was to introduce subjects "better suited to the economic and social needs of the pupils, meaning increased social efficiency of all future citizens who attend school."[83] From New Albany, Indiana, in 1911 came the conclusion expressed by its superintendent Charles B. McLinn that the school was "by its nature a social unit whose purpose is to fit for social efficiency."[84] In 1913 one of the most complete expressions of the idea, with explicit provision in it for social control, came interestingly enough from Superintendent Addison B. Poland, of Newark, New Jersey, one of the remaining survivors of the period of the Committee of Ten. Poland took exception to a statement by old-time Herbartian Frank M. McMurry about individuality as the central purpose of the school. The true purpose, as expressed by Poland, was "not individuality but social unity," and he stated his plea for the

[80] Lewis M. Terman, "Child-Study: Its Reason and Promise," *Educator-Journal* (November, 1911), pp. 124–125.

[81] Nathaniel Butler, "The Aim in the High School," *School Review* (February, 1906), p. 137.

[82] Arthur Deerin Call, "Some Problems Common to High and Grammar School," *Education* (September, 1909), p. 9.

[83] G. H. Patterson, "The Chief Aim of High School Education," *Proceedings of the Ninth Annual Convention,* Oregon State Teachers' Association (western division) (The Association, 1909), p. 63.

[84] Charles B. McLinn, "The Social Side of High School Life," *Journal of Education* (October 5, 1911), p. 345.

"unity which results in efficiency and is rarely, or never, attained except by and thru uniformity of some kind." Poland went on to denounce individuality as the assumption of aristocratic systems. "In a political and social democracy such as ours," he concluded, "children must be taught to live and to work together co-operatively; to submit their individual wills to the will of the majority; and to conform to social requirements whether they approve of them or not."[85]

In the end, social efficiency conquered all, and it absorbed even industrial education, the topic that had so long dominated pedagogical discourse. It was largely under the banner of social efficiency that school men began to talk of industrial education as only one part of a comprehensive school program. Social efficiency reinforced the growing dislike of separate high schools of commerce or manual training. It demanded what was first called the "cosmopolitan high school," where pupils from all classes would come together, if not in their classrooms, at least in the social life of the school. This did not, however, imply abandonment of the idea of "differentiated" programs for pupils of the different social or economic groups, for such differentiation could be provided within the context of a single high school plant through a definite, or even rigid, plan of election by courses.

The spread of social doctrine in education was favorable to the introduction and development of the so-called practical studies. Much of this took place in relation to industrial education, but it was applied also to such subjects as physical education and home economics. The Woman's Christian Temperance Union had a department of physical education, and its superintendent, Frances W. Leiter, urged the development of physical education in schools as a means of combating drink. Her explanation was an interesting one, involving the habit-forming uses of certain patent medicines by the sick. "It is not alone at the hotel bar," she declared, "nor at the grog shop, that drunkards are started. The prescription of the physician, the enormous list and quantity of patent medicines used, have much to account for in the progress of drunkard-making."[86] In 1908 one of the projects of the Brookline, Massachusetts, Education Society culminated in the opening of the $141,000 public gymnasium, characterized by *Education* as "without parallel in the United States."[87]

[85] Addison B. Poland, discussion, NEA, 1913, pp. 143–146.
[86] Frances W. Leiter, "Physical Education Legislation—Its Needs," NEA, 1901, p. 762.
[87] *Education* (June, 1908), p. 660.

There were, however, many public provisions being made for physical education, both in and out of the schools. Social settlements, women's clubs, churches, and youth organizations offered gymnasium facilities for youth and adults. Physical education, particularly as expressed through sports and games, was one of the most social of all pedagogical enterprises, and it was bound to thrive in an age of social reform.

Of all the practical subjects, however, the one that seemed most clearly to reflect the doctrine of social efficiency was home economics, otherwise known as housewifery or domestic science. Ellen H. Richards of the Massachusetts Institute of Technology had assumed the leadership of this movement back in the middle 1890's and had enlisted as her second-in-command Mrs. Melvil Dewey, wife of the onetime Secretary of the New York State Board of Regents. The Deweys made their summer home available for what became the Lake Placid Conferences, where leaders in home economics assembled from all sections of the country. Mrs. Richards began with the more scientific or technical aspects of the subject, but soon linked these to social implications, searching the writings of Edward A. Ross, Thorstein Veblen, and other sociologists and economists for material pertaining to the role of the family in society.[88] "Who can doubt," she asked the National Council of the NEA in 1908, "that . . . the domestic science course offers the best means to influence the lives of the people and influence them quickly?"[89] Increasingly she gave attention to the economics of consumption as part of home economics. Prevailing notions about good food, in her estimation, were incorrect, and a person could be fed on ten cents a day if necessary.[90] The trouble, as she saw it, was that people would rather spend money than save it and that everybody wanted money to spend.[91]

Other home economists also stressed the contributions of the field to social efficiency and reform. Matie P. Clark, a domestic science teacher at the Manual Training and Commercial High School of Oakland, California, pointed out that instruction in her field endeavored "to create a demand for pure foods." The real influence would be felt when the girl

[88] Ellen H. Richards to Mrs. Melvil Dewey, February 25 and April 19, 1902, Melvil Dewey Papers (Columbia University, New York, N.Y.).
[89] Ellen H. Richards, "Home Economics in Elementary and Secondary Education," NEA, 1908, p. 490.
[90] Ellen H. Richards to Mrs. Melvil Dewey, January 24, 1910, Melvil Dewey Papers (Columbia University, New York, N.Y.).
[91] Ellen H. Richards to Mrs. Melvil Dewey, March 26, 1910, Melvil Dewey Papers (Columbia University, New York, N.Y.).

being educated then became a housekeeper and used "to her fullest power the law of supply and demand in pure foods and sanitary surroundings."[92] Irene McDermott, Director of Household Economy in the Pittsburgh Public Schools, pointed out the need for teaching people how to "maintain the family as an efficient unit in society" in the face of low incomes, although she protested against the injustice of the low incomes as well. Much of this kind of discussion was centered on the unwise spending of money, and Mrs. McDermott felt there was "as much misery and crime brought about by an inordinate desire to possess clothes unsuited to one's income" as there was "in the overindulgence in strong drink."[93]

VII

There was nothing inherently antiacademic in the development of these practical subjects. Neither was there in the idea of social efficiency itself. As it happened with industrial education, however, the discussion of social efficiency set up in the minds of many educators and others who wrote and talked on the subject a sharp conflict between the academic and the practical. The "academic" or traditional subjects, by then including some of the modern subjects as well as the classics and mathematics, did not for the most part come out well in considerations of this alleged conflict. English and the sciences, it was thought, could be redeemed and made socially valuable. History was doubtful, and there was a tendency to favor the other social sciences or studies, particularly government and economics. The subjects most frequently disparaged were mathematics and the languages, ancient or modern, especially Latin. Along with this point of view came a widespread repudiation of mental training as a purpose, by then considered an exploded doctrine.

Attacks on the allegedly traditional subjects were numerous and

[92] Matie P. Clark, "The Public School Domestic-Science Department as an Influence in the Community for Enforcing Pure-Food Laws and Civic Cleanliness," NEA, 1911, p. 765.

[93] Irene E. McDermott, discussion, NEA, 1912, pp. 982–983. If Mrs. McDermott was talking about women, she may have been blaming the wrong sex. According to a member of the Mother's Assembly of the State of New York, it was the men of the lower stations of life who were at fault in wanting their wives to look like those of the higher stations. Better education of boys, she felt, would help resolve this difficulty. Mrs. D. B. Perry to M. V. O'Shea, September 16, 1915, Michael Vincent O'Shea Papers (State Historical Society of Wisconsin, Madison, Wis.).

varied. They were written off as a bookish, medieval, and aristocratic. Some of the prevailing attitude reflected the feeling that traditional subjects were unsuitable for particular groups, such as girls of any social class, or "the masses" of both sexes. Others went beyond this and questioned the value of traditional subjects for anybody; but they reluctantly consented to their survival, in view of the truculence of the colleges, as tickets for college admission. Sometimes the various points of view were mixed in the same utterance. For the most part, these expressions came from the "new men" in education, but there were a few of the old who joined in as well. Most of these "new men" were themselves the products of the traditional programs.

It was desirable in the education of women, thought Superintendent H. J. Wightman of Altoona, Pennsylvania, to weigh Latin against cooking, solid geometry against dressmaking, and algebra against household duties.[94] "Crowd out the subjects," advised Professor Arland D. Weeks of the North Dakota Agricultural College, "that are least defensible from any point of view, as Latin, and make room for the trade element."[95] It was "adolescent imitation" that favored the college-preparatory course, declared Principal William D. Lewis of the North High School in Syracuse, New York, and "boyish snobbery" that was "proud to study Latin."[96] Principal William McAndrew of the Washington Irving High School for Girls in New York City, addressing the NEA Department of Secondary Education in 1910, said he was "tired of the restrictions of an unproved curriculum." His girls, he went on, wanted "to study the social amenities that make life more pleasant and friendship more enjoyable" and wanted something in 1910 they could use in 1911. He did not care "a picayune for the horrible nightmare they called the scansion of Latin verse," although he granted a possible place to Latin literature that moved the heart. "Around us," he reminded his fellow principals, "hover problems clamoring for answer; we see crime increasing, wedded loyalty renounced without a tear, literature and drama festering with immorality, city governments weltering in corruption, business in the vise-like grip of monopoly and privilege, while we, in whose hands are

[94] H. J. Wightman, "Technical Courses in High Schools," *Pennsylvania School Journal* (March, 1907), p. 400.

[95] Arland D. Weeks, "The Two Aims of High Schools," *Education* (March, 1909), p. 421.

[96] William D. Lewis, "College Domination of High Schools," *Outlook* (December 11, 1909), p. 821.

the citizens to be, consider the character of these coming men and women as a possible by-product or neglect it altogether."[97]

A somewhat different note was struck by Ellwood Cubberley in an address to the Harvard Teachers' Association in 1911, but to much the same effect. Arguing that the introduction of new subjects did not threaten liberal culture, Cubberley conceded that the effect would be to decrease the relative enrollments in Latin and Greek. This, he said, could not be denied, and he added, "indeed, it is much to be hoped," an effect which in his opinion "would be no blow to liberal culture."[98] Thus were the classics not only denied admission to the new realm of social efficiency, but they were also hurled forth from territory once considered to be their own.

In March and April of 1912, the *Saturday Evening Post* published two vigorous assaults against the academic tradition. One of them, by William Hughes Mearns, was entitled, "Our Medieval High Schools: Shall We Educate Children for the Twelfth or the Twentieth Century?" What was wrong with the high school was "culture," and "the culture chaps" had controlled the high school for a long time. The spell of culture had even taken over manual training. Culture, said Mearns, is "an incommunicable communion with Nature; it is clean hands and a pure collar; it is the possession of great-grandparents—white, Christian preferred; it is the achievement of tolerance; it is the proper use of 'shall' and 'will'; it is a knowledge of Hegelian philosophy; it is Greek; it is Latin; it is a five-foot shelf of books; it is twenty thousand a year; it is a sight of truth and a draught of wisdom; it is a frock coat and pearl gloves." Having disposed of Harris, Eliot, and the classics, the writer of this article said the people had begun to murmur and would in the next few years be demanding a change. The high school, he predicted, would be "turned topsy-turvy several times" before it settled down. It was "a democratic institution," and it should base its studies on no plan that would not "bear the test of efficient service to the community about it."[99]

The other *Post* article came from William D. Lewis, formerly Principal in Syracuse, but then of the William Penn High School in Philadelphia. "Isn't it true," he asked, "that the high school's largest service is the best possible training for economic efficiency, good citizenship, and full and

[97] William McAndrew, "The High School Itself," NEA, 1910, pp. 455–457.

[98] Ellwood P. Cubberley, "Does the Present Trend toward Vocational Education Threaten Liberal Culture?" *School Review* (September, 1911), p. 464.

[99] William Hughes Mearns, "Our Medieval High Schools," *Saturday Evening Post* (March 2, 1912), pp. 18–19.

complete living for all its pupils?" To achieve this, he said, the high school should provide English, but not dissection of literary masterpieces under a "pedantic microscope." It should provide a wide range of mathematics, but not require algebra. Foreign languages were fine for those who wanted them, but "at present," he said, "nearly every pupil in an American high school is compelled to study at least one foreign language"[100]—a statement that was somewhat incorrect. Two years later Lewis presented an expanded version of his ideas in a book, *Democracy's High School,* to which an enthusiastic foreword was written by Theodore Roosevelt. In the first chapter, called "A Social View of the High School," Lewis called for training "in citizenship and in right social thinking," both through the curriculum and through participation in the organization and management of the school.[101] The American people, he said, had "no concern for academic traditions evolved from a scheme of education aimed to serve an aristocratic or leisure class."[102] Classical education, he conceded at one point in the book, was still needed, but the new type of education was equally necessary because of "revolutionized social and industrial conditions. . . ."[103] He did not specify those who needed the classical education.

Some of these utterances represented a point of view that was later attached, possibly with some injustice, to the stereotype of "life-adjustment" education. "Scholarship is not our chief business," declared a committee of teachers at the Washington Irving High School of New York City in 1911.[104] Edward O. Sisson, Professor of Education at the University of Washington, criticized a conference of high school teachers that had stated the purposes of English as the development of ability to write and speak, the acquainting of the pupil with the best literary products, the cultivating of a sense of style, and the inculcating of a love of literature. Commenting on these purposes, Sisson said: "The fact is that the secondary school teacher is too absorbed in the intellectual aspects of his particular subject."[105] An editorial in *Education* in

---

[100] William D. Lewis, "The High School and the Boy," *Saturday Evening Post* (April 6, 1912), pp. 77–78.

[101] William D. Lewis, *Democracy's High School* (Boston: Houghton Mifflin Co., 1914), p. 6.

[102] *Ibid.,* p. 26.

[103] *Ibid.,* p. 29.

[104] Jessie A. Beach and others, "Success in School," *School Review* (November, 1911), p. 587.

[105] Edward O. Sisson, "The High School's Cure of Souls," *Educational Review* (April, 1908), p. 362.

1911 asked, "Where does trigonometry apply in a good woman's life? Will it contribute anything toward peace, happiness and contentment in the home? Will it bake any bread, sew on any buttons or rock any cradles?"[106] Perhaps the most interesting comment came from Nellie Hattan Britan of Hanover College, Indiana, about Lady Jane Grey, who, in the account given in Roger Ascham's *The Scholemaster,* had been found reading Plato while her friends were hunting in the park. When asked why she was not out with the hunt, Lady Jane had replied that all sport in the park was but a shadow to the pleasure she found in Plato. "If such a child were found to-day," said Miss Britan, "I dare say she would be hurried off to a physician or a brain specialist."[107]

There was little room in the prevailing climate of American education after 1905 for those who preferred Plato to hunting in the park, especially for those who preferred Plato to working on projects for improving the community. Still the movement was not on the whole what might be called anti-intellectual, certainly not in the sense of being opposed to the use of intelligence—and Plato also had been concerned about community improvement. Furthermore, the movement for social efficiency should not be thought of as one directed against solid content or subject matter. In fact, the new doctrines were on the side of information in the old debate about information versus training. Snedden and Bagley, for example, placed much stress on the social usefulness of appropriate subject matter. Years later, in the period following World War I, they would be found leading the opposition to the Progressive Education Association, and its alleged disparagement of subject matter. The point in their doctrine between 1905 and 1915, as in those of many other educators at that time, was that every subject and every part of every subject had to meet the test of social usefulness or efficiency.

Perhaps the main defect in the popular utterances of this period was the sharp distinction made between the academic and the practical. It was this distinction that Nicholas Murray Butler, an earlier proponent of many new causes, attacked in 1908. "The Philistine," he said, "whether writing for a newspaper or not, uniformly uses the word academic as a term of contempt or derision."[108] His was not the only voice to be raised in protest against the trend of the times, although the protests

[106] *Education* (October, 1911), p. 118.
[107] Nellie Hattan Britan, "What Physical Education Is Doing for Women," *Education* (September, 1908), p. 35.
[108] Nicholas Murray Butler, "The Academic and the Practical," *Educational Review* (November, 1908), p. 377.

were for the most part drowned in the overwhelming volume of utterance on the other side. Many of the protests, of course, came from the professors of Latin and Greek, now faced by a much more formidable threat than had ever been presented to them by the Committee of Ten.

Some of the protests came from professors of education and from school administrators. James L. McConaughy, professor of education at Bowdoin College, criticized the notion that "algebra, because it may not help a girl to earn a bigger salary or make a more comfortable home, is to be thrown into the scrap heap." He argued for the academic subjects on the grounds of enjoyment. "Should not high school boys and girls," he asked, "go into life trained to use the wonderful pleasure giving opportunities which literature, art and history afford? How many of the pupils trained in the new vocational subjects know how to read with pleasure—and what bigger gift can education bring us?"[109] Superintendent James Harris of Dubuque, Iowa, criticized efficiency as an educational aim, contending that it ignored or possibly even condemned "the reflective and contemplative side of life." To exalt it to a philosophy of education, he said, was to do violence to intelligence and common sense.[110] On the broader issue of the individual and society, it was a school administrator, Lewis B. Avery, Assistant Superintendent in Oakland, California, who contended that the freedom of the individual was fundamental. "Neither labor nor capital, neither society nor state, neither theories of efficiency nor the acknowledged attractiveness of industrial and social solidarity," he proclaimed to the NEA Department of Secondary Education in 1915, "shall keep us from making the high school first of all the bulwark of individual freedom."[111]

[109] James L. McConaughy, "Three Popular High School Fallacies," *Education* (February, 1914), p. 372.

[110] James H. Harris, "Is Efficiency an Adequate Statement of the Aim of Education?" *Ohio Educational Monthly* (April, 1916), pp. 148–149.

[111] Lewis B. Avery, "The Future High School," NEA, 1915, p. 751.

Chapter 12

The colleges defied

"We are come to the Rubicon."

PRINCIPAL J. STANLEY BROWN,
JULY 8, 1909.

*I*n the midst of all the talk about industrial education and social efficiency, the class-room teachers of the high schools had no choice but to go on with their daily tasks. Cosmic pronouncements notwithstanding, there were still lessons to assign, exercises to correct, recitations to conduct, order to maintain, and marks to record. With more and still more pupils coming, there was more and much more of all this to be done. City high schools outgrew their capacities and spilled over into annexes and branches; many new schools had to be built. Always there was the demand for more teachers. "The high school has had to grow with the speed of a mushroom," wrote one observer looking back from the vantage point of the year 1919, "and is excusable for not having acquired the strength of an oak. . . . Faster than a thousand teachers could be trained it has had to have ten thousand."[1] Teachers and administrators, however, were not looking for excuses. They were far too busy meeting the future that was already upon them.

By 1905 the first shock of the enrollment increase had been absorbed. After that time, it was not only the rate of increase that had to be taken into account, but also the sheer magnitude of the numbers involved, with the enrollment of public high schools passing the million level in 1912, reaching a total of 1,105,360 pupils.[2] The size of the enrollment made old dilemmas—such as preparation for college and preparation for life—look like new ones, and the legend of a golden past in secondary education was already in the making. Inevitably, the doctrines of vocational-

[1] C. H. Ward, "Education Bolshevism," *Outlook* (September 24, 1919), p. 130.
[2] Commissioner, 1912, II, p. 484.

284

ism and efficiency were said to have been called forth by the new magnitude of the school enrollment and to be ways of dealing with it, as well as being desirable and good in themselves.

Still the relative enrollments in so-called traditional subjects did not begin to show marked decline until the period between 1910 and 1915. Those in Latin, for example, came to 49 percent of the number of pupils as late as 1910 and 37.3 percent in 1915. In mathematics the total relative enrollments in algebra and geometry stood at 86.9 percent in 1910, followed by a decline to 74.6 per cent over the next five years.[3]

As might be expected, there continued to be much speculation about the social and economic composition of groups both in and out of school. The traditional nature of the high school curriculum was blamed for keeping pupils away, but there was the undisputed fact that many thousands more were entering each year. Nevertheless, ran the criticisms, the needs of such pupils were not being met, and the traditional subjects were judged unsuitable for the "masses" now invading the high school. What emerged then was a two-pronged argument: first, that the program kept many pupils out of high school; and second, that there were many pupils coming who presumably should have known better in view of what was being offered.

A comprehensive study of the social and economic backgrounds of 826 pupils who entered the high schools of New York City in 1906 indicated a broad representation of various occupational groups and in about the same proportions in which these groups were represented in the city population as a whole. Artisans and contractors, for example, made up 16.4 percent of the population (presumably of the employed population), while the children of artisans and contractors made up 18.1 percent of the group entering high school. For the category of "manufacture and trade," the corresponding figures were 27.5 and 28.1. Office workers were more heavily represented in the group of high school entrants than in the city population, 12.8 percent to 7.9 percent, as were

[3] Commissioner 1910, II, p. 1139, and 1916, II, p. 487. The 1916 report contains the data for the year ending June 30, 1915. It should be noted that the relative enrollments in the 1910 report and all subsequent reports up to 1948–1949 were based not on the total population of the high school, but on the number of pupils in schools whose principals filled out the schedule pertaining to the school studies. In 1910, for example, this figure came to 739,143 pupils as contrasted with a total enrollment of 915,061. Before 1910 the total enrollment had been used as the base. Figures for 1910 and for all years up to 1948–1949, therefore, cannot be directly compared with those given in the reports before 1910.

also federal and city employees, 7.4 percent to 3.6 percent. Factory labor made up 10 percent of the population, but was represented by only 4.4 percent of the fathers of the high school entrants.[4]

The investigator, however, was surprised by the "use of the high school by the children of artisans, mechanics and other skilled hand-workers," presumably represented by the category of manufacture and trade, and speculated on the possibility that "escape from manual work" was "a strong factor in sending some boys and girls to high school." He noted furthermore that approximately every other unskilled laborer had one child in the New York high schools. His figures, he felt, might "well cause surprise because they apparently show that the high schools are used chiefly by the children of parents who themselves never, in all probability, carried their own education beyond the earliest years of the elementary schools." He raised the question he said must constantly recur, namely, "Does the curriculum which we have inherited from earlier and different social conditions still stand as the best one to meet the present situation?"[5]

This New York study was not confined to the occupations of the fathers, but included also the monthly rentals paid by the families. According to the investigator, the figure of $15 a month, "the most common one for our recorded pupils," was relatively low for New York City.[6] "If rental is taken as a criterion," he said, "we find a class of pupils, whose parents are struggling for the bare necessities of life, pursuing at high school for the greater part the remnants of an aristocratic secondary education to which are added many subjects chiefly dictated by the colleges or modern culture. We are preparing for a college to which few will ever go and for a life of ease and refinement which few will ever enjoy, the greater part of our thirty thousand pupils." Among the inappropriate elements of the curriculum mentioned by him were German, Latin, and algebra, and within the field of English, the study of "The Rime of the Ancient Mariner."[7]

The suitability of the traditional curriculum, he felt, was called into question by the large number of dropouts, but he found only a slight degree of relationship between the rents paid by the parents and the

[4] Joseph K. Van Denburg, *Causes of the Elimination of Students in Public Secondary Schools of New York City,* Contributions to Education No. 47 (New York: Teachers College, Columbia University, 1911), p. 44.
[5] *Ibid.,* pp. 46–48.
[6] *Ibid.,* p. 80.
[7] *Ibid.,* p. 82.

tendency of children to drop out of high school. Again he was surprised. "We saw," he observed, "that children remain through the elementary school and enter high school from homes of the most meagre financial resources. We now find that such children remain in high school as long or nearly as long as do children whose parents pay $40 or more a month for rent."[8] He did not, however, revise his judgments about the unsuitability of the traditional program.

Apparently each generation of school men discovered dropouts anew, just as it discovered the "masses," but the rate of school leaving for the period after 1905 was no greater than it had been during the 1890's. Graduates comprised 10.7 percent of the total enrollment in 1890, 11.9 percent in 1900, 11.7 percent in 1905, 12.1 percent in 1910, and 12.5 percent in 1912.[9] The proportions remained about the same in spite of a five-fold expansion of enrollments, with the "masses" showing no greater tendency to leave school than had their allegedly more select predecessors. The drop-out question of the period after 1905 was, therefore, a continuation of the same question that had troubled the school men of the past.

Much attention was paid in this period to school failure or "non-promotion," both as an elucidation of the drop-out question and as an indicator of the degree of the effectiveness of the schools. Elementary schools attracted most of the attention, or notoriety, on this point, but the high schools also were involved.[10] Among the proposals for dealing

---

[8] *Ibid.*, pp. 113–114.

[9] Commissioner, 1889–1890, II, pp. 1388–1389; 1899–1900, II, p. 2122; 1905, II, pp. 813, 816; 1910, II, pp. 1127, 1135; 1912, II, pp. 484, 488. Comparing the number of graduates with the total number in school was the conventional way of estimating dropouts in this period. This led to overestimates during periods of rapidly increasing enrollments, but it certainly did not lead to underestimates. Possibly there may even have been some reduction in the drop-out rate over this period.

[10] Reports on failure in high school varied widely from one place to the next. One study, published in 1907 on the basis of 39 high schools, showed an average failure rate of 16 percent in algebra, with a range from 5 percent in one school to 50 percent in another, and of 14 percent in Latin, with a range from zero to 35 percent. R. R. Grant, "Statistics of High School Requirements," *School Journal* (April 27, 1907), pp. 428–429. Another study, reported in 1908 from 16 high schools, showed an average failure rate in all subjects of 22 percent, with rates of 28 percent for algebra, 24 percent for geometry, 23 percent for Latin, 18 percent for German and history, and 20 percent for chemistry, English, physics, and French. H. E. Kratz, "How Shall We Assist Our Pupils When and Only When They Need It?" NEA, 1908, p. 592. In 1913, a study made of schools in the vicinity of Chicago showed figures both for failures and for withdrawals from subjects. First-year algebra had an average withdrawal of 12.9 percent and an

with the failure rate was one advocating a longer school day, with time for supervised study. The idea was developing also that failure of a pupil constituted failure on the part of the teacher and the school. In 1911 a committee of teachers at Washington Irving High School for Girls, New York City, called every failure of a girl to advance "a failure of her teachers" and demanded that teachers be rewarded for keeping beginners in school and "punished for letting them leave." The committee said advertising writers were judged by results and teachers should be likewise. "We suffer," concluded this group of teachers, "from lack of competition."[11] Shortly afterward a committee of teachers from Boys' High School in Brooklyn disagreed with this point of view.[12] There was no particular demand in this period for adjusting marks to the capacities of pupils, although back in 1900 Superintendent C. H. Gordon of Lincoln, Nebraska, had objected to what he called "a fixed standard" in elementary schools. Gordon recommended "effort rather than subject matter" as a basis for promotion and said that a pupil who applied himself conscientiously "should be marked 'satisfactory' no matter how many questions he [might] be unable to answer at an examination."[13]

According to some who wrote and talked about failures in the first year of high school, the fault really lay in a bad connection between the high school and the grade school. There were those like Supervisor Stratton D. Brooks of Boston, who felt in 1905 that the upper grades should adopt "high-school methods of study and instruction and high-school methods of discipline and management."[14] On the other hand, some felt the high school to be at fault in not adjusting its own practices to those of the grade school. "The first year of the high school," wrote a committee of mothers in 1912, "discourages most of our children. In the last year of the grades they are coaxed and loved to a hothouse rapidity of growth. Then suddenly they are plunged into a chilling atmosphere of

---

average failure of 17.2 percent. In first-year Latin the corresponding figures ran 14.9 and 10.8. Manual training showed a low failure rate (4.8 percent), but a high withdrawal rate (20.7 percent). Commercial arithmetic had 15.4 percent failure and 10.6 percent withdrawal. *School Review* (June, 1913), pp. 414–415.

[11] Jessie A. Beach and others, "Success in School," *School Review* (November, 1911), pp. 589–593.

[12] M. L. Bishop and others, "Success in School," *School Review* (October, 1912), pp. 559–563.

[13] C. H. Gordon, "Reorganization of the Grammar School and a Rational System of Grading," *Education* (September, 1900), pp. 21–23.

[14] Stratton D. Brooks, "The Extension of High-School Influence," *Educational Review* (May, 1905), p. 438.

tutorial indifference which causes most of them within the year to stay away from the great, new, cold, strange school."[15] It is difficult to reconcile these and similar statements with the prevailing high ratios of pupils to teachers in many grade schools and with the high rate of pupil retardation in the grades themselves. Yet it did seem clear to many that there was a difference in spirit and approach between the two levels. With all this, however, high schools were tied inevitably to the grades in a relationship that could neither be ignored nor explained away.

Neither could the administrators and teachers of high schools forget their relationship to the post-high-school plans of the pupils who did stay with them through graduation. It has been assumed that the proportions of the enrolled pupils who were bound for college declined after 1900, but the evidence is by no means clear on this point. According to the Commissioner's *Reports,* the proportions of pupils in the public high schools who were preparing for college declined from 10.8 percent in 1900 to 9.5 percent in 1905 and to 5.6 percent in 1910, while those of graduates prepared for college went up from 30.3 percent in 1900 to 35.5 percent in 1905 before falling slightly to 34 percent in 1910, still a higher figure than the one for ten years before.[16] In 1912, the *Report,* using slightly different terminology, showed 35.1 percent of the graduates in the category of college-preparatory students. For the first time, the Commissioner presented an additional category of graduates preparing gor other higher institutions, with 15.3 percent in this group, making a total of 50.4 percent aiming at further study beyond high school.[17] Even without those preparing for other institutions, the 1912 figure was higher than the one for 1900.

Beyond this, there was the persistent question of what became of high-school graduates who did not go on to further schooling. Many still went directly into teaching.[18] Others distributed themselves over a variety

[15] As quoted by Milton C. Potter, "Social Organization in the High School," NEA, 1912, pp. 183–184.

[16] Commissioner, 1899–1900, II, p. 2122; 1905, II, p. 816; 1910, II, pp. 1135, 1139.

[17] Commissioner, 1912, II, p. 488. The same kinds of figures were also presented for 1911 in *Public and Private High Schools* (U.S. Bureau of Education, Bulletin No. 22 [Washington, D.C., 1912]), Table 5, p. 18. According to these, college-preparatory students made up 34.5 percent of the graduating class of 1911, plus 15.6 percent in the category of those preparing for other institutions.

[18] One study of 735 high school graduates of the year 1908 in the state of New York showed 117 of them directly entering teaching, as compared with 122 going to the normal schools. Guy-Wheeler Shallies, "The Distribution of High-School Graduates after Leaving School," *School Review* (February, 1913), p. 90. According to an-

of occupations. In a study of the immediate activities of graduates of 596 schools in the North Central Association for 1913, Judd and Counts found that 15.1 percent of them just stayed at home. Another 10.1 percent went into business, while the categories of farming, "domestic economy and agriculture," trades, and "professions" drew less than 5 percent each.[19] This kind of scattering underscored the diverse nature of the high school population, but it did not clarify the questions whether or not to base programs specifically on vocational choice.

In 1914 Superintendent J. O. Engleman of Decatur, Illinois, surveyed the anticipated destinations of some 800 of the pupils in the high school of that city. More than half this group had not yet chosen their vocations. Of those who had, the largest single group was that of 67 prospective teachers. What struck Engleman was the difference between the choices of the pupils and the occupations of the fathers. Whereas the fathers represented 102 different occupations, the selections of the pupils who had made up their minds came to only half as many. "While 109 have fathers who are farmers," reported Engleman with misgiving, "only 23 now expect to be farmers; and while 20 fathers are grocers, only one student now looks forward to life as a grocer. But 19 lawyers are scheduled to take the place of the 7 having children in the high school, and 20 physicians and 17 musicians hope to find places now filled by one-fifth of that number. . . . Barbers, blacksmiths, carpenters, laborers, machinists, and ministers are well represented among the fathers, but no son of these men indicates a desire to follow in the

---

other study, 458 graduates went directly into teaching from a group of 2,365 in 118 high schools of the Middle West during the years 1910, 1911, and 1912. This was almost one-fifth of the group. B. F. Pittenger, "The Distribution of High-School Graduates in Five North Central States," *School and Society* (June 17, 1916), p. 904. A study in Kansas showed that of 735 graduates of 47 high schools in that state in 1914 there were 212 (or 29 percent of the group) who entered teaching "at once." F. R. Aldrich, "The Distribution of High-School Graduates in Kansas," *School Review* (October, 1916), p. 613. This, then, was direct vocational training for a substantial number of high school pupils, and there were 711 high schools in 1911 reporting "training courses for teachers" and enrolling 2,103 boys and 12,-577 girls. *Public and Private High Schools* (U.S. Bureau of Education, Bulletin No. 6 [Washington, D.C., 1912]), Table 3, p. 16.

[19] C. H. Judd and G. S. Counts, *A Study of the Colleges and High Schools in the North Central Association* (U.S. Bureau of Education, Bulletin No. 6 [Washington, D.C., 1915]), Table 32, pp. 90–91. In this study, 26.9 percent of the group was reported as going to college, 7.3 percent to normal school, and 3.7 percent to commercial school.

father's footsteps."[20] With 23 pupils indicating a career choice in agriculture and a total of 155 saying they would like to study agriculture in high school, Engleman succeeded in getting a four-year program established in that field beginning in September, 1915. He considered this one of the "first fruits" of his survey.[21] Apparently Engleman felt that many of the choices made by these pupils were unrealistic and that the introduction of more specific vocational programs might correct this state of affairs.

II

Confronted by questions of vocational choice as well as by high rates of failure, the school men of this period became increasingly concerned about what should be required for admission to college and for graduation from the high school. The older protests against "college domination" had emphasized the quantity of material in the subjects required for entrance. The new attack directed attention more specifically to the patterns of required subjects, especially mathematics and foreign languages, the chief culprits in the failure rates. Most of the recognized colleges still required preparation in both fields for admission, although in many the languages did not have to include Latin. Mathematics was required for graduation in practically all high schools except those with liberal election by subjects, as in Boston between 1901 and 1907. Foreign language was less extensively required, particularly in high schools with several courses of study.

The NEA Committee on College-Entrance Requirements in 1899 had recommended identical constants for college admission and for high school graduation. Included were one year of algebra, one year of geometry, and four years of foreign language. This was still the official expression of the NEA. Opinion shifted rapidly after 1905, however, largely in the direction of giving pupils an option between mathematics and foreign language and of applying this option both to college admission and to graduation from high school. Beyond this, the impact of the vocational movement was felt in the demand for recognition of business education, shop, home economics, and agriculture as electives for college admission.

[20] J. O. Engleman, "An Extra-Classroom Study of the Decatur High School," *Educational Administration and Supervision* (January, 1916), p. 12.
[21] *Ibid.*, p. 20.

Existing college requirements were denounced for their alleged influence on the entire high school program. When Superintendent Payson Smith of Auburn, Maine, castigated what he called "the college trust" in a speech to the NEA Department of Superintendence in 1907, he said the course of study was "framed for the whole number of students to meet the needs of the few for whom the colleges have prescribed."[22] Even college men joined the attack. In 1908 President David Starr Jordan of Stanford characterized the tendency of colleges "to specify certain classes of subjects, regardless of the real interest of the secondary schools and their pupils" as "a species of impertinence which only tradition justifies."[23] For the most part, however, the criticisms came from superintendents and from high school principals who were apparently finding this to be one issue on which they could join forces.

"We are come to the Rubicon," declared Principal J. Stanley Brown of Joliet, Illinois, in his presidential address to the NEA Department of Secondary Education in 1909. College domination, he said, was "unjust and un-American because the whole student body must be subjected to the thing which, in truth, belongs only to a few." Already the signs of a new "bifurcation," as Eliot termed it, or dualism were beginning to appear. "Shall the indefensible demands, made upon the 5 per cent. of the graduates who enter college," asked Principal Brown, "be applied to the 95 per cent. who do not go?" Evidently Brown was torn between a desire to avoid bifurcation and a willingness to settle for it as a last resort. At any rate, he said, the high school did not propose to ask for bread and get a stone. "The high school wants peaceable autonomy," he concluded, and "we must have it, even if it has to come thru legislative enactment, state by state."[24]

Another foe of college domination was State Superintendent C. P. Cary of Wisconsin, in this period engaged in conflict with the university of his own state. In an address to the NEA Department of Secondary Education in 1910, Cary called college domination "an intolerable impertinence" and said the high school men had to "fight this battle to a finish." A disciple of William T. Harris, Cary did not want to intensify the distinction between college-preparatory and non-college-preparatory

[22] Payson Smith, "Admitting That Our Schools Are Defective, Who Is Responsible for the Present Conditions?" NEA, 1907, p. 178.
[23] David Starr Jordan, "The High-School Course," *Educational Review* (November, 1908), p. 372.
[24] J. Stanley Brown, "The Autonomy of the High School," NEA, 1909, pp. 481–482.

programs. His desire was to modify college requirements and graduation requirements in the same directions and amounts. He said that many high schools, however, "in their desperation," faced with college domination, were drawing "a line of cleavage" between the two groups of pupils. "They are establishing preparatory academies within the high school itself," he said, and he called this undemocratic, wasteful, and unnecessary.[25] Finally he declared that "the best and wisest course of study" for the pupil in high school was also "the best preparation for college," thereby endorsing one of the fundamental beliefs of the Committee of Ten.[26] Cary was joined in this position by Superintendent Charles E. Chadsey of Denver, who spoke against both college domination and dualism, and who reported to the NEA in 1909 a resolution adopted by representatives of 48 Colorado high schools calling for college acceptance of four to six units in courses designed to meet "local needs."[27]

So articulate was this attack on the colleges that Commissioner Elmer E. Brown gave it special notice in his *Report* for the year ending June 30, 1910, referring to it as "an old-time controversy" that had been "revived with more than its usual intensity."[28] Brown did not commit himself about the merits of the attacks, but like Cary, he was an opponent of dualism in the high school program. In the light of the new attacks, however, the leaders of the moderate revision were not sure how to proceed. They had sought and, to a degree, had achieved recognition for the modern academic subjects, but the so-called practical subjects were another matter. Some, like Cary, were prepared to accept them, but others resisted the new demands.

One of those who resisted was Nicholas Murray Butler. "Almost every educational meeting nowadays," wrote Butler editorially in his *Educational Review* in 1911, "produces one or more attacks upon the colleges because they will not turn over their courses of study to the high schools and because they will not put bookkeeping and blacksmithing on a par with Latin and mathematics in their scheme of educational values." An early supporter both of manual training and of industrial education, Butler now felt the vocational movement was going to extremes. "We

[25] C. P. Cary, "The Opportunities of the Modern High School," NEA, 1910, pp. 458–459.
[26] *Ibid.*, p. 462.
[27] Charles E. Chadsey, "The Relation of the High School to the Community and to the College," NEA, 1909, p. 207.
[28] Commissioner, 1910, I, p. 15.

have in the United States only the colleges, and by no means all of them, to support the idea of a liberal education and to stand between our civilization and the unchallenged domination of semi-educated vocationalists," he concluded, adding that not more than one-fourth of the high school graduates were likely to benefit from a college education anyway. For the others he recommended either direct entrance into "practical life" or to "a professional school of technology," which he apparently considered to be something different from a college.[29] Butler then was ready to give up the struggle against dualism and to do so in the interests of preserving what he considered to be a liberal education.

The old split program of the high school had been based on the distinction between the classics and the modern subjects; the new one reflected the conflict, so much deplored by Dewey, between the academic and the practical. It was this new dualism that Butler and others were now preparing themselves to accept, some on the ground that college domination could not be overthrown and some in the hope that the colleges would hold the line against vocationalism. In both cases it was a counsel of despair. This is not to say that all educators in this period were ready to give up. There were many who felt that a new and adequate basis for college admission and high school graduation could be achieved, and a new NEA committee was soon to be set up for this purpose.

Neither was it the case, however, that all educators wanted to avoid dualism. "We want one class of persons to have a liberal education," declared Woodrow Wilson to the High School Teachers Association in 1909, "and we want another class of persons, a very much larger class, of necessity, in every society, to forego the privileges of a liberal education and fit themselves to perform specific difficult manual tasks."[30] It was in this speech that he identified the "majority of men" as having to be "drawers of water and hewers of wood," adding that the Germans knew

[29] "Notes and News," *Educational Review* (November, 1911), p. 431.
[30] Woodrow Wilson, "The Meaning of a Liberal Education," *Year Book of the High School Teachers Association of New York City 1908–1909* (New York: The Association, 1909), p. 23. Wilson had previously expressed similar sentiments in his address before the Indiana State Teachers' Association in Indianapolis, December 27, 1907, published under the title, "A Liberal Education," *Educator-Journal* (February, 1908), pp. 261–270. Eliot replied to this in an address to the Northern Indiana Teachers' Association, also at Indianapolis, April 3, 1908, published under the title, "The Elements of a Liberal Education," *Educator-Journal*, (June, 1908), pp. 498–505. In this address Eliot said that to "think of liberal education as the attainment only of a small minority" would be "untrue to God's conception of what the human race is for." *Ibid.*, p. 505.

how to provide their nation with "a great body of trained mechanics."[31]
There were, in addition, powerful voices in favor not only of the distinction between the "liberal" and the "practical" or "technical," but also of
a broad range of differentiation aimed at various social and economic
groups. Nevertheless, the attack on college domination in this period
came largely from those who shared the tenets of the moderate revision
to some extent and who believed these could be preserved if appropriate
changes were made.

III

One group that took a leading part in this discussion was the High
School Teachers Association of New York City. Much of the initiative
came from one man, Clarence Kingsley, teacher of mathematics at the
Brooklyn Manual Training High School, who, along with Snedden, had
been a graduate student at Columbia's Teachers College several years
before. Brisk, efficient, and businesslike, Kingsley possessed a rare spirit
of dedication to the cause of secondary education and the pupils whom it
served. As an active member of the High School Teachers Association,
he had taken part in a study calling for more high schools in Brooklyn,
particularly those of what he called the "university type," meaning what
later came to be called cosmopolitan or comprehensive high schools.

In May, 1910, the Association gave approval to a report presented by
Kingsley for its Committee on Conference with Colleges. The report was
prophetically entitled "Articulation of High School and College," with
the subtitle "The Reorganization of Secondary Education." This statement deplored the requirement by colleges of two foreign languages, but
noted that many colleges had no such requirement. It recommended that
only one foreign language be required, and, more significantly, it called
for the acceptance of limited amounts of high school credit in the vocational or practical subjects. The document contained a ringing denunciation of dualism in the high school program. "Every attempt to divide high
school students into two classes," said the report, "and to prepare one
class for college and the other class for life is unsatisfactory. Many of
those being 'prepared for college' drop out of school without proper
education for citizenship and without the industrial or commercial efficiency which society rightly demands the tax-supported high school

31 Wilson, *op. cit.*, p. 28.

should develop. Those being 'prepared for life' include many who, later in their course, would go to college if the work already done were recognized by the colleges."[32] With this reference to efficiency, the declaration represented the moderate revision brought up to date.

Four months later, Kingsley descended upon the Department of Secondary Education at the Boston NEA meeting with copies of the New York report. At its July 6 session, the Department approved a statement of beliefs in four lengthy "whereas" clauses and passed two resolutions, very similar in content and tone to the material brought from New York. It also authorized the appointment of a new national committee, this time of "nine," to study the whole question and to make recommendations for new patterns of college admission.

The first resolution passed by the Department echoed the New York report in calling for one foreign language in place of two and in supporting the recognition as electives "of all subjects well taught in the high school." In the second it was held to be the sense of the Department "that until such modification is made by the colleges, the high schools will be greatly hampered in their attempts to serve the best interests of boys and girls in the public high school."[33] These resolutions were passed with only one dissenting vote.

Unfortunately, the new committee was saddled with the main title of Kingsley's New York report, becoming known as the Committee on the Articulation of High School and College. Some tried to call it the Committee of Nine, but this did not take hold. The task of appointing the members of this grandchild of the Committee of Ten fell to the Department's president, Principal H. M. Barrett of the Pueblo, Colorado, High School. His choices included four high-school principals, two university professors, one city superintendent, one official of a state department, and one high-school teacher, Kingsley himself, who was subsequently chosen as chairman.

The four principals were William M. Butler of the Yeatman High School, St. Louis; Charles W. Evans of the high school at East Orange, New Jersey; William H. Smiley of the East Side High School, Denver; and W. D. Lewis of the William Penn High School, Philadelphia. Smiley was a veteran of the older period, the successor of James H. Baker at the

---

[32] Clarence D. Kingsley, "Report of Committee on Conference with the Colleges," *Year Book of the High School Teachers Association of New York City 1909–1910* (New York: The Association, 1910), p. 19.

[33] Department of Secondary Education, Secretary's Minutes, NEA, 1910, p. 443.

Denver High School. He had served on Nightingale's Committee and was still on the National Council's seemingly timeless Committee on the Economy of Time. Principal Lewis of Philadelphia had not yet written his famous article for the *Saturday Evening Post,* but he was already known as an outspoken critic of the allegedly academic character of the high school. Charles H. Judd, Professor of Psychology and Education at the University of Chicago, and Alexis Lange, Professor of Education and Dean of the College Faculties at the University of California, represented the only potential threats of college domination. The only city superintendent was Frank B. Dyer of Cincinnati, a pioneer in the movement for continuation schools, while state departments were represented by David Snedden's right-hand man in Massachusetts, Deputy State Commissioner William Orr.[34]

Much has been said in recent years of an alleged split between academicians and school men beginning in 1910, or even earlier. The composition of the Committee on the Articulation of High School and College may seem, on the surface, to support the idea of such a split. Kingsley, however, had been trained in mathematics at Colgate and had been a college teacher of the subject. Judd worked closely with professors of academic subjects in various projects of the North Central Association. Smiley was a disciple of James H. Baker. Lange had been Professor of English and Scandinavian Philology at the University of California until 1907. The only member of the Committee with an antiacademic bias at that time was Principal Lewis of Philadelphia. So far as the general context of protest against college domination was concerned, this was by no means new in itself. There had been fierce denunciations of college academicians in the discussion following the report of the Committee of Ten.

IV

Kingsley wasted little time getting down to work. His Committee was ready with its report at the San Francisco meeting of the Department of Secondary Education in 1911. One might suspect Kingsley of having predetermined its conclusions, but this was probably not the case. The report went beyond the New York declaration and the Department's supporting resolutions, indicating that new ideas had come in, from Kingsley himself as well as from other members of the Committee. Still,

[34] Department of Secondary Education, Secretary's Minutes, NEA, 1911, p. 559.

the spirit of the report, with its blending of traditional ideology and the new doctrine of social efficiency, was largely the same as that of the New York teachers who had taken action sixteen months before.

The report contained a long preamble about the social functions of the high school, the blending of liberal and vocational education, and the importance of making appropriate modifications in college-admission requirements. Some of the language, such as references to "exclusively bookish curricula" and "false ideals of culture" sounded more like W. D. Lewis than like Kingsley. One statement questioned "traditional ideals" of preparation for college in relation to "the actual needs and future responsibilities of girls."[35]

With these observations disposed of, the report set forth the Committee's recommendations for stipulations for the high school program itself. In all cases, these were meant to apply both to high school graduation and to college admission. First came an over-all prescription of fifteen units, not including those in physical education and chorus. Of these fifteen units, at least eleven were to be in what had by then come to be known as the "academic subjects," while the other four were to be a "margin" used for "additional academic work" or for the vocational or practical subjects, these to be unspecified, thereby avoiding the need for gaining "formal recognition . . . for each new subject."

The main body of the report dealt with the distribution of the eleven academic units. Every high school course was to require the completion of two majors of three units each, one of these specified as English, and one minor of two units. Nine of the eleven units, however, were specified as constants for all pupils, these to include three units of English, two of mathematics, two of foreign language, one of social science "including history," and one of natural science.[36] Up to this point what the Committee had done was to add one unit of English to the pattern recommended by Nightingale's Committee in 1899 and to subtract from it two units of foreign language.

After the main report came an additional statement entitled "Supplementary Report," in which provision was made for substituting "under proper supervision" an extra unit each of social science and natural science for the requirement of the two units in either foreign language or mathematics. This would make it possible for a pupil to avoid foreign

[35] Clarence D. Kingsley, "Report of the Committee of Nine on the Articulation of High School and College," NEA, 1911, p. 561.
[36] *Ibid.*, pp. 561–563.

language or mathematics (but not both) and still achieve both high school graduation and admission to college. It was the first time such a possibility had been presented by a national committee.[37]

The Committee presented a long argument to justify this position. The report pointed out how the range of college-admission subjects had been broadened by including the modern academic subjects. This had made it possible to appeal "to a much larger group of men and women." Now the time had come to appeal "to still other students," specifically through the recommended option. "Schoolmen in general," argued the Committee, are familiar with students, usually girls, who do good work in languages, history, and certain sciences, but who cannot master high-school or college mathematics. There are other students, mostly boys, who do good work in mathematics, science, and history, but who have exceptional difficulty with foreign languages." In spite of the attacks then being leveled against "formal discipline," the Committee did not disparage the objective of mental training. On this point it simply argued that mathematics and foreign languages were not "indispensable for intellectual discipline" and that the disciplinary values of other subjects had not been fully recognized.[38]

With its supplementary report, the Committee exposed itself to the possible charge of lowering standards. What it had done in fact was to adopt Eliot's doctrine of disciplinary values in any subject well organized and well taught and to give this doctrine a far more limited application than Eliot would have given it himself. Furthermore, it could be argued that the major-minor system followed the argument of Eliot, as set forth in the report of the Committee of Ten, that several subjects should be studied long enough to provide for thoroughness and depth. The entire report, then, was consistent with the moderate revision, and the only discernible impact of the movements for industrial education and social efficiency lay in the reservation of four of the fifteen units for free electives that might be used for the so-called practical subjects.

The report was adopted by the Department, with only two dissenting votes,[39] and 30,000 copies of it were soon on their way throughout the country, paid for in part by a grant of $300 from the NEA. Kingsley was enthusiastic about its reception. "The report," he told the Department at its 1912 meeting, "has been discussed by many high-school and col-

[37] *Ibid.*, p. 566.
[38] *Ibid.*, pp. 565–566.
[39] Department of Secondary Education, *op. cit.*, p. 555.

lege faculties and educational associations; it has been formally indorsed by various associations; enacted with practically no modifications by the State Board of Indiana as defining an approved high-school course; and is receiving favorable consideration by college authorities."[40] Among the associations that had indorsed the report were those of Maine and Michigan, along with the high school teachers' sections of those of New Jersey and Indiana. Kingsley also reported that the state board in Kansas had given official approval to "nearly all of the main propositions of the report." Favorable testimonials were read from various educators, including, surprisingly enough, David Snedden. The only criticism came from State Superintendent Nathan Schaeffer of Pennsylvania, one of the veterans of the moderate revision, who felt that it had not gone far enough.[41] Unlike the Committee of Ten, the Committee on the Articulation of High School and College evoked practically no criticism and was subjected to no abuse. Apparently the days of "giving it" to national committees had passed away.

Although it had presented what to many committees would have been a final report, the Committee on the Articulation of High School and College did not pass out of existence, and Chairman Kingsley was seeking ways to expand its scope and function. Up to that point it had lacked a set of subcommittees in the school subjects. Accordingly, Kingsley in 1912 recommended and gained approval for the creation of such groups, not only in the major academic fields as had been the case with previous committees but also in the practical or "non-academic" subjects such as mechanic arts, home economics, agriculture, business, and music. The NEA president appointed most of these groups in the fall of 1912. Two conferences for the subcommittees were held during the winter, and by the next July Kingsley reported that some of the groups had "already made substantial progress."[42]

It was at the summer meeting of the NEA in 1913 that the parent committee and its offspring were absorbed into the Commission on the Reorganization of Secondary Education, a title that had been used by Kingsley as the subtitle of his New York report three years before.[43] This new enterprise, a creation not only of the Department of Secondary

[40] Clarence D. Kingsley, "Report of the Committee on the Articulation of High School and College," NEA, 1912, p. 667.
[41] *Ibid.*, pp. 670–671.
[42] Clarence D. Kingsley, "Third Report of the Committee on the Articulation of High Schools and Colleges," NEA, 1913, p. 489.
[43] *Ibid.*, pp. 490–491.

Education but also of the NEA Board of Directors, had its nerve center in a "reviewing committee" made up of the chairmen of the subject groups and ten other members at large. Kingsley became Chairman of the entire Commission, an unwieldy body of shifting membership and over-lapping categories incorporating the Committee on the Articulation of High School and College and its subject subcommittees and involving 150 or more members. He had left the New York schools in the fall of 1912 to become state high school inspector in Massachusetts, a position that gave him more freedom for directing a national enterprise, although this was not necessarily the reason for the change. Ahead lay the road to the "Cardinal Principles of Secondary Education."

V

Whether or not the story of the Committee on the Articulation of High School and College was entirely a success story would depend in large measure on the response of the colleges. The University of Chicago was prepared to lead the way. In June, 1911, one month before the presenta-tion of the report, the faculty of Arts, Literature, and Science adopted new requirements to be effective in October. These stipulated fifteen units, of which three had to be in English. Beyond this, they included seven units to be drawn from the other four major academic fields—language, mathe-matics, history and social science, and science—with a major of three units in one and a minor of two units in another. This left a free margin of five units for any work credited toward graduation in the high school from which the applicant had come. Under these provisions, an applicant could omit any two of the five academic fields, and these two could be mathematics and foreign language.[44] These requirements were more liberal than those recommended by Kingsley's Committee, as was pointed out by Judd in a second supplement to the report. They granted one addi-tional unit for the free electives and made it possible for a pupil to avoid both mathematics and foreign language, instead of merely having a choice of which he preferred to avoid. The device was an ingenious one indeed. It provided for flexibility and concentration and guaranteed that a substantial part of the work would be in some, although not all, the major academic fields. The only constant left was English, the one con-

[44] C. R. Mann, "Changes in Entrance Requirements at the University of Chi-cago," *Educational Review* (September, 1911), pp. 186–191.

cession Eliot had been willing to make to the idea of common subjects for all.

Kingsley liked the Chicago requirements and praised them on several occasions. Probably he too felt that his Committee had not gone far enough. He also hailed what he considered to be the liberalizing of requirements at Minnesota and Michigan.[45] Whether these defined a trend was another matter. Kingsley optimistically felt they did. In his survey of requirements published in 1913 he said that recent changes were "almost wholly in the direction of greater insistence upon the completion of a four-year high-school course and greater flexibility in entrance requirements."[46] Much of the flexibility consisted of greater recognition of vocational or practical subjects.[47]

Surveys reported between 1912 and 1922, however, indicated little disposition on the part of colleges to abandon requirements in foreign language and mathematics.[48] Some colleges, of course, continued to admit students on condition, and there were doubtless other modifications, in practice, of the requirements printed in catalogues. Still the image of college-admission requirements continued to include both fields. The fact that some colleges did not require one or the other or either of these fields provided little help to the principal who had to advise pupils on their choice of subjects. He was virtually obliged to recommend both mathematics and foreign language for every pupil who thought he might go to college. Perhaps this was good in itself, but it was accompanied by

[45] Clarence D. Kingsley, "Report of the Committee on the Articulation of High School and College," NEA, 1912, p. 672.

[46] Clarence D. Kingsley, *College Entrance Requirements* (U.S. Bureau of Education, Bulletin No. 7 [Washington, D.C., 1913]), p. 6.

[47] Kingsley did not claim all this as a result of the report of his Committee, and some colleges had been accepting vocational or practical subjects before 1911. See A. B. Graham, "Report of Committee on Encouraging College Entrance Credit in High-School Agriculture," NEA, 1910, pp. 480–481, and Joseph H. Penniman, "Shall Industrial or Vocational Subjects Be Accepted for Admission to College?" MSM, 1911, p. 53.

[48] See C. O. Davis, "Entrance Requirements in Twenty-Five Colleges and Universities," *School Review* (September, 1912), p. 486; E. E. Lewis, "Foreign Languages and Mathematics As Requirement for Admission to, and Graduation from, American Colleges and Universities," *School Review* (January, 1918), pp. 2–4; Millard A. Black, "Changes in Entrance Requirements of New England Colleges," *Educational Administration and Supervision* (February, 1919), p. 83; Leonard V. Koos, "The Flexibility of Requirements for Admission to Colleges East and West," *School Review* (June, 1920), pp. 439–441; and George F. Zook, *Accredited Secondary Schools in the United States* (U.S. Bureau of Education, Bulletin No. 11, Part I [Washington, D.C., 1922], pp. 10–79).

an increasing tendency to drop foreign languages or mathematics or both from the requirements for high school graduation. This tendency was under way before 1911, but it was encouraged by the Committee's supplementary report.

The effect, then, was to reinforce the divergence between college-preparatory and non-college-preparatory programs. "The wide discrepancy between preparation for life and preparation for college," Kingsley had written in 1911, "is to be removed."[49] He succeeded, however, only in making it wider than before. This should not be interpreted as an intellectual or personal defeat for Kingsley and his Committee. The conditions of the times were against them and others who sought to preserve the tradition of unified programs by means of reasonable compromise. Many of the school men felt they could not wait for the colleges to act. Many defenders of the academic subjects felt the colleges represented the last line of defense. Both these groups were willing to accept dualism in preference to the recommendations of the Committee. This acceptance of dualism opened the door, in turn, to greater modifications in the requirements of high school graduation than the Committee considered necessary or desirable. Their compromise would have preserved either mathematics or foreign languages for all pupils. Even the more liberal requirements of the University of Chicago, followed in varying degrees by some other universities and colleges, stipulated for all pupils at least ten units in some selection from the major academic fields. In time of sharp conflict, however, it is difficult for reasonable compromise to find a welcome.

[49] Clarence D. Kingsley, "Articulation of High School and College: Progress in the Movement," *Year Book of the High School Teachers Association of New York City 1910–1911* (New York: The Association, 1911), p. 15.

Chapter 13

The call to judgment

"*O*ne hears continually of scientific management," proclaimed George D. Strayer of Columbia's Teachers College to the National Council in 1912, "and in the school field, no less than in other situations demanding organizing and administrative genius, the result of investments is being accurately measured."[1] With these words he announced the emerging commitment of school men to the use of terms previously more familiar in the business and industrial world. Superintendent Frank E. Spaulding of Newton, Massachusetts, having calculated the instructional costs of various subjects in the system, thought it undesirable to purchase more Greek instruction at the rate of 5.9 pupil recitations per dollar. "The price must go down," he concluded, "or we shall invest in something else."[2] It was an age of "refined organization and highly skilled specialization," declared the President of the NEA in the summer meeting of 1913, and no institution could be successful that failed "to employ twentieth-century business methods."[3]

Much has been made of the tendency among school men in this period to surround themselves with the apparatus of big business. This did not in itself mean that the school men had surrendered to objectives dictated by industrial or business interests. Whatever tendency they may have shown in these directions had not originated with the disciples of scien-

[1] George D. Strayer, "By What Standards or Tests Shall the Efficiency of a School or System of Schools Be Measured?" NEA, 1912, p. 560.
[2] Frank E. Spaulding, "The Application of the Principles of Scientific Management," NEA, 1913, p. 265.
[3] Edward T. Fairchild, President's Address, NEA, 1913, p. 35.

tific management. Furthermore, it was in the period following 1913 that school men became increasingly skeptical about the motives of manufacturers and businessmen in the movement for industrial education. Enthusiasm for scientific management paralleled the reaction against separate control of vocational schools, and indeed against separate schools of vocational training. Imitation of so-called business efficiency did not, then, necessarily imply acceptance of the pedagogical motives of big business, whatever these may have been.

Moreover, it was inevitable that school men would begin to cast about for help—finding themselves engaged, as were the superintendents in the large school systems, in the management of enterprises involving thousands of pupils and millions of dollars. Practically none of them, in this period, had been trained to assume such responsibilities. Whether a school man wanted to fancy himself a business tycoon or not, these things were now the facts of his life. Efficient operation of a school system, from the point of view of budgets, personnel, and pupil accounting, did in fact make it possible for all concerned to devote themselves more comfortably and effectively to their appropriate educational tasks.

In the popular new expression, "scientific management,"[4] the "management" part undoubtedly came from industry, but the "scientific" part, in its application to school affairs, came largely from the educators themselves. Students of education in this period needed little stimulation from the time-study movement in the industrial world in their pursuit of scientific certainty in pedagogy. Behind them lay the whole nineteenth century with its devotion to science! The administrators were by no means the first in education to make an appeal to science. Both the Herbartians and the child-study enthusiasts claimed to be supremely scientific, and the National Herbart Society, in its title, had proclaimed its dedication to "the scientific study of teaching."

Although Spaulding's pronouncement about Greek reflected what was popularly understood to be business practice, it did not reflect what was actually done in the application of scientific management to education.

[4] Other works besides Spaulding's with this term or some variant of it in the titles were J. M. Rice, *Scientific Management in Education* (New York: Hinds, Noble & Eldridge, 1913); Paul H. Hanus, "Improving School Systems by Scientific Management: Underlying Principles," NEA, 1913, pp. 247–259; and Franklin Bobbitt, "Some General Principles of Management Applied to the Problems of City-School Systems," *The Supervision of City Schools,* National Society for the Study of Education, twelfth yearbook (The Society, 1913), Part I, pp. 7–96. Rice's book was a collection of articles that had appeared as his second series in the *Forum.*

Instructional costs were computed, but few leaders in the movement proposed that they should be the criterion for evaluating portions of the school program. More to the point was the accurate measurement of what pupils learned. This called for better tests (scientifically devised) and for better statistical presentation and interpretation of test results. The conventional subjects were accepted at face value. Instruction in arithmetic was judged by what the pupils learned in arithmetic. By 1912 a number of investigations had already been made of learning in reading, spelling, arithmetic, handwriting, and composition.

A large portion of this work was directed to the program of the elementary school, as was also that of the new Committee on the Economy of Time, appointed by the Department of Superintendence in 1911. Unlike Baker's Committee that had the same name, this one did not deal with the relationships among the various levels of schooling; it devoted itself rather to the testing of results and to the modification of content within subjects on the basis of what was revealed by the tests. It sought also to remove so-called dead wood from such subjects as arithmetic, meaning by this, exercises on topics no longer relevant to everyday life, and to replace these with up-to-date materials.[5] Eliot had also complained about dead wood in arithmetic, but since he was concerned with training rather than content, he did not look elsewhere for material to replace it and was inclined to substitute algebra for arithmetic at the earliest possible opportunity. The emphasis was placed by the new Committee on Economy of Time on the identification of "minimum essentials," and it looked to scientific efforts to determine what these were.

Most of this study was relatively harmless, and much of it was useful. It was similar to technological efforts that sought to avoid waste motion and placed a premium on maximum results with minimum effort—comparable to the use of steam power to replace muscles in factories. The demands of everyday life were to serve as criteria in the revision of content—but this approach did not differ essentially from outcries for the "practical" at least as far back as the 1880's. Much of the dead wood scheduled for replacement had been viewed as practical by those who

---

[5] One of the studies, for example, based on judgments of superintendents in 1830 cities, recommended the deletion of apothecaries' weight, annual interest, cube root, cases in percentage, compound and complex fractions of more than two digits, foreign money, longitude and time, least common multiple, metric system, progression, and troy weight. Walter A. Jessup, "Current Practices and Standards in Arithmetic," *Minimum Essentials in Elementary-School Subjects—Standards and Current Practices,* National Society for the Study of Education, fourteenth yearbook (The Society, 1915), Part I, p. 118.

had introduced it in preceding generations. So far as this Committee related itself to an ideology of the curriculum, it was that of social efficiency, but it failed to grasp, or mercifully preferred not to grasp, the wider implications of what a merger of scientific management and social efficiency might achieve.[6]

Such implications, however, were soon apprehended, not by the management experts with their scales and tests or by the superintendents with a flair for business methods, but by those who gave special attention to pedagogical theory and doctrine. One broad possibility was the scientific definition of educational aims. These turned out to be centered in social efficiency, viewed in terms of citizenship, character, family living, the use of leisure, and other aspects of life. A second was that of passing judgment on the school subjects in relation to achievement of these aims. It was one thing to judge a school by what the pupils learned in arithmetic; it was quite another to demand proof that arithmetic produced better citizens, husbands and fathers, wives and mothers. True, something of the same point of view had been implicit in earlier discussions, such as Herbert Spencer's claims for science and the assertions of the classicists about the contributions of Latin to well-rounded development, but its advocates had kept largely in the realm of debate. Now the proving time had come; and the dread engines of scientific determination were to be applied to the most cherished convictions, or delusions, of the past.

II

The main object of attention was the public high school. In the minds of many critics it was still a citadel of reaction, less so perhaps than the college or the private secondary school, but at the same time more vul-

[6] This Committee on Economy of Time identified two principles for selecting content, one being its suitability to the capacities and interests of children at a given age, and the other, the ministering of the content "to the social needs common to ordinary American children." H. B. Wilson, "The Minimum Essentials in Elementary-School Subjects," *ibid.*, p. 15. What the committee meant by "social needs" were "those concepts, and principles essential in a democracy to common discussion and to the collective consideration of common problems." *Ibid.*, p. 12. Some of the contributors to the committee embraced the broader implications of scientific management as applied to curriculum, as did, for example, David Snedden in "Symposium on the Purpose of Historical Instruction in the Seventh and Eighth Grades," *Third Report of the Committee on Economy of Time in Education*, National Society for the Study of Education, seventeenth yearbook (The Society, 1918), Part I, pp. 115–118. Snedden, however, was not a member of the committee. Chairman H. B. Wilson of Topeka, Kansas, later stated the more extended point of view, but had not expressed it at the time of the first report in 1915.

nerable to attack. The academic tradition had survived the oratory of G. Stanley Hall, the onslaughts of vocationalism, the first wave of social efficiency, and the besieging of the college. It was battered, but still intact. The question now placed before the pedagogical world was whether or not the academic tradition could survive the more subtle pressures represented by social efficiency made scientific.

Among the leaders in the demand for scientific statements of purpose were William C. Bagley, who had moved to a professorship at the University of Illinois, and David Snedden, then Commissioner of Education in Massachusetts. Bagley and Snedden disagreed with each other on many points, but they were of one mind on this: "We have long had our educational 'aims,'" declared Bagley in an address before the NEA Department of Elementary Education in 1912, "but too often they have given us no aid because they have been formulated in terms too remote to connect with the situation that is here and now. . . . It is no longer sufficient to say that education must develop moral character; we must know what habits and what items of knowledge and what ideals we must engender in our pupils that moral character may be achieved."[7] Thus would disposition be made of the question with which tradition had struggled for many centuries in vain.

Snedden developed this point of view in a series of addresses given over a period of years beginning in 1913. With his strong background in sociology and his commitment to social control, it was to be expected that his application of the scientific approach would be made to socialized objectives. In 1913 he found algebra to be in a particularly hopeless state. "Not being able to formulate socially valid purposes for the teaching of algebra," he told the American Institute of Instruction at its summer meeting, "it becomes impossible to develop scientific methods of teaching the subject." The only socially valid reason for algebra, in his opinion, applied to "small numbers" who would use it as a professional tool. Other "guesses" about the purposes of algebra were on the same basis, he said, as the speculations of "our forbears who guessed about the flatness of the earth."[8] A year later, he included Latin with algebra as a subject for which no socially valid purposes could be identified. It was necessary, he told the Iowa State Teachers' Association in their annual

[7] William C. Bagley, "The Need of Standards for Measuring Progress and Results," NEA, 1912, pp. 637–638.

[8] David Snedden, "Increasing the Efficiency of Education," *Journal of Education* (July 17, 1913), p. 63.

convention, to find out what knowledge, skill, appreciation, and the like "make for efficient living" in relation to personal culture, citizenship, and vocational efficiency. Some traditional subject names might be retained, he promised, "even history," but it would be necessary to reorganize the subjects to make them "instruments in producing the educational results that seem to us most worth while in the light of our analysis of social needs and demands."[9] It was possible, of course, to state the aims of Latin and algebra in terms of learning those subjects, that is, in terms of the knowledge of the materials, but this, declared Snedden on another occasion, was precisely what had to be stopped. Subject matter was only a means "toward the attainment of higher and more real social utilities," and it was in terms of "concrete social utilities" that the aims must be expressed, a task calling for the application of the principles of "scientific efficiency."[10]

Late in 1915 Snedden made these points even more explicit in an address before the Associated Academic Principals of the State of New York. Secondary education, he said on this occasion, suffered from vague aims, such as promoting character, mental discipline, citizenship, and "self-realization." It was desirable, he declared, "to be able to demonstrate that our boys and girls actually become better citizens in part by virtue of the dry study of history which we have enforced." To do this, however, would require valid aims "through which to control the educational processes employed, and against which to measure results achieved." Traditionalists, he warned, would be against this and would "seek to block every progressive step," but scientific experimentation would clear the way.[11] The study of English literature, for example, was "surely not to be regarded as an end in itself," but scientific precision would provide answers to important questions, such as the service that the study of Shakespeare and Milton might "render to youths of twentieth-century America."[12]

Suggestions for translating such expressions of confidence into recog-

[9] David Snedden, "Some Problems of Secondary Education," *Proceedings of the Sixteenth Annual Session,* Iowa State Teachers' Association (The Association, 1914), p. 91.
[10] David Snedden, "High School Education as a Social Enterprise," in Charles Hughes Johnston (ed.), *The Modern High School* (New York: Charles Scribner's Sons, 1914), Chapter 2, p. 36.
[11] David Snedden, "New Problems in Secondary Education," *School Review* (March, 1916), p. 179.
[12] *Ibid.,* p. 182.

nizable procedure usually resolved themselves into proposals for making inventories of adult characteristics or activities, an approach that was to be later popularized by Franklin Bobbitt under the name of "activity analysis." Snedden, for example, recommended the "analysis and classi-fication of all the qualities . . . possessed by a series of selected in-dividuals of from twenty-five to sixty years of age," these being selected in relation to the standards desired for youth. In addition, he felt, studies might be made of successful people and failures, with successful defined as "successful in the best sense of the word."[13]

Also involved was the belief that sociology, or rather educational sociology, should become the basic science in determining the purposes of schooling. Back in 1908, Henry Suzzallo had dwelt on the shortcom-ings of psychology from this point of view and had called for the develop-ment of "an educational sociology."[14] In 1915 Ernest R. Groves of New Hampshire State College wrote that while psychology could not settle purposes, sociology could. Psychology, he said, was for methods, and sociology for purposes.[15] It was in 1915 also that Snedden left his posi-tion in Massachusetts to become Professor of Educational Sociology at Columbia's Teachers College. Six years later he published his *Sociological Determination of Objectives in Education,* in which he pursued the point that sociology should provide "criteria of scientific aims in all educa-tion."[16]

Given the circumstances of the times, the practical result of the move to define objectives scientifically was the reinforcement of social effi-ciency as the all-embracing educational objective into which others would be absorbed. Education for leisure was socialized by making it a response to the eight-hour day. Writing in 1917 Professor Louis W. Rapeer of Pennsylvania State College cited with approval the argument that before people could be granted "much freedom from toil," it would be neces-sary to train them to use their leisure wisely. "To throw open suddenly large periods of the day for a great population that had not previously been trained to use this leisure well," said Rapeer, "would only mean the

13 *Ibid.,* pp. 185–186.
14 Henry Suzzallo, "Education as a Social Study," *School Review* (May, 1908), pp. 338–340.
15 Ernest R. Groves, "Sociological Aspects of Public Education," *School and Society* (February 13, 1915), p. 244.
16 David Snedden, *Sociological Determination of Objectives in Education* (Phila-delphia: J. B. Lippincott Co., 1921), p. 18.

degradation of that people."[17] The problem of recreation, felt Rapeer, was "to discover the best forms, to socialize them, and to get all the people to participate reasonably in the creation of the forms which they most need."[18]

Another objective that was socialized and made scientific was the traditional one of promoting moral or ethical character—one that drew much attention in an age of reform and of campaigns against evils and corruption. Juvenile delinquency and an alleged state of unrest and bad discipline in large city school systems added further to this demand. As might be expected, Snedden argued for scientific inquiry and planned experimentation in character education, and in 1918 he called upon the NEA to form committees for the "discovery, analysis, and documentary statement of the specific problems of character education which lie ahead of us."[19]

It was Milton Fairchild of the National Institution for Moral Instruction who attempted to provide leadership in this movement for socialized character education. A former clergyman, Fairchild had speculated on the possibilities of what he called an educational church,[20] an institution presumably different from traditional schools and traditional churches. Failing to gain wide support for this idea, he turned to moral education through the schools. By 1910 he had devised a plan of teaching character through the showing of lantern slides on topics such as "The Gentleman," "Personal and National Thrift," and "The True Sportsman." These were presented to high school pupils in assemblies and followed by discussion of the principles involved. According to a report he made to the Department of Superintendence in 1910, he had shown these to more than 100,000 pupils in more than twenty states. Each set had cost $10,000 to produce; the funds had been gathered from private donors through the Moral Education Board, the organization with which he was associated at that time. He noted also that funds were being provided for a massive study in which this system of moral instruction would "be fully tried out in America."[21]

[17] Louis W. Rapeer, "Rural Recreation," *School and Society* (September 22, 1917), p. 331. At the time this article was published, Rapeer had just moved to a deanship at the University of Puerto Rico.

[18] *Ibid.*, p. 335.

[19] David Snedden, "Education toward the Formation of Moral Character," NEA, 1918, p. 83.

[20] Milton Fairchild to Edward A. Ross, May 19, 1896, Edward A. Ross Papers (State Historical Society of Wisconsin, Madison, Wis.).

[21] Department of Superintendence, Secretary's Minutes, NEA, 1910, pp. 143–

Both the scientific and the social sides of moral education were evident in Fairchild's thinking and practice. The great need, he came to feel, was for prepared lesson texts in teaching morality in the schools. At this time (1914) he believed there was nothing that furnished schools with a trustworthy basis for moral instruction. Opinions of teachers, in his view of the matter, would not serve, for they were to him a $600 crowd, and he did not think high intelligence could be expected at that price.[22] Great care was needed in all this, for it was the social motive that dictated the need for moral education. Public education, he wrote in 1918, ought to "turn out a product in boys and girls and young people who believe in the fundamental objects in life in which the intellectuals of the nation believe."[23]

By 1919 the enthusiasm had spread to Canada, and a National Conference on Character Education in Relation to Canadian Citizenship was held at Winnipeg in October of that year with 1500 delegates in attendance, representing municipal councils, boards of trade, and labor organizations. Included among the 30 speakers "of eminence" were Henry Suzzallo, by that time President of the University of Washington, and Milton Fairchild himself. This session led to the creation of a National Council for the stimulating of research on education for character and Canadian citizenship. Here again were the dual notes of scientific precision and social efficiency within which character education was to function.[24]

Much of all this, of course, was far from scientific, but the ideology of science was claimed as a basis for support. In the absence of scientific validation, the case became largely dependent on polemics. Socialized objectives gained their scientific reputation by association; they were advocated by those who believed simultaneously in social efficiency and in science.

If science could not prove social efficiency right, there was strong and sincere belief in this period that it had proved mental discipline wrong.

---

149. His work attracted much attention and was described with enthusiasm by Walter Hines Page, "Teaching Morals by Photographs," *World's Work* (March, 1910), pp. 12,715–12,725 and by Ray Stannard Baker, "How to Teach Morals to Boys and Girls," *American Magazine* (February, 1916), pp. 6–11, 70.

[22] Milton Fairchild to Michael Vincent O'Shea, June 1, 1914, Michael Vincent O'Shea Papers (State Historical Society of Wisconsin, Madison, Wis.).

[23] Milton Fairchild, as quoted in "Morality Codes Competition," *School and Society* (February 9, 1918), pp. 165–166.

[24] *School and Society* (November 29, 1919), p. 650.

True, it was psychology rather than sociology that had supposedly accomplished this, but the verdict was welcome nonetheless. One of the leading figures in this repudiation of mental discipline was Ernest Carroll Moore, who moved in this period from Harvard to the presidency of the State Normal School in Los Angeles. Moore carried on long controversy in the journals with mathematicians Charles N. Moore of the University of Cincinnati and Robert E. Moritz of the University of Washington.[25] His point of view was shared widely, and it turned up in a variety of contexts, sometimes in casual statements that indicated how much it was taken for granted. The Educational Director of the Wanamaker Store, Philadelphia, wrote to several professors about his plans for developing such qualities as original thinking, judgment, observation, and attention. From one of these correspondents he received a stern admonition to straighten out his thinking on the subject of formal discipline. Another more gently told him that the idea of formal discipline had been discarded and that no modern professor of education or psychology believed in it.[26]

Another opponent of disciplinary values was Michael Vincent O'Shea of the University of Wisconsin, who recommended in 1915 that all references to formal training be deleted in the announcement of the campus school. "For instance," wrote O'Shea, "in the discussion of the value of science, it is stated that it is taught so as to develop keenness and vigor of thought. It would be better to eliminate this general statement, because the value of science has been adequately established in the other purposes which are mentioned."[27] In 1920 O'Shea wrote with finality that "the doctrine of formal discipline is passed."[28] Others used terms such as "exploded," and one writer observed that the "steady advance of

[25] Ernest Carroll Moore, "Does the Study of Mathematics Train the Mind Specifically or Universally?" *School and Society* (October 27, 1917), pp. 481–491; "Mathematics and Formal Discipline—Again," *School and Society* (February 2, 1918), pp. 137–140; "A Reply to a Reply," *School and Society* (June 29, 1918), pp. 754–764. See also Charles N. Moore, "The Inadequacy of Arguments against Disciplinary Values," *School and Society* (December 29, 1917), pp. 767–770 and Robert E. Moritz, "The New Comedy of Errors," *Educational Review* (October, 1919), pp. 219–238.

[26] H. H. Kaeuper to Michael Vincent O'Shea, November 21, 1914, Michael Vincent O'Shea Papers (State Historical Society of Wisconsin, Madison, Wis.).

[27] Michael Vincent O'Shea to E. C. Elliott, July 7, 1915, Michael Vincent O'Shea Papers (State Historical Society of Wisconsin, Madison, Wis.).

[28] Michael Vincent O'Shea, "Dominant Educational Interests at the Cleveland Meeting," *School and Society* (March 27, 1920), p. 384.

scientific experimentation has shattered, or at least rendered less habitable the formal discipline fortress."[29]

The abandonment of mental training as an aim marked an almost complete break with the world of the Committee of Ten. During the 1890's practically nobody but the Herbartians and Lester Frank Ward had disputed the primacy of formal aims. It was in relation to mental training that Eliot and others had developed and promoted the elective principle, particularly election by subjects. Subjects were judged on the grounds of their presumed contributions to the formal values, with Eliot using such criteria as time allotments, thoroughness, and depth. Now the subjects would have to be judged either on the grounds that it was worth while to know them as such or on some other grounds.

For some reason, educators have always been loath to identify the knowledge of a subject as a reason or a purpose.[30] Relatively few have dared, for example, to say that the purpose of studying history is to learn history. Inevitably, then, other purposes are sought. The first essential of a socialized school, declared Superintendent H. B. Wilson of Topeka, Kansas, early in 1918, "is a body of right objectives for its guidance." These he found in the general objective of social efficiency and its five phases, which he identified as health, vocational, avocational, civic, and religious and moral.[31] "Neither knowledge, nor culture, nor discipline, nor even morality," concluded Superintendent Wilson, "is sought as an outcome in the socialized school just for its own sake. Any of these outcomes which are secured is sought because of its value in fitting the individual for efficient social service."[32]

III

The way was thus cleared for the second major curricular implication of the merger of efficiency and science. Subjects were to survive on the

[29] J. Crosby Chapman, "Function of Latin in the Curriculum," *Educational Review* (May, 1917), p. 487.

[30] Recent expressions to this effect are interesting, but not traditional. For example, "The high schools should have as their central aim the imparting of subject matters, bodies of knowledge: history, science, mathematics, languages, literature, some of the social sciences." Albert R. Kitzhaber, Robert M. Gorrell, and Paul Roberts, *Education for College: Improving the High School Curriculum* (New York: Ronald Press, 1961), p. 181.

[31] H. B. Wilson, "Socializing the School," *Educational Administration and Supervision* (February, 1918), p. 88.

[32] *Ibid.,* p. 94.

basis of results. Those who had shuddered at Spaulding's naïve suggestion for evaluating Greek on the basis of how much it cost now faced a far more penetrating and potentially more disastrous demand. Admittedly it was the academic subjects that were threatened the most, but not even the practical subjects were exempt from review.

It was a school man, Principal William L. Felter of the Girls' High School, Brooklyn, who early caught the significance of the new doctrines and who expressed them not only in the terminology of business but also in that of a court trial. "The paying public," he said, "is demanding of us an accounting of our stewardship. . . . Every subject must present itself at the bar of competent opinion and plead for itself. One of the first questions asked will be, 'Does it function?' Is it true that many of the subjects either do not function in themselves, or that they are presented too much with reference to their 'pure' aspects without regard to their application in contemporary life and activity?" He then became more specific. "Latin," he challenged, "justify thy presence in a twentieth century American high school curriculum! What has the prevailing study of physics, of chemistry, of biology to do with liberal education? These are the days of accounting. High school sciences, what report can you render? History, you too, are on the rack. . . . Every subject is up for discussion, for examination, for acceptance or rejection."[33]

Somewhat less passionate expression—accompanied by even more remorseless logic—was given to this view of the curriculum by Louis W. Rapeer. He began early in 1916 by breaking down the general aim of social efficiency into seven aspects—health, industrial, domestic, civic, moral, social service, and avocational—and proceeded from this to specify the minimum essentials of an education. He managed to find in this venture a place for many of the subjects, but not all. "The list is noteworthy," he pointed out, "for two great omissions covering six to eight subjects, namely, the *non-English languages* and the *non-arithmetical mathematics*. . . . They are highly specialized subjects meeting the dominant and fundamental needs of exceedingly few persons." He argued that if we were a European country close to others with different languages, if all students went into engineering, if we could depend on formal discipline, and if all students had ten to fifteen years for secondary and higher education, "we might entertain the suggestion that these five or more subjects might well be kept as the staples of

[33] William L. Felter, "On Reconstructing the Curriculum in Secondary Schools," *Educational Review* (June, 1914), pp. 46–47.

secondary education and required for entrance by all colleges." As things stood, however, high schools were forced by the "aristocratic and traditional standards" of colleges to teach "the non-essential instead of the essential."[34] The colleges, Rapeer insisted, should either base their admission requirements on the seven aspects of social efficiency or abolish all requirements save graduation from a high school course.[35]

In 1917 Rapeer drew up and published a preliminary report for a Committee of One-Hundred-Five of the High-School Department of the Pennsylvania Education Association. Here he made it even more explicit that all the subjects were on trial. "Every subject, every method, and every curriculum in the high school," he contended, "must justify itself by its relative contribution to these five aims, under which we can classify all the problems of life and the principal avenues of individual and social happiness." On this occasion the main culprits were Greek and Latin, and he asked whether these subjects promoted health, vocational ability, recreation, citizenship, or morality better than other subjects that might be put in their place. "Just what," he demanded, "are these subjects contributing to life and social efficiency?"[36]

In this report Rapeer sought to identify first of all "the core curriculum," meaning the one to be required of all pupils; second, those subjects pertinent to particular groups of pupils, such as "commercial, industrial, home-economics, normal-training, college-entrance, short-course, and general education pupils"; and third, the subjects that should be eliminated, "since no one should be permitted to waste time upon them."[37] His core program included English, physical education, music and fine arts, household arts, arithmetic, geography and elementary science, United States history, general history, penmanship, community civics and survey of vocations, general science, applied ethics and sociology, and economics.[38]

The doctrines set forth by Rapeer and those who shared his views were by no means those of soft pedagogy. Secondary education, wrote Snedden in 1917, "lacks a certain vertebrate quality, a kind of hardness and firm-

[34] Louis W. Rapeer, "College Entrance Requirements: The Judgment of Educators," *School and Society* (January 8, 1916), pp. 46–47.

[35] Louis W. Rapeer, "College Entrance Requirements: The Elimination of the Non-English Languages and the Non-Arithmetical Mathematics," *School and Society* (April 15, 1916), p. 549.

[36] Louis W. Rapeer, "A Core Curriculum for High Schools," *School and Society* (May 12, 1917), p. 543.

[37] *Ibid.*, pp. 545–546.

[38] *Ibid.*, p. 548.

ness. Its results are vague, its graduates intellectually flabby to a degree that disturbs us."[39] To the Sneddens, Bagleys, Rapeers, and Moores of this period life was indeed most real and most earnest, demanding, in their opinion, a tougher sort of education than the world had ever known.

The rigorous demands of social efficiency were taken to apply also to cultural or liberal education, terms now beginning to appear in the writings of the prophets of scientific management. Much was made of some kind of true liberal or cultural education as contrasted with the false culture of mathematics and the classical tongues. There was, however, a metallic ring to these discussions, leaving the impression that the socially efficient citizen would be expected to budget a portion of his time for cultural pursuits.

Perhaps nothing more clearly symbolized the nature of this new culture than a debate that took place in 1917 on the social functions of art. Snedden opened this debate with an article questioning the role of the arts in modern life. He identified the four fundamental activities of mankind as defense, work, worship, and mating. In all these, he said, art was being replaced by science. More people, for example, were entering marriage with open eyes and fuller understanding. "In their mating," he felt, "reason, understanding, and even science play an increasing part."[40] If men were able to control their "desired destinies" through science, "why should the world again miss the desires and strivings that formerly in the ages of faith and feeling produced a Homer, a Phidias, an Angelo, a Wren, a Palestrina, a Shakespeare?"[41] He did, however, leave place for art in what he called derivative or minor activities, such as recreation, advertising, and what he called the refining functions of human life.[42]

The reply to this article was written by a young professor, named Ross L. Finney, of the State Normal School at Valley City, North Dakota, later an educational sociologist at the University of Minnesota. Finney saw more to life than Snedden's four functions of defense, work, worship,

[39] David Snedden, "The High School of Tomorrow," *School Review* (January, 1917), p. 7. Snedden believed that a pupil should give part of this time to hard intellectual work and part of it to what he called "high-grade physical, intellectual or social play." See his "Proposed Revision of Secondary-School Subjects Looking to More Effective Education in Personal Culture and Good Citizenship," *School and Society* (February 8, 1919), p. 164.

[40] David Snedden, "The Waning Powers of Art," *American Journal of Sociology* (May, 1917), p. 815.

[41] *Ibid.*, p. 819.

[42] *Ibid.*, p. 816.

and mating, and held that art was needed to express ideals. Although he granted that psychology and sociology could greatly aid in "discovering the chief end of man," he felt they were "bound to fall short." He went on to state important "sociological reasons" for the arts, namely, that they inculcated and enforced traditional virtues, furnished wholesome pleasure as protection against vice, and contributed to "the social efficiency of the family and other fundamental social institutions." He anticipated great development of educational sociology in the following generation, but was sure that it would emphasize art.[43] Thus was the place of art in human life, and presumably in the curriculum, made secure.

This discussion illustrated what was happening in the attempt to prove the contributions of the subjects. The affair became largely one of advocacy, as had been the case also with the determination of the objectives. Still, the implication remained that the worth of subjects could and should be tested scientifically; but the burden of proof rested increasingly with those who defended subjects that were by this time considered traditional. Those who questioned history, for example, did not have to prove their doubts; those who defended it were called upon to do so scientifically. Since this could not readily be managed, history, or any subject so questioned, necessarily remained under a cloud.[44]

IV

On the administrative side of curriculum, scientific management and the efficiency movement reinforced "differentiation," particularly in relation to courses of study aimed at the supposed needs of pupils viewed as groups. This idea had been developing for some time, but it came into

[43] Ross L. Finney, "The Social Function of Art," *School and Society* (October 6, 1917), pp. 395–398.

[44] There has been much recent speculation about the possible causes in the years following 1910 of a supposed alienation of college academicians from the work of the public schools and from their own brethren in college departments of education. Possibly these demands had much to do with whatever such alienation may have taken place. The so-called academicians had learned to live with charges that their subjects were impractical and with the outcries against college domination. It was quite a different matter to stake the very existence of their subjects on what looked like an impossible test. Professors of education, of course, were not alone in voicing these demands; neither did all professors of education voice them. Still, one of them was a professor of education who said some subjects should be eliminated, "since no one should be permitted to waste time upon them." Rapeer, "A Core Curriculum for High Schools," *op. cit.*, p. 546.

full advocacy after 1912, culminating in a resolution of the Department of Superintendence, which Maxwell unsuccessfully opposed at the annual meeting of 1915. Such election by courses had come to be known as "the curriculum plan," and the various courses of study as "curriculums." A survey made in 1915 of 54 high schools in cities of 4000 or more population showed 40 of them following the curriculum plan. Of these there were 30 with college-preparatory courses, some of which were designated as academic or classical. The study of foreign language had apparently become the hallmark of the college-preparatory course, for 27 of these college-preparatory "curriculums" required at least two years of foreign language, whereas this was stipulated in only three of 26 programs designated as commercial and in only five of 16 called "general."[45]

Although extreme differentiation was mainly a phenomenon of the larger cities, it appeared in small cities as well. Mishawaka, Indiana, for example, in 1915 presented its pupils with the possibility of eight different courses of study: college-preparatory; teacher-preparatory; industrial; domestic science; art; four-year commercial; two-year commercial; and printing. "The suggested courses," said a member of the school staff, "are named and constituted for vocational ends. Students select a course on the basis of their vocational expectancy. For this purpose they are given a printed blank of instructions on how to choose a course which will most nearly prepare them for what they expect to do after leaving school." He did add that the courses permitted easy transition from one to another during the first or second year.[46]

Among the chief advocates of intensive differentiation in this period was Professor Charles Hughes Johnston of the University of Illinois. One of the "new men" in education, Johnston came to Illinois in 1913 with a background that included high school teaching and administration, a doctorate from Harvard, and professorships in education, psychology, and philosophy at several colleges and universities. Like Snedden and Kingsley, he was able, articulate, and given to much hard work in the pursuit of a cause. By 1914 he had committed himself to the curriculum plan and was prepared to assume leadership not only in its promotion but also in defining its meaning in precise and explicit terms.

A curriculum, he wrote, is a "systematic and schematic arrangement

[45] C. E. Holley, "Curriculum Differentiation and Administration in Typical High Schools," *Educational Administration and Supervision* (May, 1915), p. 337.

[46] D. W. Horton, "A Plan of Vocational Guidance," *School Review* (April, 1915), pp. 237–238.

of courses which extends through a number of years and which leads to a certificate or diploma, and which is planned for any clearly differentiated group of high-school pupils."[47] The system provided for "organization of courses into distinctive curriculums definitely planned with reference, not to each pupil's personal needs primarily, but with reference to the different educational requirements of special groups of pupils—curriculums based upon social rather than necessarily vague psychological considerations." While there would be some leeway within each curriculum, the system emphasized "chiefly the election of curriculums only" and allowed "little freedom for individual and capricious choice of studies belonging to other curriculums."[48]

The note of efficiency in all this was made quite clear. Election by subjects was an inefficient system that wasted the time of the staff in giving individual advice to pupils. "I know a high-school principal," wrote Johnston, "who spends eight weeks of his precious school year in thus 'advising' individual pupils, while all his other duties are simply not done at all. He does it from a sense of duty, and thinks that this shuffling of isolated courses will somehow work wonders for each of his over 800 advisees. This is a prevalent educational superstition." He was even critical of an utterance made by Frank Spaulding to the effect that courses should not hinder adapting work to the individual needs of every pupil, noting, however, that Spaulding's practice was better than his preaching since he maintained fourteen defined "curriculums" in the Newton, Massachusetts, Public Schools.[49]

Two years later, Johnston identified those opposed to differentiation as "absolutists," while those who favored it were designated "experimentalists." Among the "absolutists" were included the members of the Committee on Economy of Time of the Department of School Superintendence—an indication of how far removed he thought they were from the advanced curricular doctrines of the efficiency movement. They were "absolutists" because they stressed "absolute essentials" in the elementary school as common property for all Americans.[50] At the same time Johnston hastened to point out that differentiation did not mean shifting to the individual and his immediate welfare. It meant, rather,

[47] Charles Hughes Johnston, "Curriculum Adjustments in Modern High Schools," *School Review* (November, 1914), p. 583.

[48] *Ibid.,* p. 585.

[49] *Ibid.,* pp. 586–587.

[50] Charles Hughes Johnston, "What Is Curriculum Differentiation?" *Educational Administration and Supervision* (January, 1916), p. 50.

"that a socialized conception of all education is to prevail during the 20th century."[51] By this time the widely-publicized reorganization of the schools of Gary, Indiana, was under much discussion, and Johnston characterized its adherents as "experimental idealists" who removed the differences between general and vocational education. The reorganization proposed in the Gary plan, he felt, was so profound that "our artificial terms of differentiation" could no longer characterize it.[52] Whether he regarded this as a desirable form of pedagogical evolution was not made clear.

Advocates of differentiation continued to emphasize the presumed needs of different social groups. It was getting to be easy to slide into an identification of the non-college-preparatory group with the lower socio-economic groups and from this into an identification with academic dullness. Principal Jesse H. Newlon of Lincoln, Nebraska, argued that high school courses in English, as planned by collegians with preparation for college in mind, were not adapted to the "present-day" high school population. "So far as English is concerned," wrote Newlon, "there is an impassable gulf between the brilliant boy or girl coming from the cultural home and the dull pupil coming from the poor home; and yet all are put thru the same courses and in the same sections."[53] The function of the cultural high school, with its work in language, literature, history, mathematics, and science, was declared by Professor Alfred L. Hall-Quest of the University of Cincinnati, to be "lamentably obscure" as preparation for successful living on the part of the non-college-preparatory group.[54]

Differentiation sometimes was pointed to ethnic and racial groups as well. The so-called "new" immigration continued to be a favorite preoccupation in pedagogical discussions. In 1911 Eliot had protested against the tendency to think of English literature as unsuitable to the new immigrant groups as such. "Children in the same family," he contended, "often exhibit extraordinary differences. . . . The differentia-

[51] *Ibid.,* p. 53.

[52] *Ibid.,* p. 57. For recent interpretations of the Gary plan see Raymond E. Callahan, *Education and the Cult of Efficiency* (Chicago: The University of Chicago Press, 1962), pp. 126–147, and Lawrence A. Cremin, *The Transformation of the School* (New York: Alfred A. Knopf, 1961), pp. 154–160.

[53] Jesse H. Newlon, "A Stronger Foundation for, and a Better Command of, Spoken and Written English: in the High Schools," NEA, 1917, pp. 694–695.

[54] Alfred L. Hall-Quest, "Curriculum Thinking," *Educational Review* (September, 1917), p. 112.

tion must get down to the individual before we can obtain the best results."[55] It was more popular, however, to think of people as groups. Five years later, Professor Michael Vincent O'Shea of the University of Wisconsin found occasion to praise "great reforms" being initiated by Superintendent Charles S. Meek of the San Antonio, Texas, Public Schools. "There are three races in San Antonio," wrote O'Shea, "the Americans, the Mexicans, and the negroes. Supt. Meek now proposes to develop an educational program which will be adapted to the abilities, traits and needs of each race."[56]

Advocacy of "practical" or "modern" secondary education for racial groups did not in all cases necessarily imply differentiation. A massive two-volume report of the Bureau of Education in 1916, for example, deplored the survival of traditional subjects in high schools for Negroes as an instance of regrettable lag behind the progress made in schools for whites. The survey revealed large amounts of ancient languages in high schools for Negroes, especially in private schools managed "by the colored denominations." Negroes, according to the report, had clung to this "rigid curriculum" because of "lack of contact with the progressive elements of the day," as well as because of lack of funds. Also, explained the report, Negroes feared the introduction of industrial and agricultural courses as the imposition of caste education on them by the whites.[57] From the point of view of this report, all groups were entitled to some kind of new education, one that was presumably practical rather than traditional or classical. Possibly, then, differentiation represented a compromise under which practical education was assured to those not bound by the requirements of college entrance, in short, a temporary adjustment pending final victory.

V

The curricular implications of the merger between scientific management and social efficiency represented a summation of tendencies that had been developing piecemeal since 1905. They included socialized objectives (scientifically established); the judging of subjects by their

[55] Charles W. Eliot, "The Differentiation of the High School Course in English," *Education* (June, 1911), p. 644.

[56] Michael Vincent O'Shea to Abraham Flexner, April 18, 1916, Michael Vincent O'Shea Papers (State Historical Society of Wisconsin, Madison, Wis.).

[57] *Negro Education* (U.S. Bureau of Education, Bulletin No. 38 [Washington, D.C., 1916]), I, 42–43.

proved contributions to these objectives; a strong feeling against foreign languages and traditional mathematics; an equally strong feeling for vocational or practical subjects; the substitution for history of what were coming to be known as the social studies; an acceptance of English, but in "socialized" or "functional" forms; and differentiation aimed at groups, although this may in some instances have meant a desire to contain academic tradition in the college-preparatory course.

This platform represented the dominant point of view after 1910 among those who were articulate on broad matters of educational policy. Enthusiasts for the doctrines of reform were not so much concerned about the occasional protests voiced at meetings or in journals as they were about the supposed inertia or silent opposition of the great body of secondary school teachers and principals. Progress, reform, and improvement were, of course, identified with the acceptance of the doctrines and the translation of them into everyday school practice. Professor Thomas H. Briggs explained the slowness of improvement in the high school on the ground that most principals and teachers did not have a philosophy of education based on the principles of psychology and sociology.[58] There was, accordingly, much discussion of how to move this alleged mass of foot-draggers in the desired directions and how to do so with efficiency and speed.

One way seemed to be to make use of the opportunity presented by educational surveys of state and local school systems. Surveys had become popular about 1910. Four years later the National Society for the Study of Education presented a major statement on surveys, written by Superintendent H. L. Smith of Indianapolis and Charles H. Judd of the University of Chicago.[59] During the school year 1915–1916 no less than 76 surveys were in progress.[60] Surveys concentrated primarily on such matters as school finance, pupil accounting, testing of achievement, school buildings, and personnel policies, but the reports usually included statements of educational doctrine and curriculum recommendations as well. Many of these statements were clearly imbued with the doctrines of social efficiency.

[58] Thomas H. Briggs, "Secondary Education," Commissioner, 1914, I, Chapter 6, p. 128.

[59] H. L. Smith and C. H. Judd, *Plans for Organizing School Surveys with a Summary of Typical School Surveys*, National Society for the Study of Education, thirteenth yearbook (The Society, 1914), Part II.

[60] Lawrence A. Averill, "A Plea for the Educational Survey," *School and Society* (February 16, 1918), p. 187.

Among notable and widely publicized surveys were those of Baltimore 1911; New York City, 1911–1912, culminating in a sixteen-pound report of three volumes and 2573 pages; Portland, Oregon, 1913; Springfield, Illinois, 1914; the Carnegie Foundation survey of the state of Vermont, 1914; and Cleveland, 1916. The Portland survey was conducted by a team headed by Ellwood Cubberley of Stanford's School of Education and included Frank E. Spaulding of Newton, Massachusetts; Super-intendent J. H. Francis of Los Angeles; and Professor Edward C. Elliott of the University of Wisconsin. The report spoke enthusiastically of changes "of far-reaching significance" that involved "radical reconstruc-tion" of public education.[61] Regarding secondary education, the report recommended inauguration of junior high schools and more development of vocational programs, particularly in agriculture and business. Some place was left, however, for "the older types of college-preparatory sub-jects," since Portland was a city with "many beautiful homes and many attractive cottages" and "a people of good native stock."[62] Much criticism was made of alleged uniformity in the Portland schools, this being pre-sumably in conflict with differentiation. Observers throughout the country gave this survey extravagant praise. Randolph Bourne of the *New Re-public,* who regarded himself as a follower of Dewey, pronounced it "a new achievement in educational thinking," particularly as contrasted with what Bourne regarded as the inadequate surveys made of Springfield, Illinois, and of New York City.[63]

The Vermont survey was conducted by the Carnegie Foundation at the request of a commission that had been created by legislative action in 1912. Professor William S. Learned of Harvard's School of Education wrote the portion of the report dealing with secondary schools. Among other things, he was dismayed to learn that 31 percent of the fourth-year students in 1912–1913 were taking Latin although only 18 percent of the previous year's graduates had gone to college. "Latin should unquestion-ably disappear," wrote Learned, "except in such schools as are large enough to offer it as a wisely administered elective. Opportunity may be given in the central school for two years of Latin under superior condi-tions, where those who go to college and possibly have plans for studying

[61] Ellwood P. Cubberley, director, *Report of the Survey of the Public School System of School District No. 1, Multnomah County, Oregon* (November 1, 1913), p. 86.

[62] *Ibid.,* p. 91.

[63] Randolph Bourne, *Education and Living* (New York: Century Co., 1917), p. 84.

law, medicine, or philology may secure a foundation which the colleges should recognize and plan to meet."[64] The moderate revision had sought to build the modern subjects up to a level equal to that of Latin; the efficiency movement grudgingly accorded Latin nothing more than survival. Professor George D. Strayer of Columbia's Teachers College applauded Learned's report, but recorded his distress over the lack of progress in secondary education as a whole. "As one reads the report on secondary education in Vermont," said Strayer, "he is imprest with the inadequacy of the present provision for the education of youth, not only in Vermont, but thruout the United States. Most of the statements with regard to the failure of secondary education in Vermont to realize the purpose for which it should be organized, might have been made with equal truth of the secondary schools of any state."[65]

Another by-product of scientific management in this period was teacher participation in the discussion and formulation of school policy, as a means of in-service education—although the leaders did not always agree on this point, and it was not an early feature of the movement. In 1913 Bobbitt had written that the "burden of finding the best methods" was "too large and too complicated to be laid on the shoulders of teachers."[66] Shortly afterward, however, Superintendent J. O. Engleman of Decatur, Illinois, developed a course-of-study writing project that involved the cooperation of 200 teachers in his system. During the school year 1914–1915, "committees were assigned for the study of the various phases of the course, and these committees in turn divided into subcommittees for work upon still smaller units of each subject. . . . Scores of conferences and committee meetings were held during the progress of the work."[67]

The idea gained popularity and was recognized by 1919 as an integral part of the efficiency movement, one that promised much in the way of moving teachers toward the desired goals. In that year Harlan Updegraff identified his study of teacher participation "as a study in the field of management of enterprises in general," noting that the means by which

[64] Carnegie Foundation for the Advancement of Teaching, *A Study of Education in Vermont,* Bulletin No. 7 (New York: The Foundation, 1914), p. 101.

[65] George D. Strayer, "The Vermont Educational Survey," *Educational Review* (April, 1914), p. 335.

[66] Bobbitt, *op. cit.,* p. 52.

[67] J. O. Engleman, discussion, NEA, 1917, p. 215. This was not the first instance of highly-organized teacher participation in course-of-study writing. Boston had made some beginnings in this direction as far back as 1909. The major Boston project, however, was started in 1914, the same year as the one in Decatur. See Frank S. Ballou, discussion, NEA, 1919, p. 156.

"subordinates in an enterprise participate with managers in the determination and execution of policies" were now receiving attention from managers in all kinds of enterprises. He justified teacher participation on the grounds of efficiency and also on social grounds. "Cooperative endeavors," said Updegraff, "are essential in a democracy. Each member of society should work in and realize himself thru his own social group."[68] On the basis of his study he reported that "administrative cooperation" in the making of elementary school courses was approved by enough superintendents in cities of more than 25,000 population "to establish it as an accepted principle of administration of schools in such cities."[69]

Principal Lewis Wilbur Smith of the Thornton Township High School, Illinois, in 1919 reported the application of these ideas in faculty meetings in high schools. The educational process, according to Principal Smith, had to be "thoroughly integrated" to prevent "enormous waste of efficiency and effort." It was necessary, in his view, for the same objectives of education to "dominate" the principal and all the teachers. "They cannot so dominate the entire high-school faculty," he explained, "unless these objectives are discussed in the faculty meeting and concrete applications of them to the teaching in every department are thoroughly considered by the teaching body as a whole." The high school faculty was "a social machine" for the accomplishment of social results, and the faculty meetings at Thornton provided for "constant review of the fundamental principles of secondary education."[70] Evidently not all the teachers were integrated, for one of them asked, "Why not hold the meetings necessary to the proper conducting of the school, and then *after* the time consumed for such business, or else at entirely different sessions, announce that any who do not care to stay may *freely* go?"[71]

It was Superintendent Charles S. Meek of San Antonio, Texas, who in 1919 summarized the presumed benefits of this movement. "Everyone agrees," he pointed out, "that teachers cooperate more enthusiastically in administering a curriculum that is the joint product of their own work rather than in having a school policy imposed upon them." He added,

[68] Harlan Updegraff, "Report of the Committee on Superintendents' Problems," NEA, 1919, pp. 675–677.

[69] *Ibid.*, p. 714.

[70] Lewis Wilbur Smith, "The High-School Faculty Meeting," *School Review* (June, 1919), pp. 426–427. One of the topics discussed at these meetings was "the education of the masses to prevent social unrest." *Ibid.*, p. 435.

[71] *Ibid.*, p. 437.

however, that it was important to make sure the joint efforts moved not toward reaction, but progress.[72]

VI

Above all, as the newest and fondest hope for the future, there was the separate junior high or intermediate school. This was not the six-year secondary school that had been suggested as a possibility by the Committee of Ten and subsequently recommended by Nightingale's Committee on College-Entrance Requirements. The new institution, clearly identified from 1910 on, covered a limited range of grades, usually seven through nine, and was separated both from the elementary grades and from the high school. Nobody quite knew where this junior high school had come from, but there it was. Among the communities identified as having originated the term or the practices associated with it were Crawfordsville, Indiana; Ogden, Utah; Columbus, Ohio; Madison, Indiana; and Berkeley, California.[73] Its ideological context included, however, the intermediate industrial schools under discussion in 1909 and 1910; referred to by Charles De Garmo as "junior industrial high schools," these were to be terminal institutions for pupils who might otherwise leave school before finishing the grammar school course. The doctrinal ancestry of the junior high school has been sought in many quarters—and one possibility worth considering is Miss Kingsbury's report for the Douglas Commission of Massachusetts in 1906.

[72] Charles S. Meek, discussion, NEA, 1919, p. 155.

[73] The literature on the origins of the junior high school is confusing indeed. For a discussion of this matter, written not too long after the events dealt with, see Joseph Abelson, "A Study of the Junior High School Project," *Education* (September, 1916), pp. 4–8. As far back as 1898, Principal Abram Brown of Columbus Ohio, had recommended separate schools for eighth and ninth grades. NC, 1898, pp. 143–144. Early suggestions for separate schools covering grades seven through nine were made by Principal J. E. Armstrong of the Englewood High School, Chicago. NC, 1901, p. 31. Also by a Brooklyn teacher Charles S. Hartwell. "Economy in Education," *Educational Review* (September, 1905), p. 163. See William T. Gruhn and Harl R. Douglass, *The Modern Junior High School* (New York: Ronald Press Co., 1947), pp. 35–36 for discussion of the report that a separate school for grades seven and eight existed in Richmond, Indiana, beginning in 1896. According to Gilbert B. Morrison in 1909, however, the school in Richmond, Indiana, was and had been a six-year secondary school. Gilbert B. Morrison, "Third Report of the Committee on Six-Year Course of Study," NEA, 1909, p. 499. Morrison's preoccupation with the six-year secondary school may have led to his being mistaken on this point.

It was Berkeley, California, that first attracted national attention with a three-year intermediate school. The reorganization plan there, including "this introductory high school," went into effect in January, 1910. The change had been preceded by an intensive campaign, led by Superintendent Frank F. Bunker, to build "a strong sentiment in support of the same" through "improvement clubs, mothers' clubs, parent-teachers' associations, and other civic bodies." Bunker argued for the intermediate school as a means of providing for "a gradual transition" to the high school and also as a vehicle of differentiation.[74] "To force all children in the seventh and eighth grades . . . to take the same work," said Bunker, "is clearly wrong." Reorganization, he felt, would make possible the bringing together of pupils in sufficient numbers to assure variety,[75] that is, to make differentiation more feasible.

According to an editorial in *Educational Review,* however, the motive behind the Berkeley reorganization was to relieve overcrowding in the high school without the construction of new buildings. The high school had been growing so fast that not even a new building program had been able to keep up with the increase in numbers. "Reluctant to apply to the taxpayers for another bond issue for high school purposes," said the editorial, "Superintendent Bunker proposes a reorganization and a regrouping of the several grades of schools in the interest both of economy and of educational efficiency." By drawing off the ninth grade into what the editorial called "introductory high school centers," the entire school plant would "be kept working to nearly its full capacity" and congestion in the high school would be relieved.[76] Bunker himself did not stress this in his later writings, and economy probably was not a motive for such reorganization in most communities. Once the junior high schools were established, it usually cost more to run them than it did to run the conventional elementary schools, but the proponents of the new institutions argued that they were well worth the difference.[77]

[74] Frank F. Bunker, "The Better Articulation of the Parts of the Public School System," *Educational Review* (March, 1914), pp. 253–255.

[75] *Ibid.,* pp. 260–261.

[76] *Educational Review* (February, 1910), pp. 210–211. This kind of argument had been set forth explicitly by Charles S. Hartwell in 1905. Hartwell, *op. cit.,* p. 164.

[77] J. H. Francis, "Needed Reorganizations and Expansions of the School System," Cubberley, *op. cit.,* Chapter 11, pp. 191–194. It was argued in the New York City survey, however, that operating costs there were lower for the "intermediate" schools. This was admittedly because of the higher teacher-pupil ratios in the intermediate schools than in the seventh and eighth grades of the conventional

Regardless of motive, the idea spread rapidly. Los Angeles moved it along by establishing intermediate schools in 1911, and Superintendent J. H. Francis of that system became one of the leading national spokesmen for the new organization. School surveys, particularly those of Portland, Oregon, and Springfield, Illinois, recommended it. During the period following 1911, estimates of the numbers of "reorganized" school systems ran into the hundreds, with occasional skepticism expressed about the validity of the reports. By 1916, however, Charles Hughes Johnston felt able to proclaim to a general session of the NEA that the junior high school plan was sweeping the country.[78]

There was little explicit objection to junior high schools on the platforms of national debate. Bagley provided the chief resistance among educational leaders, a move costing him some popularity and probably leading to his identification as a conservative.[79] A flurry of opposition was evoked at the 1916 meeting of the Department of Superintendence by Carroll G. Pearse of Milwaukee, who claimed that the junior high school represented an attempt on the part of the universities to capture the seventh and eighth grades.[80] Pearse may have been referring to a report made on behalf of junior high schools two years before by the Faculty of Literature, Science, and the Arts of the University of Michigan.[81] At any rate, he temporarily attracted a large following at the meeting, but this probably testified more to the vitality of the old slogans about college domination than to any weakening of enthusiasm for junior high schools. An editorial writer in the *Journal of Education,* presumably Winship, declared it to be the first real opposition to the junior high school that he had heard.[82]

---

elementary schools. Frank P. Bachman, "Intermediate Schools," *Report of Committee of School Inquiry, Board of Estimate and Apportionment, City of New York* (New York: The City, 1911–1913), II, pp. 481–496.

[78] Charles Hughes Johnston, "The Junior High School," NEA, 1916, p. 145.

[79] According to one writer, Bagley was "practically the only educator of national reputation" who was against junior high schools. Marie Gugle. "The Junior High School," *Ohio Educational Monthly* (August, 1916), p. 390. Bagley was not necessarily opposed to the three-year institution as such; what he disapproved of was cutting off the elementary school at the end of the sixth grade. He did not like early differentiation and feared that it would threaten the melting-pot function of the school. See his editorial in *School and Home Education* (March, 1915), pp. 239–241.

[80] "Superintendents at Their Best: Detroit Meeting of Department of Superintendence Biggest and Best Ever," *Journal of Education* (March 9, 1916), p. 256.

[81] *School Review* (September, 1914), pp. 493–494.

[82] *Journal of Education* (March 9, 1916), p. 256.

Local resistance was more formidable. In his chapter on the Portland Survey, J. H. Francis, anticipating such opposition, said the superintendent and the board must be prepared "to turn a deaf ear" in its direction.[83] This was not always a sufficient remedy. Objections in Somerville, Massachusetts, for example, were vigorous enough to make one pedagogical journal call for facts with which to meet such "lay skepticism."[84] Opposition of any kind, however, seemed only to sting the proponents of reorganization into even more furious advocacy of their cause, and Judd declared that whoever opposed the junior high school would have to answer for it to society.[85]

Prominently put forward as advantageous features of the new institution were the advancement of practical subjects, the provision for early differentiation, and the fostering of socialized aims. In connection with the practical subjects, one superintendent declared that "the fundamental principles underlying the Junior High School" called "for a maximum of manual activities and a minimum of academic work for these years."[86] A set of resolutions presented at the 1920 meeting of the Associated Academic Principals of the State of New York, reflected the view that the program of the junior high school should include vocational education, general science, business methods and mathematics, and general social science, with foreign language as an elective.[87] The practical subjects, however, were usually regarded as features of differentiated programs rather than as constants for all pupils.

It was the prospect of early differentiation that attracted much of the favorable comment in the campaign for the junior high school. Nevertheless, many schools so designated did not embrace it.[88] Those that did

[83] Francis, *op. cit.*, p. 195.

[84] "The Junior High School Opposed," *Educational Administration and Supervision* (April, 1920), p. 232. Local controversy often involved the practice of departmentalized teaching. This was not inherently a question involving junior high schools, for such teaching could be and was introduced in the seventh and eighth grades of 8–4 systems. Nevertheless, it was with junior high schools that departmentalized teaching came to be identified.

[85] As quoted by L. A. Troumbley, *Junior High School Clearing House* (October-November, 1920), p. 51. This journal was founded by S. O. Rorem of Sioux City, Iowa, in March, 1920. Judd was one of the sponsors, as was Thomas H. Briggs of Teachers College, Columbia.

[86] *School Review* (April, 1919), p. 307.

[87] *School Review* (March, 1920), p. 171.

[88] See Aubrey A. Douglass, "The Junior High School," *Educational Administration and Supervision* (May, 1917), p. 283, and W. A. Smith, "Junior High School Practices in Sixty-Four Cities," *Educational Administration and Supervision* (March, 1920), p. 146.

were well advertised in the journals. The junior high school of Solvay, New York, for example, furnished differentiated courses of study labeled acadmic, practical arts, business, and household arts. Pupils who were to continue the same courses of study in the senior high school attended the junior high school for two years only and went directly from the eighth to the tenth grade, one of the few instances in which reorganization brought about an economy of time. The ninth grade was known as the "readjustment year for pupils changing courses."[89]

In the Sophie J. Mee Junior High School of Mount Vernon, New York, pupils chose their differentiated courses at the beginning of the seventh grade, using their "aptitudes, ambitions, and future prospects" as guides to choices. "A pupil adapted to research and book work, and financially able to pursue higher education," wrote Principal Jasper T. Palmer, "would likely choose the Academic department of the high school on Gramatan Avenue. Such pupils should take the Academic course at the Mee School." There was also a commercial course at Mee Junior High, designed to lead to the Commercial High School on South Third Avenue, this being "advised for pupils who may likely leave school early to earn a livelihood." Mechanically inclined boys had a course leading to the School of Industrial Arts, while mechanically inclined girls were offered sewing, cooking, and "housewifery." English, arithmetic, geography, history, and music were common to all three programs.[90]

Commercial or business programs were a feature of differentiation in some junior high schools, although even so ardent an advocate of business education as Cheesman A. Herrick advised against early specialization in that field.[91] The Webster Junior High School of Spokane was described as "of the commercial sort," with 200 pupils enrolled in typewriting, shorthand, bookkeeping, and commercial art and with "a commercial trend" given to the academic subjects.[92] Even in a small community like Hannibal, Missouri, the two junior high schools made their

[89] Philip W. L. Cox, "The Solvay Junior High School," *Educational Administration and Supervision* (November, 1915), pp. 619–622.

[90] Jasper T. Palmer, "Sophie J. Mee Junior High School," *Junior High School Clearing House* (March-April, 1921), pp. 21–22.

[91] Cheesman A. Herrick, "Commercial Education in American Secondary Schools," *Educational Review* (October, 1916), p. 255. See also Philip W. L. Cox, "Discussion of Mr. Cheesman A. Herrick's Criticism of the Junior High School," *Educational Administration and Supervision* (January, 1917), pp. 23–29.

[92] J. C. Boyington, "Contributions from Everywhere," *Junior High School Clearing House* (May, 1920), p. 17.

modest contribution to differentiation by providing "commercial arithmetic" and "business English" in the eighth grade.[93]

Early differentiation was clearly a part of social efficiency, but it exposed the junior high school to the criticism of disregarding other social aims. Some advocates of differentiation felt that as long as the junior high school was "comprehensive" rather than specialized there would be social experiences common to all courses. Others, however, felt there was more need for common subjects, particularly in the field then coming to be known as the social studies, and moved toward constants and electives. Both points of view were consistent with social efficiency, but the proponents of common subjects were expressing ideas similar to those used by Bagley in his opposition to the junior high school. "Unless our future citizens have a certain common basis for their thinking and doing," declared a committee on junior high schools of the state of Washington, "American democracy cannot be thoroughly integrated and united."[94] The Ben Blewett Junior High School of St. Louis was among those placing stress on common studies and common social life. It was, according to one observer in 1920, moving "in the direction of exalting social studies" as the core of the program.[95] In addition, this school awarded the Blewett "B" not only for athletics, but also for scholarship, citizenship, and activities, with several kinds of letters, including plain ones and some in Old English style.[96]

The promotion of practical subjects and the provision for differentiation and socialized aims were by no means the only advantages claimed for the junior high school. It was also advocated as affording a better transition to secondary schooling, as giving attention to the characteristics of the younger adolescents, as providing exploratory courses, vocational guidance, and enrichment of programs, and as making provision for individual differences, although the differences recognize usually turned out to be these among groups. Some of these features, of course, were associated with the idea of starting secondary education in the seventh grade and could accrue equally well from reorganization under variations

[93] L. McCartney, "The Junior High School," *School Review* (November, 1917), p. 655.
[94] Thomas R. Cole, "Organization, Administration and Course of Study for Junior High Schools in Washington," *Junior High School Clearing House* (May, 1920), p. 26.
[95] R. L. Lyman, "The Ben Blewett Junior High School of St. Louis," Part I, *School Review* (January, 1920), p. 35.
[96] *Idem.*, Part II, *School Review* (February, 1920), pp. 108–110.

of the 6–6 plan, as recommended by the Committee on College-Entrance Requirements back in 1899.

The major attraction of the separate three-year junior high school, however, was precisely that it was a new institution, one that could serve as a weapon in the campaign against tradition. "It is the name," said Charles Hughes Johnston, "we have come to associate with new ideas of promotion, new methods of preventing elimination, new devices for moving selected groups thru subject-matter at different rates, higher compulsory school age, new and thoro analyses (social, economic, psychological) of pupil populations, enrich courses, varied and partially differentiated curricular offerings, scientifically directed study practice, [and] new schemes for all sorts of educational guidance." It was also, he said, associated with a new school year, a new school day, new kinds of class exercises, new kinds of laboratory and library equipment, and new kinds of intimate community service.[97] In this catalogue of virtues, Johnston included practically everything being advocated under the heading of "reform," and many of the items bore the mark of social efficiency as a general aim.

Others made it even more explicit that so-called tradition was the main object of attack. The junior high school, said E. R. Breslich of the University of Chicago, aimed "to break away from the traditions of the past and to reorganize the subject-matter from a social standpoint." Europe, he said, had bequeathed us a system based on class distinctions, especially with the "essentially aristocratic" colleges and preparatory schools of "English ancestry," but the junior high school was "an Americanizing movement."[98] According to Thomas Warrington Gosling of the Wisconsin State Department of Public Instruction, the junior high school would be a very different school from anything we had had before. Elementary schools and senior high schools, he said, were "so strongly enmeshed in traditionalism" that they were "almost incapable of recognizing and responding to the demands," and it was better, he felt, to make a fresh start in a new type of school.[99]

It was necessary, therefore, that the unique character of this new institution be jealously guarded. Some of the advocates were beginning to fear

[97] Johnston, *op. cit.*, p. 150.
[98] E. R. Breslich, "Junior High-School Mathematics," *School Review* (May, 1920), p. 368.
[99] Thomas Warrington Gosling, "Educational Reconstruction in the Junior High School," *Educational Review* (May, 1919), pp. 384–386.

that it might lose its distinctive character and, like other schools, eventually succumb to tradition. Stern warnings were expressed against thinking that the mere separation of the grades seven through nine constituted a junior high school in the "true" sense. Calvin Davis in 1918 suspected that many of the 293 junior high schools reported to the North Central Association in that year were not authentic specimens and suggested that the Association cautiously begin standardizing the junior high school.[100] One writer in 1920 warned against the possibility that the junior high school might become an imitation of the senior high school and noted what to him was a deplorable tendency among high school principals and teachers to favor the 6–6 over the 6–3–3 plan. "Having modeled, consciously or unconsciously, the high school after the college," he observed, "they are engaged wherever they have the shaping of the intermediate school in their control, in making it in reality a junior *high school*."[101] Cyrus D. Mead of the University of California was particularly apprehensive about possible domination from above. "It will be a sad day," he wrote, "if this mossback element of the secondary field succeeds in dominating the policies of the new 'intermediate' school and makes of it a 'Junior' academy." The junior high school, he felt, would not fulfill its true mission unless it could become "an institution standing upon its own feet."[102] In 1919 D. E. Phillips of the University of Denver demanded still more, namely, that the regular high school "must be adjusted to this new shrine of the golden age, and not vice versa."[103] Phillips, however, was an old follower of electivism, and his first principle for the junior high school was almost unlimited freedom in choice of subjects under wise guidance,[104] a proposition with which few, if any, of the leaders of the social efficiency movement would have agreed.

In spite of the demand for purity of doctrine, the so-called true character of the junior high school remained elusive. By 1920 the latter-day enthusiasts for the new institution were protesting against attempts to define it at all. "The Junior High School," wrote Principal S. O. Rorem of

[100] Calvin O. Davis, "Junior High Schools in the North Central Association Territory," *School Review* (May, 1918), p. 325 and p. 336.

[101] G. L. McCulloch, "A Good Come Back," *Junior High School Clearing House* (June-September, 1920), p. 21.

[102] Cyrus D. Mead, "A Junior High School Comment," *Educational Administration and Supervision* (February, 1920), pp. 108–109.

[103] D. E. Phillips, "The Decalogue of the Junior High School," *School Review* (March, 1919), pp. 169–170.

[104] *Ibid.*, p. 163.

the East Junior High School of Sioux City, Iowa, in 1920, "cannot easily be defined; it is doubtful if there is a real one in existence except as someone has supposed that someone else has that one." The true essence of the junior high school, he declared, was simply "Opportunity and Growth," meaning that "principals and teachers may now stir themselves to find what the school shall be to the pupils of the seventh, eighth and ninth years."[105] The efficiency movement, in short, was being struck down by its favorite child. In happy words reminiscent of the less inhibited period of the1890's, Rorem went on to predict a great future for this institution that no one could define. "Two thousand schools," he exulted, "are on the trail where ten thousand more schools may sometime follow. At the head of the long line there are a few dozen sane, cautious, pioneers who bravely confront all the difficulties they encounter, while the hundreds who follow are overjoyed to have the trail made smooth and easy to traverse. These pioneers expect nothing without struggle. They ask no quarter, and give none in confronting knotty problems." In the end, however, Rorem did hazard a definition himself. "The Junior High School," he said, "is the living presence of a visioned idea which had been so dearly cherished that it had been relegated to the rare rendezvous with school folk only in the quiet hour of 'Best Moments.' "[106] Before such a definition as this, the most resolute champion of scientific management would have had to quail indeed.

[105] S. O. Rorem, "What Is a Junior High School?" *Junior High School Clearing House* (March, 1920), p. 11.
[106] S. O. Rorem, "Have We Done It?" *Junior High School Clearing House* (March-April, 1921), pp. 5–7.

Chapter 14

The reshaping of the studies

> "The study of history, for example, can no longer be regarded as an end in itself."
> —DAVID SNEDDEN,
> FEBRUARY 10, 1917.

*S*ocial efficiency called upon the school subjects to prove their right to exist. The so-called practical subjects, it was often assumed, did so by definition. Inevitably, then, the demand fell heavily on those fields by this time identified as traditional or academic, namely, the foreign languages, mathematics, history, English, and science. Part of the agitation about these subjects after 1910 was directed toward either meeting or rejecting this demand. Much of it, however, reflected general concern about improving content and method. Among those working in this direction were the members of the relevant subject committees of Clarence D. Kingsley's Commission on the Reorganization of Secondary Education (CRSE), the new NEA enterprise that was created in the summer of 1913 from Kingsley's Committee on the Articulation of High School and College. In some instances, the work of these committees was closely related to the activities of larger groups, such as the American Historical Association and the National Council of the Teachers of English.

The most traditional of all the subjects then being extensively taught was Latin. The general field of foreign languages, however, included Latin, Greek, German, and French, with Spanish making its entrance shortly before 1910. So far as enrollments were concerned, all seemed well as late as 1910. Greek had been surrendered as a hopeless cause, but Latin continued to attract many pupils, or at least their parents. Larger proportions of pupils than ever were studying German and French.

Still, the teachers of foreign languages were uneasy. Even the defenders of Latin admitted that many pupils who started the subject dropped it before finishing the second year. College professors criticized both the methods and the results of the teaching of Latin in the secondary schools. In 1907 classicist Francis W. Kelsey of the University of Michigan complained that the study of Latin in high schools was "above all a hurried cramming of facts," suffering from poorly prepared teachers and lack of time.[1] According to Professor Gonzalez Lodge of Teachers College, Columbia, a specialist in the pedagogy of foreign languages, pupils in Latin were no longer learning to write or even to read it. He advocated more oral work, not to teach pupils to converse in Latin,[2] but for its possible contribution to the reading aim. Teachers in secondary schools added their voices to the chorus of complaints. The head of the Classics Department at Boys' High School in Brooklyn found that "the condition of Latin teaching" called "for serious reflection" on the part of all who were interested in the survival of classical education. "No matter how consolatory the statistics as to the number of Latin students may sound," he warned, "there are other figures that threaten like the Mene Tekel of Belshazzar."[3] In the same meeting, John Kirtland of Phillips Exeter Academy condemned the methods of teaching Latin at that time as an example of "stereotyped incompetency."[4]

Comparable self-criticism or even self-castigation came from those engaged in the teaching of what were often referred to as the living tongues. Professor C. H. Grandgent of Harvard, who had served as Chairman of the conference on "other modern languages" of the Committee of Ten, asked in 1907 whether the teaching of modern languages was a failure. Teachers of German and French, he said, complained about the students who came to them with previous study of those languages. "The uncomplimentary references," he concluded, were "for the most part, substantially correct," and the amount of knowledge carried from one grade to the next seemed to him insignificant "in proportion to the quantity of ignorance and misapprehension."[5] At the same time, some of the modern-language people were still fighting the battle

[1] Francis W. Kelsey, "The Position of Latin and Greek in American Education," *Educational Review* (February, 1907), pp. 166–167.
[2] Gonzalez Lodge, "Can Students Be Taught to Read Latin?" MSM, 1908, pp. 27–39.
[3] Ernest Riess, "Natural and Artificial Stimuli in Teaching Latin," NEA, 1910, p. 499.
[4] John Kirtland, discussion, NEA, 1910, p. 497.
[5] C. H. Grandgent, "Is Modern Language Teaching a Failure?" *School Review* (September, 1907), pp. 513–514.

for their fields against the classics. Julius Tuckerman of the Central High School of Springfield, Massachusetts, as late as 1910 saw an " 'irrepressible' conflict" between the two kinds of languages, attributing this in part to the "assumption" of superiority made by those in the classics. Already in tune with the new demands, Tuckerman declared that modern languages would "have to prove their right to existence in the school curriculum," but reverting to older terminology, he said that the proof would be based on whether they prepared not for college, but for life.[6]

Meanwhile there continued to be attacks from the outside, not only with regard to college requirements and requirements for high school graduation but also often in more general terms. Latin and Greek probably suffered more from this criticism than did German and French. The *Wisconsin Journal of Education* in 1908 admitted that President Hall and other educators had been saying "such ugly things about Latin as have rarely been said about any other study." To the dismay of the classicists, the attacks came not only from "educators" but often also from their own academic colleagues in the sciences. Professor Paul Shorey of the University of Chicago in 1910 still found the scientists to be the major opponents of the classics. He warned both the scientists and the teachers of modern languages that the weapons being used against the classics could be turned against their fields as well. "For the practical man," he said, "Corneille and Lessing are as dead as Homer and Aristotle. His only use for French is to fight the battle of life—with waiters in French restaurants."[7] Two years later Professor Martin D'Ooge of the Greek Department of the University of Michigan warned that the loss of Greek would hurt the modern literatures which drew so much of their vitality from that source. "If Greek must go," he sadly concluded, "then we must be content to become modernized barbarians and practical Philistines."[8]

It was in the fall of 1912 that the President of the NEA appointed the subject committees to work with the Committee on the Articulation of High School and College; this revised version of the Committee became the CRSE in the summer of 1913, with Kingsley as chairman. Among them were two on foreign languages, one for ancient and one for modern. Confronted as they were by outside attacks, and tormented

[6] Julius Tuckerman, "Modern-Language Teaching in New England," NEA, 1910, pp. 519–521.

[7] Paul Shorey, "The Case for the Classics," *School Review* (November, 1910), pp. 609–610.

[8] Martin D'Ooge, "Must Greek Go?" *School Review* (March, 1912), p. 181.

to some extent by self-doubt, some of the leading figures in the foreign-language fields were receptive to the creation of these committees and even served on them. Among the fourteen members of the committee on ancient languages were five secondary school principals, three college professors, three secondary school teachers, two representatives of normal schools, and one city superintendent. One of the college professors was Gonzalez Lodge of Columbia's Teachers College. Another was Latinist Charles E. Bennett of Cornell University, a veteran of the Latin conference of the Committee of Ten. Bennett was an eager advocate of his subject, but one who as far back as 1893 had declared that not all the criticism of Latin in high schools came from the prejudiced or the ill-informed.[9]

The twelve members of the committee on modern languages included eight classroom teachers from secondary schools, three college professors, and one representative of a state department of education. Here was indeed a preponderance of secondary school teachers. The chairmen of both committees were teachers from secondary schools, Walter Eugene Foster of the Stuyvesant High School, New York City, for ancient languages, and William B. Snow of the Boston English High School, for the modern, the latter being succeeded later by Edward Manley of the Englewood High School, Chicago. There is no reason to suspect that the high school teachers had less commitment to their subjects than did the college academicians.

Both committees presented tentative statements at the meetings called by Kingsley in the winter and spring of 1913. Kingsley had earlier prepared an outline to serve as a guide for the investigations and activities of all the committees. The portion of the outline dealing with purpose ran as follows: "To which of the following ends does the subject make substantial contribution? (a) Development of specific efficiency: civic, vocational, domestic. (b) Development of general efficiency: that is, intellectual power. (c) Development of ideals: civic, vocational, domestic, personal character. (d) Development of appreciation: aesthetic, literary, scientific, social. Indicate how the dominant purpose or purposes of the

---

[9] Charles E. Bennett, "Latin in the Secondary School," *School Review* (May, 1893), p. 280. Membership lists of all CRSE committees making final reports are given in the published reports themselves. The two language committees did not publish final reports, but their membership lists are given in *Preliminary Statements by Chairmen of Committees of the Commission of the National Education Association on the Reorganization of Secondary Education* (U.S. Bureau of Education Bulletin No. 41 [Washington, D.C., 1913]), pp. 40, 58.

subject modify and control the methods of instruction."[10] The reference to "intellectual power" showed that Kingsley had not entirely abandoned the terminology of the earlier period, but the suggestions on the whole were consistent with the newer moods. Neither of the two committees on languages followed these suggestions in specific detail, although both dealt with purposes and contributions.

The committee on ancient languages sought to agree with the adversary quickly by recognizing "the threatening signs of the times" and conceding that some of the attacks against Latin were "merited." Latin should have to respond, said the report, to "profound changes" taking place in civic, social, industrial, and religious life. The high schools belonged to the people and must teach what the people wanted. If people did not want their children to take a given subject, then that subject would cease to be taught. "In these democratic institutions," went on the report, "every subject must stand or fall on its merits."[11] Latin, therefore, must be practical, and apparently the most practical thing it could do was to enrich the vocabularies of pupils in English. Here was a place for scientific investigation, and the committee cited two studies showing that pupils who took Latin improved more in their English than those who took German or French.[12] Other benefits said to derive from the study of Latin were also related to improvement in English, and several general skills or characteristics were mentioned, such as clearness and accuracy of expression and habits of industry and application. The committee also felt that the ability to read some of "the great Latin masterpieces was a justifiable objective."[13] The report made various recommendations in connection with methods and books to be read, including one reminiscent of a point that had been made repeatedly by William C. Collar, namely, the abandonment of Caesar in the second year.[14] "Like the Sabbath," concluded the committee, "Latin was made for man, not man for Latin." Chairman Foster noted, however, that some mem-

---

[10] Clarence D. Kingsley, "The Report of the Committee on the Articulation of High School and College," NEA, 1912, pp. 668–669.

[11] Walter Eugene Foster, chairman, "Statement of Chairman of the Committee on Ancient Languages," *Preliminary Statements by Chairmen of Committees of the Commission of the National Education Association on the Reorganization of Secondary Education, op. cit.*, p. 34.

[12] *Ibid.*, pp. 32–33.

[13] *Ibid.*, p. 35.

[14] *Ibid.*, p. 36.

bers of the committee were not in full sympathy with some of the views expressed in the report.[15] He did not say who these were.

On the other hand, the committee on modern languages made practically no concessions to the spirit of the times. It did recognize that many pupils who enrolled in courses in modern languages took them for only relatively short periods, and it sought to adjust the specific aims of modern-language teaching to this state of affairs. These aims, as proposed by the committee, were to teach "a reasonable degree of phonetic accuracy," to develop precision in the use of words and a clear understanding of grammatical relations, and to stimulate the pupil's interest in the "nation" of the language under study.[16] At the end of the first year's work, pupils who were "unprepared to continue modern language study in a somewhat serious and determined way" were to be eliminated.[17] Much attention was given in the report to a discussion of method, particularly to the matters involving direct and indirect method and to detailed consideration of ways of handling translations, written work, and conversational practice in everyday classroom work. Evidently the eight secondary school teachers on the committee had insisted that the report be down to earth! In it was evident neither the lofty criticism of college leaders in the field nor the demand that languages prove themselves by meeting the tests of social efficiency.

After 1913 the CRSE did little or nothing about foreign languages. A report on ancient languages did come before the reviewing committee early in 1918, but the members of that body could not agree on its acceptance. No final reports on languages were published. It was in this period that relative enrollments in foreign languages declined, going from 84.1 percent in 1910 to 73.2 percent in 1915 (about what it had been in 1900) and to 55 percent in 1922.[18] Possibly the CRSE might have done something to slow down this rate of decline, although it is doubtful that most of the members of the reviewing committee were greatly con-

[15] *Ibid.,* p. 40.
[16] William B. Snow, chairman, "Statement of Chairman of the Committee on Modern Languages," *Preliminary Statements by Chairmen of Committees of the Commission of the National Education Association on the Reorganization of Secondary Education, op. cit.,* pp. 42–43.
[17] *Ibid.,* p. 43.
[18] Commissioner, 1910, II, p. 1139; 1916, II, p. 487; *Biennial Survey of Education, 1920–22* (U.S. Bureau of Education, Bulletin No. 14 [Washington, D.C., 1924]), II, 578. Subsequent references to foreign-language enrollments in this chapter also come from these sources for the years indicated.

cerned. Nothing could have been done, however, by the CRSE to prevent the collapse of German during the war. The virtual disappearance of this subject—going from 24.4 percent of the high school enrollment in 1915 to less than 1 percent in 1922—contributed significantly to the over-all decline. Had relative enrollments in German remained at the 1915 level, the proportions of pupils taking foreign languages would actually have increased by 1922.

The silence of the CRSE did not mean that all had become quiet on the language front. Even apart from the attack on German, there was enough to keep the defenders of foreign languages fully occupied. For one thing, the persistent demand for proof of contribution to social efficiency could not be shaken off. In addition, some of the main lines of attack, especially those against Latin, had by this time become the small-talk of much pedagogical conversation and writing. Mathematics had once been associated with Latin in the Classical course of study, but by 1917 at least one defender of mathematics had found it expedient to disavow this relationship. "The association of mathematics and the dead languages," he indignantly protested, "as is so commonly done, is unjust."[19]

Classicists, however, still had much zeal for the study of their allegedly dead languages, and they managed to assemble their forces for one more counterattack. What aroused them was a series of events set off by Charles W. Eliot in a paper written for the General Education Board in the winter of 1915–1916. The paper itself, entitled *Changes Needed in American Secondary Education,* was innocent enough. It was largely a restatement of his arguments for training the senses, with emphasis on such skills as observing, reporting, and inferring. He called upon schools to provide more hand work, art, and music, and again testified to the importance of laboratory work and firsthand experimentation in the sciences.[20] There was nothing in this to upset the classicists, and they probably would have given the paper little attention had it not been for a next step taken by Abraham Flexner in another paper for the General Education Board, *A Modern School.*

Flexner was a former teacher of the classics who had leaped to national fame with a report on medical education prepared for the Carnegie Foundation in 1910. He began his paper with a reference to the one by

[19] G. A. Miller, letter to the editor, *School and Society* (December 15, 1917), p. 713.
[20] Charles W. Eliot, *Changes Needed in American Secondary Education,* Occasional Papers, No. 2 (General Education Board, 1916), pp. 11–12.

Eliot, but included in it a statement in support of early differentiation. He attacked the doctrine of mental training "in the sense in which the claim is thus made for algebra and ancient languages," but claimed that a realistic and genuine education would "produce sheer intellectual power."[21] His proposed main fields for the new curriculum were science, industry, aesthetics, and civics.[22] Mathematics would have to start fresh to include what served real needs. The modern school, moreover, would include nothing for which an affirmative case could not be made. To him this meant leaving out Latin and Greek. "A positive case," he said, "can be made out for neither."[23]

As if this were not enough, he followed it by an article in the *Atlantic Monthly* in which he rubbed salt into the wounds he had already inflicted. "Learning to read Virgil," he said, "is, of course, just as valid a purpose as learning to play a symphony, or to bake a pumpkin pie . . . and because people rarely care to read Virgil, because almost none of the thousands who study Virgil ever can or do read Virgil, therefore, in so far as they are concerned, Latin has no purpose."[24]

Words like these were bad, indeed, so far as the classicists were concerned, but the ultimate insult was delivered in more tangible form: early in 1917 the General Education Board announced the next step in the program, namely, a grant of money to Teachers College, Columbia, for the purpose of establishing a school in line with Flexner's point of view. The school was to cover the range of elementary and secondary education, although not at once. Otis W. Caldwell, Professor of Science Education at the University of Chicago, was named its director, and the prospectus of this Lincoln School stated that it would teach no Latin or Greek.

All this stung the classicists into fury. They lashed out not only at Flexner, but at Eliot, who in their eyes was guilty by association. They had partial justification for this in that the Lincoln School was being widely discussed as an outgrowth of the ideas presented in Eliot's and Flexner's papers. Eliot added further justification in part, but only in part, when he published an article, "The Case against Compulsory Latin," within three months after the new school was announced. He

[21] Abraham Flexner, *A Modern School,* Occasional Papers, No. 3 (General Education Board, 1916), pp. 8–10.
[22] *Ibid.,* pp. 10–14.
[23] *Ibid.,* pp. 17–18.
[24] Abraham Flexner, "Parents and Schools," *Atlantic Monthly* (July, 1916), p. 30.

did not, like Flexner, call for the abolition of Latin, and he even insisted explicitly on its retention as an elective subject. Nevertheless, in this article he did disparage the importance of Latin. Not only was it unnecessary for practical purposes, but it was also not indispensable for the study of ancient or modern civilization, of great literatures, or of great religious or ethical systems. Judaism and Christianity, he pointed out, were more important than the religions of Greece and Rome, and he found ancient Athens sadly deficient in ethics. Still he did grant that Latin might be studied by future poets and men of letters if they wished to do so.[25]

Neither Eliot's 82 years nor his reputation as an elder statesman spared him from the massive counterattack opened by Paul Shorey in June, 1917. Shorey accused Eliot of disregarding "distinctions that have been pertinently drawn," of ignoring "challenges that have been presented again and again," and of restating "without qualification fallacies that have repeatedly been exploded."[26] He went on to denounce Muensterberg, Flexner, and G. Stanley Hall as pseudoscientists.[27] The attackers of the classics, he warned, were just as contemptuous of Dante, Shakespeare, Milton, Racine, and Lowell. Their purpose, he declared, was "to stamp out and eradicate these things and inculcate exclusively their own tastes and ideals by controlling American education with the political efficiency of Prussian autocracy and in the fanatical intolerance of the French anticlericalists."[28] In a subsequent article Shorey said that he did not consider Eliot to be as bad as the company he chose to keep. "President Eliot's taste, his command of pure lucid English, and his early education in *real* science," declared Shorey in this more charitable mood, "distinguish him sharply from the body of his pseudo-scientific colleagues."[29]

[25] Charles W. Eliot, "The Case against Compulsory Latin," *Atlantic Monthly* (March, 1917), pp. 356–359. In the same year, Eliot also published a survey showing that 38 of 76 major colleges and universities no longer required Latin either for admission to the program of the A.B. degree or for the degree itself. He argued for one degree only, the A.B., with more options in admission and without requirement of "traditional subjects" in the colleges. *Latin and the A.B. Degree,* Occasional Papers, No. 5 (General Education Board, 1917), p. 4 and pp. 11–12.

[26] Paul Shorey, "The Assault on Humanism," *Atlantic Monthly* (June, 1917), p. 798.

[27] Paul Shorey, "The Assault on Humanism," *Atlantic Monthly* (July, 1917), p. 97.

[28] *Ibid.,* pp. 103–104.

[29] Paul Shorey, "The Modern School," *Education* (May, 1918), p. 580.

Another classicist who swung mighty blows was Professor H. C. Nutting of the University of California. He was frankly suspicious of Eliot's willingness to retain Latin as an elective subject, charging that enrollments would decline and the subject would not be offered for small classes. According to Nutting, pupils would have to take some work in Latin in order to become interested enough to pursue it further. Eliot's proposal, therefore, struck Nutting as "fair only in appearance."[30] There was an air of unreality about Nutting's argument here, since Latin had in fact become largely elective some years before and without at that time declining in enrollments. Later, Nutting identified Eliot with David Snedden as lending his weight in favor of holding to "a curriculum so circumscribed that it takes into account only the immediate commercial needs of the average or mediocre student."[31]

The classicists did not confine their counterattack to articles in journals. In June, 1917, they gathered at Princeton for a Conference on Classical Studies in Liberal Education, called for the purpose of meeting the criticisms that had culminated in Flexner's paper and in the announcement about the Lincoln School. Nor did they gather alone. Their conference included "men prominent in political, business and professional life."[32] Former presidents Taft and Roosevelt were summoned as witnesses for the classics, and the latter presented his case vigorously, as he had previously done for vocational education.

Defenders of the Lincoln School tended to deplore the controversy that had arisen and tried to play it down. The main idea behind the school, they claimed, had been misunderstood, and it was not dedicated to materialism after all. Science in the Lincoln School was not to be the science of "dead materialism," but rather that of "a rich culture."[33] Shorey was not impressed. Controversy would cease, he declared, only when the opposition ceased disparaging the classics and when they admitted that the omission of one subject did not constitute an educational experiment. "Till that happy day," he concluded, "the spilling of blood or ink must continue."[34]

[30] H. C. Nutting, "Latin and the A. B. Degree," *School and Society* (February 2, 1918), p. 125.

[31] H. C. Nutting, "Democratizing Education," *School and Society* (July 20, 1918), p. 82.

[32] "Classics the Basis of the Best Education," *Pennsylvania School Journal* (August, 1917), p. 59. The proceedings of the conference were published by Princeton University Press in a volume entitled *Value of the Classics,* 1917.

[33] *School Review* (April, 1917), p. 287.

[34] Shorey, *op. cit.,* p. 568.

With heads unbowed, the classicists nevertheless went down to defeat. The controversy about the Lincoln School revealed their lack of allies inside and outside the schools. Even the New England Association, in its 1918 meeting, passed resolutions expressing interest in and approval of the experiments at the Lincoln School.[35] In 1919 the *New York Tribune,* commenting editorially on the dropping of Latin as an admission requirement at Yale, said that the "professorial textualists and taskmasters" had made it a "desiccated and barren tongue." Latin, continued the editorial, would have its mourners, "but they will be few."[36]

The controversy about the Lincoln School, it should be noted, did not necessarily involve social efficiency as an aim. Flexner's comments were partly in the context of social efficiency, but they also reflected a number of other considerations, such as the doctrine of interest and the principles of child study. They could be regarded as a blend of social efficiency, Eliot, and G. Stanley Hall, in fact a singular kind of creative achievement. Eliot was far from the doctrines of social efficiency as understood at that time, and he did support the founding of the Lincoln School, although he considered it a mistake not to include Latin. Caldwell defended the school on a variety of grounds, but insisted that it was aimed, not at utilitarian, but at significant, education.[37] Although the creation of the Lincoln School drew applause from some of the advocates of social efficiency, it was not directly a product of that movement. Except for the omission of Latin, there was nothing particularly controversial about its program. By arousing the Latin controversy, however, it demonstrated, possibly without intention on the part of anyone but Flexner, that there were few who would defend the classics except the classicists themselves.

Even during and after the War Latin failed to pick up the pupils who were no longer taking German. It was the French and Spanish enrollments that increased, but not enough to offset the German losses. In 1919 Nicholas Murray Butler, one of the remaining friends of Latin and Greek, stated flatly that "the swing of the pendulum away from interest in the ancient classics has plainly come to an end."[38] He was wrong. By 1922 relative enrollments in Latin had declined to 27.5 percent, and the end was not yet in sight.

[35] *School and Society* (December 28, 1918), p. 769.
[36] As quoted in *School and Society* (March 29, 1919), pp. 390–391.
[37] Otis W. Caldwell, "An Experimental School," *Education* (May, 1918), p. 601.
[38] Nicholas Murray Butler, "Education after the War," *Educational Review* (January, 1919), p. 75.

II

At the NEA meeting of 1910, William E. Breckenridge, head of the Department of Mathematics at the Stuyvesant High School of New York City, expressed his worries about the immediate present and his fears of the impending future. "All over the country," he said, "our courses are being attacked and the demand is for fitting the mathematical teaching to the needs of the masses of pupils." He noted a widespread call for the practical and for giving to the non-college-bound pupils the mathematics that would fit them for efficient service. "The time is close at hand," he declared with reference to the future, "when mathematics will be called to judgment before a severe and critical tribunal and the demand will be, as each subject is called to account, 'Answer! What excuse has this subject for existence in our schools?' "[39]

Mathematics was indeed under attack, not only from the advocates of social efficiency, but also from those with humanitarian concerns about high failure rates and pressures on pupils. It was alleged in some quarters that algebra had "injured the mind, destroyed the health, and wrecked the lives of thousands of children."[40] Some critics were especially concerned about the effect of mathematics on girls. Superintendent J. H. Francis of Los Angeles was reported to have declared at the NEA meeting in 1914 that the study of algebra had caused many a girl to lose her soul.[41] Others criticized mathematics for girls on the ground that it contributed little or nothing toward peace, happiness, and contentment in the home.

In the midst of all these strictures, there were vigorous developments within the pedagogy of mathematics itself. These involved professors of education, professors of mathematics, and teachers of mathematics in the secondary schools. Much of this activity dated back to about 1900, when it had been stimulated by the movement toward correlation. By 1906 there had been established a number of strong associations of teachers of mathematics and science, and the movement culminated that year in a national meeting of seven of these groups in New York to form an American federation. These developments in the United States were part of important international developments. The International Congress

[39] William E. Breckenridge, "Applied Problems," NEA, 1910, pp. 515–516.
[40] This allegation reported by E. R. Breslich, "The Girl and Algebra," *School Review* (October, 1914), p. 563.
[41] *Ibid.*

of Mathematicians at its meeting in Rome in 1908 had a section on the Philosophy, History, and Pedagogy of Mathematics, at which Professor David Eugene Smith of Columbia proposed and gained approval for a vast project in the curriculum and teaching of mathematics from the primary schools to the university, with emphasis on correlation among the branches of the subject.[42] Four years later, participants in this project from "most of the leading countries of the world" presented some one hundred and fifty papers and reports at the fifth International Congress held in Cambridge, England. Commenting on these papers, Smith noted gladly that "the blind attack upon all mathematics, which seems to be a phase of degeneracy in some of our educational circles today" was not found in European countries.[43]

Smith and his colleagues did not ignore the attacks, and on occasion they responded to them with vigor and asperity. For the most part, however, they devoted themselves to the pedagogy of mathematics without attempting to prove the case for their subject in relation to the current demands. This is not to say that they were conservative defenders of an allegedly sterile tradition. They were seriously concerned about improving content and method in their subject, but in relation to the nature of the subject itself rather than in relation to social efficiency. Professor George W. Myers of the University of Chicago School of Education was active in the development of experimental programs at the campus high school and brought out a textbook in first-year mathematics in which he introduced a chapter on inequalities.[44] Some of the American leaders showed interest in the arguments advanced by Professor Klein of Goettingen for using the function as the central or organizing thought of mathematical work from the beginning of the secondary school course. "If this means anything to American teachers," wrote Myers of Chicago, "it must mean that the fundamental concepts of the calculus should be given in secondary-school courses in mathematics."[45] One writer had already published the first part of a course in differential calculus for the high school.[46] In 1910 a committee of the NEA Department of Second-

---

[42] Louis C. Karpinski, "Reform in the Teaching of Mathematics," *School Review* (April, 1909), p. 267.

[43] David Eugene Smith, "The International Commission on the Teaching of Mathematics," *Educational Review* (January, 1913), p. 6.

[44] George W. Myers, "The Year's Progress in the Mathematical Work of the University High School," *School Review* (October, 1907), p. 583.

[45] George W. Myers, book review, *School Review* (March, 1909). p. 208.

[46] *Ibid.* The book reviewed here was Charles N. Schmall, *High-School Course in Differential Calculus, First Lesson*, published by its author, New York, 1907.

ary Education brought out a preliminary "National Geometry Syllabus," aimed in part at developing more explicitly the logical bases and considerations of the subject.[47] This then was ferment dedicated to the future, and it produced ideas that went far beyond most that were observed in practice in secondary school mathematics at the time. Still, proposals for teaching the calculus in high school or for developing the logical bases of geometry were hardly likely to commend themselves to the critics of mathematics in the year 1910.

The attempt to bring mathematics to judgment, therefore, was made under other auspices, namely, the CRSE committee on the subject. Its membership consisted of two superintendents, two principals, two professors of education, one head of a department of mathematics in a state normal school, and one teacher of mathematics from the controversial Lincoln School. William Heard Kilpatrick of Columbia's Teachers College was the chairman; like Kingsley, he was a former teacher of mathematics. The committee worked slowly, and its report did not come up for consideration until 1919. When it did, it produced explosive results, both in the reviewing committee of the CRSE and in the Bureau of Education, which was associated with the CRSE in the publication of the reports. According to those who opposed it, the report on mathematics was not a report at all, but an attack against the field of mathematics itself.[48]

Defenders of the report called for its immediate approval and publication. Among these was William D. Lewis, Deputy Commissioner of Instruction in Pennsylvania, a leading advocate of social efficiency and the author of *Democracy's High School*. Lewis granted that traditionalists would dislike the report, but he wanted it published to help in the fight against tradition.[49] To support his contention, Lewis referred to a proposed course of study for one of the high schools in his state as the kind of program that had been forcing thousands of pupils to leave the schools.[50] Writing along the same line, a member of the committee told Commissioner Claxton that those who wanted to improve the teach-

[47] William Betz, "Preliminary Report of the 'National Geometry Syllabus Committee' and Its Practical Pedagogical Implications," NEA, 1910, pp. 511–515.

[48] J. C. Boykin to P. P. Claxton, February 14, 1919, Commissioner's Office, Reorganization of Secondary Education, 1915–1923 (National Archives, Record Group 12). Hereafter documents in this collection are indicated as RSE.

[49] W. D. Lewis to P. P. Claxton, September 22, 1919, RSE (National Archives, Record Group 12).

[50] W. D. Lewis to P. P. Claxton, October 3, 1919, RSE (National Archives, Record Group 12).

ing of mathematics were calling for the report.[51] It was finally published in 1920.

The report set forth five reasons for making an inquiry into the teaching of mathematics, the first being the current insistence "that each subject and each item in the subject justify itself." The other four were the growing skepticism about mental discipline, the belief that not all high school pupils should take the same studies, the possibility of differentiating between pupils who would and would not go on to further study, and the problem of method. In this mixture the notes of social efficiency could be clearly discerned, but there were other elements as well, such as the acknowledgment of the elective principle and the recognition of method, the latter topic being defined largely in terms of "factors" in learning, namely repetition, satisfaction, and set.[52]

Much was made in the report of the alleged needs of various groups of pupils. First the question was raised whether there were "differentiable groups among high-school pupils whose probable destinations or activities determine within reasonable limits the extent and type of their future mathematical needs." The writers of the report thought there were, but noted that "in a democracy like ours," questions of "probable destination" were difficult. "There must be," they said, "no caste-like perpetuation of economic and cultural differences; and definite effort must be made to keep wide open the door of further study for those who may later change their minds." With these qualifications, the committee was prepared to identify four groups: "general readers" of mathematics; those who needed practical mathematics for the trades; future engineers or students of certain sciences; and those who would specialize in it either for research or teaching, or for "the mere satisfaction of extended study in the subject." It was acknowledged that these groups were not sharply marked off from one another.[53]

No item of subject matter, however, was to be retained "for any specific group of pupils" unless its probable value could be shown. According to the committee, this principle, when properly applied, would prove "a grim pruning hook to the dead limbs of tradition." Disclaiming

[51] John H. Minnick to P. P. Claxton, October 16, 1919, RSE (National Archives, Record Group 12).

[52] Commission on the Reorganization of Secondary Education, *The Problem of Mathematics in Secondary Education* (U.S. Bureau of Education, Bulletin No. 1 [Washington, D.C., 1920]), pp. 10–12. Hereafter the reports of this commission are indicated as CRSE, with the appropriate title.

[53] *Ibid.*, pp. 14–15.

restriction to a "bread and butter" basis, the committee insisted that the value of any topic "be sufficiently great in relation to other topics and to the element of cost (as regards time, labor, money outlay, etc.) to warrant its inclusion in the curriculum."[54] For the first two groups, the committee stripped mathematics down to its supposedly minimum essentials. Even for the prospective engineers, the committee recommended many items for exclusion, particularly "material introduced from considerations of theory rather than of intelligent practical mastery." Among these were radical equations, the theory of exponents, "except the simplest operations with fractional and negative exponents," operations with imaginaries, cube root, and proportion as a separate topic.[55] So far as the "specializers" in mathematics were concerned, the committee did not recommend exclusions, but made a general statement on behalf of unifying algebra, geometry, and trigonometry. This was consistent with similar advocacy among many leaders in the pedagogy of mathematics.[56]

The committee recommended a common course of mathematics for grades seven, eight, and nine, referring to this as "the work of the junior high school." This was held to be sufficient for the "general reader" group and for most of those entering the "trades," although provision was made for some additional practical mathematics in "some of the trade curriculums." It would be desirable, the committee felt, to construct a separate course beyond the ninth grade for the prospective engineers, while for the "specializers" there should be elective work in grades ten, eleven, and twelve, reorganized on the basis of "experimentally determined conditions in growth, in interest, and power."[57]

In spite of its commitment to differentiation, the committee did not anticipate the later development of a choice between "general mathematics" and algebra in the ninth grade. All pupils were to take the common ninth-grade course, and differentiation was to come afterward. The ninth-grade course, as recommended by the committee, would have included a very small amount of algebra, such as literal formulas, algebraic equations in one unknown, negative numbers, the notion of functions, and the use of graphs. Much algebra and all of formal demonstrative geometry were thereby removed from the programs of pupils in the first two groups. Actually, the committee, with its common ninth-grade course, stipulated more mathematics for every pupil than had the Com-

54 *Ibid.*, pp. 15–16.
55 *Ibid.*, pp. 18–20.
56 *Ibid.*, p. 20.
57 *Ibid.*, pp. 22–23.

mittee on the Articulation of High School and College in 1911 and more than had been required for admission by the University of Chicago in its requirements of 1910.

It is difficult, therefore, to agree with those who pronounced this a report against mathematics. What probably irritated the traditionalists was not the specific content of the report, but the somewhat cavalier tone of its writing. The pages bristled with comments aimed at formal discipline and "tradition." Furthermore, while the committee apparently decided to permit mathematics to continue to exist as a subject in the secondary school, it applied its "grim pruning hook" to much of the content.

Meanwhile a new national venture in the teaching of mathematics was getting under way apart from the work of the CRSE committee. This was the National Committee on Mathematical Requirements, organized in 1916 by the Mathematical Association of America and later financed by grants of $16,000 and $25,000 from the General Education Board. The Committee consisted of six college professors, six representatives of secondary schools, and the Commissioner of Secondary Education in the California State Department of Education. The Chairman was Professor J. W. Young of Dartmouth, but the Vice-Chairman was a high school teacher, J. A. Foberg of the Crane Technical High School, Chicago. Both men were granted leaves of absence during 1919–1920 to devote full time to the work of the Committee. A report of this Committee was published by the Bureau of Education in 1921 and distributed widely throughout the country.[58] The Committee also participated in the formation of the National Council of Teachers of Mathematics at the 1920 meeting of the NEA Department of Superintendence. Here, at least, was a major instance of the continued participation of "academicians" in the development of secondary school programs. Divorced they may have

---

[58] *The Reorganization of Mathematics in Secondary Education,* a summary of the report by the National Committee on Mathematical Requirements (U.S. Bureau of Education, Bulletin No. 32 [Washington D.C., 1921]). Raleigh Schorling of Lincoln School, who had served on the CRSE committee on mathematics, was also a member of this group. Like the CRSE committee, this group recommended mathematics for all pupils through the ninth grade, with electives in grades ten to twelve, urging, however, that schools encourage many pupils to take these electives (pp. 31–32). The courses for the seventh, eighth, and ninth grades in junior high schools were of a composite character, and the Committee suggested five different plans under which these might be worked out (p. 24). The report favored what it called composite, correlated, or unified courses, but said many schools "for some time" would find it "desirable" to stay with separate courses in algebra and geometry (pp. 10–11).

been indeed from the CRSE committee on mathematics, but not from matters pertaining to the schools.[59]

III

The committee on "social studies" appointed for the CRSE in 1912 was the first of its kind since the conference on history, civil government, and political economy of the Committee of Ten. Nightingale's committee in 1899 had adopted the report of the Committee of Seven of the American Historical Association, but this dealt with history only. So did the report of the Committee of Five of that Association in 1911. The scope of the new CRSE committee therefore symbolized a return to the older form of organization.

It was history that dominated the field. By this time it had become respectable and was beginning to share in the general disrepute attached to academic tradition. The four-year sequence recommended by the Committee of Seven in 1899 was followed in many schools. It consisted of ancient history (defined to include the period up to A.D. 800), medieval and modern European history, English history, and American history and government. Some schools, in defiance of judgments made by historians, offered courses in general history. In 1911 the Committee of Five had recommended the moving of English history to the second year, the creation of a modern European history course for the third year, and the allocation of at least two-fifths of the time in the fourth-year course to the separate study of government. It also recommended three years of history as a general requirement for graduation.[60]

This, then, was the general state of affairs when Thomas Jesse Jones, a staff member of the Bureau of Education, became chairman of the CRSE

[59] From 1910 on, says one recent statement, "and until very recently the schools in this country were isolated from academic and research scientists so far as the development of courses, textbooks, and other learning aids was concerned." This "divorcement," continues the statement, resulted from the growth of secondary education and the problems "inherent in the bold effort to devise suitable educational experiences for all the nation's youth." Staff, Division of Scientific Personnel and Education, National Science Foundation, "The Role of the National Science Foundation in Course Content Improvement in Secondary Schools," *School Review* (Spring, 1962), pp. 3–4. If such "divorcement" took place, it was in the period after 1920. There is much to contradict such a view, particularly in mathematics, so far as the period between 1910 and 1920 was concerned.

[60] *The Study of History in Secondary Schools,* Report of the Committee of Five to the American Historical Association (New York: Macmillan Co., 1911), reviewed by Carlton H. Hayes, *Educational Review* (January, 1912), pp. 95–97.

committee in the fall of 1912. Jones had been a teacher at Hampton Institute with the title "Instructor in Social Studies." He had used the term "social studies" in the title of a book published in 1908 on the program at Hampton. These were perhaps the earliest instances of the use of this term in the present sense, as a generic name for the field. Possibly it was Jones who recommended the use of the term in the title of the CRSE committee.[61]

The original committee of seventeen members included seven classroom teachers from the secondary schools and three college professors, two of these professors of history. One of them was James Harvey Robinson of Columbia, prophet of the "new history" and one-time member of the conference on history, civil government, and political economy of the Committee of Ten. Robinson was a forceful personality who had much to do with the character of the committee's reports. Kingsley, Chairman of the entire CRSE, joined the committee later. His presence on it may have accounted for the speed with which the committee prepared its major report, having it completed by 1916.

Like some of the other CRSE committees, the one on social studies published a preliminary statement. This document, which appeared in 1913, outlined the committee's views about the objectives of the social studies program and the role of history in it, and there were also recommendations of courses in community civics, economics, and one called "civic theory and practice." The aim of social studies in the high school was declared to be good citizenship. "Facts, conditions, theories, and activities that do not contribute rather directly to the appreciation of methods of human betterment have no claim." This called for replacing the old civics by the new civics, defined as "a study of manner of social efforts to improve mankind."[62] Here then was one version of the doctrine of social control, closer in spirit to Lester Frank Ward than to Edward Ross and David Snedden, but social control nonetheless.

"History, too, must answer the test of good citizenship," flatly declared the committee. The old history of kings, palaces, cathedrals, and tombs was dead. "In this spirit," said the committee, "recent history is

[61] See Rolla M. Tryon, *The Social Sciences as School Subjects* (New York: Macmillan Co., 1935), pp. 399–401. Tryon cites the book by Jones, *Social Studies in the Hampton Curriculum* (Hampton, Va.: Hampton Institute Press, 1908).

[62] Thomas Jesse Jones, chairman, "Statement of Chairman of the Committee on Social Studies," *Preliminary Statements by Chairmen of Committees of the Commission of the National Education Association on the Reorganization of Secondary Education, op. cit.,* pp. 16–17.

more important than that of ancient times; the history of our own country than that of foreign lands; the record of our own institutions and activities than that of strangers; the labors and plans of the multitudes than the pleasures and dreams of the few."[63] These were the accents of James Harvey Robinson, and the report went on to include a long direct quotation from an article of his, calling upon historians to display "greater skill in hitting upon those phases of the past which serve us best in understanding the most vital problems of the present."[64] History was no longer to be "a branch of polite literature," but would be made to go to work and to fulfill its role in the quest for social efficiency.

In the period between 1913 and the publication of the final report in 1916, the committee members led busy lives indeed, coming together not only for general sessions several times each year, but meeting in subcommittees as well. The committee also met in conference with representatives of the American Historical Association and the American Political Science Association for suggestions and criticisms. This, then, was no collection of educationists working in isolation from their academic brethren, and some of these academicians were on the committee itself.

The final report of the social studies committee turned out to be one of the most successful efforts of the entire CRSE. Behind it were the driving force and restless energy of Kingsley, who by this time had abandoned mathematics to make social studies his major field of interest. It aroused much serious discussion. Some of its important recommendations came to be adopted in the schools. Beyond this, it served as an important point of reference in subsequent discussions of the social studies field.

In this final report, the committee reiterated its ideological positions and made concrete recommendations for a sequence of courses. Social efficiency, it declared, was the keynote of modern education, and "all subjects should contribute to this end." It was the social studies, however, that afforded "peculiar opportunities" for training the individual as a member of society. "Whatever their value from the point of view of personal culture," declared the committee, "unless they contribute directly to the cultivation of social efficiency on the part of the pupil they fail in their most important function." Society was interpreted as all of humanity, with emphasis on membership in a world community, but this depended, in the view of the committee, on the "realization of national

[63] *Ibid.,* pp. 17–18.
[64] As quoted in *ibid.,* pp. 23–24.

ideals, national efficiency, national loyalty" and "national self-respect."[65]

The committee again discoursed extensively on the role of history, with quotations from James Harvey Robinson and from Professor William H. Mace of Syracuse University, another committee member. There was a suggestion by Kingsley for a course in what he called the study of nations, starting with modern nations as they then existed and tracing their development from the past. This course, Kingsley felt, would cure "the tendency to claim that one nation has a sweeping superiority over others," and it would help people in the United States to develop better appreciation of "foreigners who come to our shores."[66] The report also struggled with criteria for selecting topics in history. Interestingly enough, considering the ideology of the times, it declared that selection of a topic should depend not merely on its importance from "a sociological point of view" but also, and chiefly, on the relationship of the topic to "the present life interests of the pupil" or the degree to which the pupil would find it relevant in "his present processes of growth."[67]

Two cycles of studies, both containing complicated options, were recommended, one for grades seven through nine, the other for grades ten through twelve. The main program for grade seven consisted of European history, with the possibility of a one-semester option in geography. The eighth grade was to be devoted to a semester of American history and a semester of civics. One full year of civics or a combination of civics and economic history constituted the content for grade nine.[68] The second cycle provided for a year of European history to the end of the seventeenth century, to be followed by combinations of full-year or semester courses in modern European history, in American history since the seventeenth century, and in a new venture called "problems of democracy."[69]

This "problems" course grew out of the attempt to incorporate po-

[65] CRSE, *The Social Studies In Secondary Education* (Bureau of Education, Bulletin No. 28 [Washington, D.C., 1916]), pp. 1–2.

[66] *Ibid.*, pp. 39–40.

[67] *Ibid.*, p. 44. These are overtones of Dewey. The committee quoted Dewey on "needs of present growth" on p. 11 and repeated the quotation on p. 40.

[68] *Ibid.*, p. 15.

[69] *Ibid.*, p. 35. The first course in this cycle, European history to the end of the seventeenth century, was to include "ancient and oriental civilization, English history to the end of the period mentioned, and the period of American exploration." What this course did was to absorb those in ancient history and English history, and part of the course in medieval and modern, that had been recommended by the old Committee of Seven.

litical science, sociology, and economics in the twelfth grade work. Problems "of vital importance to society and of immediate interest to the pupil" would involve content from all three fields. This required, according to the committee, a good deal of flexibility, with the problems selected varying from year to year and from class to class. The report presented immigration as an example, showing how this question could be studied in its economic, political, and sociological aspects.[70] Many schools adopted this recommendation for a "problems" course, but did not always follow the committee's theory on how it should be organized. In practice, the course often turned out to be separate blocks of government, sociology, and economics.

Although the report provided for two or three semesters of community civics in the eighth and ninth grades and for one or two semesters of "problems of democracy," it certainly did not eliminate history from the social-studies program. Its options made possible the offering of three full years of history in grades ten through twelve. Instead of promoting the other social studies at the expense of history, what it did was to try to clarify the ways in which civics, economics, and sociology might be organized and presented. The report, in fact, preserved the identity of history at a time when even historian Carl Becker was suggesting for the high schools "a carefully coordinated course in which history, economics, civics, and sociology should all find their properly related place" as a substitute for distinct courses in history and the other subjects.[71] It is true, of course, that the report emphasized modern or recent history, but this "presentism" was then a popular notion in many quarters. Even so, the committee by no means confined itself to current events.

The committee did its work in a pedagogical climate dominated by extreme interpretations of social studies and their place in the school program. In an address to the History Teachers of the Middle States and Maryland on February 10, 1917, David Snedden seriously questioned the value of history in secondary education, although he granted the possibility of its study by others than secondary school students, or "even, under some circumstances, when more pressing educational needs have been met, by some interested secondary-school students themselves." The study of history, he declared, could no longer "be regarded

[70] *Ibid.*, pp. 53–54.
[71] Carl Becker, "History in the High School Curriculum," *Educational Administration and Supervision* (June, 1916), p. 378.

as an end in itself."[72] Objectives must be directed "primarily towards social conduct," with the study of history for purely cultural reasons permitted to, or encouraged in, a few.[73] The most fundamental problem of all, he declared, was whether "we shall not be obliged in large measure to substitute social sciences, exclusive of history, for history as it has been heretofore taught."[74]

Others became so enthusiastic about this supposedly new domain of social studies that they sought to promote it at the expense not only of history, but of other fields as well. In 1919 Judd, reporting for the Committee on Social Science of the National Association of Secondary-School Principals, found "it not unlikely that some of the territory now occupied by Virgil and Euclid, by Sir Roger de Coverley and Edmund Burke, by the laws of motion and the bones of the body, will be surrendered to the allies of the Committee."[75] William D. Lewis, long known for his attacks on tradition, called for a large requirement in social studies in every high school curriculum. "We must get away," he declared, "from the superstitions left us by an essentially aristocratic education, and leave the ancient classics and higher mathematics to be chosen by those who can profit by them."[76] Some, like Principal Edmund D. Lyon of East High School, Cincinnati, came to view the social studies as a field particularly appropriate for the "submerged tenth" who presumably could not study languages and mathematics.[77]

This preoccupation with the place of social studies in the secondary school was becoming a prominent feature of pedagogical activity not only in the National Association of Secondary-School Principals, but also in other groups. Committees of the American Historical Association, the American Political Science Association, and the American Sociological Society devoted themselves with vigor to questions involving the instructional programs of their respective fields. Meanwhile, the CRSE committee on social studies, which did not disband after produc-

[72] David Snedden, "History and Other Social Sciences in the Education of Youths Twelve to Eighteen Years of Age," *School and Society* (March 10, 1917), pp. 275–276.

[73] *Ibid.* (continued March 17, 1917), pp. 308–309.

[74] *Ibid.*, p. 311.

[75] C. H. Judd, "Report of the Committee on Social Science," *Third Yearbook*, National Association of Secondary-School Principals (The Association, 1919), pp. 28–29.

[76] William D. Lewis, "Student Participators in School Organization and Government as a Training in Democracy," *ibid.*, pp. 4–5.

[77] Edmund D. Lyon, "The Submerged Tenth," *Fifth Yearbook*, National Association of Secondary-School Principals (The Association, 1921), pp. 3–4.

ing its 1916 report, kept closely in touch with some of these allied ventures.

One parallel group was the Committee on History and Education for Citizenship in the Schools of the American Historical Association. In January, 1920, Arthur Dunn, secretary of the CRSE committee, wrote with satisfaction to Commissioner Claxton about conferences that had been held with this group of historians, stating that progress had been made toward a common point of view. "There is every prospect," he wrote, "of harmonious action among these committees which will go a long way toward relieving the minds of school people of their perplexities in regard to what is really desirable in high schools." Presumably referring not only to the Historical Association Committee but also to those of other groups, he added that "other committees" were tending "to accept frankly the fundamental principles reported by our Committee in 1916."[78] The historians' Committee did recommend a course in social problems for the twelfth grade and the dropping of ancient history as a required subject, but its report was not accepted by the parent association. An editorial in the *School Review* made bitter comments on this rejection. Not only was the report of the history committee rejected, said this editorial, but "objections were raised to almost every part of it and from almost every point of view." This action would not, however, "blockade a movement which is in fact going forward in the schools," added the editorial, and the demands of modern life would end the "absurd practice of making ancient history the chief historical course of the high school." A somewhat ominous note was introduced by the editorial's suggestions that historians might take care of their own subject most intelligently by "supporting a program which allows social science to develop as an independent subject."[79]

It was the Committee on Social Science of the National Association of Secondary-School Principals that cast history into the outer darkness. According to Chairman Judd, historians had problems to solve before their subject could be considered satisfactorily organized. "If they can be encouraged," wrote Judd, "to see the importance of giving up the

[78] Arthur W. Dunn to P. P. Claxton, January 22, 1920, RSE (National Archives, Record Group 12).

[79] "Conservatism in History," *School Review* (March, 1920), pp. 166–167. The report itself was published in American Historical Association, *Annual Report for the Year 1920*, pp. 91–93. It recommended a course similar to the one set forth by the CRSE committee for tenth grade, calling it, however, one in "modern world history" rather than "modern European."

chronological principle of organization of school curricula and can be
persuaded that ancient history is less important than modern, much good
will come of their discussion." In the meantime, Judd continued, his
Committee was dealing with other matters. "Social studies, as the term
is employed in this report, includes sociology, economics, ethics, vocational guidance, and civics, not history. The field of immediate interest
here under consideration is present-day social life."[80]

In these comments and in those of the *School Review* were the possible beginnings of conflict between educationists and historians, although the barbs were aimed, not at the Historical Association's Committee, but at the American Historical Association itself for not having
adopted its Committee's report. Even this report, however, was regarded
by Judd as less "favorable" than one issued by a committee of the
American Sociological Society. The report of the sociologists was, in
Judd's opinion, "more in touch with current movements in the school in
that it recognizes the junior high school as at hand."[81]

It was not surprising that the report of the sociologists should find
favor with Judd and others who leaned toward social control. The Chairman of the committee was Ross L. Finney, who disliked hedonism, excessive individualism, and soft pedagogy.[82] Also on the committee was
sociologist Charles Ellwood, the advocate of social control through compulsory education. In a letter to Clarence Kingsley, Finney stated the
aims of sociology in high school as the creating of social intelligence, the
socializing of attitudes and ideas, and the forming of cooperative habits.
He wanted foreign languages made elective and the requirements in
mathematics reduced to one year of composite mathematics in the ninth
grade, with applied sociology and economics substituted as required subjects.[83]

The report of Finney's committee began with a reference to "the social

[80] C. H. Judd, "Report of the Committee on Social Studies in the High School,"
Fourth Yearbook, National Association of Secondary-School Principals (The Association, 1920), pp. 30–31.
[81] *Ibid.,* p. 39.
[82] Ross L. Finney, "The Sociological Principle Determining the Elementary
Curriculum," *School and Society* (March 23, 1918). At this time, Finney was still
on the faculty of the Valley City, North Dakota, Teachers College; he moved in
1919 to the College of Education of the University of Minnesota, where he was
identified with the field of educational sociology. Finney was a former clergyman
and had at one time been a professor of philosophy and economics at Illinois
Wesleyan University.
[83] Ross L. Finney to Clarence Kingsley, November 28, 1919, RSE (National
Archives, Record Group 12).

function of distributive scholarship," terminology reminiscent of Lester Frank Ward. It made the usual comments about mental discipline and "schooling as the badge of aristocratic exclusiveness." The American high school, it declared, had been "raised up during the last half century in order that it might train a citizenry for adjustment to a complex and problematical social environment." It commented favorably on the re- viewing committee of CRSE, noting with approval that the leaders of this group had developed a fuller appreciation of "scientific sociology" than was evident in the social-studies report of 1916.[84] So far as recom- mendations for courses and programs were concerned, however, these sociologists did not diverge much from what the 1916 committee of CRSE had set forth. They retained European history, but urged that it be taught with an emphasis on "social evolution." Endorsement was given to the "problems of democracy" course for grade twelve.[85] When this report was published in the *School Review*, Chairman Finney added a note about "an expert in secondary education" who admitted not un- derstanding what was meant by social religion. "No other confession," he declared, "could more shamefully uncover the nakedness of moral education in American schools. Social goals must be idealized until they appear as a kingdom of God; social responsibility must be motivated till it becomes the equivalent of a religious duty."[86]

IV

The field of English presented many contradictions and frustrations. Its friends insisted on it as a constant for all pupils, but even they criti- cized the way it was taught and the alleged barrenness of the results. Then as now, there were complaints from the colleges. Much of the criticism, said Superintendent R. B. Dudgeon of Madison, Wisconsin, in 1901, came "from young instructors and inexperienced assistants in higher institutions of learning."[87] Noncredit or "remedial" freshman English was in effect at the University of Chicago in 1910, and 13 per-

[84] Ross L. Finney, chairman, "Tentative Report of the Committee on Teaching of Sociology in the Grade and High Schools of America," *Papers and Proceedings of the Fourteenth Annual Meeting*, American Sociological Society (The Society, 1919), pp. 243–246.

[85] *Ibid.*, pp. 247–248.

[86] Ross L. Finney, *School Review* (April, 1920), p. 262.

[87] City of Madison, Wisconsin, *Annual Report of the Public Schools, 1900– 1901*, p. 45.

cent of the entering students were placed in it.[88] "Ever since I became a teacher of English," wrote Edwin L. Miller of Detroit's Central High School, "I have heard teachers of English abused. Before that, I abused them myself. Tho all sorts of people join in this chorus of detraction, the voices which are most frequently and vociferously lifted up to condemn us are those of young college professors and old business men."[89]

Although the advocates of social efficiency did not exempt English from the call to judgment, they were inclined to view it with more favor than they did foreign languages and mathematics. On the other hand, it was an academician, Woodrow Wilson, who doubted that such a subject as English did or could exist. In his presidential address to the Middle States Association in 1907, he declared that English should not be taught as a subject, but should pervade the teaching of all subjects. "The only way to learn English and to appreciate it," he said, "is to use it."[90]

Those who believed in a subject called English were not always sure what it was and what aspects of it should be taught in school. There was much confusion about the relationships among literature, composition, rhetoric, and grammar. Nightingale's Committee on College-Entrance Requirements sought to reduce the diversity of courses to two main branches, literature and composition. Four years later, a committee of the Associated Academic Principals of the State of New York valiantly insisted that English was "one indivisible subject" and should not be "broken into parts," such as grammar, composition, rhetoric, and literary interpretation.[91]

As in the case of some other fields, there was much dissension about the stipulations made by colleges in relation to entrance examinations in English, particularly with reference to prescribed books, such as *Silas Marner* and *Ivanhoe*. Yet it was the college-entrance examinations that most effectively represented the attempt to unify the various aspects of English. Almost always they required the writing of a composition on some "classic"; the same examination was designed to elicit from the pupil his knowledge of the book and his ability to express this in writing.

[88] James Weber Linn, "What the University Expects of High-School Students in English," *School Review* (February, 1911), pp. 101–102.

[89] Edwin L. Miller, "Rebuilding an English Course," NEA, 1910, p. 483.

[90] Woodrow Wilson, "School and College," MSM, 1907, pp. 85–86.

[91] E. O. Holland, "Discussion of the Report of the Subcommittee on the Course of Study in English to the Associated Academic Principals of the State of New York, December, 1903," NEA, 1904, p. 505.

This system had begun at Harvard in 1874, and it was adopted by other colleges in New England. Books for the examinations were announced in advance. The Harvard catalogue of 1882–1883, for example, contained the lists applicable to the examinations of 1883, 1884, and 1885. In these were many of the books that long survived as stock pieces in the high school curricula. The list for 1885 contained *Macbeth* and *The Merchant of Venice,* the first two books of *Paradise Lost,* Emerson's *Essay on Eloquence, Silas Marner,* and *A Tale of Two Cities.*[92]

Apparently the colleges did not agree on their lists, and school men set up a demand for uniformity. The question of prescribed books in English was therefore one of the first taken up by the Commission of Colleges in New England on Admission Examinations at the time of its formation in 1886. A comparable movement developed in the Middle States Association, and in 1894 the two efforts converged in the formation of the Conference on Uniform Entrance Requirements in English to promote uniform lists from Maine through Maryland. This coalition group adopted the cumbersome device of separating the books into two categories, one allegedly "for reading," the other "for study," these for parallel examinations of different intensity and depth. Its membership was subsequently augmented by representatives from the Southern Association and the North Central Association.[93]

This National Conference met periodically, usually every two years, to revise its lists, although the revisions usually consisted of a reshuffling of the "classics," many of which had begun their career in the Harvard lists several decades before. The lists also became the basis for the examinations in English given by the College Entrance Examination Board. Although most pupils did not go to college and many of those who did so never took an examination for admission, these lists came to define the substance of English literature in high schools throughout the country. Close attention therefore was given to the pronouncements of the Conference and to the many discussions about minute points involved in the distinctions between books for reading and books for study. In 1905 some flexibility was achieved by the provision of options in both lists.

According to Professor Francis H. Stoddard of New York University, who served for many years as Chairman of this Conference, the force exerted was entirely a moral force, without compulsion. "More than

[92] *Harvard University Catalogue, 1882–1883,* p. 67.
[93] For the origin and development of the National Conference, see Francis H. Stoddard, "The Uniform Entrance Examination in English," *Educational Review* (November, 1905), pp. 375–383.

4000 high schools," he wrote in 1909, "have adopted these regulations, and with absolute autonomy on their own part they can use part of them, or the whole of them."[94] This voluntary adoption, of course, was conditioned by the ever-present possibility that pupils from a given high school might wish to go to a college that required examinations.

Inevitably, then, the enterprise attracted unto itself much of the outcry against college domination. It was easy to forget that it had all begun as a response to the demands of school men themselves. The National Conference and its lists were held responsible for practically all the defects in the English program. Within the group itself a good deal of dissension began to take place, usually fomented by the delegates of the North Central Association, who brought with them the ideological objections of their parent body to any system based on entrance examinations.

One of the most vigorous controversies took place in the meeting of 1912. "Three full sessions," wrote one observer, "were devoted to talk. Twenty-two men unburdened themselves in a succession of speeches consuming many hours. Alas! there was no stenographer; history will be none the richer for the oratory so lavishly expended."[95] The result was the adoption of more regulations designed to promote flexibility through options and a provision that candidates might offer certificates that they had read ten books from a list of 150 the National Conference would approve. Since most colleges already accepted students on certificate, this action probably represented little more than a verbal concession to the point of view of the North Central Association. By this time, however, the National Conference had begun to decline in importance, although its pool of "classics" remained for many years in the programs of some high schools.

The decline of the National Conference was paralleled by the appearance of a new and vigorous organization. At the Boston meeting of the NEA in 1910, a delegation of teachers from New York City had stormed the English Round Table of the Department of Secondary Education demanding action against the college requirements. The outcome of this session was the creation of a committee with James Fleming Hosic, Professor of English at the Chicago Teachers College, as Chairman. A year later at San Francisco, the Round Table directed this com-

[94] Francis H. Stoddard, "Report of the Committee on Uniform Entrance Requirements in English," MSM, 1909, p. 93.

[95] James F. Hosic, "If There Were No College Entrance Requirements in English What Would We Teach in the High Schools?" NC, 1912, pp. 57–58.

mittee to organize a National Council of the Teachers of English. Hosic moved swiftly to this task, and the National Council held its first session at Chicago in December, 1911.

Back of this lay a long period of preparation for national leadership on the part of Hosic himself. In 1905 he had organized the English Club of Chicago, with 60 "chosen" members, some of them from the Chicago Public Schools, but with representatives of suburban and private schools as well, along with college professors from Northwestern and the University of Chicago. In addition to meeting each month, the Club sponsored two "mass meetings" a year to spread the new English to many teachers of Chicago and vicinity.[96] Hosic's energy and intensity almost matched that of Clarence Kingsley. He was well equipped to lead the English teachers of the nation to their new status as the best-organized and most articulate group among those representing the subjects of the secondary school.

The newly formed Council lost no time in organizing a committee for the high school course. This became the nucleus of the CRSE committee on English appointed in the fall of 1912. It picked up more members as the work proceeded and tried to establish a numerical identification for itself as the Joint Committee of Thirty. Its final cast included eight representatives of colleges, eleven high school teachers, three superintendents, two supervisors, three librarians, two principals, and a field agent of the University of the State of New York. The college representatives included four professors of English, two professors of speech, one dean of a faculty of arts, and an editor attached to a college of agriculture. One of the high school principals was William D. Lewis of Philadelphia's William Penn High School. The Chairman, of course, was Hosic.

Two reports came from this Committee, one in 1913, the other in 1917. The preliminary report was relatively brief, being devoted primarily to a list of aims and problems. On the one hand, the Committee proclaimed the lofty aim of leading pupils to "higher living," but on the other, it talked more specifically about providing pupils with a mastery of language as an effective tool. The problems also were quite specific, dealing with tangible matters such as whether or not to offer a general English course or specialized versions such as "commercial English"; the relative merits of organizing courses on full-year or half-year schedules;

---

[96] "More Chicago News," *School Journal* (November 25, 1905), p. 577.

and ways of training pupils in the use of current books and periodicals.[97]

The final report was a volume of 181 pages, virtually a textbook on all phases of the teaching of English. It included special reports of sub-committees on composition, literature, oral expression, business English, and school libraries. Sequences were provided for continuing strands of literature, composition, and oral work from grades seven through twelve. Gone were the prescribed classics as an identifiable group. In their place appeared long lists of suggested titles broadly ranging over a variety of literary types, from which, however, such familiar items as *Silas Marner* and *Julius Caesar* were not excluded.

A statement on "point of view" occupied a short, but prominent place in the report. It showed the impact of the times, although it began with a statement, reminiscent of the Committee of Ten, to the effect that preparation for college was only a minor function of the high school. From this it drew the inference that the course in English "should be organized with reference to basic social needs rather than with reference to college-entrance requirements," thus assuming a distinction between the two points of reference. It added, however, that the high school would prepare best either for college or for life "by making its own life real and complete." The high school was assumed to be "truly demo-cratic" in serving the children of all the people, this requiring "a con-siderable range of subject matter," without, however, sacrificing "uni-formity of aims and a body of common culture." Thus did the report seek to accommodate itself to differentiation, but with due regard for at least the terminology of tradition.

Social efficiency, of course, had to appear, but the report split the term into its two parts. English was social in content and social in "method of acquirement," necessarily so, since the chief function of language was communication. "No one," went on the report, "has more need to be a close student of contemporary social activities, social move-ments, and social needs than the teacher of English." Efficiency, taken separately, also received due recognition, with a distinction drawn, how-ever, between English as "training for efficiency" and English as "train-ing for the wholesome enjoyment of leisure."[98]

---

[97] James Fleming Hosic, "Statement of Chairman of the Committee on English," *Preliminary Statements by Chairmen of Committees of the Commission of the National Education Association on the Reorganization of Secondary Education, op. cit.,* pp. 11–16.

[98] CRSE, *Reorganization of English in Secondary Schools* (U.S. Bureau of Education, Bulletin No. 2 [Washington, D.C., 1917]), p. 26.

Not only in the exposition of the point of view but also in other parts of the report, there were indications of compromise. This was particularly evident in the treatment of the thorny question of "grammar," an entity that had been thrown out and brought back into the teaching of English on several previous occasions. A sane attitude toward grammar, said the subcommittee on composition in grades seven through nine, involved finding out what parts of the subject had "actual value," in short, the grammar of use. The grammar of classification was to be abandoned.[99] This rather grim notion of grammar conflicted with a point of view stated by Otto Jespersen to the New England Association of Teachers of English in 1910. Most people, said Jespersen, considered grammar dull but useful. "Now I hold," confessed this expert, "the exactly opposite view. I think that the study of grammar is really more or less useless, but that it is extremely fascinating."[100] Still, grammar viewed solely as a fascinating subject would have received short shrift in this age of efficiency.

The report gained enthusiastic applause,[101] although some of its patrons made more extreme interpretations than could be readily justified in its pages. Conservative aspects of the report tended to be overlooked. Even William D. Lewis, presumed to have prepared the section on high school literature, sounded more temperate in this statement than in many of his other statements on the work of high schools. Stripped of its possibly ceremonial use of expressions fashionable at the time, the report presented a solid six-year program in English, for the most part consistent with its two "immediate" aims of giving pupils a command of speech and writing and of teaching them "to read thoughtfully and with appreciation, to form in them a taste for good reading, and to teach them how to find books that are worth while."[102] With these aims, few traditionalists indeed would have found it possible to disagree.[103]

[99] Ibid., p. 37.

[100] Otto Jespersen, "Modern English Grammar," School Review (October, 1910), p. 530.

[101] At its 1918 meeting, the North Central Association endorsed the report and voted to send no more delegates to the National Conference. NC, 1918, pp. 78–79. Hosic stated in this meeting that 30,000 to 40,000 copies of the report had been circulated.

[102] CRSE, Reorganization of English in Secondary Schools, op. cit., p. 30.

[103] Nontraditionalists may have had some misgivings about the conservatism of the report. Jesse H. Newlon, for example, although supporting the endorsement of it by the North Central Association, thought perhaps it had not gone far enough. NC, 1918, p. 79. Possibly Newlon wanted more differentiation. In the same meeting, Newlon proposed questions to be used in determining the efficiency of a school.

Traditionalists and others, however, might have found it easier to disagree with an enthusiastic review of a new textbook, *Practical English for High Schools,* written by two members of the CRSE Committee, Chairman Hosic and William D. Lewis. "Very few illustrations," favorably commented the review, "are drawn from the classic writers. Instead quotations from the *Youth's Companion* and from Theodore Roosevelt and other noted men of the day are employed. The book as a whole is a distinct challenge to the traditions of high school English established by the earlier reports of the National Education Association and embodies the main features of the report of the Committee of Thirty on the reorganization of English in the secondary schools."[104]

Meanwhile the National Council of the Teachers of English continued to thrive. Its fifth annual meeting, held at Chicago in 1915, offered a program in which 40 speakers covered a multitude of topics, including speech training, newspaper work, libraries, versification, and, as always, formal grammar. One of the speakers advanced a new idea that was already old, but still considered, in some quarters, a new idea today. English, he declared, was a nearly grammarless tongue. "Most of our formal grammar, he added, "comes from the effort to impose the categories of Latin upon English."[105] By 1920 the Council was ready to celebrate its tenth anniversary on a note of triumph. Its joint report with the CRSE, declared an editorial in *School and Society,* was being "widely used by city and state departments of education as the foundation of their courses." The editorial noted that the Council had originated as a "revolt" against college domination. Having become unified "in their contention with the colleges," the members had since moved on to other "reforms." Its next world to conquer was to be the "application of scientific method" to the teaching of English.[106]

V

Science teachers and leaders in the field of science education in this period were greatly concerned about the state of their enrollments. Between 1910 and 1915, total relative enrollments in the natural sci-

One of these was, "Are curriculums administered with a view to meeting the needs of the varying pupil groups?" *Ibid.,* p. 21.

[104] "Recent Publications in the Field of English," *School and Society* (March 22, 1919), pp. 363–364.

[105] As quoted in *Education* (January, 1916), p. 337.

[106] *School and Society* (December 11, 1920), pp. 582–583.

ences slumped from 82.7 percent to 65.4 percent, with substantial losses in physical geography, physiology, botany, and zoology. Even the appearance of enrollments in general biology to the extent of 6.9 percent in 1915 did not offset the decline in combined botany and zoology enrollments from 24.9 percent to 12.4 percent during the preceding five-year period.[107]

This was indeed a strange state of affairs for an allegedly modern age. G. Stanley Hall and others blamed the Committee of Ten for the decline in physics enrollments that had taken place before 1910, charging this to the mathematical treatment and laboratory work recommended by the conference on physics, chemistry, and astronomy. One professor of physics who supported this criticism, although not with reference to the Committee of Ten, was Robert A. Millikan of the University of Chicago. He felt that physics should stress familiar phenomena and that only a small amount of mathematics was needed in school science.[108] These arguments were part of a loud chorus of complaint that science as taught in schools was not related to life. Science should be more practical, declared W. J. Bray, Professor of Chemistry at Kirksville, Missouri, State Normal School, and there was no room in high school for science for science's sake.[109]

Professor C. R. Mann of the University of Chicago observed that students avoided science when there was free election.[110] Professor Fred Barber of Illinois State Normal University feared that the twentieth century was less fascinated by science than had been the nineteenth. "The popular interest in science which characterized the epoch of Darwin, Huxley, and Agassiz, of Faraday, Lydell, and Tyndall has largely waned in recent years." High school science, he added, needed reorganization to make clear to students "the monumental effects of applied science upon modern life." He also thought that science courses had been more popular when "spiced through and through with details and illustrations of interest to the common people."[111]

Science teachers, obviously, would have to lead the twentieth century

[107] Commissioner, 1899–1900, II, p. 2123; 1910, II, p. 1139; 1916, II, p. 487.
[108] In discussion, *School Review* (April, 1906), p. 251.
[109] As quoted in "Enrollment in High-School Courses in Missouri," *School and Society* (March 20, 1915), p. 415.
[110] C. R. Mann, "Science in Civilization and Science in Education," *School Review* (November, 1906), p. 665.
[111] Fred D. Barber, "Fundamental Considerations in the Reorganization of High-School Science," *School Review* (December, 1916), pp. 724–725.

back to the scientific enthusiasms of the nineteenth, and to do so they would have to make their courses more practical and descriptive. Chemistry was one science course with possibilities along these lines. A committee of the New York State Science Teachers' Association recommended two syllabi, one for general chemistry, the other for applied chemistry. The applied course was to be similar to one in use for some time at Erasmus Hall High School, Brooklyn, and it was teacher William J. Hancock of that school who argued its merits. Provision was made in the applied course for the study of such practical matters as stoves and burners, cleaning compounds, fuels, fibers, germicides, and foods. It was not, he argued, "merely" an information course, but included the writing of equations as well. He reported much enthusiasm at Erasmus Hall for the projects on fire-extinguishers, baking powder, and soap. Sound mental discipline was also claimed as an outcome. "Yes," concluded Hancock, "I believe in applied chemistry. May it live long, and prosper!"[112]

The demand was not only for the practical, but also for the social. Science teachers sought ways to show their contributions to social efficiency. Here it was biology that led the way. Principal Joseph K. Van Denburg of New York City in 1907 sought to relate biology to socialized aims. "Let it remain for the college," said Van Denburg, "to make *biologists;* our effort should be to make intelligent citizens."[113] The ant and the mosquito, he declared, should receive more attention than the locust, the mosquito because of its effect on human life, the ant because its social system paralleled that of the human race. "The communal life, the division of labor, the building of homes, the storing of food, the care of the pupa, all these the youth can not only see, but appreciate some of the facts and processes which will make more intelligible the structure of *human* society." Van Denburg felt the study of biology should include the principles of evolution, partly because these had forced people to pay more attention to biology itself. "Would it not be absurd," he asked, "for the high school course in biology to discard or neglect the fairy god-mother that took it from the intellectual kitchen and carried it to the king's court?"[114]

Teacher Bertha May Clark of the William Penn High School for Girls,

[112] William J. Hancock, "The New York State Syllabus of Applied Chemistry," NEA, 1916, pp. 702–704.
[113] Joseph K. Van Denburg, "The Subject-Matter or the Year of High School Biology Should be Changed," *Year Book, 1906–07,* High School Teachers Association of New York City (New York: The Association, 1907), p. 45.
[114] *Ibid.,* pp. 48–49.

Philadelphia, used social objectives as an argument for living, as against dead, biology. Living biology, she said, would teach the interdependence of all living things. "The dead bee and ant," she observed, "are nothing to the pupil, but from the living, active ant or bee colony, he learns community life, the strength of the many as contrasted with the weakness of the few." This living biology would also be a powerful factor for "social uplift," and it would increase "efficiency in the concrete" by application of scientific laws to daily life. It would also raise "moral tone" when its lessons were related to the interdependence of society.[115]

Other advocates of biology were somewhat less spectacular in their arguments, but were equally committed to practical applications in relation to social aims. In 1918 C. F. Hodge and Jean Dawson published a textbook entitled *Civic Biology,* based on biological aspects of community problems, largely those involving destructive plants and animals, such as weeds, poisonous plants, flies, mosquitoes, rats, and bacteria. Here possibly were more overtones of one interpretation of the Darwinian theory of evolution. "It is an ugly, not a beneficent, nature that faces the pupil," wrote E. R. Downing in his review of the book. "The pupil must feel that 'nature is red in tooth and claw.' The book may make him aware of the problems of civic biology, but may also make him a confirmed pessimist."[116]

By 1919 practical and social biology seemed triumphant. According to one observer, the content had been "entirely revolutionized" during the preceding ten to fifteen years. Gone, he said, were dissections of frogs and crayfish, along with the learning of "long lists" of terms. At least they were gone from the published courses of study. On examining a "recently-issued syllabus," he had found every topic dealing in some way with hygiene or food problems or community welfare. "Thus," he concluded, "are the ends of scientific training gained while practical aims are being carried out."[117]

Of all the sciences, physics had the most difficult time meeting the

[115] Bertha May Clark, "Living versus Dead Biology," *School Review* (April, 1913), pp. 251–253.

[116] E. R. Downing, book review, *School Review* (January, 1919), pp. 75–76. The book under review was published by Ginn and Company, 1918. "Civic biology" evidently became a popular term. It was another textbook by the same title that was used by teacher Scopes in his test-case violation of the Tennessee law against the teaching of evolution. The book in question was on the state prescribed list. Ray Ginger, *Six Days or Forever? Tennessee v. John Thomas Scopes* (New York: Signet Book edition, 1960 printing [originally published by Beacon Press, 1958]), p. 22.

[117] A Teacher of Biology, "Practical Biology," *School and Society* (June 28, 1919), pp. 780–781.

new demands. Many joined in the denunciation of alleged college domination, interpreted in this field to mean insistence upon precision, rigorous laboratory work, and the use of mathematics. There was, however, no dearth of committees and projects to put things right. Sixteen educational associations were involved between 1906 and 1909 in a mass movement known as the new physics, aimed as usual against "the abstract and mathematical character of much of instruction given."[118] In 1909 the College Entrance Examination Board adopted a new definition of physics, "formulated by a competent commission of physicists and teachers of physics," and designed to correct "some of the unfortunate mistakes which have been made in the past."[119]

None of this apparently brought about sufficient reform to please the advocates of social efficiency. Addressing the New York Physics Club in 1918, David Snedden challenged his audience with characteristic questions. "What," he asked, "are your purposes in teaching this subject? Are these alleged purposes worth while? To whom and for what reasons? . . . To what extent do your present means and methods realize your alleged aims? How do you know?" It was as hard, he believed, to justify physics as taught in 90 percent of the schools as it was to justify "Latin for boys, algebra for girls, or ancient history for both."[120] He proposed examining the attainments in physics of "superior" persons in our society. Then, he declared, we would know what to teach in physics.[121]

Along with these attempts to reform chemistry, biology, and physics as separate subjects, there was under way a strong movement for a unified course called "general science," this being designed particularly for the eighth and ninth grades. This course dated back at least as far as 1900, when an example of it had been reported in practice at the high school of Lincoln, Nebraska. It was a one-semester course for the ninth grade, "constructed so as to include an experimental study of the important properties of matter and the simpler illustrations of forms of energy and chemical action, with special reference to physiography and biology and to the simple familiar phenomena of daily life."[122] By 1911 such courses were reported in Boston, Chicago, and San Francisco, and

[118] *Educational Review* (January, 1909), p. 102.

[119] *Educational Review* (May, 1909), p. 532.

[120] David Snedden, "Current Problems of Aim in Physics Teaching," *School and Society* (November 30, 1918), p. 631.

[121] *Ibid.,* pp. 632–633.

[122] Hermon C. Cooper, "An Introductory Science Course for Secondary Schools," *School Review* (September, 1901), p. 441.

there were many requests to publishing houses for appropriate texts.[123] Although one critic in 1915 referred to general science as a step toward soft pedagogy, consisting of titbits rather than solid food, the movement continued to thrive.[124] In the same year, one survey found general science to exist in about one-fifth of the reporting schools in Iowa and nearly half the reporting schools in California.[125] There were, of course, various arguments put forward by the advocates of general science. One teacher defended it as a course for potential dropouts.[126] A superintendent of schools, however, thought the entire science program should be unified, and he claimed that general science was what Spencer really had in mind when he pronounced science to be the knowledge of most worth.[127]

Still, the more science was reformed, the more its relative enrollments declined. Perhaps Eliot had been right back in 1894 when he characterized mathematics and science as "acceptable to but a small proportion of the students."[128] Eliot remained aloof from discussions about science until his "needed changes" address in the winter of 1915–1916. In this he talked of science as the observing and describing of concrete things, plus the skill of drawing correct inferences from what had been observed and described. It was still, in his view, properly an elective subject, but he urged schools to expand their offerings in science and to strengthen the teaching of it through laboratory work with adequate equipment. During the Lincoln School controversy, he veered from his former convictions sufficiently to declare science "the knowledge best worth having," but he followed this statement immediately by more discussion about its use in training the senses.[129]

It was in the general context of the demand for the practical and the

[123] George A. Cowen, "Elementary or General Science from the Standpoint of the Eastern Schoolmaster," NEA, 1911, p. 940.

[124] J. G. Coulter, "A Four-Year Course in Science in the High Schools," *School and Society* (February 13, 1915), p. 228.

[125] Aravilla Meek Taylor, "General Science Situation in Iowa and California," *School Review* (January, 1916), p. 22.

[126] Ida Welch, "General Science for the First Year of High School," NEA, 1915, p. 1022.

[127] Arthur Deamer, "General or Elementary Science in Junior High Schools," NEA, 1917, p. 543.

[128] Charles W. Eliot to Caskie Harrison, August 9, 1894, Charles W. Eliot Papers (Harvard University Archives, Cambridge, Mass.). In 1910 he wrote that "experience during the past fifty years seems to have proved that fewer minds are naturally inclined to scientific than to linguistic study." Introduction to Herbert Spencer's *Essays on Education* (New York: E. P. Dutton & Co., 1949), p. ix, Eliot's introduction dated October, 1910.

[129] Charles W. Eliot, "The Case against Compulsory Latin," *Atlantic Monthly* (March, 1917), p. 355.

social, however, that the CRSE committee on science did its work. This grew into a monster committee of 47 persons, broken into subcommittees on physics, chemistry, biology, general science, and supervision. Its chairman was Otis W. Caldwell, who moved from the University of Chicago to the directorship of the Lincoln School in 1917. The listing of the final membership in the 1920 report included nineteen secondary school teachers, five representatives of Columbia's Teachers College, five members from normal schools, and five professors from universities other than Columbia, the remainder being scattered among various categories.

In its 1920 report the committee sought to show how science contributed to six of the seven objectives stated by the CRSE two years before. Beyond this, it specified certain values, such as various interests, habits, and abilities.[130] Little was said, except in the report of the subcommittee on physics, about Eliot's favorite skills of observing, recording, describing, and inferring. On the other hand, the committee bestowed approval on "informal values," meaning "a large body of facts and principles of significance in the home, school, and community." Apparently teachers of science no longer resented the charge that theirs was a "mere" informational subject. Cultural and aesthetic values were also included.[131]

For what it called "the junior-senior high school," the committee recommended general science in grades seven and eight and biology in grade nine, with differentiated elective courses in chemistry, physics, geography or physiography, and advanced biology for grades ten to twelve. It is remarkable how this recommendation corresponded to the science sequence developed in the high schools during the late 1950's. Schools on the 8-4 plan were advised to place general science in the ninth grade and biology in the tenth, and to offer the same range of electives for the two upper years. Modifications of the range of electives were suggested for high schools of medium size and for small high schools. In both cases the advanced biology courses and the courses in general geography or physiography were deleted. Approval was given to the practice in small high schools of alternating the courses in chemistry and physics in successive years.[132] It is noteworthy that this com-

[130] CRSE, *Reorganization of Science in Secondary Schools* (U.S. Bureau of Education, Bulletin No. 26 [Washington, D.C., 1920]), pp. 12–15.
[131] *Ibid.*, p. 15.
[132] *Ibid.*, pp. 22–24.

mittee, coming out with its report at the end of a decade of supposed alienation from the scholars in the various science fields, recommended that every high school provide biology, chemistry, and physics.

The emphasis, of course, was on the practical side, particularly in the outline recommended for general science. Although social aspects of biology were dealt with, the report avoided the excesses found in many statements about socialized aims. One impact of the social-efficiency movement was revealed in the suggestions for "differentiated chemistry courses for certain curriculums."[133] The physics subcommittee offered many examples of practical applications, but it also declared that the course should lead to "a body of facts and principles set forth in an orderly manner . . . grouped under the greater principles that give unity to the science."[134] Down-to-earth advice was offered physics teachers on such matters as excursions, pupil reports, physics clubs, laboratory work by pupils, demonstrations, and notebooks.

Like the CRSE reports on social studies and English, the one on science was essentially conservative and retained much of the traditional content. It was somewhat more pedestrian than the other reports, an impression perhaps created by the determination of the committee to prove the contributions of science to the prosaic problems of everyday life. Spencer had already performed the same task many decades before, with equally uninspiring results.

In the general discussions of the field, however, there was still an occasional flame from the nineteenth-century fires lighted by scientists like Huxley. Even a scholarly physicist like Millikan was not ashamed to testify his belief that natural science had much to do with the abiding hopes and dreams of mankind. In a lecture delivered on April 19, 1915, he said he could see natural science as one of the ways to permanent peace. "The lesson which physics has to teach the world," he declared, "is that war can and must be abolished; and it will be abolished through the adoption by the nations of the earth of the method and the faith of the scientist . . . the faith that he can find a way to stay the ravages of the most hideous, most loathsome disease which has thus far blighted the lives of men, the disease of militarism, just as he has already found a way to stay the ravages of diphtheria and smallpox."[135]

[133] *Ibid.*, pp. 47–49.
[134] *Ibid.*, p. 57.
[135] Robert A. Millikan, "The New Physics," *School Review* (November, 1915), p. 620.

VI

The CRSE did not confine its attention to the academic subjects. It maintained committees in a number of the other fields as well, and published substantial reports on music, physical education, home economics, agriculture, and business education. These were, in this period, relatively noncontroversial fields, not insofar as their own internal issues were concerned, but in terms of questions about what the secondary school program as a whole should include. If some of them did not grow as rapidly as their adherents wished, this was more a matter of default than of active opposition from school administrators and governing boards.

Of these reports, one of the most complete was that of the CRSE committee on business education,[136] a field which by 1922 showed total enrollments amounting to 42 percent of the high school population.[137] It was probably this field, along with English, that absorbed many of the pupils who were no longer enrolling in courses in foreign languages and science and in the algebra-geometry sequence in mathematics. The chairman of the business committee was Cheesman A. Herrick, then President of Girard College, long a leader in the field, who had been criticized for opposing specialized business subjects in the seventh and eighth grades. His moderate point of view was reflected in the report. Attention was given not only to the business subjects, but also to the place of other fields in business curricula or courses of study. The committee recommended English for all grades from seven through twelve. It talked of "business English," but not necessarily as a separate subject. Business curricula should be so organized, felt the committee, that a pupil in it could elect four years of a foreign language. Strong endorsement was given to work in social studies, including history.

The age of efficiency, then, did not wipe out any of the instructional fields. Even the so-called academic fields, hauled before the bar of justice as they were, managed to survive. They were, in effect, allowed to do so on promise of good behavior. Whether or not they lived up to the promises was another matter; English and social studies, however, did manage to win some approval and even applause from the parole boards. There were spokesmen for all the academic fields who sought to

[136] CRSE, *Business Education in Secondary Schools* (U.S. Bureau of Education, Bulletin No. 55 [Washington, D.C., 1919]).

[137] *Biennial Survey of Education, 1920–1922,* (U.S. Bureau of Education, Bulletin No. 14 [Washington, D.C., 1924]), II, p. 578.

meet the new demands, partly by professing adherence to social efficiency as an aim, partly by recommending and effecting some modification in what was taught. In some cases this modification appeared in differentiated courses, such as applied chemistry. This, of course, sharpened the dualism between pupils preparing for college and those planning to end their formal schooling at the twelfth grade or before.

Chapter 15
Mr. Kingsley's report

> "It will be seen at a glance that these seven main objectives take care of the whole man, body, soul, and mind."
>
> —PRINCIPAL F. R. WILLARD,
> JULY 5, 1919.

*K*ingsley wanted a shorter name for the Commission on the Reorganization of Secondary Education. "The Committee of Ten," he reminded Claxton, "gained much of its prominence from its short and easily remembered title."[1] Claxton agreed, but the NEA did not. As it turned out, Kingsley was right. Few indeed remember the name of his Commission. Yet posterity has done much to compensate for this. Even today school people remember the title of the Commission's main report, *Cardinal Principles of Secondary Education,* and use it as one of the most familiar of pedagogical labels. It was to the production of this report that the reviewing committee devoted major attention between 1915 and 1918.

The organization of the Commission was as cumbersome as its name. On it were all the members of all the committees, plus ten members at large. These ten and the sixteen committee chairmen made up the reviewing committee. Prominent names, or names that were to become prominent, on the reviewing committee were those of Commissioner Claxton, President Edward O. Sisson of the University of Montana, Thomas H. Briggs and William Heard Kilpatrick of Columbia's Teachers College, Charles Hughes Johnston of the University of Illinois, Alexander Inglis of Harvard, Henry Neumann of the Ethical Culture School, President Cheesman A. Herrick of Girard College, James Fleming Hosic of the Chicago Teachers College, and Director Otis W. Caldwell of the

[1] Clarence Kingsley to P. P. Claxton, May 12, 1916; P. P. Claxton to Clarence Kingsley, May 15, 1916; Clarence Kingsley to members of the reviewing committee, July 24, 1916, RSE (National Archives, Record Group 12).

controversial Lincoln School. There were six professors of education, plus Edward O. Sisson, who had been one before becoming a university president. The composition of the reviewing committee differed in two respects from that of the subject committees. It included no university representatives from the academic fields and only two classroom teachers from the secondary schools, Edward Manley of the Englewood High School, Chicago, and Walter Eugene Foster of the Stuyvesant High School, New York.

Still, Chairman Kingsley had only recently left the classroom for his new position as Inspector of High Schools in Massachusetts. It was from the classroom and from his active participation in the High School Teachers Association of New York City that he derived his sense of wrongs needing to be put right. Moreover, Kingsley had been a teacher of mathematics, in both high school and college, and he was never one to disparage the academic fields. Possibly of equal importance had been his employment as a social worker. On all counts, Kingsley was unusual. He had stepped from the classroom to the chairmanship of the NEA's Committee on the Articulation of High School and College. He combined pedagogical evangelism with a hard-headed grasp of reality in the schools. Although he had never held a post as a school administrator, he now found himself administering a complex enterprise, with responsibility to a pair of highly critical taskmasters, the U.S. Bureau of Education and the NEA.

During 1913 and 1914 Kingsley produced articles and addresses in which he further developed his point of view and discussed the matters on which the reviewing committee was getting down to work. He was also getting used to his new job under David Snedden in the State Department of Education of Massachusetts. One of the fascinating questions of this period is how much Snedden may have influenced Kingsley. Up to this time, Kingsley had dealt mainly with flexibility in college-admission requirements. He did not abandon this interest, but he now began to assemble the elements that would later appear in the *Cardinal Principles* report.

This expansion of interest reflected a concern on his part with the place of vocational training in the larger scheme of education. In a general-session address to the NEA in 1913 he declared that specialized training was not enough. "The adjustment of the individual to life," he said, "is broader than the adjustment to vocation. It includes also the selection of avocation, the enlargement of interests, and the preparation for citizenship." Discovery of aptitudes in the individual pupil was of the utmost importance, he said, and he recommended that schools engage in systematic testing of pupils for this purpose. All this, he felt, called for the cosmopolitan or composite high school, with flexible handling of courses of study to permit changes and shifts. The work should not be too specialized, and the vocational responsibilities of the high school lay chiefly in the field of vocational guidance.[2]

A year later, in an address to the NEA Department of Secondary Education, he used the term "general education" to designate the broader responsibilities of the high school. The place of subjects in the high school of the future would depend on "their value in reaching the ends of general education." He interpreted "the present tendency "as one giving greater place to "English literature, English composition, both written and oral, socialized history, economics, community civics, general science, elementary biology, agricultural science, and household arts." Noticeably absent from this list were the foreign languages and his own field of mathematics.[3] He called also for specific aims expressed in terms of "the power to execute or in the ability to appreciate rather than in terms of subject-matter to be mastered," a point of view he said had been adopted by the CRSE. "Thus," he declared, "subject-matter becomes the means to the end rather than the end itself." As examples of this he gave, for English, the ability to write a concise business letter and, for history, the "appreciation of the development of the rights of the individual as achieved by the Anglo-Saxon."[4]

On the whole, Kingsley's expressions were more subdued than those of many of his contemporaries. In a chapter written for a symposium published by Charles Hughes Johnston in 1914, Kingsley merely said that the theory of formal discipline had been called into question, concluding that this implied recognition of "definite training for specific purposes both liberal and vocational." In the organization of the high school program he recommended the major-minor system rather than courses of study. With a degree of charity to tradition unusual for the time, he listed six fields of study, four or five of which should be represented in the program of every pupil. These were language, including English and foreign languages, natural science, social studies, mathematics, practical

[2] Clarence Kingsley, "The High-School Period as a Testing Time," NEA, 1913, pp. 50–53.
[3] Clarence Kingsley, "Problems Confronting the Commission on the Reorganization of Secondary Education," NEA, 1914, pp. 485–486.
[4] *Ibid.*, pp. 483–484.

arts, and fine arts. Beyond this the pupils should choose majors and minors. Moreover, in a period that talked much of "the needs of society," Kingsley, in this article, called for "knowledge of pupils from fourteen to eighteen years of age" as well, thereby granting the importance of child study in the adolescent years.[5]

There were occasions, however, on which he veered closer to the prevailing winds of doctrine, sometimes even reflecting Snedden's ideas of social control. It was in an address to the High School Masters' Club of Massachusetts in March, 1914, that he called for investigations to find what kinds "of boys and girls of eighteen society needs." If, for example, people with "certain attitudes toward life" made for progress, then "we," he said, must discover methods of giving boys and girls "those attitudes toward life"; similarly, if appreciation of art, music, and literature "contributes to higher living," then again "we" must introduce methods "to give this appreciation." Even the higher living apparently was to come under control, and there was a hint of Snedden's view of "culture" as something that should be budgeted into every properly conducted life. Also reminiscent of Snedden's terminology was Kingsley's use in this address of expressions such as "the rank and file," who, along with the future leaders, should be trained for their responsibilities. On this occasion, Kingsley foreshadowed the categories of objectives in the *Cardinal Principles* report, calling for aims such as "the inculcation of health habits, health ideals, and health knowledge; the development of civic pride, and intelligent interest in movements for human betterment; appreciation of good music, art and literature; and right standards of conduct in the home, in the community, and in the vocation." Again he declared that aims must be stated in terms of effects upon the boy or girl rather than as subject matter to be mastered.[6]

Here evidently was a man groping his way. Working at Snedden's elbow in Massachusetts and confronted by articulate colleagues on the reviewing committee, Kingsley had to absorb and evaluate many ideas that were delivered to him under high pressure indeed. The varying composite pictures he evolved from these, however, were his own. Kingsley was no rubber stamp for others, and he resisted, for example, the strong demand so popular at the time for fixed "curriculums" aimed at

[5] Clarence Kingsley, "The Relation of the High School to Higher Educational Institutions," *The Modern High School*, Charles Hughes Johnson (ed.) (New York: Charles Scribner's Sons, 1914), pp. 198–201.

[6] Clarence Kingsley, "New Aims of the Modern High School," *Journal of Education* (April 23, 1914), p. 458.

"groups" of pupils. His ways of resolving dilemmas, of course, could not please everybody. While he clung to "tradition" in his commitment to history as a school subject, he talked of it as "socialized history," although the content he proposed was solid enough history. Most of all he was a man with a job to be done, but in the course of this he did not propose to surrender his stubborn convictions about what was right.

II

The reviewing committee began its work in earnest at the Cincinnati meeting of the Department of Superintendence in February, 1915. Eighteen members were present when it was decided to consider secondary education as beginning in the seventh grade, thereby following the lead of Nightingale's Committee sixteen years before. Like Eliot, Kingsley believed in quick action, and the various subject committees were given until October 1 to make their reports. As soon as possible thereafter, Kingsley hoped, the reviewing committee would meet to issue its first complete report.[7] As had been the case with Eliot, Kingsley was in for disappointment and had to revise his schedules as he went along.

In July, 1915, Kingsley called a meeting of the reviewing committee to be held that November in Chicago. He prepared an outline for a general report, complete with the assignment of personnel responsible for writing the various sections. He proposed to write the first three sections himself, those dealing with the definition of secondary education, the need for reorganization, and the reasons for reorganizing on a national scale. The topic of "curriculum differentiations" was assigned to Charles Hughes Johnston and that of vocational guidance to Frank M. Leavitt and Henry Neumann.[8] Edward O. Sisson, then State Commissioner of Education in Idaho, apparently had already written a statement on "prescribed units" in secondary education.

Kingsley supplemented this outline with a broad sketch not only of his sections but also of others. He defined secondary education as all forms of education planned for pupils approximately twelve to eighteen years of age. This, he pointed out, meant all pupils of those ages, since the secondary school was no longer regarded as a selective institution.

[7] Clarence Kingsley, "Meeting of the Commission on the Reorganization of Secondary Education," *Educational Administration and Supervision* (May, 1915), pp. 330–332.

[8] Clarence Kingsley to P. P. Claxton, September 30, 1915, RSE (National Archives, Record Group 12).

Again he called for specific aims, this time including as one example "the point of view that will lead to cooperation with a charity organization society." On Johnston's topic of differentiation, he suggested that while the junior high school should offer several "curriculums," any of these should admit to any curriculum in the senior high school. Furthermore, if election was to be by "curriculums," there should be room for electives within them, with substitutions permitted.[9]

At the November meeting in Chicago, the reviewing committee approved in broad outline Kingsley's proposals for the general report, issued further instructions to the subject committees, decided to use the terms *junior high school* and *senior high school,* and authorized the appointment of the controversial committee on mathematics. The reviewing committee also had before it a memorandum, possibly written by Kingsley himself, setting forth questions for the committee on mathematics to consider. Kingsley was enthusiastic about the results of this session and pronounced it "one of the best Committee meetings that was ever held on the problems of secondary education."[10]

Sisson's paper on "prescribed units" was also under consideration during the latter part of 1915, but it did not appear in the final *Cardinal Principles* report. Kingsley had circulated it among the members of the reviewing committee; several of them gave their written opinions of it. It was unusual in that it presented constants and electives for the entire six-year span of secondary education. Of the twenty-three units considered available, fifteen were stipulated as constants and eight as electives, with the fifteen constants including four units of English, three of mathematics, four of science, three of history, and one of economics. Sisson praised natural science and social studies as "the disciplines upon which more than all others the wits of the race have been sharpened."[11] His paper, however, drew criticism from Columbia's Thomas H. Briggs, largely because no statement had been made about what the various units should contain.[12] Perhaps this paper was considered too conservative by some members of the reviewing committee, although even the three units of required mathematics amounted to no more than one

[9] Clarence Kingsley, "Topics Suggested for Treatment in the Report of the Reviewing Committee," undated, but prepared for the November, 1915, meeting, RSE (National Archives, Record Group 12).

[10] Clarence Kingsley to P. P. Claxton, November 26, 1915, RSE (National Archives, Record Group 12).

[11] Edward O. Sisson, "The 'Nine Prescribed Units,'" undated, prepared for the Chicago meeting, November, 1915, RSE (National Archives, Record Group 12).

[12] Quoted *ibid.*

unit in the old category of grades nine through twelve. Or it may have been considered conservative since it did not recommend "curriculums." Possibly the reviewing committee decided at some point that it was not appropriate to make recommendations along these lines.

The next meeting took place at the Detroit convention of the Department of School Superintendence early in 1916, with sixteen people present. By this time Kingsley had prepared manuscript for the general report, covering not only the sections for which he had already taken responsibility, but also several additional ones. Among these new sections was one called "the main objectives of public education," this eventually becoming the most widely known part of the report. The committee discussed Kingsley's work and referred several sections, including the one on objectives, to him and a special committee for revision. On this special committee were Alexander Inglis, William Heard Kilpatrick, and Cheesman Herrick. Kingsley apparently was not displeased by this development. In fact, he expressed much satisfaction with the Detroit meeting as a whole, particularly with a decision made to hold another session in New York that July. "This will make," he wrote, "eight days of strenuous work in a single year, in addition to all the correspondence and committee work which has been done in between times. Certainly there are few committees that have a record equal to ours in this respect."[13]

After consulting with Inglis, Kingsley went ahead to do the revising himself, sending the new draft to the special committee and to the reviewing committee so that it could be considered at the July meeting in New York. "I have entirely rewritten the material that I presented at Detroit," he declared, "and believe it is now much more satisfactory."[14] By this time the report had become almost entirely Kingsley's own production, although space was left for the two sections expected from Johnston and Leavitt.

The version of the report sent out by Kingsley in June, 1916, is of particular interest with reference to some of the later interpretations of the motives and the thinking involved in the work of the CRSE. The main objectives of public education were stated as "health education, home-making education, vocational education, social-civic education, education for the wise use of leisure, ethical education."[15] With some

[13] Clarence Kingsley to members of the reviewing committee, March 8, 1916, RSE (National Archives, Record Group 12).
[14] Clarence Kingsley to members of the reviewing committee, June 3, 1916, RSE (National Archives, Record Group 12).
[15] "Draft of Report of Reviewing Committee of the Commisison on Secondary

changes in words, these became six of the seven objectives set forth in the final report. Conspicuously missing from this draft, however, was any mention of the seventh, "command of fundamental processes." This was not necessarily a mere oversight. Some publicity was apparently given to the list in this form, for the report entitled *Negro Education,* issued by the Bureau of Education in 1916, cited these six objectives as a preliminary statement made by the CRSE.[16] Except for this one omission, the draft of June 3 was a briefer version of what later appeared.

Somewhere along the line of further revision, the seventh objective, "command of fundamental processes" found its way into the final report. Unfortunately the records of the CRSE are incomplete for the period after the summer of 1916. At any rate, the work of revision went forward, and it was in 1918 that the CRSE gave its *Cardinal Principles of Secondary Education* to the waiting pedagogical world.

III

The general report appeared as a modest, grey-colored, 32 page Bulletin of the U.S. Bureau of Education. Like that of the Committee of Ten, this report of the CRSE did not gain its wide publicity and response from its format in print. Neither were these gained through flamboyant rhetoric. Like Eliot, Kingsley avoided long and elaborate discourse, and his own draft of July 3, 1916, was even more restrained than the final report. So far as the verdict of history is concerned, however, the Committee of Ten and the CRSE were the "big" committees, separated from each other by a quarter of a century occupied by less significant groups. This is unfair to these intervening groups, for they did contribute elements that appeared in the CRSE report.

Education Appointed by the National Education Association," undated, but for consideration at July 2, 1916, meeting, RSE (National Archives, Record Group 12).

[16] *Negro Education* (U.S. Bureau of Education Bulletin No. 38 [Washington, D.C., 1916]), I, 41. In this connection, it is interesting to note recent efforts to clear the CRSE of "anti-intellectualism" by citing the presence of "command of fundamental processes," the objective omitted in this original draft. See National Education Association and American Association of School Administrators, Educational Policies Commission, *The Central Purpose of American Education* (Washington, D.C.: The Commission, 1961). The omission of this aim, on the other hand, does not convict the CRSE of anti-intellectualism. "Command of fundamental processes," undoubtedly a worthy objective, is not parallel to the other six. Also, Thomas H. Briggs in a letter to Walter H. Drost, October 6, 1961, stated he did not remember that "command of fundamental processes" was absent from the list at the time he joined the Committee.

Although the report presented little that was new, it was a masterly summary of doctrines current at that time, and it worked them out in a somewhat original combination. Its opening sentence proclaimed that "secondary education should be determined by the needs of society to be served, the character of the individuals to be educated, and the knowledge of educational theory and practice available." These had been no more than implied by the Committee of Ten; the CRSE report made them explicit. Moreover, the CRSE report justified its existence by pointing to changes that had taken place in these three areas of concern, all of which in the minds of the reviewing committee called "for extensive modifications of secondary education," a judgment that has been accepted by many commentators on the report.[17]

Inevitably, the report placed much stress on social change that had allegedly taken place "within the past few decades." Life had become far more complex to the individual in his capacity as a citizen, as a worker, and as "a relatively independent personality" with more leisure. The report revived the familiar theme that agencies other than the school were doing less than before, coupling this with references to changes that had been going on for more than a century, such as the substitution of the factory system for the domestic system of industry and the use of machinery in place of manual labor. Apprenticeship was still breaking down, and fathers and mothers were withdrawing from the home to the factory or store. Churches, communities, and "the State" were changing too. "These changes in American life," said the report, "call for extensive modifications in secondary education."[18]

Possibly someone other than Kingsley wrote these observations on social change for the final report. Kingsley had dealt with the same points in his version of July 3, 1916, but much more briefly, and the statement in the final report has a more cosmic ring to it than Kingsley liked to give to his own utterances. As often happens in committee productions, however, Kingsley may have felt compelled to include these points himself simply because someone had brought them up and made a strong case for including them.

So far as the other two determiners of secondary education were concerned, the report called attention to the increasing number of pupils

---

[17] CRSE, *Cardinal Principles of Secondary Education* (U.S. Bureau of Education, Bulletin No. 35 [Washington, D.C., 1918]), pp. 7–9.
[18] *Ibid.,* pp. 7–8.

in the secondary school and to "changes in educational theory" resulting from the study of educational psychology. Among these were the recognition of individual differences, the reexamination of "general discipline," the importance of applying knowledge, and the awareness of continuity in the development of children. The statement on discipline was moderate, noting merely that former conceptions of general values needed to be revised, although "the final verdict of modern psychology has not as yet been rendered." With regard to human growth, the report stated that the development of the individual was a continuous process and that "any sudden or abrupt break between the elementary and the secondary school or between any two successive stages is undesirable."[19]

The next three sections, dealing with the goal of education in a democracy, the main objectives of education, and the role of secondary education in achieving these objectives, appeared in the final report substantially as Kingsley had written them in his preliminary draft, except for the addition of the seventh objective. The statement on democracy, like so many others of its kind, noted the importance both of the individual and of society or the group. It leaned, however, toward the group side of this perennial dilemma. "The purpose of democracy," said the report, "is so to organize society that each member may develop his personality primarily through activities designed for the well-being of his fellow members and of society as a whole." This demanded, according to the report, "a high level of efficiency" and placed on the individual the responsibility of choosing "that vocation and those forms of social service in which his personality may develop and become most effective." Education therefore should develop in each individual "the knowledge, interests, ideals, habits, and powers whereby he will find his place and use that place to shape both himself and society toward ever nobler ends." This, then, was democracy as the age of social efficiency saw it.[20]

The "main objectives of education" grew out of a brief analysis of the activities of the individual. Normally, said the report, the individual was a member of a family, of a vocational group, and of various civic groups. This provided three objectives. The next consideration was that of leisure, discussed in the report as an adjunct of efficiency. Leisure, "if

[19] *Ibid.,* pp. 8–9. This was precisely the point Eliot had made in his reply to G. Stanley Hall back in 1905. "The Fundamental Assumptions in the Report of the Committee of Ten," *Educational Review* (November, 1905), pp. 343–344.
[20] *Ibid.,* p. 9.

worthily used," would enable the individual to "recreate his powers and enlarge and enrich life, thereby making him better able to meet his responsibilities." Contrariwise, "unworthy" use of leisure would impair health, disrupt home life, lessen vocational efficiency, and destroy civic-mindedness. The next objective, that of health, was important because of its effect on "the vitality of the race" and "the defense of the Nation." Ethical character, defined as "conduct founded upon right principles," gained its place in the list partly on its own merits and partly through its relationship to good citizenship, vocational excellence, and the worthy use of leisure time. So it ran with the original list of six. The seventh aim, command of fundamental processes, was viewed not as "an end in itself," but nevertheless as indispensable in the affairs of life. Included among these processes were reading, writing, arithmetical computations, and oral and written expression.[21] With this discussion in the background, the report took four lines of print to assemble the "main objectives of education" that were to establish its fame, namely, "1. Health. 2. Command of fundamental processes. 3. Worthy home-membership. 4. Vocation. 5. Citizenship. 6. Worthy use of leisure. 7. Ethical character."[22] The report gave no reasons for the order in which the objectives appeared, and the CRSE evidently did not have priorities in mind.

These objectives, said the report, applied to education as a whole—elementary, secondary, and higher.[23] The main question at hand, however, was what secondary education could and should do about them. Under the vocational aim, for example, the report grappled with the question of specific job training in the high school. This would depend on "the vocation, the facilities that the school can acquire, and the opportunity that the pupil may have to obtain such training later." Truly the vocational movement had lost much of its driving force. Vocational guidance, however, was declared essential.[24] With regard to leisure time, the report directed the high school not only to emphasize music, art, literature, and drama, but to "see that adequate recreation is provided both within the school and by other agencies in the community."[25] This was reminiscent of the idea of the school as a social center and leaned in the direction of the service side rather than the control side of the social movement.

[21] *Ibid.*, pp. 9–10.
[22] *Ibid.*, pp. 10–11.
[23] *Ibid.*, p. 11.
[24] *Ibid.*, p. 13.
[25] *Ibid.*, p. 15.

At this point, in a paragraph that had not appeared in the original Kingsley draft, the report opened the question of the school subjects. Social efficiency and scientific management had demanded that the subjects prove their right to exist. The CRSE report was more charitable, but it did call upon the subjects to make their contributions to the objectives. "Each subject now taught in high schools," declared the report, "is in need of extensive reorganization in order that it may contribute more effectively to the objectives outlined herein, and the place of that subject in secondary education should depend upon the value of such contribution."[26] In effect, it proposed to judge the subjects in terms of criteria outside the subjects themselves. On the other hand, it did not demand that every subject meet all seven objectives to the same degree.

A section on differentiated "curriculums" had been provided for in Kingsley's original outline, but no material on this point appeared in the 1916 tentative draft. The final report, however, declared "curriculums" essential in providing for individual differences in pupils and for the varied needs of society, although these were not to appear until the senior high school period. Strict differentiation was not recommended below this point, but the junior high school was to provide guidance aimed at assisting pupils twelve or thirteen years of age "to begin a preliminary survey of the activities of adult life" and of their own aptitudes "in connection therewith."[27]

This, then, was differentiation, but a less extreme version of it than the Department of Superintendence had demanded in its widely heralded resolution of 1916. In the end Maxwell's minority point of view won the day. So far as the "definite curriculum organization" of the senior high school was concerned, the report recommended the use of such terms as agricultural, business, clerical, industrial, fine-arts, and household-arts "curriculums." It also recommended provision for those having "dis-

[26] *Ibid.*, p. 16. The report did not place less emphasis on subject matter than had that of the Committee of Ten, as was suggested by the Committee on the Teaching Profession of the American Academy of Arts and Sciences in its 1955 report in the ACLS *News Letter*, Vol. V, No. 2, p. 24. With regard to the old debate between formal and substantive outcomes, the CRSE report was on the side of substance where the Committee of Ten had been on the side of form. The pupil would gain useful knowledge to apply in the activities of life represented by the objectives. The difficulty in the CRSE position is not that it fails to emphasize subject matter, but rather its demand that the subjects be judged on the basis of their contributions to the seven aims.

[27] *Ibid.*, p. 18.

tinctively academic interests and needs."[28] Mercifully, the report did not label theirs a college-preparatory curriculum.

The report, in fact, sought to consider all work in high school as potentially college-preparatory in nature. It called for the "scientific evaluation" of all types of secondary education as preparation for continued study. This "broader conception" meant that pupils who devoted "a considerable time to courses having vocational content should be permitted to pursue whatever form of higher education, either liberal or vocational, they are able to undertake with profit to themselves and to society."[29] Apparently the idea of the Committee of Ten that there should be no distinction between preparing for college and preparing for life still survived in national committees, even though it may not have survived in other quarters.

Like Nightingale's Committee and Kingsley's own Committee on the Articulation of High School and College, the reviewing committee recommended constants, but unlike these predecessors, it did not name any. Sisson's paper on "prescribed units" had been lost somewhere along the way. Instead, the general report said that constants should be determined primarily by the objectives of health, command of fundamental processes, worthy home-membership, citizenship, and ethical character. The vocational objective was to determine the "curriculum variables" appropriate to certain vocations, that is, the stipulation of subjects within "curriculums," while free electives were to make their contribution to the worthy use of leisure time.[30]

The recommendation for constants implied a concern on the part of someone, probably Kingsley, about the effects of two much differentiation through "curriculums." Further concern on this point appeared in the section entitled "recognition of the objectives in planning curriculums." The opening sentence bluntly proclaimed that no curriculum could be regarded as satisfactory unless it gave "due attention to each of the objectives of education outlined herein."[31] The seven objectives apparently were to hold the line against excessive differentiation. Perhaps this is what Kingsley had in mind when he originally devised the list.

[28] *Ibid.*, p. 22. On the administrative side, the report recommended that each curriculum have a "curriculum director," an interesting use of this term, but one that did not survive in later usage. *Ibid.*, p. 28.
[29] *Ibid.*, p. 20.
[30] *Ibid.*, p. 23.
[31] *Ibid.*, p. 20.

In another place, the report spelled out what it called the unifying function of the secondary school. The school, it said, was the one agency for bringing unity out of the diversity of American life. This was good, old-fashioned doctrine going back at least as far as Horace Mann. In the past, however, it had been mainly applied to elementary schooling. This was why Bagley had contended for the maintenance of elementary schooling through eight grades. Perhaps it was with Bagley in mind that the report called for the extension of this unifying function throughout the period of the junior and senior high schools. The elementary school, said the report, could not "alone" develop the common knowledge, ideals, and interests "essential to American democracy." It was duly noted, also, that children of immigrant parents were coming to high school in greater numbers.[32]

All of this implied a need for the high school to provide studies directly valuable "for this purpose," especially social studies, and "the mother tongue, with its literature." Here, then, was probably what the report meant by constants, namely, social studies and English. Beyond this, the report called for "the social mingling of pupils through the organization and administration of the school" and "the participation of pupils in common activities . . . such as athletic games, social activities, and the government of the school."[33] Schools had been including such activities for years, possibly for a variety of reasons or for no explicit reason at all. Now the activities were to be specifically directed to the unifying function.

Consistent with this concern for unity was the advocacy of what the report called the comprehensive high school, sometimes referred to in that period as the cosmopolitan or the composite high school. This, it said, should "remain" the standard type of secondary school. By this time specialized or differentiated high schools, especially those along vocational lines, were no longer so popular as they had been ten to fifteen years before. The comprehensive high school, declared the report, would reduce to a minimum the influences interfering with a wise choice of curriculum. It would make it easier for pupils to change from one curriculum to another. With reference to unification, the report offered arguments that have become familar through much repetition over the years. "Through friendships formed with pupils pursuing other curric-

[32] *Ibid.*, pp. 22–23.
[33] *Ibid.*, p. 23.

ulums and having vocational and educational goals widely different from their own," stated the report, "the pupils realize that the interests which they hold in common with others are, after all, far more important than the differences that would tend to make them antagonistic to others. Through school assemblies and organizations they acquire common ideas. Through group activities they secure training in cooperation. Through loyalty to a school which includes many groups they are prepared for loyalty to State and Nation." The comprehensive high school was a "prototype of a democracy in which various groups must have a degree of self-consciousness as groups and yet be federated into a larger whole through the recognition of common interests and ideals."[34]

Inevitably the report moved from these points of view straight ahead to the ideal of universal secondary education. "To the extent to which the objectives outlined herein are adopted as the controlling aims of education," declared the report, "to that extent will it be recognized that an extended education for every boy and girl is essential to the welfare, and even to the existence, of democratic society." Each of the objectives, the argument continued, required "not only the training and habit formation that the child may secure, but also the intelligence and efficiency that can not be developed before adolescence." Their realization depended on the pupils' continuing attendance through the full period of the junior and senior high schools. "Consequently," the report went on, this time in italics, "this commission holds that education should be so reorganized that every normal boy and girl will be encouraged to remain in school to the age of 18, on full time if possible, otherwise on part time."[35]

There was nothing new in the idea that the school was responsible for developing programs to hold the pupils, but placing the ideal stopping age at eighteen was going beyond much of the thinking at that time. This recommendation of the CRSE obviously invited comparisons with the statement made by the Committee of Ten that the function of high schools was to prepare for the duties of life "that small proportion of all the children in the country who show themselves able to profit by an education prolonged to the eighteenth year, and whose parents are able to support them while they remain so long in school." The comparisons, of course, were not flattering to the Committee of Ten. In defense of the Ten, however, it may be observed that the first part of their statement

[34] *Ibid.*, pp. 24–26.
[35] *Ibid.*, pp. 29–30.

constituted one interpretation of democratic education, while the second part was simply recognition of the economic facts of life in 1893.

The CRSE report recommended that schooling to the age of eighteen be made compulsory, but only on a part-time basis. This part-time education, however, was not to be offered in separate continuation schools. What the CRSE wanted, and for obvious reasons in the light of its concern for unification, was at least eight hours attendance a week in the comprehensive high school itself. "By this plan," said the report, "the part-time students and the full-time students may share in the use of the assembly hall, gymnasium, and other equipment provided for all," and this was, of course, desirable because of "the importance of developing a sense of common interests and social solidarity on the part of the young worker and those of his fellows who are continuing in full-time attendance at school."[36]

One may argue for universal secondary schooling on various grounds, but this was clearly an argument from one version of social control, although it was milder in tone than some other versions in existence at that time. Whoever wrote this section of the report—probably Kingsley himself, although it did not appear in the 1916 draft—undoubtedly was motivated by other considerations as well. Someone, however, regarded it as necessary or desirable, in the climate of the times, to state the case for universal education on the grounds set forth. It must be remembered also that the CRSE was arguing for universal secondary schooling as a necessary extension of universal elementary schooling. In so doing, it took over what it assumed to be the accepted arguments for such elementary schooling, arguments that Bagley, for example, had used in support of the eight-year system. What the CRSE said was that secondary schooling also had these functions and, in consequence of this, must also be universal.

In the end, the report did not forget the development of the individual for his own sake. "The doctrine that each individual has a right to the opportunity to develop the best that is in him," said the unidentified author of the next paragraph to the last, "is reinforced by the belief in the potential, and perchance unique, worth of the individual."[37] This was reminiscent of Eliot's address on desirable and undesirable uniformity in schools. On all occasions, however, Eliot would have left out the "perchance."

[36] *Ibid.*, pp. 30–31.
[37] *Ibid.*, p. 32.

IV

The CRSE report did not arouse "limitless desire for discussion." For one thing, it was perhaps too faithful a reflection of its own times. Also, it suffered from competition with the War. Nevertheless it did draw some immediate response, and it received its measure of applause, sometimes with interpretations that went beyond what the report itself justified.

In February, 1919, for example, the National Association of Secondary-School Principals "heartily" endorsed the seven objectives.[38] Its Committee on Curriculums grimly pursued what it considered to be their implications. "Can each subject in the present curriculum," asked this Committee, "be justified on the ground that it contributes definitely and vitally to some or all of these seven ends? If it does not, is the proper remedy reform from within or elimination?" Latin "as now taught" could not be justified, but there was hope of reform so that it could "justify itself." The Committee believed that reform was better than elimination, and it invited teachers "to test and justify their own subjects in the light of the seven fundamental aims."[39]

Several independent observers added their endorsement of the report. One of these was S. P. Duke, Supervisor of High Schools for Virginia. He rightly interpreted the report as moderate. Its guiding principles, he said, were "neither the iconoclastic vagaries of radical theorists nor yet the tradition-bound dogmas of age-fettered practitioners." He noted that the report did not give "the expected short shrift" to general discipline. Yet it was subjects with "a clearly defined relation to better, more complete living" that were "pushed to the forefront," while other subjects, "those dependent upon vague generalities, faiths, and hopes," were "relegated to the problematical period of intellectual leisure." Duke probably misunderstood the report on the latter point, for Kingsley at least did not so regard either the objective of leisure or the subjects considered to serve it. No educator, concluded Duke, could afford to neglect this "excellent report."[40]

[38] J. Alvin Snook, "Report of Committee on Resolutions," *Third Yearbook,* National Association of Secondary-School Principals (The Association, 1919), p. 84.

[39] Edwin L. Miller, "Report of the Committee on Curriculums," *ibid.,* p. 52.

[40] S. P. Duke, "Cardinal Principles of Secondary Education," *Educational Administration and Supervision* (April, 1919), pp. 207–209.

Principal F. R. Willard of the high school in Watertown, Massachusetts, waxed even more enthusiastic about the report and, like the Committee on Curriculums of the National Association of Secondary-School Principals, spelled out a few extra interpretations of his own. "It will be seen at a glance," said Willard, "that these seven main objectives take care of the whole man, body, soul, and mind." Willard sought to relate the report to the social questions of his day. "If democracy is to prevail over bolshevism and all other forms of revolution," he declared, "it must chiefly be by means of a system of education inculcating in the minds of youth the cardinal principles governing various kinds of controls—bodily, mental, social, economic, political, esthetic and moral." Unlike the writers of the report, Willard demanded that makers of curricula "put behind them" the doctrine of general or formal discipline, which he identified with the assumption that human nature was "fundamentally perverse."

Willard's interpretations also took him into the realm of social class. The "classes," he declared, understood such abstract objectives as morality and power to think, or at least they thought they did, but the "masses" never did. "The seven objectives under discussion," he felt, "are of the sort that the masses can comprehend, because they deal with the stuff life is made up of." Still, he feared not much was being done about these objectives and that so far as school men were concerned they had been caught napping.[41]

Another laudatory, but pessimistic, utterance came from Burton P. Fowler of Cleveland's Central High School. He too pronounced the seven objectives excellent and feared they were being insufficiently applied. " 'Good!' we exclaim," Fowler deplored, "and note them down for use in our next talk or forthcoming article for publication. But where in the world is there a high school that consciously, as a part of a well-defined plan, puts those objectives on the same plane as the formal course of study?"[42] Comments such as these set the tone for much subsequent discussion of the report.

The major critic of the report turned out to be David Snedden. This was surprising in view of his association with Kingsley in the State Department of Education of Massachusetts. It was not surprising in view

[41] F. R. Willard, "The Objectives of Education as a Basis for Curriculum-Making in High Schools," *School and Society* (July 5, 1919), pp. 9–12.

[42] Burton P. Fowler, "The Social Organization of a High School," *School and Society* (October 30, 1920), p. 396.

of the moderate tone of the report. Snedden did not believe in compromising with tradition. He expected unconditional surrender. Naturally he found the report disappointing.

Nevertheless, he began his criticism on a friendly note, calling Kingsley "one of the exceptional leaders of our time" and praising the CRSE for its "noteworthy work in American education." The most important service of the report, he felt, lay in its "partially successful endeavors" to find aims elsewhere than in "some mystic principles," but he hoped the CRSE would not make the mistake of traditionalists, namely, failing to trace connections between means and ends.[43]

After giving the CRSE this low pass for effort, Snedden went on to attack the results. He found the ideology uncertain and inconsistent. The statement about developing personality through activities designed for the well-being of society, he felt, would please a Prussian philosopher, while their expression about the right of the individual to develop the best within him would appeal to a philosophical anarchist. He quarreled with the words used in the seven objectives, charging there was little to be gained in differentiating among worthy home-membership, citizenship, and ethical character. The CRSE, he declared, should have used the term "social education" as parallel to health education, and the latter, preferably, should have been called "physical development and education."[44]

The main offense of the report, thought Snedden, was that of "almost completely" missing the significance of vocational education. Here was where the CRSE had fallen victim to false doctrine. "The entire philosophy of the reviewing committee," complained Snedden, "seems almost hopelessly academic in the unfavorable sense." He pounced in particular on the view expressed in the report that provision for specific vocational training should depend on the vocation under consideration, the facilities of the school, and the opportunity of the pupil to obtain such training later. "Is this to be interpreted," he asked, "as meaning that the committee would ban all public school vocational education that could not conveniently be brought within its 'comprehensive high

[43] David Snedden, "Cardinal Principles of Secondary Education," *School and Society* (May 3, 1919), pp. 517–519.

[44] *Ibid.*, pp. 519–521. In his autobiography, however, Snedden referred to his own use of what he called the "careers" followed in some degree by nearly all adults, namely, "the vocational; the family-rearing; the civistic; the cultural; the religious; the health safeguarding; the intermediate social; and the pleasure-finding." *Recollections of over Half a Century Spent in Educational Work,* privately printed, 1949, p. 54.

school'?" Only an imitation of vocational education, said Snedden, could be given in the comprehensive high school, and specialized vocational schools were essential.[45] "The members of the committee," he concluded, "are chiefly preoccupied with the liberal education of youth of secondary school age. . . . In spite of its seeming insistence to the contrary it is hard to believe that the committee is genuinely interested in any vocational education that can meet the economic tests of our time."[46] In relation to views popular at the time of this criticism, Snedden was already out of date. The threat of separate or dual control had frightened school men away from the special high school. While the vocational aim itself was not denied, the tendency was to do what the CRSE itself had done, namely, to blanket vocationalism under a host of other aims.

Kingsley replied with vigor to this attack. He denied that the statements referred to by Snedden would comfort, respectively, a Prussian philosopher and a philosophical anarchist. The report, he said, was not "individualistic," since it required the unique worth of the individual to be developed in relation to the well-being of his fellow members of society. Snedden's main objection to the report, he felt, was its endorsement of the comprehensive high school. By way of defense, Kingsley testified to the belief that every comprehensive high school "should give *real* vocational education of whatever type the community needs." He denied that the reviewing committee had been interested in "so-called liberal education at the expense of vocational education."[47] Kingsley apparently was willing to talk back to Snedden, but his article also indicates some desire to assure Snedden that he was not in favor of the wrong things. At any rate, there was little disposition to continue the debate, and it did not grow into anything like the massive conflict between Eliot and Hall about the Committee of Ten.

On the whole, Kingsley had every reason to feel pleased with the outcome of his long project. His dissatisfactions of a decade before as a classroom teacher in the Brooklyn Manual Training High School had led to the production of one of the most important statements ever made about secondary education. On learning that the CRSE report was being used and studied by educational leaders in China, he felt that his boyhood purpose of becoming a missionary to that country had been real-

[45] David Snedden, "Cardinal Principles of Secondary Education," *School and Society* (May 3, 1919), pp. 522–523.
[46] *Ibid.*, p. 527.
[47] Clarence Kingsley, "Cardinal Principles of Secondary Education," *School and Society* (July 5, 1919), pp. 19–20.

ized in part. He had written something, he felt, that might "be of real help to that great people in building a new educational system to meet the needs of a better type of living."[48]

V

The report continued to interest and occupy the attention of educators for decades, with three tendencies persisting even in the later discussions. One was that of reading extra meanings into the report, a process that had started almost as soon as the report had appeared. The second was that of centering attention on the seven objectives to the neglect of other features. The third was that of applauding the report itself, but deploring the pedagogical lag that supposedly kept it from being applied.

It was in 1928, ten years after the report came out, that the Department of Superintendence published an attempt to appraise its influence, based on replies from 1228 principals of high schools of various sizes throughout the United States. Of these, 689 said they had, within the preceding five years, undertaken reorganization of their programs in line with the cardinal principles.[49] This, of course, could mean anything, but it did reveal continuing interest in the report. Two hundred fifty-five of the principals said the report had never been called to their attention! These made up about one-fifth of those who had answered the questionnaire. Most of these were from small high schools. Nine principals said they were not in sympathy with the report.[50]

The make-up of the inquiry blank and the interpretations of the results indicated the image of the report in the minds of those who conducted the study. They apparently thought of reorganization as the adding or dropping of subjects, and placed some of these subjects in a category for non-college-preparatory pupils. "The needs of the non-college preparatory group," said the published statement of this inquiry, "have apparently been uppermost in the minds of those principals who have undertaken a reorganization of their high-school programs in line

[48] As quoted in Elizabeth S. Kingsley to Raymond E. Brooks, January 12, 1927 (Colgate University Archives, Hamilton, N.Y.). This informative and fascinating document was called to my attention by Walter H. Drost.

[49] William Martin Proctor and Edwin J. Brown, "College Admission Requirements in Relation to Curriculum Revision in Secondary Schools," *The Development of the High School Curriculum,* Sixth Yearbook, Department of Superintendence, (The Department, 1928), pp. 171–173.

[50] *Ibid.,* p. 177.

with the Cardinal Principles. The subject groups which they have most frequently added are commercial studies, social studies, industrial arts, physical and biological sciences, and home economics. The subjects which have been most frequently dropped are Latin, ancient history, French, and advanced mathematics."[51] Thus did this group read its own conclusions into the CRSE report. Kingsley's attempts to avoid bifurcation, like Eliot's, had apparently missed the mark.

The year 1928 was a banner one for the report, with recognition coming from the National Congress of Parents and Teachers, the organization that had originated back in 1897 as the National Congress of Mothers. This organization adopted the seven aims as its national platform, designating them as "The Sevenfold Program of Home and School."[52] As the special theme for its 1928 convention, the Congress chose, "the application of these seven objectives to 'The Whole Child,' from babyhood through his high school years."[53] Kingsley had not talked about the whole child, although he veered toward this idea in his education for complete living. The Congress, of course, was thinking of education as carried on both in the school and in the home, whereas the CRSE report dealt with the school only.

Increasingly the seven aims loomed large in the minds of those who considered the report. The notion grew that schools had no general aims before 1918 and that the CRSE had been created for the purpose of developing them. Perhaps the aims stood out because they appeared in a list. According to the National Congress of Parents and Teachers, they were stated in "clear, quotable phrases."[54] Quotable the phrases certainly were, but their clarity depended on what each reader saw in them for himself. Finally, the seven aims swallowed the title of the report in which they appeared and became known all by themselves as The Seven Cardinal Principles. Kingsley had effectively dramatized the seven aims, but in doing so he drew attention away from the rest of the report.

One latter-day appraisal of the report came in 1951 from Thomas H. Briggs, who had served on the reviewing committee. He noted the verbal applause the report had received, but like many others deplored the tendency to do little or nothing about it. He called this a tragic characteristic of the educational profession. Nevertheless, he felt that the

[51] *Ibid.,* p. 187.
[52] National Congress of Parents and Teachers, *Jubilee History: 50th Anniversary 1897–1947* (The Congress, 1947), pp. 95–96.
[53] *Ibid.,* p. 108.
[54] *Ibid.,* p. 95.

seven aims had had "in time a real effect." The subject committees of the CRSE, on the other hand, he thought, had "almost entirely failed in their assignment."[55]

The image of the report has shifted somewhat in recent years. There is less tendency to applaud it, and, with this, less inclination to deplore its lack of application. It has been disparaged as an anticipation of "life-adjustment" education and as a symbol of what might be called an anti-academic bias. Snedden, however, had found it too academic for his tastes. In the long run, the effect of the report may have been to support those who wished to preserve as much as possible of the academic tradition. Certainly a far different statement would have come from a committee consisting, for example, of David Snedden, L. W. Rapeer, William D. Lewis, and J. H. Francis.

VI

The report was an archeological deposit of many ideas and influences in the American tradition of education, some of them at least as old as the expressions of the founding fathers, others as close to its own times as the doctrines of social efficiency. This has, of course, stimulated much interest in the sources, or causes, of the report. Many have seen in it the American passion for Herbert Spencer; some have ascribed it to the influence of John Dewey. Others have traced it to the social settlement movement, or even to the increased impact of immigration on American schools. Some have accepted the version presented in the first several pages of the report itself, namely, that it proposed a reorganization of secondary education made necessary by social, economic, and pedagogical changes in process since the time of the Committee of Ten.

Interpretation of the report in relation to the seven aims immediately suggests, of course, the direct influence of Spencer. Supervisor S. P. Duke of Virginia pointed out the connection in his article in 1919, referring to the aims as "another complimentary endorsement of that sage philosopher."[56] Spencer had stated five categories of human activities:

---

[55] Thomas H. Briggs, "The Secondary School Curriculum: Yesterday, Today and Tomorrow," *Teachers College Record* (April, 1951), pp. 408–409.

[56] Duke, *op. cit.,* p. 208. The nature of Spencer's general influence on American education is open to debate. According to one interpretation, American educators tended to reject Spencer. See Jurgen Herbst, "Herbert Spencer and the Genteel Tradition in American Education," *Educational Theory* (April, 1961), pp. 99–110, 118.

those of self-preservation, meaning largely health; those indirectly related to self-preservation, meaning the gaining of livelihood; those of
rearing and disciplining offspring; those involved in social and political
relations; and those "miscellaneous activities which make up the leisure
part of life, devoted to the gratification of the tastes and feelings."[57] The
connection is indeed obvious, but perhaps misleading. That the reviewing committee, taken as a whole, had dedicated itself to promoting
Spencer's views may well be doubted. Certainly anyone who proposed to
categorize life activities would come out with a list not greatly different
from Spencer's or from that in the report. The fact is that many others
who have tried reformulating the list have ended up with much the same
thing.

Someone on the CRSE, however, had the idea of using such a classification in the report, and that someone in all probability was Kingsley.
Although Kingsley did not mention Spencer, he revealed his indebtedness to him by the repeated use of one of Spencer's favorite expressions,
namely, education for complete living. "To prepare us for complete living is the function which education has to discharge," the English philosopher had written nearly sixty years before, adding to this in anticipation of the efficiency movement, that "the only rational mode of
judging of any educational course is, to judge in what degree it dis-
charges such function."[58] The CRSE report modified this by adding
"worthy" as a modifier, stating that secondary education must aim at
nothing less "than complete and worthy living for all youth."[59] Once the
idea of complete living was accepted, the way was clear to the statement
about life activities. Spencer, then, probably was an "influence," at least
so far as Kingsley was concerned.[60]

[57] Herbert Spencer, *Education: Intellectual, Moral, and Physical* (New York:
Appleton-Century-Crofts, 1860), pp. 13–14. The essay, "What Knowledge Is of
Most Worth?" pp. 1–87 was reprinted from the *Westminster Review* (July, 1859),
pp. 1–23.

[58] *Ibid.,* p. 12.

[59] CRSE, *op. cit.,* p. 32.

[60] Kingsley may or may not have been a close student of Spencer's works. He
would, in any case, not have needed anything more than a reading of the *Education* essay. Possibly he picked up Spencerian expressions from close association
with David Snedden in the Massachusetts State Department of Education. Snedden
was a long-time admirer of Spencer, and his debt was obvious in the statement of
the eight "careers" of most adults (see footnote 44). As a student in Los Angeles
(before going to Stanford), Snedden had used the public library for "lavish reading" of Spencer, Huxley, and Darwin. While teaching at Santa Paula, California,
he had joined one of his colleagues in a project of reading Spencer's complete
works; these volumes, he said, had laid the groundwork for his subsequent thinking

Kingsley did not, however, accept Spencer's judgment that science constituted the knowledge of most worth. Neither did he assign leisure to the "miscellaneous activities" of life. His views on history as the study of nations, on the other hand, might well have come from Spencer's writings on this point. The notion of history as related to present problems and as service to the citizen, however, did not have to come to Kingsley through Spencer. After all, he had James Harvey Robinson as his colleague in the committee on social studies.

Undoubtedly Kingsley and his colleagues on the reviewing committee did know Dewey's writings, or some of them, and probably had various responses of their own. As Chairman of the committee on mathematics, Kilpatrick was also a member of the reviewing committee. Possibly he served as a spokesman for the Dewey position, whatever that may have been. It is difficult, however, to see Dewey as a direct influence. The first several pages on social change merely repeated commonplaces that were not unique to Dewey. Neither was Dewey alone at that time in his preoccupation with democracy. So far as the use of the term is concerned, Eliot had been giving it specific attention as far back as 1897. Furthermore, the term itself was very much in the air because of the War. Dewey's *Democracy and Education,* of course, did come out in 1916; Kingsley may have been influenced by it, but there is no need to assume this in order to account for the nature of the report.[61]

So far as the social impulses of the period were concerned, the report tended to reflect the reform movement as a whole. The specific influence of social settlements is another matter. Perhaps the mood of settlement work found its way into the report. This would depend in part on the alleged desire of social-settlement people to have the schools take over their work. Such was not always the case.[62] It would depend also

"more than those of any other philosopher or sociologist." *Recollections of over Half a Century Spent in Educational Work,* privately printed, 1948, pp. 8 and 12. In some way, Snedden managed to reconcile the views of Spencer with those he acquired from sociologists like Edward A. Ross.

[61] Henry F. May, however, has seen Dewey as a specific influence on the report. See *The End of the American Innocence* (New York: Alfred A. Knopf, 1959), pp. 147–152.

[62] Morris Isaiah Berger sees the CRSE report largely as an outgrowth of the settlement movement. *The Settlement, the Immigrant and the Public School: A Study of the Influence of the Settlement Movement and the New Immigration upon Public Education: 1890–1924* (Doctoral dissertation, Columbia University, 1956), pp. 155–156. In his abstract, Berger says also that the settlement workers wanted to transfer their program to the school. *Dissertation Abstracts,* Vol. 16, No. 7, pp. 1230–1231. For expressions from settlement workers not in agreement with this,

on the alleged tendency of school people to shift their views of education as they provided more social services through the schools. The extension of such services in the New York Schools during the 1890's and early 1900's did not in itself imply a commitment to education for complete living. Maxwell and other administrators were willing to provide whatever seemed necessary, but they did not move in the direction of the seven aims. In fact, while Maxwell was being accused by Jacob Riis of wanting to do too much through the schools, he was also regarded by the new men in education as a relic of the age of academic tradition. Kingsley, it is true, had been an agent of the Charity Organization Society of New York, but the ideologies of the charity associations and the social settlements were by no means identical. His experience, however, may have led him to seek expansion of social service in the schools, not only on the practical level but also on the doctrinal.

The work of social settlements and the extension of social services in schools inevitably suggest the related matter of immigration.[63] There are two possibilities on this point. One is that the shift in doctrine represented by the report was a necessary consequence of the presence of immigrant children in the schools. This would be difficult, if not impossible, to be sure about. The other is that school people thought this was the case. Some such thinking does appear in the report, but it is not stressed. Kingsley used the presence of the foreign-born as only one of several arguments for extending into the secondary school the traditional function of unification. Presumably he would have advocated such extension even had there been no immigrants.

Still another point of view is that the report described the kind of reorganization of secondary education demanded by over-all social and economic change, presumably either ignored by the Committee of Ten or taking place after its time. Among the changes mentioned have been the new immigration, the expansion of industry, the population shift from rural to urban areas, and the decline of apprenticeship. The report itself dealt with some of these matters. Again, it would be difficult to

---

see Mary Simkhovitch, "The School and the Family," *Social Education Quarterly* (January, 1908), p. 17, and David Rosenstein, "The National Federation of Settlements, 1917," *School and Society* (July 21, 1917), pp. 72–78.

[63] See Alan M. Thomas Jr., "American Education and the Immigrant," *Teachers College Record* (February, 1954), pp. 253–267. Thomas says the Committee of Ten "reckoned without awareness of the immigrants and their children," p. 257. His argument is that the presence of immigrants had much to do with the shift in doctrine as expressed by the CRSE report.

tell just why these inevitably led to the doctrine of education for complete living, the seven aims, and the advocacy of the comprehensive high school. It is clear, however, that Kingsley was reacting to, and interacting with, an overwhelming body of utterance on these matters and their supposed effect on the schools. Inevitably he absorbed and summarized the impacts of all these writings and speeches. The report, then, may or may not have reflected the consequences of these social and economic changes for the reorganization of the secondary school. What it did without question was to describe what many people felt to be such consequences.[64]

This suggests that the immediate sources of the report were the specific issues under consideration and discussion at the time. These could not be avoided by Kingsley and the committee. Nor did they want to avoid them. Prominent among current issues was that of vocational education. By 1916 extreme vocationalism was on the wane. Still, there were leading educators like Snedden who advocated separate vocational schools. Others, like Charles Hughes Johnston, favored comprehensive high schools with "curriculums" organized on the basis of vocational choice. This point of view ultimately emerged in the report, but Kingsley, and presumably others on the committee, did not want extreme differentiation. In particular, they did not want vocationalism as the only aim. This demanded an explicit statement of other aims, preferably practical ones, that could bind together the work of the separate vocational programs.

Also prominent in the discussions of the time was the issue of vocational differentiation in the seventh and eighth grades. The Department of Superintendence had endorsed this as late as 1915, and Maxwell had been written off as a traditionalist on the basis of his opposition. Here also the reviewing committee had to take a stand. What it came up with was the recommendation that the junior high school be used for vocational exploration and guidance, a far cry from the resolution of the Department of Superintendence only three years before. The report did not recommend "curriculums" for the junior high school. The committee's position on this point was supported by arguments for extension of the unification function into the secondary school. Such extension

[64] For a discussion of the CRSE report in relation to social and pedagogical change between 1893 and 1918, see Lawrence A. Cremin, "The Problem of Curriculum Making: An Historical Perspective," *What Shall the High Schools Teach?* 1956 yearbook, Association for Supervision and Curriculum Development (The Association, 1956), Chapter 1, pp. 6–26.

also reinforced the idea of constants in the senior high school as a partial offset to curricular differentiation.

The traditional high school also had differentiated courses of study, and Eliot's idea of election by subjects offered a far more decisive break with this tradition than did the "curriculums" of the CRSE report. Still, the new "curriculums" were not the same as the old curricula. They were explicitly set up by vocations, whereas the older courses were so only indirectly. The report endorsed such terms as agricultural, business, clerical, industrial, fine-arts, and household-arts, calling these vocational in the broad sense. Here again the report was responding to the impact of the vocational movement. What it did was to move the programs of the special high schools, disguised as "curriculums," into the comprehensive high school.

Besides taking the vocational movement into account, the report responded to issues involved in social efficiency, the term that embraced both social service and social control. The major issue was the place of the individual. Instead of ruthlessly subordinating the individual to society, however, the report sought fulfillment for the individual on the basis of his service. This was a kind of subordination, but it was supposed to develop the individual's personality as well. Moreover, the report balanced this position with its statement about the unique worth of individuals, which Snedden had characterized as philosophical anarchism.

The report, then, dealt with issues growing out of vocational education and social efficiency. Obviously the rise of cities, the expansion of industry, the coming of immigrants, and the spread of reform all contributed something to the ways these issues were formulated and understood.[65] The influence of Spencer, Eliot, Dewey, and the social workers entered in varying degrees into the ways the CRSE sought to resolve these issues.

In another sense, it was the unique personality of Clarence Kingsley that was the major source, if not indeed the major cause, of the report. Without Kingsley, there probably would have been neither a report nor a Commission to sponsor it. "He swam into prominence like a meteor,"

---

[65] There is also the question of how much the report was influenced by the War and by wartime conditions. Much of the document, however, had already been written by the summer of 1916, nine months before the entry of the United States. The remarkable thing is that Kingsley and his associates did not revise it along more extreme lines before its publication in 1918. Certainly there was powerful motivation for them to do so, but the document they produced was moderate compared to proposals then being considered and applied.

wrote Thomas H. Briggs many years later, "and his untimely death extinguished a brilliance that was needed."[66] There are many today who refer to his report without ever having heard his name. It is ironic that a generation so preoccupied with the meaning of this report should overlook the man who did more than anyone else to bring it into existence. Yet his story was a romantic one indeed, and some day it should be more fully told.

[66] Thomas H. Briggs to Walter H. Drost, October 6, 1961 (made available to me by Walter H. Drost).

Chapter 16

The impact of war

> "English teachers were never more fortunate in having a wealth of interesting and thoroughly worth while topics from which to select for composition exercises."
>
> —LOTUS D. COFFMAN,
> JANUARY, 1918.

*T*he wiping out of German as a school subject furnished a startling demonstration of education for social control and showed how swiftly a major portion of the academic program could collapse. On April 22, 1918, for example, the Montana State Council of Defense called for the suppression of German in public and private schools throughout the state. By noon of the following day, the state university at Missoula had discontinued all its classes in the subject.[1]

Here indeed was rapid change in the curriculum, and it went on throughout 1918 with little or no evidence of cultural lag. Foremost in the campaign was the National Security League, working through 281 branches to obtain the active cooperation of state and local authorities in the schools.[2] Many of them cooperated so well that by 1922 less than 1 percent of the pupils in high school were taking German, a decline from 24.4 percent in 1915.[3]

---

[1] "Teaching German," *School Review* (June, 1918), pp. 458–459. A good general account of the campaign against German is available in Wallace Henry Moore, *The Conflict Concerning The German Language and German Propaganda in the Public Secondary Schools of the United States, 1917–1919*, (Doctoral dissertation, Stanford University, 1937).

[2] "German in the Schools," *School and Society* (June 1, 1918), p. 645.

[3] Commissioner, 1916, II, p. 487; *Biennial Survey of Education 1920–22* (U.S. Bureau of Education, Bulletin No. 14 [Washington, D.C., 1924]), II, p. 578. Subsequent figures in this chapter on foreign-language enrollments also come from these sources.

Apparently there was some resistance to this in the traditionally stubborn fastnesses of Massachusetts and Vermont. The stronghold of German, noted one observer in September, 1918, seemed to be, "not Wisconsin or Nebraska, but Massachusetts." He reported that the number of pupils taking German in that state had in fact increased "within the last year," suggesting as a reason for this the requirement in that language for admission to the Massachusetts Institute of Technology.[4] In Vermont the question of teaching German was left to the local school authorities "as the result of the rejection by the Vermont Senate, by a vote of 23 to 3, of a measure prohibiting the teaching of the German language in the public schools."[5]

For the most part, educators had little choice but to acquiesce in the campaign. Some did so with enthusiasm. "The schools of Indiana," declared an editorial in the *Educator-Journal* of that state in March, 1918, "might as well make the exclusion of German unanimous." The Germans, said this editorial, with their spy system and propaganda and with "their insistence on the teaching of their mother tongue in American public schools" had imposed long enough on the American people. "It is exceedingly appropriate just now," concluded the editorial, "to kick the whole outfit out of this land forever."[6] It was impossible, said H. Miles Gordy of Elizabeth, New Jersey, to study German without being influenced to a degree by German thought, and American teachers who defended the study of that language placed themselves "in the class of German propagandists." Modern civilization, he declared, had "no need of the products of a people who are the Huns of modern times."[7]

Others acquiesced reluctantly, or only in part. German should not be completely eliminated, thought President Robert J. Aley of the University of Maine, but in the future any American who knew German "should know it for practical purposes, and not as an accomplishment." Teachers of German, he demanded, should be of undoubted loyalty, meaning "that in general they will not be of German blood, or, if of German blood, far removed from the Fatherland." He found the claims of German scholarship "grossly exaggerated" and pronounced most of the great developments in physics, biology, mathematics, agriculture, chemistry, history,

---

[4] B. L. Ullman, "Latin in Place of German," *School and Society* (September 21, 1918), p. 339.

[5] *School and Society* (March 29, 1919), p. 382.

[6] *Educator-Journal* (March, 1918), p. 370 and p. 372.

[7] H. Miles Gordy, "The German Language in Our Schools," *Educational Review* (October, 1918), pp. 262–263.

philosophy, and other fields not to have been of German origin.[8] In deciding not to offer classes in beginning German, the New York City Board of Education concluded that there would be "small need" for German scientific works in the future and that these could be read in translation. One educator came up with a proposal under which German could be taught without danger, namely, through the use of German translations of English and American authors. "Sherlock Holmes," he thought, "would probably go far toward making the course in German one of the most popular courses in the high school."[9]

Some educators even disagreed flatly with the attack on German. The National Conference Committee of Standards of Colleges and Secondary Schools, made up of representatives of the various regional associations, placed itself on record against the campaign.[10] Commissioner Claxton also disagreed and added that we were not at war with the German language and literature, citing Woodrow Wilson to the effect that we were not at war with the German people as people.[11]

Neither did the strictly pedagogical impact of the campaign pass without notice. Professor B. L. Ullman of the University of Pittsburgh, for example, feared the elimination of German as the only language he felt could be substituted for Latin in linguistic training. To substitute French or Spanish for German, he thought, would "mean a weaker grammatical foundation for the Latinless student." Beyond this, Ullman noted that the loss in German was not being made up by gains in other languages.[12] His observation was correct. The 23.8 percent loss between 1915 and 1922 in relative enrollments in German was offset by gains of only 8.9 percent in Spanish and 6.7 percent in French, while Latin continued to decline. In effect, the campaign against German weakened the general position of the foreign languages in the secondary school program.

This was, of course, not an unwelcome consequence to those who had already been expressing doubts about the study of foreign languages. Such was the point of view taken in an editorial in the *School Review*. If German was to be abandoned, said this editorial, it must not be on

[8] Robert J. Aley, "The War and Secondary Schools," *School and Society* (December 29, 1917), pp. 752–754.

[9] T. W. Todd, "German in Our Public Schools," *Education* (March, 1918), pp. 434–435.

[10] MSM, 1918, p. 41.

[11] P. P. Claxton to Robert L. Slagle, as quoted in *School and Society* (March 30, 1918), p. 374.

[12] Ullman, *op. cit.*, pp. 339–341.

account of the animosities of war, but for educational or social reasons. One social consideration was the need for English to weld together the "heterogeneous mass of widely differing elements." Accordingly, the system of language instruction in American schools was "absurd," since the schools were spending more money to teach foreign languages than to teach English to foreign-born adults. Furthermore, the editorial continued, if teaching a foreign language fosters ideals "antagonistic to those of the nation," it should be "excluded by state or federal law."[13] This presumably meant any or all foreign languages.

II

Beyond reducing the amount of foreign languages in the curriculum, the War stimulated the reorganization of subjects along practical lines and provided a favorable mood for the extension of those subjects already considered to be practical. The practice of basing English composition on the works studied in literature had been under attack for some time. Now the War provided lifelike topics indeed. "English teachers," wrote Lotus D. Coffman of the University of Minnesota, "were never more fortunate in having a wealth of interesting and thoroughly worth while topics from which to select for composition exercises." Among those he suggested were Liberty Loans, the Junior Red Cross, the YMCA, the cantonments, aviation, the shipbuilding program, the saving of food and fuel, and the iron output. "For teachers to continue to use the time-worn and threadbare topics found in many of the school books is an illustration of that useless pedantry for which they have been frequently criticized."[14]

Even more explicit was the demand for practical materials in the social studies. In a letter dated August 23, 1917, President Woodrow Wilson called upon school officers to "increase materially the time and attention devoted to instruction bearing directly on the problems of community and national life." He asked Herbert Hoover and Commissioner Claxton to organize agencies to prepare and distribute "suitable lessons" along these lines for elementary and high schools. The task was assigned to Professors Charles H. Judd and Leon Marshall of the University of Chicago, who quickly brought out three series of these lessons. Topics

[13] "The German Language," *School Review* (October, 1917), pp. 599–600.
[14] Lotus D. Coffman, "The War and the Curriculum of the Public Schools," *Educational Administration and Supervision* (January, 1918), pp. 12–13.

covered included social organization and the effects of the War, production and wise consumption, machine industry and community life, national control and food conservation, business organization and national standards, and the worker and the wage system.[15] These were widely hailed as contributions to more vital content in the social-studies field.

Many went beyond this to denounce the supposedly sterile and ineffective work in social studies, particularly in history. "Too much attention," said Superintendent C. E. Rose of Boise, Idaho, "has been paid to the history of Greece and Rome and Europe and too little to that of the American Republic. High-school pupils have spent too much time upon Punic Wars and some pope of the eleventh century, when they knew nothing and cared less of the important events and characters in our own history. . . . A more prominent place must be given to current events. In fact, current events can and should be taught in connection with all history. To do this, many teachers must be made over, but that will do them good." The War, he felt, had brought real teaching of citizenship through the food program, the Junior Red Cross, war gardens, and the War Savings Stamp Campaign, for "the essence of good civics teaching is to make the citizen aware of his duty to his state and inculcate such a strong desire to do that duty that immediately whole-souled action results." Courses of study must be arranged not in terms of events, or epochs, or men, but rather to create "ideals and right attitudes" in the pupils.[16] Superintendent Fred M. Hunter of Oakland, California, likewise saw great civic value in the War activities. The government, he felt, had forced more real training for citizenship into the schools than all the plans "or social studies have done in the past five years." All this

[15] "Lessons in Community and National Life," *School Review* (November, 1917), p. 674. The materials were published by the Bureau of Education, in cooperation with the U.S. Food Administration in 1918. This was one of the few pedagogical events in this period consistent with Wilsonian idealism as contrasted with postwar reaction. Another was Kingsley's approach to the study of nations in the CRSE social studies report. Both of these were in the context of social efficiency, but in what might be considered a liberal direction. The protests of Dewey and Eliot might be viewed as examples of Wilsonian idealism not tied to social efficiency as such. For the most part, however, educational developments during the War reflected little Wilsonian idealism. This does not mean that education was out of step with the times. The national mood during the war reflected more of what is ordinarily considered the postwar reaction than it did of Wilsonian ideals.

[16] C. E. Rose, "The Necessity for the Rearrangement of the History and Civics Program," NEA, 1919, pp. 615–616.

had brought a "new definition of the curriculum, and that definition has come to stay."[17]

One of the most widely applauded practical activities during the War was the school garden army under the direction of J. H. Francis, former Superintendent of Schools in Los Angeles and in Columbus, Ohio, who had worked with Cubberley in the famous Portland survey. Francis was a sincere disciple of social efficiency, and he left his post in Columbus to take over this project at a relatively small salary. Soon he had worked up an organization involving 1,500,000 boys and girls in military ranks.[18] Obviously this project helped greatly in the production of food, and it could have been evaluated in these terms without reference to the ideology of curriculum. This was not a likely possibility at that time.

Physical education, of course, came in for a great share of attention, both on its own merits and as a substitute for military training in the schools. The demand for military training had arisen shortly after the outbreak of the War in Europe and had become an important issue in school policy by the end of 1915. Many educational leaders, including Eliot, resisted this, and the NEA in its 1916 convention passed a compromise resolution that was fiercely debated.[19] When Woodrow Wilson said that physical training was needed, but could be had without compulsory military service, a group of educators, among whom were John Dewey, Ella Flagg Young, and Carroll G. Pearse, formed a committee to promote physical education in the public schools. A model bill was drafted by Harvard's Dudley A. Sargent, long a leader in the movement for physical education. It was entitled "a bill to upbuild national vitality through the establishment of physical education and training in the public schools of the state," meaning any state in which it might be introduced.[20] There were no military features in the bill.

[17] Fred M. Hunter, "Needed Modifications in Textbooks as Shown by the War," NEA, 1918, p. 467.

[18] J. H. Francis, *The United States School Garden Army* (U.S. Bureau of Education Bulletin No. 26 [Washington, D.C., 1919]). Francis apparently was just the man for the job. He was a popular national figure in education. Winship's *Journal of Education* ([March 9, 1916], p. 255) had described him as "the lion of the week" at the Detroit meeting of the Department of School Superintendence in 1916, saying that more people were anxious to see and hear him than anyone else in Detroit.

[19] National Education Association, "Report of the Committee on Resolutions," NEA, 1916, pp. 26–27; editorial comment in *School and Society* (July 15, 1916), pp. 110–114. For Eliot's opposition, see quotations in "Massachusetts Commission on Military Education," *School Review* (March, 1917), pp. 170–171.

[20] *School and Society* (February 10, 1917), p. 170.

One of the first states to respond favorably was New Jersey, and it was joined by seven others throughout 1917 and 1918. The campaign did not slacken off at the end of the war, five more states entering the fold between January, 1919, and the time of the NEA convention in July.[21] By this time, physical education was being advocated in large social terms. Many people, said E. Dana Caulkins of the National Physical Education Service, hoped to stop the spread of un-American political propaganda through prohibitory legislation. He doubted the effectiveness of this and believed physical education to be a better antidote. "Did you ever hear," he asked, "an unhealthy, un-American doctrine proceed from a normal, healthy body?" He welcomed the cooperation of leading educators in the movement for universal physical education, but feared that the classroom teachers had not yet been effective in "hearty promotive work" for the subject.[22]

With all these developments taking place, there was naturally much interest in what education should become after the War. Some merely predicted the future, while others sought to define it. Commissioner Claxton felt that the old subjects would continue, but that many of them would be redirected. "There will be," he said, "a larger demand for teachers of science and of sociological subjects, including definitely those things that pertain to citizenship in the enlarged democracy."[23] Superintendent C. E. Chadsey of Detroit hoped the schools would not return to the limited aims and efforts characteristic of the period before 1914. He called on them to remain broader and less academic "than in those days which from now on will be known as the period 'before the war.' "[24] Superintendent Walter R. Siders of Pocatello, Idaho, asked his fellow school men to put out of their minds the school as it was. "Let us forget," he declared, "that such an institution exists or has ever existed." Then the school could be redesigned, he said, as "an institution for the purposes of citizenship," and teachers who refused to read the signs of the times might "expect to read the handwriting on the wall."[25] Eliot also,

[21] E. Dana Caulkins, "The Promotion of Physical Education thru State Legislation," NEA, 1919, p. 320.

[22] Ibid., pp. 319–320.

[23] P. P. Claxton to J. A. Pitman, November 1, 1918, Commissioner's Office, Various Meetings and Conferences, 1909–1922 (National Archives, Record Group 12).

[24] C. E. Chadsey, "After the War," Educational Administration and Supervision (January, 1919), p. 40.

[25] Walter R. Siders, "War-Modified Education, the Teachers, and the Schools," NEA, 1918, p. 116.

84 years of age at the close of the War, hoped the future would provide more fully for the principles he had maintained throughout the years, namely, the development of intelligence, personal initiative, well-trained senses, sound reasoning, and skill. Relative to the draft rejections, he saw the need for better medical services and provisions for public health. Above all, the schools should discourage uniformity, providing, however, for the voluntary, free cooperation of free individuals through such means as part-singing, folk dancing, and acting in plays.[26]

For the most part, however, the demand was that the schools not regress from the practical toward the so-called academic side of the curriculum. In the minds of many, great gains had been made through such activities as the thrift program, the school garden army, and the Junior Red Cross. This was practical but not selfishly materialistic. Superintendent Rose of Boise pointed out that children had worked to relieve the sufferings of those whom they had never seen. "Cannot these feelings," he asked, "be transferred to their immediate surroundings and to the sufferers in their midst whom they have seen?"[27] Few indeed, academicians or others, would not have concurred in the retention of these practical works of compassion. There was also, however, the point of view of Superintendent Hunter of Oakland, who hoped that practical activities would lead to "the obliteration of school subjects as such, except in the realm of scientific research and specialization."[28]

III

Industrial education, along with other kinds of vocational subjects, was still the main symbol of practical activity in the schools, although it never won its way back to the place it had occupied in the hearts of school men in the period between 1905 and 1912. Nevertheless, it did prosper during the war. "It is safe to affirm," said the Commissioner's *Report* for 1919, "that no special phase of education has more strikingly justified itself in the crisis than vocational education."[29]

The passing of the Smith-Hughes Act on February 23, 1917, just two months before the entry of the United States into the War, was the cul-

[26] Charles W. Eliot, "Defects in American Education Revealed by the War," *School and Society* (January 4, 1919), pp. 6–10.
[27] Rose, *op. cit.*, p. 616.
[28] Hunter, *op. cit.*, pp. 469–470.
[29] Commissioner, 1919, I, p. 24.

mination of a long campaign waged by the advocates of specific job training. By the early fall of that year, the newly created Federal Board for Vocational Education, with Charles A. Prosser as Director, had formulated and published its policies for the distribution of funds. From then on, it swung rapidly into its task of reviewing the plans for vocational education submitted by the states and of granting the funds made available under the Act, amounting to $1,860,000 for the first fiscal year. The fields of instruction provided for were trade and industrial education, agriculture, and home economics.

In spite of the enthusiastic reception of this act in some quarters, school men were still uneasy about separate vocational education and the possibility of dual control. Three days before the Act was passed, John Dewey addressed the Public Education Association in Baltimore, warning against what he called narrow trade education. It was necessary, he argued, to be clear whether vocational education was designed for the benefit of the worker or for helping the United States in its competitive struggle for world commerce. Was the main purpose to increase profits or to increase "the industrial intelligence and power of the worker for his own personal advancement"? He advocated the study of history and civics as part of vocational education, but he warned against the kinds of social studies that would emphasize "duties to the established order and a blind patriotism which accounts it a great privilege to defend things in which the workers themselves have little or no share."[30]

These were strong words indeed in a country on the verge of war. Nevertheless the *School Review* backed them up with an editorial in its May issue, after War had been declared. The editorial expressed the fear that the Smith-Hughes Act pointed toward dual control and was designed to promote "unadulterated trade education" of the type warned against by Dewey.[31] Evidently it was not alone in these fears, for the NEA in 1918, in the midst of endorsing propositions aimed at various kinds of social control, called for amendments to the Smith-Hughes Act to prevent the possibility of establishing a dual system in any state. A similar resolution had previously been passed by the Department of Superintendence at its winter meeting of that year.[32] These actions were remarkable in that they constituted the only instance in which the NEA or its affiliated organiza-

[30] John Dewey, "Learning to Earn," *School and Society* (March 24, 1917), pp. 332–333.
[31] *School Review* (May, 1917), pp. 364–366.
[32] National Education Association, "Report of the Committee on Resolutions," NEA, 1918, p. 26. For Department of Superintendence, see p. 476.

tions questioned something regarded as a wartime measure. They testify dramatically to the very real apprehensions about vocational education felt by the school men of that time.

David Snedden, however, continued to move further away from many of his fellow educators, not only in his enthusiasm for vocational education, but also in his advocacy of highly specialized forms of it, preferably conducted in special rather than comprehensive high schools. He was critical of undifferentiated vocational education in agriculture and called for programs directed to specialized farming, such as in rice or poultry. Without this he feared that agricultural education would become bookish, academic, and sterile.[33] He was sensitive, on the other hand, to changes in factory work running counter to traditional trades training.[34] In 1918–1919 he began to call for compulsory education on at least a part-time basis to the age of eighteen. Unlike the CRSE, he favored continuation schools for those not attending full time, with general and vocational aims identified for particular groups of pupils.[35] With his thinking running along lines such as these, Snedden was necessarily critical of what he regarded as the weak position taken on vocational education in the *Cardinal Principles* report.

In 1918 the National Society for the Promotion of Industrial Education changed its name to the National Society for Vocational Education. The *School Review,* however, remained suspicious and was not convinced that the change in name really meant any change in heart. Advocacy of dual control was still the major offense. Even now, declared the writer of the editorial, the organization was unrepentant in its refusal "to think of industrial education as a part of the general plan for American education."[36]

The War, then, did not shift the mood of educators with respect to vocationalism. They willingly accepted the ideology of the *Cardinal Principles* report, namely, that of containing vocational education within the context of six clearly nonvocational aims. The advocates of extreme vocationalism had lost their case with the school men by raising the issue

[33] David Snedden, "Agricultural Education—What Is It?" *School and Society* (January 19, 1918), pp. 66–70.

[34] David Snedden, "The War and Vocational Education," *Educational Administration and Supervision* (January, 1918), p. 38.

[35] David Snedden, "Vocational Education after the War," *School and Society* (December 28, 1918), pp. 751–758.

[36] "Society for Vocational Education," *School Review* (December, 1920), p. 722.

of dual control. Even the pressures of the War did not reverse this decision.

IV

Quite otherwise was the response of educators to the national campaign for Americanization. They took part with enthusiasm in the "National Conferences on Americanization through Education" held in 1917 and 1918 under the auspices of the U.S. Bureau of Education and Commissioner Claxton. What was being encouraged was, in part, an intensified version of the traditional role schools had assumed in the assimilation of immigrants. Beyond this, the campaign for Americanization reflected the apprehensions, whether justified or not, about the so-called "new immigration" from countries with ideals supposedly in conflict with those of the United States. There was, of course, one large element of contradiction in these fears. It was Germany against whom the ideological war was being fought, but the Germans in the United States had been part of the "old immigration," presumably responsive to American ideals. The "new immigration" largely represented countries with which the United States was allied in the war.

The campaign for Americanization took many forms, both inside and outside the schools, but the most tangible objectives were the stamping out of illiteracy and the conversion of foreigners to the use of the English tongue. The speaking not only of German but also of other foreign languages came to be regarded as a symptom of disloyalty. School systems were urged to expand previously existing facilities for evening classes or to create them where they did not exist. This was a laudable effort to help individuals overcome the handicap of illiteracy and to provide literate foreigners with a chance to learn the language of the country to which they had come.

Enthusiasts in the campaign, however, began to cast about for indirect and direct means of compulsion. Principal Lewis Wilbur Smith of the Thornton Township High School in Harvey, Illinois, organized the leaders of local industries into a committee for the sponsorship of the night-school program. "Practically all of the managers of the various industries," said Principal Smith, "promised energetic assistance. They even declared that they would give preference in employment to those who attended the night school. One firm went so far as to inform its employees that it would retain no one who did not make specific plans toward naturalization."³⁷ The state of New Hampshire applied direct pressure through its Americanization and Educational Law that went into effect May 1, 1919. This law required youth between 16 and 21 years of age who could not read or speak English and who lived in districts with evening or special day schools to attend such schools, and employers were forbidden, beginning in October of that year, to employ those not so enrolled.³⁸ A similar bill in Massachusetts drew severe criticism from Boston's Superintendent Frank V. Thompson, who declared it unconstitutional and against "the Bill of Human Rights."³⁹ Eliot also opposed the bill. ⁴⁰ Perhaps because of the opposition of these and other educators, the Massachusetts bill was not enacted.⁴¹

In its larger dimensions, the campaign for Americanization went beyond the immigrants and beyond the mere use of the English tongue. Guy Stanton Ford of the Committee on Public Information assured the NEA in 1918 that his agency stood ready to join the schools in their common wartime task of making "an Americanized, nationalized American nation."⁴² This mood persisted at least into 1920. "Within the last two years, as never before," said Calvin O. Davis of the University of Michigan to the National Association of Secondary-School Principals in that year, "there has echoed and re-echoed across our country a demand for full-blooded Americanism everywhere. The nation has . . . accepted without reservation the Biblical precept that he who is not for

³⁷ Lewis Wilbur Smith, "Americanization in the Thornton Township High School," *School Review* (November, 1920), p. 659.

³⁸ *Laws of New Hampshire,* sessions of January 1–May 28 and September 9–11, 1919, c. 106, sec. 17.

³⁹ Frank V. Thompson, discussion at 28th annual meeting of the Harvard Teachers' Association, April 12, 1919, *School and Society* (December 20, 1919), pp. 722–723.

⁴⁰ Charles W. Eliot, discussion at 28th annual meeting of the Harvard Teachers' Association, April 12, 1919, *School and Society,* December 20, 1919, p. 737.

⁴¹ *School and Society* (December 20, 1919), footnote, p. 723. Some educators, such as Thompson and Eliot, did resist these pressures. Only rarely did educators initiate them, although some of them applauded and approved. The *Educator-Journal* ([July, 1918], p. 597) gave its editorial approval to a proclamation by the governor of Iowa ordering that English be the only language spoken in public throughout the state. Even the campaign for Americanization, however, was considered too mild by the president of a county school directors' association in the state of Washington, who declared himself against "this soft-pedal, pussy-foot, half-hearted method of Americanizing the foreigner, be they native-born or otherwise." J. S. Freece, "Adoption of Program of Constructive Measures as a Forward Step in School Administration," NEA, 1920, p. 327.

⁴² Guy Stanton Ford, "A New Educational Agency," NEA, 1918, p. 208.

our state is against it, and has set itself the task not alone of rooting out existing forms of anarchy and hyphenism, but also of protecting itself in the future against the unchallenged development of anti-American doctrines and of divided national allegiances."[43] In this long-term program, Davis saw a large role for the schools, and he had a questionnaire ready to find out what 1180 high schools in the North Central Association were planning to do about it.

Inevitably there arose questions about the loyalty of teachers. Prominent among the dismissals of university professors were those of Professors J. McKeen Cattell and Henry Wadsworth Dana of Columbia University for pacifism and peace activities. The Boston *Journal* expressed its disapproval of this action and placed the blame on Nicholas Murray Butler.[44] Professor Charles Beard of Columbia resigned in protest against these dismissals and later found himself along with Jane Addams and Lillian Wald on a list of persons suspected of activity in movements not helpful to the United States in the War.[45]

Other teachers found themselves suspect, not because of outside activities, but because of what they taught in their classes. "It is time to read the riot act to some of these teachers," said one member of the New York City Board of Education. "They are just as dangerous," he declared, "just as guilty of treason as the man who blows up the White House." Drunkenness, he pointed out, was a cause for dismissal under the regulations of the Board, and a teacher who taught pacificism, he felt, was "a thousand times more dangerous to the welfare of the city than the teacher who gets drunk and lies in the gutter."[46] In Washington, D.C., social-studies teachers contended they were carrying out their duty of teaching current topics, but one of them was suspended for a week without pay for touching on the League of Nations and on Bolshevism, topics on which the Board declared the teacher to be "clearly an amateur." In commenting on this, the *School Review* deplored the "amateurish ignorance of most teachers," saying, however, that intelligent people must cooperate in "careful preparation of suitable material for school instruction."[47]

Even the most carefully prepared material sponsored by national

[43] C. O. Davis, "Training for Citizenship in the North Central Association of Secondary Schools," NC, Supplement, 1920, p. 26a.
[44] Editorial reprinted in *School and Society* (October 16, 1917), p. 442.
[45] Beryl Williams, *Lillian Wald* (New York: Julian Messner, 1948), p. 189.
[46] *School and Society* (April 28, 1917), p. 495.
[47] *School Review* (June, 1919), pp. 466–467.

leaders at the highest levels, however, did not escape attack. Judd and Marshall had written their *Lessons in Community and National Life* at the express request of Woodrow Wilson and Commissioner Claxton. Nevertheless, Magnus W. Alexander, Managing Director of the National Industrial Conference Board, charged that the lessons contained unwarranted propaganda favoring social insurance, industrial insurance, labor unions, and government control of private activity. An editorial in the *School Review* expressed disapproval of this criticism, noting indignantly that the manufacturers had been guilty of favoring separate administration for vocational schools.[48]

V

The attack on German and the more compulsory features of the Americanization campaign proceeded from an intellectual climate in which the doctrines of social control through education had already been established. This does not mean that individual advocates of social control necessarily favored the removal of German from the schools or the denial of employment to those who did not learn English. These specific actions, however, were fully consistent with pedagogical ideas that subordinated the individual to the group; and the War provided ample opportunity for the extension and application of these doctrines to the schools.

One of the first to see the explicit possibilities in the wartime mood was Charles A. Prosser, the Secretary of the National Society for the Promotion of Industrial Education. In an address to the Harvard Teachers' Association in March, 1916, a full year before the United States entered the War, Prosser criticized the immediate past as an age of the "unrestrained ego," in which schools had "fanned the flame of personal ambition and personal achievement" and had "laid large stress upon rights and opportunities." The time had come, he declared, when the trend was away from democracy as freedom to democracy as conservation.[49] He cited Germany as an example of patriotism in the sense of

---

[48] *School Review* (March, 1919), pp. 211–212.

[49] Charles A. Prosser, "Education as Preparedness," *School and Society* (June 3, 1916), pp. 797–798. In this address, Prosser said that adjustment of the individual to life was merely a rephrasing of preparation for life, which he characterized as a shibboleth of individualistic education, a noteworthy comment in view of his later use of the term "life-adjustment education." Prosser did not necessarily get his social enthusiasm from the movement for industrial education. He may have caught some of it from his interpretations of the pedagogical doctrines of the

"living and working for the country." While granting the possibility that German education had subordinated the individual too much to the state, he found it "probably equally true" that American education had asserted the rights and ambitions of the individual at the expense "of true patriotic service to the state." The ideal, he thought, lay in middle ground between what prevailed in Germany and what he felt had prevailed up to that time in the United States. He deplored the eagerness of some American school men to condemn the German system because of the War, saying that while he did not advocate transplanting German schools to our soil, it would be desirable to "winnow" from them what was good for us.[50]

It was also in 1916 that G. Stanley Hall used the German model in pointing out what he considered to be some of the benefits of War. "We are told," he proclaimed to a general session of the NEA, "that the most thrilling slogan in Germany is the cry, 'Deutschland über Alles.' What about the same slogan, 'America above all,' here? Are we not each and all called to rise to a higher moral and religious plane and to find new points of connection here between a patriotism and religion, since a republic is after all more or less a theocracy?"[51] Two years later, Hall was still celebrating the comradeship and higher unity growing out of the War, welcoming also "the splendor and glory of 'the day' that has come to us Americans!"[52] In a speech to an NEA meeting on the twenty-fifth anniversary of the founding of the Department of Child Study (by this time known as the Department of Child Hygiene), Hall discussed the view of authority as centered on the father, noting the presence in the world of those who had developed "morbid symptoms at every suggestion of control, constraint, command," these being "negativists who respond to any hint of compulsion by protesting their readiness to die for liberty." From this group, he said, came the incorrigibles, the anarchists, and the conscientious objectors—although he granted that negativists of the better type also made inventors and pioneers.[53]

New Harmony movement in Indiana. As Superintendent of the New Albany, Indiana, Schools in 1905, he had taken a leading part in the study of New Harmony as a topic for that year in the Indiana Teachers' Reading Circle and had written a series of articles on the subject. See, for example, his "The Harmony Movement," *Educator-Journal* (December, 1905), pp. 144–150.

[50] *Ibid.*, pp. 805–806.
[51] G. Stanley Hall, "The War and Education," NEA, 1916, p. 91.
[52] G. Stanley Hall, "Some Educational Values of the War," NEA, 1918, p. 97.
[53] G. Stanley Hall, "A General Survey of Child-Study," NEA, 1918, pp. 333–334.

In somewhat less colorful language, other educators also grimly pursued the social ideal. "If we are now to develop social efficiency through progressive adaptation of the individual to his social environment," said Walter Robinson Smith of the Kansas State College, Emporia, in 1917, "it will be necessary to pour into the curriculum a mass of socializing materials and organize them for the definite purpose of socializing the individual pupil."[54] A year later he declared that individuals "must be educated into group consciousness, group intelligence and group service."[55] Sociologist Charles Ellwood of the University of Missouri called for education that would "inculcate values, standards, and ideals, as soon as sufficient scientific knowledge of facts has been attained on which to base scientific social standards and ideals." It was the nation, he felt, that should be the unit of "socialized education," and the agency of the federal government "must be invoked for its final establishment."[56]

Since democracy played so large a part in the ideology of the War, it was inevitable that discussions of social control would involve attempts to define, or perhaps rather to redefine, what democracy should mean. It was in 1918 that sociologist Ross Finney criticized Dewey's *Democracy and Education* as too individualistic. "While it is true," granted Finney, "that citizens of a democracy need to be taught to think, it is even more important, especially in the present crisis, that they be trained to revere and to obey." Fortunately, he thought, *Democracy and Education* was so hard for the average school man to read that its influence would "be greatly handicapt." Finney commended G. Stanley Hall for saying that children of a certain age would profit from regimen and drill, noting that Hall might have added "And so will our social order!"[57] Democracy turned up in many calls to action in this period. "In the Prussian school," said one writer, "the paramount aim of every lesson is to teach 'Kaiserism.' The teacher finds or makes the opportunity. In the American school let the paramount aim of every lesson be to teach Democracy. The teacher shall find or make the opportunity."[58]

[54] Walter Robinson Smith, "The Value and Scope of Educational Sociology," *School and Society* (July 14, 1917), p. 46.
[55] Walter Robinson Smith, "The Fundamentals of a Socialized Educational Program," *School and Society* (July 13, 1918), p. 36.
[56] Charles A. Ellwood, "The Reconstruction of Education upon a Social Basis," *Educational Review* (February, 1919), p. 101.
[57] Ross L. Finney, "Sociological Principles Fundamental to Pedagogic Method," *Educational Review* (February, 1918), pp. 109–110.
[58] Edward P. Gilchrist, "Teaching Democracy," *School and Society* (September 28, 1918), p. 380.

The National Council of the NEA took up the study of democracy as part of the work of its Committee on Superintendents' Problems. With A. Duncan Yocum of the University of Pennsylvania as Chairman, the subcommittee assigned to this project declared democracy to be incomplete "in the more dangerous sense that on the side of individual freedom and the right to individual development it may be carried too far." To correct this, the subcommittee presented six essential propositions in democracy, namely, limitation of individual rights, compensation for rights through service, leveling-up as the only means to permanent equality, self-achievement, equality through highest individual effort, and common compulsion of all essential equalities not individually self-achieved. The subcommittee proposed asking leaders in each social field to identify the contributions of that field to democracy, "for example, not how much democracy must let religion alone, but what, if anything, democracy for its own sake must compel of and thru religion."[59]

At the 1920 session of the National Council in Cleveland, the subcommittee reported that it had presented to the Religious Education Association of America a questionnaire with the title, "What Democracy Should Compel through Religion." One of the objects of this was to investigate the contribution of religious teaching to democracy and the attitude of the churches toward a firmer insistence on the fundamental forms of religion and morality essential to democratic living. "A similar cooperation of other agencies," continued the report, "will be necessary to satisfactory study of increasing compulsion upon the individual for the sake of the common welfare, exerted in the fields of health, industry, and citizenship."[60]

Meanwhile the NEA as a whole had moved toward more specific recommendations with regard to social education. Among the resolutions for 1919 was one calling for a year of civic training under federal auspices. "We urge the government of the United States," read the resolution, "to institute and maintain a full twelve-month year of instruction, training, and discipline for each young man and young woman between the ages of seventeen years and six months and twenty, such training to be carried on at such place and in such manner as may result to the particular advantage of the individual in the development of civic responsi-

---

[59] A. Duncan Yocum, "Preliminary Report on the Democracy Questionnaire," NEA, 1919, pp. 730–731.

[60] A. Duncan Yocum, "Report of the Sub-Committee on Curriculum of the Committee on Superintendents' Problems," NEA, 1920, p. 175.

bility and vocational efficiency, and to bear the entire expense of this undertaking."[61] This was an extension of the idea of compulsory and universal schooling, and the 1919 resolutions also called for state laws to make schooling compulsory to the age of sixteen, with provision for compulsory continuation schooling to the age of eighteen. The *Cardinal Principles* report had made a similar proposal, but with the part-time education to be offered in the comprehensive high school.

Perhaps the most sweeping endorsement of the high school as a supervisor of youth was that presented by Superintendent Ernest A. Smith of Salt Lake City in his discussion of the Utah law of 1919 on compulsory education. The law itself required all boys and girls up to eighteen years of age to be in school or at work. It went into effect on September 1, 1919, with the application of it by the State Department of Education involving the registration of all youth in the pertinent age groups. "The location of each youth is known," said Superintendent Smith, "and record follows, if removal elsewhere in the state occurs." Under the application of this law, local school districts were to provide a full twelve-month period of schooling each year, with school credit for Junior Red Cross work, thrift stamp activity, clean-up campaigns, and community service. Three sets of reports were devised for checking vocational activities, health habits, and out-of-school activities. "Complete and specific details are covered," noted Smith, with the health report including the use of narcotics, care of person, sleeping habits, and kind and amount of recreation. As understood by Smith, the policies developed under this law meant that Utah had abandoned "the traditional

---

[61] National Education Association, "Report of the Committee on Resolutions," NEA, 1919, p. 24. Superintendent Fred Hunter of Oakland, California, a vigorous advocate of social efficiency, was Chairman of this committee, and Principal William D. Lewis of Philadelphia was one of the members. Earlier versions of this idea, but with some provision for military training, had been set forth by Randolph Bourne in *Education and Living* ([New York: Century Co., 1917], p. 72), and Charles A. Prosser in "Training for Citizenship through Service," *School and Society* (September 7, 1918). Possibly some support for the idea came from a desire to find a substitute for required military training. Dewey had on several occasions asked why universal training should not be directed toward social service rather than military service. See his "Universal Service as Education," *New Republic* (April 22 and 29, 1916), pp. 309–310 and 334–335. Two years later, however, Dewey made a strong statement on behalf of "a national scheme of socialized education applying to the youth between the older ages, just as we have already made our elementary system universal and conscriptive." John Dewey, *Vocational Education in the Light of the World War*, Bulletin No. 4, Vocational Education Association of the Middle West (Chicago: The Association, January, 1918), p. 3.

scheme" of caring for the pupil only a thousand hours a year in the class-room and had undertaken the direction of the child "for the other three thousand active, wakeful hours of the year." Smith reported that the superintendents of the state hailed this policy "as a call to civic and moral righteousness for all the youth."[62]

In comparison with the point of view evinced by Smith in his interpretation of this law, the *Cardinal Principles* report was not moderate, but anemic. So were any of the expressions of Dewey. There is little to be wondered at in Yocum's complaint that Dewey did not with "clean-cut realization seize upon a completer democracy as our supremist immediate aim."[63]

VI

By no means did all this pass without protest. Dewey in 1916 warned a general session of the NEA against the tendency to identify Americanism with a uniform set of cultural characteristics. Our nation, he said, was "complex and compound . . . inter-racial and inter-national in its make-up . . . composed of a multitude of peoples." No single ethnic group could define the American ideal. "No matter how loudly any one proclaims his Americanism, if he assumes that any one racial strain, any one component culture, no matter how early settled it was in our territory, or how effective it has proved in its own land, is to furnish a pattern to which all other strains and cultures are to conform, he is a traitor to American nationalism."[64] In the same address, he called upon the public school to become "an energetic and willing instrument in developing initiative, courage, power, and personal ability in each individual,"[65] a statement of aim virtually identical to Eliot's expressions over a period of three decades. Even in 1918, when he advocated conscription for a national scheme of social service, Dewey remained critical of those who called for "Germanizing our own system of education" and who wanted methods of teaching and discipline that would produce docility.[66]

[62] Ernest A. Smith, "Compulsory Character Education," NEA, 1920, pp. 472–473.
[63] A. Duncan Yocum, "Existing Democratic Factors in American Life and Education," NEA, 1919, p. 718.
[64] John Dewey, "Nationalizing Education," NEA, 1916, pp. 184–185.
[65] *Ibid.,* p. 188.
[66] John Dewey, *Vocational Education in the Light of the World War, op. cit.,* p. 3.

Eliot also maintained the New England tradition of stubborn protest. He disagreed with the compulsory features in the Massachusetts bill on the learning of English by foreigners. Similarly he had expressed disagreement with the idea of compulsory military training in the schools, particularly from the point of view of teaching obedience. "I have heard a great deal of talk lately," said Eliot, "about the importance of a boy's acquiring the habit of implicit obedience: that is the worst habit a boy can acquire after he ceased to be an infant, because it implies the subjection of the boy's own will."[67] Eliot had never joined in the uncritical admiration of Germany before the war; he refused to take part in the reversal of this admiration. In 1909 he had accepted without enthusiasm the Royal Order of the Prussian Crown,[68] but in 1918 he rejected the suggestion that he should return it. "It does not seem to me expedient or dignified," he said when asked to explain himself, "for Italians, Frenchmen and Englishmen, men of science and letters, to revoke membership in German scientific and learned societies, or to return medals." He added that the object of the War with Germany was not to be promoted by denying the past achievement of the German people in science and letters.[69]

Others warned against the tendency to imitate some of the characteristics in Germany against which the United States was fighting. One of these was Professor Joseph Jastrow of the University of Wisconsin, who specifically protested against the imitation of German intolerance. The "dykes of reason" must be kept intact, he declared, for the danger was always present that an emotional flood might overflow its banks. Noting that in Germany intolerance was a cult, he said that in America it was "a controllable menace" and urged that it be controlled.[70]

Also among those who warned against believing that we had to adopt Germany's methods to defeat Germany was Professor Charles Hughes

[67] As quoted in *School Review* (March, 1917), p. 170. Eliot later supported for defense purposes the Swiss system of military training, consisting of two or three months at age twenty, with annual training periods of ten days to a fortnight. Henry James, *Charles W. Eliot* (Boston: Houghton Mifflin Co., 1930), II, 277–278.

[68] *Ibid.*, pp. 141–143. Back in 1902, finding himself reluctantly awarding an honorary degree to Prince Henry of Prussia, Eliot congratulated the recipient on his being Queen Victoria's grandson. *Ibid.*, p. 139.

[69] Edward H. Cotton, *The Life of Charles W. Eliot* (Boston: Small, Maynard & Co., 1926), pp. 360–361.

[70] Joseph Jastrow, "War and Sanity: An Appeal to the Teaching Profession," *Educational Review* (September, 1918), p. 105.

Johnston of the University of Illinois.[71] Johnston had previously identified himself with some aspects of social control. Now he was beginning to fear the extreme interpretations of this doctrine. In 1917 he asked whether it was necessary to sacrifice individualism in wartime. "Where has individualism still a place?" he asked, and the answer he gave was "in education if anywhere." He warned against what he called "blind collectivism," although he thought "collectivism" was necessary to make the world safe for democracy and to establish "still more firmly a fundamental individualism."[72]

There were also those who deplored what they regarded as a tendency in American life to cut itself off from intellectual kinship with the rest of world civilization. In the midst of his struggles to defend the classics against the threat of the Lincoln School, Princeton's Andrew F. West appeared before a general session of the NEA to criticize the desire for a purely American national education. "Is there," he asked, "an American multiplication table?" It was particularly important, as he saw it, for the United States not to "impair the vital unity of our international civilized freedom."[73]

Perhaps the element most missing from the doctrines of social control was what Eliot had called "joy and gladness in achievement." Education had come to be regarded exclusively as a duty, a form of service to the state. It was, feared Arthur C. Barrows of Providence, Rhode Island, in 1919, "no longer a privilege to be sought, but a kind of military service to be endured."[74] Duty and joy, of course, were not necessarily in conflict, as Eliot himself recognized on many occasions. Extreme versions of social control, however, left little place for learning as joy. It may well have been this feature of the times that called forth a common protest from such diverse persons as Dewey, Eliot, and West.

[71] Charles Hughes Johnston, "War and the Schools," *Educational Administration and Supervision* (June, 1917), p. 377.

[72] Charles Hughes Johnston, "One Educational Issue of War Time," *Educational Administration and Supervision* (September, 1917), p. 434.

[73] Andrew F. West, "The Immortal Conflict," NEA, 1918, p. 90.

[74] Arthur C. Barrows, "Shifting Ideals of Education," *Education* (March, 1919), p. 423.

Chapter 17

The venture reaffirmed

"I think it best for us all to refuse to contemplate the possibility of that failure."
—CHARLES W. ELIOT,
APRIL 30, 1921.

*B*ack in 1897, the city of Buffalo, New York, had opened a new high school, the Masten Park, with Frank W. Fosdick as its Principal. This was just four years after the Committee of Ten. The 1200 pupils that year included the Principal's son, Raymond, later President of the Rockefeller Foundation and the General Education Board.

Raymond Fosdick liked high school. In his autobiography, he spoke with much appreciation of his studies and found the debating society "vivid in recollection." Particularly did he recall his father's talks to the entire school in the assembly hall each morning.[1] He felt the school "would have been called progressive by the standards of those days" and noted the acceptance of its certificates by colleges in the East. He mentioned the large German and Polish populations in Buffalo at that time, but said "they attended the public schools not only with no social discrimination but with little awareness on our part that they were 'different.' " The few Negro pupils "were absorbed into the life of the school without question." His father, he said, ran the school on the principle of "the dignity and potential worth of all of the sons and daughters of men, regardless of the color of their skins."[2]

This was what would later have been called a traditional school. Yet as a community devoted to academic learning, it was open without favor or discrimination to those who could meet its standards, regardless of their

[1] Raymond B. Fosdick, *Chronicle of a Generation: an Autobiography* (New York: Harper & Row, 1958), pp. 27–28.
[2] *Ibid.*, p. 30.

race, national ancestry, or social class. Economic circumstances undoubtedly affected the opportunities of youth in Buffalo to attend high school, but these were conditions not set by the school itself. Those who were critical of schools like this probably would have discounted Fosdick's favorable appraisal. He represented, they would have observed, the kind of pupil for whom this school was designed, not because he was the principal's son, but because of his abilities and interests and the background of learning represented in his home. "Around the green-shaded 'student lamp' we gathered every evening," wrote Fosdick, "each person with his book. I do not remember our parents reading aloud to us, or even determining what we should read. Ours was a home in which personal independence was cherished and encouraged, and this extended to our choice of books. The only limitation was the narrow supply."[3] The home was not a wealthy one, but like the school, it constituted a little community of book learning where great value was placed on such things.

What then, ran the questions of critics who discussed such matters in the 1890's, about the thousands of youth who came from homes without books, without family dedication to learning, and without commitment to ideals of scholarship? These were then, as now, difficult questions to face. So far as individual pupils were concerned, however, the answer may have been suggested by Mary Antin, who came from a Boston slum to John Tetlow's classical high school, finding there something that met her "needs" as much as or more than it did those of the residents of Beacon Hill.[4] It was a simple answer, namely, that pupils were individuals and not, as was later to be held, members of groups for whom "curriculums" had to be designed.

More recent critics would perhaps note Raymond Fosdick's statement that at the time he entered Colgate in 1901 he had never "seen an automobile or an airplane or a moving picture" and had not "listened to a radio or heard a phonograph record."[5] Some of these, of course, were still being invented, but the world around the Masten Park High School was in fact bursting with technological change, with much more to come.

[3] *Ibid.,* pp. 22–23.

[4] "For I love literature above all noble and beautiful things of which man is master," wrote Mary Antin with youthful enthusiasm, "and poetry has been my favorite ever since I began to read." Mary Antin to John Tetlow, March 2, 1899, John Tetlow Papers (Houghton Library, Harvard University, Cambridge, Mass.). See also her book, *The Promised Land* (Boston: Houghton Mifflin Co., 1912).

[5] Fosdick, *op. cit.,* p. 34.

These circumstances, it has been argued, erased the validity of the assumptions on which the program of the Masten Park High School was based. The school itself and the moderate revision it represented were already out of date, at least, according to this point of view.

It was in 1909 that Rexford Guy Tugwell entered the Masten Park High School. This was twelve years later, but the school had not been greatly changed. At this time, however, Tugwell did observe what he called the beginnings of separation between college-preparatory pupils and others in the school,[6] a state of affairs presumably not characteristic before. Tugwell's background was similar to Fosdick's, and his family also respected books and learning. They had taken active part in the Chautauqua movement, and Tugwell appreciated its contributions, although he also characterized it as "a gathering ground for the semi-learned," the learning being "superficial perhaps, but not by any means useless."[7]

Tugwell's response to his schooling, including that at the Masten Park High School, was mixed. His teacher of Latin and Greek at Masten Park had "at odd moments, sometimes even after classes were over for the day and he must have been longing to get away . . . talked to a few of us in ways that opened windows on an antiquity we had not guessed at." From a course in ancient history, taken at the suggestion of this teacher, Tugwell gained "the picture of a rational, gracious civilization on the shores of that dark and wine-red sea which was so far from Buffalo in time and space as hardly to seem credible at all."[8]

Still there was something Tugwell felt the schools of that era had failed to do. In his autobiography, he spoke favorably of Dewey's ideas and deplored the "glacial deliberation" with which these and what he called "the progressive methods" had spread.[9] For the new world of airplanes, electricity, and new means of communication, "we were grossly unprepared when we got through our high schools."[10] The texts of his time, he felt, "no longer explained the world we would find when we graduated. They did little more than elaborate and defend the myths which were growing farther and farther away from reality."[11] Philoso-

[6] Rexford Guy Tugwell, *The Light of Other Days* (Garden City, N.Y.: Doubleday & Co., 1962), pp. 312–313.
[7] *Ibid.*, pp. 19–20.
[8] *Ibid.*, p. 315.
[9] *Ibid.*, pp. 106–107.
[10] *Ibid.*, p. 225.
[11] *Ibid.*, p. 230.

phers, he felt, had a vision of "an educational system directed to social ends, finding out and developing individual talents, setting young people on the way to making a contribution while they also express their own minds," but this was not something "consented to by actual educational authorities."[12]

Traditional schools certainly did not suffer from lack of critics in the period after 1900. There were, however, different kinds of criticisms, each tied to some vision of a better world to come. The better world contemplated by the social efficiency movement threatened to be a grim and cheerless place. Dewey's criticisms, on the other hand, reflected the vision of a world that would be "worthy, lovely, and harmonious."[13] In *Democracy and Education* he sought to reconcile natural development and social efficiency by correcting the errors in both. "Social efficiency, even social service," he said, "are hard and metallic things when severed from an active acknowledgment of the diversity of goods which life may afford to different persons, and from faith in the social utility of encouraging every individual to make his own choice intelligent."[14] The democratic criterion, he felt, was violated by the attempt "to fit individuals in advance for definite industrial callings, selected not on the basis of trained original capacities, but on that of the wealth or social status of parents."[15] This inference would probably have been denied by the advocates of social efficiency; yet some of the statements made by Newlon, Snedden, and, in his earlier expressions, Charles Hughes Johnston did veer dangerously toward what Dewey was warning against.

Eliot's better world was one of joy and gladness in achievement.[16] Consistently throughout his career, he criticized anything in schooling seen by him as failing to help every individual develop his fullest powers through subjects and activities chosen on the basis of interest and talent. Mass methods and uniformity of studies, he felt, killed off the development of individual skill. Even Dewey, with all his compassion and humanity, did not often talk of joy. So thoroughly committed was Eliot to this ideal that he might well have become the chief target of those who

[12] *Ibid.,* pp. 310–311.

[13] John Dewey, *The School and Society* (Chicago: University of Chicago Press, 1899), p. 40.

[14] John Dewey, *Democracy and Education* (New York: Macmillan Co., 1916), p. 141.

[15] *Ibid.,* pp. 139–140.

[16] Charles W. Eliot, "Status of Education at Close of Century," NEA, 1900, p. 198.

denounced the doctrine of interest and of happiness in learning. Yet to Eliot this did not mean soft pedagogy. He was talking of joy and gladness in achievement, not in failure to achieve. When children and youth worked on subjects of interest to them, they should be held to the highest standards of achievement. Contrariwise, no child should be held accountable for standards in subjects in which he had neither interest nor talent. This implied, of course, that every individual had some talent within him to be found.

Behind Dewey and Eliot lay a long trail of criticism of conventional schooling. Almost every philosopher of pedagogy from Plato to Dewey himself had protested against the imposition of unpleasant tasks, against rote learning and drill, and against harsh and repressive discipline. Even William T. Harris, for all his belief in disciplining the will, rejected corporal punishment. The child study movement and the stereotype of the so-called child-centered school were late comers to this ancient company. Child study did not, however, necessarily imply child-centeredness or even the doctrines of interest and individual choice. Many of the early participants in child study saw themselves as rigorous scientists objectively describing the nature and growth of children. Still the overtones of the movement were favorable to the tradition of protest against harsh discipline and meaningless drill.

In the period following 1905, Dewey and Eliot were among the few major figures who gave expression to this perennial criticism. Most of the prominent critics of schooling were preoccupied with vocational education, or with its larger contexts of social efficiency and control. Several articulate observers, such as Ella Flagg Young and Randolph Bourne, tried to merge the two lines of criticism not by seeking a new synthesis, as had Dewey, but adding one to the other. This mixture of doctrines was represented in the controversial Gary plan and to a degree in the program of the Lincoln School.

There were, however, some teachers actively at work in the older tradition of protest. For the most part, they did not set forth philosophies of education. Rather they were busily engaged in schools, often private schools, seeking spontaneity, freedom, and joy in learning, perhaps adding to these the quest of the shared associations and interests to which Dewey had pointed in the laboratory school of the University of Chicago. Some of these were possibly unsuccessful or even inept, but they clung nonetheless to their efforts to break the crust of the conventional school.

It was one of these comparatively unknown people who in 1918, surrounded by the furious din of social control, kept dreaming of a new venture, designed to bring together those who were in sympathy with these efforts. An instructor in English at the United States Naval Academy, Stanwood Cobb represented, as did also Clarence Kingsley, a combination of dedicated commitment and the organizing ability to realize it in practice. Just as Kingsley had started from his classroom to reorganize secondary education on a national basis, so did Cobb venture from his to call into being the Association for the Advancement of Progressive Education. With his term *cardinal principles,* Kingsley bestowed upon American pedagogy the most familiar of its household words. Cobb's enterprise reached even farther, and the term *progressive education* was destined to capture world-wide attention from multitudes not connected with schools at all.

The beginnings, so far as numbers of people were concerned, were on the modest side. In mid-January of 1919, Cobb wrote that the Association was "at present" being organized in Washington, D.C., and that Eliot was to be its honorary president. It was, said Cobb in this letter, to be "chiefly a lay association, to arouse the interest and co-operation of parents in the latest and most ideal forms of education."[17] In this it was perhaps similar to the National Congress of Mothers that had, since its organization in 1897, grown into the National Congress of Mothers and Parent-Teachers Associations. Cobb, however, had visions of an enterprise comprehensive enough to include many kinds of groups. Only a few people were involved at that time, but there was, Cobb wrote on January 23, 1919, "no limit" to what the association could become, and nothing could "stop its ultimate growth into one of the most powerful forces in the educational world, except faulty management." The Association, he declared, could be based on the ideas of no one person, not even of those of a small group. "What we want is the broadest and most universal and harmonious co-operation of all the progressive forces in education." On the practical side, he planned "to place our publicity in the hands of Lee, Harris and Lee, one of the best firms in the country."[18]

[17] Stanwood Cobb to Michael Vincent O'Shea, January 15, 1919, Michael Vincent O'Shea Papers (State Historical Society of Wisconsin, Madison, Wis.).
[18] Stanwood Cobb to Michael Vincent O'Shea, January 23, 1919, Michael Vincent O'Shea Papers (State Historical Society of Wisconsin, Madison, Wis.). In this letter Cobb mentioned some of the people associated with him in the enterprise. One of these was Mrs. Laura Williams, mentioned here as "one of the chief supporters of Mrs. Johnson" (Marietta Johnson of the Organic School of Fairhope,

The first public meeting was held in Washington, D.C., in the middle of March. Cobb worked hard on the advance publicity for this meeting, providing materials to go out as news stories from the press bureaus, and making suggestions for special feature articles for the Sunday editions.[19] At this first meeting, Louis F. Post, Assistant Secretary of Labor, presided and read a message from Eliot. Speakers included Otis Caldwell of the Lincoln School; Marietta Johnson; Anne George of the Montessori movement; Eugene R. Smith, headmaster of the Park School, Baltimore; and Cobb himself.[20] An "authorized statement" was issued, declaring the aims of the Association, namely, to bring together all the forces working on progressive lines and "through a large lay organization of parents and others interested in education, to give wider publicity to the more recent experiments in the education field." Schools mentioned as examples were the Montessori Schools; the Francis Parker Schools at Chicago and San Diego; the Organic Schools at Fairhope, Alabama, Greenwich, Connecticut, and Montclair, New Jersey, and the Park School of Baltimore. All these schools, said the authorized statement, sought "to develop initiative and resourcefulness in the pupil and to make him master of his environment, rather than to cram him with undigested information, in order that he may pass examinations and acquire degrees, while his soul is fettered by the many demands of the system."[21]

This statement placed the Association squarely within the context of the perennial protest against regimentation and rote learning and on behalf of freedom, spontaneity and interest. So did the "platform" that was written and adopted some time during the winter of 1918–1919. The first three points of this platform—freedom, interest as the motive of all work, and the teacher as a guide, not a taskmaster—must indeed have

---

Alabama). Others mentioned were Mrs. Parsons, widow of a former Librarian of Congress, "a woman of means, broad intelligence, and ability"; Mrs. Ayres, sister-in-law of Leonard P. Ayres; Anne George of the Washington Montessori School; and Eugene Randolph Smith of the Park School, Baltimore, "one of the most remarkable educators in the country." According to Lawrence A. Cremin, it was Mrs. Johnson who suggested that Cobb form an association and who gave him a list of people in and around Washington, D.C. Lawrence A. Cremin, *The Transformation of the School* (New York: Alfred A. Knopf, 1961), p. 242.

[19] Stanwood Cobb to Michael Vincent O'Shea, March 5, 1919, Michael Vincent O'Shea Papers (State Historical Society of Wisconsin, Madison, Wis.).

[20] "The Association for the Advancement of Progressive Education," *School and Society* (March 22, 1919), p. 353.

[21] Quoted *ibid.*

delighted Eliot, although nothing was said in this document about joy and gladness.

The organization of the new movement developed slowly throughout 1919, and Cobb seemed worried. In June he wrote that Mrs. Laura Williams of Washington, D.C., had offered to be one of twenty to guarantee an annual fund of ten thousand dollars. "I hope," he said, "we can find the 19 others."[22] He managed to get an article into the *Baltimore Sun* and was busily engaged in trying to interest national magazines such as *Good Housekeeping* and *Delineator*. By July he had started what he called the "endless-chain system," under which each person to whom he wrote was asked to furnish new names.[23] His hopes for a journal conducted by the Association itself did not materialize at this time, and the magazine *Progressive Education* did not appear until 1924. With all this, he persisted in his efforts, and he did keep the Association alive as a basis for its future expansion and influence.[24]

It was indeed remarkable that the Association survived at all. The doctrines of its authorized statement and platform must indeed have been foolishness to most of the articulate leaders in education at that time. Especially where the secondary school was concerned, the popular notes remained those of efficiency and control. The new Association, on the contrary, preached freedom, spontaneity, and interest. Even Dewey did not join at first, perhaps because he felt the Association placed too much stress on one side of the dualism between natural development and social efficiency.

Eliot apparently had no doubts. His message read at the first meeting of the Association on March 15, 1919, reaffirmed his long-felt convictions and was entirely consistent with the ideals of the new group. The message ran along familiar lines: reduce class work and size of classes;

---

[22] Stanwood Cobb to Michael Vincent O'Shea, June 11, 1919, Michael Vincent O'Shea Papers (State Historical Society of Wisconsin, Madison, Wis.).

[23] Stanwood Cobb to Michael Vincent O'Shea, July 5, 1919, Michael Vincent O'Shea Papers (State Historical Society of Wisconsin, Madison, Wis.).

[24] Apprehension about the survival of the Association was expressed by Mrs. Williams in October, 1919. The executive committee had met and agreed there was no cause for discouragement even though the Association was not growing rapidly. Laura C. Williams to Michael Vincent O'Shea, October 14, 1919. O'Shea was glad to hear that "our Association is not moribund." Michael Vincent O'Shea to Laura C. Williams, October 20, 1919. By this time Cobb had left the Naval Academy and had opened a progressive school himself. Michael Vincent O'Shea Papers (State Historical Society of Wisconsin, Madison, Wis.).

increase individual work; reduce book work and mere memorizing; make training of the senses a prime object daily; cultivate power to see and describe accurately; connect each lesson with something in the life of the child; make sure every child learns to enjoy reading; teach related subjects in natural groups; enlist interest; stimulate competition such as in games; give every pupil practice in determining facts and judging evidence; develop skill of eye, ear, or hand. He closed with Pasteur's definition of democracy—"that form of government which best enables and sets free each individual citizen to do *his* best for the common welfare."[25]

In the thirtieth annual meeting of the Harvard Teachers' Association, held at Cambridge, April 30, 1921, Eliot praised the work of "progressive" schools, declaring that the pioneers in the movement were "acting on the principles which alone can make elementary and secondary education in the United States the firm support of political and industrial freedom, and the true safeguard of democracy." It was, he felt, much more difficult to make headway in 1922 than it had been 60 years before, because the teaching profession in the elementary and secondary schools was even more conservative than the university teachers had been in the earlier period. "The campaign for freedom and attention to the powers and rights of the individual child," he said, "is difficult at this moment in the legislatures and boards of education in this country."[26] Perhaps he was thinking of the still-powerful forces acting on behalf of education for social control, or possibly harking back to the laws for compulsory Americanization proposed in Massachusetts at the end of the war.

The Association did not, in this period, deal specifically with matters pertaining to the high school. What it did, however, was to provide a rival ideology of protest against so-called conventional schooling. Before 1919 nearly all the organized criticism had come from those who urged social efficiency and scientific management. In fact, the Association might be interpreted as a protest movement not only against conventional schooling, but also against the doctrine of social efficiency itself. It certainly did not repeat the slogans of social efficiency. It did not propose to haul the academic subjects before the bar of justice to prove their right to life. There was no advocacy of differentiated "curriculums"

[25] Charles W. Eliot, "Reforms in American Schools," *School and Society* (April 26, 1919), pp. 510–511.
[26] Charles W. Eliot, "The Progressive Movement in Education," *School and Society* (January 21, 1922), pp. 77–78.

aimed at "groups" of pupils. There was no trace of subordination of the individual to the group. This is worthy of note because of the later tendency to attribute all criticism of the conventional school to the ideology represented by the Association. What the Association did was to reaffirm the perennial and ancient protest against uniformity, rote learning, and repressive discipline and to restate the ideals of freedom, spontaneity, interest, and joy. Eventually the Association expanded its doctrines and took up some that were close to social control, but this was not true in the early period.

Meanwhile the NEA marched on to a membership of 30,000 in 1918, and State Superintendent Mary C. C. Bradford of Colorado was calling upon all teachers to join.[27] Still, not all was well with the NEA. Butler had been thundering away for years about the alleged decline of intellectual quality in its leadership. Now the *School Review* added its criticism, declaring that the NEA was exhausting itself on trivial matters and political bickering.[28] "Let us have once more, as in the days when Eliot and Harris led the National Education Association in the ways of intelligence, discussions of the course of study," exhorted this journal in an editorial late in 1918.[29] A year later it stated flatly that "the Association is threatened with dissolution." The Department of Superintendence, it declared, would soon be more influential than the NEA itself; its winter meeting was becoming the most important educational gathering in the country. The Department, advised the *School Review,* should "throw off its inhibiting affiliation with the moribund Association."[30]

During the War and in the period immediately following the War, the NEA committed itself heavily to education for social control. Beyond this it issued spectacular pronouncements on the level of higher statesmanship, such as its demand for a cabinet post in education. Some of these came from the Commission on the Emergency in Education and the Program for Readjustment during and after the War, created in 1918. The Commission did, however, identify some important projects, such

[27] Mary C. C. Bradford, "The Work of the Commission on the Emergency in Education," NEA, 1919, p. 80.

[28] "The National Education Association in 1919," *School Review* (September, 1919), p. 547.

[29] *School Review* (December, 1918), p. 778.

[30] "The National Education Association in 1919," *School Review* (September, 1919), pp. 546–547.

as the improvement of school facilities for rural children and youth.[31]

With regard to secondary schooling, the NEA seemed to have spent its force on the CRSE general report, the most important subject reports having appeared before this time. Although the CRSE continued its existence on a somewhat spasmodic basis after 1918, it apparently had little left to say. Even the *Cardinal Principles* report had been more a product of the personal commitment of Clarence Kingsley than of driving force within the NEA itself.

It was to be decades before the NEA as a whole again set forth a point of view on secondary schooling. As the *School Review* had predicted, the Department of Superintendence picked up the function of leadership.[32] The ideology of the Department remained that of social efficiency and scientific management, tempered somewhat by the moderating influence of the *Cardinal Principles* report. Some antiacademic bias persisted, not as it had flourished back in the days of the campaign for vocational education, but rather as a mood taken for granted without argument. The storms were over, and only a grey overcast remained.

Under these circumstances, it was not surprising that Stanwood Cobb's new Association, stumbling along in its precarious existence during the first several years, eventually became the arena for discussion that the NEA meetings had been for nearly four decades. With its Eight-Year Study of the 1930's, a project of The Commission on the Relation of School and College, the Association succeeded for a time in dramatizing the issues of secondary schooling and recapturing the spirit of the 1890's and early 1900's. By this time, however, the Association had become an eclectic organization indeed, and many were the birds of the air that had come to nest in its branches. In this process, it tended to lose its distinctive missionary commitment. Nevertheless, its collapse in the 1950's left a vacuum in pedagogical discussion that has not yet been adequately filled.

[31] See George D. Strayer, "The National Emergency in Education," NEA, 1918, pp. 129–131; "The National Education Association Program of Work," NEA, 1919, pp. 41–46; and "A Final Report of the Commission on the Emergency in Education, Presented by Its Chairman," NEA, 1920, pp. 41–48.

[32] Some leadership on the secondary school program was also exercised by the newly formed National Association of Secondary-School Principals, an NEA department formed as an offshoot of the Department of Superintendence in 1916. See Jesse H. Newlon, "The National Association of Principals of Secondary Schools," *Educational Administration and Supervision* (June, 1917), pp. 351–353.

II

Neither criticism nor controversy had slowed down the sheer physical expansion of the public high schools. By 1920 they enrolled 1,851,965 pupils in grades nine through twelve and were well on their way to the ideal of universality called for by the *Cardinal Principles* report. True, there was some unfinished business. Pupils continued to drop out in large numbers, and girls, comprising 55.7 percent of the total enrollment, still outnumbered the boys.[33] These difficulties, however, were confidently expected to disappear under more widespread application of the doctrines of social efficiency and other doctrines that had been evolving over the period of the preceding ten to fifteen years.

There were more public high schools than ever before, 14,326 of them in 1920 as contrasted with 10,213 in 1910, and the average number of pupils per school had risen during this period from 89.6 to 139.5. Still, about half these schools enrolled fewer than 50 pupils each. In some parts of the country, the small high school was not a choice, but a necessity. There could be small high schools or none. The state of Idaho in 1916 had 1300 school districts, but less than 100 of these had as many as 100 children each, with this number yielding an average of only 10 to 12 of high school age. Many of these districts could not maintain high schools at all, and there were only 70 districts in the state with four-year courses.[34]

The small high school was then as now an object of worry and concern. Where the leaders of the present, however, worry about the inability of the small high school to offer academic subjects, particularly foreign languages, those of the past deplored it as the last refuge of the academic program. One of these critics noted with apprehension the fact that of eighteen rural high schools in Idaho, there were seventeen teaching algebra, twelve geometry, and ten Latin. "To many," he complained, "the distinguishing notes of a high school, without which it is not, are algebra,

[33] *Biennial Survey of Education 1918–1920* (U.S. Bureau of Education, Bulletin No. 29 [Washington, D.C., 1923]), p. 497. Subsequent references in this chapter to nationwide statistics on pupils, teachers, and schools are also taken from this source.

[34] Edward O. Sisson, "Some Characteristics of the High-School Movement in Three Far Northwestern States," *School and Society* (January 15, 1916), p. 85. For the most part, district reorganization was still in the future. In states like Idaho, however, there were practical limits to the geographical size of districts.

Latin, ancient history, and so on. Out on the prairies, in the woods, among the mountains, in mining and lumbering regions, there are scores of pitiful little schools marked by these branches."[35] To the author of a Bulletin of the Bureau of Education in 1923, it was "only too evident" that preparation for college was "the chief object" in many small high schools. "Then, too," he pointed out, "greater emphasis is placed upon the older or more traditional subjects, such as Latin and mathematics, rather than upon many of the newer subjects for which many colleges give credit."[36]

Except in the very small schools, however, the practical subjects and activities were well represented in offerings throughout the country. This was true even in the cities of thinly populated regions, and the high school of Twin Falls, Idaho, for example, as far back as 1912 had laboratories, shops, a gymnasium, a lunch room, and an assembly room seating 750 people.[37] Of the 1032 accredited public high schools in the North Central Association in the spring of 1917, 79 percent offered at least one year of manual training and 15 percent offered as much as four years. With regard to the two major categories of household arts, 83 percent of these schools offered cooking and 79 percent sewing. Typewriting was taught in 68 percent of the schools and stenography in 71 percent. Occupying the limbo classified neither as academic nor as practical, music and art turned up in 63 percent and 42 percent, respectively, of the schools under study.[38]

Meanwhile the so-called academic studies had not suffered, this probably to the disappointment of the critics. All the schools in the North Central survey offered English, algebra, and geometry, while practically all provided Latin, ancient history, American history, and physics. Thirty-seven of these schools, or 3.59 percent of the total number, were still teaching Greek, a surprisingly high proportion in view of the long assault on the classics.[39] On the whole, the expansion of the practical subjects, although substantial, had not yet brought a decline in academic offerings;

[35] *Ibid.,* p. 90.

[36] W. S. Deffenbaugh, *Secondary Education in 1921 and 1922* (U.S. Department of Education, Bulletin No. 12 [Washington, D.C., 1923]), p. 20.

[37] Sisson, *op. cit.,* p. 86.

[38] Calvin O. Davis, *The Accredited Secondary Schools of the North Central Association* (U.S. Bureau of Education, Bulletin No. 45 [Washington, D.C., 1919]), Table 109, p. 107.

[39] *Ibid.,* Table 93, p. 95.

obviously there were, as previously noted, shifts in relative enrollments, particularly in foreign languages.

More pupils and more schools had, of course, demanded more teachers, and the number rose from 41,667 in 1910 to 97,654 in 1920, the latter figure including 6,430 teachers in junior high schools. Since 1890 the number of high school teachers had increased tenfold. How this could come about was suggested by a survey showing that nearly one-sixth of all the graduates of the University of Washington between 1876 and 1915 had entered high school teaching.[40] The expansion of high schools evidently provided a major job market for those who went to college. This was reinforced by the requirement of college graduation as the norm for beginning high school teachers, particularly in the larger schools found in the accredited lists. By 1917, 69 percent of the teachers in the 1032 accredited public high schools of the North Central Association had college degrees, with the percentages varying from 61 percent in Wisconsin to 88 percent in Nebraska.[41]

The public high school had indeed come a long way from its uncertain status of 40 years before, and the domain of secondary education was thrusting itself against both the elementary school and the college. Great efforts had been made to promote the idea that the seventh and eighth grades were part of secondary education, not only in the separate junior high school, but in the six-year secondary school as well. This was by no means always acceptable or even clear to the public at large. Had the emphasis been placed on the six-year secondary school, the result might have been clear, although not necessarily more acceptable. The separate junior high school broke the continuity of the program from grade seven through grade twelve, and it was consequently difficult to identify as a part of secondary education.

At the other end of the range, the high school had for the most part claimed and occupied the eleventh and twelfth grades. The efforts of the various regional associations and of the Carnegie Foundation had been successful in drawing the line below which the college was not supposed to go. Less successful were the contentions of those who sought to extend the secondary school into the traditional domain of the college. William Rainey Harper, James Greenwood, J. Stanley Brown, and many others had favored work beyond the twelfth grade in the local high

[40] *School and Society* (January 15, 1916), pp. 95–96.
[41] Davis, *op. cit.,* Table 110, p. 109.

schools, even to the extent of taking over the first two college years. Whatever merits these proposals may have had, they were not widely adopted.

Some local systems, however, had offered postgraduate work even before 1910, in some instances applying to it Harper's term, *the junior college*. Between 1910 and 1920 there was a mild upsurge of interest in the junior college idea, especially in California, where a state law of 1911 authorized high schools to establish two years of lower-division university work. A Bulletin of the U.S. Bureau of Education in 1919 identified 39 junior colleges in local public school districts, of which 21 were in California. These competed with, but did not replace, the first two college years. Beyond these there was a confusing assortment of schools called junior colleges, including the lower divisions of universities, normal schools accredited for the first two years of college work, and small private colleges that had reduced their programs to two years.[42]

Fortunately, many colleges accepted junior college work for transfer. This made it possible for some students to get part of their college education at home and at less expense, but it aroused the criticism of those who felt the junior college should provide a terminal program. At another level it raised the old question of bifurcation between those who did, and did not, plan to get further schooling. "In other words," said James Rowland Angell in 1915, "we have over again here the old schism with which we are so familiar." Angell thought the junior colleges could perform both functions.[43] Dean Frederick E. Bolton of the University of Washington College of Education, while granting the provision of the first two years of college work as a laudable aim for public education, felt this hardly justified the establishment of junior colleges.[44] Cubberley of Stanford, on the other hand, not only defended this purpose of the junior college, but also went back to the older hope that the universities would be led to dispense with freshman and sophomore work.[45] Some of the leaders in the movement, such as Dean Alexis Lange of the Univer-

---

[42] F. M. McDowell, *The Junior College* (U.S. Bureau of Education, Bulletin No. 35 [Washington, D.C., 1919]), p. 100.

[43] James R. Angell, "The Junior College and the Senior High School," NC, 1915, pp. 86–87.

[44] Frederick E. Bolton, "What Should Constitute the Curriculum of the Junior College or Extended High School," *School and Society* (December 21, 1918), p. 728.

[45] Ellwood P. Cubberley, "Some Recent Developments in Secondary Education in California," *Education* (October, 1916), pp. 84–85.

THE VENTURE REAFFIRMED   443

sity of California, made valiant efforts to have the junior college defined
as part of secondary schooling, in fact, as the culmination of that
period.[46] It has not proved possible, however, to convince recent generations that an institution called a college is really a secondary school.
The term *junior college* itself effectively disposed of the idea that the two
years beyond the twelfth grade were part of secondary education.

The central enterprise of secondary education had become and was
destined for many years to remain the four year high school, covering
grades nine through twelve. This was a recognizable institution, plainly
to be seen throughout the land. Even districts limited to programs of two
or three years thought the four year high school the ideal toward which
to work. It was the institution the American people had been fashioning
and expanding over a period of 40 years. The idea of secondary education remained abstract and elusive, but the local four year high school
was real and visible indeed.

III

No matter what winds of doctrine swirled about the loftier altitudes of
the NEA, the local high school sat solidly on its allotted ground, ready to
open each August or September with classes to be held and another nine
months of daily routine ahead. Its teachers responded slowly to the
various cosmic missions set forth by critics. Most of the time, they simply
did what seemed to be their work. The nature of this work was defined
by the doing of it.

Part of this work, whether in 1890 or 1920, was to provide a supervised environment for an aggregation of youth approximately fourteen
to eighteen wears of age. Long before the orators proclaimed the socialized high school and the doctrines of social control, the high school was in
fact socialized and had certain functions of social control to perform.
It had a group life and spirit, much of which went on outside the classroom. As far back as the 1880's and even before, there had been
athletics, debates, school socials, and clubs—and anxious pedagogues
who wrung their hands about the dangers of overemphasis.[47] Gradually

[46] Alexis Lange, "The Junior College—What Manner of Child Shall This Be?!"
School and Society (February 23, 1918), p. 213.

[47] For some of the discussions for and against, see C. W. French, "School
Government," *School Review* ([January, 1898], pp. 35–44); Florence Milner,
"School Management from the Side of Social Life," *School Review* ([April, 1899],
pp. 215–221); Reuben Post Halleck, "The Social Side of High-School Life," NEA,

the idea emerged that extracurricular activities too were part of the process of education, and the *Cardinal Principles* report explicitly recognized them in relation to the seven aims. In any case, whether its activities were many or few, the high school served the youth as a definite place to go, five or six hours a day, five days a week, nine or so months of the year, a place to see and talk with friends, a setting with assigned and not unduly burdensome tasks, and a home away from home.

For another thing, the high school was a promised route to getting ahead in a competitive world. This impression was at variance with the criticism that the high school was impractical and did not help young people to earn their living, but it was firmly fixed nevertheless. Eventually the idea would develop that a worthwhile career could not be attained at all without the stipulated high school diploma. Beyond the high school lay the college, equally criticized as impractical, but regarded in the everyday affairs of life as an even more dependable road to social and economic advancement. Educators might decry this as selfish individualism, but surely parents could not be blamed in seeking it for their children. Moreover, they had even John Dewey on their side. It was this champion of social education who asserted that there was a difference

1902, pp. 459–461; F. D. Boynton, "Athletics and Collateral Activities in Secondary Schools," NEA, 1904, pp. 206–214; Paul G. W. Keller, "Open School Organizations," *School Review* ([January, 1905], pp. 10–14); Spencer R. Smith, "Report of the Committee on the Influence of Fraternities in Secondary Schools," *School Review* ([January, 1905], pp. 1–10); Gilbert B. Morrison, "Social Ethics in High-School Life," NC, 1905, pp. 116–130; Louise R. Gibbs, "Making a High School a Center of Social Life," *School Review* ([November, 1909], pp. 634–637); Franklin Winslow Johnson, "The Social Organization of the High School," *School Review* ([December, 1909], pp. 665–680); Alice Sinclair Botkin, "The Relation of Outside Interests to Major Subjects in the High School," *Education* ([October, 1910], pp. 103–107); Helen Louise Guise, "Recognition of Social Instincts in High School Pupils," *Ohio Educational Monthly* ([December, 1910], pp. 612–615); Rufus C. Bentley, "Extra-Classroom Activities in High School: Their Place and Their Importance," NEA, 1911, pp. 581–586; Charles B. McLinn, "The Social Side of High School Life," *Journal of Education* ([October 5, 1911], pp. 345–346); Mrs. Clarence L. Atwood, discussion, NEA, 1914, pp. 875–876; Elmer Harrison Wilds, "The Supervision of Extra-Curricular Activities," *School Review* ([November, 1917], pp. 659–673); Olivia Pound, "The Need of a Constructive Social Program for the High School," *School Review* ([March, 1918], pp. 153–167); H. T. Steeper, "The Extra-Curriculum Activities of the High School," *Education* ([February, 1919], pp. 367–373); Thomas H. Briggs, "How to Encourage a High Standard of Scholarship," *Fifth Yearbook,* National Association of Secondary-School Principals ([The Association, 1921], pp. 29–30, discussion, pp. 30–38). See also Jesse B. Davis, *The Saga of a Schoolmaster* (Boston: Boston University Press, 1956), for accounts of school activities at the Detroit High School in the late 1880's and later at the Grand Rapids, Michigan, High School.

"between the happiness which merely means contentment with a station and the happiness which comes from the struggle of a well-equipped person to better his station"[48]—and approved the latter.

Along with this were the studies, representing selected portions of the intellectual achievements of civilized humanity. The complex wisdom of institutionalized accreditation had agreed that four major portions of these at a time was the desirable amount and distribution for all pupils. Among these studies were the subtleties of human language, including its mathematical forms, the historical memories of the race, the secrets of nature, the arts by which nature could be modified and subdued, and the awesome processes of man's humanity and inhumanity to man in social institutions and arrangements. Practically all educators except Eliot and Nightingale felt that some of these should be pursued by every pupil, and even Eliot made the concession of stipulating some work in English. Just which ones these were and how they should be arranged in relation to studies not pursued in common became the occasion of the fierce debates that occupied the educators in the journals, in their regional associations, and in the NEA.

There were, of course, and always would be diverse notions about what these studies were designed to accomplish. As Jespersen had once said of grammar, the consideration of pedagogical aims may be more or less useless, but it has also been endlessly fascinating. Like grammar, it has often turned out to have its uses after all. At any rate, it was with almost incredible ingenuity that educators of the period between 1880 and 1920 pursued the many variants of the question.

Most of the school men of the 1890's agreed that the purpose of the schools was to furnish mental training or training of the will. Mere information was disparaged, although concessions were made at times to something called the furniture of the mind. Eliot agreed with mental training, but even more, he regarded the subjects as the means of capturing the interest of pupils and setting them afire in at least one or two fields suited to their capacities and talents. From this, he believed, would individual power be developed. To Lester Frank Ward, the studies were the undistributed capital of the race; the distribution of this capital would tend to equalize opportunity and help solve the problems of society.

After 1900 some of the dormant competitors to these ideas began to assert themselves. Explicit in the campaign for vocational education was

[48] John Dewey, "Learning to Earn," *School and Society* (March 24, 1917), p. 333.

the expected contribution of the studies to national prosperity and strength. In the vocational campaign of that time, it was the practical studies of industrial education that were so favored; more recently these have been joined and surpassed by the physical sciences and mathematics, studies earlier considered to be impractical and academic. The motive, however, has remained much the same. In it is represented the eternal blending of the utilitarian and romantic sides of the nature of man, for technology has never been pursued solely for either personal or national gain.

Vocationalism in its naked form soon frightened the educators into accepting other approaches to judging the studies on the basis of their useful deeds. It was, they then declared, the mission of the subjects to produce socially efficient citizens. The subjects were called upon to prove themselves before the high court of scientific management. No subject has ever done so, but the idea has registered permanent impact on the minds of educators. Few advocates of any subject are comfortable unless they assert its merits in socially useful terms and make the expected testimony that the subject does not exist solely for its own sake.

The same idea persisted in the *Cardinal Principles* report, although the scope of the aims was widened beyond both vocationalism and social efficiency. Like Spencer, Kingsley proposed to have the subjects accomplish the purposes of complete living. To this he added worthy living, perhaps being motivated to do so by Dewey. What Kingsley set forth, however, was not so much a threat to the right of subjects to exist as a missionary call for the teachers of every subject to direct themselves to the strenuous pursuit of the seven aims. In the long run, this led to absurdities from which some subjects have not yet recovered. Nevertheless, when applied with discrimination and common sense, the seven aims have proved useful instruments in the making of some curricular decisions, and there are subjects to which some of the aims directly apply.

Meanwhile Eliot had continued to preach his version of mental training and to refine it in relation to the skills of making accurate observations, recording these in clear and simple language, and drawing from them valid inferences applicable to a wide range of human affairs. This, in his mind, was what the subjects were supposed to do. Another name for what he advocated was *reflective thinking,* a term that became popular with many who joined and stayed with the newly formed Association for the Advancement of Progressive Education. Like the older notion of mental discipline, reflective thinking was a formal objective rather than an objective of substance. In this strange way did the most allegedly reactionary and the most allegedly progressive views of the subjects come together. Opposed to them both was the point of view of those who maintained the necessity of learning specific subject matter for every possible task from the saving of society to the repairing of the window screens.

From all this, teachers could make their various choices. Perhaps the academically inclined among them sought most of all to share with pupils their own love for the subjects they were teaching. Tugwell's teacher who "opened windows on an antiquity we had not guessed at" must have been one of these. The literature about "great teachers" has tended at times to drown itself in sentimentality. At its best, however, and possibly even at its worst, it provides a needed corrective to the doctrine that subjects must prove themselves in relation to external aims.

Still, there was a Masten Park High School in which Tugwell's teacher could open his windows on antiquity. Like other high schools, it had been created by social action, and it was maintained by a community at substantial expense to itself. The 14,000 high schools across the land in 1920 represented a social investment of no small dimensions. Educators and general public alike must have gasped in wonder at what they had created; certainly they had every reason to ponder its value for the public welfare. Inevitably and rightly, many sought the meaning of the high school in relation to the democratic way of life. As Kingsley had pointed out in the *Cardinal Principles* report, education for democratic citizenship could no longer be comprehended by the elementary school alone. Within this context, the high school was of necessity committed to both individual and social aims.

This, of course, demanded high faith in the possibilities of man—and throughout his long career of criticizing the schools, Eliot repeatedly testified to his own personal faith not only in the general capacity of humankind, but also in the good sense and good will of its individual members. At the age of 85, he quoted James Russell Lowell's statement that democracy must produce and foster all the finest and loftiest types of human capacity, or democracy would fail. "I think it best," Eliot said on this occasion, "for us all to refuse to contemplate the possibility of that failure."[49] Here was optimism truly representative of the forty-year-long impulse behind the expansion of the high school. Throughout that campaign there had been many critics, but few pessimists.

[49] Charles W. Eliot, discussion at 28th Annual Meeting of the Harvard Teachers' Association, April 12, 1919, *School and Society* (December 20, 1919), p. 739.

Bibliographical Note

*U*npublished correspondence and memoranda of participants in the affairs of secondary education during the period 1880–1920 are available in various manuscript collections. The Charles W. Eliot Papers in the Harvard University Archives contain exchanges of letters between Eliot and other educators during the 1890's and early 1900's, dealing with such matters as the Committee of Ten, the New England Association of Colleges and Preparatory Schools, and the College Entrance Examination Board. Eliot's own letters on a variety of topics in education bring out clearly the convictions he applied to the secondary schools. In these letters are evident the qualities found in his educational articles and speeches, namely, simplicity, directness, economy in the use of words, naked honesty and frankness, and a tendency to suffer fools with something less than enthusiasm.

The John Tetlow Papers at The Houghton Library, Harvard University, include a document entitled, "The Classical and non-Classical High Schools," covering events leading to the creation of the New England Association and of the Committee of Ten. Also pertaining to these matters is a small, but valuable correspondence between Tetlow and Eliot. For those interested in criticisms of the schools, there is a lively set of letters between Tetlow and Charles Francis Adams, Jr., at that time a member of the Harvard Board of Overseers.

Two important groups of documents are housed at the Michigan Historical Collections of the University of Michigan. The James B. Angell Papers include correspondence pertaining to the Committee of Ten as well as letters from high school principals in Michigan and other midwestern states describing the circumstances and programs of their schools, some of them with printed circulars or announcements. The second group, consisting of the Records of High School Accreditation, Bureau of School Services of the University of Michigan, contains reports of visits made by faculty members to high schools and correspondence involving the accreditation of these schools. Similar records on university accreditation of high schools are to be found in the archives of the University of Wisconsin.

Located in the Labor and Transportation Branch of the Social and Economics Records Division of the National Archives are documents pertaining to Commissioner William T. Harris and to the work of the Commission on the Reorganization of Secondary Education. The Harris correspondence includes material on the Committee of Ten and on the controversy between Harris and the Herbartians over the Report of the Committee of Fifteen. There are other materials on Harris in the William T. Harris Papers in the Library of Congress. Although this vast collection is lacking, for the most part, in unpublished correspondence, it assembles manuscripts for articles and speeches published by Harris in journals not always easily obtained at the present time.

The documents in the National Archives on Kingsley's Commission are gathered under the category, "Reorganization of Secondary Education, 1915–1923." These contain correspondence between Kingsley and others on the reviewing committee, as well as with Commissioner Claxton and staff members of the Bureau of Education. Here may be found support for the opinion expressed by many in this period that the *Cardinal Principles* report was largely a creation of Kingsley himself. Of special interest is the tentative draft of the report made in the summer of 1916, containing only six of the seven aims and omitting the one on fundamental processes. Also in the collection is an early draft of the report of the committee on mathematics, along with vigorous correspondence about the evaluation of this report.

Although sparse on matters pertaining to the Committee of Ten, the Nicholas Murray Butler Papers in the Columbiana Library of Columbia University offer a variety of letters between Butler and other educators on a great range of topics, all of interest to the student of pedagogical matters in the 1890's. Among these are letters between Butler and Harris on the Herbartian controversy and on the child study movement. Other correspondents of Butler in this collection include Charles De Garmo, Elmer Ellsworth Brown, Richard H. Jesse, and Andrew F. West.

Also of use in the study of this period are the Melvil Dewey Papers, Columbia University Libraries; the Michael Vincent O'Shea Papers in the State Historical Society of Wisconsin; and the James C. Mackenzie Papers at the Lawrenceville School, New Jersey. In addition to correspondence pertaining to his work as Secretary of the New York State University Regents, the Melvil Dewey Papers contain letters from Ellen H. Richards to Mrs. Melvil Dewey on the development of home economics as a school subject. The O'Shea Papers contain much interesting material on the child study movement, including correspondence with leaders in organized child welfare, such as Mrs. Frederic Schoff of the National Congress of Mothers. Also of value in this collection are letters between O'Shea and Stanwood Cobb on the founding of the Association for the Advancement of Progressive Education. John Dewey, William C. Bagley, Milton Fairchild, Abraham Flexner, and L. W. Rapeer are among others with whom O'Shea carried on correspondence. The Mackenzie Papers contain several letters of interest from Eliot and Harris on the Committee of Ten.

Unfortunately, much of the once-extensive collection of documents at the headquarters of the National Education Association no longer exists, having deteriorated physically to the point where it could no longer be used. The remains, which have been saved and transferred to steel cabinets, include correspondence involving Henry Sabin, Irwin Shepard, H. H. Seerley, and other leaders of the NEA in the 1890's.

II

Government publications—national, state, and local—furnish not only general and routine statistics, but also reports of special studies, recommendations of school officials, and actions of various administrative bodies. The annual *Reports* of the U.S. Commissioner of Education are indispensable to the student, but require some caution in their use. Prior to 1889–1890 they are unreliable guides to the numbers of public high schools in existence.[1] Statistics on higher education in the *Reports* before 1900 are confusing and contradictory. With much patience and some guesswork, the student may extract generalizations from the mystifying and sometimes overlapping categories represented in the tables. An editorial in the *World's Work* referred to these *Reports* as the dullest books in the world and as whole thick volumes of dullness.[2] Perhaps they were saved from dullness by the tantalizing perplexities they often present to the student.

The Circulars of Information of the U.S. Bureau of Education for the period up to 1906 and the Bulletins, beginning in 1906, supply material on an almost incredible variety of pedagogical topics. Among the Bulletins on matters of interest in secondary schooling are Henry Turner Bailey, *Instruction in the Fine and Manual Arts in the United States,* 1909, No. 6; International Commission on the Teaching of Mathematics, *Mathematics in the Public and Private Secondary Schools of the United States,* 1911, No. 16; Clarence D. Kingsley, *College Entrance Requirements,* 1913, No. 7; Charles H. Handschin, *The Teaching of Modern Languages in the United States,* 1913, No. 3; Will Earhart, *Music in the Public Schools,* 1914, No. 33; C. H. Judd and G. S. Counts, *A Study of the Colleges and High Schools in the North Central Association,* 1915, No. 6; *Negro Education,* 1916, No. 38; *Vocational Secondary Education,* 1916, No. 21; Calvin O. Davis, *The Accredited Secondary Schools of the North Central Association,* 1919, No. 45; and H. P. Barrows, *Development of Agricultural Instruction in Secondary*

---

[1] There were general complaints in this period about the supposed unreliability of the Commissioner's statistics. "The statistics prepared by the National Bureau of Education," said State Superintendent Fred Dick of Colorado in 1890, "are in a degree unreliable and misleading." In discussion, NEA, 1890, p. 385. Some of this complaint was probably exaggerated. During the same meeting others said the statistical materials were being improved. Figures on public high schools in the 1880's, however, were admittedly undependable.

[2] *World's Work* (December, 1903), p. 4174.

Schools, 1919, No. 85. During the period after 1915 the Bureau conducted various surveys of local and state systems and published Bulletins on the findings: The systems surveyed include San Francisco, California, 1917, No. 46; Elyria, Ohio, 1918, No. 15; and South Dakota, 1918, No. 31. The reports of the subject committees of the Commission on the Reorganization of Secondary Education appeared as Bulletins of the U.S. Bureau, as did also the main report, *Cardinal Principles of Secondary Education,* 1918, No. 35.

Reports issued by state superintendents of education tend to emphasize attendance, financial provisions, and building construction, all of these being of value in tracing the expansion of high schools. The reports for Massachusetts beginning in 1913 supply records of the activities and utterances of Clarence D. Kingsley as State High School Inspector. In these are distinct overtones of the *Cardinal Principles* report—in some cases virtually the same language. The reports of the state superintendents of Indiana provide interesting examples of the tendency to divide and subdivide high schools into categories, with varying standards and prescriptions applied to each. In addition, the Indiana report for 1911–1912 contains a record of the action of the state board in adopting the recommendations of the NEA Committee on the Articulation of High School and College for what it called the commissioned high schools.

Almost any of the great multitude of reports of local school districts may be studied with interest and profit. Those of the St. Louis, Missouri, Public Schools in the 1880's, for example, provide data on the growth of high schools in a city system on the eve of the Committee of Ten. Of special interest are those of the Lake View Township, Illinois, High School, during the period before its merger with the Chicago system. Written by Augustus F. Nightingale in his capacity as Principal, these colorful reports not only show the characteristics of the program and the student body but also reveal the development of the man who became chairman of one of the NEA's most important committees.[3] After the merger, Nightingale served as Assistant Superintendent in Chicago, with special responsibility for high schools; his sections of the annual reports of the Chicago Board of Education through 1901 constitute a record of his attempts to apply the elective principle to a large city system. Another document of interest along these lines is the statement of Superintendent E. P. Seaver of Boston in the annual report of the School Committee for 1901, showing one of the most extreme applications of election by subjects.

Much additional material on local schools and school districts is to be found in numerous articles in the journals; in reports made to the NEA and other associations; and for the period from 1910 to 1920, in reports of

---

[3] A set of these is available at the Ravenswood–Lake View Historical Association (Frederick H. Hild Regional Library, Chicago).

surveys, such as the widely praised Portland, Oregon, survey published by Ellwood Cubberley and his associates in 1913, entitled *Report of the Survey of the Public School System of School District No. 1, Multnomah County, Oregon.*

III

By any means of calculation, the greatest torrent of recorded words on education in this period came from the NEA and from the regional, state, and local associations. The annual volumes of the *Addresses and Proceedings* of the NEA contain not only the speeches made to the general sessions and to the various departments, but also, in many cases, the discussions as well. Sometimes the discussions consisted solely of short papers prepared in advance and given at the conclusion of a speech, but at other times they included the give-and-take of vigorous differences of opinion. In any case, what was recorded seemed to depend on the characteristics of the secretary and the policy of those responsible for editing the volumes in given years.[4] The main difficulty is that they were edited, and it is impossible to guess in many instances what may have been left out. There are mysterious references throughout to apparently important items that did not get into the published volumes at all. In some cases, omission may have been deliberate. This was perhaps what happened to Nightingale's peppery criticism of the Committee of Ten at the Richmond meeting of the Department of School Superintendence in 1894. Actions taken by the various NEA departments are sometimes difficult to interpret or even to follow. Particularly confusing is the sequence of events in the National Council leading to the creation of the Committee of Ten.[5]

[4] "Every effort," said Secretary Irwin Shepard in 1901, "has been made in editing the volume to exclude useless material, to secure the abridgement of papers and discussions of excessive length, and to limit the matter as far as consistent with a fair representation of the valuable papers and discussions presented in the general sessions and the eighteen departments now organized." First Annual Report of the Permanent Secretary to the Board of Trustees, NEA, 1901, p. 47. William T. Harris complained bitterly about the editing done by N. A. Calkins on the *Proceedings* of 1893, the International Congress of Education. Harris to Calkins, May 22, 1894, and Harris to Butler, May 31, 1894, plus other correspondence in the Nicholas Murray Butler Papers (Columbia University, New York).

[5] Beyond the matter of editing, there was the question about the accuracy of the stenographic reports. In some cases these were checked by the people who had given the addresses or had taken part in the discussions. According to James M. Greenwood in 1914, the National Council had taken great pains along these lines. "History and Achievement of the National Council of Education," NEA, 1914, pp. 366–367. The difficulty with the proceedings of the National Council for 1892 lies not in the addresses, but in the haphazard reporting of the events. Eliot apparently was sensitive to the possibility of error in the reporting of his speeches

The reports of major NEA committees constitute the basic documentary literature of national policy on secondary schooling in the period 1880–1920. Essential in any consideration of the subject are the *Report of the Committee of Ten on Secondary School Studies,* issued first by Harris through the U.S. Bureau of Education and quickly reprinted with an analytical index by the American Book Company, 1894; the *Report of the Committee of Fifteen on Elementary Education,* also published for the NEA by the American Book Company, 1895; the *Report of Committee on College-Entrance Requirements,* published by the Association itself, 1899; the *Report of the Committee of the National Council of Education on Economy of Time in Education,* published by the U.S. Bureau of Education in its Bulletin series, 1913, No. 38; the "Report of the Committee of Nine on the Articulation of High School and College," published by the NEA in its *Addresses and Proceedings* of 1911, pp. 559–567; and the reports of the Commission on the Reorganization of Secondary Education published as Bulletins of the U.S. Bureau of Education.

In the published proceedings of the regional associations of colleges and secondary schools may be traced some of the most important developments in secondary schooling throughout the four decades of this study. All these associations—New England, Middle States and Maryland, North Central, and Southern—published their own proceedings. In addition, those of the New England Association appear in the *Academy* (1888–1891), *School and College* (1892), and the *School Review* (1893–1902). The Association of Colleges and Preparatory Schools of the Middle States and Maryland was preceded by the College Association of Pennsylvania (1887–1888) and the College Association of the Middle States and Maryland (1889–1892). The other regional associations had no parent organizations as such, although the initiative to form the New England Association came from the Classical and High School Teachers' Association of Massachusetts, as did that of the North Central from the Michigan Schoolmasters' Club.

Proceedings and reports of state teachers associations were in some cases published by the associations in separate volumes. Otherwise they appeared in the journals of the associations or in independent journals. The *Ohio Educational Monthly,* although independently owned, was identified as the

---

and on one occasion elicited a somewhat anguished letter on this subject from Ray Greene Huling, secretary of the New England Association. Huling said that the work of various stenographers, including some with experience as reporters of the Rhode Island and Connecticut Supreme Courts, had turned out to be unsatisfactory. The reporting of meetings, concluded Huling, was a difficult task. Ray Greene Huling to Charles W. Eliot, November 6, 1896, Charles W. Eliot Papers (Harvard University Archives, Cambridge, Mass.). Huling's letter, however, made it clear that some of the speakers at the New England Association had the opportunity to check the stenographic reports before publication.

organ of the Ohio State Teachers' Association and published the proceedings of that group. The *Pennsylvania School Journal* was identified as the organ both of the Pennsylvania State Teachers' Association and the Department of Public Instruction. Although the *Journal of Education* had no official status, it carried the proceedings of the Massachusetts State Teachers' Association and of the Classical and High School Teachers' Association of that state. The *Academy* was founded by the Associated Academic Principals of the State of New York and published the proceedings of that organization through 1891.

One of the most active and enterprising local groups was the High School Teachers Association of New York City. From this group came the impulse that led to the NEA Committee on the Articulation of High School and College and ultimately to the Commission on the Reorganization of Secondary Education. The yearbooks of this group from 1906–1907 through 1910–1911 carry the record of Kingsley's leadership in several projects, including one on the planning of new high schools in Brooklyn.

In addition to these general organizations of teachers, the American pedagogical scene abounded in a variety of boards, foundations, commissions, and societies, more specialized in function, but often national in scope. The yearbooks of the National Herbart Society for the Scientific Study of Teaching (1895–1898) contain speeches and articles which, although characterized by William T. Harris as "a dreary sort of stuff," reflect the concerns and interests of the Herbartians themselves, as well as those of some of the people involved in child study. Its successor organization, the National Society for the Scientific Study of Education, addressed itself to a broader range of topics and began in 1901 to publish its long-sustained series of yearbooks. The *Fourteenth Yearbook,* Part I, published in 1915, carried the first report of the Committee on the Economy of Time in Education of the Department of School Superintendence. Like the subsequent reports of this Committee, appearing in the yearbooks of 1917, 1918, and 1919, respectively, this was a far more "dreary sort of stuff" than the papers of the National Herbart Society, but it served as an important reflector of one aspect of scientific management in the period following 1910.

The College Entrance Examination Board began issuing annual reports in 1901. These were independently published, but for the period through 1908 appeared also in Butler's *Educational Review.* Digests of these reports were included in *The Work of the College Entrance Examination Board 1901–1925,* published by the Board in 1926.

In the annual reports of the President of the Carnegie Foundation for the Advancement of Teaching in the period 1906 through 1911 may be seen the efforts of that organization to define the boundary between the high school and the college, with material on development of the unit, known inaccurately but controversially as the Carnegie unit. Another important publication of the Foundation was its Bulletin No. 7, 1914, *A Study of Education in Vermont,* with Chapter 4 devoted to the secondary schools of that state.

Indispensable in the study of the vocational education movement are the proceedings of the National Society for the Promotion of Industrial Education, beginning with Bulletin No. 1 in 1907 on the organization meeting held in November, 1906, and its special studies and bulletins. The same may be said of the Report of the Massachusetts Commission on Industrial and Technical Education (the Douglas Commission) published in 1906, containing not only the general conclusions of the Commission but also the special paper by Susan M. Kingsbury on the relation of children to industries. Its successor, the Massachusetts Commission on Industrial Education, with Paul Hanus as Chairman, issued annual reports in 1907 and 1908. Also of importance on this topic are the reports of the Committee on Industrial Education of the National Association of Manufacturers for 1909, 1910, and 1911, included in the published proceedings of the Association for those years. The point of view of the American Federation of Labor may be found in the proceedings of that organization. Its publication in 1939 of *Labor and Education* made available in convenient form the resolutions and actions of the Federation on industrial education and other pedagogical topics as far back as 1881, with the period from 1908 to 1917 being of special interest in this study.

Also engaged from time to time in matters pertaining to secondary education were the American Philological Association, with the report of its Committee of Twelve included in the NEA *Report of Committee on College-Entrance Requirements* in 1899; the American Historical Association, with the report of its Committee of Seven published independently as well as part of the NEA 1899 *Report,* and that of its Committee on History and Education for Citizenship in the Schools presented in the annual report for the year 1920, pp. 91–93; the American Political Science Association, Committee on Instruction, *The Teaching of Government,* published by the Macmillan Company, 1916; the Mathematical Association of America, with the publication of *The Reorganization of Mathematics in Secondary Education* as Bulletin, 1921, No. 32, of the U.S. Bureau of Education; and the American Sociological Society, with the report of its Committee on Teaching of Sociology in the Grade and High Schools of America, included in Volume XIV of the *Publications of the Society,* 1919, pp. 243–251.

IV

Pedagogical journals in the period under study were hard-hitting, controversial, and uninhibited. Crammed with articles on every level of thought, provocative editorials, acrimonious exchanges of correspondence, appraisals of competing journals, book reviews, and frank expressions about the NEA and other associations, the journals spread before the reader a vivid panorama of thought and action pertaining to the schools. This was a period of wide-open journalism, and the educational magazines did not fall far behind the model set by newspapers and some of the popular periodicals.

The *Journal of Education*, the *School Journal,* and the *American Journal of Education* were well established by 1880. During the 1890's and later, A. E. Winship developed the *Journal of Education* as the gadfly of prominent educators and committees. His were perhaps the most caustic of the many uncomplimentary expressions about the Committee of Ten. On the other hand, he virtually idolized William T. Harris, and his goading of the Herbartians may have had much to do with the intensity of the controversy about the report on correlation of the Committee of Fifteen. Ossian Lang's editorship of the *School Journal,* while national in coverage, was marked by special attention after 1900 to the development of social services through the New York City Public Schools. The *American Journal of Education* warmly defended the Committee of Ten, but shared with the *Journal of Education* its unbounded admiration of William T. Harris. It aroused strong feelings in some quarters, the editor of the *Ohio Educational Monthly* charging it with two marked characteristics, "self-laudation" and "harsh and unkind criticism of others."[6]

The first of the new journals in the period of this study was *Education*, founded by Thomas W. Bicknell in 1880. After his spectacular triumph with the NEA convention at Madison, Wisconsin, in 1884, Bicknell turned over the editorship of *Education* to William A. Mowry, who left it to become Superintendent of the Salem, Massachusetts, Public Schools in 1891. Among the editors after that period were Frank Kasson, Frank Palmer, and Richard G. Boone.

In contrast to *Education* with its rapid changes in editorship, *Educational Review* enjoyed the continuous services of Nicholas Murray Butler through 58 semiannual volumes from 1891 to 1919. At the beginning, however, Butler shared the editorship with William H. Maxwell, Addison B. Poland, and E. H. Cook. *Educational Review* provided Butler a medium for the expression of his many strongly held views; it also brought down upon his head the thunderbolts of competitors, particularly Winship, for his alleged attempt to gain exclusive rights to the publication of the *Report of the Committee of Fifteen*. After 1905 Butler used his journal as a means of attacking the leadership of the NEA. In the midst of his many pressing duties as President of Columbia University after 1901, Butler continued to give close personal attention to the journal and to take pride in it as one of his major

[6] *Ohio Educational Monthly* (January, 1891), p. 33.

accomplishments. At all times, Butler opened the *Review* to articles expressing points of view quite in conflict with his own.

Emerging from its precedecessors, the *Academy* (1886–1891) and *School and College* (1892), the *School Review* announced itself in January, 1893, as "a journal of secondary education." In the period 1893–1906, it was probably the most informative of all the journals on matters specifically pertaining to high schools. The January, 1906, number, however, announced that while it would continue to emphasize secondary education, it would broaden its scope to include other matters as well. Charles H. Thurber and George Herbert Locke had successively, and for part of the time concurrently, carried the editorship during that period, after which it was assumed by a board of editors in the Department of Philosophy and Education of the University of Chicago, with associate editors from other universities.

The year 1915 marked the appearance of *Educational Administration and Supervision* and *School and Society*. An offspring of the movement for social efficiency, the first of these contained articles largely, but not exclusively, representative of this point of view. Charles Hughes Johnston of the University of Illinois was managing editor, serving with three associates, David Snedden, L. D. Coffman, and James H. Van Sickle. All of these except Van Sickle were disciples of social efficiency, as were also Bobbitt, Cubberley, C. O. Davis, William McAndrew, E. C. Moore, H. C. Morrison, Jesse Newlon, Charles A. Prosser, Frank Spaulding, and G. D. Strayer in the group of collaborating editors. Johnston provided brilliant editorship, and the journal proved to be an admirable medium for the ideology represented and expressed.

School and Society dealt with a broader range of educational topics and carried articles by a variety of authors representing many views and interests. Editor James McKeen Cattell did not allow his dismissal from the faculty of Columbia University to dominate or distort his policies for the magazine. The extensive coverage of news items on education and the practice of reproducing editorials from newspapers make *School and Society* one of the most useful sources for students of this period.

Other pedagogical journals containing material on secondary education and related topics were the *American School Board Journal, Intelligence and the Schoolmaster: a Journal of Education, Pedagogical Seminary*, the *Public-School Journal*, and the *Journal of Pedagogy*. The very end of the period covered in this study witnessed the appearance of the *Junior High School Clearing House*, founded by Principal S. O. Rorem of the East Junior High School, Sioux City, Iowa. There were, in addition, many and varied regional and state journals dealing with education. Among those with items of interest on secondary schools were the *Ohio Educational Monthly*, the *Pennsylvania School Journal*, and the *Educator-Journal* (Indiana).

Reference material on journals is provided in Sheldon Emmor Davis'

Educational Periodicals during the Nineteenth Century, Bureau of Education Bulletin, 1919, No. 28. The appendix contains lists of periodicals founded before 1876, of the more important ones founded between 1876 and 1900, and of the ones in publication in May, 1917. The student will also profit by consulting Frank Luther Mott, *A History of American Magazines: 1885–1905*, Harvard University Press, 1957, pp. 267–273.

Among the general magazines that carried articles from time to time on matters pertaining to secondary schools were the *Arena*, the *Atlantic Monthly*, the *Dial*, the *Forum*, the *New Republic*, the *North American Review*, the *Outlook*, the *Survey*, and the *World's Work*.

V

Books written on secondary education and related matters throughout this period serve as indicators of the thinking of those who wrote them, and, in some cases, of the schools of thought these authors represented or reflected. Among these were books on the developing social emphasis, dealing with social service or social control or both. In Chapters 13 and 14 of his *Dynamic Sociology*, Appleton-Century Crofts, 1883, Lester Frank Ward set forth his views on schools as agencies for the distribution of knowledge, extending this in his *Applied Sociology*, Ginn and Company, 1906, to a criticism of formal objectives and the work of the Committee of Ten. His disciple, Edward A. Ross, went further with Ward's ideas in his *Social Control*, the Macmillan Company, 1901, particularly in Chapter 14 on education as social suggestion. More from the point of view of education as social service, Samuel Train Dutton's *Social Phases of Education in the School and the Home*, the Macmillan Company, 1899, not only appeared in the same year as John Dewey's *The School and Society*, but also expressed views similar to the ones in that more famous publication.

The social emphasis was continued in Michael Vincent O'Shea's *Education as Adjustment*, Longmans, Green & Company, 1903; William C. Bagley's *The Educative Process*, the Macmillan Company, 1905; David Snedden's *Administration and Educational Work of American Juvenile Reform Schools*, Faculty of Philosophy, Columbia University, 1907; Colin A. Scott's *Social Education*, Ginn and Company, 1908; Irving King's *Education for Social Efficiency*, Appleton-Century-Crofts, 1913; Randolph Bourne's *Education and Living*, the Century Company, 1917; and David Snedden's *Sociological Determination of Objectives in Education*, J. B. Lippincott Company, 1921.

Books in this period dealing specifically with high schools included Paul Hanus' *Educational Aims and Educational Values*, the Macmillan Company, 1900; Charles De Garmo's *Principles of Secondary Education, a Text-Book: The Studies*, the Macmillan Company, 1907; John Franklin Brown's

The American High School, the Macmillan Company, 1909; Julius Sachs' *The American Secondary School and Some of its Problems,* the Macmillan Company, 1912; William D. Lewis's *Democracy's High School,* Houghton Mifflin Company, 1914; John Elbert Stout's *The High School,* D. C. Heath and Co., 1914; David Snedden's *Problems of Secondary Education,* Houghton Mifflin Company, 1917; and Alexander Inglis' *Principles of Secondary Education,* Houghton Mifflin Company, 1918. Three important books in the nature of symposia were *High School Education,* Charles Scribner's Sons, 1912, edited by Charles Hughes Johnston; *The Modern High School,* Charles Scribner's Sons, 1914, also edited by Johnston; and *Principles of Secondary Education,* the Macmillan Company, 1914, edited by Paul Monroe.

The numerous utterances of Charles W. Eliot and Nicholas Murray Butler appeared in a great variety of journals, proceedings, and reports. Some of Eliot's most important statements have been collected in his *Educational Reform,* the Century Company, 1898, and *A Late Harvest,* Little, Brown and Company, 1924; in *Charles W. Eliot: The Man and His Beliefs,* Harper & Row, 1926, edited by William Allan Neilson; and in *Charles W. Eliot and Popular Education,* Classics in Education No. 8, Teachers College, Bureau of Publications, Columbia University, 1961, edited by Edward A. Krug. In *The Meaning of Education,* Charles Scribner's Sons, 1915, Nicholas Murray Butler assembled and published a collection of his previously written articles and addresses.

Autobiographies of participants in this period include *Charles Francis Adams 1835–1915: An Autobiography,* Houghton Mifflin Company, 1916; James Burrill Angell, *Reminiscences,* Longmans, Green & Company, 1912; Nicholas Murray Butler, *Across the Busy Years,* Charles Scribner's Sons, 1919; Jesse Buttrick Davis' *The Saga of a Schoolmaster,* Boston University Press, 1956; Abraham Flexner's *I Remember,* Simon and Schuster, 1940, and *An Autobiography,* Simon and Schuster, 1960; G. Stanley Hall's *Life and Confessions of a Psychologist,* Appleton-Century Crofts, 1923; Paul Hanus' *Adventuring in Education,* Harvard University Press, 1937; William A. Mowry's *Recollections of a New England Educator 1838–1908,* Silver Burdett Company, 1908; and David Snedden's *Recollections of Over Half a Century Spent in Educational Work,* privately printed, 1949.

Memories of their own schooling are often included in the autobiographies of those who were not in this period directly engaged in the work of secondary education. Mary Antin's *The Promised Land,* Houghton Mifflin Company, 1912, provides a sympathetic portrayal of the work at the Boston Girls' Latin School and of its Principal, John Tetlow. Henry Seidel Canby's *The Age of Confidence,* Farrar & Rinehart, Incorporated, 1934, contains acid comments on the work of the academy he attended in the 1890's. Raymond B. Fosdick, in *Chronicle of a Generation,* Harper & How, 1958, and Rexford Guy Tugwell, *The Light of Other Days*, Doubleday & Company, Incorporated, 1962, write with appreciation of their work at the Masten Park High School, Buffalo, New York, although Tugwell adds some general criticism of schooling in that period. In his *More Lives Than One*, William Sloane Associates, 1962, Joseph Wood Krutch recalls his high school days in Knoxville, Tennessee. Her high school work in Newton, Massachusetts, as well as her teaching at Somerville High School in that state before she entered social work are mentioned by Mary Kingsbury Simkhovitch in *Neighborhood: My Story of Greenwich House*, W. W. Norton & Company, Incorporated, 1938. The *Autobiography of Upton Sinclair*, Harcourt, Brace & World, Incorporated, 1962, contains the author's recollection of the secondary school work in the City College of New York in the 1890's.

Biographies of leading educators in this period contain much interesting material not only on the people themselves, but also on the contexts in which they lived and worked. Shirley W. Smith's *James Burrill Angell: an American Influence*, University of Michigan Press, 1954, says relatively little about high schools, but provides a full account of Angell's career in university administration and in diplomacy. I. L. Kandel's *William Chandler Bagley: Stalwart Educator*, Bureau of Publications, Teachers College, Columbia University, 1961, includes material on Bagley's early career as well as on his later work in the essentialist movement. An excellent account of the pedagogical career of Nicholas Murray Butler is available in Richard F. W. Whittemore, *Nicholas Murray Butler and Public Education 1862–1911*, doctoral dissertation, Columbia University, 1962. A broad overview of many aspects of American education, made possible by the varied activities of his subject, is provided by Charles Lee Lewis in *Philander Priestly Claxton: Crusader for Public Education*, University of Tennessee Press, 1948. A sympathetic presentation of the career of Ellwood Cubberley is offered in *Cubberley of Stanford* by Jesse B. Sears and Adin D. Henderson, Stanford University Press, 1957. In *Samuel Train Dutton: A Biography*, the Macmillan Company, 1922, Charles Herbert Levermore presents a substantial treatment of Dutton's own schooling, his work as a schoolmaster at New Haven and Brookline, his part in the movement for social service through the schools, his career at Teachers College, Columbia, and his participation in the movement for international peace. Kurt E. Leidecker's *Yankee Schoolmaster: the Life of William Torrey Harris*, the Philosophical Library, 1946, portrays Harris in his larger role as philosopher and scholar, but says relatively little about his work with the Committees of Ten and Fifteen.

Donald M. Love's *Henry Churchill King of Oberlin*, Yale University Press, 1956, covers many aspects of King's work, but presents a confusing and somewhat inaccurate report of the events surrounding the Committee of Ten. *Chancellor Kirkland of Vanderbilt*, by Edwin Mims, Vanderbilt University Press, 1940, contains an excellent account of the formation and the work of the Southern Association. There is a good biographical sketch of George Henry Martin, Chairman of the Douglas Commission, in *Essentials of Education,* edited by Joseph Asbury Pitman, Richard G. Badger, 1932. John T. McManis' laudatory *Ella Flagg Young and a Half-Century of the Chicago Public Schools* contains much interesting material on this controversial superintendent and people with whom she was associated.

Merle Curti's *The Social Ideas of American Educators,* Charles Scribner's Sons, 1935, offers lively and challenging sketches and interpretations of Harris, Parker, Hall, Thorndike, and Dewey. Additional interesting material on Parker is included in Robert Eugene Tostberg's *Educational Ferment in Chicago, 1883–1904,* doctoral dissertation, University of Wisconsin, 1960. There are substantial articles in the *Dictionary of American Biography* on Angell, Elmer Ellsworth Brown, Eliot, Harris, Jesse, King, Taylor, and Mackenzie. A biographical sketch of Clarence Kingsley appears in Volume XX of the *National Cyclopaedia of American Biography.*

The major biography of Eliot, *Charles W. Eliot: President of Harvard University 1869–1909,* by Henry James, Houghton Mifflin Company, 1930, contains many excerpts from correspondence and is rich in fascinating anecdotes, but says little about Eliot's work in public schools. A fuller account of this aspect of Eliot's career is presented by Edward H. Cotton, *The Life of Charles W. Eliot,* Small, Maynard & Company, 1926. An interesting sketch of Eliot as well as other Harvard personalities appears in Rollo Walter Brown's *Harvard Yard in the Golden Age,* Current Books, Incorporated, 1948. Eugen Kuehnemann's *Charles W. Eliot,* Houghton Mifflin Company, 1909, presents a favorable appraisal of Eliot from the point of view of a German educator who had taught as an exchange professor at Harvard. Perhaps the most unfavorable comment on Eliot's ideas was that offered by Irving Babbitt, "President Eliot and American Education," the *Forum,* January, 1929, pp. 1–10.

The standard work on the earlier development of American secondary education is Elmer Ellsworth Brown's *The Making of Our Middle Schools,* Longmans, Green and Company, 1902. With its emphasis on the period before 1890, this book is rich in material on grammar schools and academies. John Elbert Stout's *The Development of High-School Curricula in the North Central States from 1860 to 1918,* the University of Chicago Press, 1921, presents courses of study and subject offerings for the period and the region indicated. Walter S. Monroe and M. E. Herriott give brief overviews of broad trends in the high school curriculum in their *Reconstruction of the Secondary School Curriculum: Its Meaning and Trends,* Bureau of Educational Research, Bulletin No. 41, University of Illinois, 1928. They are mildly critical of the Committee of Ten and favorable to the *Cardinal Principles* report. Interesting and provocative analyses of enrollment data from the Commissioner's *Reports* are provided in John Francis Latimer's *What's Happened to Our High Schools?* Public Affairs Press, 1958, along with favorable interpretation of work of the Committee of Ten. For an interpretation of American secondary education in relation to anti-intellectualism see Richard Hofstadter, *Anti-Intellectualism in American Life,* Alfred A. Knopf, 1963, pp. 325–358.

Accounts of the Committee of Ten and other major NEA committees appear in Mildred Sandison Fenner's *The National Education Association 1892–1942,* doctoral dissertation, George Washington University, 1942. Edgar B. Wesley's *NEA: The First Hundred Years,* Harper & Row, 1957, presents a colorful account of that organization, particularly of the convention at Madison, Wisconsin, in 1884. It offers the conventional interpretation of the Committee of Ten as an agency of college domination and tends on the whole to view the school as a victim of the college. Further accounts of the NEA committees are available in Gordon M. Seely, Jr., *Investigation Committees of The National Education Association: A History of the Years 1892–1918,* doctoral dissertation, Stanford University, 1963, and Gladys A. Wiggin, *Education and Nationalism: An Historical Interpretation of American Education,* McGraw-Hill, 1962, pp. 153–198. Specialized treatments of the Committee of Ten and controversies related to it are provided in two recent doctoral studies, Bernard Mehl's *The High School at the Turn of the Century,* University of Illinois, 1954, and Theodore Sizer's *The Committee of Ten,* Harvard University, 1961. Noah Gayle Simmons' *The Emerging Design for the Comprehensive High School,* doctoral dissertation, Washington University, 1960, is comparable in scope and treatment for the Commission on the Reorganization of Secondary Education.

Relationships between high schools and colleges and the development of regional associations are covered by Edward Cornelius Broome, *A Historical and Critical Discussion of College Admission Requirements,* the Macmillan Company, 1903; Claude M. Fuess, *The College Board: Its First Fifty Years,* Columbia University Press, 1950; Edwin Fred Mengersen, *The Quantitative Standardization of Secondary Education, 1890–1910,* doctoral dissertation, Washington University, 1959; William K. Selden, *Accreditation: a Struggle over Standards in Higher Education,* Harper & Row, 1960; and Calvin O. Davis, *A History of the North Central Association of Colleges and Secondary Schools 1895–1945,* the Association, 1945.

Among useful historical accounts of given instructional fields in the school program are Jessie Graham's *The Evolution of Business Education in the United States and Its Implications for Business-Teacher Education,* University of Southern California Press, 1933; Edna Hays's *College Entrance Requirements in English: Their Effects on the High Schools, an Historical Survey,* Bureau of Publications, Teachers College, Columbia University, 1936; Paul DeHart Hurd's *Biological Education in American Secondary Schools 1890–1960,* American Institute of Biological Sciences, 1961; Solberg Einar

Sigurdson's *The Development of the Idea of Unified Mathematics in the Secondary School Curriculum, 1890–1930,* doctoral dissertation, University of Wisconsin, 1962; and Rolla M. Tryon's *The Social Sciences as School Subjects,* Charles Scribner's Sons, 1935.

Some of the movements and forces directly and indirectly affecting secondary schooling in this period have become objects of special inquiry in recent studies. Raymond E. Callahan's *Education and the Cult of Efficiency,* the University of Chicago Press, 1962, describes the ideology of scientific management in relation to budgets, personnel, school buildings, and supervision. Lawrence A. Cremin's *The Transformation of the School,* Alfred A. Knopf, 1961, presents the social and intellectual forces behind progressive education, broadly defined. Morris Isaiah Berger's *The Settlement, the Immigrant and the Public School,* doctoral dissertation, Columbia University, 1956, sets forth a challenging expression of the idea that the social-settlement movement was a major cause of changes in doctrine and practice of the public schools. A useful overview of social work, as identified in the discussions and actions of the National Conference of Social Work, is provided in Frank J. Bruno's *Trends in Social Work 1874–1956,* Columbia University, second edition, 1957. Robert Ripley Clough's *National Society for the Promotion of Industrial Education: Case History of a Reform Organization, 1906–1917,* master's thesis, University of Wisconsin, 1957, describes the activities of that purposeful and aggressive organization. Psychological theories in relation to educational doctrines are treated in Sherwood Augur's *E. L. Thorndike's Educational Psychology and the American Educational Program of the Period 1890–1915,* doctoral dissertation, University of Michigan, 1961, and in Geraldine M. Joncich's *Psychology and the Science of Education: Selected Writings of Edward L. Thorndike,* Classics in Education No. 12, Teachers College, Columbia University, 1962. New interpretations of the psychological and social doctrines of G. Stanley Hall appear in Charles O. Burgess' *The Educational State in America: Selected Views on Learning As the Key to Utopia, 1800–1924* and Charles E. Strickland's *The Child and the Race: Theories of Culture Epochs and Recapitulation in the Rise of the Child-Centered Ideal in American Educational Thought, 1870–1900;* both of these are doctoral dissertations, University of Wisconsin, 1962. An overview of the child study movement is provided in Wilbur H. Dutton's *The Child-Study Movement in America from its Origin (1880) to the Organization of the Progressive Education Association (1920),* doctoral dissertation, Stanford University, 1945.

Because of the broad range of activities engaged in by the organization it describes, Leslie A. Butler's *The Michigan Schoolmasters' Club: a Story of the First Seven Decades, 1886–1957,* University of Michigan, 1958, serves also as general treatment of secondary schooling in that state. A substantial portion of Calvin O. Davis' *Public Secondary Education,* Rand McNally &

Company, 1917, is also devoted to Michigan. Other state histories include Clarence Ray Aurner's *History of Education in Iowa,* Volume III, the State Historical Society of Iowa, 1915; Richard G. Boone's *History of Education in Indiana,* Appleton-Century-Crofts, 1892; Walter John Gifford's *Historical Development of the New York State High School System,* Faculty of Philosophy, Columbia University, 1922; Alexander J. Inglis's *The Rise of the High School in Massachusetts,* Teachers College, Columbia University, Contributions to Education No. 45, 1911; and James Mulhern, *A History of Secondary Education in Pennsylvania,* Science Press Printing Company, Lancaster, Pennsylvania, 1933.

Among histories of local schools and school systems are John Wesley Bell's *The Development of the Public High School in Chicago,* University of Chicago Libraries, 1939; Charles W. Blessing's *Albany Schools and Colleges Yesterday and Today,* Fort Orange Press, Incorporated, Albany N.Y., 1936, with material on Oscar D. Robinson, member of the Committee of Ten; Hannah B. Clark's *The Public Schools of Chicago: a Sociological Study,* the University of Chicago Press, 1897; Franklin Spencer Edmonds' *History of the Central High School of Philadelphia,* J. B. Lippincott Company, 1902; Richard Walden Hale, Jr., *Tercentenary History of the Roxbury Latin School 1645–1945,* Riverside Press, 1946, with material on William C. Collar, one of the founders of the New England Association; Gladys A. Midura's *A Critical History of Public Secondary Education in Springfield, Massachusetts,* doctoral dissertation, University of Connecticut, 1961; Pauline Holmes, *A Tercentenary History of the Boston Public Latin School 1635–1935,* Harvard University Press, 1935; Olive B. White's *Centennial History of the Girls' High School of Boston,* the Samuel Eliot Memorial Association of the Girls' High School, 1952; and Lucy R. Woods's *A History of the Girls' High School of Boston 1852–1902,* Riverside Press, 1904. Both volumes on the Girls' High School contain material on John Tetlow.

VI

In addition to the *List of Publications of the United States Bureau of Education 1867–1907,* Bulletin, 1908, No. 2, and *Index to the Reports of the Commissioner of Education: 1867–1907,* Bulletin, 1909, No. 7, the Bureau issued general bibliographies of education for the years 1907 through 1910–1911 as well as specialized bibliographies such as those covering child study for 1908–1909 and 1910–1911 and the *Bibliography of the Relation of Secondary Schools to Higher Education,* Bulletin, 1914, No. 32. Publications of the Bureau for the period after 1910 are itemized in Bulletin, 1937, No. 22, *List of Publications of the Office of Education, 1910–1936 Including Those of the Former Federal Board for Vocational Education from 1917–1933.*

Other bibliographies for portions of this period include "References on the Report of the Committee of Ten," *School Review*, November, 1894, pp. 558–561; Elmer E. Brown's "The History of Secondary Education in the United States—Bibliography," *School Review*, February, 1897, pp. 59–66, and March, 1897, pp. 139–147; Isaac B. Burgess' "A Selective Bibliography for Use in Framing Classical Programmes for Secondary Schools," *School Review*, November, 1897, pp. 625–635; Will S. Monroe's *Bibliography of Education*, Appleton-Century-Crofts, 1897; Henry Ridgely Evans's "A list of the Writings of William Torrey Harris," Commissioner's *Report for the Year Ending June 30, 1907*, pp. 37–73; Louis N. Wilson's "Bibliography of the Published Writings of G. Stanley Hall: 1866–1924," *Biographical Memoir*, National Academy of Sciences, Volume XII, 1929; and Milton H. Thomas's *A Bibliography of John Dewey, 1882–1939*, Columbia University Press, 1939.

Index

Abbott, Augustus Nightingale, 139 n.
Abelson, Joseph, 327 n.
"Academicians" vs. "educationists," 297, 318 n., 352–353
Academies, 3–5, 7
Academy, 8, 19, 183, 454, 458
Accreditation, 151–163, 463
Activity analysis, 310
Adams, Charles Francis, Jr., 9, 32–33, 96, 449, 460
Adams, Charles Kendall, 53, 134, 163
Adams, H. C., 15 n.
Addams, Jane, 223, 229, 419
Adolescence, 116–121, 332, 381
Adolescence, 120–121
Adrian (Mich.) High School, 13
Agriculture, study of, 217–218, 376, 416
Aims, 176, 339, 341, 365–366, 374, 380, 383, 389, 445–447
    of mental discipline, 21, 22–23, 57, 63, 87, 203–208, 313–314, 343, 445–447
    moral, 99, 311–312, 388
    scientific determination of, 307–314
    seven, in *Cardinal Principles of Secondary Education*, 381, 387–388, 390
    social, 213–214, 249–260, 274–283, 307–314, 330, 332–333, 355–356, 360, 370–371, 448
    substantive, 99, 102, 203–204, 208
    vocational, 199–201, 219, 225–227, 241–243
Aiton, George B., 137, 153
Albany (N. Y.) Public Schools, 465
Aldrich, F. R., 290 n.
Alexander, Magnus W., 420
Aley, Robert J., 408, 409 n.
Altgeld, John Peter, 210

American Federation of Labor, 235, 247, 456
American Historical Association, 336, 355
    Committee of Five, 353
    Committee of Seven, 140–141, 353, 356 n., 456
    Committee on History and Education for Citizenship in the Schools, 358–360
American Institute of Instruction, 76, 85, 259, 308
American Journal of Education, 71, 103, 457
American Philological Association, Committee of Twelve, 81–83, 139–140, 141, 456
American Political Science Association, 355, 358, 456
American School Board Journal, 458
American Social Science Association, 108
American Sociological Society, Committee on Teaching of Sociology in the Grade and High Schools of America, 358–360, 456
Americanization, campaign for, 417–419
Anarchism, 10, 210
Angell, James B., 4, 34 n., 134, 151, 152, 449, 460, 461, 462
    member of the Committee of Ten, 38, 40–41, 43, 55, 56 n., 57, 58 n.
Angell, James Rowland, 442
Antiacademic tendencies, 278–283, 307–310, 314–316
Anti-intellectualism, 282, 385, 463
Antin, Mary, 429, 460
Arena, 269–270, 459

Arithmetic, 20, 90, 94, 306–307
Armstrong, J. E., 327 n.
Art, 317–318, 440
Associated Academic Principals of the State of New York, 8, 309, 330, 362, 455
Association for the Advancement of Progressive Education, 282, 433–438, 446, 450
Association of Colleges and Preparatory Schools of the Middle States and Maryland, 41, 89, 127–129, 158–159, 363, 454
founding of the College Entrance and Examination Board, 148–150
Association of Colleges and Preparatory Schools of the Southern States, 127, 129–133, 158, 160, 461–462
Association of Colleges of New England, 147
Association of Collegiate Alumnae, 272
Atherton, George W., 127
Atkinson, Fred W., 117–118, 188
Atlantic Monthly, 121, 343, 459
Atwood, Mrs. Clarence L., 444 n.
Augur, Sherwood, 464
Aurner, Clarence Ray, 465
Autobiographies, 460–461
Averill, Lawrence A., 323 n.
Avery, Lewis B., 283

Babbitt, Irving, 462
Bacheler, A. W., 179
Bachelor of Arts, degree of, 29, 344 n.
Bachelor of Philosophy, degree of, 29
Bachelor of Science, degree of, 29
Bachman, Frank B., 238 n.
Bacon, George A., 8
Bagley, William C., 274, 282, 308, 317, 329, 332, 391, 393, 450, 459, 461
Baker, James H., 18, 27, 29, 32, 33, 123, 144, 153, 196–197, 297
Chairman of Committee on Economy of Time in Education (National Council of Education), 166–168
member of the Committee of Ten, 40–41, 43, 57, 74–76, 78
rôle in creation of the Committee of Ten, 35–38
Balliet, Thomas M., 218, 270

Ballou, Frank S., 325 n.
Barber, Fred, 369
Bardeen, C. W., 105
Barnes, Earl, 110–111
Barnum, Mrs. O. Shepard, 273
Barrett, H. M., 296
Barrows, Arthur C., 427
Bartlett, S. C., 166
Baths, school and public, 260–262
Beach, Jessie A., 281, 288 n.
Beard, Charles A., 21 n., 419
Beard, Mary R., 21 n.
Becker, Carl, 357
Beedy, Mary E., 10 n.
Beggs, R. H., 107
Bell, John Wesley, 195 n., 465
Bellamy, Edward, 213
Bennett, Charles E., 339
Bentley, Rufus C., 444 n.
Benton, George W., 178, 228 n.
Berger, Morris Isaiah, 402 n., 464
Berkeley (Calif.) Public Schools, 240, 328
Betz, William, 349 n.
Bibliographies, 465–466
Bicknell, Thomas W., 7, 8, 21, 27, 457
Biographies, 461–462
Birge, E. A., 185
Birney, (Mrs.) Alice McLellan, 272
Bishop, J. Remsen, 78–79, 82 n., 86, 137, 229
Bishop, M. L., 288 n.
Bittle, (Mrs.) Gertrude B., 247
Black, Millard A., 302 n.
Blessing, Charles W., 465
Bliss, Frederick L., 134
Blodgett, James H., 14 n.
Bobbitt, Franklin, 305 n., 310, 325, 458
Bolshevism, 395, 419
Bolton, Frederick E., 185–186, 442
Bonner, H. R., 170 n.
Bookkeeping, 4, 6, 14
Boone, Richard G., 196, 457, 465
Boston (Mass.) Girls' High School, 465
Boston (Mass.) Latin Grammar School, 465
Boston (Mass.) Mechanics Arts High School, 184
Boston (Mass.) Public Schools, 14, 93, 96, 183–184, 194, 195, 215 n., 235, 241–242, 452

Botkin, Alice Sinclair, 444 n.
Boundary between high school and college, 3, 124, 129–133, 159–168, 441–443
Bourne, Randolph, 324, 424 n., 432, 459
Boyington, J. C., 331 n.
Boykin, J. C., 349
Boynton, F. D., 174, 444 n.
Boys, secondary education and, 11–12, 171–172, 299
Bradford, Mary C. C., 437
Bray, W. J., 369
Brearley, H. C., 249 n.
Breckenridge, William E., 347
Breslich, E. R., 333, 347 n.
Briggs, Thomas H., 86, 323, 330 n., 378, 383, 385 n., 399, 405–406, 444 n.
Britan, Nellie Hattan, 282
Brookline (Mass.) Education Society, 213, 276
Brookline (Mass.) Public Schools, 212–213
Brooklyn (N. Y.) Public Schools, 97, 185
Brooks, Edward, 98, 165, 198–199
Brooks, Raymond E., 398 n.
Brooks, Stratton D., 172, 215 n., 242 n., 288
Broome, Edwin Cornelius, 124 n., 463
Brown, Abram, 327 n.
Brown, Edwin J., 398 n.
Brown, Elmer Ellsworth, 4 n., 11 n., 106–107, 142, 187, 189, 272 n., 293, 450, 462, 466
Brown, George P., 105
Brown, Goodwin, 261 n.
Brown, J. Stanley, 164–165, 186, 292, 441
Brown, John Franklin, 85, 86 n., 459–460
Brown, Walter, 462
Bruno, Frank J., 464
Buchanan, John T., 137
Buffalo (N. Y.) Masten Park High School, 428–431, 447
Bunker, Frank F., 240, 328
Burgess, Charles O., 464
Burgess, Isaac B., 466
Burnham, William H., 117–119
Burstall, Sara A., 115

Business education, 4, 6, 14, 142–143, 185, 216, 217, 331–332, 376, 399, 440, 463
Butler, Leslie A., 134 n., 464
Butler, Nathaniel, 275
Butler, Nicholas Murray, 18, 26, 28–29, 67, 93, 104, 105, 106, 111, 115, 122, 129, 153–154, 203, 214, 215, 216, 223, 267, 282–283, 293–294, 346, 419, 437, 450, 457–458, 460, 461
  defender of the Committee of Ten, 70–71, 75–76, 91
  rôle in creation of the Committee of Ten, 36–38
  rôle in founding of the College Entrance Examination Board, 146–149
  rôle in selecting members of the Committee of Ten, 39–40
Butler, W. R., 198, 201
Butler, William M., 296

Caldwell, Otis W., 342, 346, 374, 378–379, 434
California, accreditation of secondary schools in, 152
  general science in, 373
  junior colleges in, 442–443
  proportions of one-teacher high schools in, 183
Calkins, N. A., 67 n., 101, 453 n.
Call, Arthur Deerin, 275
Callahan, Raymond E., 321 n., 464
Cambridge (Mass.) Public Schools, 95, 184
Canby, Henry Seidel, 460
Cardinal Principles of Secondary Education, 91, 216, 424–425, 447, 452, 462
  criticism of, 395–396, 400, 416
  influence of, 398–399
  overview of, 385–393
  preparation of, 382–385
  reputation of, 395–399
  seven aims, as stated in, 384–385, 387–388, 399
  sources of, 400–405
Carman, G. N., 134
Carnegie Foundation for the Advancement of Teaching, 160–162, 324–325, 455

Carnegie unit, 161–162
Carpenter, Frank O., 228 n.
Cary, C. P., 292–293
Catholic Child Study Congress, 110
Cattell, James McKeen, 419, 458
Caulkins, E. Dana, 413
Certificate system of college admission, 31, 41, 146, 151–156
Chadsey, Charles E., 293, 413
Changes Needed in American Secondary Education, 342
Chapin, Charles S., 115
Chapman, J. Crosby, 314 n.
Character education, 311–312
Charles Scribner's Sons, 274
Charles W. Eliot Papers, Harvard University Archives, 449
Chicago (Ill.) English High and Manual Training School, 184
Chicago (Ill.) Public Schools, 90, 96, 139, 183, 194, 195, 452, 462, 465
Chicago, University of, admission requirements, 301–303, 351–352
Child and the Curriculum, The, 112
Child labor, 221–222, 236, 266–267
Child study, 108–122, 464
Child Welfare Conference, 116, 271–272
Cincinnati (Ohio) Public Schools, 234
Civic Biology, 371
Civics, 356–357
Clark, Bertha May, 370–371
Clark, Hannah B., 465
Clark, Matie P., 277–278
Clark, O. D., 125 n.
Classical Conference, Ann Arbor (Mich.), 134
Claxton, Philander P., 214, 349, 350 n., 359 n., 378, 382 n., 383 n., 409, 410, 413, 420, 450, 461
Clay, Charles Marsh, 96 n.
Cleveland, Mrs. Grover, 272
Cleveland (Ohio) Public Schools, 238
Cleveland (Ohio) Technical High School, 231–232
Clough, Robert Ripley, 464
Cobb, Stanwood, 433–435, 438, 450
Coffman, Lotus D., 410, 458
Cogswell, Francis, 196
Coit, Stanton, 260
Cole, Lucy K., 271

Cole, Thomas R., 332 n.
Collar, William C., 2, 3 n., 29–31, 82, 124, 125, 126, 128, 158, 340, 465
College, admission requirements for, 7, 89–90, 124–125, 131–134, 140–145, 159–163, 291–303, 463
  in English, 362–364
  in foreign languages, ancient and modern, as general category, 291–292, 295, 298–299, 301–303
  in Latin and Greek, 28–31, 64–65, 79–81, 131–132
  in mathematics, 124, 131
  recognition of vocational and practical subjects in, 291, 298
  entrance examinations for, 7, 29–31, 146–151, 153–156
  preparatory function and programs for, 4, 6–7, 11, 27–29, 64–65, 84, 86, 89, 127, 140–144, 177–178, 198–203, 291–295, 319, 440
College Association of Pennsylvania, 127, 454
College Association of the Middle States and Maryland, 127, 454
College domination of the high school, allegations of, 84–86, 291–293
College Entrance Examination Board, 91, 129, 146–151, 153–154, 157, 158, 161, 216, 363, 449, 455, 463
Colleges and universities, advanced-standing credit for high-school work, 164–165
  enrollments in, 123, 177 n.
  numbers of, 123–124
Colorado, University of, 123
Commercial Club of Chicago, 235
Commercial education, see Business education
Commercial high schools, 185
Commission of Colleges in New England on Admission Examinations, 90–91, 363
Commission on the Emergency in Education and the Programs for Readjustment during and after the War, NEA, 437–438

Commission on the Relation of School and College, Progressive Education Association, 438
Commission on the Reorganization of Secondary Education, NEA, 91, 265, 341–342, 438, 449–450, 454, 455, 463
  Committee on Ancient Languages, 338–341
  Committee on Business Education, 376
  Committee on English, 365–367
  Committee on Mathematics, 349–352
  Committee on Modern Languages, 338, 341
  Committee on Science, 373–375
  Committee on Social Studies, 353–357, 358–359
  creation of, 300–301, 336, 338
  reviewing committee, membership of, 378–379
  See also Cardinal Principles of Secondary Education
Commissionership of Education, U. S., 18, 26, 214
Committee of Conference between Colleges and Secondary Schools, National Council of Education, NEA, member institutions of, 36–37
Committee of Fifteen on Elementary Education, NEA, 23, 73, 97–106, 450, 454, 457
  elementary-school curriculum recommended by, 102
Committee of Ten on Secondary-School Studies, NEA, 159, 168, 213, 313, 378, 385, 386, 389 n., 392–393, 403, 449, 450, 453, 454, 457, 462, 463, 466
  background of, 27–34
  college-admission requirements and, 64–65, 79–81
  conferences of, 52–56
  creation of, 35–38
  criticism of, 68–87, 94, 190, 192, 214, 250–251, 297
  influence of, 88–92
  membership of, 37–38, 39–43
  recommendations of, 58–65, 191, 203, 299

Committee of Ten on Secondary-School Studies (*Continued*)
  reputation of, 39, 86–88
  survey of offerings by, 47–49
Committee on College-Entrance Requirements, NEA, 137–146, 153, 159, 161, 191, 193, 203, 291, 327, 332–333, 362, 454, 456
  membership of, 137–138
  recommendations of, 141–142
Committee on Economy of Time in Education, Department of Superintendence, NEA, 167 n., 306–307, 320, 455
Committee on Economy of Time in Education, National Council of Education, NEA, 166–168, 454
Committee on the Articulation of High School and College, NEA, 216, 296–301, 336, 338, 351–352, 452, 454, 455
  membership of, 296–297
  response to, 299–303
Comprehensive high school, 186, 243, 276, 391–392, 396–397, 405
Compulsory attendance, 96, 170 n., 266–267, 416, 424
Conference on Classical Studies in Liberal Education, Princeton University, 345
Congress of Secondary Education, 125
Connecticut State Board of Education, 95
Constants, in secondary-school programs, 135–136, 153–154, 193–195, 291, 298, 316, 382–384, 390
Continuation schools, 234–236, 423
Cook, E. H., 457
Cooley, Edwin G., 195 n., 235
Cooper, Hermon C., 372 n.
Corbett, Henry R., 180, 214
Correlation of studies, 54, 98–105, 347, 352 n.
Corson, O. T., 111
Cosmopolitan high schools, *see* Comprehensive high schools
Cotton, Edward H., 426 n., 462
Cotton, Fassett A., 181 n., 182 n.
Coulter, J. G., 373 n.
Counts, George S., 290

Courses of study, 5–6, 141–143, 319–320
  Classical, 5, 6, 58, 60–61, 69, 74, 80, 198–199, 200
  English, 5–6, 58, 60, 62–64, 198, 204
  Latin-Scientific, 6, 29, 58, 61, 74, 198–199, 200
  recommended by the Committee of Ten, 58–65, 69, 77, 191
Cowen, George A., 373 n.
Cox, Philip W. L., 331 n.
Coy, E. W., 27–28, 31 n., 134, 144
Crawley, Edwin S., 159
Cremin, Lawrence A., 321 n., 404 n., 434 n., 464
Cross, W. L., 201–202
Cubberley, Ellwood P., 280, 324, 328 n., 442, 453, 458, 461
Curricula or curriculums, see Courses of study
Curti, Merle, 462

Dana, Henry Wadsworth, 419
Darwin, Charles, 72, 108, 121
Daughters of the American Revolution, 272
Davis, Calvin O., 152 n., 302 n., 334, 418–419, 440 n., 458, 463
Davis, Jesse B., 242, 444 n., 460
Dawson, Jean, 371
Deamer, Arthur, 373 n.
Decatur (Ill.) Public Schools, 290–291, 325
Deffenbaugh, W. S., 440 n.
DeGarmo, Charles, 88, 99, 100, 103, 106, 114 n., 122, 185, 239, 450, 459
Degrees, college and university, 29, 344 n.
Democracy, 45, 250, 387, 391–392, 422–423
Democracy and Education, 402, 422, 431
Democracy's High School, 280–281
Denver (Colo.) Public Schools, 184–185
Department of Business Education, NEA, 185
Department of Child Study, NEA, 110, 118, 121
Department of Elementary Education, NEA, 308

Department of Higher Education [Instruction], NEA, 33, 82, 137, 143
Department of Music Education, NEA, 270
Department of National Organizations of Women, NEA, 272–273
Department of School Patrons, NEA, 273
Department of Secondary Education [Instruction], NEA, 27, 34, 82, 137, 139, 143, 282, 292, 296–301, 348–349, 364
Department of Superintendence, NEA, 18, 19, 24, 97, 114, 224, 267, 311, 352, 389, 398, 404
  Cleveland meeting on the Report of the Committee of Fifteen, 101–104
  resolution for early differentiation, 240
  Richmond meeting on the Report of the Committee of Ten, 68–71
Devine, Edward T., 265
Dewey, John, 107, 122, 229, 235, 243, 248, 294, 356 n., 405, 411, 412, 415, 424, 425, 430–433, 444, 450, 462, 466
  child study and, 113–114
  influence on Cardinal Principles of Secondary Education, 400, 402
  Michigan Schoolmasters' Club and, 134
  social service and, 255–256, 259–260
Dewey, Melvil, 178, 450
Dewey, Mrs. Melvil, 277, 450
Dexter, Edwin G., 91, 187
Dial, 71, 459
Dick, Fred, 451
Differentiation of programs, for groups of pupils, 198–203, 237–240, 292–296, 303, 316, 318–322, 324, 330–332, 350–351, 375, 382–383, 389–390, 398–399, 404–405
Diploma system, see Certificate system of college admission
Domestic science, see Home economics
Donnan, Laura, 210 n.
Donnelly, Samuel P., 223
D'Ooge, Martin, 338
Douglas, Charles H., 187

Douglas Commission, *see* Massachu-
    setts Commission on Industrial
    and Technical Education
Douglass, Aubrey A., 330 n.
Douglass, Harl R., 327
Downing, E. R., 371
Draper, Andrew S., 69–70, 98, 153–
    155, 231
Dropouts from elementary schools, 96,
    221–223
    from secondary schools, 13–15, 172–
    175, 286–289
Drost, Walter H., 385 n., 398 n., 405 n.
Dualism of college-preparatory and
    noncollege - preparatory pro-
    grams, 28–29, 64–65, 198–203,
    237, 292–296, 303, 377, 398–399
Dudgeon, R. B., 361
Duke, S. P., 394, 400
Dunn, Arthur, 359
Dutton, Samuel Train, 212–214, 255,
    459, 461
Dutton, Wilbur H., 464
Dyer, Frank B., 224, 234, 297

Eau Claire (Wis.) Public Schools, 14
Economy of time, 44, 95, 166–168
Edmonds, Franklin Spencer, 465
Education, 7, 8, 10, 71, 210–211, 266,
    270, 281–282, 457
*Educational Administration and Super-
    vision*, 458
Educational Review, 70, 93, 124, 140,
    147, 184, 209, 328, 455, 457–
    458
Educator-Journal, 408, 459
Election by courses and by subjects,
    191–197, 319–320
Elective principle, 20–21, 46, 63, 77–
    78, 135–137, 140–142, 144–145,
    190–203
Elementary schools, 44, 55, 77–78, 90,
    93–98, 159, 165, 167, 220–223,
    237–239, 393
    criticisms of, 95–97
    departmentalization in, 93, 102
    dropouts, 96
Eliot, Charles W., 2, 3 n., 18–23, 80–
    81, 93, 95, 121, 122, 139, 160–
    161, 165, 179–180, 198, 203,
    204–205, 209–210, 212, 214,
    215, 216, 280, 294 n., 299, 306,

    314, 321–322, 373, 387 n., 393,
    405, 411, 412, 413–414, 418,
    425–427, 431–433, 433–436,
    445, 447, 449, 450, 453 n., 460,
    462
    Chairman of the Committee of Ten,
    39–40, 43–47, 52–53, 55–60,
    63–65, 67, 71–72, 74–75, 90
    College Entrance Examination Board
    and, 146–150
    defense of the Committee of Ten,
    76–77, 84–85, 92, 120
    electives and, 20–21, 46, 63, 77–78,
    136–137, 145, 190–192, 197
    elementary education and, 44–45,
    77–78
    Lincoln School controversy and,
    342–346
    membership in reform organizations,
    271
    rôle in creation of the Committee of
    Ten, 36–38
    social aims and, 250
    social service and, 256
    views on uniformity, 44–46
    vocational education and, 225–228,
    234, 241, 245
Elliot, John R., 270
Elliott, Edward C., 324
Ellwood, Charles A., 253–254, 255,
    422
Elson, William H., 231 n., 238 n.
Emery, William T., 2 n.
Engleman, J. O., 290–291, 325
English, 4, 29, 30, 52, 141, 145, 201–
    202, 281, 309, 361–368, 376,
    410, 440, 463
    college-admission requirements in,
    362–364
    criticism of, 361–362
    study of grammar in, 367–368
English Club of Chicago, 365
Enrollments, relative, in school sub-
    jects, 441
    business education, 376
    foreign languages, combined, 341
    German, 407
    Latin, 176–177, 285
    mathematics, 285
    science, 368–369
Equivalence of studies, 74, 78, 84–85,
    197

Erie (Pa.) High School, 12
Eugenics, 254
Evans, Charles W., 296
Evans, Henry Ridgely, 466
Expansion of public high schools, reasons for, 169–171
Extra-class activities, 391–393, 443–444

Failure rates in high-school subjects, 287–289
Fairchild, Edward T., 271, 304 n.
Fairchild, Milton, 311–312, 450
Fall River (Mass.) Public Schools, 174
Farrand, Wilson, 89 n., 124 n., 129
Faulkner, Harold U., 170 n.
Fay, Charles E., 80 n.
Federal Board for Vocational Education, 415
Fellows, George, 158
Felter, William L., 315
Fendley, J. M., 93 n.
Fenner, Mildred Sandison, 39, 463
Fine, Henry B., 138
Finney, Ross L., 317–318, 360–361, 422
Fitchburg (Mass.) Plan for vocational education, 233–234
Fitzgerald, M. E., 96 n.
Flexner, Abraham, 322 n., 450, 460
  Lincoln School controversy and, 342–346
Forbes, S. A., 152–153
Ford, George B., 257
Ford, Guy Stanton, 418
Foreign languages, ancient and modern, as general category, 315, 319, 336–342; see also, French, German, Greek, Latin, Spanish
  college-admission requirements in, 291–292, 295, 298–299, 301–303
  relative enrollments in, 341
Form-and-content distinction, 57, 74, 87, 99–100
Formal discipline, see Mental discipline
Forum, 66, 459
Fosdick, Frank W., 428
Fosdick, Raymond B., 428–429, 460
Foster, Walter Eugene, 339, 340–341, 379
Foster, William T., 201, 203

Fowler, Burton P., 395
Francis, J. H., 240 n., 324, 328 n., 329–330, 347, 400, 412
Free high schools, opposition to, 9, 178–179
Freece, J. S., 418
French, 4, 33, 52, 237, 336, 337, 338, 340, 346, 399, 409
French, C. W., 443 n.
Frieze, Henry S., 151
Fuess, Claude M., 463

Galesburg (Ill.) Public Schools, 194
Gary (Ind.) Public Schools, 321, 432
Gay, George E., 172
General education, 380
General Education Board, 269, 342–343, 352
General Federation of Women's Clubs, 272
Geography, 52
George, Anne, 434
German, 4, 33, 52, 90, 236, 336, 337, 338, 340, 346
  attack against, in World War I, 342, 407–410
  relative enrollments in, 342, 407
Germany, educational theories and practices of, 33, 75, 99, 234, 294–295, 420–421, 426
Gibbs, Louise R., 444 n.
Gibson, Carleton, 239
Gifford, Walter John, 465
Gilchrist, Edward P., 422 n.
Gilman, Daniel C., 166
Ginger, Ray, 371 n.
Girls, secondary education and, 11–12, 171–172, 229–230, 279, 299
Gladden, Washington, 271
Glenn, G. R., 104
Goodwin, Edward J., 194 n.
Goodwin, William W., 82
Gordon, C. H., 288
Gordy, H. Miles, 408
Gorrell, Robert M., 314 n.
Gosling, Thomas Warrington, 333
Graduates, secondary school, numbers of, 13–14
  vocational status of, 289–290
Graham, Jessie, 463
Grand Rapids (Mich.) Public Schools, 242

Grandgent, C. H., 337
Grant, R. R., 287 n.
Greek, 4, 5, 6, 22, 134, 139, 144, 197,
    204, 213, 280, 282, 304–305,
    315, 316, 336, 440
  college-admission requirements and,
    28–30, 33–35, 64–65, 128, 131–
    132
  Committee of Ten and, 52, 60, 79–83
  criticism of, 9, 32, 338
  in high schools of Mississippi, 131–
    132
Greenwood, James M., 68–69, 94, 98,
    173, 196, 441, 453 n.
Greer, John N., 196
Groves, Ernest R., 254–255, 310
Gruhn, William T., 327
Gugle, Marie, 329 n.
Guise, Helen Louise, 444 n.

Haeseler, Louise H., 176 n.
Hailmann, W. N., 113, 114 n.
Hale, Richard Walden, Jr., 465
Hall, G. Stanley, 177, 203, 259, 272,
    308, 338, 344, 346, 369, 387 n.,
    421, 422, 460, 462, 464, 466
  child-study movement and, 108–110,
    113, 116, 118–122
  criticism of the Committee of Ten,
    75–76, 83–85, 119–120, 201
Halleck, Reuben Post, 443 n.
Hall-Quest, Alfred L., 321
Ham, Charles H., 26
Hancock, William J., 370
Haney, James Parton, 223, 228, 238,
    246
Hannibal (Mo.), junior high schools in,
    331–332
Hanus, Paul H., 86, 137–138, 221, 230,
    231, 234, 242 n., 268, 305 n.,
    456, 459, 460
Harper, William Rainey, 164, 441
Harris, Ada Van Stone, 268
Harris, James, 282
Harris, William T., 16, 18, 22–23, 67,
    72, 76, 87 n., 108, 111–112, 119,
    120, 122, 204, 209, 212, 214,
    215, 216, 280, 292, 432, 449–
    450, 453 n., 457, 462, 466
  controversy with Herbartians, 98–
    107

Harris, William T. (*Continued*)
  manual training and, 23–26
  member of the Committee of Ten,
    39–40, 43, 58 n., 63, 69, 70
Harrison, Caskie, 373 n.
Hart, Albert Bushnell, 53, 54, 96 n.,
    101
Hartwell, Charles S., 173 n., 327 n.,
    328 n.
Harvard Teachers' Association, 72, 148,
    259, 436
Harvard University, 29, 79
  admission requirements in English,
    363
  College Entrance Examination Board
    and, 149–150
  three-year course, 165
Harvey, Lorenzo D., 224, 228
Hathaway, J. A., 152
Hayes, Carlton H., 353 n.
Hays, Edna, 463
Hearst, (Mrs.) Phoebe Apperson, 272
Heller, Harriet H., 121 n., 188 n.
Henderson, Adin D., 461
Herbart Society, *see* National Herbart
    Society for the Scientific Study
    of Teaching
Herbartians and Herbartianism, 99–
    108, 114–116, 314
Herrick, Cheesman A., 331, 376, 378,
    384
Herriott, M. E., 462
Higgins, Milton P., 223, 247
High School Masters' Club of Massa-
    chusetts, 381
High School Teachers Association of
    New York City, 295–298, 379,
    455
High schools, public, enrollments in, 5,
    11, 13, 169–170, 284
  entrance examinations, 94–95
  numbers of, 5, 168–169, 186, 439
  sizes of, 86, 176 n., 182–183, 186,
    439
Higher education, 7, 123–125, 161–166
  proposals for shortening period of,
    164–167
Hillhouse High School, New Haven
    (Conn.), 118
Hine, Charles D., 95
Hinsdale, Burke A., 107, 137–138,
    206–207

History, 4, 5, 141, 278, 309, 315, 353–361, 382, 399, 411, 440
   college-admission requirements in, 29–30
   Committee of Ten and, 52, 53–55, 60
History, civil government, and political economy, Committee of Ten conference on, 53–55
History Teachers of the Middle States and Maryland, 357
Hitchcock, Alfred H., 201–202
Hodge, C. F., 371
Hofstadter, Richard, 463
Holland, E. O., 362
Holley, C. E., 319 n.
Hollingshead, A. B., 249 n.
Holmes, Pauline, 465
Home economics, 6, 229–230, 277–278, 331, 376, 399, 440
Horton, D. W., 319
Hosic, James Fleming, 364–365, 366 n., 368, 378
Household arts, see Home economics
Howe, Julia Ward, 271
Hubbard, Charles W., 236 n.
Huling, Ray Greene, 2, 3 n., 15, 53, 54, 78 n., 125, 126, 137, 454
Hunter, Fred M., 411–412, 414, 424 n.
Hunter, S. J., 180–181
Hunter, W. B., 233 n.
Hurd, Paul DeHart, 463
Hyde, William DeWitt, 65 n., 79

Idaho, public high schools in, 439–440
Illinois, conflict over separate administration of vocational schools in, 235–236
   rural high schools in, 181–182
Immigrants and immigration, 10–11, 87, 209–211, 260–263, 391, 402 n., 403, 417–419, 428, 464
Indiana, accreditation system in, 152
   approval of Report of the Committee on the Articulation of High School and College, 300
   development of secondary education in, 465
   reports of State Superintendent, 452
   rural high schools in, 181, 182
Individualism and education, 250, 254–255, 283, 320–321, 393, 447

Industrial arts, see Manual Training
Industrial education, see Vocational education
Industrial Education Association of New York, 26
Inglis, Alexander, 378, 384, 460
Intelligence, 71, 73, 103, 104, 140, 458
Interest as Related to Will, 107
Intermediate schools, see Junior high schools
International Congress of Education, 42, 66
International Congress of Mathematicians, 347–348
International Congress on the Welfare of the Child, 272
Iowa, development of secondary education in, 465
   general science in, 373
Iowa State Teachers' Association, 308–309
Ithaca (N. Y.) Public Schools, 174
Ittner, Anthony, 247

Jackman, Wilbur S., 99, 106, 107
James, Edmund J., 138, 143, 185, 200
James, Henry, 271, 462
James, William, 114
James B. Angell Papers, Michigan Historical Collections, University of Michigan, 449
James C. Mackenzie Papers, Lawrenceville School, New Jersey, 450
Jastrow, Joseph, 426
Jefferson Township (Ill.) High School, 6 n.
Jespersen, Otto, 367, 445
Jesse, Richard H., 163–164, 450, 462
   member of the Committee of Ten, 38, 41, 52 n.
Jessup, Walter A., 306 n.
John Tetlow Papers, Houghton Library, 449
Johnson, Ben W., 240
Johnson, Franklin Winslow, 444 n.
Johnson, Marietta, 434
Johnston, Charles Hughes, 237 n., 241, 258 n., 260 n., 319–321, 329, 333, 378, 380, 382, 404, 426–427, 431, 458, 460
Joliet Township (Ill.) High School, 164–165, 182

Joncich, Geraldine M., 464
Jones, R. W., 89 n.
Jones, Thomas Jesse, 353–354
Jones, William Carey, 137–138, 143
Jordan, David Starr, 292
Journal of Education, 70, 71–72, 80, 81, 82, 144, 246, 270, 329, 455, 457
Journal of Pedagogy, 458
Journals, in education, 456–459
Joynes, Edward S., 17
Judd, Charles Hubbard, 121, 239, 290, 297, 323, 330, 358–360, 410, 420
Junior College, 164–165, 441–443
Junior high school, 239–240, 327–335, 383, 389, 404, 441
Junior High School Clearing House, 458
Junior Red Cross, 411, 414

Kaeuper, H. H., 313 n.
Kandel, I. L., 461
Kansas, approval of Report of the Committee on the Articulation of High School and College, 300
    rural high schools in, 180
Kansas City (Mo.) Public Schools, 172–173
Karpinski, Louis C., 348 n.
Kasson, Frank, 457
Keller, Paul G. W., 444 n.
Kelsey, Francis W., 337
Kennedy, John, 73
Kentucky "Committee of Ten," 89
Kerschensteiner, Georg, 234–235
Keyes, Charles H., 218
Kilpatrick, William Heard, 349, 378, 384, 402
King, Henry C., 461, 462
    member of the Committee of Ten, 38, 41, 43
King, Irving, 459
Kingsbury, Susan M., 221–223, 224, 227, 232, 233, 240, 245, 327, 456
Kingsley, Clarence, 265, 319, 349, 360, 365, 411 n., 433, 438, 447, 450, 452, 455, 462
    activity in the High School Teachers

Kingsley, Clarence (*Continued*)
    Association of New York City, 295–296
    Chairman of the Commission on the Reorganization of Secondary Education, 300–301, 336, 338, 339–340, 378–397, 399, 401–406
    Chairman of the Committee on the Articulation of High School and College, 296–303
    controversy with David Snedden, 395–397
    Dewey and Spencer as possible influences on, 401–402
    rôle of, in preparation of *Cardinal Principles of Secondary Education,* 384–385, 401–402, 404–405
    social studies and, 354–356
Kingsley, Elizabeth S., 398 n.
Kirkland, J. H., 129–131, 133, 144, 461
Kirtland, John, 337
Kitzhaber, Albert R., 314 n.
Kneeland, George J., 262 n.
Koos, Leonard V., 302 n.
Kratz, H. E., 287 n.
Krug, Edward A., 460
Krutsch, Joseph, 461
Kuehnemann, Eugen, 462

Lake View Township (Ill.) High School, 12, 13 n., 181, 183, 452
Lancaster, E. G., 118, 121
Lane, Albert G., 90, 98
Lang, Ossian, 457
Lange, Alexis, 297, 442–443
Latimer, John Francis, 462
Latin, 4, 5, 22, 144, 182, 197, 203, 204, 213, 229, 236, 282, 315, 316, 399, 409, 440
    college-admission requirements in, 28–29, 34–35, 43, 64–65, 79–81, 128, 131, 149–150
    Committee of Ten and, 52, 60, 63–65, 82–83, 90
    criticism of, 32–34, 84–85, 278–280, 308–309, 324–325, 337–338, 342–346, 394
    relative enrollments in, 176–177, 346
Lawson, Victor, 10
Learned, William S., 324–325

Leavitt, Frank M., 235 n., 237–240, 382
Leidecker, Kurt E., 461
Leisure, education for, 310–311, 387–388
Leiter, Frances W., 276
Lenfest, B. A., 218
Levermore, Charles Herbert, 21 n., 461
Lewis, Charles Lee, 461
Lewis, E. E., 302 n.
Lewis, William D., 279–281, 349, 358, 365, 400, 424 n., 460
    member of the Committee on the Articulation of High School and College, 296–298
Liberal education, 185, 186, 200, 280, 294–295, 317
Life-adjustment education, 87, 238, 281, 420 n.
Lincoln (Neb.) Public Schools, 372
Lincoln School, Columbia University, 343, 345–346, 432
Linn, James Weber, 362 n.
Locke, George Herbert, 458
Lodge, Gonzalez, 337, 339
Looking Backward, 213
Los Angeles (Calif.) Public Schools, 237, 240, 329
Love, Donald M., 461
Lyman, R. L., 332 n.
Lyon, Edmund D., 358
Lyons Township (Ill.) High School, 195
Lyttle, Eugene W., 85 n.

McAndrew, William, 246, 270 n., 279, 458
McCartney, L., 332 n.
McCaul, Robert L., 268
McClure, S. R., 179 n.
McConaughy, James L., 283
McCulloch, G. L., 334 n.
McDermott, Irene E., 278
Macdonald, J. W., 16
MacDonald, John, 105
McDowell, F. M., 442 n.
Mace, William H., 356
Mackenzie, James C., 129, 164, 450, 462
    member of the Committee of Ten, 38, 42, 56 n., 75, 78
MacLean, George E., 153, 157

McLinn, Charles B., 275, 444 n.
McManis, John T., 462
McMurry, Charles, 99, 103, 106, 112
McMurry, Frank, 99, 106, 107, 112, 119 n.
Maine, approval of the Report of the Committee on Articulation of High School and College, 300
    proportions of college graduates among high school teachers in, 187
Manley, Edward, 339, 379
Mann, C. R., 369
Mann, Horace, 72, 219, 228
Manual training, 6, 14, 15, 23–26, 142, 216, 219–220, 399, 440
Manual-training high schools, 184–185, 231
Marble, A. P., 104
Mark, E. H., 196
Marrinan, John J., 217 n.
Marshall, Leon, 410, 420
Martin, Mrs. A. B., 95
Martin, George Henry, 5 n., 218–220, 230, 462
Martindale, W. C., 196
Massachusetts, college-preparatory pupils in, 178
    development of secondary education in, 465
    high-school enrollments in, 174
    numbers of high schools in, 5 n.
    reports of State Superintendent, 452
    teaching of German in, 408
Massachusetts Classical and High School Teachers' Association, 1–3, 7, 11, 73, 455
Massachusetts Commission on Industrial and Technical Education, 217–223, 456
Massachusetts Commission on Industrial Education, 221, 230, 456
Massachusetts State Teachers' Association, 19, 259, 455
Massachusetts Teacher, 95
Mathematical Association of America, 352, 456
Mathematics, 4, 5, 95, 124, 141, 182, 204, 213, 281, 308–309, 342, 347–353, 399, 440, 463–464
    Committee of Ten and, 52, 60, 90
    criticisms of, 347–349

Maxwell, William H., 68, 69, 73, 76, 93, 97, 105, 211, 240–241, 261–262, 264, 266, 267, 270, 319, 389, 403, 457
May, Henry F., 402 n.
Mayo, A. D., 130
Mead, Cyrus D., 334
Meaning of Education, The, 154
Mearns, William Hughes, 280
Meek, Charles S., 322, 326–327
Mehl, Bernard, 463
Meiklejohn, Alexander, 207
Melvil Dewey Papers, Columbia University Libraries, 450
Mengersen, Edwin Fred, 463
Mental discipline, 21, 22–23, 57, 63–64, 86, 87, 99, 203–208, 278, 299, 313–314, 343, 350, 380, 445–447
Merrill, Moses, 33
Metcalf, D. D., 11 n.
Michael Vincent O'Shea Papers, State Historical Society of Wisconsin, 450
Michigan, approval of the Report of the Committee on the Articulation of High School and College, 300
college-preparatory pupils in, 178
Michigan, University of, accreditation system, 41, 151–152
Michigan Schoolmasters' Club, 134, 464
Middle States Association, *see* Association of Colleges and Preparatory Schools of the Middle States and Maryland
Midura, Gladys A., 15 n., 465
Military training in schools, 195, 412
Miller, Edwin L., 362, 394
Miller, G. A., 342 n.
Miller, Herbert, 228 n.
Millikan, Robert A., 369, 375
Milner, Florence, 443 n.
Mims, Edwin, 133, 461
Minimum essentials, scientific determination of, 306–307, 320
Minneapolis (Minn.) Public Schools, 14
Minnesota, accreditation system in, 152
proportions of college graduates among high-school teachers in, 187

Minnesota (*Continued*)
proportions of one-teacher high schools in, 183
Minnick, John H., 350
Mishawaka (Ind.) Public Schools, 319
Missimer, H. C., 13 n., 14 n.
Mississippi, Committee of Ten and, 89
Greek in high schools of, 131–132
Mississippi, University of, 131–132
Missouri, Committee of Ten and, 89
Moderate revision, movement for, 190, 214–216, 293–294, 299
Modern foreign languages, 4, 29, 52, 338–342
See also French; German; Spanish
Modern Language Association, 140, 141
Modern School, A, 342
Monroe, Paul, 460
Monroe, Walter S., 462
Monroe, Will S., 466
Monroe (Mich.) High School, 34
Montana State Council of Defense, 407
Montclair (N. J.) Public Schools, 14
Moore, Charles N., 313
Moore, Ernest Carroll, 313, 317, 458
Moore, F. W., 158 n.
Moore, Wallace Henry, 407 n.
Moral Education Board, 311
Morgan, H. M., 80
Moritz, Robert E., 313
Morrison, Gilbert B., 327 n., 444 n.
Morrison, Henry C., 225 n., 458
Mount Vernon (N. Y.) Sophie J. Mee Junior High School, 331
Mowry, William A., 13 n., 16–17, 457, 460
Muensterberg, Hugo, 111 n., 344
Mulhern, James, 465
Munich (Germany) Plan for Continuation Schools, 234–235
Munroe, James P., 178–179
Music, 195, 270–271, 376, 440
My Pedagogic Creed, 213
Myers, George W., 348

National Archives, documents on Commission on the Reorganization of Secondary Education, 449–450

National Association of Manufacturers, 235, 247, 456
National Association of Secondary-School Principals, Committee on Curriculums of, 394
  Committee on Social Science of, 358–360
  creation of, 438 n.
National Association of State Universities, 157, 158
National Committee on Mathematical Requirements, 352–353
National Conference Committee of Associations of Colleges and Preparatory Schools, see Williamstown Conferences
National Conference of Civic and Social Center Development, 257–258
National Conference of Social Work, 464
National Conference on Character Education in Relation to Canadian Citizenship, 312
National Conference on Uniform Entrance Requirements in English, 363–364
National Conference on Vocational Guidance, 242
National Conferences on Americanization through Education, 417
National Congress of Mothers, 272, 433
National Congress of Parents and Teachers, 272, 399
National Council of Education, NEA, 8, 18, 25, 27–28, 32, 35–38, 67, 97, 119, 423, 453
  creation of the Committee of Ten, 36–38
  meeting on the Report of the Committee of Ten, 74–76
National Council of Jewish Women, 272
National Council of Teachers of English, 336, 364–365, 368
National Council of Teachers of Mathematics, 352
National Education[al] Association, 8, 67, 215, 437–438, 450–451, 453

National Herbart Society for the Scientific Study of Teaching, 106–107, 455
National Institution for Moral Instruction, 311
National Security League, 407
National service, compulsory, 423–424
National Society for the Promotion of Industrial Education, 223–224, 226, 235, 242, 246, 416, 455, 464
National Society for the [Scientific] Study of Education, 107, 323, 455
National Vocational Guidance Association, 242
Nebraska, proportion of college graduates among high-school teachers in, 441
  proportion of one-teacher high schools in, 183
Nebraska State Teachers' Association, 121
Negroes, education of, 209, 322
Neilson, William Allen, 460
Neumann, Henry, 378, 382
New education, the, 9, 121
New England Association of Colleges and Preparatory Schools, 3, 38, 79–81, 84, 89, 117, 119, 125–126, 128, 129, 346, 449, 454
New England College Entrance Certificate Board, 156–157, 158
New Hampshire, Americanization and Educational Law, 418
  proportions of college graduates among high-school teachers in, 187
New Jersey, approval of the Report of the Committee on the Articulation of High School and College, 300
New Republic, 324, 459
New York Bureau of Municipal Research, 268
New York Charity Organization Society, 264, 403
New York (N. Y.) Public Schools, 261–264, 457
  school survey, 268, 324, 328 n., 329 n.

New York (N. Y.) Public Schools (*Continued*)
social and economic status of high-school pupils in, 285–287
vocational education in, 232–233
New York (N. Y.) Washington Irving High School for Girls, 279, 281, 288
New York Physics Club, 372
New York State, development of secondary education in, 465
high-school enrollments in, 174
proportion of college graduates among principals of high schools and academies in, 188
New York State Science Teachers' Association, 370
New York Tribune, 346
Newark (N. J.) Public Schools, 14
Newlon, Jesse H., 321, 367 n., 431, 438 n., 458
Newton (Mass.) Public Schools, 193, 197, 320
Nicholas Murray Butler Papers, Columbiana Library, Columbia University, 450
Nightingale, Augustus F., 34, 80 n., 181–182, 203, 214, 445, 452, 453
Chairman of the Committee on College-Entrance Requirements, 137–146
criticism of the Committee of Ten, 70–71, 82
electives and, 135–136, 194–196
in North Central Association, 134–136, 153–154
Nightingale, Jessie Irma, 139 n.
Nineveh Township (Ind.) High School, 182
Norris, John O., 12 n.
North American Review, 459
North Central Association of Colleges and Secondary Schools, 133–137, 146, 156, 157, 158, 161, 364, 418–419, 440–441, 463
Commission on Accredited Schools, 152–156, 158, 160, 185
Nutting, H. C., 345

O'Connell, Archbishop William, 259

Ohio, continuation-school law in, 234, 235
high-school dropouts in, 13–14
Ohio Educational Monthly, 454, 457, 458
Ohio State Teachers' Association, 455
Oregon, proportion of one-teacher high schools in, 183
Oregon State Teachers' Association, 275
Orr, William, 297
O'Shea, Michael Vincent, 113 n., 115, 187, 274 n., 278 n., 312 n., 313, 322, 433 n., 434 n., 435 n., 450, 459
Outlook, 459

Packard, John C., 202
Page, Walter Hines, 312 n.
Palmer, Frank, 457
Palmer, Jasper T., 331 n.
Parker, Francis W., 9, 68, 88, 93, 99, 100 n., 103, 105, 106, 107, 112, 207, 212, 462
Parsons, James Russell, Jr., 174
Patterson, G. H., 275
Patton, F. L., 148
Pearse, Carroll G., 329, 412
Pedagogical Seminary, 150, 458
Pennsylvania, college-preparatory work of high schools in, 127–128
rural high schools in, 181
Pennsylvania, University of, 159
Pennsylvania Education Association, 316
Pennsylvania School Journal, 454, 458
Pennsylvania State Teachers' Association, 455
Periodicals, *see* Journals, in education
Perrin, John W., 266 n.
Perry, Arthur C., 258 n.
Perry, Mrs. D. B., 278 n.
Peru (Ill.) Public Schools, 14
Philadelphia (Pa.) Central High School, 465
Phillips, D. E., 195–196, 334
Physical education, 195, 276–277, 376, 412–413
Pickard, J. L., 115
Pitman, Joseph Asbury, 219 n., 413 n., 462

Pittenger, B. F., 290 n.
Pletcher, Milford F., 181 n.
Poland, Addison B., 275–276, 457
Port Huron (Mich.) High School, 34
Portland (Ore.) school survey, 324, 329, 453
Post, Louis F., 434
Potter, Milton C., 289 n.
Pound, Olivia, 444 n.
Powell, E. B., 4 n.
Powell, W. B., 98
Practical English for High Schools, 368
Preparatory schools, endowed, 6 n.
Pritchett, Henry S., 160–162, 223
Private secondary schools, numbers of, 3–5
Problems of democracy, study of as school subject, 356–357
Proctor, William Martin, 398 n.
Programs, *see* Courses of study
Progressive Education, 435
Progressive Education Association, *see* Association for the Advancement of Progressive Education
Prosser, Charles A., 238–239, 242–243, 414, 420–421, 424, 458
Psychology and education, 310, 313, 387, 464
Public health and education, 265–266
Public School Journal, 105, 210, 458
Pupils, boys, numbers and proportions of, 11–12, 171
 college-preparatory and noncollege-preparatory, 6, 27–28, 53–54, 90, 127, 177–178, 198–203, 289, 290 n., 398–399
 girls, numbers and proportions of, 11–12, 171
 numbers of, in private schools, 5
 numbers of, in public high schools, 5, 11, 13, 169–170, 284, 439
 quality of, alleged changes in, 175
 selection factors, 12–14, 173–175
 social and economic status of, 12–14, 170–171, 175–177, 285–287, 321
 survival rates of, *see* Dropouts
 vocational plans of, 290–291
Pure Literature League, 271

Quincy (Mass.) Public Schools, 9

Ramsay, Charles Cornell, 122 n.
Rapeer, Louis W., 310–311, 315–317, 400, 450
Ravenswood-Lake View Historical Association, Chicago (Ill.), 452
Records of High School Accreditation, University of Michigan, 449
Reform and education, 16–17, 211–212, 245, 249, 266–273
Regents Convocation (N. Y.), 73
Religious Education Association of America, 423
Reports, annual, of the United States Commissioner of Education, 451
Rice, Joseph M., 66, 96, 305 n.
Richards, Charles, 223, 224, 246
Richards, Ellen H., 229–230, 277, 450
Richards, Z., 8 n.
Richman, Julia, 211, 261–262
Riess, Ernest, 337 n.
Riis, Jacob, 264, 403
Roberts, Paul, 314 n.
Robeson, Henry J., 34 n.
Robinson, E. V., 239
Robinson, James Harvey, 53, 54, 354–356, 402
Robinson, Oscar D., 10, 191
 criticism of the Committee of Ten, 73, 75, 82
 member of the Committee of Ten, 37, 39, 42, 43, 56–57, 60 n., 465
Robinson Crusoe, 103
Rochester (N. Y.) Public Schools, 256–257, 268
Rockefeller, John D., 269
Rogers, Henry M., 136
Roosevelt, Theodore, 225, 267, 272, 275, 281, 345
Rorem, S. O., 330 n., 334–335, 458
Rose, C. E., 411, 414
Rosenstein, David, 264–265, 403 n.
Ross, Edward A., 249, 251–253, 255, 268–269, 277, 311 n., 354, 459
Roxbury Latin School, 465
Rural high schools, 12, 174–175, 180–183, 439–440
Russell, James Earl, 116–117, 137–138, 176, 228–229, 270

Sabin, Henry, 451
Sachs, Julius, 118, 129, 172 n., 460

Saginaw (Mich.) Trade School, 233
St. Louis (Mo.) Ben Blewett Junior High School, 332
St. Louis (Mo.) Public Schools, 452
St. Stephen's College, 159
Salmon, Lucy M., 30, 188 n.
San Antonio (Tex.) Public Schools, 322
Sargent, Dudley A., 412
Saturday Evening Post, 280–281
Saunders, Paul Hill, 132–133
Schaeffer, Nathan C., 181, 300
Schmall, Charles N., 348 n.
Schmitt, C. D., 197 n.
Schoff, Mrs. Fredric, 450
School, 147
School and College, 454, 458
School and Society, 368, 458
School and Society, The, 113, 213, 259–260, 459
School Bulletin, 104, 105, 178
School garden army, 412, 414
School Journal, 115, 262, 457
School Review, 73, 118, 195, 243, 359, 360, 361, 409, 415, 416, 419, 420, 437, 438, 454, 458
School surveys, 323–325, 329, 452
Schorling, Raleigh, 352 n.
Schurman, J. C., 129
Science, 4, 52, 60, 141, 204–205, 313, 315, 368–375, 399, 440
    alleged decline of enthusiasm for in twentieth century, 369–370
    biology, 370–371, 374–375, 463
    chemistry, 370, 374–375
    general, 372–374
    physics, 119–120, 202, 369, 371–372, 374–375
    relative enrollments in, 368–369
Scientific management in education, 304–327, 389, 464
    application of, to theory of curriculum, 307–317, 322–323
    differentiation and, 318–322
    school surveys and, 323–325
Scott, Colin A., 259–260, 459
Scott, F. N., 155
Scudder, Horace E., 213, 255–256
Scudder, Myron T., 118–119
Search, Preston W., 118
Sears, Jesse B., 461
Seaver, Edwin P., 73, 98, 195 n., 452

Secondary education, ideal of universal, 382, 392–393
Seely, Gordon M., Jr., 463
Seerley, H. H., 451
Selden, William K., 463
Sex education, 270
Seymour, Thomas D., 165
Shaler, Nathaniel, 72, 91
Shallies, Guy-Wheeler, 289 n.
Shaw, Marie Adele, 261 n.
Shaw, Mrs. Quincy A., 241
Shepard, Irwin, 67 n., 451, 453 n.
Sheppard, James J., 185 n.
Shipman, W. D., 41 n.
Shorey, Paul, 109, 199, 338, 344–345
Siders, Walter R., 413
Sigurdson, Solberg Einar, 463–464
Simkhovich, Mary, 264, 461
Sinclair, Upton, 461
Sisson, Edward O., 281, 378, 382, 383, 439 n.
Six-year secondary school, 142, 327, 332–334
Sizer, Theodore R., 87, 463
Skinner, Charles R., 175
Slagle, Robert L., 409 n.
Slaton, W. F., 196
Small, Albion W., 249 n., 251, 255, 274
Smiley, William H., 78 n., 137, 296
Smith, Charles Forster, 129
Smith, Clement, 149
Smith, David Eugene, 348
Smith, Ernest A., 424–425
Smith, Eugene Randolph, 434
Smith, H. L., 323
Smith, Lewis Wilbur, 326, 417–418
Smith, Payson, 292
Smith, Shirley W., 461
Smith, Spencer R., 444 n.
Smith, W. A., 330 n.
Smith, Walter Robinson, 422
Smith-Hughes Law, 229, 414–415
Snedden, David, 251–253, 255, 265, 282, 295, 311, 316–318, 319, 345, 354, 379, 381, 395–397, 400, 401 n., 405, 416, 431, 458, 459, 460
    scientific determination of aims, 307 n., 308–310
    views on study and teaching of history, 357–358

Snedden, David (*Continued*)
    views on study and teaching of physics, 372
Snook, J. Alvin, 394 n.
Snow, William B., 339, 341 n.
Social aims, *see* Aims, social
Social and economic status and education, 10, 12–14, 68, 74, 85, 88, 170–171, 175–177, 207, 260–264, 285–287, 321–322, 395
Social and economic views of educators, 10–11, 208–213
Social-center movement, 255–259
Social change and education, 280–281, 386, 403–404
Social control, 249–255, 381, 393, 405, 420–421, 426–427
Social Education Association, 259
Social Education Congress, 259
Social education movement, 259–260
Social Education Quarterly, 259
Social efficiency, 249, 274–283, 308–318, 347, 355–356, 366, 370–371, 375, 389, 405, 422, 431, 436–437, 458
Social Phases of Education in the School and in the Home, 213
Social service, 249, 255–265, 388, 405
Social settlements and education, 260, 263–265 402–403
Social studies, 353–361, 399, 410–411, 464
    origin of term, 354
Sociological Determination of Objectives in Education, 310
Sociology and education, 249–255, 310, 317–318
Solvay (N. Y.) Junior High School, 331
Somerville (Mass.) Public Schools, 330
South, secondary education in, 129–133
Southern Association, *see* Association of Colleges and Preparatory Schools of the Southern States
Southern Association of College Women, 272
Spanish, 336, 346, 409
Spaulding, Frank E., 304–305, 315, 320, 324, 458
Specialized high schools, 184–186, 237
Spencer, Herbert, 83 n., 204, 307, 373 n., 375, 400–402, 405

Spokane (Wash.) Webster Junior High School, 331
Springfield (Ill.) school survey, 324, 329
Springfield (Mass.) Public Schools, 15, 93, 465
Stacy, Chester R., 121 n.
Standardization, 159–163, 463
Steele, W. L., 194
Steeper, H. T., 444 n.
Steere, E. A., 175
Stern, Bernhard J., 250
Stevens, Thaddeus, 72
Stevenson, Mrs. Adlai, 272
Stewart, John A., 34 n., 152 n.
Stewart, Joseph, 133
Stoddard, Francis H., 363–364
Stout, John Elbert, 460, 462
Straubenmuller, Gustave, 232 n.
Strayer, George D., 304, 438 n., 458
Strickland, Charles E., 464
Stuart, George, 11 n.
Students, *see* Pupils
Substantive aims (as contrasted with formal), 87, 102, 203–204, 208, 250–251, 282, 380
Survey, 459
Suzzallo, Henry, 310, 312

Taylor, Aravilla Meek, 373 n.
Taylor, James M., 127, 462
    member of the Committee of Ten, 38, 41, 56–57
Teachers, numbers of high school, 441
    preparation of high school, 182, 186–189, 441
    social and intellectual status of high school, 188, 189
Teaching, direct entrance into, from high-school graduation, 289, 290 n., 291 n.
Technology and secondary education, 170–171
Tennessee, public high schools in, 130
Terman, Lewis M., 274
Tetlow, John, 1–3, 36–38, 53, 79–81, 126, 128, 183–184, 215 n., 429, 449, 460, 465
    member of the Committee of Ten, 38, 42, 46, 67
    papers of, 449

Textbooks, 182, 348, 362–363, 368, 371, 372–373
Thomas, Alan M., Jr., 86, 87 n., 403 n.
Thomas, Isaac, 156
Thomas, Milton H., 466
Thompson, Frank V., 418
Thorndike, Edward L., 86, 109, 120–121, 176 n., 182–183, 186, 206–207, 462, 464
Thornton Township (Ill.) High School, 326, 418
Thurber, Charles H., 117, 125, 137–138, 143, 195, 458
Thurber, Samuel, 19 n., 33, 43, 176–177, 192–193
Todd, T. W., 409 n.
Toledo (Ohio) Public Schools, 15, 184
Tomlinson, E. T., 17
Tostberg, Robert Eugene, 462
Township high schools, 180–182
Trade schools, 218, 224, 231–234
Troumbley, L. A., 330 n.
Trout, H. E., 247 n.
True, A. C., 247–248
Tryon, Rolla Milton, 463
Tuckerman, Julius, 338
Tugwell, Rexford Guy, 430–431, 447, 461
Twin Falls (Ida.) High School, 440

Ullman, B. L., 408 n., 409
United States Bureau of Education, Circulars of Information and Bulletins of, 451–452, 465
Updegraff, Harlan, 200, 325–326
Utah, compulsory-attendance law in, 424–425
Utica (N. Y.) Public Schools, 93, 174

Vacation schools, 260–262
Van Denburg, Joseph K., 285 n., 370
Vanderbilt University, 130
Van Dyke, Henry, 271
Van Liew, C. C., 99, 106
Van Sickle, James H., 196, 458
Van Tufty, Esther W., 139 n.
Veblen, Thorstein, 277
Vermont, proportion of college graduates among high-school teachers in, 187
  teaching of German in, 408
Vermont school survey, 324–325

Vincent, George E., 249 n.
Vocational education, 14–16, 186, 200–201, 217–248, 319, 379–380, 388, 396–397, 404, 440, 445–446
  child labor and, 221–223
  continuation schools and, 234–236
  differentiation and, 237–241
  Douglas Commission and movement for, 219–224
  endorsed by Social Education Congress, 259
  girls and, 229–230
  guidance and, 241–243, 245, 288
  impact of movement for, 243–245
  junior high schools and, 239–241, 331–333
  selection or identification of pupils for, 225–230
  separate administration of, 230–231, 235–236, 243, 397, 415–416, 420
  trade schools in, 218, 224, 231–234
  World War I and, 414–417
Vocational guidance, 241–243, 245, 388

Wald, Lillian, 419
Ward, C. H., 284 n.
Ward, Edward J., 255 n., 256–258, 268
Ward, Lester Frank, 87 n., 250–251, 314, 354, 361, 445, 459
Warfield, Ethelbert D., 148–149
Warner, C. F., 218
Warriner, E. C., 164, 233 n.
Washington University, Manual Training High School, 14–15, 24, 25, 184
Weaver, Eli, 241
Webster, R. H., 196
Weeks, Arland D., 279
Weinberg, Arthur and Lila, 269 n.
Welch, Ida, 373 n.
Wendell, Barrett, 212
Wesley, Edgar B., 68 n., 463
West, Andrew F., 66, 134, 163, 197, 427, 450
Western School Journal, 105
White, Andrew D., 166
White, E. E., 106
White, Olive B., 465
White, Richard Grant, 9, 96
Whitney, A. S., 151, 152 n., 153

Whittemore, Richard F. W., 461
Wiggin, Gladys A., 463
Wightman, H. J., 279
Wilder, Burt C., 270
Wilds, Elmer Harrison, 444 n.
Willard, F. R., 395
Williams, Beryl, 419
Williams, (Mrs.) Laura, 433 n., 435
Williamstown Conferences, 158, 161–162
Wilson, H. B., 307 n., 313
Wilson, Louis N., 466
Wilson, Woodrow, 53, 54, 129, 257, 294, 362, 409, 410, 412, 420
Wiltse, Sarah E., 110 n.
Winship, A. E., 72–73, 79, 82, 94, 102, 144, 147, 215 n., 246, 270–271, 329, 412 n., 457
Wisconsin, high-school dropouts in, 13
    proportions of college graduates among high-school teachers in, 187, 441
    vocational education in, 235
    University of, accreditation system of, 152
Woman's Christian Temperance Union, 272, 276

Women and reform, 272–273
Woods, Lucy R., 465
Woodward, Calvin M., 14–15, 23–26, 74–75, 183, 200, 224
Woodworth, R. S., 207 n.
Worcester (Mass.) Public Schools, 174
World War I, 407–427
    Americanization program, 417–420
    education for democracy and, 422–423
    impact on teaching of German, 407–410
    physical education and, 412–413
    vocational education and, 414–417
World's Work, 451, 459
Wright, Carroll D., 218
Wright, D. S., 211

Yale Report, 205–206
Yocum, A. Duncan, 423, 425
Young, Ella Flagg, 86, 412, 432, 462
Young, Walter H., 156 n.
Youth, proportions of in secondary school, 173–175
Youth's Companion, 368

Zook, George F., 302 n.